H.E. PANTELEIMON LAMPADARIOS,
METROPOLITAN OF ANTINOES
(Retired Metropolitan of the Greek Orthodox Patriarchate
of Alexandria and All Africa)

THE CATECHESISM OF THE ORTHODOX CHURCH

(IN 374 QUESTIONS AND ANSWERS)

LONDON 2022

akakia

H.E. PANTELEIMON LAMPADARIOS, METROPOLITAN OF ANTINOES
(Retired Metropolitan of the Greek Orthodox Patriarchate
of Alexandria and All Africa)

The Catechesism of the Orthodox Church
(In 374 Questions and Answers)

ISBN (UK): 978-1-915848-06-2
© 2022-2023 PANTELEIMON LAMPADARIOS

His Eminence PANTELEIMON LAMPADARIOS,
METROPOLITAN OF ANTINOES
Mobile: +30-684-415-3114 (Metropolitan Panteleimon)
Email: metropolitanantinoes@gmail.com

Printed by European Printers Ltd
Published by AKAKIA Publications

December 2022

46 Warberry Road, N22 7TQ, London, UK
T. 0044 208 2457 849

publications@akakia.net
www.akakia.net

IN MEMORY OF MY BELOVED FATHER

PANTELIS M. LAMPADARIOS

&

WITH LOVE TO MY BELOVED MOTHER

KALIOPPE LAMPADARIOS

NOTE BY THE AUTHOR

The *"The Catechesism of the Orthodox Church (In 375 Questions and Answers)"* is the summary of my previous book *"Orthodox Teachings. The Catechism of the One, Holy, Catholic and Apostolic Church According to Holy Scriptures and Sacred Apostolic Tradition".* This new publication was requested for the benefit of the all English speaking Orthodox Christians, as well as those who desire knowledge of the True Christian Faith.

I believe that the *"The Catechesism of the Orthodox Church"* will be of great help for all those who teach the Orthodox Faith because the whole context is based upon the two Sources of Divine Revelation: Holy Scripture (Old and New Testament) and Apostolic Tradition. Following the Teachings of the Holy Apostles and the Fathers of the Orthodox Church, this book assures the reader the clear Teachings of the Orthodox Faith as it is enriched by many biblical references and opinions of the great and Holy Fathers.

Anyone who truly wishes to love God must know as much as possible about Him and anyone who professes true love of Christ will practice His Commandments. But how can anyone practice God's Commandments if he ignores His Teachings? To know Christ means that one knows His Teachings. Ignorance of the Teachings of Holy Scripture means ignorance of Christ. If we ignore our own Lord and Saviour, how can we achieve our Salvation and Sanctification in Christ?

I wish to express me heartfelt gratitude to all the members of the **"Holy Cross Press"** for this publication.

I pray that this humble effort will bring forth its fruits for the glory of our God, the Father and the Son and the Holy Spirit and the benifit of His people.

+PANTELEIMON, Metopolitan of Antinoes
(Retired Archbishop of the Greek Orthodox Patriarchate of Alexandria and All Africa)

Kalymnos-Greece, 16th November, 2022

INTRODUCTION
CHAPTER ONE.

Question 1: What is the meaning of the word "Dogma"?

Answer: The Greek word *"dogma"* (*"δόγμα"* = *"doctrine"*) means a *"precept,"* a *"decree,"* an *"opinion,"* or a *"law."* As a fundamental philosophical principle, the members of a society or a school of philosophy were bound to accept its validity and authenticity. Among the ancient Greeks and Romans the word *"dogma"* was used to refer to:

1) philosophical conceptions, and

2) directives, which were to be precisely fulfilled.[1]

In the Old Testament Greek (Septuagint; LXX) the word *"dogma"* (*"decree"*) is used to predicate a decree of legal authority or decisions of kings.[2] In the New Testament the word is found five times. In Luke 2:1 and Acts 17:7 it is used to express a royal decree; in Colossians 2:14 and Ephesians 2:15 it is applied to the precepts of the Mosaic Law; and in the Book of Acts 16: 4 the word is used to signify the decision of the Holy Apostles, which they took under the Guidance of the Holy Spirit at the Apostolic Council (49 AD). [3]

The True Path of Faith that has always been carefully preserved in the history of the Church was called *"straight"* or *"right"* (*"ορθός"* – *"orthos"*). In early Christian literature there is constant mention of the keeping of *"the Rule of Faith"* or the *"Rule of Truth."* Orthodoxy therefore means the straight, the right, the true way of Christian Faith.

The Doctrines of the Orthodox Church are strictly based upon Holy Scripture and Holy Apostolic Tradition.[4] St Basil the Great (379 AD) says, *"the Doctrine of Faith has as its foundation our Lord Jesus Christ."* [5]

---

[1] Xenophon, *Anabasis,* III, 3, 5. Polybius, III, 27, 7. St Justin, the philosopher and martyr, *1 Apology,* ch. 26, 46, in *B*, v. 3, p. 175. Cf. Ibid, *1 Apology,* ch. 26, 46, in Migne, *P.G.,* 6, 369. St Isidorus of Pelusion, in Migne, *P.G.,* 78, 185. "Sapientia neque de se ipsa deputare debet, neque de suis decretis, quae philosophi vocant dogmata, quorum nullum sine scelere prodi potest" (Cicero, Quaestiones academicae, IV. 9).
[2] Dan. 2:12-13; 6:8-9. Esther 3:9. II Maccab. 10:8; 15:36. Luke 2:1. Acts 17:7. Ephes. 2:15. Col. 2:14, 20.
[3] Acts 15:1-29. Cf. Evdokimov, *Orthodoxia,* p. 235.
[4] 2 Tim. 2:15.
[5] St Basil the Great, *To Isaiah,* ch. 5, 152, in Migne, *P.G.,* 30, 368A-B. Theodoretus of Cyrus, in Migne, *P.G.,* 82, 249.

Teachings that are not founded upon the above two Sources cannot claim any place amongst the Doctrines of the Orthodox Church.[6]

The Doctrines are not any rational conceptions, nor images or symbols, which interpret personal feelings or religious opinion of individuals.[7] The Doctrines are the authentic declarations of Faith necessary to Salvation, the precise clarification of Holy Scripture and Holy Apostolic Tradition, harmoniously combined together into a single and organic whole.

God has revealed the Doctrines not for theoretical or intellectual purposes, but for man's Salvation.[8] The Doctrines present the authentic interpretation of Divine Revelation through the Guidance of the Holy Spirit Who, as promised by our Lord and Saviour Jesus Christ, the Son of God, *"will guide you to all the Truth."*[9]

The need to secure the Truths revealed by God through Divine Revelation, led the Orthodox Church to investigate, compare, formulate, develop and define the Teachings of Holy Scripture through legitimate theological speculation in Local, Ecumenical, and General Councils. Doctrines are not just official statements of the content of Christian Faith, which are scientifically presented,[10] they are all the Teachings of the Orthodox Christian Faith, which are contained in Holy Scripture and Holy Apostolic Tradition. These Teachings of the Faith have been experienced within the life of the Orthodox Church and have been defined, explained and formulated in part by her Holy Councils.[11] It is impossible to define the Doctrines without reference to their context, for they are the Operations of God within and through His Church.[12]

The whole heart of the Orthodox Church is established on the new status of man with God.[13] This Relationship was initiated by the loving Act of God[14] and yet depends upon the response of man and his cooperation.[15] The Orthodox Christian Religion is the elimination of discord between God and man made possible by and functioning through sacred fellowship ("*koinonia*") founded by our Lord and Saviour Jesus Christ, the Son of God,

---

[6] Trempelas, *Dogmatique,* v. I, p. 5.

[7] Ibid., p. 7.

[8] Androutsos, *Dogmatique,* p. 26.

[9] John 16:13.

[10] Androutsos, pp. 2, 3 and 20-31. Balanos, *Is Theology science,* Athens, 1906. Skaltsoune, *Religion and Science.*

[11] Androutsos, *Dogmatique,* pp. 1-2. Trempelas, *Dogmatique,* v. I, pp. 6-7. Pomazansky, *Theology,* p. 25. Karmires, *Synopsis,* p. 5. Bratsiotes, «The meaning», v. 28, t. 4. Makarios, *Enchiridion,* p.11.

[12] Rhosse, *System,* p. 28

[13] Matth. 26:28. Mark 14:24. Luke 22:20. 1 Corinth. 11:25. He. 8:8-13; 9:15, 20; 12:24.

[14] John 3:16.

[15] Matth. 17:4; 19:17, 21. Mark 8:34-35; 10:43-44. Luke 9:23-24. Mesoloras, *Practical Theology,* pp. 1-18. *Symbolique,* v. III, pp.1-33.

and the re-establishment of the correct relationship of man to God.[16] As the Living Body of Christ, the Orthodox Church is called not only to confess her Faith to Jesus Christ before the whole world,[17] but also to live according to His Teachings.[18]

The Orthodox Church acts through a reflective process of human insight and human reasoning. She presents that which has been defined and taught by herself as the authentic and infallible interpreter of Holy Scripture and Holy Apostolic Tradition. The Orthodox Church formulated the Teaching of our Lord necessary to Salvation in unchangeable terms and statements called *"Doctrines."*[19]

The aim of Orthodox Theology is not to demonstrate the logical necessity of Doctrines, which would then subvert the true conception of *"Doctrines,"*[20] but to present the faith of the Orthodox Church as an organic whole.[21]

We must note that besides Doctrines there are also *"pious opinions"* that are allowed to circulate freely among the members of different schools of thought as their own personal conclusions and speculations, provided that they do not violate or oppose any of the Doctrines of the Church. These are called *"theological opinions,"* or *"theologoumena"*[22] (*"matters open for discussion"*).

Question 2: What are the essential characteristics of the Doctrines?

Answer: Each Dogma has two essential characteristics:

a) *The internal and objective characteristic.* Each Dogma originates from and is based upon the two Sources of Holy Scripture and Holy Apostolic Tradition. It is the Truth that is revealed by God to man (objective view), an

b) *The external-ecclesiastic and subjective characteristic.* The Church as the infallible Interpreter and Guardian of Divine Truth, investigates,

---

[16] Androutsos, *Dogmatique*, p. 21.
[17] Matth. 10:32. Luke 12:8. Heb. 13:15.
[18] Matth. 28:20. John 13:34-35; 14:15, 21, 23-24; 15:10, 12. 1 Corinth. 14:37. 1 John 2:3-6; 3:22-24; 4:21; 5:2-5. 2 John 6-9. Rev. 12:17; 14:12; 22:14.
[19] Gavin, *Orthodox Thoughts,* p. 5. Trempelas, *Dogmatique,* v. I, p. 8. Androutsos, *Dogmatique,* pp. 3, 9 and 12.
[20] Gavin, *Orthodox Thoughts,* p. 10. Androutsos, *Dogmatique,* p. 31.
[21] Gavin, *Orthodox Thoughts,* p. 7. Androutsos, *Dogmatique,* p. 22.
[22] Ibid, p. 3. Cf. Gavin, *Orthodox Thoughts,* p. 17.

compares, correlates, explicates and interprets with authenticity and infallibly the Teachings of Christian Faith (subjective view).[23]

Holy Scripture and Holy Apostolic Tradition contain the Divine Truths. The formulation of these Truths into systematic Doctrines is not the work of any faithful, but that of the Church.[24] Holy Scripture stresses this in the following words of St Peter: *"No prophecy of the Scripture is of any private interpretation. For the prophecy came not in old time by the will of man: but Holy men of God spoke as they were moved by the Holy Spirit."*[25]

The Orthodox Church as the Guardian and Interpreter of Divine Revelation, had received the instruction from our Risen Lord *"to teach"* the faithful the Word of God with authority and authenticity.[26] The Church does not reveal a new Revelation but unfolds and interprets the Teachings of the one unique Divine Revelation.[27] These Teachings remain unchangeable and it is essential that they be accepted by all those who wish to be members of Christ's Body and thereby to be saved. The Truths of the Orthodox Church define her *"catholic consciousness,"* a consciousness that is guided always by the Holy Spirit.[28]

The term *"catholic"* means *"universal"* as referring to the Orthodox Church of all times, *"where there is neither Greek nor Jew, circumcision nor uncircumcision, Barbarian, Scythian, bond nor free: but Christ is all and in all."*[29] The Teachings of the early Church have been preserved in the Orthodox Church, which is the One, Holy, Catholic and Apostolic Church.

Question 3: What is the relation between Truths of Faith and Logic?

Answer: Religious Truths cannot be examined under the microscope of science as any other object or phenomenon of this material world. The spiritual world is revealed only to our souls, if and when the Light of Faith enlightens them.

Religious Truths remain unapproachable to man's reasoning, because man is incapable of fully understanding God Who is the only Infinite Being,[30] the Cause of Divine Revelation and the Source of all logic.[31] Man

---

[23] Trempelas, *Dogmatique*, v. I, pp. 7-8. Cf. Gavin, *Orthodox Thoughts*, pp. 5, 11. Boulgareos, *Theologicon*, pp. 22-23. Androutsos, *Dogmatique*, p. 2. Makarios, *Enchiridion*, pp. 19-20.
[24] Androutsos, *Dogmatique*, p. 9.
[25] 2 Peter 1:20-21.
[26] Androutsos, *Dogmatique*, p. 9.
[27] Ibid, p. 13.
[28] Pomazansky, *Theology*, p. 25.
[29] Col. 3:11.
[30] St Basil the Great, *To Psalm 115(116):1*, in Migne, *P.G.*, 30, 104B.
[31] Androutsos, *Dogmatique*, p. 12.

uses images from this visible world in order to compare and describe the things that are in heaven[32] and yet they remain for him a Mystery, which can be understood only through faith.[33]

Some Truths are called *"articula mixta"*[34] because they are approachable by man's mind and can be approximately understood. One must never forget that whatever pertains to the invisible world cannot be proven mathematically in order to convince man's mind to accept its results without any questions or doubts.[35]

It is without any doubt that God reveals Himself to man and at the same time He is the Source and Creator of True Logic (*"ορθός λόγος"* = *"orthos logos"*). Logic or reasoning can prepare the way to faith but it is never the source of faith. Logic and Christian Life assist the faithful in their search for an essential understanding of the Essence of Faith. This combination of true reasoning and true faith leads man to a sound assurance of God's Revelation. It assists the Orthodox Church as well to examine the credibility of the sources and the carriers of Divine Revelation and to formulate correctly the articles of true Orthodox Christian Faith.[36]

Our Lord and Saviour Jesus Christ, the Son of God, used examples of this visible world in order to guide man, through true reasoning, to the understanding of the Truths of the invisible world.[37]

Logic is not blinded by faith. It is enlightened through experience and the radiance of Divine Revelation, which, although it is accepted by faith, does not cease to offer knowledge that is objectively true. Clement the Alexandrian supports the principal that *"neither knowledge without faith, nor faith without knowledge."*[38] Therefore, the Doctrines of the Orthodox Church are not just teachings of Christian Faith but also knowledge received within and experienced through faith.[39]

The Truth of Orthodox Christian Doctrine contains a Mystery that is approachable only by faith but inevitably always remains a Mystery even to the pious.[40] Faith continues to be based on Divine Authenticity and is never

---

[32] Heb. 11:1.

[33] 1 Corinth. 13:12.

[34] Trempelas, *Dogmatique,* v. I, pp. 11-12. Makarios, *Enchiridion,* p. 15. Androutsos, *Dogmatique,* p. 12-20.

[35] Trempelas, *Dogmatique,* v. I, p. 11.

[36] Trempelas, *Dogmatique,* v. I, p. 12.

[37] Owen, *Theology,* p. 4. Cf. John 10:30, 37-38.

[38] Clement the Alexandrian, *Stromata,* V, ch. 1, in *B*, v. 8, p.110. Theodoretus of Cyrus, *Homily 1 about Faith,* in Migne, *P.G.,* 83, 816A. Origen, *About Principals,* book IV, ch. 1, in Migne, *P.G.,* 11, 249.

[39] John 7:17.

[40] Androutsos, *Dogmatique,* p. 18.

displaced by knowledge.[41] Nevertheless, the information and assurance of the context of Divine Revelation, experienced through true faith, becomes sound and steadfast by the assistance of knowledge and consequently *"strong and undoubted proof of what we have received by faith."* [42]

Doctrine becomes part of man's knowledge. Man embraces Divine Truth and clarifies its context by using correct words and by formulating its Teachings with the precise articles of faith.[43] This development is not something that changes Divine Truth but is a progress that does not change its Essence.[44]

Knowledge and faith grow together and affect one another. Through faith one achieves full consciousness of the Knowledge of Divine Revelation.[45] Full consciousness means to have a wide and precise knowledge of all things concerning God's Revelation.[46] The faithful comes to the full knowledge of faith by using his intellectual capability (logic), through which he is able to examine, understand, accept and formulate the Truths revealed by God through His Orthodox Church to him.

The Truths of Faith do not contradict man's logic even though they are above man's understanding. They become the pure Light that enlightens the mind and the understanding of man.

As Orthodox Christians we must *"be ready always to give a defence to everyone who asks you a reason for the hope that is in you, with meekness and fear."* [47] When we know and understand our Orthodox Faith, we prevent heresies (false teachings) entering from within the flock of Christ.[48] The Power of True Knowledge is like a protective wall that does not allow the Doctrines to become corrupted by those who wish to change the Divine Truths entrusted to us by God.

---

[41] Trempelas, *Dogmatique, v.* I, p. 13. Boulgareos, *Theologicon,* p. 21.
[42] Clement the Alexandrian, *Stromata,* VII, ch. 10, 57. in *B,* v. 8, p. 271.
[43] Boulgareos, *Theologicon,* p. 19.
[44] Androutsos, *Dogmatique,* p. 14.
[45] Ephes. 4:13.
[46] Trempelas, *Dogmatique, v.* I, p. 14. Androutsos, *Dogmatique,* p. 9-12. Rhosse, *System,* p. 61.
[47] 1 Peter 3:15.
[48] Clement the Alexandrian, *Stromata,* I, ch. 20, in *B,* v. 7, p. 275. St John Damascenus, *Catechesis,* I, 5, in Migne, *P.G.,* 94, 801. Boulgareos, *Theologicon,* pp. 20-21.

CHAPTER TWO
DIVINE REVELATION

Question 4: What is Divine Revelation?

Answer: It was an absolute necessity that God, the Creator of all things, visible and invisible, reveal Himself after man's Fall to him whose mind and conscience had been darkened by sin[49] and thus was unable to restore his relationship with his Creator. God is not only superior to His Creation but He also works in it. In accordance with His Divine Nature and Character, God, Who is the Source of Revelation, reveals the Mysteries of His Existence and His Divine Will to man[50] who is the receiver.[51] Man, being created in God's *"image and likeness,"* [52] is capable of receiving Revelations concerning Almighty God. This Act whereby God makes Himself known to man is called *"Divine Revelation "*[53] and although it is one, it has been revealed to man in many ways. We can distinguish this Revelation between the *Natural Revelation* and the *Supernatural Revelation*.

Question 5: What is Natural Revelation?

Answer: Natural Revelation is on one hand, the miracle of nature itself and the sphere in which it unfolds. On the other hand, it is man's inner and spiritual world. King David cries out saying: *"O Lord, how manifold art Thy works! In wisdom hast Thou made them all: the earth is full of Thy riches."*[54]

God always reveals Himself to man who is favoured by God's Divine Energies. Man becomes the receiver of Divine Revelation, not in a passive condition nor as a simple spectator. By using all his intellectual ability of understanding everything that is revealed to him, man is able to see whatever God reveals and hear whatever He instructs. The complex inner world of man does not consist only of his logic that enables him to examine

---

[49] Rom. 1:21.
[50] He. 1:2-3; 9:26; 11:3. Rom. 1:19-20; 9:4-5. Acts 2:17-21; 14: 15-17; 17:27. 1 Peter 1:20. Col. 1:16. Gal. 4:4-6. John 1:3. Num. 12:6, 8. Deut. 5:2-3. Is. 55:6. Jer. 23:23. Psalm 2:8; 32(33):6.
[51] Trempelas, *Dogmatique*, v. I, pp. 79-80. Plato of Moscow, *Orthodox Teaching*, p. 68.
[52] Gen. 1:26.
[53] Rhosse, *System*, p. 447. Mesoloras, *Symbolique*, v. III, pp. 17-21, 26-32. Trempelas, *Dogmatique*, v. I, p. 79. Romanides, *Dogmatique, v. 1*, p. 121. Mitsopoulos, *Themata*, p. 20.
[54] Psalm 103(104): 24.

God's Work in nature and in life, but also consists of his conscience that *"bears witness"* to God's Works and *"the Law written"* in his heart.[55]

Natural Revelation offers the fundamental basis of all forms of religion, faith in a Higher Being, Who is the Creator and Governor of all, visible and invisible, His Justice and Providence, to Whom all logical creatures – Angels and man - are accountable. [56] Many theories have been developed amongst the diverse religions concerning the teachings of *"good"* and *"evil,"* *"virtue"* and *"sin."*

Question 6: What is Supernatural Revelation?

Answer: Undoubtedly Natural Revelation is the forerunner of the Supernatural Divine Revelation by which God spoke directly to His elect - the Prophets (Old Testament) and the Apostles (New Testament). They are His conscious instruments who received His Divine Will and who, through the enlightenment of the Holy Spirit, understood the Divine Mysteries revealed to them. But the fullness and complete Revelation of God to the world is revealed in the Person of His Son, our Lord and Saviour Jesus Christ.[57]

God reveals His Divine Revelation for the Salvation of mankind in Holy Scripture, Apostolic Tradition and within and through His Holy Orthodox Church.[58] The Revelation is a Truth that is manifested through a miracle by God's Almightiness.[59] The Holy Fathers of the Orthodox Church, through their unanimous Teachings, explain and interpret the Divine Mysteries.[60]

God's Revelation takes place in the following ways:

God reveals Himself in man's history through extraordinary and supernatural events.[61] Man's Salvation is achieved in history, having Christ as its centre. Holy Scripture (Old Testament) contains historical events that prophesy of the Coming of the Messiah and are fulfilled in the Person of the God-Man, Jesus Christ (New Testament).

---

[55] Rom. 2:15; 14. 2 Corinth. 3:3. Psalm 103(104): 24.
[56] Matth. 12:36-37; 5:21-22; 10:15; 11:20-24; 12:18, 31-32; 23:33; 25:31-46. Mark 3:28-30. Luke 10:14-15. John 3:18; 5:22, 24-30; 8:15-16; 12:31, 48; 16:8,11. Acts 10:42; 17:31. Rom. 2:16; 3:6. 1 Corinth. 11:31-32. 2 Thess. 1:5. 1 Tim. 5:24. 2 Tim. 4:1, 8. Heb. 9: 27; 10:26-31; 12:23; 13:4. James 2:13; 5:9, 12. 1 Peter 4:5-6. 2 Peter 2:4-22. 1 John 4:17. Jude 6, 15. Rev. 14:7; 16:7; 18:10; 19:2; 20:12-13.
[57] 1 John 1:1-3.
[58] Boulgareos, *Theologicon,* p. 22.
[59] Plato, *Orthodox Teaching,* p. 24.
[60] Boulgareos, *Theologicon*, p. 23. Androutsos, *Dogmatique*, p. 11.
[61] Frangopoulos, *Christian Faith,* pp. 15-16. Mitsopoulos, *Themata*, p. 21.

God reveals His Will to His elect *"in spirit."* When the Prophets received God's Revelation, they were *"in spirit."* [62] This means that their understanding and senses are put aside completely[63] or partially for a short period of time.[64] Being freed from worldly things, God reveals His Will[65] and the things which He promises to them. Their minds and their understanding, enlightened by the Holy Spirit, were opened and elevated to a higher level of understanding and at the same time their full conscience and intellectual abilities were preserved.[66]

God is revealed in dreams, visions and words. These types of Revelations are assisted in many cases by the bodily senses. The Spirit of God reveals Himself to the spirit of man who hears the Voice of God with his physical senses and sounds or sees the Mysteries of God with his physical eyes. God assures man of the Divine Revelation through which He Teaches and Reveals the Mysteries of His Divine Will through His Prophets.[67]

Question 7: Who are the instruments of God's Revelation?

Answer: In order for God to reveal Himself and His Will to the world, He choses certain people who are suitable to be His Instruments. God *"at various times and in various ways"* has communicated with man *"and spoke in time past to the fathers by the Prophets,"* [68] but *"in these last days (He has) spoken to us by His Son, Whom He had appointed Heir of all things."*[69] The Son of God, our Lord and Saviour Jesus Christ, is not any instrument of God's Revelation like the Angels, Prophets or Apostles. On the contrary, He Himself Who reveals the Name of God the Father to mankind is God's Revelation to the world.[70] The Knowledge of the Divine

---

[62] Rev. 1:10. Ez. 11:24. Zach. 7:12..

[63] 2 Corinth. 12:2-4. Acts 10:11. St Ecumenius, in Migne, *P.G.,* 118, 180.

[64] Acts 12:6-11. 1 Samuel (1 Kings) 9:19. Is. 6:1-3, 9-10; 7:14-16. Jer. 1:4-9. Ez. 1:1, 4-28; 2:1-2; 8:4-18; 40:2-49; 43:2-7; 44:2; 47. Daniel 7:1-14. Hos. 1:1-2. Joel 2:28-32. Amos 9:1. Jonah 1:1-2; 3:1-2; 4:9-11.

[65] Theodorus Mopsuestias, *To Naoum 1:1,* in Migne, *P.G.,* 66, 401B-D, 404A. Theodoretus of Cyrus, *To Ezekiel 3:22,* in Migne, *P.G.,* 81, 852; Ibid, *To Naoum, Argument,* in Migne, *P.G.,* 81, 1789A. Origen, *Against Celsus,* book VII, 4, in Migne, *P.G.,* 11, 1425B. St John Chrysostom, *To Psalm 44:1-2,* in Migne, *P.G.,* 55, 183α, 185β.

[66] Didemus the Blind, *To 2 Corinthians,* in Migne, *P.G.,* 39, 1677A, 1704.

[67] Nu. 12:6-8. Is. 2:1. Jer. 1:1, 11,14; 2:2,5; 3:12; 13. Ez. 1:3; 6:1; 7:1. Dan. 7. Amos 7:1. Hos. 1:2. Joel 1:1. Jonas 1:1. Mich. 1:1. Soph. 1:1. Zach. 1:1. Acts 10:4. Rev. 1:10. Matth. 1:20; 2:12-13. Luke 1:11-12, 28; 2:9-10, 13, 26. Acts 2:17; 16:9; 18:9. Theodorus Mopsuestias, *To Naoum 1:1,* Migne, *P.G.,* 66, 404.

[68] Heb. 1:1.

[69] Heb. 1:2.

[70] John 17:6. Cf. Romanides, *Dogmatique,* v. 1, pp. 122-124.

Mysteries are by nature known to Him because He is the Source of all Divine Knowledge.[71] This is the reason why Christ proclaims to be the only Teacher[72] Who speaks with authority[73] as no one else has ever done before.[74]

In Jesus Christ the Messiah Who was awaited by the Jews, God's Revelation is fulfilled and perfected. The Prophets and Apostles taught what was revealed to them and what the Holy Spirit had unfolded, thereby Guiding them *"to all the Truth,"*[75] but Christ reveals Himself as well as what He has heard from the Father to the world.[76]

It is obvious that we cannot speak of God-inspired Scripture without Revelation, either objectively or subjectively.[77] St Paul received Divine Revelation before he preached the Gospel that was revealed to him.[78] God spoke to the Prophets even before He gave the Law to Moses and in other cases Divine Revelation was written many years after the time of its manifestation.[79]

Question 8: What is Internal and External Revelation?

Answer: The Action of the Spirit of God communicating directly with the human spirit is a Revelation called *"Inspiration,"* or *"internal Revelation."*[80] At the moment of the Revelation man's free-will and actions are not precluded, for he acts as an agent of the Holy Spirit.[81] Man is in full possession of his intellectual abilities and consciousness. When the Spirit of God acts along with human understanding, the Revelation is referred to as *"external."* Such manifestations of God's Energies act as validation and guarantee of the inner Revelation made to man's spirit.[82]

The source from which we receive our knowledge concerning God's Revelation can be identified as *"external"* or *"internal."* The former uses philosophy and history as the source of its arguments, whereas the latter has

---

[71] Col. 2:3.
[72] Matth. 23:8.
[73] Matth. 7:29.
[74] John 7:46.
[75] John 16:13. Cf. Theophylactus of Bulgaria, *To John,* in Migne, *P.G.,* 123, 1236D.
[76] John 8:26.
[77] Trempelas, *Dogmatique,* v. I, p. 97.
[78] 2 Corinth. 12:1-4. Gal. 1:11-12.
[79] Acts 1:1. 2 Corinth. 12:1-4. St John Chrysostom, *To Isaiah 2:1*, in Migne, *P.G.,* 56, 27. Theodoretus of Cyrus, *To Ezekiel 10:2*, in Migne, *P.G.,* 81, 821. St Irenaeus, *Heresies*, II, 33, 3; III, 1, 1, in Migne, *P.G.,* 7, 832, 844. Ibid, Hadjephraimides, pp. 185, 190.
[80] Gavin, *Orthodox Thoughts,* p. 11.
[81] Col. 1:29.
[82] Rhosse, *System*, p. 444-445, 462.

the revealed Truth from Holy Scripture and Sacred Tradition.[83] Tradition in its widest meaning includes Revelation or the Teachings of our Lord and His Apostles that have been meticulously handed down from one generation to the next, preserved as sacred Treasure in Holy Scripture and other monuments of the past.[84] In its narrower meaning it is applied to the Teachings of the Church that have not been recorded in Holy Scripture.[85] The Holy Bible takes the oral Tradition for granted, for the Christian Faith was preached at first only by word of mouth.[86] *"Holy Tradition is not only the continuation of the Word of God contained in Holy Scripture, but also the trustworthy guide and interpreter of it."*[87]

Question 9: What is Internal Revelation?

Answer: It is the Uncreated Energy of Divine Grace by which man's mind and understanding are opened to the Truth,[88] which is accepted only by those who are pure in heart and spirit.

Question 10: What is the difference between the objective manifestation and the subjective Revelation?

Answer: There is a difference between the objective manifestation and the subjective Revelation. The former is offered by God as a Promise or a Prophesy to His Elect, the Prophets, whereas the latter takes place in the heart of man when the veil of sin has been lifted.[89] Only when this veil is removed can man understand Heavenly things[90] because sin is an obstacle that prevents him from ascending into Heavenly places and partaking of Divine Knowledge. Also in many cases, objective manifestation and subjective Revelation occur simultaneously in order for God's instruments to reveal His Divine Will to the world. Thus the *"external manifestation"* entering man's heart becomes at that very moment *"internal Revelation."*[91]

It must be emphasized that the external Revelation is complete and has no need of any additional teachings to its Truth. God reveals His Truth

---

[83] Boulgareos, *Theologicon,* p. 22. Cf. Gavin, *Orthodox Thoughts,* p. 17. Balanos, *Orthodox Catechesis*, p. 4. Pomazansky, *Theology,* pp. 24-25.
[84] Androutsos, *Dogmatique,* pp. 6-7, note 7.
[85] Gavin, *Orthodox Thoughts,* p. 17.
[86] 2 Thess. 2:14. 1 Corinth. 11:2. 2 Tim. 1:13-14; 2:2. 2 John v. 12.
[87] Mesoloras, *Practcal Theology*, p. 29.
[88] Luke 24:16, 31. Acts 9:17-18. 2 Corinth. 3:14, 16-18. Rev. 3:7.
[89] Trempelas, *Dogmatique,* v. I, p. 92. Boulgareos, *Theologicon*, pp. 14-15.
[90] John 3:12.
[91] Trempelas, *Dogmatique,* v. I, p. 92.

in time, especially through His Son, our Lord and Saviour Jesus Christ. This Truth is passed down from one generation of man to the next, who, as members of the Mystical Body of Christ – the Orthodox Church - teaches and clarifies it. The internal Revelation is the Grace of God that acts upon each individual,[92] and is manifested throughout all time. Our Lord assured us that *"No man can come to Me, unless the Father Who hath sent Me draws him."*[93] It is obvious that the internal Revelation, by which man is attracted to God and acquainted to Divine Illumination and Sanctification, is subjective, whereas the many manifestations by which God's Truth is revealed, are objective.

Revelation may be examined by two criteria: external and internal. The external criterion is that of a miracle as an indication of the Divine Will, Power and Love of God.[94] The internal criterion is both positive and negative: positive in that the Truth *"satisfies the religious and ethical ideals of man, and works towards his holiness and happiness"*[95] and negative in that it is capable of being shown consistently with other Revelation and is not averse to reason.[96]

Question 11: What are the fundamental notes of genuine Revelation?

Answer: 1. Original, Creative and New. God works with man in his religious life, and His Spirit shares the activity of reaching Him with the human soul. This distinct and new act of God's Revelation to man is not to be appropriated by the individual to whom the Revelation is made. On the contrary, it must be proclaimed abroad as it is a Truth for all mankind. The individual acts as an agent for the promulgation of the new Revelation and his guarantee is the evidence of the miracle. There is an exact correlation and parallel between the Revelation to the human soul through God's Inspiration and the occurrence of a miracle in the order of natural phenomena. Both are supernatural.[97]

2. Self-consistency. Each new Revelation serves to explain better and to unify the content of sacred Truth. It comes to supplement and to complete, not to subvert. It must form part of an ordered whole, yet the

---

[92] Matth. 16:17.
[93] John 6:44. St Cyril of Alexandria, *To John 6:44, 45*, in Migne, *P.G.*, 73, 552, 553. Theophylactus of Bulgaria, in Migne, *P.G.*, 123, 1305.
[94] 1 Corinth. 2:4.
[95] Rhosse, *System*, p. 446.
[96] Gavin, *Orthodox Thoughts*, p. 11-12.
[97] Gavin, *Orthodox Thoughts*, p. 12.

method of its introduction is always extraordinarily subjective as well as being an objective declaration of God's Will.[98]

It is only because of our limited understanding that such extraordinary events may be regarded as contradictory to the order of nature. The terms *"natural"* and *"supernatural,"* *"rational"* and *"superrational,"* are only relative and coined by man with limited experience of his own finite plane.[99]

Man uses the word *"superrational"* to describe the illumination of man's mind by God's Illuminating Grace, meaning the Revelation of the Truth to which man's reasoning could not attain. Whereas on the other hand, we apply the term *"supernatural"* to an extraordinary occurrence in the realm of the physical world, the causes of which are not the ordinary secondary causes resident in the world of experience.[100] The two spheres of *"natural"* and *"supernatural,"* *"rational"* and *"superrational"* are logically helpful and legitimately useful because of our limited and finite range of knowledge.[101]

3. Positive Character. Divine Revelation has the characteristic of a gradual and progressive development.[102] This development does not violate the finality or positive character of any previous Revelation. Each successive step in the process is conditioned by the Divine Will of God foreordaining the given sequence of the gradual Illumination on God's part, and of the response, acceptance and appropriation on man's part. The relationship of the two functioning properly, forbids the refusal of hearing a new Revelation by a too literal adherence to the letter of past Revelation. At the same time it inhibits an unregulated and unfettered evolution of novel and uninspired developments by means of the fixed content of past Revelation.[103]

Question 12: What is External Revelation?

Answer: The external manifestation of the Divine Will of God, in the order of natural phenomena, acts as a validation and guarantee of the subjective Inspiration vouchsafed to man. There is a close and intimate relationship

---

[98] Gavin, *Orthodox Thoughts*, pp. 12-13.
[99] Ibid, *Orthodox Thoughts*, p. 13.
[100] Ibid, *System*, p. 451.
[101] Gavin, *Orthodox Thoughts*, p. 13.
[102] Rhosse, *System*, p. 452.
[103] Gavin, *Orthodox Thoughts*, p. 14.

between the external and the internal, the objective and subjective forms of Revelation.[104]

The Revelation to the spirit of man acts upon that which in Creation is closest to God. Subjective Revelation or Inspiration is of a higher order. The subjective Revelation is higher than the objective Revelation, or a miracle.

External Revelation seals, guarantees, validates, and authenticates the subjective Revelation given to man directly from God. The Illumination of man's spirit by God is not a mechanical, magical, or automatic domination of man by the Holy Spirit. The Illuminated man cooperates with God in order that the Revelation may become a fact to mankind. Man does not abandon either his reasoning, conscience, or will.[105]

The most complete Revelation of God to man was manifested in the Person of our Lord and Saviour Jesus Christ. The Son and Word of God the Father was always God before all eternity.[106] He became perfect Man by the Holy Spirit and of the Ever-Virgin Mary, the Theotokos, and has united the two Natures, that of perfect God and perfect Man, in the one Person of Jesus Christ. Jesus Christ is the climax of God's Revelation to the world. The Prophets and the Holy people of the Old Testament were united in spirit with God only for a period of time as conveyors of His Divine Will whereas the Son of God was always united with His Father by Nature from all eternity. The Incarnation of the Word of God is the perfect and final Revelation of God to man. It is the unique Miracle and the greatest of all miracles.[107]

CHAPTER THREE
APOSTOLIC TRADITION

Question 13: What is Apostolic Tradition?

Answer: Apostolic Tradition is the *"unwritten word"*[108] of our Lord and Saviour Jesus Christ, the Son of God, and His Holy Apostles, which has been preserved and experienced by the faithful in the inward Life of the Orthodox Church and was written in their hearts by the Grace and Power of the Holy Spirit. At the beginning of the Christian era, for more than twenty years, the Church had no written Scripture (New Testament) and *"Tradition*

---

[104] Gavin, *Orthodox Thoughts*, p. 15.
[105] Rhosse, *System*, pp. 461-462.
[106] John 17:5. Gavin, *Orthodox Thoughts*, p 16.
[107] Ephes. 4:13. Rhosse, *System*, pp. 463-466.
[108] Boulgareos, *Theologicon*, p. 39. Evdokimov, *Orthodoxia*, pp. 265-268. Kefalas, *Catechesis*, pp. 177, 260-264. Frangopoulos, *Christian Faith*, pp. 21-23. Mitsopoulos, *Themata*, p. 28.

was the standard of faith, first in time as well as in importance."[109] When converts were taught, they did not study from books but were instructed by word of mouth.[110] These Teachings, during the first half of the first century AD, were either oral or written Apostolic Tradition. After the deaths of the Holy Apostles, the written Tradition, Gospels and Epistles were considered God-inspired and new when compared to the oral Teaching of the Holy Apostles.

The oral Apostolic Tradition, under the Illumination and Guidance of the Holy Spirit, formed the catholic ecclesiastical conscience and Apostolic prudence of the faithful. This Tradition has been preserved and passed down from one generation to the next, until this day, within the One, Holy, Catholic and Apostolic Church (the Eastern Orthodox Church) and is equal to Holy Scripture and one of the two Sources of Divine Revelation.[111]

The centre of Holy Tradition is Christ and Communion with Him as well as the Testimony of His friends, the Prophets, Apostles and the Saints.[112]

Apostolic Tradition differs from all Ecclesiastical Traditions. Nevertheless, the former has been incorporated in the ancient Creeds of the Orthodox Church, in the writings and interpretations of Holy Scripture by the Holy Fathers (*consensus Patrum*), the Decrees and Articles of Faith issued by the Holy Ecumenical or Local Councils (Synods), in the Divine Mysteries (Holy Sacraments) and in the life of the universal Orthodox Church.

The Holy Apostles never considered it a priority to chronicle all they had learnt from Christ but rather to teach all nations according to His Commandment. For this reason most of them did not immediately record His Teachings although some later wrote down part of them because of certain problems that had arisen within the Church. But not everything concerning our Lord's many Teachings and miracles could be written down as stressed by St John the Evangelist.[113]

These instructions of *"sound words"*[114] highlight the importance of the oral Apostolic Tradition, which is the first Source of Divine Revelation and the main Source of preservation, transference and spreading of its

---

[109] Rhosse, *Dogmatique*, p. 481. Mesoloras, *Symbolique*, III, pp. 63-77.

[110] For an illustration of this method and its developments, Cf. The History of the Catechetical School of Alexandria, P.M. Papadopoulos, *The Catechetical System in the ancient ecumeny;* Papadopoulos, *St Dionysius the Great,* Alexandria, 1918.

[111] Cf. Mitsopoulos, *Themata*, p. 32.

[112] Romanides, *Dogmatiques,* v. 1, p. 121.

[113] John 20:30-31.

[114] 2 Tim. 1:13. Theodoretos of Cyrus, *To 2 Timothy,* in Migne, *P.G.,* 82, 836.

Truth.[115] Thus, in the very early stage of the Church's life, the *"form of teachings,"* the way of pious life and belief were established. Their common agreement was a Testimony to a common Tradition received unchanged from the past.[116]

This unified *"form of Teachings"* made up the one Gospel preached by the Holy Apostles and their co-workers to the one united Church.[117] This Tradition contained the basis of the Teachings, pastoral guidance and administration of the Orthodox Christian Communities as well as the Doctrines, Moral Principles and Teachings.

The context of Divine Revelation revealed in Christ, the word of the Holy Apostles and the first preachers of the Gospel, were spread amongst the faithful who constituted the Church by the Teachings and Tradition. The Books of the New Testament received their context from Apostolic Tradition.

The literature of the Teachings of the Holy Apostles, entrusted to the Church, both orally and written, is a sacred trust that does not accept any addition or reduction. Apostolic Tradition is guarded and interpreted only by the Church and has an objective and subjective aspect.

The objective aspect means that Apostolic Tradition, being the Teaching of the Holy Apostles, is treasured by the Church and remains unchangeable without any additions or reductions. The subjective aspect means that these Teachings have been accepted by the faithful.[118]

Apostolic Tradition has been preserved and guarded by the Orthodox Church and the very fact that it has been kept unalterable by the Orthodox Church, becomes the Tradition of the Church herself: it *"belongs"* to her, it testifies to her and, parallel to Holy Scripture, it is called by her *"Holy Tradition."*[119]

Question 14: What sources embodied Apostolic Tradition?

Answer: The oral and living Teachings of the Holy Apostles that were passed down by word of mouth, began to differentiate from Holy Scripture during the second century. This comprised the Apostolic Tradition that was recorded and embodied within:

(a) The official interpretations of Scripture.

---

[115] Trempelas, *Dogmatique,* v. I, p. 122-123. See also note 8, p. 123.
[116] Gavin, *Orthodox Thoughts,* p. 26.
[117] 1 Corinth. 15:11.
[118] 2 Corinth. 3:3.
[119] Pomazansky, *Theology,* p. 34.

(b) *The Symbols or Confessions of Faith.* The interpretations of the Symbol of Faith of the Orthodox Church, in the common meaning of this term, are those expositions of the Christian Faith which are given in the:

1.   *Book of Canons of the Holy Apostles.*
2.   *The Holy Local and Ecumenical Councils .*
3.   *The Holy Fathers.*
4.   *The Confession of the Orthodox Faith,* compiled by Dositheus, Patriarch of Jerusalem in 1672.
5.   *The Encyclical of the Eastern Patriarchs on the Orthodox Faith,* compiled by Dositheus, Patriarch of Jerusalem in 1732.
6.   *The Orthodox Confession* of Peter Mogilas, Metropolitan of Kiev, which was examined and corrected at two local councils, that of Kiev in 1640 and Jassy 1643.
7.   *The Orthodox Christian Catechism* of Metropolitan Philaret of Moscow.

(c) *In Worship.*
(d) *The Decisions of the Holy Ecumenical or Local Councils.*
(e) *In the so-called "Consensus Patrum".*
(f) *The Acts of the Christian Martyrs.*
(g) *The Ancient Records and History of the Church.*

CHAPTER FOUR
HOLY SCRIPTURE

Question 15: What is Holy Scripture?

Answer: Holy Scripture is the Book that contains Divine Revelation in conjunction with Apostolic Tradition, the unique Source from which we learnt of Divine Revelation. Holy Scripture, containing the Word of God, has with and within the Orthodox Church absolute Authority, whereas the Orthodox Church has to lead her Life and Teachings according to Holy Scripture.[120] The Orthodox Church bears witness to the authenticity of Holy Scripture and is its faithful Guardian and safe Interpreter.[121] She cannot remove or change any word from the Holy text nor can she give to any man-written document the validity and authenticity equivalent to that of Holy

---

[120] Kefalas, *Catechesis,* pp. 22-23. Frangopoulos, *Christian Faith*, pp. 17-21. Mitsopoulos, *Themata,* pp. 21-24.
[121] 1 Tim. 3:15.

Scripture. It is most important to stress that the Authority of the Orthodox Church as the authentic Witness and Interpreter of Holy Scripture cannot be ignored or put aside.[122]

Holy Scripture's God-given Inspiration is witnessed by the Holy Apostles and by Christ Himself.[123] At the moment of Divine Inspiration, the Holy Spirit descended, enlightened and guided the Holy men but at the same time they maintained their intellectual freedom and conscience. All the Books of Holy Scripture are God-inspired. In other words, we can assuredly say that they are the Work of the Holy Spirit.

Question 16: What is the importance of Holy Scripture?

Answer: Holy Scripture as mentioned above, distinguishes itself from Divine Revelation. We learn about the events of Divine Revelation after they had taken place and had been recorded in Holy Scripture, which is the authentic and God-inspired Source. We would have remained ignorant of Divine Revelation if we did not have Holy Scripture.

Holy Scripture should not be identified as one with Divine Revelation but this does not mean that another source exists from which we could receive the Life-giving Water of Divine Revelation. We confess that everything concerning our Salvation is contained in Holy Scripture and Holy Apostolic Tradition, which are the unique and God-given Divine Sources that grant us the Light of Divine Revelation.

From the above therefore one can realize the importance of Holy Scripture as the Source of Divine Revelation. Without Holy Scripture Divine Revelation would not have been known to mankind. The Light of Divine Revelation would have remained as a temporary event and its radiance would have been long forgotten. But God revealed Himself to His servants so that the Light of His Revelation might shine its Life-giving radiance as a bright sun upon all mankind. Therefore God directly instructed His servants to write down whatever they had seen or heard[124] although in some cases He commanded them not to write what they had witnessed.[125]

The Orthodox Church is older than the New Testament itself, bearing in mind that the Church existed before the writing of the New Testament Books. People living in the East had very reliable memories and were

---

[122] Matth. 5:18.
[123] 2 Tim. 3:16. 2 Pet. 1: 20-21.
[124] Ex. 17:14; 34:1, 27. Nu. 5:23; 17:2-3. Is. 8:1; 30:8. Jer. 43:2. Ez. 24:2; 37:16. Hab. 2:2; Rev. 1:11, 19; 2:1, 8, 12, 18; 3:1, 7, 14; 14:13, 19:9, 21:5.
[125] Rev. 10:5.

capable of accurately passing down knowledge by word of mouth from one generation to the next. Thus were God's Revelations from the time of Noah until Moses faithfully passed on. An example of this is the Talmud, which before it had been written down, existed as an oral Teaching and Tradition.[126]

Question 17: What is the authority of Holy Scripture?

Answer: In the Holy Books God speaks and, because of this, it has the absolute Authority according to which the Orthodox Church is obliged to pursue her Life and Teachings. This absolute Authority of Holy Scripture is not drawn from the Authority of the Orthodox Church but directly from God Who speaks in and through her.

The Orthodox Church did not create Holy Scripture. Being the Guardian that received the valuable Covenant from God through His servants the Church keeps it safe. The Orthodox Church is the true witness to the Divine Origin of the Sacred Books. She infallibly and authentically interprets, through the Guidance of the Holy Spirit and the living Apostolic Tradition, the God-inspired Revelation and Teachings of Holy Scripture.

Any ecclesiastical decision is valid only and when it is based on God-inspired Holy Scripture and Apostolic Tradition. Neither the Orthodox Church nor any of her members have any authority to alter, change or remove any word, phrase or verse from the original text of Holy Scripture. Nor can the Orthodox Church give to any man-written book the same authority as that of the God-inspired Books. Even the Decrees of the Ecumenical Councils that we accept as having interpreted Divine Truth infallibly and having received high ecclesiastic Authority, can under no circumstances be called Holy Scripture or be included in its text.[127]

The Authority of Holy Scripture was recognized and proclaimed by the Holy Fathers and the ecclesiastic writers of the Orthodox Church from the beginning.

Question 18: What is the authority of Holy Scripture in relation to the Church's authority?

Answer: Parallel to the Authority of Holy Scripture, one must not underestimate the Authority of the Orthodox Church that bears witness and interprets its Teachings with authenticity. We must bear in mind that Holy

---

[126] Hastoupis, *Introduction*, pp. 84-158.
[127] Trempelas, *Dogmatique,* v. I, p. 102-103.

Scripture does not contain all knowledge. Holy Scripture was not given to us in order for us to learn everything about the physical world surrounding us but to offer us the appropriate knowledge with which to achieve our Salvation in Jesus Christ, the Son of God.

This Christian Knowledge of the Truth must always be examined in the Light of Apostolic Tradition, which is alive within the Orthodox Church and which existed before the composition of the New Testament Books. For this reason Holy Scripture does not exclude the Church's Authority as being the authentic and safe interpreter of its Teachings. In the Orthodox Church, which is the original New Testament Church and the Mystical Body of Christ, the Holy Spirit lives, acts and guides *"into all Truth."*[128]

Question 19: What is the Church's testimony concerning the authenticity of the Books of the Holy Bible?

Answer: The Authority of the Orthodox Church bears witness to the authenticity of the Books of Holy Scripture and their inclusion amongst the Canonical Books of the Old and New Testament[129].

> *Internal Presumptions*:
> a. *The Internal Unity of the Holy Bible.*
> b. *The "Spiritual Grace" of Each Book.*
> c. *The Authors' Testimony.*

External Presumption. This external presumption originates from the authenticity of the Orthodox Church not only because of the importance of its testimony but because the internal presumptions of the Books of the Holy Bible are not unassailable. The importance of this external presumption is based on the fact that it incorporates the testimony of the first Christian Community concerning the origins of the Books of the New Testament written by the Holy Apostles and the collection of the Canon of the Old Testament. It represents the experience of the entire Body of the Orthodox Church, which refers to the God-given unity of the Bible and to its spiritual and genuine Grace.[130]

---

[128] John 16:13.
[129] Cf. Romanides, *Dogmatique,* v. 1, pp. 157-172.
[130] Ibid, *Dogmatique,* v. I, p. 106.

Question 20: What is the *"Inspiration of God"* of Holy Scripture?

Answer: God Commanded His servants to whom He revealed Himself, to write down whatsoever He had shown or spoken in order that these Divine Revelations are known by others. Through God's Divine Grace, these Holy men were inspired and guided by the Spirit of God. They became worthy of carrying out God's instructions. Consequently the Holy Bible is characterized as being the *"Inspiration of God."*[131] In Holy Scripture we find only two direct testimonies concerning the *"Inspiration of God"* of the Holy Bible: 2 Timothy 3:16 and 2 Peter 1: 19-21. Indirect testimonies are found in: John 10:35; Matthew 5: 18; 15:3, 4; 22:31-43; Luke 16:17; 24:44; Acts 1:16; 2:17; 3:21; 15:28; Hebrews 1:5, 13; 4:7; 1 Corinthians 9: 1; 14:37; Galatians 1:7-8, 16; 1 Thessalonians 2:13.

Question 21: What is the nature and meaning of the term *"Inspiration of God"*?

Answer: In order to understand the true nature and meaning of the term *"Inspiration of God,"* we must realize that God's servants were not used as simple instruments, as many in the past believed, they also used their own knowledge and ability to compose the Books that God had instructed them to write. In Holy Scripture we find indications that the Holy Spirit allowed the holy authors to use knowledge that they possessed naturally or had achieved through study. The Grace bestowed upon them did not release them from the need to gather extra information.[132] The authors seem to speak of their own experiences,[133] as St Luke refers to this while accompanying St Paul on his Apostolic journeys,[134] or as St Mark refers to his during the night when Christ delivered Himself to the Jews.[135]

Regardless of the various differences in language and narrations of events that do not contradict each other although they do not appear to be

---

[131] StAthanasius the Great, *Epist. to Marcellinus,* in Migne, *P.G.,* 27, 12. St Gregory of Nyssa, in Migne, *Against Eunomius,* Homily VII, *P.G.,* 45, 744. St John Chrysostom, *All Scripture is god-inspired,* Homily IX, in Migne, *P.G.,* 62, 649. Theophylactus of Bulgaria, *Exposition II to Timothy,* ch. III, in Migne, *P.G.,* 125, 125A. Didymus the Blind, *About the Holy Trinity,* book II, in Migne, *P.G.,* 39, 644A. Origen, *To the Song of Songs,* Homily II, in Migne, *P.G.,*13, 56. Mitsopoulos, *Themata,* pp. 24-28.

[132] 2 Samuel 1:18 (see in Septuagint O', Old Testament Greek): 2 Kings 1:18) and 2 Kings 12:9 (see in Septuagint O', Old Testament Greek): 4 Kings 12:9).

[133] Jer. 35 (28). John 18:15-16; 19:27.

[134] Acts 16:10-17; 20:5-15; 21:1-18; 27:1-28. Galites, *Interpretations,* p. 198.

[135] Mark 14:51-52.

identical, it shows that the authors maintained their freedom of conscience and action.

The Holy Spirit had spoken through the Prophets and Apostles and the Word of God moved the Prophets to speak because the Word is God's Spirit Who descended upon the Prophets through whom He spoke. Therefore Holy Scripture can be characterised as the Writings of the Holy Spirit because the Prophets and Apostles did not speak or write by their own authority. The Grace of God and the Holy Spirit moved them and thus they spoke or wrote.[136]

The Holy Fathers of the Orthodox Church, parallel to the *"Inspiration of God"* of the Prophets and the Holy authors, emphasize that their souls were purified and their bodies became more virtuous. Consequently they became the worthy instruments of God and were able to speak His Words.[137]

"Inspiration of God" is a special *"Charisma"* granted by the Holy Spirit Who fulfills the whole existence, wills, thoughts and lives of inspired men without abolishing either their conscience, Free-will, personalities, or themselves as people.[138] The Holy Spirit raises them up to a higher level of morality and virtue, transforming them into *"synergous"* (co-operators, co-workers) with God who are able to write down *"God-inspired"* Sacred Books. Therefore the Holy Scripture's *"Inspiration of God"* is the result of the *"Inspiration of God"* upon the authors of the Holy Scripture, which was expressed not only in their writings but also in their speech and Holy lives.[139]

Question 22: What is the Orthodox term of *"Epistasia"* (*"Supervision"*)?

Answer: The Bible is the Revelation of our Salvation in the form of history. In the Bible all the Truths have been sealed under the cover of historical

---

[136] Theodoretus of Cyrus, *To 2 Timothy*, in Migne, *P.G.*, 82, 849. St Justin, the philosopher and martyr, *1 Apology,* in Migne, *P.G.*, 6, 386. Theophilus of Antioch, *To Autolycus*, II, in Migne, *P.G.*, 6, 1065. Origen, *To Song of Songs,* book II, in Migne, *P.G.,* 13, 121-122. St Basil the Great, *To Psalm 1:1.* in Migne, *P.G.*, 29, 209A. St Gregory of Nyssa, *Against Eunomius*, Homily VII, ch. 1, in Migne, *P.G.*, 45, 741. St John Chrysostom, *To Genesis,* Migne, *P.G.*, 53, 65. Ibid, *To Holy Week,* Homily 3, in Migne, *P.G.*, 55, 520. Evdokimov, *Orthodoxia*, pp. 260-261.

[137] Clement the Alexandrian, *Stromata*, article II, in Migne, *P.G.*, 9, 1425. St John Chrysostom, *To Psalm*, in Migne, *P.G.*, 55, 183. St Cyril of Alexandria, *Against Julianus*, in Migne, *P.G.*, 76, 913.

[138] St John Chrysostom, *To John*, Homily 1, in Migne, *P.G.*, 59, 25-26. Ibid, *To 1 Corinthians*, Homily 29, in Migne, *P.G.*, 61, 241. St Cyril of Jerusalem, *Catechesis*, XVI, in Migne, *P.G.*, 33, 941. St Cyril of Alexandria, *To Romans*, in Migne, *P.G.*, 74, 813, 817. Theodoretus of Cyrus, *To Ezekiel 3:22,* book II, in Migne, *P.G.*, 81, 852.

[139] Trempelas, *Dogmatique*, v. I, p. 112.

events, which lead altogether to the historical Person of our Lord and Saviour Jesus Christ, the Incarnated Word and Son of God.[140]

God's Revelation enlightened the Patriarchs less, and made Moses and the Prophets stronger, and reached its climax with the *"Epiphany"* (*"Manifestation"*) of the Messiah, our Lord and Saviour Jesus Christ, the Son of God. This progress of the Divine Revelation did not move from lies to Truth, but from the lesser to the complete, as in the natural growth of the body. The difference of the level of the *"Inspiration of God"* is the result of the difference of level of the outpouring and Energy of the Holy Spirit in the Old and New Testament. Also the difference of the level of the *"Inspiration of God"* depended on the instruments' ability to receive the Holy Spirit's Divine Inspiring Grace.[141]

Question 23: To what extent is the *"Inspiration of God"*?

Answer: The *"Inspiration of God"* extends throughout Holy Scripture. According to the Teachings of St Paul *"all Scripture is given by Inspiration of God."*[142] We confess that the Wisdom of God is throughout all Holy Scripture including even the less important letters.[143]

The Divine aspect is that the Truth, which has been revealed by God, rules throughout the Sacred Books. The human aspect is the literary form according to which the Heavenly Treasure has been recorded.[144] Human mistakes in literature do not affect either the *"Inspiration of God"* or the ideas that are expressed. The anthropomorphic expressions found in Holy Scripture concerning God *"if taken literally lead us to blasphemy,"*[145] yet they express a deeper meaning which is clothed with some Divine Majesty and cannot be expressed any other way but in human terms only.[146]

Holy Scripture is not a science book. Its purpose is to teach men about Divine Truth in the form of ideas according to human understanding. It aims to glorify God and to praise His Perfection.[147]

---

[140] Oosterzee, *Dogmatics*, p. 185.
[141] St Athanasius the Great, *Epist. to Marcellinus*, in Migne *P.G.*, 27, 17.
[142] 2 Tim. 3:16.
[143] Cf.: St John Chrysostom, *To Genesis*, XV, in Migne *P.G.*, 53, 119. St Basil the Great, *About faith*, in Migne *P.G.*, 31, 692. Ibid, *To Exahemerus*, VIII, in Migne *P.G.*, 29, 184. Socrates, *De vita et Scriptis*, in Migne *P.G.*, 67, 17 and St Makarius of Egypt, Homily 5, in Migne *P.G.*, 35, 504.
[144] St Gregory of Nyssa, *Against Eunomius*, XII, in Migne, *P.G.*, 45, 976. Didymus the Blind, *To Psalms*, in Migne, *P.G.*, 39, 1293. Theodoretus of Cyrus, *To Ezekiel*, book II, in Migne, *P.G.*, 81, 853. Origen, *To Ezekiel*, in Migne, *P.G.*, 13, 801.
[145] St Athanasius the Great, *To Matthew*, in Migne, *P.G.*, 27, 1384.
[146] St Gregory of Nyssa, *Against Eunomius*, XII, in Migne, *P.G.*, 45, 976.
[147] Trempelas, *Dogmatique*, v. I, p. 118.

In conclusion, all Holy Scripture is *"God-inspired"* and none of its parts can be separated from the *"Inspiration of God."* We notice that there is a verbal *"Inspiration of God"* in the words. Although the Holy Spirit did not dictate them word by word, the Holy men used their freedom by expressing the Divine Truths using the most appropriate words from their own vocabulary, always under the enlightenment of the Charisma of the *"Inspiration of God."*[148]

Question 24: What is the *"Inspiration of God"* in relation to the criticism of Text of Holy Scripture?

Answer: Within the Orthodox Church, from the first centuries, efforts were made to correct the literary errors in the different manuscripts of the Holy Bible. It is evident from the work of Origen, Hesychios and Lucianos on the translation of the Greek Old Testament (Septuagint), as well as on the text of the New Testament, that the ancient Orthodox Church did not hesitate to allow such criticism. The Orthodox Church never forbade even the philological and historical criticism that deals with the problems of authenticity, the origin, the unity and the integrity of the Sacred Books.[149]

It is most important to emphasize that the scholar must never change or add or subtract from the original text according to his own opinion because this will be considered blasphemy! For in such a case the scholar claims for himself the Charisma of the *"Inspiration of God"* and considers his words as of the same importance and authenticity as those of the Word of God, which are inscribed in the Holy Scripture.[150]

---

[148] Trempelas, *Dogmatique,* v. I, p. 119. Oosterzee, *Dogmatics,* p. 179. Cf. St John Chrysostom, *To Genesis,* Homily 15, in Migne, *P.G.,* 53, 119. Origen, *To Psalms,* in Migne, *P.G.,* 12, 1081. St Basil the Great, *To Eunomius about the Son,* in Migne, *P.G.,* 29, 601.
[149] Trempelas, *Dogmatique,* v. I, p. 120.
[150] Ibid, *Dogmatique,* v. I, p. 121.

PART ONE
GOD
CHAPTER ONE

Question 25: Is there a possibility of knowing God?

Answer: According to Holy Scripture and the Holy Fathers of the Orthodox Church, it is possible for man to know God. The Holy Fathers believe, although God is incomprehensible, indescribable and infinite, He does not completely escape the sphere of our understanding and knowledge. God reveals Himself and Who cannot be known without Divine Revelation.[151] To know God is the first level of wisdom.[152] This Knowledge of God is possible only because of Revelation and directly puts an end to every logical method concerning its unutterable existence.[153]

It is necessary to distinguish between the full Knowledge of God and that of His Essence. To a certain level man can achieve Knowledge of God[154] but His Essence remains unfathomable.

Question 26: Do Holy Scripture bear witness concerning man's ability to know about God?

Answer: St Paul the Apostle teaches that man can achieve Knowledge of God by seeing the works of Creation, the manifestations of Divine Providence and man's internal inclinations[155] Although Creation has no voice, yet, it speaks of the Creator.[156] Furthermore the Law that is written in man's heart,[157] leads him to seek the Supreme Law-giver.

God did not remain unknown because of His Divine Providence and His Dominion upon all things through which He could be acknowledged by all.[158] In conclusion, St Paul emphasizes three aspects that assist man in knowing about God:

a)   The order of nature.[159]
b)   The inborn Moral Law and conscience.

---

[151] Lossky, *Theology,* p. 20.
[152] Plato of Moscow, *Orthodox Teaching,* p. 34.
[153] Evdokimov, *Orthodoxia,* p. 70. Mitsopoulos, *Themata,* pp. 52-53.
[154] St Symeon, the New Theologian, *Euriskomena,* Homily XXX, pp. 150-154.
[155] Rom. 1:20.
[156] St Ecumenius, *To Romans,* I, in Migne, *P.G.,* 118, 340.
[157] Rom. 2:15.
[158] St Irenaeus, *Heresies,* book II, ch. VI, in Migne, *P.G.,* 7, 724.
[159] Cf. Mitsopoulos, *Themata,* pp. 53-106.

c)   The manifestations in man's history of Divine Providence.

Although man can receive Knowledge of God by examining the things of nature, this knowledge is imperfect, dim and indefinite; it can be easily interpreted in various ways.[160] However, in this natural search for God, man was not left alone.

From the above it is understood that Holy Scripture teaches us that man has the ability to know about God and especially when he uses his intelligence, he is capable of reaching Knowledge of God in conjunction with faith.[161]

Question 27: Can man know about God?

Answer: God is incomprehensible by His Nature and exists beyond any creative matter.[162] Man being creative and living in a world amongst others who have been created, can understand Him Who is beyond any matter and Who cannot be compared to anything of this world.   God's Will is unsearchable and His Ways are inscrutable, *"for who has known the mind of the Lord? Or who has become His counselor?"*[163]

God is unapproachable not only to those who have not experienced Divine Revelation, but also to those who are like Moses or who have ascended into the third heaven like St Paul and heard *"inexpressible words, which it is not lawful for a man to utter."*[164] Even if they surpassed those holy men and became worthy of an Angelic or Archangelic Rank, God will always remain unapproachable to them, like the distance that exists between heaven and earth, Angels and humans, spirit and matter. God's Essence is Unapproachable even to the Archangels.[165]

Holy Scripture speaks of Visions that the Prophets had seen in which the Lord was sitting on a Throne of Glory,[166] except what they had seen was not God Himself, but the Glory of God. God is simple, uncompounded and unformed, the Prophets saw different forms of His Glory that were revealed to them. Hence God is anonymous and has many Names at the same time.[167]   Because God is unintelligible,[168] He is completely

---

[160] Frangopoulos, *Christian Faith,* pp. 38-44.
[161] St Basil the Great, *Epist.* 233, in Migne, *P.G.,*32, 868. Ibid, *Epist.* 235, in Migne, *P.G.,* 32, 872.
[162] St Athanasius the Great, *Against Greeks*, in Migne, *P.G.,* 25, 69.
[163] Rom. 11:34.
[164] 1 Corinth. 12:4.
[165] St Gregory of Nazianzus, *Theologicus II, About Theology,* Homily 28, in Migne, *P.G.,* 36, 29. Clement the Alexandrian, *Stromata*, VI, 7, in ***B***, v. 8, p. 199.
[166] Is. 6:1.
[167] Boulgareos, *Theologicon*, p. 71.

unnamed.[169] Holy Scripture identifies God by using many names, such as "*Judge,*" "*Just,*" "*Powerful,*" "*Forbearing,*" "*Truth,*" "*Merciful,*" etc. Thus He Who is anonymous receives many names from men. Even these names are imperfect because God's qualities are far greater than all those put together.[170]

Question 28: Can we prove the existence of God?

Answer: The existence of God cannot be proved. To prove the existence of God we must emphasize the reason and the cause of His existence. Because God is Infinite and the One Who absolutely Exists (O ΩN), He has the reason for His existence not outside Himself nor above Himself but absolutely and only in Himself. God, as the Infinite Being, can be known by man to a limited extent only and although He reveals Himself, it is impossible for Him to be proven like a scientific experiment.[171]

Question 29: What are the theories of proof concerning the existence of God?

Answer: 1. The proof based on **the movement of the world**, according to the principle "*whatever moves, moves by something else.*" Searching for the cause of the movement in the universe we find a long line of causes, of which each and every one has its cause of movement from another. But this cannot be infinite and therefore we are forced to accept the First Cause, which gave movement to all.

2. **The appearance of new beings** that had not existed before, appear today in order to be replaced in future by others. This proof claims to have its first cause within it and not elsewhere. But the Creation of an infinite line cannot be accepted. Thus we have to accept the existence of the First Cause from which everything originated.

3. The proof of **dependency** means that "*Everything which can be moved does not exist because of its essence, but because of another necessary being.*" According to this theory, everything before us exists only as a possibility. They might or not exist. Nothing makes their existence necessary, since they do not have the cause of their existence within them.

---

168 St John of Damascus, *Catechesis,* I, 12, in Migne, *P.G.,* 94, 845.
169 Clement the Alexandrian, *Stromata*, book V, ch. 12, in *B*, v. 8, p. 146.
170 Trempelas, *Dogmatique,* v. I, pp. 152-153.
171 Ibid, *Dogmatique,* v. I, p. 155.

4.	The three abovementioned proofs can be united in one **cosmological proof,** according to which the existing beings have different levels of perfection. This difference occurs according to the level on which they become closer to the perfect Being Who gave them, accordingly, their perfection.

5.	The proof deriving from **Mankind's general belief in God**. The Holy Fathers of the Orthodox Church do not ignore proof obtained from the general belief of mankind that there is a God.[172] This general belief in God by all men was not ignored by the Greek nor Latin philosophers.[173] This phenomenon proves that all men, especially those who deal intellectually with higher thoughts, have received a Divine outpouring by which they confess, even if they are not willing, to the existence of one God Who is without beginning.[174]

From the above we are led to acknowledge that the soul has the capability of turning towards God and having a relationship with the Divine. Man's soul was created in *"the image and likeness"*[175] of God according to which, when man turns towards evil, idolatry and becomes a slave to carnal sins and pleasures, he immediately recovers through true repentance as from drunkenness, automatically turns to God and with desire calls upon Him.[176]

CHAPTER TWO

Question 30: What is the true idea concerning God?

Answer: The Orthodox Church upholds the Truth and does not search for the Truth. Although man has a limited mind and is incapable of understanding the fullness of the Divinity, he can still obtain solid and true knowledge of God. This Knowledge is not compared to God's Knowledge of Himself, but is the Knowledge of God as He reveals Himself to man.

The Revelation found in Holy Scripture is the only safe and infallible Source from which every man can obtain the True Idea concerning God. Being enlightened by the Names that are given to God, we know God as the

---

[172] Kefalas, *Catechesis,* pp. 36-37.
[173] Ciceron, *De natura Deorum*, book I, ch. XVII.
[174] Clement the Alexandrian, *Protrepticos*, VI, 59, in **B**, v. 7, p. 52.
[175] Gen. 1:26.
[176] Trempelas, *Dogmatique,* v. I, p. 162. Tertullian, *De Testimonium Animae,* c. 2, in migne, *P.L.,* 1,685; *Apologet.,* c. 1, 17, in migne, *P.L.,* 1, 433.

Absolute Being, as the infinite and transcendental Spirit, distinguished from His Creation on the one hand as the infinite and perfect Person ("Πρόσωπον" - *Prosopon*) and on the other hand always providing and guiding the Cosmos through His Divine Providence.

Question 31: What do the Names given to God express?

Answer: In order to establish a true idea of God we must bear in mind that no name should be given to God except those that were ascribed by Moses, the Prophets and our Lord and Saviour Jesus Christ, the Son of God; and with the understanding that even these names cannot precisely describe God's Attributes and Essence, which remains unapproachable even to the Angelical Hosts in Heaven because *"the Essence of God cannot be comprehended by the mind of men; nor it can be contained by any name."*[177] But if we see through the eyes of faith the external Energies and relationship of God towards the world, then we can give names in order for our limited mind to comprehend.

Question 32: What are the Names given to God?

1.   The Name **"I AM THE BEING"**[178] (= «Ο ΩΝ») is the most fitting Name for God, because by this the whole Being is expressed as being alike unto God, neither related with something before Him nor to anything else after Him. This Name was given by God Himself[179] when He appeared to Moses at Choreb *"in flaming fire out of the bush"* and *"the bush burned with fire, - but the bush was not consumed."*[180]

2.   **The Name "SPIRIT".** Our Lord and Saviour Jesus Christ, the Son of God, when speaking to the Samaritan woman (St Photini) about the Father said that *"God is Spirit."*[181] Calling God the Father *"Spirit,"*[182] He defined God as bodiless, Whose Nature is unchangeable and not like anything else in nature as He is the absolutely perfect Spirit: *"He is infinite*

---

[177] St Gregory of Nyssa, *Againsts Eunomius*, XII, in Migne, *P.G.,* 45, 1108. St Gregory of Nazianzus, *Homily* 30, 18, in Migne, *P.G.,* 36, 125 and 128. Lossky, *Theology,* p.49.
[178] Ex. 3:14. Cf. Frangopoulos, *Christian Faith,* p. 44.   Sophrony, *His Life,* pp. 24-31. Lossky, *Theology,* p. 22.
[179] Ex. 3:14.
[180] Ex. 3:2. Cf. Kefalas, *Catechesis,* p. 48. Mitsopoulos, *Themata,* p. 111.
[181] John 4:24.
[182] For the definition of the word "Spirit" see: Tsakonas, *Paracletus,* Athens, 1978.

in Power, unlimited in size, incalculable in time and in addition to these He is in Essence 'Spirit.'[183]

Question 33: What other Biblical Names are given to God?

Answer: In the Old Testament (Hebrew text) we find many other names ascribed to God, such as:

1.   *"Elohim"*[184] (=Lord) is found in the first verse of the Book of Genesis[185] in plural form. We find also the names *"El"* (60 times), *"Eloach"* (23 times), *"Elohin"* (192 times), *"Elohe Sebaoth"* (3 times), *"Gebier"* (2 times), *"Mare"* (4 times), *"Shalin"* (once) which refers to God.[186]

      The abovementioned words were translated by the Septuagint (LXX) as *Mighty,"*[187] *"Almighty,"*[188] *"Pantocrator"*[189] and *"Lord of Sabaoth."*[190] These names included the meaning of God as being the *"King"* [191] of Israel.

2.   *"Adon – Adonai"* (=Lord)[192] is the name that was used to replace the unspoken Name *"Jahve,"*[193] which, out of respect, the Jews never pronounced. It has the same meaning as that of Elohim.

3.   *"Goel"* = *("Saviour").*[194]

4.   *"Just."*[195]

5.   *"Beginning and the End."*[196]

---

[183] St Basil the Great, *About the Holy Spirit,* Homily 9, 22, in Migne, *P.G.,* 32, 107. Damalas, *Catechesis,* p. 5. Frangopoulos, *Christian Faith,* p. 45.
[184] Hastoupis, *Introduction,* pp. 193-194.
[185] Gen. 1:1.
[186] Galites, *Interprtations,* p. 254.
[187] **Gen.** 49:24. **De.** 7:21; 10:17; 11:2. **Josua** 4:24. **Psalm** 24:8; 50:1; 132:2, 5. Is. 1:24; 9:6; 28:2; 30:29; 42:13; 49:25-26; 60:16. **Jer.** 20:11; 32:16; 32:19. **Dan.** 8:24. **Hab.** 1:12. **Zep.** 3:17. **Luke** 9:43. **1 Peter** 5:6.
[188] **Gen.** 17:1; 28:3; 35:11; 43:14; 48:3; 49:25. **Ex.** 6:3. **Nu.** 24:4, 16. **Job** 5:17; 6:4, 14; 8:3, 5; 11:7; 13:3; 15:25; 21:15, 20; 22:3, 17, 23, 25-26; 23:16; 24:1; 27:2, 10-11, 13; 29:5; 31:2, 35; 32:8; 33:4; 34:10, 12; 35:13; 37:23; 40:2. **Psalm** 68(69):14; 91:1. **Is.** 13:6. **Ez.** 1:24; 10:5. **Joe** 1:15. **2 Corinth.** 6:18. **Rev.** 1:8; 4:8; 11:17; 15:3; 16:7, 14; 19:15 and 21:22.
[189] 2 Corinth. 6:18. Rev. 1:8; 4:8; 11:17; 15:3; 16:7, 14; 19:6, 15 .
[190] Is. 1:9; 6:3. Rom. 9:29. James 5:4.
[191] Psalm 89(90):18. Galites, *Interpretations,* pp. 268-269.
[192] Galites, *Interpretations,* pp. 253-267.
[193] Hastoupis, *Introduction,* pp. 190-192.
[194] **Psalm** 106(107):21. **Is.** 43:3; 45:15, 21; 49:26; 60:16; 63:8. **Luke** 1:47. **Acts** 5:31. **1 Tim.** 4:10.
[195] **Is.** 45:21. **Zep.** 3:5. **Acts** 3:14; 22:14.
[196] Psalm 111(112):10. Rev. 1:8; 21:6; 22:13.

6.   *"I Am the first and I Am the hereafter."*[197]

7.   *"I Am the first, and I endure for ever"*[198]

8.   *"I God, the first and to all futurity, I AM."*[199]

9.   *"the Alpha and the Omega,"*[200]

10.   *"Who is and Who was and Who is to come, the Almighty."*[201]

11.   *"I AM the First and the Last"*[202]

12.   *"Qadosh" (="Holy").*[203]

13.   *"All-powerful,"*

14.   *"Lord of Hosts,"*

15.   *"Lord of Arms,"*

16.   *"Lord Almighty."*[204]

17.   *"El-Roeh" (="He Who sees").*[205]

All the names given to God are in order for us to understand God's external relationship with His Creation and especially with His intellectual

---

[197] Is. 44:6.

[198] Is. 48:12.

[199] Is. 41:4. Galites, *Interpretations,* pp. 314-315.

[200] Rev. 1:8; 21:6; 22:13.

[201] Rev. 1:8.

[202] Rev. 1:17.

[203] **Le.** 11:19:2; 20:7, 26; 21:8. **Josua** 524:19. **1 Samuel (1 Kings)** 2:2. **2 Kings (4 Kings)** 19:22. **1 Chron.** 16:10. **Job** 6:10. **Psalms** 22(23):3; 32(33):21; 71(72):22; 78(79):41; 89(90):18; 99(100):9; 102(103):1; 105(106):3; 145(146):21. **Is.** 1:4; 5:16, 19, 24; 6:3; 10:20; 12:6; 29:19, 23; 30:11-12; 31:1; 37:23; 40:25; 41:14, 16, 20; 43:3, 14-15; 45:11; 47:4; 48:17; 49:7; 54:5; 55:5; 57:15; 60:9, 14. **Ez.** 39:7;43:7-8. **Ho.** 11:9. **Amos** 2:7. **Hab.** 1:12.

[204] Origen, *Against Celsus,* V, 45, in *B*, v. 10, pp. 64 and 45.

[205] **1 Samuel (1 Kings)** 16:7. **Job** 28:10. **Ez.** 8:12. **Psalms** 94(95):7; 103(104):21, 20; 113(114):5; 147(148):16. **Pr.** 24:18. **Is.** 37:17. **La.** 1:11.

beings: Angels and men. But under no circumstances do they describe His Divine and Infinite Essence.[206]

Question 34: What is the absolute Divine Unit?

Answer: Examining the meaning of God, we realize the Truth that there is only One, Unique God. Throughout the entire Holy Scripture it is emphasized that the living God is One Who opposes all false and lifeless gods of idolatry.[207]

In the Old Testament it is written, *"Hear, O Israel, the Lord our God is one Lord"*[208] and *"there is none beside Him."*[209] In the New Testament the Truth that God is One is proclaimed and it renounces the idols of the world.[210] *"For there is One God"* Who gave us *"One Mediator between God and men, the Man Christ Jesus."*[211]

Although God is One in Essence, He is Three in Persons. This unity is related to the One Undivided Essence of God. God is bodiless, spirit, simple, invisible, unchangeable, untouchable and One by His Nature.[212]

Question 35: What proof do we have that God is One?

Answer: 1. St John of Damascus teaches us that if we accept the existence of many gods, differences must exist among them. If there are no differences between them, then they should be considered as one rather than many. Conversely, if there are differences, then where is the perfection? Again, if there is uniformity, then we have one and not many because how can many gods preserve the indescribable? Since there is One God, there are no others.[213]

2. St Athanasius the Great of Alexandria teaches us that God's Oneness and Unity can be justified by the order and harmony that rules the Universe because if there were many gods, there would not be such harmony, but disorder and chaos since each of them would want everything for

---

[206] Kefalas, *Catechesis,* pp. 42-43.
[207] Psalm 135(136):15-17; 115(116):4-7.
[208] Deut. 6:4.
[209] Deut. 4:35.
[210] 1 Corinth. 8:4, 6.
[211] 1 Tim. 2:5.
[212] Origen, *About Principals,* book I, ch. 1, § 6, in Migne, *P.G.,* 11, 123-126.
[213] St John of Damascus, *Exposition, About the Word and Son of God,* book I, ch. VI, in Migne, *P.G.,* 94, 801.

themselves and would fight one another. The complexity of the Universe cannot be ruled except by only One Ruler Who guides it harmoniously.[214]

3.   In Creation there are no independent universes. The numerous heavenly bodies compose the one Cosmos. If there were many gods, we should have had many universes because why would they create only one? Because of their weakness? This would prove their imperfection and to say there is imperfection in the Divine is not merely disrespectful but certainly blasphemous! Consequently the vainglory of these false gods would have been totally inappropriate.[215]

CHAPTER THREE

Question 36: What are God's Attributes?

Answer: By using the terms *"being"* or *"existence"* we refer to those characteristics of each being, according to which it is distinguished from the other beings. It is that which it is. The terms used to describe God are therefore called *"Attributes,"* *"virtues"* or *"perfections"* of His Divine Nature, through which the simple but not synthetic Essence of God is distinguished from the world and is revealed to us as the absolute and infinite *"BEING."* God's Essence is unapproachable and inconceivable. Thus when we speak of God's Attributes we must never forget that no word can describe Divine Nature, nor can we obtain complete knowledge of God's Essence. Even all the names in Holy Scripture do not contain the meaning of the Divine Essence, but each and every one of them are interpreting the surrounding and external Energies of God's Nature. For example the terms: *inoffensive, immortal, invisible, wrathless, apathetic, impeccable, bodiless, unborn, without beginning, unalterable, untouchable, imperishable, unchangeable, indescribable, incomprehensible, unequivocal, unlimited, untold, boundless, incorruptible, inseparable, undated, timeless, irreproachable.* Names that describe Divine Nature in a positive way are: *good, just, light, life, etc.* However, these terms do not precisely describe the Nature of God. They are applied to Him according to our limited and weak nature.

These many Attributes offer us a limited knowledge of God because they are unable to describe the invisible and incomprehensible Essence of God. Consequently we know that God is Wise but we ignore how Wise He

---

[214] St Athanasius the Great, *Against Greeks,* in Migne, *P.G.,* 25, 80.
[215] St Athanasius the Great, *Against Greeks,* in Migne, *P.G.,* 25, 77.

is. We know that He is Magnificent yet we do not know the measure of His Majesty. We know that He is All-present yet we do not know how. This is why St Paul the Apostle wrote: *"For we know in part and we prophesy in part."*[216]

Question 37: What are the Divine Attributes in relation to the Simplicity of the Divine Essence?

Answer: When we ascribe different Attributes to God, we must never forget that the Essence of God is *simple*. How these Attributes are expressed must be understood in such a way that we must never touch the Simplicity of God's Essence, nor should we say that It consists of many elements.

It is blasphemous to think that God is synthetic or that there are things that exist around His Essence that complete Him. Synthesis is the cause of division and dissolution, which are alien to God. The many names ascribed to God's countless Attributes should be understood as describing the one, simple and incomprehensible Essence of God. The absolute simplicity of God's Essence remains undivided, unformed and unchangeable and is made known to us through its different relationship and Energies towards the Cosmos.

Question 38: What do the anthropomorphistic terms express?

Answer: The Attributes that we have ascribed to God are incomplete and unable to describe the fullness of His Divine Essence since we use images and examples from our own limited understanding. It is natural therefore that these will always bear human characteristics. This explains why in Holy Scripture we find anthropomorphistic and humanistic expressions Attributed to God.

Question 39: What methods of teachings are used?

Answer: The first is the *Abductive method ("απαγωγική")* according to which one chooses one of God's basic Attributes - for example the Self-existence or the Self-essence - and upon this we come gradually to the knowledge of the rest.

The second is the *Inductive method ("επαγωγική")* according to which one always seeks the Divine Attributes one by one through the visible world, as they are revealed through the Cosmos.

---

[216] 1 Corinth. 13:9.

Question 40: What classification & division of the Divine Attributes do we have?

a)   *Positive and Negative.*

Positive Attributes are those that describe God as being the Absolute Perfect and Infinite BEING. For example: *Good, Just, Light, Life etc.*[217]

Negative Attributes are those that deny any imperfections of God. For example: *inoffensive, without anger, impeccable, inscrutable, forebearing, inexplicable, unexplored, inexhaustible, unhindered, etc.*[218]

b)   *Transitional or Transmittable, Persistent or Intransitive Attributes.*

Intransitive Attributes are those that can be ascribed to the Divine BEING. For example: *simplicity, infinity, unintelligible, self-existence*, etc.

Transitional correspond to the positive Attributes. For example: *Holiness, Goodness, Truth, Love, etc.,* which can be transmitted to the intellectual beings, the Angels and men, but only to a certain level.[219]

c)   *Natural and Energetic Attributes.*

Natural Attributes present God as the Absolute and Blessed Being.

Energetic Attributes characterize the Energies and the Manifestations of His Life in the Creation. These Divine Energies are divided into *moral* and *intellectual* Energies.

d)   *Relative and Absolute Attributes.*

Relative Attributes signify that there is some type of relationship between God and His Creation, whereas the *Absolute Attributes* can be characterized as transcendental. Nevertheless, the relative Attributes

---

[217] Theodoretus of Cyrus, *Evangelic Truth. About Principal,* Homily II, in Migne, *P.G.,* 83, 856.
[218] St Gregory of Nyssa, *Against Eunomius,* XII, in Migne, *P.G.,* 45, 953, 957. St Basil the Great, *Against Eunomius,* I, 10, in Migne, *P.G.,* 29, 533.
[219] Boulgareos, *Theologicon,* p. 83.

(*creativity*) are Eternal and exist in the Essence of God, even if we presume that God did not want to create the world.

e) *Internal and Hypostatic Attributes.*

Internal and *Hypostatic Attributes* of God are the *Fatherhood* of God the Father, the Son *being a Son* and the *Procession* of the Holy Spirit only from the Father.

f) *Personal and Essential Attributes.*

Personal Attributes are those that refer to the three Persons of the One Godhead. Thus, God the Father as a Person cannot be God the Son, nor can the Holy Spirit as a Person be the Father or the Son. Each Person of the Holy Trinity differs from the other two according to their *Hypostases*.[220]

Essential Attributes are those that refer to each Person of the Holy Trinity being the One True God. For example: *without beginning, Endless, Goodness, Kindness, Almightiness, Creator, Providence, Omnipotence, Omniscient, All-present, Indescribable, All-knowing, etc.*[221]

CHAPTER FOUR
THE DIVINE ATTRIBUTES
IN RELATION TO THE WAY OF THE DIVINE EXISTENCE

Question 41: What are the Divine Attributes in relation to the way of the Divine Existence?

Answer: The Attributes of God that are related to the Divine Existence are those that refer to the Divine Nature itself without any relation to the Creation. Their basis is that God is the *"Absolute Being,"* the *"Self-existing,"* the *"Perfect,"* the *"existing beyond any boundaries of space or time,"* the *"Needless,"* the *"Blessed,"* the *"Invisible"* and *"Incomprehensible"* to any intellectual mind. In other words, God being Perfect is *"beyond any limitation"* and *"want,"* having absolutely *"all perfection."* He is *"Self-existing"* not only because *"He is that He is,"* but because He does not receive His existence from anyone else. He is the One Who gave the existence to everything that exists outside Himself, which He

---

[220] Karmeris, *The dogmatics*, v. I, pp. 364-365.
[221] Ibid, v. II, pp. 598-599. Kefalas, *Catechesis,* pp. 47-48.

created from nothingness and brought into being. Being beyond time, He is *"without beginning"* and *"without end,"* *"Eternal,"* not distinguishing within Himself past, present or future, but always present. Thus God is unalterable and unchangeable because any alteration is the result of a change of events, which creates time. Being beyond space, He cannot be contained by any creation and yet He is All-present without being confused with the Creation. Being the Absolute and Perfect Spirit, God is invisible and incomprehensible even by the Angels. Finally, God being the Perfect Being is the Absolute Blessed One.

Question 42: What is the Unlimited and Infinity of God?

Answer: God is unlimited as He cannot be restricted by any boundaries. He is free from all limitations and want, and having Absolute Perfection His Essence is infinite and unlimited.[222] God is for Himself unlimited and the Absolute Being Who distinguishes Himself from Himself through His natural, logical and moral Eternal Energies.[223]

The Holy Fathers of the Orthodox Church characterize God as being the Absolute Infinite Being Who is impossible to be seen or comprehended. The only perception of Him is His infinity and incomprehensibility because as God is unlimited by Nature, He cannot be limited nor restricted by any boundaries.[224]

The Infinite Attribute of God reveal His unlimited Perfection. God is infinitely Perfect in all things and is the Source of all Virtues. He is Perfect in seeing, Perfect in creating, Perfect in majesty, Perfect in foreknowledge, Perfect in goodness, Perfect in justice, Perfect in philanthropy. God is Perfect in all His Attributes and there is no part of His Divine Essence where one Attribute is lesser than another, but all are equal and absolutely Perfect. He is neither greater in Philanthropy and smaller in Wisdom, nor greater in Foreknowledge and smaller in Justice, but all His Attributes are equal.[225]

---

[222] Plato of Moscow, *Orthodox Teaching,* pp. 40-41.
[223] Rhosse, *System,* pp. 305-306. Mitsopoulos, *Themata,* pp. 115-116.
[224] St Gregory of Nazianzus, *Homily* 38, in Migne, *P.G.,* 36, 317. St Gregory of Nyssa, *That there are not three gods,* in Migne, *P.G.,* 45, 129. Ibid, *Against Eunomius,* Homily III, ch. 7, in Migne, *P.G.,* 45, 601. Ibid, *Against Eunomius,* Homily IX, ch. 1, in Migne, *P.G.,* 45, 808. St John of Damascus, *Exposition. About the Word and Son of God,* book I, ch. VI, in Migne, *P.G.,* 94, 801.
[225] St Cyril of Jerusalem, *Catechesis,* VI, 8, 5, 10, in Migne, *P.G.,* 33, 552, 542, 553.

Question 43: What is the Self-existence of God?

Answer: Self-existence is an Attribute that is related to the infinity of God and cannot be ascribed to anyone else but only to the infinite and self-existing God Who is the only Source of Life, Who *"has life in Himself"*[226] and does not receive it from some other source, but rather *"gives to all life."*[227]

Question 44: What is the Self-sufficiency of God?

Answer: Inseparable from the above Divine Attributes is the Self-sufficiency of God. According to Holy Scripture the Lord is Self-sufficient and has no need of anyone.[228] God has no need of any worship and glory that we offer Him. We offer these because we need to do so. Through this means of communication we participate in His Divine Grace and Gifts.[229] The Self-sufficiency of God is an endless Fountain of Life that flows with love to all, requiring no replenishment or renewal whatsoever. God has no need of anyone or of anything. He is self-sufficient, giving to all everything necessary, being the Creator of all,[230] *"for in Him we live and move and have our being."*[231]

Question 45: What is the Without Beginning & Eternal of God?

Answer: God is *without beginning* and *without end*, not created by another being, nor having begun life in a certain period of time. He does not come to an end nor has He a successor.[232] The time of this world is like split-seconds to God when compared to Eternity.[233] Because we are limited beings moving in time, we cannot have a perfect concept of Eternity. God as the Absolute Being is neither bound within nor part of time. Therefore we should not say that God *"was always and is and shall be,"* but rather that He *"is always."*[234] Time only began when God created the visible world.[235] It

---

[226] John 5:26.
[227] Acts 17:25.
[228] Acts 17:25. Psalm 50(51):12-13.
[229] II Maccabees 14:35.
[230] St John Chrysostom, *Against Greeks,* in Minge, *P.G.,* 25, 56.
[231] Acts 17:28. Psalm 113(114):6-7. Is. 57:15.
[232] St Cyril of Jerusalem, *Catechesis,* IV, § 4, in Migne, *P.G.,* 33, 457. Frangopoulos, *Christian Faith,* pp. 49-50. Mitsopoulos, *Themata,* pp. 113-114. Psalm 90(91):2. Psalm 102(103):12, 26, 27. 1 Tim. 6:16.
[233] 2 Peter 3:8. Pslam 90(91):4.
[234] St Gregory of Nazianzus, *Homily* 38, ch. 7 and 8, in Migne, *P.G.,* 36, 317, 320.
[235] Gen. 1:1.

did not exist before the Creation and is the result of the movement of matter and the constantly changing events within Creation. Therefore God Who looks down upon His Creation with love and compassion is the Cause of all time, directing all events to the final destination of man's Salvation in Jesus Christ.

Question 46: What is the Unchangeable Attribute of God?

Answer: The Unchangeable Attribute[236] excludes any change or alteration or *"variation or shadow of turning"*[237] of His Existence. God is unchangeable and unalterable, neither being decreased nor increased but remaining always what He is,[238] as He says through the Prophet Malachi, *"for I Am the Lord your God, and I Am not changed."*[239] The Love of God towards man remains unchangeable, because the Salvation offered on the Cross by the Son of God, our Lord and Saviour Jesus Christ, existed in the Will of God before all ages and was not a result of any additional action by God. God did not begin to love us after Christ's Crucifixion because He always loved us, even before the creation of the Cosmos.[240]

Question 47: What is the All-presence of God?

Answer: God is All-present. The All-presence is a relative Attribute and one can refer to it mainly ever since Creation occurred. It is related to the Unlimited Attribute of God and we can say that the All-presence is the qualification of the Unlimited Attribute of the Divine Essence in relation to the limited world. In relation to Creation God is Uncontainable. He is not restricted or limited to physical places, neither is He contained by anyone because He is beyond and above all space.[241]

The All-presence of God should not be understood as though the Divine Existence is confused or mixed with the Cosmos. God is present everywhere and undivided. It is not as though one part of Him will be here and another part elsewhere. God acts everywhere simultaneously through

---

[236] Frangopoulos, *Christian Faith,* pp. 50-52. Mitsopoulos, *Themata,* pp. 114-115. Bryennios, *Paralipomena,* ch. XVIII, v. III, p. 86.
[237] James 1:17.
[238] St Cyril of Jerusalem, *Catechesis,* IV, §§ 4, 5, in Migne, *P.G.,* 33, 457, 460. St Gregory of Nyssa, *Against Eunomius,* I, in Migne, *P.G.,* 45, 435.
[239] Mal. 3:6.
[240] Rom. 5:8.
[241] Clement the Alexandrian, in *B,* v 8, p. 261. St Athanasius the Great, *Epist. about the Nicene Council,* in Migne, *P.G.,* 25, 433. St John of Damascus, *Exposition. About the place of God and that only the divine is indescribeable,* book I, ch. XIII, in Migne, *P.G.,* 94, 852.

His One simple Energy but in different ways because He is All-present.[242] God is All-present throughout the Universe but He is above and beyond it and cannot be contained by it. He is fully present throughout the entire Cosmos but cannot be restricted by any space.[243]

According to Eugenios Boulgareos[244] God is All-present according to:

1. His *All-knowing*, because nothing can be hidden from Him.
2. His *Almightiness*, because in Him we live and move and exist
3. His *Essence*, because He cannot be described or limited.

Question 48: What is the Invisibility and Unintelligibility Attribute of God?

Answer: God being the Absolute Spiritual Being is Invisible and Unintelligible. God's invisibility is the natural result of the spirituality of the Divine. God is bodiless, invisible and untouchable by Nature.[245] The Prophets had not seen the Lord Himself except what God had revealed to them, which was a small radiance of His Divine Glory.[246] God does not appear as He is but as He Wills. God makes Himself known to whomever He wills.[247] Only the Son of God with the Holy Spirit can see and know the fullness of God the Father.[248] He who knows the Son knows the Father because he who has seen the Son has seen the Father, for the Son is in the Father and the Father in the Son[249] and *"no one comes to the Father except through"*[250] Jesus Christ, the Son of God, *"and the one to whom the Son Wills to reveal Him."*[251]

---

[242] St John of Damascus, *Exposition. About the place of God and that only the divine is indescribeable,* book I, ch. XIII, in Migne, *P.G.*, 94, 852. St Athanasius the Great, *Against Arians,* III, § 22, in Migne, *P.G.*, 26, 369.

[243] St John of Damascus, *Exposition. About the place of God and that only the divine is indescribeable,* book I, ch. XIII,, in Migne, *P.G.*, 94, 856.

[244] Boulgareos, *Theologicon,* p. 103.

[245] St Athanasius the Great, *Against the Greeks,* § 26, in Migne, *P.G.*, 25, 56. St Gregory of Nazianzus, *Homily* 28, § 7, in Migne, *P.G.*, 36, 33.

[246] **Is.** 6:1-3. **Ez.** 1:4-28; 2:10; 44:1-3. **Dan.** 7:9-10. **Amos** 9:1. **Zach.** 3:1; 4:1-3.

[247] Ex. 25:22.

[248] St Cyril of Jerusalem, *Catechesis,* VI, § 7, in Migne, *P.G.*, 33, 545.

[249] John 14:7, 9-11.

[250] John 14:6.

[251] Matth. 11:27.

Question 49: What is the Blessedness of God?

Answer: The Lord our God Who is needless and self-sufficient, unalterable and unchangeable, is *"the fullness of joy"*[252] and His Peace *"surpasses all understanding."*[253] He is the Absolute Blessed One and thus the Self-Blessed.

CHAPTER FIVE
GOD'S ATTRIBUTES IN RELATION
TO THE WAY OF GOD'S ENERGY

Question 50: What are God's Attributes in relation to the way of His Energy?

Answer: The first Attribute ascribed to the Divine Intellect is the *All-knowing*. God knows Himself through Absolute Knowledge, as Absolute is His Divine Essence. As the Absolute Being God is *independent* and *free*. God's Almightiness is related to His Will and Freedom and nothing is impossible because *"whatever the Lord pleases He does."*[254]   Divine Holiness is relative to the Almightiness of God, according to which He is free from all moral imperfections, spurns wickedness, never uses His Power to perform evil and loves whatever is just and good.   God is Absolutely Holy by Nature and the Source of all Holiness.

Related to the Holiness of God is His Justice.[255] God loves justice[256] and has manifested His Love through the assurance that His *"yoke is easy"* and His *"burden is light."*[257] God's Almightiness is characterized as being *Power of Love*, like His All-knowingness is portrayed as *Knowledge* and *Wisdom of virtue* and *Mercy;* and His Justice as *Justice of Love* and *Blessedness,* which is spread to all by God out of His love towards His Creation. This Absolute Divine Love of God is expressed as *"Goodness,"* *"Philanthropy,"* *"Forbearance"* and *"Mercifulness"* towards man. Finally, God is *"Truthful"* and *"Faithful"* to His Promises, but alienated from any lies.

---

[252] Psalm 16(17):11.
[253] Phil. 4:7.
[254] Psalms 134(135):6; 114(115):3.
[255] Gen. 18:19. Is. 56:1.
[256] Is. 61:8.
[257] Matth. 11:29. Jer. 6:16.

Question 51: What is the Divine All-knowing?

Answer: The first Attribute ascribed to the Divine Intellect is *All-knowing.*[258] God knows Himself and everything that exists outside Himself through His Absolute Knowledge.[259] The High Being is a Personal God and as an Absolute Spirit He has Self-conscience. This Personal Knowledge of God does not restrict Him, neither does it contradict the infinity or limitlessness of God because as His Essence and His Existence are infinite so is His Knowledge.

Our Lord and Saviour Jesus Christ, the Son of God, assured us that *"no one knows the Son except the Father. Nor does anyone know the Father except the Son, and the one to whom the Son wills to reveal Him."*[260] St Paul teaches of the Holy Spirit that *"no one knows the things of God except the Spirit of God"*[261] as He is not alien to the Deity and Essence of God.

Question 52: What is the Divine Foreknowing?

Answer: God knows everything that exists outside Himself, not only the logical beings, Angels and man, but also everything that occurs in the visible and invisible world. He knows before all time the acts of all intellectual beings, what each and everyone will do and what they might have done. He knows exactly each and every detail from before the creation of time, not having received this knowledge afterwards.[262] God's All-knowing is not as a result of a progressive knowledge, as with men but because of the simplicity of His Essence, He knows all and sees all, the past and the future as being present before Him, even before they are realized.[263]

It is incomprehensible how God can know everything before all time.[264] He knows all thoughts of men and Angels, even the most secret things of their hearts, not only at present but even before all time began.[265]

Although God foreknows men's actions that are performed by their free-will, He is not responsible for any evil deeds of mankind.[266] Even our prayers addressed to God requesting the change of the path of our lives are

---

[258] Mitsopoulos, *Themata,* p. 118.

[259] Plato of Moscow, *Orthodox Teaching,* p. 38.

[260] Matth. 11:27.

[261] 1 Corinth. 2:11.

[262] Clement the Alexandrian, *Stromata,* VI, 17, in **B**, v.8, p. 238.

[263] St John of Damascus, *Catechesis,* I, 14, in Migne, *P.G.,* 94, 860. Clement the Alexandrian, *Stromata,* VI, 17, in **B**, v.8, p. 238.

[264] St Augustine, in migne, *P.L.,* 36, 576.

[265] Karmeris, *The dogmatics,* v. II, p. 601.

[266] St John of Damascus, *Against Manichees,* 79, in Migne, *P.G.,* 94, 1577.

under God's All-knowing as He foreknows whose prayers He will hear because they are sincere and whose He will renounce because they are unworthy, not having been addressed correctly.[267]

God knows His Creation: the irrational, rational and intellectual not indirectly but directly; not imperfectly but perfectly and in all its fullness; not indefinitely and dimly but clearly, accurately and exactly, not to a level that could accept addition but absolutely perfectly. God knows everything, always, simultaneously, by Him and through Him. Everything is completely exposed before Him.[268]

Question 53: What is the Divine All-wisdom?

Answer: The Attribute of *All- wisdom*[269] is God' s Attribute by which He places perfect goals and uses perfect ways to achieve perfect purposes. His All-wisdom is His All-knowing when it is to be seen:

1.   in relation to the aims that God planned when creating the world and

2.   in relation to the ways used for the fulfillment of *"the Eternal Purposes."*[270]

The Wisdom of God found ways to destroy moral evil that entered into the world through Satan, the inventor of evil. This was accomplished through Jesus Christ by the Plan that God the Father had before all time. Consequently mankind has been restored to the righteous condition in which he was created before the Fall and therefore the Wisdom of God finds ways for the Salvation of all humanity.

Question 54: What is the Independent and Free-will of God?

Answer: God is ascribed as Independent and Free. God acts independently and by His own Free-will that is unlimited.[271]

Christ assured us that God, being the Extreme and Absolute Good,[272] does not act by force but acts independently and gives freely to those who

---

[267] Origen, *About prayer,* 6, 4, in **B,** v. 10, p. 244.
[268] Trempelas, *Dogmatique,* v. I, p. 211.
[269] Frangopoulos, *Christian Faith,* pp. 54-57. Mitsopoulos, *Themata,* pp. 121-122.
[270] Ephes. 3:11.
[271] St John of Damascus, *Catechesis,* III, 57, in Migne, 94, 1033, 1041. Plato of Moscow, *Orthodox Teaching,* p. 39.

ask. He assists those who seek and opens His door to those who knock upon it.[273] God does not act out of sympathy nor out of need nor by force. Neither does He act by blind instinct, as within the animal world but out of true Love for His Creation.[274] He always acts with Justice and without partiality.[275] The Attribute of freedom as an inner act of His Will can be considered identical to His Essence, which being simple, excludes any divisions.

Although in the Absolute and Simple Essence of God there can be no differentiation or synthesis of acts from a human point of view, we can distinguish God's Will in the following:

1.   *The natural* **or** *necessary Free-will of God.*

2.   *The foregoing and the following Will of God.*

The *foregoing Will of God* is also called **"good pleasure"** (*ευδοκία)* and the **following Will of God** is called **"concession"** (*παραχώρηση).*[276] The **concession Will** of God is differentiated into the **"economia"** and the **"pedagogic"** according to which it is used as the means of man's Salvation.

3.   *The absolute and relative or under conditions Will of God.*

4.   *The effective and the inoperative Will of God.*

Question 55: What is the Almightiness of God?

Answer: In Creation three Attributes reign: the Will of God, the Wisdom of God and the Almightiness of God.[277] The Will of God is pleased with the results; the Wisdom of God directs and the Almightiness of God perfects Creation.[278] Nothing is impossible for God.[279] Everything that He Willed He created in Heaven and on earth.[280]

---

[272] Matth. 19:17.
[273] Matth. 7:7-8.
[274] Rom. 9:18-19.
[275] 1 Peter 1:17. Acts 10:34.
[276] Trempelas, *Dogmatique,* v. I, p. 214.
[277] Mitsopoulos, *Themata,* pp. 117-118.
[278] Boulgareos, *Theologicon,* p. 145.
[279] Luke 1:37. Gen. 18:14. Cf. Frangopoulos, *Christian Faith,* pp. 52-54.
[280] Psalm 134(135):6. Cf. Plato of Moscow, *Orthodox Teaching,* p. 40. Psalm 32(33):9. Psalm 32(33):6. Psalm 76(77):13-14.

God is the One Who calls the non-being into being and merely by His Word creates everything from nothingness and brings them into existence.[281] In addition, as easy as it is for Him to create anything from nothingness, with the same ease He can return to nothingness everything He has created. God can do even more of whatever He has done through His faithful servants and within His Church.[282]

Although God can do whatever pleases Him, He cannot act upon or realize something that opposes His Divine Nature and character, simply because it is impossible for Him to will so.[283] Whatever God Willed He created but He does not want everything that He could create. God has the Power to create thousands of worlds like ours but He does not wish to do so.[284] This indicates the greatness of God's Power, as He is the Father of Truth.[285]

Question 56: What is the Holiness of God?

Answer: Holiness is the Attribute of God according to which God is free from all moral imperfections, loves whatever is just and good, and despises whatever is evil and bad.[286] Thus His Divine Will always elects the good, whereas His Almightiness acts in all Holiness.

The *Holiness* of God is not a condition whereby God has been cleansed from all moral evil or that He has achieved all virtues progressively. For God He is by His infinite and perfect Nature and Existence the only *Holy One*. He is absolutely and truly Holy by Nature, the Source by Whom everyone is Sanctified.[287]

Question 57: What is the Righteousness of God?

Answer: The Divine Righteousness derives from God's Holiness. One can clearly see that God loves righteousness but despises evil and sin.[288] He is the God Who judges the works of all men with Justice and without

---

[281] Rom. 4:17.
[282] John 14:12-14.
[283] Heb. 6:18.
[284] Karmeris, *The dogmatics*, v. II, p. 599.
[285] 2 Tim. 2:13. Clement the Alexandrian, *Stromata*, book IV, in **B**, v. 8, p. 263. St Isidorus of Pelusion, Book III, *Epist.* 335, in Migne, *P.G.*, 78, 993.
[286] Plato, *Orthodox Teaching*, pp. 39-40. Frangopoulos, *Christian Faith*, pp. 56-57. Mitsopoulos, *Themata*, pp. 123-124.
[287] St Cyril of Jerusalem, *Catechesis Mystagogic V*, ch. XIII, § 7, in Migne, *P.G.*, 33, 1124.
[288] Psalm 10(11):7, 5. Cf. Frangopoulos, *Christian Faith*, pp. 57-58. Mitsopoulos, *Themata*, pp. 124-125.

partiality.[289] Being the Only True Righteous, He judges everything according to righteousness that exists in the world.[290] Therefore Holy Scripture proclaims God as the God of Justice Who loves righteousness[291] and is Righteous in all His Ways,[292] He will Judge all the nations and all the earth with righteousness.[293] God being Righteous as the Law-giver is also Just as the Judge. God will judge the world through His Son.[294] He will judge the living and the dead on that Day that God the Father has placed in His own Authority.[295]

Question 58: What is the Love and Kindness of God?

Answer: Who can speak of God's Love and who can find words to describe the greatness of His Kindness and Mercies?[296] God's Love is considered to be the Attribute that unites all the other Attributes. Thus, all Qualifications of God can be considered as Qualifications of God's Love. His Almightiness is considered as the Almightiness of Love. His All-knowing and All-wisdom is Knowledge, Wisdom of Virtue and Mercies that leads all men to their final destination and for the intellectual creatures this final cause is to inherit Divine Blessedness. God's Righteousness is Righteousness of Love that desires the return to the path of joy and peace of all those who went astray. His All-presence joins and governs everything with Love and Kindness. His infinite Blessedness grants Eternal Blessedness to those who will inherit His Kingdom. In other words God is the Supreme Good Who does not restrict His Love to Himself but disperses it from His own Richness and Blessed Life to all His Creation.

God's Love is expressed towards Creation accordingly: to Creation as Kindness and to creatures as providing them with every good thing.[297] God shows especially to the intellectual beings the richness and abundance of His Kindness. God does not neglect the sinners either, nor does He abandon those who have fallen. Instead He is Merciful towards them and raises them up thereby revealing His great Mercy and Longsuffering. To those who prove to be ungrateful, He does not immediately send His Divine Wrath

---

[289] 1 Peter 1:17.
[290] Clement the Alexandrian, *Protrepticus,* VI, in **B**, v. 7, pp. 52-53.
[291] Psalm 11(12):7.
[292] Psalm 145(146):17.
[293] Psalms 67(68):4; 96(97):10, 13; 9(10):8.
[294] John 5:27.
[295] Acts 1:7.
[296] Cf. Frangopoulos, *Christian Faith,* pp. 58-59. Mitsopoulos, *Themata,* pp. 125-126. Bryennios, *Paralipomena,* ch. II, v. III, p. 74.
[297] Psalm 104(105):21, 27-30. Matth. 5:25-34.

upon them but offers them His Tolerance, Forbearance and Longsuffering in order to lead them to repentance[298] because He desires that *"all men be saved and come to the knowledge of Truth."*[299]

God's Love and Goodness is beyond any measure being infinite and unsearchable to man's mind. One must be careful not to place the Love of God in opposition to His Righteousness. Mercy and Justice are joined together in a perfect harmony. This perfect union is manifested clearly in the Sacrifice that was offered by Christ, the Son of God, on the Cross. The Divine Love of God delivers the Only Begotten Son to death for the Salvation of all mankind and at the same time, through Christ's obedience,[300] the Divine Righteousness and Holiness of God were satisfied, after He had been insulted by man at the time of the Fall (man blamed God for his own Fall).[301]

Question 59: What is the Truthfulness and Faithfulness of God?

Answer: According to St John the Apostle and Evangelist, God *"is True"* and *"His words are True."*[302] Since God's Power is unlimited, His Kindness infinite and His All-knowing unsearchable, He knows all that He has promised, and has not only the Will but also the Power to fulfill them in the proper time. His Promises are the Promises of the Divine Kindness and Wisdom, the Promises by Whom the *"yes"*[303] and the *"amen"*[304] have assurance and are immoveable.

God is faithful in His words and it is impossible for Him to lie. It is utterly impossible for God to lie, not only because He gave the Commandment *"not to bear false witness,"*[305] but because He Himself is the Holy and Just One Who cannot lie. Nothing is impossible for God except to lie. His words are pure and free of lies, as molten gold and silver are cleansed of all false metals. Thus, the Lord assured us that *"heaven and earth will pass away, but My words will by no means pass away."*[306]

---

[298] Rom. 2:4.
[299] 1 Tim. 2:4.
[300] Phil. 2:8.
[301] Gen. 3:13.
[302] John 3:33; 17:17. Rev. 3:7. Cf. Frangopoulos, *Christian Faith,* pp. 59-60.
[303] Rev. 14:13. 2 Corinth. 1:19.
[304] 2 Corinth. 1:20. Rev. 1:7; 3:14; 22:20.
[305] Ex. 20:16. Matth. 5:37.
[306] Matth. 24:35.

CHAPTER SIX
THE DOCTRINE OF THE TRIUNE GOD

Question 60: What is the Doctrine of the Triune God?

Answer: The specific and unique characteristic of the Christian Doctrine is that ***God is One in Trinity and Trinity in One.***[307] God is One according to His unique and undivided Essence. God is also Trinity according to His Hypostases (Persons) who differ from one another, being co-eternal Persons Who have no beginning and are of the same Essence and Energy.[308]

The Truth concerning the Triune God was in the Old Testament but strictly monotheistically with only a few indications concerning the Trinity. The Doctrine of the Holy Trinity and the Incarnation of the Word were made known to the Prophets and the Apostles through Christ in the New Testament.[309] These indications were not clear in the Old Testament and they would have remained obscure if the Light of Divine Revelation did not shine in the New Testament through the Incarnation of the Word and Son of God in the Person of the God-Man, the Messiah, our Lord and Saviour Jesus Christ.

The Orthodox Church proclaims that God is One in Deity but Three Persons in Hypostases.[310] The Three Persons or Hypostases are distinguished from one another as co-existing before time and without beginning but at the same time they are declared to be inseparable and undivided. It was also declared that beside the Hypostatic Attributes of each Person of the Trinity, they have One and the same Energy, Will and Essence. Thus, the Father through the Son in the Holy Spirit creates everything. In this way the Unity of the Holy Trinity is preserved and One God is proclaimed *"Who is above all, and through all, and in all."*[311] *"Above all"* refers to the Father Who is the Beginning and the Source of all. *"Through all"* refers to the Son Who is the Word of God the Father. *"In all"* refers to the Holy Spirit Who perfects and sanctifies all that the Father and Son do.

---

[307] Bryennios, *Paralipomena,* ch. XVI, v. III, p. 84.
[308] Plato of Moscow, *Orthodox Teaching,* pp. 96-98. Kefalas, *Catechesis,* p. 85. Damalas, *Catechesis,* pp. 10-11. Frangopoulos, *Christian Faith,* pp. 61-64. Labadarios, *Sermons,* pp. 19-21. Ware, *Way,* pp. 33-39. Lossky, *Theology,* pp.36-39
[309] Romanides, *Dogmatique,* v. 1, p. 194.
[310] Bryennios, *Paralipomena,* Homily XVI, v. I, p. 259.
[311] Ephes. 4:6.

Question 61: What are the indications concerning the Holy Trinity found in the Old Testament?

Answer: In the Old Testament one finds God speaking in the plural form[312] instead of the singular form. The use of the plural form *"let Us"* indicates that God is speaking to Others Who are equal in Authority to Him.[313] God is not speaking to Himself as one Person because this would be considered madness. Neither is He speaking to Angels because Angels cannot create and God is not obliged to give an account of His actions to His own Creation. The Angels are certainly not equal to God but stand in awe before Him, glorifying Him ceaselessly for all the wonders He has performed. The use of the word *"Holy"* three times in Isaiah[314] and the appearance of the three Angels at Mamre[315] Who were addressed as one Person, were considered to be indications of three Hypostases of the One Deity. Furthermore, in Proverbs the Wisdom appears to have Its own personality with self-conscience, activity, existing from the beginning with God, reflecting the Light of God's Knowledge and participating in the work of Creation. All we can say with regard to the Teachings of the Old Testament, is that during the times of the ancient authors, the world was prepared for faith in the Holy Trinity but it was not revealed to the Israelites, who knew and were taught Monotheism as a way of worship of the One True and Personal God.

Question 62: What are the teaching of the New Testament concerning the Holy Trinity being the One God?

Answer: The solid foundations concerning the Teaching of the Holy Trinity are founded in the New Testament, whereas, at the same time the oneness of the Deity and its unity is proclaimed. The Mother of God and Ever-Virgin Mary, the Theotokos, was informed by the Archangel Gabriel that *"the Holy Spirit will come upon you, and the Power of the Highest will overshadow*

---

[312] Gen. 1:26; 2:18; 3:23; 11:7.

[313] St Basil the Great, *To Exahemerus*, ch. VIII, in Migne, *P.G.*, 29, 205. *Barnabas*, V, 5, in Lightfoot, *Apostolic Fathers*, p. 167. Theophylactos of Bulgaria, in *B*, v. 2, p. 230, 232 and v. 5, p. 34. St Cyril of Jerusalem, *Catechesis*, X, § 7, in Migne, *P.G.*, 33, 668. St Athanasius the Great, *Against Greeks*, § 44, in Migne, *P.G.*, 25, 93. St Gregory os Nyssa, *To Genesis 1:26*, Homily 1, in Migne, *P.G.*, 44, 260. St Irenaeus, *Heresies*, IV, in Migne, *P.G.*, 7, 1032. St Cyril of Alexandria, *About the Holy Trinity*, Homily 1, in Migne, *P.G.*, 75, 25. St John Chrysostom, *To Genesis*, Homily 8, in Migne, *P.G.*, 53, 71.

[314] Is. 6:3. St Athanasius the Great, *About the Incarnation*, in Migne, *P.G.*, 26, 1000. Ibid, *To "all has been given to Me…"*, in Migne, *P.G.*, 25, 220. Ibid, *Against Arians*, Homily II, in Migne, *P.G.*, 26, 312. St Ambrosius, *De fide*, in Makarios, *Enchiridion*, v. I, p. 211, note 2.

[315] Gen. 18:1-4.

you; therefore, also, that the Holy One Who is to be born will be called the Son of God."[316] When Christ was baptized, the Holy Trinity was clearly manifested: the Holy Spirit descended *"like a dove"* and the Father witnessing from above that He Who is baptized is His *"beloved Son"* in Whom He is *"well pleased."*[317] Furthermore, when Christ took His three Disciples, Peter, James and John with Him and went up Mount Tabor, He was Transfigured before them. Simultaneously the Holy Spirit *"overshadowed them"* in the form of *"a bright cloud"* and the Father assured them that *"this is My beloved Son, in Whom I Am well pleased. Hear Him."*[318] In His last prayer before His deliverance to the Jews, Christ differentiated Himself from the Holy Spirit Whom He referred to as *"another Helper"*[319] and Whom He *"will send from the Father, the Spirit of Truth Who proceeds from the Father."*[320] This Holy Spirit Who proceeds only from the Father, will testify concerning the Son, will remind them of everything and will guide them into all the Truth.[321] When Christ called the Holy Spirit *"another Helper,"* He indicated by use of the word *"another"* the difference of the Hypostasis of the third Person from the other two Persons of the Holy Trinity, whereas, by using the word *"Helper,"* He indicated the relationship to the Divine Essence according to which the Holy Spirit performs whatever the Son does.[322]

The last Commandment that Christ gave to His Holy Apostles before He ascended into Heaven[323] proclaimed not only the Trinity of God's Hypostases but the oneness and undivided nature of the Holy Trinity. By commanding them to baptize the people NOT *"in the names"*, but *"in the Name"* He indicated the one Nature of the Holy Trinity.[324]

Question 63: What are the teachings of the Orthodox Church concerning the Holy Trinity?

Answer: The Truth of the Divine Revelation concerning the Holy Trinity was proclaimed by the Orthodox Church from the beginning[325] since anyone

---

[316] Luk. 1:35.
[317] Matth. 3:16-17. Mark 1:9-11. Luk. 3:22. Psalm 2:7. Is. 42:1. 2 Peter 1:17. John 1:33.
[318] Matth. 17:1-8. Mark 9:2-8. Luk. 9:28-36.
[319] John 14:16-17.
[320] John 15:26; 16:26.
[321] John 14:26; 15:26.
[322] St Cyril of Alexandria, *To John,* book IX, Homily 1, in Migne, *P.G.,* 74, 257. St John Chrysostom, *To John,* Homily 75, § 1, in Montfaucon, v. 8, p. 502.
[323] Matth. 28:19-20.
[324] St Ambrosius, *De Spiritus Sanctus,* I, ch. 3, § 40, in migne, *P.L.,* 16, 742. St Augustine, in migne, *P.L.,* 35, 1429.
[325] Romanides, *Dogmatique,* v. 1, pp. 173-175.

becoming a member of the Orthodox Church has to be baptised in the Name of the three Persons: the Father and the Son and the Holy Spirit. The Orthodox Church incorporated the use of the Names of the three Persons of God within its worship and made it an essential part of the Confession of Faith, which opposed any false doctrines and heresies.

Question 64: What clarifications were used for the Trinitarian terminology?

Answer: The Fathers of the Orthodox Church clarified the terms concerning the Doctrine of the Holy Trinity. In the West Tertullian introduced the terms *"Natura" ("Nature"), "Substantia" ("Substance")* and later the term *"Essentia" ("Essence"),* which refer to the common Divine Essence of the Holy Trinity. These terms represented the terms used in the East: *"Nature"* and *"Essence."* Very few scholars used the terms *"Natura"* and *"Substantia"* to define the Divine Persons for which later on the term *"Hypostasis"* was used. Furthermore, other Fathers used the terms *"Substantia"* and *"Hypostasis"* as synonymous.

When the term *"Hypostasis"* was used to express the term *"Person,"* the Fathers of the West hesitated to accept it because, according to them, this term having the equivalent term *"Substantia"* expressed the same meaning as the term *"Essence."* To clarify this difference, a Synod was held in the Great City of Alexandria (Egypt) and the decisions were sent to Antioch.[326] Finally, the term *"Hypostasis" ("Substantia")* was distinguished from the terms *"Nature" ("Natura")* and *"Essence" ("Essentia").* The Nature and Deity of the Father and of the Son and of the Holy Spirit is One but at the same time the Identity of the one Nature is distinguished into the three perfect *"Hypostases"* and thus is the One God known.[327]

The term *"of the same Essence" (homoousios-ὁμοούσιος)*[328] was accepted after many discussions. The 1st Ecumenical Synod (325) condemned the term *"something like the Essence" ("homoiousios"-"ὁμοιούσιος")* which was used by the heretic Arius who proclaimed that *"there was a time that the Son had not existed"* and that the Son is neither equal to the Father nor a perfect God but He was made and is *"something like"* God (*"homoiousios"*). The Holy Synod, adopting the term *"of the same Essence" ("homoousios"-"ὁμοούσιος"),* proclaimed that the Son is of

---

[326] Ibid, *Tomos to the Antiochians,* in Migne, *P.G.,* 26, 801.
[327] St Basil the Great, *Epist. 2,* in Migne, *P.G.,* 32, 773 and 776. Isidorus of Pelusion, *Book III, Epist. 112,* in Migne, *P.G.,* 78, 817.
[328] Lossky, *Theology,* p. 40.

the same Essence as the Father and not made. The Word of God is the Image of God the Father, the same and identical in all things with Him, unchangeable and undivided, existing before all time with Him.[329]

The Holy Synod also proclaimed that the Word and Son of God is different from all other Creation, not only because He is of the same Essence as the Father but because He remains undivided from the Essence of the Father in such a way that He is one with the Father.[330] The Son is the Image of the Father[331] and always exists in the Father and the Father in the Son,[332] as in the relation of brightness to the light.[333] Finally, the terms "*not made*" (αγένητος) and "*not born*" (αγέννητος) were clarified.

Question 65: What do we mean by saying: *"Trinity in One and One in Trinity"*?

Answer: According to the above, One and Undivided is the Essence or Nature of the Deity and One Deity is in the Trinity. In the One Deity there are three Hypostases or Persons but they are One and the three Persons have the same Nature and Identity. Each Person is the fullness of the Deity of the Father and the Son is True God, as is the Holy Spirit. Whatever refers to the Deity of the Father refers to the Son and to the Holy Spirit, without them being called "*Father.*"[334] According to the Attributes of infinity, unsearchability and uncreativeness they are the same because in the Divine Nature there is no difference between the Father and the Son and the Holy Spirit. They are one and undivided communion.

Under no circumstances can there be any kind of split or division within the Divine Essence. Neither can we imagine that the Son could exist without the Father nor can the Holy Spirit be separated from the Son. Within the three Persons there is an incomprehensible Communion in which the differentiation of the Hypostases neither divides the unity of the Nature nor confuses their personal characteristics and Hypostatic Attributes.[335] There is One Deity because One is the Essence of the three Persons.

In the Holy Trinity there is no minor Person, nor did one Person exist before the Other. The Persons are not divided by will or by force. In the three Hypostases the Will, Power and Energy is One. The Father does

---

[329] Heb. 1:3. St Athanasius the Great, *About Dionysius bishop of Alexandria*, in Migne, *P.G.*, 25, 505.
[330] John 17:11.
[331] 2 Corinth. 4:4. Col. 1:15.
[332] John 14:10; 17:21.
[333] St Athanasius the Great, *Synods*, in Migne, *P.G.*, 25, 425.
[334] St Athanasius the Great, *Against Arians,* III § 4, in Migne, *P.G.*, 26, 328 and 332.
[335] St Basil the Great, *Epist.* 38, in Migne, *P.G.*, 32, 332. St Symeon, *Euriskomena,* Homily LXII, pp. 323-326.

nothing on His own and neither does the Son do anything without the Holy Spirit. All the Divine Energy that guides Creation comes from the Father, is realized through the Son and is perfected by the Holy Spirit.[336]

The Father has His Existence and has no need of anything. He is the Cause and Source of the Deity of the Son and the Holy Spirit, as being the unique Source of the One Godhead. The Son is also perfect God being the Word of God and Begotten of the Father before all ages. The Holy Spirit is perfect God as well, being neither part of the Father nor of the Son. The Son is united with the Father and the Holy Spirit inseparably, as the Holy Spirit is united inseparably with the Son and the Father.

The three Hypostases or Persons do not divide the One Divine Essence of God, so therefore God is One and not three Gods. We believe that from the Nature of God the Father rises the Son and the Holy Spirit, as from the fire comes the light and the warmth. As the fire always radiates light and heat, likewise, before the Creation of all things, the Word of God and His Spirit existed with God the Father before all time. Thus, One is God Who is glorified in Trinity and His Deity is the Source and Root of the Deity of the Son and the Holy Spirit. God is One in Nature and Essence but three in Hypostases: Father, Son and Holy Spirit; and whatever is the Father in Nature likewise is the Son and the Holy Spirit.[337] God is One in Trinity, Trinity in One and One and simultaneously Trinity.[338]

CHAPTER SEVEN
THE TRINITATRIAN DOCTRINE

Question 66: What is the Trinitarian Doctrine?

Answer: In the Old Testament the Fatherhood of God is not ignored. He is mainly referred to as the Father of the people of Israel Who provides them with a Father Who shows love and affection to all who fear Him. In the New Testament the Fatherhood appears to have a new meaning because God as Father expands His affection to all mankind, especially to those who imitate Him through virtue but even more to those who are regenerated through the Faith in Christ and the Holy Spirit and who become sons of God by Grace and Adoption. However, these sons of God by Grace, although regenerated, are still mortal and different from the Son of God Who is the

---

[336] St Gregory of Nyssa, *That there are not three gods*, in Migne, *P.G.*, 45, 125. St John of Damascus, *About the two wills in Christ*, in Migne, *P.G.*, 95, 136. Ibid, *Exposition. About the Holy Trinity*, VIII, in Migne, *P.G.*, 94, 825.
[337] Karmeris, *The dogmatics*, v. I, p. 365. Ibid, *The dogmatics*, v. II pp. 500, 595-596.
[338] Mitsopoulos, *Themata*, pp. 58-60.

Only Begotten Son of God by Nature and not by Grace. The first Person of the Holy Trinity in relation to the second Person is the Father. God is proclaimed as the *"One God, the Father of Whom are all things"* [339]and *"from Whom the whole family in Heaven and earth is named."*[340]

God from the beginning is characterized as being the only Father Who is *"not born"* (*"αγέννητος"*). Only He exists without any cause or reason. He did not pre-exist before the Son in order to become the Father afterwards, as it is with humanity. He existed before all time and He forever is Father to His co-eternal and inseparable Only Begotten Son.

The second Person of the Holy Trinity is the Son of God the Father. The Son is not considered as being the Son of God in the same manner as the Angels, the people of Israel or those who are regenerated by Grace, who are also called *"sons of God."* The Son is by Nature the Son of God, *"not made"* (*αγένητος*), Who exists before all time, infinite in nature like the Father and *"of the same Essence"* (*"homoousios"*-*"ομοούσιος"*) with the Father. The Son knows the Father and is known by the Father. Being equal to the Father and being His identical and living Image, He is worshipped equally with the Father, having the same honour as the Father. The Son is the Creator of all things cooperating with the Father through Whom all things were made.

The Holy Spirit is referred to as the *"other Helper"*[341] Who proceeds only from the Father,[342]Who will replace Christ as He departs from this world and Who will guide the Disciples in all the Truth, reminding them of all that the Lord had spoken.[343] Christ Himself bears witness that the Holy Spirit is an individual Person in the Deity, and warns us that *"he who blasphemes against the Holy Spirit never has forgiveness but is subject to eternal condemnation."*[344]

The Holy Spirit proceeds only from the Father and is sent into the world by the Father in the Name of the Son.[345] He speaks not on His own Authority but whatever He hears from the Father, He speaks and tells of things to come.[346] The Holy Spirit searches the depths of God,[347] distributs various *Charismata* or Gifts to each one individually as He Wills,[348] dwells

---

[339] 1 Corinth. 8:6.
[340] Ephes. 3:15. Cf. Kefalas, *Catechesis,* pp. 85-86.
[341] John 14:16, 26; 15:26; 16:7.
[342] John 15:26.
[343] John 14: 26; 16:13.
[344] Mark 3:29. Matth. 12:32. Luk. 12:10
[345] John 14:26.
[346] John 16:13.
[347] 1 Corinth. 2:10. Rom. 11:33-35.
[348] 1 Corinth. 12:4, 7-11.

within us[349] and has the human body as His living temple,[350] regenerates man in Jesus Christ[351] and speaks through God-inspired men.[352]

Question 67: Who is God the Father?

Answer: In the Old Testament[353] God is referred mainly as the Father of the people of Israel[354] Who made them and provides for them as a Father Who shows love and affection to all who fear Him[355] God had always shown His Mercy and Affection to those who suffered and lacked protection.[356] In the New Testament God the Father reveals Himself in a new light. He reveals Himself as Father, not only because He created everything in the world, providing and protecting the helpless and those in need but mainly in a moral aspect as the Father of all, without differentiating between Jews and other ethnicities. All those who through repentance return to God become His children as He becomes their Father once again.[357]

The Only Begotten Son of God is the only One Who is of the same Essence as the Father.[358] He is the Son of God by Nature[359] and because He has whatever the Father has[360] and whosoever sees the Son has seen the Father.[361]

The Father has a unique and pure metaphysical relationship with His Only Begotten Son Who is by Nature of the same Essence as Him. All those who through faith are regenerated but they cannot achieve the Nature of God and neither can they be like the Only Begotten Son except through imitation and by Divine Grace. For what the Son is by Nature, men are by adoption and *philanthropia.*[362]

The Holy Fathers of the Orthodox Church refer to the first Person of the Holy Trinity as Father, being the Father of all, the Beginning and the

---

[349] Rom. 8:9.

[350] 1 Corinth. 3:16; 6:19.

[351] 2 Corinth. 4:16. Col. 3:10. Rom. 12:2. 1 Peter 1:22-23. John 3:5-8.

[352] Ephes. 3:5. 1 Peter 3:12. 2 Peter 1:21.

[353] Mitsopoulos, *Themata,* pp. 130-132.

[354] Deut. 32:6. Mal. 2:10. Is. 63:16; 64:8.

[355] Psalm 103(104):13.

[356] Psalm 68(69):5. Prov. 3:12.

[357] Luk. 15:11-32.

[358] Zigabinos, *To Psalms*, in Migne, *P.G.,* 129, 1124. St Gregory of Nyssa, *Theologicus IV about the Son,* Homily 30, § 20, in Migne, *P.G.,* 36, 128.

[359] John 14:10-11; 10:38; 5:19-2.

[360] St Basil the Great, *Homily 15 concerning faith*, § 2, in Migne, *P.G.*, 31, 468.

[361] John 14:9.

[362] St Cyril of Alexandria, *To John*, ch. IX, in Migne, *P.G.*, 73, 153.

Cause of all things, the Source of Life from Whom the Son is Begotten before all ages. For this reason, the Father is the Natural Cause and the Principal of the Son because there is only One Principal and not two in the Godhead. Therefore the Head of the Son is the Father.[363] God the Father is the only One Who is without beginning and not born, Who has this Hypostatic Attribute alone and cannot be shared with the other two Persons. God the Father is the Principal and Source of the Deity and from Whom the third Person of the Holy Trinity, the Holy Spirit, proceeds.[364]

The Eternal Fatherhood of the First Person of the Holy Trinity, although it is incomprehensible, when it is related to the two main Attributes of Love and Blessedness, then and only then can it be understood by our limited logic. God's Love seeks someone to love. Concerning the Infinite Love of God, the subject of His Love must be also Infinite. The second Person of the Holy Trinity fulfills the infinite ocean of Divine Love and proves that the Deity is Self-sufficient and Blessed. The Son is the Living and Perfect Image of God, in which the Father seeing His own Image is pleased.[365]

Question 68: Who is God the Son?

Answer: The Son is from the same Essence and is Begotten of the Father before all time and without beginning.[366] The Son did not take His existence in time like the rest of all Creation that has limited nature. He was Begotten before all time by the Father and has the same Nature and Essence as Him, being the Only Begotten of the Essence of the Father. Thus, the Son being Infinite and Equal by Nature like His Father.[367] The three Persons of the Holy Trinity know equally the depths of one another because they are Equal in Knowledge and of the same Essence.[368]

In the New Testament we find few verses[369] in which it seems that the Son is minor in relation to His Father but these verses refer only to the human nature of Christ as He took up flesh and the likeness of a servant. Through His humility He drew the attention of His Father to look down with mercy upon all men and through His Sacrifice on the Cross, we became His brothers as He participated in our flesh and blood.[370]

---

[363] Lossky, *Theology,* pp. 46-47.
[364] St Cyril of Alexandria, *To Habbakuk*, ch. III, in Migne, *P.G.,* 71, 897.
[365] Prov. 8:30. St Athanasius the Great, *Against Arians,* I, 20, in Migne, *P.G.,* 26, 53.
[366] John 8:58.
[367] Matth. 11:27. Luk. 10:22.
[368] John 5:19.
[369] John 5:19; 14:28; 17:3
[370] Heb. 2:14-15, 17.

These are the following verses:

1.   In John 14:28 Christ says: *"My Father is greater than I."* This statement refers to the human nature of the Lord, as it is indeed minor to the Divine Nature.

2.   In John 5:19 Christ says: *"Most assuredly, I say to you, the Son can do nothing of Himself, but what He sees the Father do; for whatever He does, the Son also does in like manner."* This verse does not reveal dependency of the Son upon the Father being minor to Him but it manifests the Absolute Equality and Harmony that exists in their Divine Will and Action, having one Will, one Authority and one and the same Equal Power. When the Lord says that He *"can do nothing of Himself,"* He reveals that He is Equal to His Father and that they both have the same Will for all things. Thus it appears that the Father and the Son have one Mind and one Will for all things and consequently, the Father and the Son act as one since *"what He sees the Father do; for whatever He does, the Son also does in like manner."* Furthermore, the Essence of the Father and the Son is One. Their acts and Essence are One because there can be only One Essence, One Power and One Action in the Deity of the Father and of the Son.[371]

3.   In John 17:3 Christ says: *"And this is Eternal Life, that they may know Thee, the only true God, and Jesus Christ Whom Thou hast sent."* This verse does not exclude the Equality of the Son's Deity because the expression *"the only true God"* is said in opposition to the false gods. The fact that to inherit *"Eternal Life"* one must *"know"* about the Son, manifests the Equality between the two Persons of the Holy Trinity.[372]

4.   When Christ referred to Himself as being the *"Son of Man"*[373] it is obvious that He emphasized His human nature. Therefore, it

---

[371] St John Chrysostom, *Homily* 38 § 4, in Montfaucon, v. 8, p. 256. St Cyril of Alexandria, *To John,* Homily II, ch. VI, in Migne, *P.G.,* 73, 349. StBasil the Great, *Against Eunomius,* Homily IV, in Migne, *P.G.,* 29, 676. Theophylactus of Bulgaria, *To John,* in Migne, *P.G.,* 123, 1268.

[372] St Basil the Great, *Against Eunomius,* Homily IV, in Migne, *P.G.,* 29, 705. St Athanasius the Great, *Against Arians,* Homily II, in Migne, *P.G.,* 26, 337.

[373] **Matth.** 8:20; 9:6; 11:19; 12:8, 32,40; 13:37, 41, 55; 16:13, 27, 28; 17:9, 12, 22; 18:11; 19:28; 20:18, 28; 24:27, 30, 37, 39, 44; 25:13, 31; 26:2, 24, 45, 64; 27. **Mark** 2:10, 28; 8:31, 38; 9:9, 12, 31; 10:33, 45,; 13:26, 34; 14:21, 41, 62. **Luke** 5:24; 6:5, 22; 7:34; 9:22, 26, 44, 56, 58; 11:30; 12:8, 10, 40; 15:17,22, 24, 26, 30; 18:8, 31; 19:10; 21:27, 36; 22:22, 48, 69. **John** 1:51; 3:13, 14; 5:27; 6:27, 53, 62; 8:28; 12:23, 34; 13:31.

is not illogical if the Father appears to commit *"all Authority to execute Judgment"* to the Son because *"He is the Son of Man;"*[374] or to grant Him *"to have Life in Himself;"*[375] or to give Him *"Authority over all flesh, that He should give Eternal Life;"*[376] or to give Him *"all Authority in Heaven and on earth"*[377] to Judge the living and the dead. Furthermore, the term *"born"* refers to the in time Incarnation of the Son.[378]

5.   Finally, when St Paul calls Christ *"the First Born of all Creation,"*[379] he proclaims the Truth that the Lord is not created but Begotten of the Father because he did not say *"the first created"* but *"the First Born"* not because the Cosmos is related to Him but because He is Begotten before all Creation.[380]

The 1st Ecumenical Synod that convened at Nicene (325) investigated Holy Scripture and the living Apostolic Tradition of the Church before proclaiming Jesus Christ as *"the Son of God, the Only-Begotten of the Father before all worlds, Light of Light, Very God of Very God, Begotten, not made; of one Essence with the Father; by Whom all things were made."*[381]

Question 69: Who is God the Holy Spirit?

Answer: In the Old Testament does the Holy Spirit appear as an individual Person. On the contrary, He is always inseparable from the Lord God and He never acts on His own. The Teachings of the New Testament concerning the Spirit seem to follow the same method. The Spirit appears in the beginning to be a Principal of Divine Power, which cannot be identified clearly as personal but is always referred to as *"the Holy Spirit"*[382] Who gives Supernatural Gifts, as in the case of St John the Forerunner and Baptist,[383] St Elizabeth,[384] St Zacharias[385]and St Simeon[386] who were all

---

[374] John 5:22, 27.
[375] John 5:26.
[376] John 17:2.
[377] Matth. 28:18.
[378] Rom. 1:3. Gal. 4:4. Heb. 1:5.
[379] Col. 1:15.
[380] St Athanasius the Great, *Exposition of faith,* in Migne, *P.G.,* 25, 205. St John Chrysostom, *Homily* 3 § 2, in Montfaucon, v. 11, p. 398. Theodoretus of Cyrus, *To Colossians,* ch. VII, in Migne, *P.G.,* 82, 597.
[381] The Nicene Creed. Cf. Mitsopoulos, *Themata,* pp. 135-137.
[382] Tsakonas, *Paracletus,* pp. 201-207.
[383] Luke 1:15.
[384] Luke 1:41.

filled with the *"Holy Spirit"* and even more importantly, the Most Honorable, Pure, Blessed Lady and Ever-Virgin Mary, the Theotokos (*"Mother of God"*) at the time of the Annunciation when the Archangel Gabriel announced to her: *"The Holy Spirit will come upon you, and the Power of the Highest will overshadow you."*[387] According to St John the Baptist, the Messiah would baptize those who believe in Him *"with the Holy Spirit."*[388] The Holy Spirit descended upon Jesus Christ *"like a dove"* during His baptism by St John the Baptist in the River Jordan. [389] The Holy Spirit led Jesus Christ into the wilderness to be tempted by the devil[390] and He appeared as *"a bright Cloud"* at Mount Tabor when Christ was Transfigured before the very eyes of His Holy Apostles, Peter, James and John.[391] In the fourth Gospel the Grace of God is compared to the *"Living Water,"*[392] which refers to the Holy Spirit *"Whom those believing in Him would receive"*[393] and out of their hearts *"will flow rivers of Living Water."*[394] In the abovementioned verses the Holy Spirit is referred to as a Personal Factor and a Hypostatic Source of Divine Life and Supernatural *Charismata.*[395]

Our Lord and Saviour Jesus Christ, the Son of God, very clearly witnesses that the Holy Spirit is an individual Person of the Deity and warned: *"Anyone who speaks a word against the Son of Man, it will be forgiven him; but to him who blasphemes against the Holy Spirit, it will not be forgiven."*[396] Christ had assured those who believed in Him and who, during the persecutions were brought before the civil authorities, that they should *"not worry about how or what they should answer, or what to say. For the Holy Spirit will teach you in that very hour what you ought to say."*[397] Christ differentiated Himself from the other *"Helper, the Holy Spirit Whom the Father will send"* in His Name and Who *"will teach all things,*

[385] Luke 1:67.
[386] Luke 2:26.
[387] Luke 1:35.
[388] Matth. 3:11. Luke 3:16.
[389] Matth. 3:16. Mark 1:10. Luke 3:22.
[390] Matth. 4:1. Mark 1:12. Luke 4:1.
[391] Matth. 17:1-9. Mark 9:2-10. Luke 9:28-36.
[392] John 4:10; 7:38. Ammonius, *Fragments to John,* in Migne, *P.G.,* 85, 1421.
[393] John 7:39.
[394] John 7:38. St John Chrysostom, *Homily* 51, § 1, in Montfaucon, v. 8, p. 345.
[395] Tsakonas, *Paracletus,* pp. 258-261.
[396] Luke 12:10. Matth. 12:31-32. Mark 3:28-29.
[397] Luke 12:11-12; 21:12. Matth. 10:19-20. Mark 13:11.

and bring in remembrance all things."[398] This Holy Spirit testifies to the Son[399] and guides the disciples *"into all Truth."*[400]

Blasphemy against the Holy Spirit is not considered as blasphemy against some impersonal Divine Force but against a Personal and Hypostatic Being. This was clarified when Christ assured us: *"The Holy Spirit will teach you in that very hour what you ought to say"*[401] *"as though He is a Teacher dwelling within us."*[402] To proclaim blasphemy against the Holy Spirit as inexcusable whereas blasphemy against the Son of Man is forgivable, indicates that the Holy Spirit is of a higher status when compared to the Son Who speaks at that moment as a human Being.

According to the fourth Gospel the Holy Spirit undoubtedly is witnessed as a Person because when the Lord assured His Disciples that He will send them *"another Helper,"* the *"Paracletus,"*[403] He indicated by these words the relationship of their Essence. This other *"Helper"* will *"teach,"* *"bring in remembrance all things,"*[404] *"testify"* the Son[405] and *"guide"* the Disciples *"into all Truth."*[406] As a Teacher, Guide and Witness of Christ, it is obvious that the Holy Spirit has His own Personal Hypostasis. Thus He is sent by the Father and the Son into the world to *"convict the world of sin, and of righteousness, and of judgment."*[407] The characteristic of these verses with regard to the Holy Spirit is that Christ speaks in masculine gender whereas in all other verses He is addressed in neuter gender. Adding to all the aforementioned, Christ declared that the Holy Spirit *"proceeds from the Father"*[408] and therefore the Holy Spirit is not a creation of God but of the same Essence as the Father because the procession is the Spirit's Natural Way of Existence[409] and His Hypostatic Attribute.

The Orthodox Church received the Teachings concerning the Holy Spirit from the Holy Apostles and always preserved them until they were completely clarified at the Second Ecumenical Synod, which took place in

---

[398] John 14:26.
[399] John 15:26.
[400] John 16:13.
[401] Luke 12:12.
[402] St Cyril of Alexandria, *To Luke*, in Migne, *P.G.*, 72, 732.
[403] Tsakonas, *Paracletus,* pp.184-191.
[404] John 14:26.
[405] John 15:26.
[406] John 16:13.
[407] John 16:8.
[408] John 15:26.
[409] Theodorus Mopsuestias, *Fragments to John*, in Migne, *P.G.*, 66, 780. Theophylactus of Bulgaria, *To John*, in Migne, *P.G.*, 124, 205. Theodoretus of Cyrus, *About the Holy Spirit*, Homily V, ch. III, in Migne, *P.G.*, 83, 456.

Constantinople (381). This Holy Synod faced the heresy of Macedonius and all those who denied the Holy Spirit as True God.[410]

CHAPTER EIGHT
THE CHARACTERISTICS OF THE DIVINE HYPOSTASES' ATTRIBUTES

Question 70: What are the characteristics of the Divine Attributes of each Person of the Holy Trinity?

Answer: From the One, Simple, Undivided Essence of God derives the differentiation of the three Hypostases of the Deity. They have the same Cause and are not infinite in number being only two: Eternal and without beginning:

> a) the Father is without begging
> b) the Father begets the Son and
> b) the Holy Spirit, proceeds only from the Father.

These Attributes differentiate from one another being individual Hypostases or Persons Who are equal and inseparable from one another, having the same Essence and all the Divine Attributes. They have only the Personal or Hypostatic Attributes as their own, which distinguishes the Father as the Cause and Source of the Deity, the second Person being Born before all ages and the third Person proceeding only from the Father.

These Hypostatic Attributes are not *part* of the Divine Essence but *"ways of existence"* of the Hypostases or Persons. They also manifest the relationship of one to another. The Birth of the second Person, as well as the Fatherhood of the first Person of the Holy Trinity should not be understood in human terms.

The Father exists as Father always, before time and for all Eternity, never having been a Son as it is with mankind who are sons before they become fathers. Although having been Begotten of the Father, the Son is not minor to the Father, as it is with man, the sons being minor to their fathers and their fathers being senior in age to their sons.

The Son is born before all time from the Father and is Co-eternal with the Him. The Son is inseparable from the Father, being His Co-eternal Brightness from Eternal Light, Equal to Him as His living Image and Character of His Hypostasis.

---

[410] See: Meyendorff, *Legacy,* pp. 153-165.

The Procession of the Holy Spirit and the Birth of the Son before all time remain inconceivable to man who is unable to understand them. Nevertheless, these Divine Attributes remain unmixed and unconfused in their relationship to one another. The Holy Spirit Proceeds only from the Father, just like the Son is Begotten only of the Father.

Question 71: What are the personal Attribute of the Father and that of the Sonship of the Son?

Answer: The personal Attribute of the first Person of the Holy Trinity is Father. To the Father, the Holy Fathers of the Orthodox Church ascribed the terms: *"not born," "Cause," "wanton"* and in relation to the Holy Spirit *"Projector."*[411] The verb *"to give birth"* is used absolutely concerning the relationship of the Father to the Son, whereas the verb *"to Proceed," "to come forth"* and *"to shine"* are used to ascribe the Procession of the Holy Spirit from the Father and His being sent into the world.[412]

Concerning the relationshi between the Father and the Son, we must never forget that the Fatherhood and the Sonship were not ascribed by us to the Blessed Trinity.[413] Under no circumstances should we ever compare the relationship between the Father and the Son in human terms.[414] God is not like man nor is it permissible to understand Him as being of male or female gender because He is addressed as *"Father."* Neither is the Holy Spirit to be regarded as neuter gender. Concerning the Holy Trinity, the Father exists forever as Father and the Son exists forever as Son before all time and there never was a period of time that the Father was not Father nor did the Son come into existence in time, having always existed with the Father without beginning.[415]

God, Who is the Absolute Spirit, has no need in order to bring forth His Only Begotten Son Who is Born of the Father *"without passion"*

---

[411] St Justin, the philosopher and martyr, *1 Apology*, 49, 5; Ibid, *2 Apology*, 6, 1, in *B*, v. 3, pp. 187 and 203. St Gregory of Nyssa, *That there are no three gods,* and *Against Eunomius*, I, in Migne, *P.G.*, 45, 133, 336 and 369. St John of Damascus, *Exposition. About the Holy Trinity,* IX, in Migne, *P.G.*, 94, 809, 817 and 821. St Gregory of Nazianzus, *Homily* 29 and *Homily* 31, in Migne, *P.G.*, 36, 76 and 140.

[412] St Athanasius the Great, *To Serapion, Epist.* 38, 4, in Migne, *P.G.*, 26, 580. Ibid, *About faith*, in Migne, *P.G.*, 32, 329 and 31, 468. St Gregory of Nazianzus, *Homily* 29 and *Homily* 31, in Migne, *P.G.*, 35, 1077 and 1224. St Gregory of Nyssa, *Against Eunomius*, I, in Migne, *P.G.*, 45, 369.

[413] Ephes. 3:15.

[414] St John of Damascus, *Exposition. About the Holy Trinity,* IX, in Migne, *P.G.*, 94, 820. St Gregory of Nazianzus, *Homily* 31, in Migne, *P.G.*, 36, 140.

[415] St Athanasius the Great, *To Serapion*, I, in Migne, *P.G.*, 26, 569.

("ἀπαθῶς") before all ages.[416]   God being simple in His Nature, is the Father of the Only Son Whom He begat without being divided, from Whom the Son is not part of the Father but the Perfect and whole Image and Brightness of the Father.[417]

The "without passion" Birth of the Son from the Father is expressed more precisely with the term "Word." As the word is born from the mind without passion, in a similar manner the second Person of the Holy Trinity is Born of the Father "without passion" ("ἀπαθῶς"). Similarly, through the term "Word" is declared not only the term "without passion" ("ἀπαθῶς"), but also the infinity ("το αΐδιο") of the Word. The Word of God is not created, neither is He part or the result of passion. Wherever there is the Father, there is the Son and Christ is the Word and the Wisdom of God the Father.[418]

The Co-eternity of the Word with the Father and the Inseparability of the Word from the Father are manifested through the term "Brightness." God is the Eternal Light Who has neither a beginning nor an end.   Likewise the Son "being the Brightness of God's Glory and the express Image of His Person"[419] is also Co-eternal and Co-exists with the Eternal Light, the Father. Just as one cannot see a light without its source, similarly there was never a time when the Son did not exist. The term "Brightness" also indicates the *inseparability* from and the closeness to the Father.

The undivided Essence, the Birth without beginning and the Equality of the Son are emphasized through the biblical expressions: "*the express Image*" of the Father and "*the character of His Hypostasis.*"   The term "*express Image*" manifests that the Son is identical to the Father having the exact characteristics as Him. The Son is not a lifeless Image, neither is He handmade nor a work of art but the living Image and in Essence the "*express Image*" of the Father. God the Father has given to His Only Begotten Son His Majesty, being the Image of the invisible God, in order to

---

[416] Ibid, *Against Arians*, I, in Migne, *P.G.*, 26, 41 and 69. St Gregory of Nyssa, *Against Eunomius*, I, in Migne, *P.G.*, 45, 444-445. St John of Damascus, *Exposition. About the Holy Trinity,* IX, in Migne, *P.G.*, 94, 816.

[417] St Athanasius the Great, *Synods*, in Migne, *P.G.*, 25, 436. Ibid, *To Serapion*, in Migne, *P.G.*, 26, 569.

[418] Theophelactus of Bulgaria, *To John*, in Migne, *P.G.*, 123, 1137. St John Chrysostom, *Homily 2* § 4, in Montfaucon, v. 8, p. 141. St Athanasius the Great, *Against Greeks,* in Migne, *P.G.*, 25, 69. Ibid, *Epist. to monks who record the impieties of the Arians*, in Migne, *P.G.*, 25, 765. St Gregory of Nazianzus, *Homily 30*, in Migne, *P.G.*, 36, 129.   St Athanasius the Great, *About Dionysius of Alexandria*, § 15, in Migne, *P.G.*, 25, 502.

[419] Heb. 1:3.

preserve the Image of the Father.[420] In addition, the term *"the character of His Hypostasis"* manifests the identical Image of the Son to the Father and that the Son is in the Father and not part of Him. As the Father is an individual Hypostasis and has no need of anything, so is the Son Who does not differ in anything.[421].

The Birth of the Son is beyond any intellectual conception and is incomparable to the births of men. The incomparability creates the permanent, unalterable, non-transferable and unsociable Personal Attributes of the Fatherhood and Sonship, the result of which is that the Father and the Son always remain Father and Son and the Son never becomes Father, nor was the Father was ever Son. In addition to this, the Birth of the Son is incomparable to the births of men because it is *"without passion"* (*"απαθές"*–*"apathes"*), *"without being divided"* (*"άτμητον"*–*"atmeton"*) and *"inseparable"* (*"αχώριστον"*–*"ahoriston"*). The Father did not transmit part of His Essence to the Son but begot the Son timelessly and from all Eternity. The Son is identical in everything to the Father and Co-exists always with Him without being divided, being inseparable.

God the Father Begets the Son not by Will but by Nature. The Son was Born of the Father by Nature and not by Will although this does not mean that the Father did not want the Son. On the contrary, the Father wants the Son as the Son declares *"the Father loves the Son."*[422]

The expression *"Brightness"* used to characterize the Son, indicates that He is Begotten of the Father by Nature.[423] We must never forget that if the Will and Ways of God are unsearchable, even more unconceivable to the human mind is the inner Life of the Deity. It is enough for man to know that the Son is Begotten but the explanation is impossible to be known even by the Angelic Hosts. When someone asks the question: *"How was the Son Born"*? the only reasonable answer is: Only *" the Father and the Only Begotten Son know; because a thick cloud covers this matter and it escapes our short-sighted understanding."*[424]

---

[420] St John Chrysostom, Homily 3 § 1, in Montfaucon, v. 11, p. 395. Theodoretus of Cyrus, *To Colassians*, VII, in Migne, *P.G.*, 82, 597. St Basil the Great, *Against Sabellius and Arius*, in Migne, *P.G.*, 31, 608. Origen, *Against Celsus*, in ***B***, v. 10, p. 112.
[421] Heb. 1:3. St Gregory of Nyssa, *Against Eunomius*, II, in Migne, *P.G.*, 45, 485. Theophelactus of Bulgaria, *To Hebrews*, XIV, in Migne, *P.G.*, 125, 192.
[422] John 3:35.
[423] Heb. 1:3. St Ecumenius, *To Hebrews*, in Migne, *P.G.*, 119, 281.
[424] St Gregory of Nazianzus, *Homily 29*, in Migne, *P.G.*, 36, 84.

Question 72: What is the Procession of the Holy Spirit?

Answer: The Hypostatic Attribute of the third Person of the Holy Trinity is that He Proceeds only from the Father.[425] The Procession is an unapproachable Mystery to man's limited mind. Since we ignore many things, we bow down our heads before the Mystery of Faith and without shame we acknowledge our ignorance concerning the way of existence of the Holy Spirit. As we are unable to understand that the Father is not Born, nor can we describe the Birth of the Son, likewise with regard to the Procession of the Holy Spirit, we cannot search the Mysteries of God.[426]

The Procession of the Holy Spirit[427] occurred Eternally and without beginning within the internal Life of the Deity, just like the Birth of the Son. This Procession must never be understood as a mission but as the Natural Existence of the Spirit[428] and as the Son is Begotten from the Father in a Mysterious manner, similarly the Holy Spirit Proceeds only from the Father.

Since the Holy Spirit Proceeds only from the Father, He is not made and because He is not born, He cannot be the "*Son.*" The Spirit Proceeds only from the Father not by birth but by Procession and He cannot become "*Father*" because He is also God. Neither can He become "*Son*" because He "*Proceeds*" from the Father and is "*not Born.*" The Hypostatic Attribute of each Person of the Holy Trinity remains "*unmovable*" ("*ακίνητον*"– "*akineton*"). The Procession must be differentiated from the Birth and must not be confused or identified with it.[429]

Question 73: What does the expression that the Holy Spirit proceeds "*from the Father through the Son*" mean?

Answer: Special attention must be given to the expression that the Holy Spirit "*Proceeds from the Father through the Son,*" which was adopted by many Holy Fathers. The term "*from*" expressing the first creative Cause of all Creation, the Father from Whom everything originates and the term "*through*" referring to the Son as the Cause through Whom all things were made. The Son is not a servant, minor to the Father, but equal in all aspects.

[425] St John of Damascus, *Catechesis,* in Migne, *P.G.,* 94, 816.

[426] St Basil the Great, *Homily 24, Against Sabellius,* in Migne, *P.G.,* 31, 613. St Gregory of Nazianzus, *Homily 31,* in Migne, *P.G.,* 36, 141.

[427] Theophanus, *History about the difference concerning the procession of the Holy Spirit,* in Bryennios, *Paralipomena,* v. III, pp. 181-279. Tsakonas, *Paracletus,* pp. 208-213.

[428] Theophylactus of Bulgaria, *To John 15:26-27,* in Migne, *P.G.,* 124, 205.

[429] St Basil the Great, *Homily 24, Against Sabellius,* in Migne, *P.G.,* 31, 616. St Gregory of Nazianzus, *Homily 31,* in Migne, *P.G.,* 36, 144 and 348. St Athanasius the Great, *To Serapion,* in Migne, *P.G.,* 26, 569.

The expression that the Holy Spirit Proceeds *"from the Father through the Son"* means that the Holy Spirit Proceeds only from One Source and not two separate Sources. He Proceeds from the Father Who is the first and principal Source of the Deity and He is sent into the world by the Son.

Without the Enlightenment of the Holy Spirit it is impossible to know either the Son or the Father. Knowing the Son and being united with Him, we receive Knowledge of the Holy Spirit. Thus, the Holy Spirit has the Father as the Cause of His existence from Whom He Proceeds. This Personal Attribute is the characteristic of the Spirit's Hypostasis. Our way of knowing the one God is from the one Holy Spirit, through the one Son, to the one Father. There is no need for the Son to intervene concerning the Procession of the Holy Spirit because as the Word of God is Begotten of the Father before all time, likewise the Holy Spirit Proceeds only from the Father's Essence.

In conclusion:

a)   If the Holy Spirit Proceeds from the Father, then He is sent into the world through the Son to perfect the Work of Salvation.[430]

b)   If the Birth and the Procession come from the Father Eternally, then time cannot exist between Birth and Procession although the Son is considered to be before the Holy Spirit according to the known order, according to which the Holy Spirit is the third Person of the Holy Trinity.[431]

CHAPTER NINE
THE HYPOSTATIC ATTRIBUTES
IN RELATION TO THE IDENTITY OF THE DIVINE ESSENCE

Question 74: What is the relationship of the Hypostatic Attributes in relation to the identity of the Divine Essence?

Answer: The Hypostatic Attributes on the one hand, manifest the relationship between the three Persons and they do not divide the unity of the Divine Essence; whereas on the other hand, they differentiate each Person clearly one from the other and cannot be transmitted.[432] Refusal to

---

[430] John15:26.
[431] Androutsos, *Symbolique,* p. 155.
[432] Ware, *Way,* pp. 39-43.

accept the differentiation of the three Persons and that their Hypostatic Attributes cannot be transmitted, leads directly to Judaism and Sabellianism, transforming the Trinity into three forms of appearance of the one God, as if under three masks. Although the Son is born and He is a different Person from the Father, as is the Holy Spirit Who proceeds only from the Father, the common Essence of the Son as God is the same as the Father and the Holy Spirit.

The Essence of the Deity is one and undivided, but differentiates in Three perfect Persons. The Three Persons differentiate in reality one from another, but they are neither divided nor do they consist of three gods. The commonality of their Essence excludes any division within the Divine Nature and we do not consider the Divine Essence to be above the three Persons or that the latter are the result of the production of the former. The Deity neither by will nor by force can be divided, but remains undivided and at the same time differentiates in three Hypostases, united, equal and perfect regardless of their order in the Trinity.

In the divinity the unity of Essence is real and is manifested in the common of Will, Authority, Power and the rest of the Divine Attributes. This unity is also manifested in the unity of the Divine actions and will, and is united undividedly by containing the three Persons the one within the other.

Question 75: Are the Hypostatic Attributes transmittable?

Answer: The relationship of the Hypostatic Attributes to the Divine Essence must be understood in that: preserving the differentiation of the Hypostases, we must not divide the unity of the Essence. Undoubtedly, although the naming '*Father*' is not vivid of the Essence, but manifests the relationship of the first Person to the Son, and the naming '*Projector*' manifests His relationship to the Holy Spirit, nevertheless, the Hypostatic Attributes of the Divine Persons within the Trinity are distinguished very clearly[433]. Thus, the Hypostatic Attribute of '*not being born*', which is ascribed only to the Father, is His personal Hypostatic Attribute and it cannot be transmitted to the other two Persons. The Son, although has the common Attributes with the Father and the Holy Spirit that He '*is not made*', yet, His own and personal Hypostatic Attribute is, that He is the '*Son*' *and* '*the only Begotten*', which cannot be transmitted neither to the Father nor to the Holy Spirit. Finally, the Holy Spirit, because of the common Divine Nature, having all the Divine Attributes with the Father and

---

[433] St Gregory of Nyssa, *Against Eunomius,* I and II, in Migne, *P.G.,* 45, 404 and 473.

the Son, is distinguished from the two Persons in that His Hypostatic Attribute is that He '*proceeds*' only from the Father and is send into the world by the Son.

Question 76: Does the undivided Sameness of the Divine Essence consists the equality of the Three Persons?

Answer: One is the Nature of the Persons in the Holy Trinity. For, if the Persons of the Deity are three in number, they are not divided in their Nature. So, he who confesses, that they are three Persons in the Deity, neither introduces alienation between them, nor accepts three gods; because the Son is the same to the Father, as the Holy Spirit is identical to the Nature of the two other Persons. The Son is different from the Father as being '*born*', but He is at the same time God. For, that which is born is the same with Him Who begets Him. Neither do we see another deity in the Father and another in the Son, but they are One in their Nature and have the sameness of Essence.[434] The same refers for the Holy Spirit Who differentiates from the two other Persons, as proceeding from the Father, but is accounted within the Trinity, which is the One God, undivided and of the same Essence, as one Deity. God is the Father, God is the Son, God is the Holy Spirit; One Nature in three Persons, who are spirit, perfect, self-existing, divided in number but not divided in Deity, nor the one is considered to be higher and the other lesser God.[435]

When we speak about the '*Sameness of Essence*' and '*One Essence*' in the three Persons of the Deity, under no circumstances should we acknowledge, that the three Persons are '*parts of One Being*' or have derived from '*a Higher*' compared to them Essence. But the Deity neither by will nor by force is divided, but remains undivided, as in the example of three suns, which have one light.

The equality of the Persons also remains intact. For God is complete and has no need of anything and the only thing which differs is the relationship between the three Persons, the first in relation with the other two being Father to the Son and Projector to the Spirit; the second because of this relation is called Son and the third being known as He Who proceeds from the Father. But these names do not declare difference in the Nature,

---

[434] St Basil the Great, *Against Sabellius,* in Migne, *P.G.,* 31, 605. St Athanasius the Great, *Against Arians,* III, in Migne, *P.G.,* 26, 328. St Cyril of Alexandria, *Homily 1 about the Trinity*, in Migne, *P.G.,* 75, 697.

[435] St Athanasius the Great, *To Serapion,* in Migne, *P.G.,* 26, 570. St Gregory of Nazianzus, *Homily* 31 and *Homily* 34, in Migne, *P.G.,* 36, 148 and 236.

but manifest only the personal Hypostatic Attributes.[436] The Son lacks in nothing, because He is not Father. Neither anything is lacking from the Father, because He is not Son, nor anything is lacking from the Holy Spirit in order to receive it and become Son. But the '*not born*', '*born*' and '*procession*' manifest the Father, the Son and the Holy Spirit, in order to maintain the unmixed of the three Hypostases in the One Nature and Divinity.[437]

If in the order of the Trinity the Father appears to be counted as first, second the Son, third the Holy Spirit, this order of numbers must not mislead us to accept inequality amongst the Persons of the Trinity. We proclaim the three Persons to be each one perfect God, preserving each one of them their personal Hypostatic Attributes.[438]

Question 77: Is the unity of the Divine Essence real and not theory?

Answer: Concerning the three Hypostases in the Deity, we must not understand them as being the result division of the united Essence of the Deity. The common and oneness of the Essence is real, because of the co-existence, of the sameness of Essence, action, agreement of the Will and of the sameness of the Authority, Power and Goodness. The Hypostases differentiate one from the other only in theory, but in reality they are not divided, as men are. This occurs because there is no space, nor difference in Will or Opinion or Action or Power or anything else, which can bring real division.[439] Speaking about men, we speak about many, counting them separate one from another; but concerning God we cannot speak about three gods, but we confess the Holy Trinity to be the One and only True God, Father, Son and Holy Spirit. "*Three in One is the Deity and One in Three, undivided and inseparable. For it is divided inseparably and united dividedly.*"[440]

Question 78: Is the Will and Action of the Holy Trinity the Same?

Answer: The unity of the Trinitarian Divinity and the undivided sameness of the Divine Essence, manifest the unity of the Divine Action and Will, as well as their co-existence of the three Hypostases within each other.

---

[436] St Gregory of Nazianzus, *Homily* 31, in Migne, *P.G.,* 36, 141, 148 and 152. St Gregory of Nyssa, *Against Eunomius,* II, in Migne, *P.G.,* 45, 472.
[437] St Gregory of Nazianzus, *Homily* 31, in Migne, *P.G.,* 36, 141-144.
[438] Ibid, *Homily* 40, in Migne, *P.G.,* 36, 417.
[439] St John of Damascus, *Exposition. About the Holy Trinity,* VIII, in Migne, 94, 828.
[440] St Gregory of Nazianzus, *Homily* 39, ch. 11, in Migne, *P.G.,* 36, 345.

Concerning the unity of the Divine Action we notice that the Action of the Father and the Son and the Holy Spirit is One and does not differ nor varies in anything.[441] This Action is neither divided in many actions nor each Person acts on His own; but whatever is done, it is done by the three Persons simultaneously and not in three actions.[442]

God the Father becomes the Saviour of all in the Son who realizes the Salvation of the world through the Grace of the Holy Spirit. Although we confess that the Salvation came from the Holy Trinity we do not confess that they are three saviours.[443] Concerning the Holy Trinity, because we have the sameness of Action and Will, we have One movement of the three Hypostases and not three same movements, One Will, One Action and One Authority.[444] Thus, we have sameness of Action united with their Nature. The Father and the Son and the Holy Spirit sanctifies, gives life, enlightens and everything else.[445]

The co-existence or habitation of the three Divine Persons within one another ("περιχώρισις" or "ενοίκησις") presupposes that there is no difference in the Life-giving Nature of the Father and the Son and of the Holy Spirit, but whatever is said about the infinite perfection of the one Divine Person must be said also for the other two. Because of the sameness of the Divine Nature, the three Persons co-exist and live within one another and their unity is undivided without any form of mixture or confusion.[446] Each one of them exists within the others in an undivided and continuous communion, like the example of three suns which contain inseparably one another, but having one light. It is impossible to separate the Son from the Father and the Holy Spirit, or the Holy Spirit from the Son and the Father, or the Father from the Holy Spirit and the Son. The three Persons co-exist within an undivided communion without having anything else interfering or existing except the Divine Nature. Also no 'non-hypostatic space' exists within the Divine Essence in order to create emptiness within and to dilate the continuous of the Divine communion.[447] Classical New Testament references are: John 10:30; 14:7, 9-11; 16:15; 17:9-11.[448]

---

[441] St Basil the Great, *Epist.* 189, in Migne, *P.G.,* 32, 693.

[442] St Gregory of Nyssa, *That there are not three gods,* in Migne, *P.G.,* 45, 125.

[443] St Gregory of Nyssa, *That there are not three gods,* in Migne, *P.G.,* 45, 129.

[444] St John of Damascus, *Exposition. About the Holy Trinity,* VIII, in Migne, *P.G.,* 94, 828.

[445] St Basil the Great, *Epist.* 189, in Migne, *P.G.,* 32, 693.

[446] St John of Damascus, *Exposition. About the Holy Trinity,* VIII, in Migne, *P.G.,* 94, 828.

[447] St Basil the Great, *Epist.* 38, in Migne, *P.G.,* 32, 332.

[448] St Cyril of Alexandria, *To John,* Homily VII, Homily XI, ch. 2 and 7, in Migne, *P.G.,* 74, 24D, 452C-D and 509. St Athanasius the Great, *Against Arians III; To Serapion,* in Migne, *P.G.,* 26, 328; 565 and 577. St Gregory of Nyssa, *Against Arius and Sabellius,* in Migne, *P.G.,* 45, 1293. St Gregory of Nazianzus, *Homily* 40, in Migne, *P.G.,* 36, 417.

Question 79: Can the Mystery of the Holy Trinity be comprehened through images?

Answer: Concerning the attempts which many had made in order to make the Mystery of the Holy Trinity more understandable through examples and images used from our daily life, we must never forget that which St Gregory of Nyssa had said: "*It is impossible through words to clarify the inexpressible Mystery, because of the absolute unity of the Divine Essence; how can it be seen divided and at the same time be understood in oneness; and again that it differentiates in hypostases, but is not divided in the Essence.*"[449] He emphasied that, after many attempts, he was unable to find neither the right image nor the correct images to express this great Mystery; and neither the example of the fountain of a river and the running water nor the image of the sun and its light and radiance were correct.[450]

The same can be said for all those who attempted to clarify the Mystery of the inner Life of the Holy Trinity according to the words of St John, the Apostle and Evangelist, that "*God is love.*"[451] According to them God expands Himself as the Father Who loves the Son Who is loved and the Holy Spirit Who unites the two others in mutual Love.[452] As it has been mentioned the explanation of the Holy Trinity is the "*explanation of the unknown by the unknown*" since the Nature of God's Love is incomprehensible to our understanding and it remains an unapproachable Mystery to all. It has been said that "*it is not permitted for anyone to speak or think about those things concerning the divinity, which are not mentioned in Holy Scriptures.*"[453]

In conclusion, the Mystery of the Holy Trinity remains an incomprehensible Mystery for any intellectual being, either from the angelic hosts or from the human race.

---

[449] St Gregory of Nyssa, *Catechesis,* in Migne, *P.G.,* 45, 17.
[450] St Gregory of Nazianzus, *Homily* 31, ch. 31 and 32, in Migne, *P.G.,* 36, 169.
[451] 1 John 4:8.
[452] St Gregory Palamas, *Chapters natural, theological, moral and practical,* in Migne, *P.G.,* 150, 1144-1145. Boulgareos, *Theologicon,* p. 271. Martensen, *Dogmatique,* p. 174. Jugie, *Theologia,* v.II, pp. 253-295.
[453] Boulgareos, *Theologicon,* pp. 279 and 318.

PART TWO
THE CREATION

PART ONE
CHAPTER ONE
THE CREATION OF THE WORLD

Question 80: Who created the World?

Answer: God created the visible and invisible world from nothingness. Being the Absolute, Infinite and Almighty Lord, He did not adapt or change pre-existing matter, but brought it from non-existence into existence through His Almighty Will. God created the limited world in time, always the same without it ceasing to be unalterable.[454]

The fact that the three Persons of the Holy Trinity co-operated in the creation of the world from nothingness, especially the Son, is stressed throughout the Holy Scriptures. The world was created in time and could not have existed on its own as an individual reality. It appeared simultaneously with the first manifestations of creation. Even the Angels did not co-exist nor are they co-eternal with God. They were created before the creation of the visible world. The creation of the creative beings surpasses natural knowledge. Only God can reveal why and how He created the Cosmos.[455]

Although the creative action of God concerning the visible world took place in time, the plan and the exact time of the realization of the creation existed eternally in the Mind of God. If God had Willed it, then a change would have taken place within the unchangeable God. Nevertheless, when God created the world, He created it by His Free-will[456] and not by any external cause or force. God's freedom of action with the creation of the world is witnessed throughout the Holy Scriptures and was proclaimed by all the Holy Fathers of the Orthodox Church. Also the creative action of God bears the Seal of His Goodness, Almightiness and All-wisdom that eternally planned creation realized in time and which was *"very good."*[457] The fact that God made the creation because of His infinite Goodness does not exclude its purpose of being glorified in His Works, His infinite

---

[454] Cf. Plato of Moscow, *Orthodox Teaching,* pp. 41-43. Evdokimov, *Orthodoxia,* pp. 115-117. Kefalas, *Catechesis,* pp. 49-50. Damalas, *Catechesis,* p. 14. Frangopoulos, *Christian Faith,* pp. 65-66. Mitsopoulos, *Themata,* pp. 61-62.

[455] Evdokimov, *Orthodoxia,* p. 115

[456] Lossky, *Theology,* p. 51.

[457] Gen. 1:31. Cf. Dositheus of Jerusalem, *Confession,* ch. 4, p. 30.

Wisdom, Power and Goodness, and generally speaking, in all His Perfection, as understood by intellectual beings. For through this knowledge of the only True God, intellectual beings find their Blessedness and Eternal Life, which are realized through our Lord and Saviour Jesus Christ, the Son of God in the heavenly Kingdom of God.

I. GOD THE CREATOR OF ALL

Question 81: What do the Holy Scripture and Holy Tradition teach?

Answer: The creation of heaven and earth as the Work of God is manifested in Holy Scripture. In the first verses of the first Book of the Old Testament it is written: *"In the beginning God made the heavens and the earth."*[458] King David stated in the book of Psalms: *"He spoke, and it was done; He Commanded, and it stood fast."*[459] He is the One Who *"made the earth by His Strength, Who set up the world by His Wisdom, and by His Understanding stretched out the sky, and set abundance of waters in the sky, and brought up clouds from the ends of the earth; He made lighntings for the rain, and brought forth light out of His Treasures."*[460] God has no need of any assistance from anyone or anything else.[461] Being eternal He created the ends of the earth *"by the Power of His Might."*[462] It was not difficult for God to create the universe.[463]

In the early testimonies is the faith that God, Father Almighty, is the One Who created heaven and earth, the seas and all that is therein.[464] This testimony was incorporated later in the Nicene Creed. It was projected as the Canon of Faith that there is only One God and none other beside Him, Who is the Creator of the world and Who brought the universe out of nothingness through His Word.[465]

---

[458] Gen 1:1.
[459] Psalm 33(34):9.
[460] Jer. 10:12-16.
[461] Psalm 104(105):2. Is. 44:24. Job 9:8.
[462] Is. 40:26.
[463] Psalm 33(34):6.
[464] St Irenaeus, *Heresies,* book I, ch. 10, § 1, in Migne, *P.G.,* 7, 550. Cf. Ibid, in Hadjephraimides, p. 64.
[465] Tertullian, *De praescriptione haereticorum,* ch. XIII, in migne, *P.L.,* 2, 26.

Question 82: What is the role of the Son of God in the Work of Creation?

Answer: It is a clear and reliable Teaching of Holy Scripture and the Holy Fathers of the Orthodox Church that God created the world through His Son and Word. The fourth Gospel proclaims: *"All things were made through Him, and without Him nothing was made that was made."*[466]

When we say that the world was made through the Son, we must never forget that the Father does nothing without the Son. Neither does the Son do anything without the Holy Spirit. All Divine Action concerning the world derives from the Father through the Son and is perfected by the Holy Spirit.[467] Divine Action can neither be divided nor described separately to each of the Divine Persons. Whatever is done by God is done by the three Persons together, in unison, and not by three separate actions. Therefore, Holy Scripture sometimes refers to the creation as being of the Father while in other cases they refer to it as being of the Son.[468] In relation to the Holy Spirit, St Basil the Great noted that the Holy Spirit is also the Creator, as He is not simply a word in God nor a spirit of air that diffuses or scatters. He is alive and existing and active. He is Power of Sanctification, Substantial, Self-existing and Hypostasis.[469] The creation has always been considered the Work of the three Persons of the Holy Trinity.

II. THE CREATION FROM NOTHINGNESS

Question 83: What do Holy Scripture teach about the creation from nothingness?

Answer: A fundamental Teaching of the Orthodox Doctrine concerning the creation of the world is that:

a) everything was created from nothingness;
b) is limited and
c) is distinguished from the infinite Essence of God.

---

[466] John 1:3.
[467] St Gregory of Nyssa, *That there are not three gods,* in Migne, *P.G.,* 45, 125.
[468] Luke 10:21. Acts 4:24. 1 Corinth. 8:6. Psalm 102(103):26.
[469] St Basil the Great, *Against Eunomius,* book V, ch. 2, in Migne, *P.G.,* 30,

In other words God the Creator neither made the cosmos from a pre-existing matter nor did it proceed from His Essence, but He Created everything from nothingness.[470]

It is certain that the matter from which the world was made was not visible, for the heavens and earth and all the matter from which the beings are made, came into existence out of nothingness by the Word of God. It is through faith that we are able to understand these things, not only because we cannot see the Creator creating, but only through faith have we learnt of these matters.

Obviously one who believes that matter pre-existed as co-eternal with God, submits Him to matter and exalts the position of matter as being above God, since it pre-describes the boundaries in which God's creativity must act.[471]

III. THE CREATION IN RELATION TO TIME.

Question 84: When was Time created?

Answer: The terms *"time"* and *"cosmos"* are relative and undivided. Time begins with the Cosmos, but the Cosmos does not begin *in* time but *with* time. For time cannot pre-exist before the Cosmos.[472] Eternity and time differentiate in that time does not exist and no change takes place within Eternity. Since there were no creatures, which through their movements could bring change and different conditions, time was impossible to begin. Time before the creation does not exist, but only God existed. As the creation took place, so did time. Time is relative to the Cosmos, to the living creatures and to the plants. And as those that were created with time pass away, so does time pass without ceasing. The present becomes past and exists no more. The future is not present and the present, before it is known, passes by and becomes the past.[473] Time began at the moment when God gave the first creative Commandment, when His creative Will was expressed at the beginning of Creation. Thus time was created by God, Who created all things and even the order of the centuries was made by God, Who is the Maker and Founder of the worlds.[474] Time does not exist

---

[470] Lossky, *Theology,* pp. 53-54.
[471] Tertullian, *Adversus Hermogenem,* in migne, *P.L.,* 2, 228.
[472] Cf. Damalas, *Catechesis,* pp. 21-22. Frangopoulos, *Christian Faith,* pp. 68-69. Lossky, *Theology,* pp. 58-63.
[473] St Basil the Great, *Hexaemerus,* Homily 1, § 5, in Migne, *P.G.,* 29, 13.
[474] St Augustine, *Confessio,* XI, 13, in migne, *P.L.,* 32, 815.

as an independent reality since it appeared at the first manifestation of Creation. Thus God is also the Creator of time.

Question 85: What are the teachings of Holy Scripture concerning the beginning of Time and the in Time Creation of the world?

Answer: When Holy Scripture proclaims: "*In the beginning God made the heavens and the earth,*"[475] this suggests that the Cosmos was created in time and the things in creation at a certain period of time.[476] Our Lord and Saviour Jesus Christ, the Son of God, in His prayer addressed to His Father before His Passion and Suffering on the Cross, asked: "*That they may behold My glory which You have given Me; for You loved Me before the foundation of the world.*"[477] Here our Lord differentiates His eternal relationship to His Father to that which began in time. He makes the same differentiation when speaking about the Love of the Father towards Himself.[478] St Paul in the Epistle to the Colossians concerning the Son stated "*He is the Image of the invisible God, the Firstborn over all Creation. For by Him all things were created that are in heaven and that are on earth, visible and invisible   All things were created through Him and for Him. He is before all things, and in Him all things consist.*"[479] He exists before the creation of the invisible world, which was created before the visible Cosmos, and thus He created the Angels.[480] Christ is the "*Firstborn*" and not the "*first-created.*" Born of the Father and existing before all things.

All things and creatures are characterized in that they were non-existent before they were brought into existence. Only the Word of God is without beginning and as the Father Who begat Him is Eternal, so is the Son. The creatures cannot be eternal, as they have a beginning and came into being from nothingness.

Question 86: Did the Plan of Creation exist in God from all Eternity?

Answer: Although the creative Action of God was expressed in time, the plan of creation existed in the Divine Mind of God before all ages. We must never think that God suddenly decided to create the world and man

---

[475] Gen. 1:1.

[476] St Ambrosius, *In Hexaemerus,* I. I, c. 6, § 20, in migne, *P.L.,* 14, 143.

[477] John 17:24.

[478] John 17:5.

[479] Col. 1:15-17.

[480] St John, Chrysostom, *Homily* 1, § 2, in Montfaucon, v. 11, p. 5. Zigabinos, *To Matthew,* in Migne, *P.G.,* 129, 640. Theodoretus of Cyrus, *To Colossians,* VII, in Migne, *P.G.,* 82, 597.

and then fulfilled the plan that He conceived before time existed. For this presupposes change and alteration in the unalterable God[481] Who always had the plan of creation in mind and Who always wanted to create the world at a specific time that He Himself had determined before time.[482]

Thus, the Creation is not co-eternal with God because He was always the Lord. He ruled from the beginning over all and when He wanted to He brought everything from nothingness into being. He has the Power to create through His Word and in the spirit of His Mouth; and being the Eternal Creator, when He wants to He creates through His Consubstantial Word and the Holy Spirit.[483] God is the Creator, because He has within Him whatever is required to be the Creator: the Plan of Creation and its changeability. The new titles such as Creator, Governor and Master that describe God after the Creation, do not bring any alteration to the Essence of the Deity. Before the Creation God was perfect and after the Creation He did not increase or change.[484]

IV. THE CHARACTERISTICS OF GOD'S CREATIVE ACTION

Question 87: Did God create by His Free-will?

Answer: The Creative Action of God was a free action. The freedom of God to create was perfect and infinite. God was free to create or not to create. It was up to God's Free-will to create this world or another. And only because of His Goodness and Holiness, He did not create an evil world.[485] God had no need of anyone or anything in order to create, since nothing existed before the Creation; but, by His own Will, He freely made everything, being the only True God and Lord, the only Creator and Father, Who contains and provides for everything in order for them to exist[486] God was not moved by anything that existed outside His Divine Essence, nor by any inner force or procession, as Pantheism claims, but by His own Free-will.[487]

God always acts as He Wills, doing whatever He pleases, as and whenever He pleases; not without His Will, but wanting and knowing that

---

[481] St Augustine, *De civitate Dei,* I. XII, c. 14, in migne, *P.L.,* 41, 362.

[482] Psalm 33(34):11.

[483] St John of Damascus, *Against Manichaenians,* § 9, in Migne, *P.G.,* 94, 1513. St Maximus, *Chapter about love,* IV, 3, in Migne, *P.G.,* 90, 1048.

[484] Heb. 1:10-12.

[485] Cf. Dositheus of Jerusalem, *Confession,* ch. 4, p. 30.

[486] St Irenaeus, *Heresies,* in Migne, *P.G.,* 7, 710.

[487] Clement the Alexandrian, *Stromata,* VII, 7, in *B,* v. 8, p. 264. St Basil the Great, *Hexaemerus,* Homily 1 § 7, in Migne, *P.G.,* 29, 17.

He made everything.[488]   God's Will is the measure of all things and everything is based upon His Will; for His Will is the foundation of the Universe.[489]   It is considered a great heresy to say that God was forced to create all that He has made.

Question 88: Was the Creative Action of God an act of Love?

Answer: The Creative Action of God bears the Seal of His Love. God being the only True Blessed One, not having any need of anything or anyone, but giving to all everything and being by Nature Good, He was pleased to create creatures that benefit from His Love and Goodness. Thus He created the Cosmos, the invisible and the visible world. But before God created the Cosmos, He was moved by seeing His own Goodness and Infinite Perfection; and His Life, Glory and Majesty is unutterable.[490]

Being the Source of Goodness and wanting to share His Goodness with other creatures, God created the world out of nothingness.[491]   Holy Scripture seals the various stations of the Creation with the expression "*and God saw that it was good.*"[492]   This expression reveals that God did not create for His own benefit, but rather out of Love and Goodness, just because that which was made was good.[493]

Question 89: Was the Energy of God always possible?

Answer: The Creative Energy of God bears the Seal of His Almightiness.[494] For God it was enough just to want and immediately it was made. God is not under stress nor exhausted or weakened when He creates. He wanted to create the world and it was created. Whatever He wants, it is done. His Will is action and the result of this is called World.[495] God has the Power to

---

[488] Aristides, *Apology,* IV, § 1, in **B,** v. 3, p. 136. St Hippolytus, *Noetus,* VIII, in **B,** v. 6, p. 16. St Irenaeus, *Heresies,* in Migne, *P.G., 7,* 735 and 736. Psalm 135(136):6.

[489] St Ambrosius, *In Hexaemerus,* lib. I, c. 6, § 22; lib. II, c. 2, § 4, in migne, *P.L.,* 14, 145 and 158.

[490] 1 Tim. 6:15. Acts 17:25. 2 Corinth. 8:9. Psalm 16(17):21. St John of Damascus, *Catechesis,* in Migne, *P.G.,* 94, 864. St Gregory of Nazianzus, *Homily 45 to holy Pascha,* in Migne, *P.G.,* 36, 629. St Ecumenius, *To 2 Corinthians,* in Migne, *P.G.,*118, 1012.

[491] St Athanasius the Great, *Concerning the incarnation of the Logos,* in Migne, *P.G.,* 25, 101. St Gregory of Nazianzus, *To holy Pascha,* in Migne, *P.G.,*36, 629. Karmeris, *The dogmatics,* pp. 513 and 749.

[492] Gen. 1:4, 8, 10, 12, 18, 21, 25, 31.

[493] St Augustine, *De civitate Dei,* I. XI, c. 24, in migne, *P.L.,* 41, 338. St Gregory of Nyssa, *Catechesis,* in Migne, *P.G.,* 45, 21.

[494] Psalm 33(34):9.

[495] Clement the Alexandrian, *Protrepticus*, IV, 63, in **B,** v.7, p. 49. Ibid, *Pedagogus,* in **B,** v. 7, p. 92. St Athanasius, *Against Arians,* II, § 24, in Migne, *P.G.,* 26, 197. St John of Damascus, *Exposition. About providence,* II, 43, in Migne, *P.G.,* 94, 964.

create tens of thousands of worlds like the one in which we exist, but He did not wish to do so.[496]

Question 90: Was the Energy of God All-wise?

Answer: The Creative Energy of God bears the Seal of His All-wisdom. The Commands *"let there be"* and *"bring forth"* in relation to the different stages of Creation and that *"God saw that it was good"* presupposes the capability of the existence of an Absolute, Supreme Mind and thoughts or ideas of the Creator that enable Him to bring forth His Plan of Creation.[497] These thoughts or ideas do not exist outside God. They pre-exist within Him. These ideas are as eternal and timeless as God is. It would be considered blasphemous to say that external ideas entered His Mind, not having pre-existed within Him.[498]

It is evident that the ideas of God existed within Him.[499] Whatever was made was known to God because He did not receive the knowledge of their existence after they were created. Before the creatures were made, they both existed and did not exist because they existed in the Knowledge of God but they did not exist in their nature.[500] They existed intellectually but not perceptibly until they were realized afterwards through the Creation. For God is simple and within Him are the images and examples of what He will make. In other words they are contained within His Eternal Will.[501]

Question 91: Is the perfection of the Cosmos relative?

Answer: The Creative Energy of God that bears the Seal of God's Goodness, All-wisdom and the freedom of His Almightiness raises the question: Is this world, which is the result of the Divine Perfection of God, as perfect as He had intended, or does it have imperfections? The answer is in the Book of Genesis: *"God saw all the things that He made, and, behold, they were very good."*[502]

By saying that the present world is the most perfect of all:

---

[496] Mogilas, A' 14, in Karmeris, *The dogmatics,* v. II, p. 599.
[497] St Gregory of Nazianzus, *Homily* 38, § 9 and 10, in Migne, *P.G.,* 36, 320 and 321. St Maximus, *Chapter about love,* IV § 4, in Migne, *P.G.,* 90, 1048. Rhosse, *System,* p. 342.
[498] St Augustine, in migne, *P.L.,* 40, 30.
[499] Boulgareos, *Theologicon,* p. 154.
[500] St Augustine, lib. V, c. 18, § 36, in migne, *P.L.,* 34, 334.
[501] St John of Damascus, *Apologiticus to those those who slander the holy Icons,* Homily 1, § 10, in Migne, *P.G.,* 94, 1240-1241.
[502] Gen 1:31.

1) One restricts the freedom of God,
2) God's Actions are limited to certain boundaries of the creation,
3) one ignores the existence of evil in the world, and finally,
4) one ignores "*His Promise of new Heavens and a new earth in which Righteousness dwells.*"[503]

The present world is "*very good*" but it is not the perfect one since it will pass away. Our Lord and Saviour Jesus Christ, the Son of God, assured us saying "*assuredly, I say to you Heaven and earth will pass away, but My words will by no means pass away.*"[504] It is impossible by nature to incorporate the perfections of the infinite into that which passes away. Since this world will pass away, it is obvious that God is able to make other more perfect worlds.

Question 92: What is moral evil?

Answer: When God created this world, He had in mind the moral evil that would enter through Satan, the fallen angel and inventor of sin. His All-wisdom, Goodness and Justice permitted it so that the moral evil of the world and natural imperfections (natural evil) would be conquered by God's All-wise Providence. Therefore after the conquest of moral evil, it is necessary to regenerate the world into a higher existence. As this present life has a worldly nature, so the Life to come must have a similar condition after the end.[505]

Concerning the existence of moral evil we must bear in mind that this does not exist as a live essence with a soul, or as a second principal, existing eternally and opposing good. Moral evil is the disposition within the soul or any intellectual being that opposes virtue and leads the indolent astray. It is the freedom of choice of each individual and intellectual being to remain either good, as God created us from the beginning, or to rebel and stray from the natural condition of goodness by being led into sin. Thus evil becomes reality within intellectual beings when they permit it and thereby misuse their free-will, the freedom of choice. This is rebelliousness against

---

[503] 2 Peter 3:13.
[504] Matth. 24:35.
[505] St Basil the Great, *In Hexaemerus*, Homily 1, § 4, in Migne, *P.G.*, 29, 12.

God, poverty of soul, lack of goodness, distortion of morality and real enslavement of intellectual beings.[506]

Question 93: Since God knew before He created the World that the intellectual beings will rebel and invent the evil, why then did He create the World and why did He not prevent them from falling?

Answer: If God did not create the world because of the moral evil that entered therein, then He would have deprived Creation from the countless numbers of intellectual beings that would have remained in virtue, His Blessedness and Blessed Life. This would then be considered a defeat of God's Goodness.

Concerning the fallen angel Satan, God gave him his existence to show that He is not afraid of the rebellion of servants; and above all to teach us that He is Merciful even to those who choose evil. Truly God gave Lucifer his existence and the freedom to choose either to remain in holiness with God or to rebel against Him. Although God has the Power to destroy the devil and all his wicked angels, and even to annihilate them by sending them back to non-existence, He did not do so. Instead God tolerated his stupidity and granted him his existence out of His Love and Goodness.[507] In other words God, in His Divine Goodness, gave existence to Satan and the angels who had followed him, so that they may still participate in His Blessedness. They remain by their own free-will in their darkness, which they prefer rather than being cast out into non-existence. God allows Satan to exist in order to prove his evilness to the whole universe. Ultimately Satan will be condemned to Eternal Condemnation[508] on the Day of the Final Judgment.

V. THE PURPOSE OF CREATION

Question 94: What is the primary and secondary purpose of Creation?

Answer: Since the world is the result of God's Free-will and Love, and not that of a blind fate or necessity, it is obvious that it was created to fulfill a certain Purpose. According to Holy Scripture God is not only the cause

---

[506] Ibid, *In Hexaemerus*, Homily 2, § 4, in Migne, *P.G.,* 29, 37. St John of Damascus, *Exposition. That God is not the cause of evil,* IV, 22, in Migne, *P.G.,* 94, 1197; Ibid, *Angainst Manichaeus,* §§ 14 and 32, in Migne, *P.G.,* 94, 1517 and 1540. Androutsos, *Dogmatique,* p. 119.
[507] St John of Damascus, *Exposition. That God is not the cause of evil,* IV, 22, in Migne, *P.G.,* 94, 1197. Ibid, *Angainst Manichaeus,* §§ 14 and 32, in Migne, *P.G.,* 94, 1517 and 1540.
[508] Matth. 25:41.

"*by*" Whom all things have their existence, but "*through Him*'" and "*to Whom*" "*are all things.*"[509] "*Through Him*" is the Distribution and Providence and "*to Him*" all things aspire. Everything is "*through Him*" being the only Begotten Son of God and "*to Him*" everything was created. In this biblical verse, St Paul presents the beginning of the existence of all things "*from Him*," and the coherence "*through Him*" and finally "*to Him*." It is proclaimed that everything was made for God, being the final Purpose of all things.[510]

The second Purpose of Creation is the intellectual man who was made in the "*image and likeness*"[511] of God. To man whom God created from the "*dust of the earth,*"[512] He gave the authority to "*have dominion over the fish of the sea, and over the flying creatures of heaven, and over the cattle and all the earth, and over all the reptiles that creep on the earth.*"[513] When God created the first couple, He "*blessed them*" and said to them "*increase and multiply, and fill the earth and subdue it, and have dominion over*" all the things upon the earth.[514] And all things God subjected under man's feet, making him the recognised ruler of the earth and of all Creation, which "*was subjected to futility, not willingly,*"[515] but because of the Fall of man.

Question 95: What do the holy Fathers of the Orthodox Church teach?

Answer: The holy Fathers proclaimed that the main Purpose of Creation is to make known "*through the works the Majesty and Greatness of God.*"[516] Tertullian stressed that "*God produced from nothingness the world in order to decorate His Majesty.*"[517] With particular regard to man's creation it is proclaimed "*that the primary and common cause that God made everything for Himself is reflected in the goodness and wisdom of man's creation.*"[518] Parallel to the primary Purpose is a secondary purpose, which refers to the benefits that man would receive from the Creation. Thus it is proclaimed that the sun, the moon and the stars were created by God "*for signs and for*

---

[509] Rom. 11:36.
[510] 1 Corinth. 15:28.
[511] Gen. 1:26.
[512] Gen. 2:7.
[513] Gen. 1:26, 28.
[514] Gen. 1:28.
[515] Rom. 8:20.
[516] Theophilus of Antioch, *1 Autolycus,* § 4, in *B*, v. 5, p. 14.
[517] Tertullian, *Apologeticus,* c. 17, in migne, *P.L.,* 1, 432.
[518] Athenagoras, *About resurrection,* § 12, in *B*, v.4, p. 320.

seasons and for days and for years,"[519] not because He needs these things, but to assist man. This was emphasized to avoid idolatry, since Creation was made for man and it must not be worshipped.[520]

VI. THE ORDER OF CREATION

Question 96: What is the order of Creation?

Answer: In Genesis, the first Book of the Old Testament, God created the unformed matter from nothingness. From this matter the heavenly bodies of the stars and the earth were made and from this earth life appeared, beginning with the most simple form of life and gradually proceeding, in order, to the most perfect of all creatures.[521]

The author of the book of Genesis presents the beginning of the earth as being in a chaotic condition.[522] The unformed matter was covered by water[523] and in six days the earth took its form with all its fullness as we know it now. The *"six days"*[524] of Creation must be understood as being six long periods of time in which, step by step, according to the laws of nature, everything developed in an orderly way, according to the Will of God. Referring to the *"seventh day"*[525] - Saturday or the Sabbath - the God-inspired author has in mind the division of the year into weeks and one week into seven days.

It is also important to notice that the heavenly bodies, the stars, the sun and the moon, which divide the time into periods of day and night, appear only on the fourth day of Creation.[526] Thus the three previous days[527] were not determined according to the movement of the earth around the sun. Nevertheless, the plants that were necessary for preserving animal life, appeared on the fifth day,[528] completely developed and covering the entire surface of the earth.[529]

---

[519] Gen. 1: 14.
[520] Theophilus of Antioch, *1 Autolycus,* § 6, in *B,* v. 5, p. 15. Tatianus, *Homily to the Greeks,* § 4, in *B,* v. 3, p. 244.
[521] Cf. Frangopoulos, *Christian Faith,* pp. 70-71.
[522] Gen. 1:1.
[523] Gen. 1:6-8.
[524] Gen. 2:1-2.
[525] Gen. 2:3.
[526] Gen. 1:14-19.
[527] Gen. 1:1-13.
[528] Gen. 1:20-25
[529] Gen. 1:11-13.

This orderly progress of Creation, whereby life proceeded from the simple form of plants (*"herb of grass"* and *"fruit-tree"*)[530] to that of life in the seas (*"reptiles," "great whales"* and *"winged creatures"*),[531] and then to the life on dry land (*"the living creatures," "reptiles"* (amongst them the dinosaurs), *"wild beasts"* and *"cattle"*),[532] was necessary because the simplest forms of life provided the means of existence to the more advanced creatures.

God does not just create the laws of nature, He also oversees the work of Creation, intervening during the different stages by His Life-giving Almightiness. Thus, the plant kingdom prepared the way for the appearance of the animal kingdom; and later, but **NOT from it**, man appeared as the crown of all Creation through the special intervention of God.[533]

CHAPTER TWO
THE PROVIDENCE OF GOD

Question 97: What is the Providence of God?

Answer: Once God had created the Universe, He did not withdraw His interest and governance but continues to bestow His Divine Providence. In the Book of Genesis, God appears to have completed the work of Creation before *"resting"* on the seventh day.[534] However, this should certainly not be understood as though God had become inactive or unconcerned because that would be considered blasphemy. In the Old and New Testaments the fundamental Doctrine concerning God's Providence is widely proclaimed and it embraces all things,[535] being revealed in many forms but remaining inscrutable and incomprehensible to the human mind.

Parallel to Holy Scripture, all the ecclesiastic Scholars and Holy Fathers of the Church proclaimed not only the Truth concerning the Divine Providence of God, but also explained and formulated it in its fullness. They were the first to distinguish between Providence that concerns inanimate and irrational creation and that which extends to all humanity, especially those who fear and seek the Lord. The Providence of God, according to the Orthodox Christian Faith, is the Work of the three Persons

---

[530] Gen. 1:11.
[531] Gen. 1:20, 21.
[532] Gen. 1:24.
[533] Gen. 1:26-28; 2:7, 21-22.
[534] Gen.2:2.
[535] Cf. Dositheus of Jerusalem, *Confession,* ch. 5, p. 30. Ibid, *Decree V,* in Link, *Apostolic Faith Today,* p. 56. Mitsopoulos, *Themata,* pp. 64-65.

of the Holy Trinity, for the Will of the Trinity is one. In the New Testament the Son is proclaimed as having everything under His Authority while the Father appears to nurture all Creation, knowing every need and the Holy Spirit distributes various Gifts as He wills.

Question 98: What is the definition of Divine Providence?

Answer: The Doctrine of Divine Providence is that it is related directly to the Creation because it is the continuation of the same Divine Act. Divine Providence began with the Creation so the expression: *"God is the Creator and the Provider"* is correct as it expresses the reliable and continuing care of God for everything that exists outside of Him but which were created by Him.[536]

Question 99: What do the Holy Scripture teach?

Answer: In the Old Testament God is depicted as *"resting"* on the seventh day from all His Works[537] but we must not understand this as being that God had stopped working. Instead it means that He had stopped forming new creatures. The order of Creation had been solidly established whereas the chaos, which appeared on the first day, was controlled.[538]

God's Providence is proclaimed in the Old Testament and especially in the Book of Psalms.[539] In the New Testament the The words of Christ in the New Testament: *"My Father has been working until now, and I have been working"*[540] refer to the Providence of God. The Son of God appears to uphold *"all things by the Word of His Power"*[541] and that *"all things were created through Him and for Him "*[542] The Divine Providence of God includes the care of *"birds of the air" "the lilies"* and *"the grass of the field"* and even much more for men[543] whose *"very hairs"* of their heads *"are all numbered."*[544]

---

[536] Plato of Moscow, *Orthodox Teaching,* pp. 46-48. Damalas, *Catechesis,* p. 27. Frangopoulos, *Christian Faith,* pp. 72-73.
[537] Gen. 2:2-3.
[538] Clement the Alexandrian, *Stromata,* VI, 16, in **B,** v.8, p. 232. St Augustine, *De Genesis ad litteram,* IV, c. XII, in migne, *P.L.,* 34, 304.
[539] Psalm 113(114):5-9.
[540] John 5:17.
[541] Heb. 1:3.
[542] Col. 1:16, 19-20.
[543] Matth. 5:26-34.
[544] Matth. 10:30.

Thus in the Old and New Testament the Providence of God touches even the simplest matters of man's life and nothing exists without Divine Providence or merely by accident.[545]

It is understood from the actual words of our Lord and Saviour Jesus Christ that the Providence of God is multifaceted and varied according to the nature of those who receive it. Divine Providence includes all things although not always distributed in the same manner and to the same degree. For, if God bestows the lilies of the field with such beauty, how much more does He bestow upon mankind? If He feeds the birds and all the animals, how much more does He provide for mankind? The Lord spoke of man alone concerning His Heavenly Kingdom. As the sun shines on good and evil alike or the rain falls on the just as well as the unjust, God assures us that *"for the elect's sake those days will be shortened"*[546] and that only the righteous will inherit His Kingdom.[547]

Thus, the separation of Divine Providence into *"general Providence"* that includes all Creation and *"special Providence"* that includes the rational creatures, especially the righteous and elect who fear God, is based upon the Words of Our Lord and Saviour, Jesus Christ, and upon Holy Scripture. It is obvious, therefore, that God has a different relationship with His rational beings to that of the irrational world. Furthermore, the Providence that God has for His elect people differs from those who do not know Him and who worship idols instead of our Creator.

Question 100: What do the Holy Fathers teach?

Answer: St Justin the Philosopher and Martyr relied upon the Prophecies as solid proof of God's Providence and completely excluded the existence of fate. Through the Prophecies God is revealed as Foreknowing the things to come. His Will for humanity's Salvation, fulfilled in due time, was revealed through the Holy Prophets.[548]

St Irenaeus proclaims that God is the Providence of all things. He believed that all rational beings must know their Provider and Governor.[549]

St Athanasius the Great of Alexandria, with regard to the Almightiness and Perfection of the Word of God, noted that *"He has spread*

---

[545] Esther 6:1-2. 1 Samuel (1 Kings) 22:29-35, 23. Acts 23:16. Acts 27:1-28:10.
[546] Matth. 24:22.
[547] Psalm 91(92):1, 11.
[548] St Justin, the philosopher and martyr, *1 Apology*, 43 and 44, in *B*, v. 3, p. 183-184; Ibid, *Dialogue*, 7, in *B*, v. 3, p. 215.
[549] St Irenaeus, *Heresies,* book III, ch. 25, § 1, in Migne, *P.G.,* 7, 968. Cf. Ibid, in Hadjephraimides, p. 259-260.

His Powers everywhere and has Enlightened those who are visible and those who are invisible, which He sustains to Himself, not leaving anything aside without His Power, but all and through all and for each and everyone gives Life and Protection."[550]

St John Chrysostom, explaining God's Providence, gave the example of a river that divides itself into many tributaries and thus quenches the thirst of the land. He comes to the conclusion that no one remains without the benefit of God's Divine Providence.[551]

Question 101: Is Divine Providence the work of the Holy Trinity?

Answer: Divine Providence is the combined Work of the three Persons of the Holy Trinity.[552] Holy Scripture states that the Son as well as the Father are working *"until now,"*[553] feeding the birds,[554] knowing all that we need[555] and giving good things to those who ask Him. Without the Father's Will, not even a sparrow falls down upon the face of the earth,[556] while everything is Constructed and Regenerated by the Holy Spirit Who proceeds from the Father,[557] being the One Who divides and distributes the variety of Gifts *"to each one individually, as He Wills."*[558]

CHAPTER THREE
THE PRESERVATION OF CREATION

Question 102: What is the Preservation of Creation?

Answer: It is the positive and continuous act of God that sustains all beings, secures the order of nature and maintains the Universe. As with the Providence of God, likewise the Preservation of Creation differs from the Creation in that no new Creation is produced. All creatures that already exist are protected from falling into non-existence and yet this Preservation differs from the Governing of the world that secures the perfect end thereof

---

[550] St Athanasius the Great, *Against Greeks,* § 42, In Migne, *P.G.,* 25, 84.
[551] St John Chrysostom, *Psalm 46,* § 1, in Migne, *P.G.,* 55, 205. Ibid, *In Matthew Homily 28,* § 3, in Migne, *P.G.,* 57, 354.
[552] Col. 1:16-17.
[553] John 5;17.
[554] Matth. 6:26.
[555] Matth. 6:32.
[556] Matth. 10:29.
[557] John 16:26.
[558] 1st Corinth. 12:4-11.

as planned by the Divine Will. However, this difference is a concept of our limited minds as it does not exist in reality.

God's intervention in order to sustain the Cosmos does not remove the power of the laws of nature. On the contrary, even nature seeks God's intervention so that it is not led into disorder (in Greek: *"αταξία"-"ataxia"*) or extinction.

Question 103: What is the definition of the Divine Preservation?

Answer: When we use the term *"Divine Preservation"* we do not simply mean God's consenting to the continuous existence of the Universe, but that through His intervention, He causes the preservation of the Cosmos, guarding through His Almighty Will not only the whole Universe, but every atom of every element from which the Universe is composed. It is understandable, however, that this Divine Intervention does not exclude the synergy of the natural powers that do not exist independently, but through God's creative Will.

The synergy of secondary causes does not exclude God's Preservation nor does it prevent one creature from being under the influence of another because although God is the main cause of the conservation of everything in the world, the creatures are real and exist as beings whose existence is continuously preserved by God. The Preservative Action of God is incessant and contributes directly to the perpetuation of their existence.

According to the above, although the Preservation of the Universe is connected to the Creation, both being the result of the one Action of God, it is different to the Creation. This is easily understood when we acknowledge that the Creation was the cause of Universe and the reason for its existence. Nonetheless, Divine Preservation does not produce any new creatures and those that already exist are preserved and do not revert to the nothingness out of which they were created.

Divine Preservation could be considered as a continuous Creation whereby all that has been brought into existence from non-existence, continues to exist and is preserved by the Divine Power that created them from nothingness. Thus, the Creative Action of God brought everything from nothingness into being whereas the Preservative Action of God presupposes their existence. And although in the Creation God Acted alone, in Divine Preservation the Creative Action of God co-operates with the laws of nature that He had established so that the Universe will continue without reverting to non-existence.

Divine Preservation of the world must be distinguished from the Divine Governing of the Cosmos. Undoubtedly, with regard to God, the

Governing of the world is inseparable from the Preservation, as both are inseparable from Divine Providence. However, due to our limited understanding, Divine Preservation is distinguished from Divine Governing so that we may examine each aspect systematically. Furthermore, Divine Preservation secures the natural order and preservation of creatures whereas Divine Governing secures the progress of the Cosmos to its final and perfect end as predetermined by God.[559]

Question 104: What are the teachings of Holy Scripture?

Answer: A few classical verses of Holy Scripture that witness the preservation of the world as being directly due to Almighty God are Colossians 1:17, in which St Paul stated that *"all things consist"* of God; Acts 17:28 in which St Luke wrote: *"we live and move and have our being"* in God and Psalm 104(105):27-30 wherein King David wrote *"these all wait for Thee, that Thou may give them their food in due season Thou sendest forth Thy Spirit, they are created; and Thou renewest the face of the earth."*

The world in general and especially the spiritual world are destined to exist forever. This Truth is not undermined by the fact that some plants or animals that existed on earth thousands or millions of years ago, are now extinct. Only spiritual beings are not subject to extinction, as they are the main concern of Divine Providence.[560] Holy Scripture confirms that God uses natural and spiritual forces as well as the general laws of nature to preserve the Cosmos.[561]

Question 105: What are the teachings of the Holy Fathers?

Answer: The Teachings of the Holy Fathers and ecclesiastic scholars of the Orthodox Church are in full agreement with the Teachings of Holy Scripture.

Theophilus of Antioch, addressing Autolycus, noted that God is called *"Pantocrator, because He upholds and sustains everything."* Continuing, he urged all men to comprehend *"the Providence of God Who prepares food for all things."*[562]

The Preservation of each species is fulfilled according to their different natures and that of minerals and inanimate Creation is

---

[559] Trempelas, *Dogmatique,* v. I, pp. 372-374.
[560] Androutsos, *Dogmatique,* p. 116.
[561] Psalm 147(148):8-9. Matth. 5:45. Acts 14:15-17. Acts 17:25. 1 Corinth. 12:6. Psalm 145(146):15-16. Job 10:8, 12.
[562] Theophilus of Antioch, *1 Autolycus,* §§ 4 and 6, in *B,* v. 5, pp. 14 and 16.

accomplished by the cooperation between Divine Providence and the laws of nature. The galaxies, the suns, the planets and their moons, are thereby maintained in keeping with their established order and movement. In addition, God preserves the different kinds of species of plants and animals since they, too, play an important role in the conservation of their realm.

The Preservation of mankind is a special concern of God's Providence, for he is the centre and goal of all Creation, his existence being extended beyond death. God intervenes directly and indirectly. He strengthens the vital powers of man directly through food that is offered by means of plants or animals. Beneficial weather conditions cause vegetation to grow and multiply, as well as all life dependent thereon. The manner of God's direct intervention in order to sustain and preserve all things is beyond any rational understanding and all we know is that this Divine Preservation does not cause weariness to or reduction of the Deity.

Question 106: Is God's Intervention necessary?

Answer: God's direct or indirect Intervention in preserving the world is considered an absolute necessity. This fact originates from the mortality of the creatures that God Created. For the Source of their existence does not originate from themselves, but from the Absolute Being. Therefore, they continue to exist because of their continuous and uninterrupted communion with the Source of Life. If God released His Work of the Creation, just as an Architect, having completed his work, leaves the structure he has designed, then as soon as Divine Providence no longer supported its existence, Creation would become extinct along with the entire Cosmos.[563]

CHAPTER FOUR
I. THE GOVERNMENT OF THE WORLD IN GENERAL

Qyestion 107: What do we mean that God governs the World?

Answer: God, being the Lord of all things that He created, does not restrict Himself to only preserving them, but also governs all things, guiding them to their perfect and final Goal, that He had planned before eternity. Holy Scripture refers to the Government of God not only in general terms but also as affecting even the smallest details of men's lives. The Will of God is fulfilled in this Divine Government, revealed not only as Divine Power but

---

[563] St Augustine, *De Genesis ad litteram,* IV, 12; V, c. 20 § 40 and VIII, c. 26, in migne, *P.L.*, 34, 304; 333 and 391.

as the Holy and Good Will of God. Divine Will is not revealed as the will of a Governor Who governs the Cosmos with arbitrariness and spite but as the Will of an Omniscient, Holy and All-good King Who governs the world according to His perfect and absolute moral Nature. Thus, since everything within the world is Governed by God, then *"fate,"* *"blind coincidence"* or the *"arbitrarily acting will"* are excluded. Everything takes place because of the Free-will of God Who acts according to the eternal order that He planned before all time and which concerns the final Goal of Creation. However our limited understanding is unable to comprehend the manifold expressions of the governmental action of God.[564] The acceptance of the Government of God upon all Creation[565] assures us of the possibility of Miracles. It also gives us the assurance that our prayers are not addressed to some deaf governor who does not hear but are heard with favour and goodwill by our Lord Who oversees and supervises all Creation with Compassion and Wisdom.

Question 108: What is the meaning and definition of the Government of God?

Answer: The Government of God upon all things is the act of the Divine Will through which God as the Lord and Master of all things created by Him, Governs and Rules, controlling the entire Universe with Compassion, Wisdom and Holiness.

This control concerns not only the whole world, but every minute element of the Universe. The Goal is to guide everything to its final and perfect end, thus fulfilling the eternal Plan according to God's perpetual Will whereby in due time He Created the Cosmos. Thus, everything that occurs in the Universe happens either due to God's free Action that aims at fulfilling His eternal Plan or because God consents, allows or tolerates the interference of rational beings so that the fulfillment of His Divine Plan not only is accomplished but also served, even by those who are opposed to it.

Question 109: What are the teachings of Holy Scripture?

Answer: Throughout Holy Scripture we are guaranteed that the Government of God includes even the smallest of details. Through this Government the Will of God never remains unrealised but is always

---

[564] Rom. 11:33-35.
[565] Frangopoulos, *Christian Faith,* pp. 75-76.

gloriously fulfilled as it is written in the Book of the Prophet Isaiah: "*All My Counsel shall stand, and I Will do all things that I have Planned.*"[566]

When we say that "*..the Will of God is fulfilled*" we speak not only of His Divine Power that nothing can resist, but also of His Holy Will that is expressed through His Divine and supreme Power that determines the events of the Cosmos. God is neither inactive nor shows any indifference. Rather, He governs all things with His Compassion and omniscient Will and also "*works all things according to the Counsel of His Will.*"[567] He is the Supreme Master Who extends His Almightiness and interest throughout the Cosmos in general, as well as in particular to each and every thing separately, acting as a Wise, Good and Holy Governor.

Question 110: What are the teachings of the holy Fathers?

Answer: Origen exalted the indescribable Technique of Divine Wisdom by means of which everything is led to a common benefit, progress, metamorphosis and correction according to the Teachings of Holy Scripture. Although they are extremely varied, they are called to one agreement and to one perfect end. This unique Perfection of God sustains all the differences of the Cosmos and guides their diverse activities to the one act.[568]

St John Chrysostom, Theophilus of Antioch and Theodoretus of Cyrus used the metaphor of a ship sailing towards a safe port to express how Divine Wisdom and Divine Will leads the entire Cosmos to a final and safe destination. Through this imagery, they made the Divine Government of God more understandable.[569]

Question 111: Are the events in Creation accidental or according to "*Fate*"?

Answer: Nothing occurs in the Universe without Divine Government. Nothing is unforeseen or unknown to Divine Providence. No one should believe anything happens according to "*fate*" or coincidence, or even due to "*bad timing*" because these concepts are those of the ignorant and unenlightened. As Christ our Lord clearly stated: " *not one of them falls to the ground apart from your Father's Will. But the very hairs of your head*

---

[566] Is. 46:10.
[567] Ephes. 1:11.
[568] Origen, *About Principles,* II, c. 1, § 1.
[569] St John Chrysostom, in Migne, *P.G.,* 47, 365. Ibid, *To Statues,* Homily 10, in Migne, *P.G.,* 49, 114. Theophilus of Antioch, *1 Autolycus,* § 5, in *B,* v. 5, p. 15. Theodoretus of Cyrus, *Homily* I and *Homily* II, in Migne, *P.G.,* 83, 564 and 576.

are all numbered"[570]   That is the Divine Eye of God Whose attention nothing escapes![571]

"*Fate*" is the perception of irrational forecasts of astrologists, mediums, wizards, sorcerers, magicians, spell-binders and fortune-tellers and therefore has absolutely no place in the lives of true Orthodox Christians. Only those who are not of the true Christian Faith or who are not solidly founded Orthodox Christians believe in such madness and foolishness for they lack true Faith in the One and True God, the Father, and the Son and the Holy Spirit.

Divine Providence acts in such a manner that whatever is free acts freely, whatever is necessary is done by necessity and whatever is accidental occurs accidentally. Nevertheless, the meaning of "*accidental*" has no subjective meaning as the limited mind of man is unable to comprehend and perceive the Action of the Divine Government of God as it is extremely complex and mysterious.

Question 112: What are the Miracles and Prayers?

Answer: Miracles must be understood as being extraordinary phenomenons in nature or Spiritual Life that are beyond explanation according to laws of nature or any scientific rationalization or theory. A Miracle is caused by the direct Action of God Who acts extraordinarily within the world to serve a higher purpose.[572] The laws of nature are set aside for a moment while God's Power Acts. This Miraculous Action of God does not abolish the laws of nature but being Supernatural, it is above them although neither abnormal nor against nature. Just as the laws that govern mineral and inanimate nature are not abolished with the appearance of life and the laws that govern living beings, plants and animals, likewise, the Supernatural Action of God intervenes extraordinarily to perform the Miracle, without disrupting the order of nature.

Those who accept and believe in God as the Governor of all, agree that the Intervention of God in the Act of a Miracle is, on the one hand, due to His Omnipotence, whereas on the other hand, it is due to His Goodness and Wisdom. Divine Omnipotence is in agreement with His Miraculous Intervention because God placed the laws of nature as powers not above Him but as totally unchangeable and necessary acting powers that are always subject to Him Who alone can interfere if and when He considers it

---

[570] Matth. 10:29-30.
[571] Psalm 33(34):13-15.
[572] Cf. Damalas, *Catechesis,* pp. 33-35. Frangopoulos, *Christian Faith,* pp. 76-78.

necessary. The Goodness of God is required because it awakens sinful man to the realization of the Presence of God. In addition to this, the Wisdom of God is not contradictory because His Miraculous Action may be characterized as being creative. God never corrects any of His Work, nor does He add anything essential to the whole system of the Universe but He does perform Miracles in order to teach man who disturbed the Work of Creation that *"was very good.."* and to remind him of God's Majesty. Finally, the unalterability of God is not affected by Miracles because they have been proclaimed by God from all eternity and are included in His eternal Plan of Creation. Thus, those who deny Divine Miracles do not defend the inalterability of God but proclaim thereby that God remains completely unmovable.

Generally speaking, there is no conflict between God's Action and the laws of nature in Miracles and neither are they abolished for they remain untouched. In Miracles the Actions of God is expressed that are beyond the laws of nature and which are Supernatural and unintelligible. Divine Miracles are the Actions of God's Love towards His Creation and especially towards mankind.

Question 113: What is prayer in relation to the Government of all?

Answer: God Who Governs all things does not remain indifferent to the prayers of those who seek His Mercy and Help, otherwise the Communication between man and God would not be alive, but a religious hoax and meaningless. Many prayers beseech God's prevention of certain events from taking place and call upon Divine Providence to change the natural path of those events, which in many circumstances seem to be unchangeable. The solution to this question is the Foreknowledge of God that Governs the world taking into account the events of free beings, which were known by God before all time.

Miraculous Intervention and the acceptance of man's prayer by God must always be hoped for on condition that it serves a higher Purpose of the Divine Plan and only if it is in full agreement with the Holy and Good Will of God the Pantocrator. Thus the request *"..let Thy Will be done"*[573] must be included in all prayers of pious Orthodox Christians, who believe in the Power of prayer and the Miracles of God but do not demand them or ask for proof.

Miracles may be realised only if people have solid faith in God's Divine Power. They must place their trust in God's Will and not allow any

---

[573] Matth. 6:10.

doubtful thoughts to enter their hearts, otherwise they put obstacles in the path God's Power causing the prevention of the Miracle taking place due to their skepticism.

II. THE GOVERNMENT OF GOD
IN RELATION TO MAN'S FREEDOM AND SYNERGY

Question 114: What is the relation of the Government of God to man's freedom?

Answer: The Government of God extends to the world of men who, as rational and free beings, actively interfere in history. Nevertheless within this free world the Will of the Lord rules. This is witnessed by Holy Scripture and by the Holy Saints who, although they faced many obstacles while serving the Will of God, accomplished His Plan. This means that man's role is essential and not eliminated. Man cooperates freely, offering his efforts to fulfill the Divine Will although sometimes he may achieve it unconsciously. Through the Divine Government of God everything is presided over by Him Who allows some events to be achieved by mankind or because His Good Will consents to or concedes or even abandons man either temporarily for correction and pedagogic reasons, or definitely for the realisation of loss.

Natural evil as well as moral evil committed by wicked men, must be understood as follows: due to the Good Will of God natural evil is allowed for pedagogic reasons whereas He always despises moral evil, having foreknown it without having predestined it. Thus, the evil of free beings is not prevented and yet the fulfillment of God's Will is fully realised, even unconsciously by those who do evil.

However, the various Actions of the Divine Government of God reveal many problems and present many Mysteries that remain impenetrable. Only through faith can one approach the Mystery of the impenetrable Will of our Great God to a certain point. Man remains amazed before the magnificent Wonders of Divine Providence that are approachable by his intellect, realising at the same time the infinite distance between Divine Wisdom and his poor human mind.

Question 115: What is the role of the Government of God and Man?

Answer: Mankind has a unique position in Creation requiring special treatment, guidance and enlightenment by God. He is a being of free intellect in antithesis to the material world that is driven by blind natural laws. It is obvious then, that man who interferes in the Government of the world, needs the Governing Action of God, for *"man's way is not his own"*[574] but the Counsel of God *"shall stand"* and He *"will do all things."*[575]

In many cases obstacles originated by human activity prevented the career of others who had been chosen by Divine Providence. However, these were incapable of cancelling God's Divine Plan, as in the history of Joseph, Moses, David and so many others. It is true that no one's success throughout history was only due to personal characteristics, capabilities, or achievements because it is always mainly due to the synergy with Divine Providence. As it is written in the Book of Psalms: *"Unless the Lord builds the house, they labour in vain who build it; unless the Lord guards the city, the watchman stays awake in vain."*[576]

We must not mistakenly believe that the human factor is either removed or forced into passivity. On the contrary, in the Old and New Testament we find examples that witness the synergy between God's Divine Providence and the human factor.

Question 116: What are the teachings of the holy Fathers?

Answer: Clement the Alexandrian stated that those things that one would consider as originating from man's intellect, have their beginning from God. Consequently, such things as health from medicine, a strong body from gymnastics and wealth from financial success, owe their existence to Divine Providence and in accordance with the synergy of man.[577] The Divine spark that activates the human factor, makes Divine Providence accessible as when the midwives of Egypt disregarded the decree of the Pharaoh to kill all male Hebrew children at birth. These women became renowned for their courage and were duly rewarded by God. Such events are considered as being the Work of Divine Providence.[578] Furthermore from Holy Scripture evidence of Divine Inspiration by means of which the hearts of men received salvation or destruction from Above is apparent.[579]

---

[574] Jer. 10:23.
[575] Is. 46:10.
[576] Psalm 127(128):1.
[577] Clement the Alexandrian, *Stromata*, VI, 17, in **B**, v. 8, p. 338.
[578] St John Chrysostom, *To Psalm 135(136)*, § 4, in Migne, *P.G.*, 54, 392.
[579] Job 12:22-25. Esther 4:17. 1 Samuel (1 Kings) 25:32, 34.

Question 117: How did Evil appeared?

Answer: The answer to the question is found in the Teachings of Holy Scripture whereby the Prophet Isaiah, through the Inspiration of the Holy Spirit, explained how evil came into the world:

> *"How has Lucifer who rose in the morning, fallen from Heaven! He who sent orders to all the nations is crushed to the earth. But you said in your heart, 'I will go up to Heaven; I will set my throne above the stars of Heaven: I will sit on a lofty mount, on the lofty mountains towards the north: I will go up above the clouds; I will be like the Most High."*[580] Furthermore, our Lord stated: *"I saw Satan fall like lightning from Heaven."*[581]

We must never think that God created evil, for there is no evil in nature. Sin is the only evil that exists in the world. Everything that man considers evil, such as death, illness and other afflictions similar to these, are referred to as being "evil" simply because they cause suffering, sorrow and grief that we would prefer to avoid. Nonetheless, for God these painful experiences are not evil, but rather have the power of potential goodness.[582]

Thus the evil in nature, no matter how distressing and mournful it might be, is consequently good to such extent that St James the Adelphotheos (the Brother of God) said: *"My brethren, count it all joy when you fall into various trials, knowing that the testing of your faith produces patience."*[583]

Generally, one must realise that if there was no natural evil, things would have been far worse for sinners and the sinful world, for although they have distanced themselves from God, they are prevented from doing worse through suffering caused by natural evil. God provides for all Creation, acknowledging our free-will and wishing us no evil. Not everything is done only according to His Will, but also according to our own free-will. What is from God is not from us although some circumstances are caused by our free-will. Whatever is accomplished without the participation of our free-will, is from God. Additionally, whatever is good comes from the synergy of our free-will and God. This synergy is Justified because it desires good with an appropriate conscience in accordance to God's Foreknowledge. However, when evil is caused by

---

[580] Is. 14:12-14.
[581] Luke 10:18.
[582] Mogilas, in Karmeris, *The dogmatics,* p. 606.
[583] James 1:2-3. James 1:12-15.

wicked men, God justly abandons all those who desire to alienate themselves from Him. He grants their abandonment with forbearance, respecting their free-will and subsequent choices.[584]

God, Who despises and punishes evil, could have abolished sin once and for all but this would have caused the annihilation of humanity's free-will and would have been done by means of force and violence. Consequently, *"whatever is done by force is not rational nor of virtue."*[585] In view of the fact that when God created man, He gave him free-will, He does not want forceful prevention through His Divine Power of consequences caused by the Fall of His rational beings because this would be considered equal to the Catastrophe of His own Work.

God infinitely Wills goodness and virtue. In addition to this He wants everything to be done freely because if goodness and virtue are forced, they loose their authenticity and incentive. God is not pleased by beings who are unwillingly obligated to do good because the Divine Plan of His Creation aims to establish a spiritual Kingdom in which only rational and moral personalities can participate. Since God has granted this precious Gift of freedom to His rational beings of being able to choose between good and evil, He tolerates and permits their actions until such time as when His Son, our Lord and Saviour Jesus Christ, will Judge the world.

Question 118: What is Foreknowledge, Predestination and Concession?

Answer: Divine Foreknowledge is not identical to predestination of events although relatively similar because evil deeds are foreknown by God yet have not been executed by those who may bring them to fruition in due time. Even though evil deeds are foreknown by God they are not predestined by Him to be fulfilled because then God would be responsible for them.

Evil deeds have been committed not because they were predicted by God but because they were fulfilled by liberated rational beings as their own free acts of will. God allows this to occur. Nevertheless this concession differs completely from predestination. For example, God anticipated the Fall of angels and of mankind even before He had created them and, whereas they had fallen even though under the control of Divine Providence, at the same time they had fallen due to their own freedom of choice. Consequently, owing to this fact as well as having willingly alienated themselves from God, they are justly held responsible.

---

[584] St John of Damascus, *Exposition. About providence,* II, 43, in Migne, *P.G.,* 94, 968.
[585] Ibid, *Exposition. About providence,* II, 43, in Migne, *P.G.,* 94, 969.

According to the forementioned, although Divine Foreknowledge is not identical to predestination of events, it is relatively similar. This Foreknowledge of God predestines the consequences of moral evil and establishes boundaries in which they may occur, so that God's Plan will not be hindered. Neither will evil be corrected, or negatively, become instruments of goodness. Furthermore evil will not be harshly punished until its total destruction on the Day of Judgement.

The Holy Fathers of the Orthodox Church distinguish between two types of Divine Abandonment: by *"economy"* or for *"pedagogic"* reasons and complete desperation. Abandonment by *"economy"* or for *"pedagogic"* reasons is used by God for the correction, salvation and glory of those who suffer. Some are healed more rapidly as a result of their evil deeds and offences because they are easier to cure.[586] Nevertheless, they may fall repeatedly into the same errors causing them to remain irredeemable and incurable. For this reason God allows longer suffering, in order that the wicked may comprehend the damage caused by their sins and subsequently loathe their evil deeds so willingly committed. In this manner, they may be healed physically and spiritually. In difficult circumstances God may postpone His Divine therapy, and although it may appear that He is not helping sinners, in reality He is most certainly doing so. Furthermore God permits shameful deeds in order to prevent worse passions. For example, when we are proud of our virtues or achievements, God allows us to fall into some type of error so that we recognise and acknowledge our own weakness, humble ourselves and approach the Lord for forgiveness.

The falls of the two great Apostles, St Peter and St Paul, are relative to the aforementioned. As recorded in the New Testament, St Peter renounced Christ three times because of personal pride and self-preservation. As a result he was in danger of becoming unworthy of the Apostolic Work.[587] St Paul had persecuted the Church with excessive zeal[588] but with ignorant conviction. However, afterwards he struggled more than any of the other Apostles to spread the Holy Gospel. The realisation that he had persecuted the Church of Christ was always before him and this constantly humbled him.[589] These are only two examples of the pedagogic abandonment of God Who always works for the Salvation of men. *"Complete abandonment takes place when God does everything for man's Salvation, but he remains unmoved and uncured in his heart; and by his*

---

[586] Origen, *About prayer,* 29, 13, in **B,** v. 10, p. 297.
[587] Matth. 26:33-35, 69-75. Mark 14:29-31, 66-72. Luke 22:31-34, 54-65. John 18:16-17, 25-27.
[588] Gal. 1:14.
[589] 1 Corinth. 15:9.

own free-will he remains in sin and without repentance, as in the case of Judah."[590]

Question 119: Does the Government of God in Wisdom restricts Evil?

Answer: Although God tolerates evil with infinite patience, He does not remain inactive but instead restricts it within certain boundaries that Divine Providence demands, or guides it with His Almighty Wisdom to achieve goodness, regardless of the evil intention of the wicked. Thus God "*tolerates Satan, not because God is weak*" but because He "*allowed him to exist, in order for two things to take place.*" Firstly "*that Satan in doing more evil will be defeated*" and secondly, so that men who are tempted by the evil one, might defeat him and, as a consequence, be "*crowned*"[591] and glorified.

God restricts Satan's power and authority with absolute Justice, as demonstrated in the therapy of the Gadarene demoniac[592] whereby the demons had no authority to enter into the herd of swine until they were permitted to do so by Christ.[593] It is obvious that Satan and his demons hate the human race more than the animals or the entire Universe because they destroyed the herd of swine without the least hesitation.[594] Therefore how much more hatred and destruction would they have brought upon humanity if they had the slightest authority? Satan would have destroyed the whole Universe in a split second but because of "*God's Guardianship, the power of the demons is restrained.*"[595]

The Divine Plan of Salvation, not only for those who love God but even for the predestined before all time, is served not only by positive events through which God acts, but also through deeds of the inventor of evil and those he uses as wicked instruments in his futile efforts to prevent or cancel God's Plan. In this manner, the Jews, used by Satan as his willing instruments and despite their absolutely evil intentions of destroying the Messiah, worked unconsciously in collaboration with God's Providence to achieve the greatest event in man's history: the Salvation of the human race by means of the condemnation of the Son of God. In their actions "*against God's Anointed One*"[596] "*Herod and Pontius Pilate with the nations and the*

---

[590] St John of Damascus, *Exposition. About providence*, II, 43, in Migne, *P.G.*, 94, 968.
[591] St Cyril of Jerusalem, *Catechesis*, 8, § 1 and 2, in Migne, *P.G.*, 33, 628-629.
[592] Luke 8:26-39.
[593] Luke 8:32.
[594] Luke 8:33.
[595] St John Chrysostom, *To Matthew, Homily* 28, § 3, in Migne, *P.G.*, 57, 354.
[596] Psalm 2:1-2.

people of Israel" performed "*whatever the Hand and Will of God had predestined to take place.*"[597] It is essential to remember, that God despises all forms of evil and never predestines man to work any evil at all. Nevertheless, evil occurs because of man's free-will. Thus in order to fulfil God's Will the actions of those who crucified the Son of God were restricted. The triumph of God over evil is accomplished without man simply becoming an instrument yet preserving his freedom. In other words the evil intentions of man remain while the prevailing good is the act of God's Divine Providence.

Question 120: How do we explain the existence of unrighteousness in the World (Theodicy)?

Answer: Throughout the generations many attempted to justify the Government of God and the existence of unrighteousness in the world. Thus the theory of "*Θεοδικία*" (Theodicy) strives to prove, as far as possible, that although unrighteousness exists in the world, God's Government is achieved with great Wisdom and Justice.[598] This struggle is not only legitimate, but originates from deep piety and is in agreement with the Teachings of the Holy Fathers and Holy Scripture. In the Book of Job, in Psalms 37(38), 73(74) and 77(78), as well as in the Letter of St Paul to the Romans (chapters 9-11) the question of "*Is there unrighteousness with God?*"[599] arose which St Paul answered correctly.

Only with the Light of Faith can we understand the "*Economia*" of Divine Providence and uncover the mysterious veil that covers the problem of unrighteousness. Without Faith that assures us of the reality of Life after this existence which is our destiny, the problem of the apparent wellbeing of the ungodly during this life contrary to the sufferings of the Just, will always remain an unsolved Mystery.

Question 121: How do we explain Natural Evil?

Answer: Faith solves the difficulties of explaining the existence of natural evil. The decay, death and disasters that the earth faces occurred even before the appearance of man. God, foreknowing the Fall of man, predestined the things of Creation in such a way that He would not be caught unaware by moral evil but instead He guided everything according to His Divine Will.

---

[597] St John of Damascus, *Exposition. About providence,* II, 43, in Migne, *P.G.,* 94, 965.
[598] Trempelas, *Dogmatique,* v. I, p. 401.
[599] Rom. 9:14.

Only the faithful can fully understand what Holy Scripture states concerning natural evil that prepares the future glory for the Just, which will be revealed as an expression of the special Love of God for His servants who now suffer but who will then be glorified.

We must never forget the length of man's life and the time of death are determined by God.[600] He gives a specific number of years to each one's life[601] so no one dies before the time appointed by God. Those who die due to personal carelessness or an undisciplined way of life or who have committed suicide thereby ending their own lives or who have been murdered by others, depart this life because God has allowed it to happen. Nevertheless questions always arise concerning the length of man's life which human intellect cannot understand.

Questions 122: How and why do many die as soon as they are born or as infants or at a young age whereas others live for so many years and fall into so many sins, or are twisted and become criminals?

Answer: These and many other Mysteries have to considered when examining the Dispensation of the process of God's All-wise Government. Nevertheless, the faithful who are always amazed by the richness of Divine Providence are neither puzzled by nor wonder at them. They consider the infinite distance that separates Divine Wisdom from that of man's and humbly acknowledge: *"For who has known the Mind of the Lord? Or who has become His counsellor?"*[602]

If the methods of Divine Providence were comprehensible to man's limited mind, then they would no longer be Supernatural but instead would be completely diminished to the level of material things. Also, we must never forget that in order to examine the Supernatural Work of the Divine Government of God, we must keep in mind the whole Work of Creation and not only a miniscule part of it. Only God has the entire history of Creation in His Sight with every detail and possibility, not only past and present but also the future of each individual creature, either rational or irrational, to the end of the present world as well as afterwards to the Eternal Kingdom.

---

[600] Daniel 5:23..
[601] Is. 38:5.
[602] Rom. 11:34.

PART TWO
THE SPIRITUAL WORLD

Question 123: What is the Spiritual World?

Answer: God did not only create the material and visible world. Since His eternal Plan was to create a Kingdom in which the citizens would participate in all the good things of His Blessed Life,[603] it is obvious that the crown of His Creation would be the intellectual beings. These beings, gifted with free-will and submitting by their own free choice to their Creator, would acknowledged Him as their King and, in doing so they would become *"partakers of the Divine Nature"*[604] and of the Blessed Life.[605]

Man is obviously counted among the intellectual beings and for this reason he can be considered as the Crown of all Creation. However, man is not the only intellectual being with free-will and neither is God referred to as *"God the Father of spirits."* Nonetheless, throughout Holy Scripture it is witnessed that there is a spiritual world that consists of higher spiritual beings. Consequently, these beings are above man in moral perfection, wisdom, power and immortality. Thus Holy Scripture characterises man as being *"lower than the Angels."*[606]

CHAPTER FIVE
THE WORLD OF THE ANGELS

Question 124: What is the world of the Angels?

Answer: The Angels received their name from the work of their mission. They bring forth the Message of and fulfill God's Divine Will. They exist in the spiritual world, which is witnessed by Holy Scripture and the Holy Tradition of the Orthodox Church. The existence of Angels was denied by the Sadducees, Deists, Pantheists and Rationalists, but their denial is completely unfounded as proved by the fact that the oldest Books of Holy Scripture, written before the Babylonian captivity, mention the existence of Angels. The reality of such intellectual and spiritual beings cannot be proved by logic as Divine Revelation is beyond any rational conception.

---

[603] Matth. 25:34. Rom. 8:17.
[604] 2 Peter 1:4.
[605] Cf. Plato of Moscow, *Orthodox Teaching,* pp. 99-100. Kefalas, *Catechesis,* pp. 51-56. Damalas, *Catechesis,* p. 15. Frangopoulos, *Christian Faith,* pp. 82-83. Mitsopoulos, *Themata,* p. 65.
[606] Psalm 8:5.

We know nothing more of the beginning or the numbers of these Heavenly Hosts other than that they consist of different categories and were created by God before the creation of the visible world including the stars. Their dwelling place is neither perceptible nor material, but intellectual and spiritual since they are spirits. And although many of the Holy Fathers described them as having some kind of airy body, they are regarded as bodiless, intellectual, free beings, who are unalterable, have no need of material food or reproduction and who are immortal and therefore eternal beings.

Being Gifted with free-will, Angels had the choice of progressing in goodness or turning towards evil rebellion and consequently falling from the holiness received right from the beginning of their creation from nothingness. However, Angels were not created perfect but with the possibility of either remaining in a state of holiness or to turn their nature towards evil. Holy Scripture describes the rest of the Angels' Attributes as being powerful and intellectual, moving automatically towards greater knowledge than man yet contained within boundaries, since they ignored the Divine Dispensation of the Mystery of the Incarnation of the Word and Son of God. They now know the Infinite Wisdom of God through the Church. Nonetheless, Angels completely ignore the near future as well as the secrets of man's heart that only God knows. Their numbers are beyond any human concept although they appear to be divided into different categories of Hosts. St Dionysius the Aeropagite divided them into nine Angelical Hosts of three decorations (groups).

Their primary work is to watch over the beauty of God's Glory and to glorify Him ceaselessly. This consists of the progression towards the Blessed Life that constantly increases as well as for the enjoyment of the Divine Majesty. Furthermore, they bring God's messages to men and call them to repentance. Each person has his own Guardian Angel and every nation and every church also has a designated Guardian Angel.

Question 125: What does the name "*Angel*" means?

Answer: The meaning of the word "Angel" expresses a general connotation and in some instances it signifies the Carrier of a Message (a Messenger) or the one who is sent. In later times it signified a special Order of the Heavenly Powers and, finally, it is used to signify the whole spiritual world. This name is used to differentiate spiritual beings from human beings, to whom they are sent by God in order to serve His Will in respect of man's Salvation. It does not represent their nature or essence, but it is a name related to their function and work towards the Salvation of man.[607] For this reason it is not a paradox that this name is also ascribed to those who are sent by the Lord, Prophets,[608] Priests[609] and Bishops,[610] in order to proclaim the Will of God to the people. The name *"Angel"* is specifically used to described the Messiah Who is referred to as the *"Angel of the Covenant"*[611] and *"Messenger of Great Counsel."*[612] Furthermore it is used to described St John the Forerunner and Baptist who *"shall survey the way before"* the Lord.[613]

In the first Book of Genesis the name *"Angel"* is mainly ascribed to spiritual beings who are invisible and bodiless. Thus *"Cherubs and the fiery sword that turns about.."* were placed by God *"to keep the way of the Tree of Life."*[614] An Angel of the Lord spoke to Agar.[615] Angels visited and saved Lot.[616] An Angel of the Lord prevented Abraham from offering Isaac as a sacrifice to God.[617] Angels of God appeared to Abraham at Mamre, ascending and descending upon the Ladder that Jacob beheld in his dream at Charrhan.[618] Angels appeared to the Prophets Elijah, Zechariah, Isaiah, Ezekiel and Daniel.[619] An Angel of the Lord appeared in the furnace at Babylon to protect the three children Sedrach, Misach and Abdenago.[620] Sometimes their names are mentioned as being *"Archangel Michael"*[621] *"Gabriel"*[622] and *"Raphael."*[623] In the New Testament there are many verses in which Angels of the Lord are mentioned.[624]

Among the numerous references to the existence and work of Angels, we particularly note the words of our Lord and Saviour Jesus Christ Who cautioned us to *"Take heed that you do not despise one of these little ones, for I say to you that in Heaven their Angels always see the Face of My*

---

[607] Origen, *Against Celsus,* V, 4, in **B,** v. 10, p. 10 and 13. St John Chrysostom, *Concerning the unintelligible,* in Migne, *P.G.,* 48, 724.
[608] Hagg. 1:13..
[609] Malach. 2:7.
[610] Rev. 1:20; 2:1, 8, 12, 18; 3:1, 7, 14.
[611] Malach. 3:1-3.
[612] Is. 9:6.
[613] Malach. 3:1. Matth. 3:3; 11:10. Mark 1:2. Luke 3:4. John 1:23. Is. 40:3-5.
[614] Gen. 3:25.
[615] Gen. 16:7-12.
[616] Gen. 19:1-22..
[617] Gen. 22:11.
[618] Gen. 28:12.
[619] 1 Samuel (1 Kings) 1:3-15. Zach. 1:9; 6:4-8. Is. 6:2-3; 11:2. Jez. 1:4-18. Daniel 7:10.
[620] Daniel 3:25.
[621] Joshua 5:13-16. Daniel 10:13, 21; 12:1. Judah 9. Rev. 12:7.
[622] Daniel 8:16; 9:21. Luke 1:19.
[623] Tobit 12:15.
[624] Matth. 1:20. Luke 1:26; 2:9, 13. Acts 12:7-11; 27:23; 10:3-7, 22, 30; 27:23.

Father Who is in Heaven.[625] At the Second Coming of the Son of God, Christ will come *"in His Glory"* accompanied by *"all the Holy Angels with Him."* [626] The Angels always rejoice when a sinner repents.[627] Furthermore, they have no need of reproduction because *"in the Resurrection"* men *"neither marry nor are given in marriage, but are like Angels of God in Heaven."*[628]

Question 126: Do the Apostolic Fathers and Ecclesiastical Scholars witness the existence of Angels?

Answer: *The Shepherd of Hermas* characterised Angels as being *"Holy Angels of God who were created first of all"*[629] and that *"there are two Angels with man: one of righteousness and one of wickedness."*[630] Athenagoras, Tatianus and Theophilus of Antioch and especially St Justin the Philosopher and Martyr[631] referred to the belief of Angels. Tertullian mentioned *"spiritual essences, which have thin bodies"* [632] while St Irenaeus expressed his belief of seven Hosts of Angels.[633]

Question 127: Who denied the existence of Angels?

Answer: The existence of Angels was denied in antiquity by the Sadducees who declared *"there is no resurrection and no Angel or spirit"* [634] while the Deists refused to acknowledge any intervention of God in the world. The Pantheists identified God with the material world whereas the Rationalists of each generation proclaimed that there is no other world except the one that we see. Finally, the contemporary Rationalists attempted to explain the ideas of Judaism concerning Angels as though they originated from the personalisation of Divine Attributes and Actions, or as being the remnants of ancient polytheism that had entered into the Jewish religion, having been borrowed from the Parsees or the Babylonians.

---

[625] Matth. 18:10.

[626] Matth. 25:31. Mark 13:27.

[627] Luke 15:7, 10.

[628] Matth. 22:30.

[629] *Shephered of Hermas*, Vision 3, 4, 1-2, in Lightfoot, *Apostolic Fathers*, p. 203.

[630] Ibid, Mandate 6, 2, 1-9, in Lightfoot, *Apostolic Fathers*, pp. 222-223.

[631] St Justine, the philosopher and martyr, *1 Apology* 6, § 2, in *B*, v. 3, p. 164. Athenagoras, in *B*, v. 4, p. 288. Tatianus, *Homily to the Greeks*, 7, in *B*, v.4, p. 246. Theophilus of Antioch, *2 Autolycus*, 28, in *B*, v.5, p. 40.

[632] Tertullian, *Apologeticus*, 22, in migne, *P.L.*, 1, 465; Ibid, *De carne Christi*,6, in migne, *P.L.*, 2, 810.

[633] St Irenaeus, *Heresies*, book II, in Migne, *P.G.*, 7, 818.

[634] Acts 23:8.

Nevertheless, belief in the spiritual world even outside Judaism confirms that this is based upon an ancient Tradition that was passed down from the first created man. The general belief of various religions, regardless of the different influences that disfigured the original belief, is solid proof of its Truth.

Question 128: How were the Angels created?

Answer: We find an indirect indication of God's creation of Angels in the Book of Exodus: *"For in six days the Lord made the Heaven and the earth, and the sea and all things in them."*[635] St Paul also taught that *" by Him all things were created that are in Heaven and that are on earth, visible and invisible, whether Thrones or Dominions or Principalities or Powers."*[636]

The Holy Fathers of the Orthodox Church note that Holy Scripture does not mention the way in which Angels were created. About the *"when"* and *"how"* they were created, nothing is mentioned.

The only indication we have concerning the time of their creation, is that from the Book of Job according to which *"when the stars were made, all My Angels praised Me with a loud voice."*[637] In accordance to this, all the Holy Fathers agree that the creation of Angels took place before the creation of the visible world. God first created the Angelical Hosts of Heaven and then the visible world and man *"who is the image of the Higher Power."*[638]

Question 129: Is the nature of the Angels spiritual, bodiless and immortal?

Answer: Many Holy Fathers support the belief that Angels are in a certain *"place"* and hold certain *"positions."*[639] St John of Damascus taught that: *"because the Angels are intellectual beings, they are in spiritual places, not described corporeally."* They *"exist in airy places in a light and movable nature."* They are not bound by specific, perceptible or material places, yet they are not ever-present as God is. Instead *"when they are in Heaven, they are not on earth, and when they are sent to earth by God, they do not*

---

[635] Ex. 20:11.
[636] Col. 1:16.
[637] Job 38:7.
[638] St Gregory of Nyssa, *Catechesis,* 6, in Migne, *P.G.,* 45, 28. St Gregory of Nazianzus, *Homily* 38, § 9, in Migne, *P.G.,* 36, 320.
[639] St Basil the Great, *About the Holy Spirit*, XVI, 38, in in Migne, *P.G.,* 32, 137. St Ignatius, *To Trallians,* 5, 2, in Lightfoot, *Apostolic Fathers,* p. 99.

remain in Heaven." They are *"always moving"* having the whole Universe at their disposal, moving with ease and without any obstacles restricting them such as *"walls and doors and locks and seals."*[640]

We cannot speak of perceptible and material places where Angels dwell since *"we do not know precisely the essence of the Angels; and even if we philosophise ten thousands of reasons, we will be unable to find even one."*[641]

Although we cannot know the exact nature of Angels, we are enlightened by Holy Scripture that God *"makes His Angels spirits"*[642] and that the Spirit of Divine Wisdom goes *"through all understanding, pure and most subtle spirits"*[643] and that there are *"..seven spirits who are before the Throne"* of God.[644] Subsequently, the nature of Angels is spiritual, free from any matter or flesh, as manifested by Holy Scripture when referring to the fallen angels who, in the New Testament, are characterised as *"unclean spirits."*[645]

Angels are characterised as *"intellectual beings and thin as the mind,"* *"bodiless and intellectual natures,"* *"bodiless and invisible and needless,"* *"thin, rational and always moving essence,"* *"essences, intellectuals, always moving, bodiless"* of whose *"kind and number only the Creator knows."* They appear in Holy Scripture as flames of fire to reveal *"the light and fiery and warmth and quickness and sharpness concerning their Divine aptitude and service."* By manifesting as *"the fiery"* and *"the Heavenly intellect's Divinity as well as their ability to imitate the Divine"* as the anthropomorphism signifies, *"the intellectual and, according to their nature, the primacy and ruling,"* *"the nakedness and without sandals,"* *"the assimilating to the Divine simplicity"* is according to their capabilities.[646]

The majority of Holy Fathers believe that Angels have some kind of *"airy body, thin and immortal,"* when compared to us humans. For this reason they are called *"bodiless and immaterial"* although when compared

---

[640] St John of Damascus, *Exposition. About fore-knowledge and destination,* II, 34, in Migne, *P.G.,* 94, 869.

[641] St John Chrysostom, *Concerning the unintelligible,* 5, § 3, in Migne, *P.G.,* 48, 74.

[642] Psalm 104(105):4.

[643] Wisdom, 7:23.

[644] Rev. 1:4.

[645] Matth. 8:16; 10:1; 12:43, 45. Mark 1:23, 26-27; 3:11, 30; 5:2, 13; 7:25; 9:25. Luke 6:18; 8:29; 9:42; 11:24, 26. Acts 5:16; 8:7. Rev. 16:13.

[646] St Gregory of Nazianzus, *Homily* 38, § 10, in Migne, *P.G.,* 36, 321. St Gregory of Nyssa, *To prayer,* in Migne, *P.G.,* 44, 1165. Ibid, *Catechesis,* 6, in Migne, *P.G.,* 45, 25. St John of Damascus, *Exposition. About angels,* II, 17, in Migne, *P.G.,*94, 865 and 868. St Dionysius, *About the heavenly hierarchy,* XV, §§ 2 and 3, in Migne, *P.G.,* 329.

to God Who is the Absolute Simple, Immaterial and Incorporeal Being, they are *"thick and material."*[647]

This matter was finalised at the 7th Ecumenical Council, which declared at the 4th meeting that Angels are *"bodiless."* During the 5th meeting a 7th century writing by John, Bishop of Thessalonica, was read in which he supported the opinion that only God is Infinitely Bodiless, while the Angels, the Archangels and the Higher Powers have thin, airy and fiery bodies according to Psalm 104(105):4. This is the belief of the majority of Holy Fathers. The Holy Council concluded that it is not sinful to represent them in images, to honour them and give them human form because that is how they appeared on innumerous occasions. The Holy Council did not deal with this matter in great detail nor did it proclaim a special decree. Nevertheless St Tarasios, Patriarch of Constantinople and President of the Council, remarked: *"Do you hear what this Father says we should paint the Angels because they are describable"* and also because they appeared to so many people. The Holy Council responded positively.[648]

Nevertheless, Angels are bodiless and intellectual powers. St Basil the Great confirmed that *"they do not change"* in their bodies in the same manner as the human body that ages. For there is no *"child or youth or elder amongst the Angels."* Instead *"they remain in the condition"* in which *"from the beginning they were created"* as *"their composition"* remains *" whole and unchangeable."*[649]

Some Holy Fathers believe that the mysterious *"manna"* is the *"Heavenly food of the Angels"* and they declare that as irrational men are fed, likewise must we consider that the Angels are fed, for they are not completely needless. Man has therefore eaten *"the bread of the Angels."*

The spiritual nature of Angels ensures their immortality which in turn is guaranteed by the Son and Word of God, our Lord and Saviour Jesus Christ Who promised us that *"those who are counted worthy to attain that Age, and the Resurrection from the dead, neither marry nor are given in marriage; nor can they die anymore, for they are equal to the Angels and are sons of God, being sons of the Resurrection."*[650]

St John of Damascus proclaimed that each Angel *"is not immortal by nature, but by Grace"* because *"only God exists always,"* *"for whatever has a beginning also has an end according to its nature."* Clarifying the term *"by Grace,"* he explained that *"we think about the bodiless and invisible in two ways: on the one hand according to their essence; on the other hand by*

---

[647] St John of Damascus, *Exposition. About angels,* II, 17, in Migne, *P.G.,* 94, 865 and 868.
[648] Mansi, v. XIII, col. 132, 164 and 165.
[649] St Basil the Great, *To Psalm* 45, § 1, in Migne, *P.G.,* 29, 388.
[650] Luke 20:35-36.

Grace. Speaking about God, He is by Nature (Immortal) *whereas the Angels and demons and souls are* (immortal) *by Grace.*"[651]

Question 130: Do the Angels have free-will?

Answer: The Angels, as spiritual beings,[652] are Gifted with free-will, having the *"authority and the freedom either to remain and to progress in goodness and virtue, or to turn to evil."*[653] St Basil the Great believed that it is possible for Angels to turn to evil because *"the Heavenly Powers are not by nature Holy"* as the *"Holiness"* is from *"outside of their nature"* and *"they receive it by being careful and hard-working." "Through the Communion of the Holy Spirit, God grants them the perfection"* and they are able to *"hold to their Order by insisting on remaining in goodness."* He then uses the imagery of iron that, when it is in contact with fire, becomes warm and hot and receives the colour and energy of the fire. Likewise, the Holy Powers, not having holiness by nature, receive it through their communion with the Holy Spirit Who by Nature is Holy. And because they receive their holiness from outside their nature, it is possible for their nature to change. This is proven by the example of Lucifer who would not have fallen if his nature was not capable of changing.[654]

The fact that bodiless Angels receive their holiness from their communion with the Holy Spirit does not mean that they were created at the beginning as *"infants and afterwards, through progress, they became worthy of receiving the Holy Spirit."* Instead, they received their holiness right from the beginning.[655]

When we say that Angels had received holiness right from the beginning of their creation from nothingness, we must not think that they were perfected in holiness. Their perfection was accomplished by the Holy Spirit and it depended on the good use of their free-will. Although there was no imperfection in their nature inclining them towards evil, the Creator implanted seeds of holiness in them that made it more difficult to move or to change, but it did not make them unable to move towards evil. They were able to progress and become perfect in holiness.[656]

---

[651] St John of Damascus, *Exposition. About angels,* II, 17; *About man,* II, 26, in Migne, *P.G.,* 94, 868 and 925.

[652] Damalas, *Catechesis,* pp. 15-16. Mitsopoulos, *Themata,* p. 66.

[653] St John of Damascus, *Exposition. About angels,* II, 17, in Migne, *P.G.,* 94, 868.

[654] St Basil the Great, *About the Holy Spirit,* XVI, § 38, in Migne, *P.G.,* 32, 137. Ibid, *Against Eunomius,* 3, § 2, in Migne, *P.G.,* 29, 660.

[655] Ibid, *To Psalm* 33(34), § 4, in Migne, *P.G.,* 29, 333.

[656] St Gregory of Nazianzus, *Homily* 38, § 9, in Migne, *P.G.,* 36, 320. Ibid, *Homily* 28, § 31, in Migne, *P.G.,* 36, 72.

The progress and perfection in holiness of Angels is verified by the fact that they were "..*made to be steadfast..*" by the Holy Spirit and subsequently it became more difficult to fall from Goodness. They became steadfast after the Great Test when their wills were tested at the time of Lucifer's rebellion against God and after other angels had fallen with him. The rest of the Angels could also have fallen but they were saved because of their love, faithfulness and devotion to God, whereas Satan's "*departure from God made him an outcast.*" Thus, because of their free choice of virtue, the Angels became unshakeable in their faith and loyalty through the Grace of God.[657]

However, if Angels were to be become perfect by progressing in Holiness, would their progress open the way to higher Angelical Orders? In other words, would the lower Orders of Angelical Hierarchy be raised through their perfection to higher Orders? As a matter of fact, the Alexandrian Fathers do accept this idea of the lower Orders of Angels being raised to higher Orders by their perfection in Holiness.[658] Other Holy Fathers are very cautious on this subject as we cannot draw conclusions based on allusions. St John of Damascus concluded that Angels "*differ from one another in brightness and position; either according to their brightness they have the position or according to their position they participate in the brightness.*"[659]

Question 131: Are the Angels supernatural and superior in power and knowledge?

Answer: Angels stand above all intellectual beings with freedom combined with greater power than man and thus enter the sphere of the Supernatural. Holy Scripture proclaims that Angels are "*strong in power*" and "*in power and force they are greater.*" In addition, Holy Scripture refers to some instances in which their power is manifested.[660] No human means of defence can prevent their activities as revealed when the Angel freed St Peter from prison.[661]

---

[657] St Basil the Great, *About the Holy Spirit,* XIX, § 49, in Migne, *P.G.,*32, 157. Ibid, *That God is not the cause of evil,* § 8, in Migne, *P.G.,* 31, 348. St John of Damascus, *Exposition. About fore-knowledge and destination,* II, 44, in Migne, *P.G.,* 94, 977.
[658] Clement the Alexandrian, in *B,* v. 8, p. 348.
[659] St John of Damascus, *Exposition. About angels,* II, 17, in Migne, *P.G.,* 94, 872.
[660] 2 Kings (4 Kings)19:35.
[661] Acts 5:19 and 12:7.

It is understandable that Angels, as intellectual and logical beings, move automatically and quickly towards Knowledge with which the Holy Fathers accept that God enlightens them.[662]

According to St Augustine, as soon as Angels were created, they were made as created Light, which is attracted by the Word, the Light Who creates, and they watch Him, seeing themselves in Him and each other.[663] In comparison to other creatures, Angels have two types of knowledge: the "*scientia infusa*" through which they see the creatures in the Creator - in the Word Who is the unalterable Cause of everything that exists - and the other type of knowledge gained through their direct supervision of Creation. Angels know themselves even better through the Word rather than through themselves, although through themselves and within themselves they are known.[664]

We are informed of the extent and depth of their knowledge from the words of Christ Who revealed that they have a higher knowledge in many ways compared to that of all men. They are placed between God and man although their knowledge is restricted[665] Their knowledge of God is limited according to their capability and nature and in many ways they disregard His Divine Acts. God is unintelligible "*not only to the Cherubim and the Seraphim, but*" also "*. to the Principalities*" and "*to the Authorities*" and "*there is no other created power which has exact knowledge of God*" "*.even from among the Cherubim or the Seraphim,*" "*if they wished to know something*" of God, they would only be able to hear "*that Heaven and earth is full of His Glory.*" Although Angels see God, they do not see Him as He is except in accordance with their capabilities[666] that enable them to see the Glory and Divine Energies of God. However they do not see His Essence.

The Event of the Divine Dispensation of the Incarnation of the Word and Son of God was unknown to Angels as witnessed by the two great Apostles, St Paul and St Peter.[667]

Angels do not know future events or what is in the hearts of men. St John of Damascus wrote that "*the future is not known by the Angels of God*" and the forecast "*is revealed to them by God.*"[668] The fact that Angels also ignore the thoughts of men is supported by St Hilarius and St Cyril of

---

[662] Ibid, *Homily* 38, § 9; *Homily* 28, § 31, in Migne, *P.G.*, 36, 320 and 72.

[663] St Augustine, *De Genesis ad litteriam*, IV, § 41, 50, in migne, *P.L.*, 34, 313 and 317.

[664] Ibid, *De civitate Dei*, XI, § 29, in migne, *P.L.*, 41, 343.

[665] Matth. 24:36. Acts 1:7.

[666] St John Chrysostom, *Concerning unintelligible*, 3, §§ 2, 4 and 6, in Migne, *P.G.*, 48, 725 and 729. Ibid, *To John Homily* 15, § 1-2, in Migne, *P.G.*, 59, 98. St Cyril of Jerusalem, *Catechesis*, VI, § 6 and 11, § 11, in Migne, *P.G.*, 33, 545 and 704-705.

[667] Ephes. 3:9-10. 1 Peter 1:12.

[668] St John of Damascus, *Catechesis*, II, 3, in Migne, *P.G.*, 94, 877.

Alexandria who remarked that the Angels know *"that God is the only One Who knows the secrets of men's hearts."* [669]

Question 132: What is the number and hierarchy of the Angels?

Answer: According to the Book of Daniel, the number of Angels were *"thousand thousands* [who] *ministered to Him, and ten thousands of myriads attended upon Him"* [670] whereas the Prophet *"beheld in the night vision one coming with the clouds of Heaven as the Son of Man."*[671] In the Book of Revelation we read: *"Then I looked, and I heard the voice of many Angels around the Throne, the living creatures, and the Elders; and the number of them was ten thousand times ten thousand and thousands of thousands."* [672] Furthermore Christ referred to the innumerability of the Angels when He gave Himself up to the Jews at Gethsemane.[673] Also, the use of the term *"clouds"* is used many times in Scripture to express the immeasurable number of Angels or Saints of the Lord.

St Cyril of Jerusalem, interpreting the Parable of the Lost Sheep,[674] concluded that the number of Angels is *"indescribable"*. In addition he observed that from the number *"one"* symbolising humanity, one could understand the incalculable numbers of Angels symbolised by the number *"ninety-nine."*[675]

The different names and Orders of the Angelic Hosts support the Teachings that they are different in Hierarchy and Ranks. In the book of Tobit we read of the *"seven Holy Angels which present the prayers of the Saints, and which go in and out before the Glory of the Holy One."*[676] They are the ones mentioned by Hermas, *"who were created first of all"*[677] and of whom Clement the Alexandrian had in mind when he spoke of *"..the seven first Angels who have the greatest of power."*[678] Furthermore, Holy Scripture speaks of *"Cherubim and the fiery sword that turns about"* which God stationed *"against the Garden of Delight to keep the Way of the Tree of Life"*[679] and of the six-winged Seraphim who stand *"round about"* God's

---

[669] St Cyril of Alexandria, *To John*, book II, ch. 1, in Migne, *P.G.,* 73, 224.

[670] Dan. 7:10. Cf. Damalas, *Catechesis*, p. 17.

[671] Dan. 7:13. Matth. 25:31. Mark 13:26. 1 Thess. 4:16.

[672] Rev. 5:11; 9:16; 19:1, 20.

[673] Matth. 26:53.

[674] Matth. 18:10-14.

[675] St Cyril of Jerusalem, *Catechesis,* 15, § 24, in Migne, *P.G.,* 33, 904.

[676] Tobit 12:15.

[677] *Shepherd of Hermas*, Vison 3, 4, in Lightfoot, *The Apostolic Fathers*, p. 203.

[678] Clement the Alexandrian, *Stromata,* 6, § 16, in *B*, v.8, p. 232. Rev. 8:2.

[679] Gen. 3:25.

Glory and who *"with two wings covered their faces, and with two* [wings] *covered their feet, and with two flew"* while glorifying the One Who sat on the *"high and exalted Throne."*[680] St Paul mentioned *"Thrones, Dominions, Principalities, Powers"* and *"Might,"* as well as *"Angels"* and *"Archangels,"*[681] while St Jude named one of them, *"Michael."*[682]

The books ascribed to the authorship of St Dionysius the Aeropagite and St John of Damascus, divide the Angelic Hosts into nine Orders and three Decorations:[683]

1)   The first decoration is composed of Seraphim, Cherubim and Thrones who stand round about God and have a close communion with Him.

2)   The second decoration is composed of Dominions, Authorities and Powers.

3)   The third decoration is composed of Principalities, Archangels and Angels.

There is no agreement amongst the Holy Fathers concerning the number of Orders and their Divisions.[684] This differentiation of Ranks, between the lower and higher levels is real and is supported not only by the writings ascribed to St Dionysius the Aeropagite, but by many other Holy Fathers and ecclesiastical Scholars. The writings of St Dionysius the Aeropagite supports the opinion that *"the Order of the Holy Cherubim partakes of a higher level of knowledge and understanding; the lower decorations partake also in wisdom and knowledge, but partial and lower compared to them"* and that the lower Orders receive their brightness from the higher Orders.[685]

St Dionysius the Aeropagite expressed the opinion that the services to mankind and to the world in general are performed by the lower decorations, the Angels, whereas the higher decorations and especially the first *"are always around God."* However, it is not so because according to the Epistle to the Hebrews, the Angels are *"all ministering spirits sent out to*

---

[680] Is. 6:1-3. Jez. 10:1-19.

[681] Col. 1:16. Ephes. 1:21. Rom. 8:38. 1 Thess. 4:16. Josuah 5:14.

[682] Jude 9. Dan. 10:13, 21; 12:1. Rev. 12:7-9.

[683] St Dionysius, *About divine names,* VI, § 2; VII, §§ 1 and 4; VIII, § 1 and IX, § 1, in Migne, *P.G.,* 3, 200, 205, 240 and 257. St John of Damascus, *Exposition. About angels,* II, 17, in Migne, *P.G.,* 94, 872. Damalas, *Catechesis,* pp. 17-18. Mitsopoulos, *Themata,* p. 67.

[684] St Basil the Great, *Homily,* XV, § 1, in Migne, *P.G.,* 31, 465. St Cyril of Jerusalem, *Catechesis,* 23, § 6, in Migne, *P.G.,* 33, 1113. St Cyril of Alexandria, *To Leviticus,* in Migne, *P.G.,* 69, 549.

[685] St Dionysius, *About heavenly hierarchy,* VIII, § 1; *About divine names,* XII, in Migne, *P.G.,* 3, 240 and 292.

minister to those who will inherit Salvation."[686] Thus in the case of the Prophet Isaiah, one of the Seraphim was sent with a live coal taken from the Altar with which he touched the Prophet's mouth.[687]

Question 133: What is the ministry and work of the Angels?

Answer: St John Chrysostom remarked that the Angels *"glorify and worship"* God *"by praising Him constantly with Mystical Odes and much fear."*[688] This is confirmed by Holy Scripture when we read that *"an Angel of the Lord stood before"* the shepherds or *"with the Angel a multitude of the Heavenly Host"* praised *"God saying: Glory to God in the highest,"*[689] whereas the Seraphim exclaim: *"Holy, Holy, Holy"* while turning their faces because they cannot look directly at God.[690] St John the Apostle, Evangelist and Theologian mentioned in the Book of Revelation that he saw the Cherubim surrounding the Throne of God and exclaiming: *"Blessed and Glory and Wisdom!"*[691] while others present the prayers of the Saints or attend to the Will of God.[692]

This endless Glorification of God by the Holy Angels is the result of their Blessedness in God. Their knowledge of the infinite Perfections of God continuously increases and therefore they stand in awe before His Divine Majesty. The repetition of the Thrice Holy Hymn is not by any means a monotonous or tiring duty. Instead it is an expression of their admiration, which is constantly renewed because of the boundless Majesty of God Whom they always see, praise and worship. This is one of the many expressions of the Blessed Life that they enjoy according to the words of our Lord and Saviour Jesus Christ Who said that *"this is Eternal Life, that they may know Thee, the only True God, and Jesus Christ Whom Thou hast sent."*[693]

However, if the main Ministry of the Angels is to Glorify God in order that they become more blessed, then their Ministry to mankind must be considered as being only partial and is performed by them, certainly not because God is unable to do so, but for their own benefit. Thus St Peter and

---

[686] Heb. 1:14.
[687] Is. 6:6-7.
[688] St John Chrysostom, *Concerning unintelligible*, 1, § 6, in Migne, *P.G.*, 48, 707.
[689] Luke 2:9, 13-14.
[690] Is. 6:1-3. Jez. 10:1-19. Rev. 4:8.
[691] Rev. 4:7-11; 5:8-14; 7:11-12. Psalms 103(104):20-22; 148(149):1-2, 4.
[692] Rev. 5:8, 11, 13; 7:11-12; 8:2, 7-9:1, 13, 16; 10:1-7, 9; 11:1, 15; 12:7; 14:6-9, 15, 17-20; 15:1, 7-8; 16:1-17; 17:1, 7; 18:1, 21, 19:1, 4, 14, 17; 20:1; 21:9; 22:1, 6, 10 .
[693] John 17:3.

St Paul proclaimed that *"the manifold Wisdom of God"*[694] is made known to the Angels through the Church and that they *"desire to look into"*[695] the Holy Mysteries (Sacraments) through which man is Sanctified.

Angels' supervision of man is a general Teaching of Holy Scripture and of the Holy Fathers of the Orthodox Church. In the Book of Psalms we read: *"The Angel of the Lord encamps all around those who fear Him, and delivers them."*[696] Jacob spoke of an *"Angel"* who delivered him *"from all evils."* [697] Daniel, after his liberation from the pit of the lions proclaimed that *"God has sent His Angel, and stopped the lions' mouths"* [698] similar to when the three children were thrown into the *"midst of the burning furnace"* and the Angel *"delivered His servants, because they trusted in Him."* [699] Furthermore, our Lord and Saviour Jesus Christ, referring to the role of the Guardian Angel, warned us: *"Take heed that you do not despise one of these little ones, for I say to you that in Heaven their Angels see the Face of My Father Who is in Heaven."* [700] What is more, in the Book of Acts the release of St Peter was accomplished by an Angel whom the Lord had sent to free him.[701]

The Holy Fathers and ecclesiastical Scholars referred to Angels of nations[702] as written in Holy Scripture when, for instance, God promised to send His Angel before Israel so that he would guide them correctly, taking them into the land that God had prepared for them.[703] Furthermore, *"when the Most High divided the nations, when He separated the sons of Adam, He set the bounds of the nations according to the number of the Angels of God."*[704]

CHAPTER SIX
THE FALLEN ANGELS

Question 134: Who are the fallen Angels?

Answer: The Holy Scriptures and Apostolic Tradition witness that besides the good Angels there are evil angels. In the Book of Genesis the evil one,

---

[694] Ephes. 3:10.
[695] 1 Peter 1:12.
[696] Psalm 34(35):7.
[697] Gen. 48:16.
[698] Dan. 6:22, 28.
[699] Dan. 3:23, 25.
[700] Matth. 18:10.
[701] Acts 12:7-11, 15
[702] Clement, *Stromata*, 7, 2 and 6, 17, in *B*, v. 8, pp. 246 and 238. Origen, *To Genesis, Homily* IX, § 3, in Migne, *P.G.,* 12, 213.
[703] Ex. 23:20.
[704] Deut. 32:8.

as a serpent, appears to seduce Eve to disobey God's Commandment.[705] This evil serpent is called by our Lord and Saviour Jesus Christ, the Son of God, as the "*great dragon, that serpent of old, called Devil and Satan, who deceives the whole world.*"[706] Many of the Books of the Old Testament refer to the existence of Satan, especially in the oldest Book, that of Job, where the evil one appears as a tyrant demanding the sufferings of man.[707] In the New Testament our Lord and His Holy Apostles assured us of the existence of Satan, also giving us information concerning his evil Attributes and thoughts, as well as the catastrophic influences and attempts, which are aimed against man and his destruction. Satan's existence is denied by the Rationalists, but it is proclaimed by all the Holy Fathers and ecclesiastical Scholars of the Orthodox Church.

Concerning the beginning and the origin of the evil spirits, it is a common belief by all the Holy Fathers, based on Holy Scriptures, that they were created at the beginning as good Angels, who fell from their first station because of pride and the desire to be placed above the Throne of God. Other Angels fell from Grace because they envied man, who was made in the "*image and likeness*" of God, and who they subsequently led to the Fall, caused to sin and thereby alienated from God. And it is true that because of Satan's envy of man, humanity fell into sin after Satan himself had already fallen from Heaven. As an evil spirit he invented the wicked plan to mislead man. The opinion that the Angels desired sexual intercourse with women according to Genesis 6:2 is not acceptable.

In accordance to the origin of the evil spirits, it is obvious that they are bodiless, immortal and eternal, just like the good Angels. They have free-will and by their own free-will they alienated themselves from the Holiness with which God had decorated them, and becoming the inventors of evil, they became the source and the beginning of evil. Henceforth, as a deceitful liar and malicious spirit, Satan hates, without any valid reason, the creatures of God but especially mankind as being in the "*image and likeness*" of the Creator. Satan has the power to prevent and overthrow the Work of God by sabotaging the Plan of man's Salvation. The Divine Wisdom, however, restricts him to certain boundaries and limits, not allowing him to test men over their abilities. God uses Satan's devious actions to lead people to goodness. God assists pious and virtuous individuals, encouraging them to do good deeds and strengthening them through His Divine Grace. Thus the

---

[705] Gen. 3:1-6.
[706] Rev. 12:9; 20:2.
[707] Job 1:6-12.

faithful are victorious against the evil spirits and prove themselves to be worthy of the Eternal Crowns and glory.

Although Satan and his evil spirits are deceitful and powerful, he is defeated by the faithful in Christ and since his mind has alienated him from the Divine Light, he remains blind and in complete Spiritual Darkness, incapable of knowing or understanding the Divine Truths. Even more, he is incapable of knowing the Divine Actions and Will of God concerning Salvation.

Question 135: Do Evil Spirits exist?

Answer: In the oldest Books of Holy Scripture we do not find the name "*Satan*" or "*diabolos,*"[708] but right from the beginning, in the Book of Genesis we read of the Fall of man that was caused by Satan. The evil force, which appeared as speaking, thinking and acting,[709] is not like the irrational, animal beings, but experienced and older than the new, simple and inexperienced man. The consequent punishment of the tempter by God[710] would be inexplicable if he was a natural snake and not some intelligent and acting being. The explanations and clarifications given by our Lord and Saviour Jesus Christ, the Son of God, and His Holy Apostles, does not leave any doubt of this. The author of the Books of the Pentateuch sees Satan under the symbolism of the serpent but avoids clear explanation. The Book of the Wisdom of Solomon proclaims that "*through envy of the devil came death into the world.*"[711] Our Lord and Saviour Jesus Christ, the Son of God, assured us that the devil "*was a murderer from the beginning, and does not stand in the Truth for he is a liar and the father of it.*"[712] St Paul in 2 Corinthians says: "*The serpent deceived Eve by his craftiness.*"[713] These three verses, in combination with the narration in Genesis concerning Eve's deception, clarify the Fall of Adam and Eve being caused by Satan, who in the Book of Revelation is called the "*the great dragon, that serpent of old, called the Devil and Satan.*"[714]

If we bear in mind the prohibitions and differentiations in the Book of Leviticus[715] concerning ventriloquists and mediums, which are related

---

[708] Kefalas, *Catechesis,* pp. 238-240. Damalas, *Catechesis,* pp. 18-20. Frangopoulos, *Christian Faith,* pp. 86-87. Mitsopoulos, *Themata,* p. 68.
[709] Gen. 3:2, 5.
[710] Gen. 3:15-16.
[711] Wisdom 2:24.
[712] John 8:44.
[713] 2 Corinth. 11:3.
[714] Rev. 12:9; 20:2.
[715] Lev. 19:31 and 20:6.

directly to ideas and faith of evil spirits, the information found in 1 Samuel (1 Kings)[716] and 1 Chronicles,[717] as well as the Book of Job,[718] we can see that belief in the existence of the devil is wide spread in the oldest books of the Old Testament. King David in Psalm 95 (96):5 proclaimed that *"all the gods of the peoples are idols (demons)."* In Tobit it is also mentioned that *"Asmodeus, the evil spirit, had killed the seven husbands of Sarah,"* as well as describing the way that Sarah would be set free from the influence of the evil spirits on her wedding day.[719]

The New Testament's Teachings concerning the devil and his evil actions are manifested very clearly by our Lord and Saviour Jesus Christ, the Son of God. Frequently He speaks to His disciples about the devil, the evil one, the tempter, Satan or Beelzebub.[720] Satan appears to have knowledge of Holy Scripture, speaking and inventing lies, totally alien to the Truth and fallen far apart from it. He turns against man with hatred and is called by Christ, the *"murderer of man."*[721] He snatches away from the hearts of men God's Word, in order for them not to be saved.[722] He is the enemy who spreads *"tares"* in the world.[723] When cast away from the heart of man, he returns with other spirits *"more wicked than him"*[724] and possesses the human soul with innumerous demons.[725] As the ruler of the world[726] he cannot find anything against the Lord.[727] At the end Satan will be cast out *"into the Everlasting Fire."*[728]

St John the Apostle, Evangelist and Theologian states that *"the devil has sinned from the beginning."*[729] The manifestation of sin began with the Fall of Satan, being its father and inventor. St Jude refers to *"angels who did not keep their proper domain, but left their own abode, He has reserved in everlasting chains under darkness for the judgment of the great day."* [730] St Peter also states, *"God did not spare the angels who sinned, but cast them*

---

[716] 1 Samuel (1 Kings)16:14.

[717] 1 Chronicles 21:1.

[718] Job 1:6-12.

[719] Tobit 3:8; 6:7, 14-17.

[720] Matth. 4:3-11; 10:25; 12:24-27; 16:23. Mark 1:13; 3:23; 4:15. Luke 4:2-13; 10:18; 22:3, 31.

[721] John 8:44.

[722] Matth. 13:19. Mark 4:13-20. Luke 8:11-15.

[723] Matth. 13:25.

[724] Matth. 12:43-45.

[725] Mark 5:9. Luke 8:30.

[726] John 16:11.

[727] John 12:30.

[728] Matth. 25:41. Rev. 20:10.

[729] 1 John 3:8.

[730] Jude 6.

down to hell and delivered them into chains of darkness, to be reserved for judgment."[731]

Question 136: What was the sin of the Angels?

Answer: The Prophet Isaiah also referred to the fall of Lucifer saying: *"How has Lucifer that rose in the morning fallen from Heaven! He that sent orders to all the nations is crushed to the earth. But you said in your heart, 'I will go up to Heaven, I will set my throne above the stars of Heaven: I will sit on a lofty mount, on the lofty mountains toward the north: I will go up above the clouds; I will be like the Most High."*[732] Thus pride was the reason for the Fall of the angels. This was also the first sin committed by the Adam and Eve who were deceived by the devil,[733] as with the first killing of a brother.[734]

Question 137: What is the place of the fallen Angels?

Answer: The place of the fallen angels is described as *"Hell"* and *"chains of darkness"* but until the appointed Day of Judgment they enjoy some kind of freedom, living in the Heavenly places from whence they attack men.[735] This Spiritual Warfare is not *"against flesh and blood, but against Principalities, against Powers, against the rulers of the darkness of this age, against Spiritual Hosts of Wickedness in the Heavenly Places."*[736] St Peter instructs the faithful to *"be sober, be vigilant; because your adversary the devil walks about like a roaring lion, seeking whom he may devour."*[737] The betrayal by Judas[738] as well as the thoughts that prevent the Work of Salvation is ascribed to the devil.[739] But whatever the devil invents to prevent the Salvation of man at the end he will be *"cast into the Lake of Fire and Brimstone where the Beast and the false prophet are. And they will be tormented day and night forever and ever."*[740]

The Faithful are advised to be watchful, sober and vigilant, concerning the assaults of the devil, for when they resist his attacks, he will retreat

---

[731] 2 Peter 2:4.
[732] Is. 14:12-14.
[733] Gen. 3:2-14.
[734] Gen. 4:8.
[735] 1 John 3:12. 2 Corinth. 2:11.
[736] Ephes. 6:12.
[737] 1 Peter 5:8.
[738] John 13:2.
[739] Matth. 16:22-23.
[740] Rev. 20:10.

because his power against man is restricted, regardless of his anger or strength, for the Lord our God is with all those who are faithful and who love Him.[741]

Consequently it is most essential that *"for this purpose the Son of God was manifested, that He might destroy the works of the devil."*[742] Had the devil not existed, it would not have been necessary for the Son of God to have been Incarnated, to have suffered, to have died on the Cross, to have Risen on the third day, to have Ascended into Heaven and to sit on the Right Hand of God the Father for the Salvation of mankind. If the devil did not exist, then how can man, being the source and inventor of evil, be capable of correction? The Salvation in Christ is based on the belief that men were not completely alienated from God but *"became futile in their thoughts, and their foolish hearts were darkened."*[743] It was therefore necessary for the Son of God to become Man in order to Redeem mankind from the bonds and slavery of Satan and thereby become *"sons by adoption."*[744]

Question 138: What is the Fall of the Angels?

Answer: The demons were created by God *"without having any impurity,"*[745] *"neither with an evil nature, but as good and without any sign of evilness"*[746] but by *"misusing their life and freedom, they had the authority either to remain with God or to be alienated from the good."* However, they *"did not remain in the state that God created them but blasphemed,"*[747] *"falling from the Heavenly Places."*[748]

The Holy Fathers of the Orthodox Church present Satan as the inventor of evil, *"the first born demon,"* *"the leader of the evil demons"* who is *"called the dragon and satan and diabolos,"* *"the criminal demon who is called Satan,"* and he *"who first rebelled from goodness and became evil"* and who, through his influence, detached innumerous other angels. Thus he became the leader of the army of the evil demons who rebelled against God.

It is a common belief amongst the Holy Fathers that the sin committed by Lucifer and his angels was caused by their puffed up pride in opposition to their Creator.[749] Thus the bright Lucifer became darkness and due to his

---

[741] 1 John 4:4; 5:18. 1 John 3:8. 1 John 3:10.
[742] 1 John 3:8.
[743] Rom. 1:21.
[744] Gal. 4:4-5; 3:13. Ephes. 5:16. Col. 4:5.
[745] St Basil the Great, *To Isaiah,* ch. 14, § 278, in Migne, *P.G.,* 30, 608.
[746] Ibid, *That God is not the cause of evil,* § 8, in Migne, *P.G.,* 31, 345.
[747] St John of Damascus, *Exposition. About Diabolos and Demons,* II, 18, in Migne, *P.G.,* 94, 876.
[748] Athenagoras, *Deputation,* 24, 25, in *B,* v.4, p. 301.
[749] St John of Damascus, *Exposition. About Diabolus and Demons,* II, 18, in Migne, *P.G.,* 94, 876.

pride and that of the angels who followed him, they became creators of evil.[750]

The Divine Revelation does not speak in more detail of the conditions of the Fall of the Angels, so it is impossible for us to determine them. Holy Scripture witnesses that *typhus* and *pride* was the sin of Lucifer. Also, the fact that he wished to deify himself and to sit on a high throne to be like God, is clearly manifested in the Fall of man who was deceived into falling into the same sin as Satan.[751] Satan falsely accused God, presenting Him as a liar, and urged them to partake of the Fruit of the forbidden Tree of *"knowing good and evil,"* promising them that they would become *"as gods."*

The Fall of Lucifer and his angels took place before the Fall of man. Satan, as a fallen angel, conceived the evil plan against man, according to the Book of Wisdom of Solomon: *"through envy of the devil came death into the world."*[752]

The opinion that the demons are the result of a sexual union between Angels of God and daughters of men,[753] is unacceptable, although supported by some Fathers.[754] St Athanasius of Alexandria, St Basil the Great and St Gregory consider this theory not worthy even of being mentioned. St John Chrysostom observed that Satan and his angels had fallen before the creation of mankind and if Satan was still a good Angel, then how could it be possible for a bodiless Angel, *"having such honour and glory,"* to envy man who is *"surrounded by a body"*? *"But, because, he fell from the highest glory into the lower disgrace, seeing man who was created with body and with such glory, he was overcome by envy."*[755]

The rebellion against God made Satan and his angels competitors of the Divine Majesty. This was the first sin that caused their downfall from the Angelical Hosts. Their Fall was complete and the moral condition that was created in them, was beyond any restoration. Satan and his angels became vessels of all evil, receiving the illness of envy. They turned against man because of the honour and glory with which God had decorated him.

---

[750] St Gregory of Nazianzus, *Homily* 38, § 9, in Migne, *P.G.,* 36, 320.
[751] Gen. 3:5-6.
[752] Wisdom 2:24.
[753] Gen. 6:2.
[754] St Justin, the philosopher and martyr, *2 Apology,* 5, § 2, in *B,* v. 3, p. 202. Athenagoras, *Deputation,* 24, 25, in *B,* v. 4, p. 301. Tatianus, *Homily to the Greeks,* § 12, in *B,* v.4, p. 250. St Irenaeus, *Heresies,* book IV, ch. 16, § 2, in Migne, *P.G.,*7, 1016. Cf. Ibid, in Hadjephraimides, p. 292. Tertullian, *De idol.,* § 9, in migne, *P.L.,* 1, 671; *De cult. Fem.,* I § 2, in migne, *P.L.,* 1, 1305; *De virg. vel.,* § 7, in migne, *P.L.,* 2, 899. Clement the Alexandrian, in Migne, *P.G.,* 118, 800; *Pedagogus,* 3, 2, in *B,* v. 7, p. 196; *Stromata,*book V, ch. 1, in *B,* v. 8, p. 114.
[755] St John Chrysostom, *To Genesis, Homily* 22, § 2, in Migne, *P.G.,* 53, 188.

Not being able to bear seeing the earthly beings rise up through Virtues to the glory of the Angels, Satan deceived mankind into disobedience. Thus Satan and his evil angels increased their evilness although they know that on the final Judgment Day they will be condemned to the Eternal Fire without any chance of repentance. For, *"as death is for men, likewise is the Fall for the angels; and after the Fall there is no repentance, as for men after death."*[756]

Question 139: What is the Nature of the Demons?

Answer: Ethereal and thin bodies are ascribed to the good Angels as well as to the demons, which, when compared only to mankind, are considered as being *"bodiless."*[757]

It is obvious that because of free-will with which intellectual beings, including all Angels, were gifted by God, even Satan *"had the authority over his life either to remain with God,"* as a result of which he could progress in goodness and move to a higher level of Holiness, *"or to be alienated from goodness."* But as soon as he invented evil and had fallen from his Order, he became enslaved to his own sin, according to the words of Christ: *"whoever commits sin is a slave of sin."*[758] As a consequence, Satan became the source and beginning of evil for all Eternity.[759]

According to his free-will Satan progresses from evil to evil. Blinding and being blind, in order to mislead men, he chooses the worst of evil and the most tempting ways. He differs from irrational creatures and wild beasts in that, although they were created wild, they act within the boundaries into which they were placed from the beginning, not as evil beings, for God created them *"very good."* On the contrary, Satan and his angels always seek wickedness and as a consequence of their Fall, they hate mankind without any reason, desiring his destruction.[760] Thus Holy Scripture

---

[756] St John of Damascus, *Exposition. About Diabolus and Demons,* II, 18, in Migne, *P.G.,* 94, 877. St Basil the Great, *That God is not the reason of evil,* § 8, in Migne, *P.G.,* 31, 348. Theodoretus, *Heresies,* Homily 5, in Migne, *P.G.,* 83, 477. Tatianus, *Homily to the Greeks,* § 14, in *B,* v.4, p. 251. St Justin, the philosopher and martyr, *1 Apology,* 28, in *B,* v. 3, p. 175. St Athanasius, the Great, *About virginity,* § 5, in Migne, *P.G.,* 28, 257. St Basil the Great, *To Isaiah* , ch. 14, § 279, in Migne, *P.G.,* 30, 609.

[757] St John of Damascus, *Exposition. About Diabolus and Demons,* II, 18, in Migne, *P.G.,* 94, 876. St Basil the Great, *That God is not the reason of evil,* § 9, in Migne, *P.G.,* 31, 352. Athenagoras, *Deputation,* 25, in *B,* v. 4, p. 301.

[758] John 8:34.

[759] St Basil the Great, *That God is not the reason of evil,* § 8, in Migne, *P.G.,* 31, 345.

[760] Ibid, St Augustine, *De civitate Dei,* VIII, 22, in migne, *P.L.,* 41, 246.

describes Satan as a wolf or as *"a roaring lion, seeking whom he may devour."*[761]

The devil's hatred of man is manifested in the tragic condition of the demon-possessed.[762] St Justin the Philosopher and Martyr witnesses that during his time *"many in the world and in the city"* of Rome were demon-possessed. The devil aroused cruel persecutions against the Church and *"the deadly Martyrdom"* that was *" turned by the demons and the army of the devil against those who confessed their Faith to God and the Mystery of the Cross."*[763]

The demons were the cause in ancient times of men worshipping as gods *"Dionysius, Semelis and Apollo, who committed dishonouring acts of sex amongst men, which are shameful even to mention; and Persephone and Aphrodite."* Even *"after the Ascension of Christ into Heaven, the demons again manifested themselves to men as being gods."* The crafty and seductive evil spirits who, as *"the ruler of the world"*[764] in our contemporary days, through heresies and sexual desires deceive those who are empty of Faith and seduces them into sin.[765]

Satan's power and strength is according to his nature and, as in the case of Job, when *"a great wind came from the desert, and caught the four corners of the house, and the house fell upon the children,"* they died.[766] This power of Satan is restricted by the Lord Who does not allow him to tempt man with more than that with which man can cope. God can at any time annihilate his power and banish him from existence but He chooses not do this for He always provides for us. Just like a doctor may use the venom of a snake to cure snakebite and to save the ill from death, likewise does God use the wickedness of the devil to exercise our souls. The tempter has the authority only to tempt us; he cannot force anyone to follow him. Therefore, to give into temptation means that we have co-operated with him. To gain victory over Satan makes him extremely angry because solely through the temptations may the Faithful become stronger and rise to a higher level of Virtue.

---

[761] 1 Peter 5:8.

[762] Matth. 4:24; 8:16, 28; 9:32-34; 10:8; 12:22-24; 15:22. Mark 1:32-34; 3:15; 5:12, 15; 6:13; 9:38; 16:9, 17. Luke 4:41; 8:2, 30, 36; 9:1, 49; 10:17; 11:15; 13:32. Tatianus, *To the Greeks,* 16, in *B*, v.4, p. 252.

[763] St Justin, the philosopher and martyr, *2 Apology*, 6, § 6; *Dialogue*, 131, § 2, in *B*, v. 3, p. 203; 329. Athenagoras, *Deputation,* 26, in *B*, v. 4, p. 302. Theophilus of Antioch, 2 *Autolycus*, in *B*, v. 5, p. 40.

[764] John 14:30; 16:11.

[765] St Justin, the philosopher and martyr, *1 Apology*, 25, § 1 and 26, § 1, in *B*, v. 3, p. 174. St Basil the Great, *That God is not the reason of evil*, § 9, in Migne, *P.G.*, 31, 352. St Cyril of Alexandria, *To John*, ch. 14, 30, in Migne, *P.G.*, 74, 329. Theodoretus of Cyrus, *To Ephesians,* 6, 12, in Migne, *P.G.*, 82, 553.

[766] Job 1:13-19.

Satan, although renowned as the father of lies, inventor of evil, professor and teacher of deceitful schemes, remains blind to the Truth and whatever concerns the future of those whom he tempts. Because of his Fall, he has lost his brightness and became alienated from the Divine Light. Thus, according to the observation of Clement the Alexandrian, *"the devil tempts us knowing who we are"* and according to our weaknesses he realises that he assaults us *"not knowing if we will resist"* and not knowing the results of his attacks.[767]

It is obvious then that Satan cannot understand the Love of God towards man nor the greatness of Divine Humility in the Divine *Economia* of the Incarnation of the Word of God. Satan had a suspicion of what took place but he did not know that the Son and Word of God became Flesh. For this reason he tempted Christ in the desert, but remained absolutely alienated from the Mystery of Divine *Economia*. Only he who has a clean and pure heart is able to see God. If, therefore, two people are in a similar situation but one has a clean heart, whereas the other has an impure heart, only the former will see God, because God cannot be seen except by one who has *"a pure heart."* Sadly, those with impure hearts are unable to see God.

CHAPTER SEVEN
THE ORIGIN OF MAN AND HIS PRIMITIVE CONDITION

I. THE CREATION OF MAN

Question 140: How was man created?

Answer: According to Holy Scripture, man was created by God last of all creatures on Earth as the crowning perfection of all visible Creation.[768] Man was created by direct Intervention and Action of God in His *"image and likeness"*[769] and the creation of the human body from the soil of the earth and the soul from the Breath of Life.[770] Thus Adam, the first man, was placed by God in the Garden of Delight as the king of the visible Creation where he received the woman as a helpmate for him. So the first couple was made whom God blessed as the root and genarchs of the human race.[771]

---

[767] Clement the Alexandrian, *Stromata,* 4, 12, in *B,* v.8, p. 78.
[768] St Symeon, *Euriskomena,* Homily XLV, pp. 206-208.
[769] Gen. 1:26. Cf. Lossky, *Theology,* pp. 70-73.
[770] Ware, *Way,* pp. 64-68.
[771] Cf. Kefalas, *Catechesis,* pp. 56-58. Damalas, *Catechesis,* pp. 36-38. Frangopoulos, *Christian Faith,* pp. 88-89. Mitsopoulos, *Themata,* pp. 68-69, 179.

Holy Scripture does not indicate the exact age of mankind and the genealogies mentioned in the various Books differ from one another. This subject remains open to modern science. Nevertheless, the important fact is not when man appeared on earth but that man was created by God.[772]

Question 141: What are the Biblical narrations concerning man's creation?

Answer: In the Book of Genesis we have two narrations concerning man's creation,[773] of which the first is brief in comparison to the second, yet they could be combined. The biblical narrations do not only have the authority of the God-inspired author of the Pentateuch but are also witnessed by many other Books of the Old Testament and especially by our Lord and Saviour Jesus Christ, the Son of God.

In the Book of Job,[774] as well as in Psalms, it is written: *"Thy Hands have made me and fashioned me."*[775] In the Wisdom of Solomon it is written: *"for God created man to be immortal, and made him to be an image of His own Eternity."*[776] Ecclesiasticus (or Wisdom of Sirah) notes: *"The Lord created man of the earth, and turned him into it again."*[777]

Our Lord and Saviour Jesus Christ, proclaimed that God *"created at the beginning and made them male and female"*[778] and then referred to the exact prophetic words of Adam in Genesis 2:24 concerning the formation of Eve.[779]

St Paul characterized the first Adam as being *"earthly"* from the fact that he was taken from the soil of the earth.[780] Concerning his relationship to Eve, he stated that *"for man is not from woman, but woman from man. Nor was man created for the woman, but woman for the man"*[781] and that *"Adam was formed first, then Eve."*[782]

---

[772] Meyendorff, *Theology,* pp. 140-143.
[773] Gen. 1:26-30 and 2:7-8, 21-23.
[774] Job 10:8.
[775] Psalm 119(120):73.
[776] Wisdom 2:23.
[777] Eccl. 17:1.
[778] Matth. 19:4.
[779] Gen. 2:24. Matth. 19:5.
[780] 1 Corinth. 15:47.
[781] 1 Corinth. 11:8-9.
[782] 1 Tim. 2:13.

Question 142: How was man created?

Answer: In the narration of the Book of Genesis, God does not Command man to come out of the sea or earth, as He Commanded the fish, birds, reptiles and all living creatures. Instead, when He Created man, God said: *"Let Us make man in Our image and likeness"*[783] and then He gave them the authority over all living creatures.[784] God did not Command: *"Let there be man"* although even if He had done so, man would still have been created. However, God formed the human body with special care and through His Divine Breath bestowed the soul[785] upon it causing man to become a living soul.

Man is presented as being the purpose of the whole Creation and the most perfect of all creatures, king of the earth and the only being ruled from Above.[786] Thus man becomes the link that unites the visible and material world with the spiritual and invisible world. Man appears to be earthly although at the same time heavenly, mortal and immortal, visible and intellectual, supervisor of the visible Creation and initiator of intellectual as well as pilgrim of the Divine Majesty. Made from two essences, matter and spirit, he is related to Heaven and earth. And through the intellectual essence he communicates with the Heavenly Powers, whereas through matter he is related to earthly things.[787]

It is sufficient to present the superiority of man because of his bodily structure and his intellectual capabilities when compared to those of animals, in order to see his unique relationship to his Creator. He appears not only as flesh but also as spirit, in between majesty and humbleness. He is like a different type of angel who combines earth and Heaven. Furthermore, although man may lack in size, strength or flexibility of movements when compared to many animals, he is superior to the entire animal world since he stands up-right, enabling him to look towards Heaven, and in the construction of his bodily parts such as his brain and hands he is able to form civilizations, participate in and recall history, create

---

[783] Gen. 1:26. Cf. Evdokimov, *Orthodoxia*, pp. 111-114. Sophrony, *His Life*, pp. 77-78.
[784] Gen. 1:26, 28. Cf. St Symeon, *Euriskomena*, Homily XLV, p. 208.
[785] Tertullian, *Adversus Marcianem*, II, 4, in migne, *P.L.*, 2, 314. St Basil the Great, *About the creation of man*, Homily 1, § 2 and Homily 2, § 1, in Migne, *P.G.*, 30, 13 and 40. Theophilus of Antioch, *2 Autolycus*, § 18, in *B*, v. 5, p. 34. St John Chrysostom, *To Genesis*, Homily 13, § 1, in Migne, *P.G.*, 53, 105-106. Plato of Moscow, *Orthodox Teaching*, pp. 44-45. Kefalas, *Catechesis*, p. 237. Frangopoulos, *Christian Faith*, pp. 95-98. Mitsopoulos, *Themata*, pp. 69, 180-182.
[786] Ware, *Way*, p. 65.
[787] St Gregory of Nazianzus, *To the holy Pascha*, Homily 45, § 7, in Migne, *P.G.*, 36, 632. St Basil the Great, *About the creation of man*, Homily 2, § 12, in Migne, *P.G.*, 30, 57. St Gregory of Nyssa, *About the soul and the making of man*, in Migne, *P.G.*, 46, 28. St John Chrysostom, in Migne, *P.G.*, 56, 182.

art, develop science, etc. Generally, he appears to have a harmonious development of his organism, according to which he is capable of adapting to different climates of the earth throughout its different periods. Consequently mankind appears to dominate the animal world as he is able to domesticate them for his own use, whereas his intellect raises him to the heights of Heaven, differentiating him from the irrational animals. The ability to speak distinguishes man and characterizes his intelligence that is incomparable to that of the animal kingdom. Only man has the absolute privilege of being intellectual, moral and religious. Therefore, the theory of man originating from ape is considered as the most foolish of theories and a blasphemy against God.

Question 143: What do the anthropomorphistic expressions regarding man's creation express?

Answer: Holy Scripture manifests man's superiority to the irrational and inanimate world by declaring: "*God formed the man of dust of the earth, and breathed upon his face the Breath of Life, and man became a living soul.*"[788] Here we find the use of expressions that fit our requirements, which the Holy and God-inspired author used in order to give the people of his time the understanding of the direct Intervention of God in man's Creation. Considering that these terms are used in reference to God, we must understand the words of Holy Scripture with regard to God and ascribed to God such as "*bodily form and composition of members*" "*in a Divine way. For the Divine is simple, without synthesis and without form.*" If we take these expressions literally then we would be forced to ascribe "*a mouth to God*" because He "*Breathed,*" as well as "*hands*" because He "*formed.*" Subsequently the question arises: Did God create man in the same way as the potter makes his pots or the sculpture his statues? But they form only the outside shape being unable to shape the inner parts, whereas in the case of man's formation, God's creative Energy entered into the depths of man's body and organised not only the veins and arteries but also the heart, the lungs, the stomach, the intestines and all the admirable parts of the human organism, which are united in one harmonious body.[789]

We must consider these expressions of Holy Scripture in a Divine Manner such as when it is said that God "*made*" man, it is understood as being the same Power as in the Divine Commandment "*Let there be*" for we

---

[788] Gen. 2:7.
[789] St John Chrysostom, *To Genesis*, Homily 13, § 2, in Migne, *P.G.*, 53, 107.   St Basil the Great, *About the creation of man,* Homily 2, § 12, in Migne, *P.G.*, 30, 56. St Gregory of Nyssa, *About the soul and the making of man,* Homily 2, in Migne, *P.G.*, 45, 293.

should understand that God's "Hands" means His Creative Power and that He took special care with man's creation. We must not think that God actually has hands. And again, when we hear that God *"breathed,"* we should not think that God has lungs from whence the breath of air issued forth, neither that the soul is part of God's Essence, for God is bodiless and not synthetic. We must understand this expression in terms of God commanding the body to have living power and which then became a living soul. We must also understand the nature of the soul as being a spirit that is intellectual and rational. Furthermore, as God created the Heavenly Bodiless Powers, likewise He created the human body from the soil of the earth and ordered it to have a rational soul that is able to dwell in the body.[790]

Question 144: Where did the woman come from?

Answer: St John Chrysostom urged us to understand the words of Genesis not by its letter but in a Divine manner. Holy Scripture concerning Eve's formation does not use the term *"made"* but *"filled up"* because God used part of Adam's flesh that already existed and He *"filled up"* the missing flesh.[791] Regarding the details of Eve's formation, St John Chrysostom believed that it is only through the eyes of true Faith that one can understand such work of Creation. In order for Adam not to think that Eve was merely another creation, God *"brought a trance upon Adam and he slept"* He then *"took one of his ribs and filled up the flesh instead thereof. And God formed the rib which He took from Adam into a woman, and brought her to Adam."* [792] God therefore put Adam into a deep trance so that he felt no pain when He removed the rib, thus preventing Adam from hating the woman when he recalled the pain of the process. God, in this manner, painlessly gave Adam his companion.[793]

The origin of Eve from the side of Adam has deeper meaning. The Creator did not want to signify only the close relationship and union of man and woman, who are united through marriage into one flesh, but in addition that she would communicate with her husband and that Adam would not see her as having a different nature, resulting in her taking a different path. Instead He wanted to stress the Mystery of the Monarchy of God, in order

---

[790] Theodoretus of Cyrus, *Heresies*, 5, 9; *About the nature of man,* in Migne, *P.G.,* 83, 477 and 941. St John Chrysostom, *To Genesis*, Homily 13, § 2, in Migne, *P.G.,* 53, 107.

[791] St Symeon, *Euriskomena,* Homily XLV, p. 210.

[792] Gen. 2:21-22. Cf. Damalas, *Catechesis,* pp. 38-39.

[793] St John Chrysostom, *To Genesis*, Homily 15, § 2 and 3, in Migne, *P.G.,* 53, 120-122.

that it would not be said that one God created man and another created woman.[794]

Holy Scripture teaches the union of the human race. The whole narration of the Creation of the first couple leads to the conclusion that the human race is derived from them. It is also literally assured in the Book of Genesis that before the Creation of Adam there was no man to cultivate the earth and even the name of Eve, which means *"Life,"* is *"because she was the mother of all living things."*[795] In the New Testament we have a clear witness to this when St Paul informed the Athenians: *"and He has made from one blood every nation of men to dwell on all the face of the earth."*[796] Finally, our Lord and Saviour assured us that *"He Who made them at the beginning made them male and female."*[797]

The importance of this Teaching concerning the origin of mankind is manifested by man being directly created by God with special care. Furthermore, due to the brotherhood and equality of all, regardless of race, language or skin tone, having the same Father in Heaven, all humanity is commanded to love one another. In particular, the spreading of sin is clarified[798] through these Teachings that explain the necessity for the Word of God to have been Incarnated, becoming perfect Man for the Salvation of all mankind.[799] The Work of Salvation that was offered by Christ on the Cross is based on the fact that all men are from one origin.

Question 145: How old is the human race?

Answer: Concerning the age of mankind, this should be left to science because Holy Scripture does not consist of books of science or exact records. Holy Scripture records and thereby makes known God's Revelation to us. They are not books of Archaeology, Paleontology or any such sciences. They are the Revelation of God revealed to man, in order that he learns of his Creator Who brought everything from nothingness into being and that Salvation came from the One and only True God: the Father and the Son and the Holy Spirit.

Holy Scripture does not mention any specific age although it is estimated by the researchers according to the chronologies that are found scattered here and there, as well as from existing genealogies. It is also

---

[794] Theophilus of Antioch, *2 Autolycus,* § 28, in *B,* v. 5, p. 40.
[795] Gen.3:21.
[796] Acts 17:26.
[797] Matth. 19:4.
[798] Rom. 5:12.
[799] John 1:14; 3:16-17.

obvious that during the copying of manuscripts some parts, such as names that were difficult to read or interpret, were left out and thus lost.

Accordingly these researchers estimate that from the time of Creation to the Birth of Christ there is a period of 3,483 years while in other cases it is estimated as being 6,984 years. According to the texts of Hebrew and Bulgata, the period from Adam to Noah is 1,656 years whereas according to the Samarian text it is 1,307 years and according to the Old Testament Greek text (the Septuagint, LXX) between 2,242 and 2,262 years. Also from the time of the Great Flood until Abraham, according to the Hebrew text, 290 years passed whereas the Samarian text brings the number of years up to 940 and according to Old Testament Greek (the Septuagint, LXX) to 1,170 years! Thus between the two official translations, that of Bulgata and the Old Testament Greek (the Septuagint, LXX), we have a difference of 1200-1500 years.[800]

No matter what the age of the human race is, it is obvious that Holy Scripture assures us that man is the newly established inhabitant of the earth and the result of the special care of God and not the development of evolution.

Question 146: What was Paradise?

Answer: According to the Book of Genesis *"God planted a garden eastward in Eden, and placed there the man whom He had formed."*[801] It was necessary for man to see God creating in order for him to know the Creator and that before him God created Paradise, a Garden that was harmonious in all aspects and full of every pleasant beauty and Divine plants full of admiration. In addition to all that, God did not let man partake only of the fruits of the earth but of the knowledge of each species as well.[802] The expression *"planted"* is used in an anthropomorphistic manner, which we must understand in a Divine way, otherwise we might fall into great error. This expression must be understood as being that God *"commanded a Garden to be."*[803] Some of the Fathers supported the theory that Paradise was in Heaven but Theophilus of Antioch observed that the expressions used in Scripture, such as *"and God made to spring up every*

---

[800] Trempelas, *Dogmatique*, v. I, p. 467.
[801] Gen. 2:8. Cf. Bryennios, *Paralipomena*, ch. XIII, v. III, p. 82.
[802] Kritopoulos, in Karmeris, *The dogmatics*, v. II, pp. 514-515. Kefalas, *Catechesis*, pp. 59-60. Frangopoulos, *Christian Faith*, pp. 99-102. Mitsopoulos, *Themata*, pp. 70-71.
[803] St John Chrysostom, *To Genesis*, Homily 13, § 3, in Migne, *P.G.*, 53, 108. St John of Damascus, *Catechesis*, II, 11, in Migne, *P.G.*, 94, 912 and 913.

tree beautiful"[804] and "*eastward*"[805] clearly teach us that Paradise was on this earth and not in Heaven.[806]

Nevertheless, Paradise was prepared for Adam as a special place for him. Man did not appear on earth before the Creation of all things on it but afterwards when God had prepared for him this kingdom and in order for him to live in it as "*a king and ruler.*"[807] Adam was placed in Paradise not to enjoy a luxurious life but "*to cultivate and keep it.*"[808] By cultivating a virtuous life and faithfulness to God his Creator, man was to rise to a higher level of Holiness and Deification.

II. THE ELEMENTS OF MAN

Question 147: What are the elements of man?

Answer: Man consists of two elements: soul and body.[809] This is witnessed by the Creative Words of God in the narration of Genesis. Man's body, although connected to mortality, remains the element with which the immortal soul is united. Both elements are derived from the Creative Commandment of God and are the essential elements of man's nature. Neither to the soul without the body, nor to the body without the soul, has God given life except through the union of both when He created one man.[810]

Two theories of the way in which souls are born during reproduction and multiplication of the human race - that of pre-existence of souls and that of the souls flowing from God's Essence, have also been condemned. One of two other theories whereby souls are created directly by God or that they are planted, are supported by some of the Holy Fathers. The Teaching of the planting of souls in association with the Eternal Plan of God for each individual person seems more acceptable.[811] This theory teaches that just as the body is formed from the parents, so also the soul is planted by the parents' souls during conception.

---

[804] Gen. 2:9.

[805] Gen. 2:8. Cf. Bryennios, Paralipomena, ch. XIII, VIII p.82

[806] Theophilus of Antioch, *2 Autolycus,* § 24, in *B,* v. 5, p. 37.

[807] St Cyril of Jerusalem, *Catechesis,* II, 4, in Migne, *P.G.,* 33, 389. St John Chrysostom, *To Genesis,* Homily 14, § 3, in Migne, *P.G.,* 53, 114. St Gregory of Nyssa, *About the creation of man,* ch. 2, in Migne, *P.G.,* 44, 132.

[808] Gen. 2:15.

[809] Kefalas, *Catechesis,* pp. 241-243. Frangopoulos, *Christian Faith,* pp. 89-90.

[810] Athenagoras, *Concerning the resurrection of the dead,* ch. 5, in *B,* v. 4, p. 322.

[811] Trempelas, *Dogmatique,* v. I, pp. 469-470.

Question 148: What is the true meaning of the Biblical verses referring to the three elements of man?

Answer: In two Biblical verses of Holy Scripture the term *"spirit"* appears to differentiate from the term *"soul"*[812] and thus we have the theory that man consists of three elements: *body, soul* and *spirit.*[813]

In the first verse we read: *"For the Word of God is Living and Powerful, and sharper than any two-edged sword, piercing even to the division of soul and spirit, and of joints and marrow, and is a Discerner of the thoughts and intents of the heart."*[814]   Here the Word of God is characterized as being *"sharper than any two-edged sword"* that pierces *"even to the division of soul and spirit, and of joints and marrow."* Concerning the terms *"joints"* and *"marrow,"* as we cannot speak of separate and distinguished elements but only of elements of the one and same body, in a similar vein, the terms *"soul"* and *"spirit"* are not distinguished from one another as separate elements but are one element consisting of the human personality. However, as *"joints"* and *"marrow"* are inseparable parts of the body, likewise the *"spirit"* is the highest moral power of the one soul, which gives life to the body.

The second verse states: *"Now may the God of peace Himself Sanctify you completely; and may your whole spirit, soul, and body be preserved blameless at the Coming of our Lord Jesus Christ."*[815]   Other Scholars understood the term *"spirit"* as referring to the spiritual Charisma [Gifts] that are given to each one through Holy Baptism. Hence it was observed that *"these three were never referred to the unbelievers, but only to those who have believed, who have the soul and body by nature but receive the spirit by Beneficence. In other words it is the Charisma of those who believe."*[816]

The Holy Fathers of the Orthodox Church support the teaching that man consists of only two elements of soul and body. Athenagoras further assured us that the human nature consists of *"an eternal soul united with the body."* In addition, the soul oversees the functions of the body, deciding what is proper, whereas the body moves according to the changes of its nature.[817]   The crown of Patristic Teachings is the Decree of the 4th Ecumenical Council, which declared Christ to be perfect Man *"with*

---

[812] Kefalas, *Catechesis,* pp. 58-59.
[813] Ware, *Way,* pp. 60-64.
[814] Heb. 4:12.
[815] 1 Thess. 5:23.
[816] Theodorus monk, in Migne, *P.G.,* 28, 80.
[817] Athenagoras, *About resurrection,* ch. 12 and 15, in ***B,*** v. 4, p. 320-321 and 322-323.

intellectual soul and body." As St John of Damascus witnessed, God "*created man from visible and invisible nature. From the dust He formed the body, the rational and intellectual soul He gave from His own Breath.*"[818]

Question 149: Is the Soul immortal?

Answer: As stressed above, man consists of two elements of soul and body. When the soul is separated from the body, death occurs and the body stops functioning. It decomposes and becomes dust that returns to the earth from whence God had taken it. However, the soul, even after death, remains alive and preserves its conscience.[819]

This is witnessed throughout Holy Scripture. In Genesis when Abraham and Ishmael died, they were counted as dead, but Abraham "*was added to his people*"[820] while Ishmael "*was added to his fathers.*"[821] When Jacob was mourning over Joseph, he said: "*I will go down to my son, mourning to Hades.*"[822] This reveals not only that the souls live after death but that they meet in Hades. King David said, concerning Christ: "*For Thou will not leave my soul in Hades, nor will Thou allow Thy Holy One to see corruption.*"[823]

In the New Testament the appearance of the two Prophets, Moses and Elijah, at the Transfiguration of our Lord on Mount Tabor and their dialogue with Christ,[824] as well as His assurance that "*God is not the God of dead, but of living*"[825] clearly proves that those who depart from this life continue to live in the After-life. This we can see from the Parable of the "*Rich Man and Poor Lazarus*"[826] wherein the rich man although "*being in torments in Hades*" recognized Poor Lazarus being comforted in the "*bosom*" of Abraham. Furthermore, the Promise of Christ to the repentant thief on the cross that: "*Assuredly, I say to you, today you will be with Me in Paradise,*"[827] literally witnesses that souls who pass away in repentance and virtues enter into Eternal Life.

---

[818] St John of Damascus, *Exposition. About man,* II, 26, in Migne, *P.G.,* 94, 920.
[819] Cf. Kefalas, *Catechesis,* pp. 61-64. Frangopoulos, *Christian Faith,* pp. 93-94.
[820] Gen. 25:8.
[821] Gen. 25:17.
[822] Gen. 37:34.
[823] Psalm 16:10.
[824] Matth. 17:1-5. Mark 9:2-13. Luke 9:28-36.
[825] Matth. 22:32.
[826] Luke 16:19-31.
[827] Luke 23:43.

A second difference in the opinions concerning the immortality of the soul refers to the question: *"Are the souls by nature and essence immortal, or are they born mortal, and then become immortal 'because God wants them to live'?"* The latter answer to this question is supported by St Justin the Philosopher and Martyr,[828] Tatianus and St Irenaeus.[829] St John of Damascus also appears to support this theory up to a certain point.[830]

Nevertheless, the difference between the two Teachings is not serious because according to both theories the soul is immortal. If we believe that the soul was created immortal, do we not mean that it was created through the Will and Grace of God or, if we accept that by nature it is immortal, if God removes His Divine Providence, it is impossible for the soul, created immortal by nature, to return to nothingness?

Question 150: What theories of the multiplication of souls were expressed?

Answer: Holy Scripture remains silent with regard to the beginning of each soul and the way of its union with the body.[831] Thus different theories have been expressed, of which two are completely denied.

a) The Theory of the Pre-existence of Souls:[832] According to this theory: The souls were created before all time and because they sinned they were punished by being embodied as though imprisoned. This opinion was condemned in 543 by the Holy Council that had gathered in Constantinople, as well as by the Holy Council of Praga in 561. Furthermore St Gregory of Nazianzus, St Gregory of Nyssa,[833] St Augustine and St Leo I[834] condemned this theory.

b) The Theory of *"Emanatismus"*: According to this theory, souls derive from the Divine Essence by means of emanation. Because it abolishes the absolute simplicity of the Divinity, it too is condemned.

c) The Theory of Creation of each Soul at the time of Conception (*"Creatianismus"*):[835] St Augustine, with some uncertainty and hesitation, spoke of this theory although he was unable to link it to the inheritance of

---

[828] St Justin, the philosopher and martyr, *Dialogue,* 6, § 1, in **B,** v. 3, p. 215.
[829] St Irenaeus, *Heresies,* book II, ch. 34, §§ 1-4, in Migne, *P.G.,* 7, 835. Cf. Ibid, in Hadjephraimides, pp. 186-187.
[830] St John of Damascus, *Exposition. About man,* II, 26, in Migne, *P.G.,* 94, 924.
[831] Mitsopoulos, *Themata,* pp. 182-191.
[832] Ibid, p. 189.
[833] St Gregory of Nyssa, *About the creation of man,* ch. 28, in Migne, *P.G.,* 44, 229-232.
[834] St Augustine, *Epist.* 217, 5, 16; Leon I, *Epist.* XV, 10, in migne, *P.L.,* 54, 684-685.
[835] Mitsopoulos, *Themata,* p. 190.

Original Sin.[836] Truly, if each soul is directly created by God, then how can anyone suggest that the soul bears the stain of Original Sin? Also it presents God as participating in sin by creating the souls of those children who are born without the blessing of marriage and who are therefore of sinful relationships.

d) **Finally, the fourth theory is that of Transplantation (*"Traducianismus"*):**[837] According to this theory, the souls derive from the souls of parents like a cutting or piece of a plant for propagation. This theory not only explains the inheritance of Original Sin by all men but also the psycho-characteristics of the parents passed down to the children.

Another form of this theory is *"Generatianismus,"* according to which both parents' souls, because of the Creative Commandment to *"increase and multiply,"* give the soul to the conceived fetus through spiritual semen (*"semen spirituale"*) or spiritual creative power at the moment of the insemination of the woman's ovum.

CHAPTER EIGHT
THE FALL AND ITS RESULTS
I. THE TEMPTER, THE FIRST DISOBEDIENCE & DIRECT ONSEQUENCES

Quetsion 151: What was the Fall of man?

Answer: The Law that was given by God to the first couple, provided the opportunity for man's free-will to exercise virtue and to be established in Goodness. God was certainly able to create man unchangeable and sinless right from the beginning but then he would have had the innocence of an infant and would have been an automatic creation of God without any moral value. The fact that God foresaw the Fall of the first-created is without any doubt. This Event occurred not because He had foreseen it and simultaneously predestinated it, but because it was a free act of man and was foreseen by God Who did not want it to happen although He allowed it while providing the means for its correction.

Holy Scripture is a valuable Source with regard to the events of the first Fall although its narration should not be taken either allegorically or as a myth incorporating philosophical ideas but rather as a historical text in its broad outlines. The importance of its history is clearly assured and witnessed by our Lord and Saviour Jesus Christ, the Son of God, as well as

---

[836] St Augustine, *De anima, IV, in migne, P.L.,* 44, 526.
[837] Mitsopoulos, *Themata,* pp. 190-191.

by St Paul, the Apostle of the Nations. This account informs us that the beginning of the Fall was due to an external force: Satan in the form of a serpent who urged Eve to taste the Forbidden Fruit that God had instructed them not to eat or even touch. The serpent, however, convinced Eve that disobeying God was easy because His Commandment was so simple to carry out. Satan slandered the Creator and Benefactor of man and incited Eve *"to become equal to God"* which is a rebellious act against God. The tasting of the Fruit of the Tree of the Knowledge of Good and Evil that followed the temptation, was a most serious act that included all the elements similar to the cause of the Fall of Lucifer. It is obvious that Eve should have resisted the temptation right from the beginning but from the moment she paid attention to Satan's lies, her inner cosmos began to be soiled, and thus to her eyes the Fruit of the Tree of the Knowledge of Good and Evil appeared to be *"pleasant to the eyes to look upon and beautiful to contemplate."*[838]

Henceforth, the consequences that followed were according to the seriousness of the Disobedience. Immediately innocence was lost and they realized that they were naked.[839] As they withdrew from the Grace of God, the guilt of their conscience made them experience fear.[840] At the same time their logic and intellect was darkened and so they imagined that they could hide from the sight of their Creator.[841] Their life, which was now full of pain, groaning and suffering,[842] became even worse as their hearts were enslaved to sinful desires and lustful thoughts. In addition to these, the animals that were subject to them before, became a threat. However, the worst result of the Fall was physical death[843] that followed their spiritual death.

Nevertheless, human nature was not completely wiped out because man was not the inventor of evil, having been deceived by an external impulse.[844] Hence God offered the First Promise of Hope, (*"Proto-evangelion"* = *"first Good News"*), that in the future the Seed (the Incarnated Word) of the woman (the Ever-Virgin Mary, the Theotokos) would defeat the serpent[845] (the Sacrifice on the Cross).

---

[838] Gen. 3:7.
[839] Gen. 3:8.
[840] Gen. 3:11.
[841] Gen. 3:9, 11.
[842] Gen. 3:17.
[843] Gen. 3:20.
[844] Gen. 3:14.
[845] Gen. 3:16.

Question 152: What were the conditions of the Fall?

Answer: God gifted man with free-will and instructed him not to partake of the Fruit from *"the Tree of knowing Good and Evil"* in order to test him and to establish virtue within him. Although man was created sinless, he had to express a steadfast willingness by means of his own free-will and choice in upholding the Divine Commandment so as to be strengthened. Free-will is the voluntary act of the will of man and is the result of his intellect doing good or evil.[846]

Question 153: Why did God not create man's nature sinless so that he would be incapable of sinning?

Answer: Had God done so, man would simply be an instrument without any moral value, acting strictly out of necessity. *"Virtue is accomplished through the free-will and not by force."*[847] For if we did not have our free-will then we would be like automatons of the Divinity and even our perfection, glory and honour would have been God's and not ours. Man would have remained undeveloped in his moral conscience, not knowing the value of moral good and virtue. Man would have been as an innocent infant. Man, on the contrary, was created to be in the *"likeness"* of God. He was gifted with free-will that offered him the freedom of choice between evil and good. Consequently, he had the *"authority to remain and progress in good, as well as to turn from good and to become evil, whereas God allowed this because of the free-will."*[848] Since immovability and unchangeability are ascribed only to the Beginningless and Uncreated Deity, man was created moveable and changeable although it was also possible for him, with the Power of God, not to change.[849] Man's Fall brought about the Fall of the events of Divine Grace and added the materialistic way of life[850] to man.

---

[846] Cf. Mogilas, 1, 27, in Karmeris, *The dogmatics,* p. 607. Plato of Moscow, *Orthodox Teaching,* pp. 105-107. Evdokimov, *Orthodoxia,* pp. 95-102. Kefalas, *Catechesis,* p. 60. Mitsopoulos, *Themata,* pp. 193-195.
[847] St Basil the Great, *That God is not the cause of evil,* § 7, in Migne, *P.G.,* 31, 345.
[848] St John of Damascus, *Exposition. About man,* II, 26, in Migne, *P.G.,* 94, 924.
[849] St Symeon, *Euriskomena,* p. 32.
[850] Evdokimov, *Orthodoxia,* p. 121.

Question 154: Since God foreknew, why was the Fall not prevented?

Answer: St Augustine's reply is that no one would dare to believe or say that it was not by the Authority of God for the Angels or man who sinned, not to fall. Nevertheless God conceded and the Fall occurred. How and why? Surely not because He wanted it to serve His Plan nor because He wanted to manifest the Grace of His Love towards the pride and wickedness of man?[851] However, this type of opinion would make God responsible for man's fall. It happened, not because God predestined it although He foresaw it, but it occurred as a free act of man. God included it in His Plan, simultaneously providing Divine Dispensation (*Economia*) for its correction through Salvation in Christ If God had prevented the Fall, it is obvious that He would have restricted man's free-will, thereby removing his freedom. Under no circumstances did God want man to be forced or by necessity become His likeness.

Man had fallen due to his own foolishness and not because God foresaw it. God certainly did not want Adam's Fall although He accepted it. Consequently Divine Holiness that always turns away from all wickedness, remained completely blameless and trustworthy, whereas immediately after the Fall God requested Adam to account for his actions.

We must take care not to suppose that although the Fall of man was the reason for having a Saviour, the Fall occurred so that the Saviour would come. Christ came because sin was committed. In other words, we do not believe that the Fall of Adam took place in order that Christ would come, because then it would have been as a consequence of Adam's Fall, predestined as a requirement for the Salvation in Christ, which had to happen so that Christ would come to redeem mankind. On the contrary, we accept that, although Adam alienated himself from God, God is never unprepared to compassionately and wisely confront the insult and disrespect shown by man who received so many Divine Blessings. God, having foreseen man's Fall before all time, prepared the Salvation through Christ, which grants an infinite wealth of good things to fallen man.

One must also cautiously approach the opinion expressed by St John Chrysostom according to whom the first-created couple, even if they had not been tempted by Satan to partake of the Forbidden Fruit, would not have remained faithful because Adam was so easily convinced by Eve, that even without Satan, he would have quickly fallen into sin.[852] However, according to this view, the Fall of Adam appears unavoidable, presenting

---

[851] St Augustine, *De civitate Dei,* XIV, 27, in migne, *P.L.,* 41, 436.
[852] St John Chrysostom, *To Stageiron,* I, § 5, in Migne, *P.G.,* 47, 435.

the first-created couple as being without any defence against evil. On the contrary, because of primitive Justice, they were free of the tendency towards sin and were inclined towards Good, strengthened by Divine Grace. This true belief is evident in those descendants of Adam, who, after the Fall, obstinately rejected the Salvation in Christ offered to them, preferring to remain in sin.[853]

In conclusion, the Biblical narration of the Fall of the first-created couple has an historic basis[854] upon which the Doctrines concerning Original Sin and Salvation in Christ are based and therefore we cannot accept the allegoric interpretation of Philo, Origen[855] or any other symbolic interpretations.

Among all the Books of the Old Testament, only the Apocryphal Books in the Old Testament Greek (Septuagint, LXX) mention that sin began through the woman and through that sin we all die. Furthermore, due to Satan's envy, death entered the world.[856] In the New Testament, our Lord and Saviour Jesus Christ, the Son of God, characterized Satan as being a *"murderer from the beginning"* who *"does not stand in the Truth, because there is no Truth in him"* since *"he speaks lies from his own resources."*[857] He too referred to Satan's deception of the first-created couple. St Paul the Apostle of the Nations, when expressing his concern for the faithful of Corinth, that they might not be deceived *"as the serpent deceived Eve by his craftiness"*[858] and when he reminds us that *"Adam was not deceived, but the woman being deceived, fell into transgression"*[859] he is clearly referring to the central points of the Biblical narration as being historical. Elsewhere in his Epistle to the Romans,[860] he referred to Original Sin as being transmitted from Adam to all mankind as a consequence of the first Transgression mentioned in the Book of Genesis.

Question 155: Who is the Tempter?

Answer: According to the Biblical narration, the source of the first Transgression should not be sought in God or in man, but rather in an external suggestion and instigation, in an evil and crafty force that incited and deceived Eve into committing the Offence. According to the narration

---

[853] Trempelas, *Dogmatique,* v. I, p. 518.
[854] Kritopoulos, in Karmeris, *The dogmatics,* v. II, p. 516.
[855] Origen, *Against Celsus,* IV, 40, in *B,* v. 9, p. 264.
[856] Wisdom, 25:24; 2:24.
[857] John 8:44.
[858] 2 Corinth. 11:3.
[859] 1 Tim. 2:14.
[860] Rom. 5:12.

in Genesis, Satan, in the form of a serpent, deceived Eve. It is therefore understandable that the closeness of all animals was quite natural for Adam and Eve, so the presence of a serpent was no threat to her, neither did it seem strange to Eve that the serpent spoke to her, whether literally or intellectually,[861] for it was the most *"prudent"* of all the animals upon the earth.

Question 156: How serious was the transgression?

Answer: The Offence into which Eve was deceived by Satan and, by following her, Adam, is far more serious than it first appears to be, since the Commandment of God was so easy to obey and therefore no excuse is possible.[862] The Instruction came from man's Creator Who had bestowed so much care and protection upon them, as well as benefiting them with so many other things. God did not demand from the first-created couple anything equal to His Beneficences except to ask them to observe a very small Commandment. Adam and Eve should have shown their gratitude to God by obeying His Commandment merely because of His Grace and Love that honoured them as *"masters."* Therefore, no one should consider their disobedience in Paradise as being insignificant. The Fall occurred through the tasting of the Forbidden Fruit, which did not incorporate evil in its nature, but rather included disobedience[863] through which man violated and scorned God's Commandment. He Who created in His *"image and likeness"* the offenders whom He placed as rulers over all the animals in Paradise, offering them the wealth of all good things, had not given them many difficult Rules with the exception of only one whereby they would have become accustomed to obedience to their Benefactor and Lord, as had the rest of all Creation.[864] Moreover the consequences of the Offence present it as being *"a great sin,"*[865] bearing the wounds of rebellion against God, relative and similar to those of the fallen angels that cast the Tempter into Eternal Darkness. First of all, we must realise that Eve was not tempted but allowed herself to be tempted, and by delaying through successive thoughts, cooperated with the Tempter, making the ensuing Offence the fruit of evil

---

[861] Theophilus of Antioch, *2 Autolycus,* § 28, in **B**, v. 5, p. 40. St John Chrysostom, *To Genesis,* Homily 16, § 2, in Migne, *P.G.,* 53, 127.
[862] Cf. Mitsopoulos, *Themata,* p. 71.
[863] St John Chrysostom, *To Genesis,* Homily 16, § 6, in Migne, *P.G.,* 53, 133.
[864] St Augustine, *De civitate Dei,* XIV, 15, in migne, *P.L.,* 41, 422.
[865] St Augustine, *Opus imperfectum contra Julianum,* I, 105, in migne, *P.L.*

and sinful will and decision. *"She would never have to come to this action, if the evil and crafty would not have proceeded."*[866]

Question 157: How did the Tempter slandered God?

Answer: The Tempter, continually[867] being *"envious, slanders the Creator"* for, since the moment Eve listened to his slander against her Creator and Benefactor without protesting and did not cut off the conversation, she entered into the sphere of the Offence.[868] As St John Chrysostom asked: *"Was the serpent, who was discussing with her, from the same kind as she herself?"* No! He was from the animal kingdom and therefore *"subject to her."* Nevertheless, Eve *"believed in the words of the serpent and thought that his advice was more credible"* rather than *"the Commandment which was given by the Creator."* Therefore, *"she was deceived in such a deceit that she was not worthy to be forgiven."* [869]

    The serpent's admonition led to Apostasy and Rebellion against God because it caused Eve to partake of the Forbidden Fruit with the intention, by tasting it, of becoming *"like God."*[870] Thus the Offence occurred in anticipation of becoming *"equal to God"* because the starting point of this great sin was pride, by means of which the first man chose to deify himself in his imagination[871] and to be under his own authority rather than to be deified due to obedience to God.[872] It is obvious that the Offence into which the serpent drew the woman was an act of Apostasy, similar to that which had caused his own fall.[873] Lucifer had desired to place his throne above the Throne of God and likewise he urged Eve to stretch out her hand to grab the Forbidden Fruit, thereby becoming *"equal to God"* and rising above the Majesty of her Creator. Eve *"imagined becoming equal to God, rushed to partake, stretched forth her thoughts and mind, not seeing any alternative except to drink from the cup that was offered by the devil."*[874] Man has since then accommodated evil in his will and has introduced it into the world.[875]

---

[866] Ibid, *De civitate Dei*, XIV, 13, in migne, *P.L.*, 41, 441 and 420.

[867] Frangopoulos, *Christian Faith*, pp. 164-168. Mitsopoulos, *Themata*, pp. 196-198.

[868] Damalas, *Catechesis*, pp. 42-44. Frangopoulos, *Christian Faith*, p 103.

[869] St John Chrysostom, in Trempelas, *Dogmatique*, v. I, p. 522.

[870] Gen. 3:2.

[871] Gen. 3:6. Cf. St Symeon, *Euriskomena*, pp. 29-30.

[872] St John Chrysostom, *To Matthew*, Homily 65, § 6, in Migne, *P.G.*, 58, 626. St Augustine, *De civitatis Dei*, XIV, 13, in migne, *P.L.*, 41, 441 and 420. Ibid, *Enchiridion ad Laurentium, c. 45,* in migne, *P.L.*, 40, 254.

[873] Is. 14:12-13.

[874] St John Chrysostom, *To Genesis,* Homily 16, § 3, in Migne, *P.G.*, 53, 129. St Symeon, *Euriskomena,* Homily XXXVII, pp. 174-178.

[875] Lossky, *Theology,* p. 80

Eve, from that moment on was no longer an innocent and sinless woman. She had already been very seriously polluted within her inner world. Consequently, she saw the Forbidden Fruit as being *"pleasant to the eyes to look upon and beautiful to contemplate."*[876] The inner world of Eve had been contaminated and had given birth to desire, which from that moment became the inner tempter within the hearts of all Adam's descendants, urging and enslaving them into sin.[877]

The Fall of the first-created couple appears to have all the characteristics of sin from the moment it violently entered the world. It is firstly a desecration of the Law given to the first-created couple whereby *"whoever commits sin also commits lawlessness, and sin is lawlessness."*[878] Due to this violation, the will of man was enslaved and his heart was filled with evil desire. From that exact instant *"out of the heart proceeded evil thoughts, murders, adulteries, fornications, thefts, false witness and blasphemies."*[879] Love for God was pushed aside and replaced by beastly pride that substituted it with the human idol where once the Altar of God's Worship stood. The devil said to Eve, *"You shall be like gods"* and to accomplish this, the first-created took and ate of the Forbidden Fruit. *"And with the hope of deification the devil tempts"* Eve *"and leads her to his own chasm."*[880]

Before the Fall, Adam and Eve's thoughts, emotions, decisions and actions were *"God-centred"* but the moment the Offence was committed, they became *"ego-centred."* Man became selfish and egotistic, worshipping himself, demanding that everyone else should turn to him and his self-deified person. In the darkness of man's selfishness, he was led astray from God, falsely believing that he loves himself although in reality everything he thinks, desires and acts upon is contrary to the true meaning of Love.

The consequences that followed the violation of God's Law by the first-created couple proved that nothing more could have been so catastrophic for them as their own selfishness and the desire to deify their own egos without the Grace and Love of their own Creator.

---

[876] Gen. 3:7.

[877] St John Chrysostom, in Trempelas, *Dogmatique,* v. I, p. 523.

[878] 1 John 3:4.

[879] Matth. 15:19.

[880] St John of Damascus, *Exposition. About fore-knowledge and destination,* II, 44, in Migne, *P.G.,* 94, 980.

Question 158: What were the direct consequences?

Answer: Holy Scripture informs us of the consequences of man's Fall, whether directly or indirectly. Thus, as soon as the first-created couple partook of the Forbidden Fruit, *"the eyes of both were opened, and they perceived that they were naked."*[881] This was due to the loss of their innocence as well as the loss of their vestment of holiness,[882] at which point they vested themselves with *"fig leaves."*[883] The Grace that overshadowed and strengthened them, enabling them to stand and progress in goodness, justice and virtue, was withdrawn from them. Their freedom from all passions and their innocence was lost forever, depriving them from communicating directly with their Creator.[884]

The source of evil is found in the heart where good and evil are together, side by side: the heart became the workshop of the just and unjust.[885] The fact that when they heard the Voice of God while walking in the midst of the garden, they hid themselves,[886] bears witness to their guilty consciences.[887] Man's logic was darkened, whereas before it enjoyed the Vision of the Creator and possessed the Knowledge of Truth. Now it had been overshadowed by the erroneous belief that they could hide from the Sight of God. That sin darkened man's intellect is shown by the attempt of the first-created couple to justify themselves before God, imagining that they could hide their guilt before the All-knowing Lord, while indirectly blaming Him for their Fall.[888] *"The Fall deeply alienated the 'image' of God without destroying it; that which was harmed was the 'likeness.'"*[889]

The Decision and Condemnation of the Creator imposed upon Adam, was that *"by the sweat of your face you shall eat your bread until you return to the earth out of which you were taken"*[890] while the woman was condemned to a life of *"pains" "groanings"* and *"submission to her*

---

[881] Gen. 3:8.

[882] St Irenaeus, *Heresies,* book III, ch. 23, § 5, in Migne, *P.G.,* 7, 963. Cf. Ibid, in Hadjephraimides, pp. 256-257. Kritopoulos, ch. 2, in Karmeris, *The dogmatics,* v. II, p. 516. Mogilas, 1, 23, in Karmeris, *The dogmatics,* v. II, p. 605. Dositheus, *Confession* 6, in Karmeris, *The dogmatics,* v. II, pp. 750 and 756. Androurtsos, *Symbolique,* v. 2, p. 182.

[883] Gen. 3:8.

[884] Cf. Damalas, *Catechesis*, pp. 45-52. Frangopoulos, *Christian Faith,* pp. 109-113. Mitsopoulos, *Themata,* pp. 71-72. Ware, *Way,* pp. 76-81.

[885] Evdokimov, *Orthodoxia,* p. 123.

[886] Gen. 3:9-10.

[887] St John of Damascus, *Exposition, About Paradise*, II, 25, in Migne, *P.G.,* 94, 913.

[888] Gen. 3:13-14.

[889] Evdokimov, *Orthodoxia,* p. 120.

[890] Gen. 3:18. Cf.: St Irenaeus, *Heresies,* book III, ch. 23, § 3, in Migne, *P.G.,* 7, 962. Cf. Ibid, in Hadjephraimides, p. 255. Boulgareos, *Theologicon,* p. 391.

husband."[891]   Consequently, when the first-created man chose to obey the deceit of the tempter who wished to destroy him, immediately after committing the Offence, his body became not only mortal but also subjected to suffering. Hence that which was created Immortal became mortal and was exiled to the land of "*thorns and thistles.*"[892]

Man who was previously intellectual by nature, free in thought, having no experience of evil, knowing only good, suddenly had the desire of evil ruling in his heart. The devil implanted sinful thoughts in man's intellectual nature, which enslaved him. Thus the "*irrational desire*" was raised to power "*ruling the intellectual mind*" of Adam who was stripped of God's Grace[893] and although he was created to rule as a king, he is subsequently dominated by many evil and sinful passions,[894] thus becoming mortal.[895]   Although man previously had the animals under his dominion, submitting to him as their king, now, because of sin, they frightened him. Finally, man is to return to the earth from which he was taken. "*By the sweat of your face you shall eat your bread until you return to the earth out of which you were taken, for earth you are and to earth you shall return.*"[896] Physical death did not occur immediately after the Offence and his exile from Paradise, as Adam lived "*nine hundred and thirty years.*"[897]

Question 159: What is the darkening of the "*In the Image*"?

Answer: Although man's Offence against God was serious and the consequences were inherited by all Adam's descendants, human nature was not completely abolished.[898] Adam was not the inventor of evil as in the case of Lucifer but was deceived into it. Consequently he lost the primitive Justice of Grace, the possibility of being sinless, innocent and Immortal but preserved his "*in the image*" even though in a wounded condition that was capable of being restored. The hope that God gave to the first-created

---

[891] Gen. 3:17.

[892] Gen. 3:19.

[893] St Isidorus of Pelusion, *book IV, Epist. 204*, in Migne, *P.G.*, 78, 1292. St Gregory of Nyssa, *To the Beatitudes,* Homily 3, in Migne, *P.G.,* 44, 1223. St Athanasius, the Great, *Against Apollinarius,* Homily 2, § 6, in Migne, *P.G.*, 26, 1141. St John of Damascus, *Exposition, About Paradise*, II, 25, in Migne, *P.G.,* 94, 909 and 981. Kefalas, *Catechesis,* pp. 66-67.

[894] St Gregory of Nyssa, *Against Eunomius,* II, in Migne, *P.G.*, 45, 545. Theophilus of Antioch, *2 Autolycus,* § 17, in *B*, v. 5, p. 33. St John of Damascus, *Catechesis,* II, 11, in Migne, *P.G.*, 94, 913. Androutsos, *Symbolique,* v. II, pp. 184-185.

[895] St Symeon, *Euriskomena,* Homily V, p. 48.

[896] Gen. 3:20.

[897] Gen. 5:5.

[898] Mitsopoulos, *Themata,* p. 199. Dositheus of Jerusalem, *Decree XIV,* in Link, *Apostolic Faith Today,* pp. 58-59.

couple is known as the *"Proto-evangelion"* (*"First Good News"*). *"And I will put enmity between you and the woman and between your seed and her seed; he shall watch against your head, and you shall watch against his heel."*[899]

In these words of the *"Proto-evangelion,"* God gave His Promise that the serpent (Satan) would be completely defeated by Eve's descendant (Christ) Who would crush his head (Crucifixion), whereas the devil would cause a small injury to Him (death on the Cross). In addition, the Divine Promise revealed that the Fall of the first-created couple was not irreparable because within man there were still powers and qualities capable of restoring him to his original condition.[900]

Hence the Holy Fathers of the Church saw the manifestation of God's Mercy and Love within the punishments, especially in the penalty of death,[901] for God did not want sin to be Eternal and for this reason permitted man to taste death, thereby restoring him to his first glory.

The Holy Fathers who proclaimed that Christ descended into Hades and granted both Adam and Eve Salvation, challenged the opinion of Tatianus that Adam, after the Fall, was condemned to Eternal Condemnation.[902]

II. THE HEREDITY OF ORIGINAL SIN

Question 160: Is the Original Sin inhered by all men?

Answer: The Offence in which the first-formed had fallen, created guilt within them for which they were punished by being exiled to the land of pains, mortality and death as well as being in a condition of sinfulness. Keeping in mind that Adam was the father of the human race and therefore all humanity came from him, with his Fall the entire human race fell as well. Mankind was contaminated and henceforth all inherit Original Sin, which drowns humanity in wickedness and which is manifested in each individual in the internal divisions and disagreements, the frigidity and enmity amongst

---

[899] Gen. 3:16.

[900] Kritopoulos, ch. 2, in Karmeris, *The dogmatics,* v. II, p. 516. Mogilas, 1, 23, in Karmeris, *The dogmatics,* v. II, p. 605. Dositheus, *Confession,* in Karmeris, *The dogmatics,* v. II, p. 756.

[901] St Gregory of Nazianzus, *Homily* 38, § 12, in Migne, *P.G.,* 36, 324. St Isidorus of Pelusion, *Book III, Epist. 195,* in Migne, *P.G.,* 78, 880. Theophilus of Antioch, *2 Autolycus,* in *B,* v. 5, p. 39. St Symeon, *Euriskomena,* Homily 4, p. 41.

[902] Ibid, *Heresies,* book III, ch. 23, § 8, in Migne, *P.G.,* 7, 690. Cf. Ibid, in Hadjephraimides, pp. 257-258. Tertullian, in migne, *P.L.,* 2, 72 and in migne, *P.L.,* 1, 1248. St Hippolytus, *Heresies,* VIII, 16, in *B,* v. 5, p. 343. Origen, *To Matthew,* 8, 126, in Migne, *P.G.,* 13, 1777. St Gregory of Nazianzus, *Homily* 37, § 7, in Migne, *P.G.,* 36, 289. St Augustine, in migne, *P.L.,* 44, 183.

people, the estrangement of mankind and God and generally speaking, the alienation of peace from our inner world. We are sinners and within us a powerful tendency rules, which draws us towards evil.[903]

The feeling of guilt is generally manifested not only in all men but also through their offered sacrifices by means of which all religious men seek to make peace with the Divine. The Teaching of the heritage of Original Sin is the main basis of Salvation in Christ Who is the new Adam. It is proclaimed as one of the most important Doctrines of the Orthodox Christian Faith.

Question 161: What do Holy Scripture teach?

Answer: Holy Scripture bears witness to the fact that all mankind is under the tyranny of sin and the shadow of death. In the Book of Genesis, God warned us that *"every one in his heart is intently brooding over evil continually."*[904] Job wondered: *"Who shall be pure from uncleanness? Not even one; if even his life should be but one day."* [905] Similarly King David, complaining of his sinfulness, besought God *"not to enter into Judgement"* with His servant, for in His *"Sight no one living is righteous."*[906] Elsewhere he stated: *"They have all turned aside, they have together become corrupt; there is none who does good, no, not one."*[907] In agreement with King David is his son, King Solomon, who prayed: *"For there is not a man who will not sin."*[908]

Hence our Lord and Saviour Jesus Christ cautioned us that *"out of the heart proceed evil thoughts, murders, adulteries, fornications, thefts, false witness and blasphemies"*[909] and He emphasized the importance of every man being Regenerated because *"that which is born of the flesh is flesh, and that which is born of the Spirit is spirit"*[910] and consequently *"unless one is born of Water and the Spirit, he cannot enter the Kingdom of God."* [911]

St John the Apostle, Evangelist and Theologian, in his 1st Epistle wrote: *"If we say that we have no sin, we deceive ourselves, and the Truth is*

---

[903] Plato of Moscow, *Orthodox Teaching,* p. 107. Kefalas, *Catechesis,* pp. 243-246. Frangopoulos, *Christian Faith,* pp. 113-115. Mitsopoulos, *Themata,* pp. 72, 202-205.
[904] Gen. 6:6; 8:21.
[905] Job 14:4-5.
[906] Psalm 13(14):3.
[907] Psalm 142(143):2.
[908] 1 Samuel (1 Kings) 8:46.
[909] Matth. 15:19.
[910] John 3:6.
[911] John 3:5.

not in us."[912] St James the Adelphotheos (the stepbrother of our Lord), said: *"we all stumble in many things"*[913] while St Paul proclaimed that *"we have previously charged both Jews and Greeks that they are all under sin"*[914] and that *"all have sinned and fall short of the Glory of God."*[915] In his Epistle to the Ephesians, he reminded the Christians of Ephesus that *"you He made alive, who were dead in trespasses and sins"*[916] *"in which you once walked according to the course of this world, according to the prince of the power of the air, the spirit who now works in the sons of disobedience."*[917]

The sinful corruption of human nature is our heritage from the fallen Adam.[918] *"For God created man to be immortal, and made him to be an image of His own Eternity. Nevertheless through envy of the devil death entered the world."*[919] King David confessed: *"Behold, I was brought forth in iniquity, and in sin my mother conceived me."*[920] However, the classical Biblical references are those of St Paul found in his Epistle to the Romans, which states: *"Therefore, just as through one man sin entered the world, and death through sin, and thus death spread to all men, because all sinned."*[921] *"For if by the one man's Offence death reigned through the one, much more those who receive abundance of Grace and of the Gift of Righteousness will reign in life through the One, Jesus Christ. Therefore, as through one man's Offence Judgement came to all men, resulting in Condemnation, even so through one Man's Righteous Act the free Gift came to all men, resulting in Justification of Life. For as by one man's Disobedience many were made sinners, so also by one Man's obedience many will be made righteous."*[922]

In conclusion, as sin and death entered mankind through Adam and through him we all became sinners, likewise through Christ Who is the new Adam of the New Creation, Life came into the world and to all who believe in Him. And as through Adam mankind inherited sin and death, likewise through Christ we become inheritors of Justice, Sanctification, Salvation and partakers of the Resurrection and Immortality.

---

[912] 1 John 1:8.
[913] James 3:2.
[914] Rom. 3:9.
[915] Rom. 3:23.
[916] Ephes. 2:1.
[917] Ephes. 2:2.
[918] Cf. Plato, *Orthodox Teaching*, p. 56-59.
[919] Wisdom 2:23-24.
[920] Psalm 50(51):5.
[921] Rom. 5:12.
[922] Rom. 5:17-19. Kalogerou, *Maria*, p. 59. Theodoretus of Cyrus, *To Romans*, in Migne, *P.G.*, 82, 100. St Cyril of Alexandria, *To Romans*, in Migne, *P.G.*, 74, 789.

III. THE ESSENCE OF ORIGINAL SIN

a) ORIGINAL SIN AS A CONDITION

Question 162: What is the essence of the Original Sin?

Answer: The Offence committed by Adam brought sorrowful consequences upon him that made his condition sinful and permanent. This condition of sinfulness deprived him of Divine Grace that Sanctified him, removed his primitive condition of holiness and thereby allowing evil desires of the flesh to rush into his nature and, as a result, through him, causing these sins to be inherited by all his descendants. Thus man became naked, being separated from God's Grace and wounded in nature.

The loss of primitive justice and the desire of the flesh (*concupiscentia*) darkened but did not destroy the "*image*" of God in man. As his mind was darkened, he became unable to understand or to approach the Divine and Heavenly Truths. His will became weak and was easily dragged into sin and evil and finally, the reign of sexual desires enslaved him to the flesh.

Question 163: What is the darkening & the weakening of man's logic & will?

Answer: St Paul cautioned us of the darkening of man's logic when he spoke of the "*natural man*"[923] who lives "*according to the flesh and has only the inborn and natural prudence*"[924] for he believes that "*the things of the Spirit of God*" " *are foolishness.*"[925] The man who bears the nature of Adam because of the inherited corrupted nature and the increasing persistence and habit of wickedness, became incapable of receiving the Enlightenment of the Holy Spirit, just as the ailing eye is unable to clearly see the light of the sun.

This darkening of man's mind does not make the descendants of Adam completely incapable of reaching out to search logically for their Creator[926] because "*since the creation of the world His invisible Attributes are clearly seen, being understood by the things that are made, even His*

---

[923] 1 Corinth. 2:14.
[924] St Cyril of Alexandria, *To Romans,* in Migne, *P.G.,* 74, 789.
[925] 1 Corinth. 2:14.
[926] Cf. Kefalas, *Catechesis,* p. 70.

Eternal Power and Godhead, so they are without excuse."[927]   Furthermore, *"although they knew God, they did not glorify Him as God, nor were thankful, but became futile in their thoughts, and their foolish hearts were darkened."*[928]

Man subsequently worshipped the Creation rather than the Creator, opening the doors to idolatry and so mankind bowed down before false gods. This does not mean that man was completely lost and incapable of receiving Divine Enlightenment. Instead God granted that man be restored by Divine Grace, in order for him to be raised up and to rediscover his Creator from Whom he had distanced himself and thereby to renew the previous joyful Communion that had been discontinued because of the Offence.

Concerning the weakening of man's will and its enslavement under the desire of flesh, it is stressed by St Paul to the Romans.[929] Even after the Offence, the moral instinct and the Divine *"image"* that were not completely destroyed, remain within man. Man does not preserve his free-will only *"in power to do evil, lying and sinning"*[930] Neither does his free-will only commit evil nor are the virtues of the pagan splendours evil, (*"splendida vitia"*) these being expressions used by St Augustine that are clarified in his writings.[931]

The great personalities of the Old Testament, through God's Grace, proved worthy of those who lived under the Grace of the New Adam, although they lived afar from the Grace in Christ And yet they were exalted: Abel for his faith in offering a sacrifice to God, Enoch for pleasing God, Noah for his righteousness, Abraham for his obedience and faith, Moses for his faith, Joshua for his faith that conquered Jericho, Gideon, Barak, Samson, Jephthah, David and Samuel and all the Prophets,[932] *"who through faith subdued kingdoms, worked righteousness, obtained promises, stopped the mouths of lions, quenched the violence of fire, escaped the edge of the sword, out of weakness were made strong, became valiant in battle, turned to flight the armies of the aliens."*[933]

Mankind, without the Incarnation of the Word and Son of God, our Lord and Saviour Jesus Christ, would have remained cursed because death would have been an eternal tyrant from which neither the just nor the

---

[927] Rom. 1:20.
[928] Rom. 1:21.
[929] Rom. 7:14-24. Cf. St Symeon, *Euriskomena*, Homily 5, pp. 48-51.
[930] St Augustine, *Sermo* 156, § 12, in migne, *P.L.*, 38, 856.
[931] Ibid, *De civitate Dei*, 18, in migne, *P.L.*, 41, 161.
[932] Heb. 11:4-31.
[933] Heb. 11:32, 33-34.

righteous of the Old Testament could have escaped.[934]   However, through God's Divine Providence they were not destined to perish.[935] Therefore, for the sake of the righteous people, God would not have destroyed the city even if He had found only *"ten"* righteous souls.[936] Furthermore, *"since we are surrounded by so great a cloud of witnesses"*[937] God could not ignore those righteous ones.

Because of Original Sin mortality ruled over mankind who was unable to reach moral Perfection without Salvation in Christ The virtues that man achieves through his natural capabilities are not only imperfect but also contaminated by selfish and egoistic intentions. The fact that these virtues cannot be characterized as *"..splendid evils"* is apparent when one is justified through faith in Christ although he has not yet been perfected in holiness. His acts of good deeds and virtues still appear to be imperfect and not free of egoism and the exaltations of vainglory.   Perfection in holiness is achieved only after many years of hard struggle against sin and its wicked passions.

b) ORIGINAL SIN AS GUILT

Question 164: What is the inheritance of Original Sin?

Answer: Original Sin consists of true and real guilt, not only in the punishment imposed as a result of Adam's Offence. Adam's sin was not committed by his descendants, and consequently for them it had nothing to do with their own will, merely being inherited as a sinful condition. Sin is not only the separate inner or external acts (*"peccatum actuale"*). It is especially the condition of sin (*"peccatum habituale"*), due to specific sinful deeds that further strengthens and cultivates it. Original Sin is the heritage of a sinful condition for all mankind, which is imputed to us not as personal sin (direct imputation), but as the sinful condition of each person (*"vitiositas"*). Between Adam's guilt and the guilt of his descendants there *"exists a great difference: in Adam the Offence of God's Law was committed by his own will whereas in his descendants it is by inheritance and unavoidable."*[938]   *"The Original Sin in the first-created should be understood as their own sin as well as the sinful condition of their nature in which the Offence led them. Whereas in Adam's descendants it is the sinful*

---

[934] Cf. Plato of Moscow, *Orthodox Teaching,* p. 62.
[935] Gen. 18:26.
[936] Gen. 18:32.
[937] Heb. 12:1.
[938] Androutsos, *Dogmatique,* v. I, pp. 156-157.

condition of man's nature with which he is born into the world."[939] Holy
Scripture does not explain how men inherit Original Sin.

Question 165: What happens to the unbaptised infants after death?

Answer: The question of what happens to unbaptised infants after death has
always troubled the Holy Fathers of the Orthodox Church and has been the
subject of many different opinions. God has great compassion towards those
who have not yet expressed the tendency towards sin as descendants of
Adam but brings His *"Wrath"* upon those who willingly participate in the
Offence of their forefather.

St Gregory of Nazianzus believed that infants who die unbaptised,
although having been born under Adam's sinful nature, have not yet
expressed that sinful tendency when overtaken by early death and
consequently *" are neither glorified nor condemned by the Just Judge, being
unsealed and naïve, although harmed by the damage (of Adam's offence)
rather than their actions, they are unworthy of punishment or honour."*[940]

St Gregory of Nyssa noted that *"we must not imagine that the
immature death of infants brings equal punishment of pains as to those who
died sinning nor that they are equal in glory to those who struggled for all
virtues."*[941] He also characterized the infant as being *"infinitely pure"* and
having *" no infection of the soul's eyes in order not to participate in the
light."*[942]

Question 166: Did the Ever-Virgin Mary partake of the Original Sin?

Answer: St Paul proclaimed that *"we all have sinned"*[943] this means that
there can be no exceptions concerning the consequences derived from the
ancestral Offence. On the contrary, it is declared that God is *"the Saviour of
all men"* through the Ever-Virgin Mary, the Ever Blessed Theotokos, who
also acknowledges Him as her own Saviour.[944] The Theotokos is
proclaimed by the Church as also being guilty of Original Sin as are all men
and that she was conceived and born naturally in the manner of all men.
However the Holy Spirit came upon her before she conceived the Word of
God, in order to cleanse her and make her a vessel worthy of hosting the

---

[939] Makarios, *Enchiridion*, I, pp. 589-599.
[940] St Gregory of Nazianzus, *To the holy Baptism*, Homily 40, § 23, in Migne, *P.G.*, 36, 389.
[941] St Gregory of Nyssa, *About the infants which are taken before their time*, in Migne, *P.G.*, 46, 192.
[942] Ibid, *About the infants which are taken before their time*, in Migne, *P.G.*, 46, 177.
[943] Rom. 5:12.
[944] Luke 1:47.

Word and Son of God. She therefore required cleansing from the Original Sin.[945]

IV. THE PUNISHMENTS AGAINST SIN

Question 167: What are the punishments against sin?

Answer: The warning by God to the First-created that *"in whatsoever day you eat of it, you shall surely die"*[946] was realised after the Offence when misery became an inseparable and unavoidable consequence of sin. The privations, the groans, the pains, the hardships of human nature resulting in the death of Adam's descendants are the retaliation and the *"wages of sin."*[947] The complete fulfillment of this Divine warning will occur after death for all who remain in the evil heritage of the First- created. Then sin will be crushed for all eternity, which is referred to as *"the second death"* in Holy Scripture.[948]

Question 168: What is the meaning and the differentiation of the punishments of sin and the misery caused by it?

Answer: When we speak of the sentence and punishment of sin, we mean in general the suffering and sorrow that followed the Offence, which first Adam and then all his descendants afterwards had to face, according to the just but painful price of disobedience to God's Law. Although these punishments in the long term are used as pedagogic ways of restoring the fallen but goodhearted man, nevertheless their direct character is the satisfaction of Divine Justice, which was offended by the violation of God's Law given in the Garden of Delight.

The extent of the punishments are divided into *"temporary"* and *"eternal"* conditions. The temporary punishments are split into those that are *"natural"* or those that directly result from sin and those that are *"positives"* having been directly imposed by God.

It was correctly stated that all punishments are *"positives"* because they have their reason in God Who is the Creator and Provider of the natural and moral order.[949] However, for example, the historic worldwide

---

[945] Kritopoulos, *Confession* XVII, in Karmeris, *The dogmatics*, p. 550. Boulgareos, *Theologicon,* p. 431. Trempelas, *Dogmatique,* v. I, pp. 559-561.
[946] Gen. 2:17; 3:4.
[947] Rom. 6:23.
[948] Rev. 2:11; 20:6, 14; 21:8.
[949] Androutsos, *Dogmatique,* v. I, p. 162.

catastrophe of the Great Flood,[950] the destruction of Sodom and Gomorrah[951] as well as the terrible afflictions that were imposed upon Pharaoh,[952] were as a result of direct Divine Wrath upon sin.

The relationship between sin and suffering is understandable and no one can seriously doubt it because surely if there was no sin, no crime would have existed nor would there be callous abandonment of the weak and poor. There would be no illness or death and consequently no misery or suffering. This connection could be characterized as direct, since sin immediately separates us from God in Whom true happiness exists. Accordingly our separation from Him creates chaos and a great chasm of unhappiness. Sin brings forth wretchedness and vice versa, which again creates new levels of unhappiness as the sinner falls from one gulf of misery to another even worse. Sin is the seed and unhappiness its fruit containing more seeds. Unhappiness increases through impatience and worries that are created within the sinner and which drive him to other, greater sins. Not only the punishments and sufferings imposed by God but also the troubles that others bring upon people as well as the trials we create ourselves, must be the fruit of sin. The evil, guilty and sinful conscience makes the unhappiness of the sinner heavier and weakens his resistance further.

Concerning the burden of the conscience, we must recall that when Adam sinned, he was overcome by fear and hid himself when he heard God walking in Paradise.[953] Every descendant of Adam is conquered by the same fear and voice of conscience, which always reminds him of the Offence, justly condemning and strictly rebuking him.[954]

The easiness of falling from one sin into another is manifested by the examples of King David[955] and Jeroboam who was killed together with his household by Baasa because of sins that he had committed against Israel.[956] The alienation from God of the unrepentant sinner increases due to his complete abandonment by God and by his falling into *a debased mind* as well as into sinful passions *which are not fitting.*[957]

It is obvious that this progress towards evil of the unrepentant sinner makes him an object of God's Just Wrath. The story of Aman, which is recorded in the Book of Esther,[958] Pontius Pilate who washed his hands of

---

[950] Gen. 6:6-9:17.
[951] Gen. 19:24-25.
[952] Ex. 2:17-18, 20-21; 3:2, 6, 17; 9:3, 10, 18, 23; 10:4, 13-15, 21-22; 11:5, 12, 29.
[953] Gen. 3:9.
[954] Gen. 42:21-22. Matth. 14:2.
[955] 2 Samuel (2 Kings)11:1-12:31.
[956] 1 Kings 15:25-30.
[957] Rom. 1:28.
[958] Esther 7:9-10; 9:13

the Blood of the Innocent One,[959] Ananias and Sapphira who by lying to the Apostle Peter found death,[960] Elymas the Sorcerer[961] and so many other catastrophic events that are mentioned throughout history such as the Great Flood, the annihilation of Sodom and Gomorrah, Pharaoh's terrifying afflictions and the destruction of Jerusalem all bear witness to the fact that many times God intervenes as the Just Judge of those who commit evil. Therefore the fear of the pagans was not mere superstition when they faced such enormous disasters. However, there have been particular occasions when *"the goodness, forbearance, and longsuffering"* of God conceded certain punishments in order to lead the sinner *"to repentance;"*[962] or the Lord has chastened some so that the sinners would *"not be condemned with the world."*[963] Furthermore, when God chastens those whom He loves *"and scourges every son whom He receives"*[964] He does so in order that the genuineness of their faith *"may be found to praise, honour, and glory at the Revelation of Jesus Christ"*[965]

What awaits the unrepentant sinner at the end of his life is eternal suffering and punishment. Before his death, he struggles to forget about death, the fear of which makes him feel guilty and which becomes a nightmare for him. However, when he faces death, his agony is increased. Darkness overshadows his soul and he has no hope of Divine Mercy to which the repentant sinner and the just look forward. If for the just death is considered as a bridge from this world of suffering to the world of Joy and Blessedness, for the unrepentant sinner death is the horrible, fearful executioner who will deliver him to the Supreme and Just Judge.

Question 169: What is the life of the sinners after death?

Answer: If the fruits of sin are so painful in this temporary life, how much more painful will it be in the Afterlife? Our Lord and Saviour Jesus Christ, the Son of God, assured us of Eternal Hell that awaits *"the devil and his angels"*[966] and all those who died in sin, being unrepentant. They *"will go away into Everlasting Punishment."*[967] All those who do not accept Christ will not participate in the Everlasting Life of Blessedness because *"he who*

---

[959] Matth. 27:24
[960] Acts 5:1-11.
[961] Acts 13:6-11.
[962] Rom. 2:4.
[963] 1 Corinth. 11:32.
[964] Heb. 12:6, 7-8.
[965] 1 Peter 1:7.
[966] Matth. 25:41. Rev. 20:10.
[967] Matth. 25:46.

believes in the Son has Everlasting Life; and he who does not believe the Son shall not see Life, but the Wrath of God abides on him."[968]   St Paul stated that God will punish the sinners *"in Flaming Fire, taking vengeance on those who do not know God, and on those who do not obey the Gospel of our Lord Jesus Christ.   These shall be punished with Everlasting Destruction from the Presence of the Lord and from the Glory of His Power.*"[969]

When comparing the two types of death, that of natural separation of the soul from its body and that of Eternal Condemnation, the former seems secondary and less important. The natural or biological death will end and be no more[970] whereas the *"Second Death"*[971] shall continue for all Eternity. Also all those who, before the General Resurrection and Second Coming of our Lord and Saviour Jesus Christ, had pleased God, such as the Prophets, Apostles, Martyrs and all the Just, and who had lived in Christ, within them the *"Second Death"* has ceased and they, having drank from the Cup of Death, await the Common Resurrection.

We do not have a complete knowledge of the nature of the punishments that follow death because in Holy Scripture they are simply described with images of this world. Nevertheless, in reality there is no similar image with which they can be compared. Even our Lord and Saviour Jesus Christ, used expressions, examples and images from daily life to express Heavenly Truths. Terms such as *"Hell of Fire,"*[972] *"where the worm does not die and the Fire is not quenched"*[973] the place of *"torment"*[974] and *"Lake of Fire"*[975] are but a few examples.

From the Parable of the Rich Man and Poor Lazarus, we are informed of the two existing conditions of Paradise and Hell.   The souls are completely conscience of their existence and are able to experience pain or happiness. Souls recognize one another even if they are in different conditions. The souls in Hell can communicate with God but the prayers of those who are in Eternal Torment are never fulfilled. Those who struggled in their life will be rewarded, whereas those who have done evil will be thrown into Eternal Punishment without any hope or comfort.[976] The fact that the punishments will last for all Eternity surpasses human

---

[968] John 3:36.
[969] 2 Thess. 1:8-9.
[970] Rev. 21:4. 1 Corinth. 15:26.
[971] Rev. 2:11; 20:6, 14; 21:8.
[972] Matth. 5:22, 29; 10:28; 18:9; 23:15, 33; Mark 9:43, 45, 47. Luke 12:5. John 3:6.
[973] Mark 9:44.
[974] Luke 16:24, 25.
[975] Rev. 19:20; 20:10, 14, 15; 21:8.
[976] Luke 16:19-31.

understanding, for just as the Righteous will inherit Eternal Life for all Eternity, likewise those who will be condemned will suffer for all Eternity.[977]

Those who describe Eternal Punishments as being cruel, do not take into consideration that the sinful man, blinded by his guilty conscience, is always lenient towards himself, imitating his forefather's justification of his deeds. They also do not consider the impossibility of anyone being more compassionate and merciful than God Who loves mankind and Who judges each and everyone accordingly.

It is obvious that those who have been freed from Original Sin through Salvation in Christ, also partake of the sufferings and trials of this world although these trials have lost their character as punishments having become a Paternal pedagogic system.[978] St James urges all brethren to *"count it all joy when you fall into various trials, knowing that the testing of your faith produces patience."*[979] Our Saviour Jesus Christ, encouraging His Apostles and Disciples, said: *"In the world you will have tribulation"*[980]

---

[977] Mark 3:28-29.
[978] Heb. 12:7-8.
[979] 2 Corinth. 5:1-4.
[980] John 16:33.

PART THREE

JESUS CHRIST FOUNDER OF THE KINGDOM OF GOD

CHAPTER ONE
THE MYSTERY OF SALVATION

Question 170: What is the Mystery of Salvation?

Answer: Man, who was deceived into sin, did not fall without the possibility of restoration, nor was he condemned to Eternal Death. But, within him, there was hope and he was not abandoned by the Divine Love of his Creator. God, before all time, had foreseen the Fall of man. To cure the mortality that sin enforced upon man and in order to realize the work of Regeneration and Recreation, God sent into the world, according to His Eternal and Mysterious Will, as the Saviour and Deliverer, His own Begotten Son.[981]

The Incarnated Word and Son of God was born for us by the Wisdom, Justice, Holiness and Salvation of God, and through His Teachings He enlightened and guided us into the true Knowledge of God. Through His Death and our incorporation and Regeneration within His Body through Holy Baptism, He freed us from all guilt, Justifying us and making us Saints by offering Himself as a *"ransom"*[982] for the Salvation of the world.

Through Jesus Christ, our nature became capable of becoming partakers of Divine Nature. Hence the Salvation in Christ is the central Doctrine and main subject of the Holy Gospel. Nevertheless it remains a Mystery, hidden from all generations and even from the Heavenly Hosts being the secret Will of God and existing in the depths of His Wisdom. The Mystery of Salvation has remained incomprehensible to our limited mind.

Salvation, as Regeneration of the fallen and corrupted nature of man, is inseparably connected to the Creation as the Will of God, existing before all time and being inseparable from the plan of Creation.

Question 171: Is the fallen man susceptible to Salvation?

Answer: Fallen man has to his credit the fact that he did not invent evil himself but was deceived by the devil.[983] Man was corrupted because of the

---

[981] St Symeon, *Euriskomena,* Homily X, pp. 65-67.
[982] Matth. 19:28.
[983] St John of Damascus, *Against Manicheans Dialogus,* § 33, in Migne, 94, 1540.

Offence and did not remain in the natural condition in which he was created. Man was corrupted to the extent that the wickedness, which invaded his nature, did not transform him into complete evil. This is the differentiation between the devil and man. The devil's nature was transformed completely and when he lies, *"he speaks of his own resources."*[984] He speaks from the bottom of his corrupted nature, which is completely possessed by deceit and is the primary and inexhaustible source of evil. On the contrary, when man lies, he speaks as an enslaved person influenced by the devil who is the father of deception. The groaning and suffering is hidden in the sinner because of the Offence. Man's conscience awakens and becomes the instrument by which God raises him up.

When man fell, he did not fall into the condition of the animals, nor did his nature take on that of the devil. His heart became like a field of thorns and thistles, but it did not change into insensitive granite, unable to receive the Enlightenment of Divine Grace. And surely by man's moral powers, which remained in him, it was impossible for him to be restored to the previous state. He was susceptible to God's attention and Salvation.[985] It was necessary for man to be Regenerated, but not to be changed, because through the Offence evil rushed into him, but it did not become the essence of his spiritual nature.

Hence the sinful man, feeling the pollution of wickedness that infected and alienated him from God, and because of the accusations of his conscience that awakened him, searched for the means to become friends with God and to be free from guilt and unhappiness. He therefore offered sacrifices, suffered punishments of the body, took up spiritual pilgrimages and went through purifications, through which he sought expiation with the Divine or cleanliness from the stain of immoral deeds.

Considering that sin is a power that soils man and alienates him from God, only through an inner Regeneration and the outpouring of a new moral life,[986] which transforms him from a son of darkness, disobedience and wrath[987] into a son of Light and Divine Blessedness,[988] is it possible to achieve restoration and Salvation from the slavery of evil. This desirable Salvation does not consist of a natural transformation of the body, nor is it some kind of lifeless morality that enlightens the mind. It is the rising and moral transfiguration of the inner man that is achieved by his freedom from

---

[984] John 8:44.
[985] Cf. Frangopoulos, *Christian Faith,* pp. 117-118.
[986] John 3:5.
[987] Ephes. 2:2; 5:6. Col. 3:6.
[988] 1 Thess. 5:5. Heb. 2:10. Rom. 8:14; 9:26. Col. 3:26.

the slavery of sin[989] and the beginning of a new Life,[990] which makes him a partaker of the Divine Nature[991] in Jesus Christ.

Question 172: How was the restoration of man achieved through Christ?

Answer: The Creation of the world finalized the vertical movement of the Acts of God: from the Father through the Son in the Holy Spirit. On the contrary, the ascent of man, the *Economia* of Salvation, follows the opposite order: from the Holy Spirit through the Son to the Father. In this ascent the Holy Spirit is revealed to be the "*Spirit of Life*" from Whom Love is derived.[992]

It is obvious that this essential change in every sinner is impossible to achieve only by means of man's powers and struggles. It is vitally necessary for a special intervention of the *Philanthropia* and Love of God Who wants the Salvation of all sinners. This Act has been manifested by God Who sent into the world His Only-begotten Son "*Who became for us Wisdom from God – and Righteousness and Sanctification and Redemption.*"[993] In other words, the Incarnated Son of God through His Teachings "*taught us the Divine Knowledge of God*" "*making us wise by freeing us from the error of the idols.*"[994] He freed us from guilt and made us "*Just and Saints*" by becoming the Head of the human race and being the New Adam.[995] Hence Christ became our true "*freedom freeing us from sin*" by giving "*Himself as ransom for the cleansing of the whole world.*"[996] This is the most joyful announcement that makes the Christian message so real and utterly truthful. It is the Holy Gospel.

Our Lord and Saviour Jesus Christ, the Son of God, was not our physical forefather as Adam was, from whom all humanity originated.[997] But He was the most Holy member of the human race, which had fallen into the slavery of sin, and for this reason He surpasses the first Adam. Because of His close relationship with mankind, having assumed flesh and blood[998]

---

[989] 1 Corinth. 7:22.
[990] Rom. 6:4.
[991] 2 Peter 1:4.
[992] Evdokimov, *Orthodoxia*, p. 150.
[993] 1 Corinth. 1:30. Cf. Mitsopoulos, *Themata*, pp. 208-209.
[994] Theophilus of Antioch, *To Corinthians 1:30*, in Migne, *P.G.*, 124, 584.
[995] St John Chrysostom, *To 1 Corinthians Homily 5*, § 3, in Montfaucon, v. 10, p. 42.
[996] St Gregory of Nazianzus, *Homily 30*, § 20, in Migne, *P.G.*, 36, 132.
[997] Rom. 8:3.
[998] Heb. 2:14.

and having been *"made like His brethren"*[999] in everything of their nature, with the exception of sin, Christ is not ashamed to call them His *"brothers."*[1000] He became *"the new beginning of the human race,"* *"our Brother for the similarity of our body, but He is also called 'the Firstborn,'*[1001] *because all men were lost according to the offence of the first, His Flesh was saved and freed as being the Body of the Word."*[1002] And because all other brothers of Christ were guilty and *"responsible to death, He presented His own Body and as everyone died through him (Adam), everyone through Him (Christ) became free"* and *"everyone according to the relationship of the flesh was freed"* and *"as one body conjoined in Him for the sameness of the flesh"* *"we are joined to the Word"* and through Him *"to God,"* being deified and *"partakers of the Divine Nature,"* according to the capability of our nature, without being absorbed or wiped out by participating in the Infinite Nature (Theosis).[1003]

"Christ became the beginning and the root of our race which is re-created towards immortality through the union with God."[1004] Thus the Word of God Who took on flesh and blood, became the same as us, although as God, He remains perfect *"having the real and true identity of nature with the Father."* However, because *"He vested Himself with our body,"* *"we all have vested (ourselves with) His."* Through Him we are united with the Father becoming *"one"* in the Father and the Son *"Whose identity we shall also have,"* similar to the Word Who has this identity with the Father by Nature, whereas we receive it by *"imitation and Grace,"* according to the Spirit Who dwells within us.[1005] Consequently our Lord and Saviour Jesus Christ, the Son of God, as the new and heavenly Adam and the Head of His Mystical Body, *"summed up"*[1006] the human race and brought it back to the ancient condition from which it had fallen. He became the Leaven that leavens the whole lump[1007] of the human race, which was incorporated in Him and united to Him. Thus He was able to loosen the curse of mankind.[1008]

---

[999] Heb. 2:17.

[1000] Heb. 2:11.

[1001] Rom. 8:29.

[1002] St Cyril of Alexandria, *To John 16:6-7,* in Migne, *P.G.,* 74, 432.

[1003] St Athanasius the Great, *Against Arians,* II, §§ 61, 69 and 74, in Migne, *P.G.,* 26, 277, 293 and 305.

[1004] St Cyril of Alexandria, *About the in spirit and truth,* Homily IX, in Migne, *P.G.,* 68, 617.

[1005] St Athanasius the Great, *Against Arians,* III, §§ 22 and 25, in Migne, *P.G.,* 26, 368 and 376.

[1006] Rom. 13:9.

[1007] 1 Corinth. 5:6. Gal. 5:9. Matth. 13:33. Luke 13:21.

[1008] St Gregory of Nazianzus, *Homily 30,* § 21, in Migne, *P.G.,* 36, 132.

Hence it is understood that the new Revelation, which has been granted to mankind by God in Jesus Christ, is the true Salvation that offers the Life-giving Light concerning the true God, the nature and the destination of man. The centre of this Divine Revelation is Salvation and Deification of our human nature in Christ, in Whom and to Whom we are united. For the purpose of the Holy Gospel is not just to lead us to the Knowledge of the true God, but also to make man perfect in virtue and in the likeness of God, freeing him from the stain of sin and all sinful passions.[1009]

Question 173: What is Salvation as the New Creation?

Answer: The Revelation is a new Creation, since it derives from the new Creation in Christ. This Creation is more important, because on the one hand it takes place on the moral field, which is higher than the natural field, whereas on the other hand, it aims for the Regeneration of the intellectual Creation. The old Creation must be replaced by a new one. It is also the higher goal of Divine Providence, which watches over the Universe and takes an interest in human history, intervening for the benefit of each man's destination. It also aims for the Salvation and Regeneration of the human race and its freedom from the disastrous consequences of the Offence and their restoration as children of God.

No matter how close the Doctrine of Salvation is to those of Creation and Providence, one must never forget that Salvation, as a Gift of the Free-will of God, which was fulfilled by the Incarnation of the Son of God, consists of *"the Mystery which has been hidden from ages and from generations"*[1010] and which cannot be understood in all its details by the limited human mind. Surely *"God is Love"*[1011] and is a free action of God's goodness, which explains the sending of His Son to save man.[1012] This Mystery *"which from the beginning of the ages"* was hidden even from the Angelic Hosts.[1013]

The *"formation"* of Christ in man - the Christ-making of man - is neither an irritation – an impossible fact – nor a realization in man of the Incarnation, but a projection within man of the Incarnation itself, which acts in and continues with the Eucharistic Mystery.[1014]

[1009] Cf. Frangopoulos, *Christian Faith*, pp. 120-121.
[1010] Col. 1:26.
[1011] 1 John 4:16.
[1012] Ephes. 1:7-10.
[1013] Ephes. 3:9-10.
[1014] Evdokimov, *Orthodoxi*, p. 153.

The Mystery of Christ being beyond any human understanding needs simple and uncorrupted faith.[1015] Because, if man ignores the union that unites his soul to his body, how much more is it impossible for him to comprehend the Incarnation of the Word and Son of God?[1016]

The Mystery of the Salvation in Christ requires solid and unshakeable faith as we examine the Incarnation and the extreme humbleness of the Word and Son of God, which is beyond any human conception and interpretation.[1017] It was because of the love expressed by God towards mankind, who alienated themselves from Him.[1018]

Question 174: Was the Salvation of man within the eternal Divine Will?

Answer: If Salvation is related inseparably to the Creation, it is obvious that the Will of God concerning Salvation existed before all time inseparably with the plan of Creation. In other words God did not wait for the Fall of man to take place and then planned his restoration. As the Will of God concerning the creation of the world and man existed eternally, without any change in the simplicity of God, and the plan of the Salvation of man existed as *"the Mystery which has been hidden from ages and from generations,"*[1019] - meaning from above and from the beginning, before all Creation and Eternally - He worked out the Salvation as He created.

Analysing the above, we understand that God decided to save man, since He foresaw his Fall. But in God there is no changing of decisions and actions and thus the Eternal Will of God concerning Salvation coincided directly with His Eternal Will concerning the creation of the world. God at the time of Adam's Fall announced the Salvation that would come from the woman's seed - a victory over the devil[1020] who had deceived her.[1021] Thus, the Holy Apostles speak about the Saviour Who *"chose us in Him before the foundation of the world,"*[1022] Who *"indeed was foreordained before the foundation of the world, but was manifest in these last times"*[1023] and as the *"Lamb slain from the foundation of the world."*[1024]

[1015] St Cyril of Alexandria, *Against Nestorius,* III, in Migne, *P.G.,* 76, 112.
[1016] St Gregory of Nyssa, *Catechesis,* II, in Migne, *P.G.,* 45, 44.
[1017] St Gregory of Nyssa, *Catechesis,* II, in Migne, *P.G.,* 45, 44.
[1018] Theodoretus of Cyrus, *Homily* VI, in Migne, *P.G.,* 83, 988.
[1019] Col. 1:26.
[1020] Gen. 3:16.
[1021] Gen. 3:14.
[1022] Ephes. 1:4.
[1023] 1 Peter 1:20.
[1024] Rev. 13:8.

Hence it is assured by the Holy Fathers and ecclesiastic Scholars that *"at the Incarnation it was predestined and the Mystery of the Gospel and the electing from on High of those who will believe"*[1025] and *"that before the law and that God before the creation of the world predestined the Economia"*[1026] and *"from these the antiquity of the Gospel is manifested."*[1027]

CHAPTER TWO
PREPARATION OF SALVATION BY DIVINE PROVIDENCE

Question 175: How was Salvation prepared?

Answer: The Will for Salvation is related to the Doctrine of Divine Providence, which foresaw, determined and prepared the proper time according to which it would be realised. Immediately, after the Offence in the Garden of Delight, God gave His first Divine Promise of the re-elevation of mankind to the first-created couple.[1028] The Covenants between God and Noah[1029] as well as all the other the Patriarchs[1030] contained Prophesies of the Salvation of the whole world. However, the admirable *"Economia"* establishing Monotheism in the one family and tribe of Abraham,[1031] clearly manifested the preparation for Salvation by Divine Providence.

Although it seemed that for a while God had abandoned His chosen people in the land of Egypt,[1032] it was instead a paternal pedagogic way by means of which the people of God were freed. The Mosaic Law[1033] that followed, can only be described as the Fruit of the special Intervention of God in man's history. Through the ritual purifications and sacrifices the need for redemption was made aware and prepared the people of Israel for the coming of the Messiah Whose royalty and Work of Salvation were exalted and prophesied by His forefather according to the flesh, King David, in the Royal and Messianic Psalms. The numerous Prophets followed and presented the image of the Saviour through clear Prophesies, declaring His Work of Salvation as extending beyond the boundaries of Israel. The work of the Prophets was confirmed by the preaching of St John, the Baptist and

---

[1025] Zigabinos, *To Ephesians 1:4.*
[1026] Kalogeras, II, 3.
[1027] Theodoretus of Cyrus, *To Colossians 1:26,* in Migne, *P.G.,* 82, 604.
[1028] Gen. 3:16.
[1029] Gen. 9:11-17.
[1030] Gen. 17:2-14; 22:16-18; 26:2-4; 28:10-13; 35:10-11; 34:10-11. Judges 2:1-2.
[1031] Gen. 12:1-3.
[1032] Ex. 1:10-14.
[1033] Ex. 20:1-17.

Forerunner,[1034] the greatest of all Prophets,[1035] who prepared the way for the Messiah.[1036]

While Divine Providence was preparing the Israelites, it also prepared the other nations, whom God did not leave without evidence of[1037] His Wisdom and Almightiness through the Creation, implanting the unwritten Law within their hearts[1038] so that the desire of being free from the burden of sin increased amongst all nations.

When the fullness of time came,[1039] when morality dropped to its lowest level and the political and social conditions had united the known world, the Message of the Gospel was welcomed as the only Anchor of Hope and Salvation. Thus the entire history of mankind led to the Saviour. The Doctrine of Salvation appeared as being central to not only the Christian Faith but also of the whole history of man. God in His All-wisdom and Providence intervened right from the beginning in man's history as an All-wise Steward Who controls His household, founding on earth His Eternal and Heavenly Kingdom.[1040]

Question 176: What was the work of Divine Providence until the time of Moses?

Answer: The manifestation of the Mystery of the Divine Will, which looks for the uplifting of fallen man, was not revealed immediately after the Fall of Adam but was gradually revealed according to the preparation of Divine Providence for the coming of the Saviour. A bright radiance of Salvation was promised by God through the *"Proto-evangelion" ("First Good News"),* the First Promise, which was given to man whereby through the seed of a woman evil would be crushed.[1041] Hence until the medicine of Salvation through the Incarnation of the Word[1042] was granted, God gave many different cures to men through the Creation and nature as well as through the Law and Prophets.[1043]

Until the Flood that came as a punishment of the wickedness of men, there was no other Divine Promise except the *"Proto-evangelion"*

[1034] Matth. 3:1-2. Mark 1:4. Luke 3:3.
[1035] Matth. 11:11. Luke 1:15; 7:28.
[1036] Matth. 3:3. Mark 1:2-3. Luke 3:4-6. John 1:23. Is. 40:3-5.
[1037] Rom. 1:19-21
[1038] Rom. 2:15.
[1039] Gal. 4:4-5.
[1040] Matth. 4:17. Mark 1:14-15.
[1041] Gen. 3:16.
[1042] John 1:14.
[1043] Theodoretus of Cyrus, *Homily* 6, in Migne, *P.G.,* 83, 988.

concerning the Mystery that was hidden in God. God made a Covenant with Noah[1044] who was saved as a new forefather of the human race after Adam and in him one can see the three Offices:

1) **The Royal** in that from him came the new human race.[1045]

2) **The Prophetic**, as being *"a preacher of righteousness"*[1046] and

3) **The High Priest**, as building an Altar to the Lord and offering from all the clean birds and beasts *"a whole burnt-offering."*[1047]

The Covenant with the promise of Noah clearly referred to the desirable Salvation that was renewed by God with Abraham who was called to leave his country and his relatives in order to settle in the unknown land of Canaan.[1048] This Covenant was contracted with Abraham and his descendants as well as with infinite forecasts concerning the entire world. It is the final Covenant of God with the entire human race.

Through Moses who was raised as the mediator between God and the people of Israel,[1049] the Law that was given on Mount Sinai,[1050] was renewed and confirmed without any new additions. The Promises in this Covenant are those that refer to the Messiah and which have been fulfilled in the New Testament.

In three different cases these Promises are repeated:

1)   To Abraham,[1051]

2)   to Isaac[1052] and

3)   to Jacob.[1053]

St Paul refers to this Promise being realised on the descendants of Abraham, *"who by faith"*[1054] are *"blessed with the faithful Abraham"* and referring directly to Christ, since it speaks of *"Abraham's seed,"* which is Christ. Hence St Peter referred to the descendants of the Patriarchs as *"sons*

[1044] Gen. 9:11-17.

[1045] Gen. 9:1.

[1046] 2 Peter 2:5.

[1047] Gen. 8:20.

[1048] Gen. 12:1.

[1049] Ex. 20:19.

[1050] Ex. 20:1-17.

[1051] Gen. 12:3; 17:2-14; 18:18; 22:18.

[1052] Gen. 26:2-4.

[1053] Gen. 28:13-14.

[1054] Heb. 11:4-38.

of the Prophets, and of the Covenant" who were called to believe in Jesus Christ Whom God had *"sent to bless"*[1055] all the nations of the world.

The separation of Abraham from his family and his restriction to living with Isaac and Jacob in isolation consists of an admirable *Economia* of Divine Providence to establish Monotheism in one family and in one generation which under no circumstances would be uprooted, but would remain the heritage of all Israel for all generations. Abraham did not submit to the idolatry of the Canaanites, neither was he tempted when he was told by God to sacrifice his beloved son, Isaac.[1056] Although Abraham lived in a strange and alien land, he did not lose his trust in God but had his faith and hope in the Promise that from his seed the Messiah would be born,[1057] *"who rejoiced to see"* His day *"and he saw it and was glad."*[1058]

And although it seems that for a while Israel in the land of Egypt was deprived of God's Protection, as was proved through their miraculous freedom, God had not abandoned His people but had used a wise pedagogic means of Divine Providence that purposely separated His elect people from those of the idolatrous world who could endanger them through their alienation from the True God.

Question 177: What was the work of Divine Providence until the time of the Messiah?

Answer: Mosaic religion is revealed in history as the Fruit of the special Intervention of God Who was made known to Moses, as previously to the Patriarchs, and elevated him as the mediator of the Old Testament.[1059] As Monotheism was in Israel, likewise the personality of Moses and the Law given by him cannot be understood through rational presuppositions. Only those who believe in Divine Providence could explain these events that prepare the way for the Divine *Economia* in Christ

St Paul being God-inspired, proclaimed that " *before faith came, we were kept under guard by the Law, kept for the faith which would afterward be revealed. Therefore the Law was our tutor to bring us to Christ, that we might be justified by faith,*"[1060] "*by Him everyone who believes is justified*

[1055] Acts 3:25, 26.
[1056] Gen. 22:2, 10-12. Heb. 11:17.
[1057] Heb. 11:8-10.
[1058] John 8:56.
[1059] Kritopoulos, ch. 3, in Karmeris, *The dogmatics,* v. II, p.517.
[1060] Gal. 3:23-24.

from all things from which you could not be justified by the Law of Moses.[1061]

The Law prevented man from committing moral sins, awakening in his conscience the feeling of guilt and the need for a Saviour and Redeemer. The ritual purifications and sacrifices supported the need of redemption from God, particularly on the Day of Sacrifice and Redemption when all the people gathered together and besought Divine Mercy.

When the period of the Judges had passed the hope of the coming of the Messiah. This hope was increased even more when Israel had lost its glory and the following generations looked back, desiring a new King worthy of King David and Who would renew the admirable achievements of His forefather. This opinion was supported also by the Promise given by God to King David through the Prophet Nathan that *"His Throne shall be set up for ever.*[1062]

The majority of Prophets foresaw, prophesied and prepared for the dawning of the new Day of Salvation. They described the personality and the sufferings of the Messiah as well as the glory of His Kingdom.[1063] At the same time they prepared the transmission from the Old to the New Testament. They combined the protests and criticisms against the errors of their people, stressing the magnificence of the Nature of the One and only True God, as well as the spirituality of the Divine Law and Divine Worship. The Prophets also emphasised the assurance of the eternity of God's Covenant with Israel, which would be extended to all nations.

The Prophets proclaimed the Mission and the characteristics of the Messiah as being like that of a Shepherd guarding all nations and[1064] becoming the Light of the nations as well as the Salvation of Israel.[1065] He would offer His Life to redeem all mankind. Through His wounds we would all be healed and through His passions and death the nations would return to God.[1066] The Messiah would appear as the Son of Man and would receive from His Father the Kingdom of the world.[1067] Through His Mission He would fill the world with the True Knowledge of God,[1068]

[1061] Acts 13:39.
[1062] 2 Samuel (2 Kings) 7:13, 16.
[1063] Kefalas, *Christology,* pp. 329-330.
[1064] Jez. 34:11-16, 23, 31.
[1065] Luke 2:32.
[1066] Is. 49-55, 61, 63, 65-66.
[1067] Daniel 7:9-14.
[1068] Is. 11:9.

peace, justice, holiness[1069] and Divine Gifts or *Charismata* by the outpouring of the Holy Spirit.[1070]

The crowning achievement of the Prophets was the preaching of St John the Baptist and Forerunner[1071] who was praised by the Messiah, our Lord and Saviour Jesus Christ, the Son of God, as the greatest of all Prophets.[1072] To St John, God the Father had given the Mission to prepare the way of the Messiah[1073] as it was foretold by the Prophet Isaiah[1074] *"..and all the ends of the earth shall see the Salvation that comes from our God."*[1075] Many believed that St John was the expected Messiah while others believed that he was the Prophet Elijah[1076] whose second coming was foretold by the Prophet Malachi.[1077] St John attracted the piety and trust of the people and was regarded with great respect. His fiery speech invited everyone to repentance and exhorted his generation to be cleansed through Baptism. One thing that attracts our attention is the fact that St John the Baptist and Forerunner, who is the greatest of all the Prophets and the holiest of all men, did not perform even one Miracle.[1078]

Question 178: How were Nations prepared?

Answer: The preparation of the nations[1079] should not be considered as a less important subject although it cannot be regarded on the same level as the preparation of the Old Testament. St Paul speaking of how God prepared the nations, emphasised that *"since the creation of the world His invisible Attributes are clearly seen"*[1080] and that the work of the Law *"is written in their hearts, their conscience also bearing witness."*[1081] With regard to the nations *"although they knew God, they did not glorify Him as God, nor were thankful"*[1082] *"God gave them over to a debased mind, to do those things which are not fitting."*[1083]

[1069] Ezek. 37:26.
[1070] Joel 2:28-32. Acts 2:17-21.
[1071] Matth. 3:1-2. Mark 1:4. Luke 3:3.
[1072] Matth. 11:11. Luke 1:15; 7:28.
[1073] Matth. 3:3. Mark 1:2-3. Luke 3:4-6. John 1:23. Is. 40:3-5.
[1074] Is. 40:3-5. Mal. 3:1.
[1075] Is. 52:10.
[1076] John 1:21
[1077] Mal. 4:5.
[1078] John 3:27-28, 30-31.
[1079] Kefalas, *Christology,* p. 330.
[1080] Rom. 1:20.
[1081] Rom. 2:15.
[1082] Rom. 1:21.
[1083] Rom. 1:28.

Amongst the Greeks, through their philosophers, Divine Providence prepared for the acceptance of the Saviour. Clement the Alexandrian stated that *"from Above was given to men"* to prepare the path for the Royal Teachings of the Truth and *"the Perfection in Christ"*[1084]

The influence on the pagan world by the Israelites can be seen in the cases of Daniel who was highly respected by many Kings of Babylon, the three Youths in the land of Babylon, Esther, Cyrus, the King of Babylon who issued a Decree in favour of the Israelites and Alexander the Great who showed respect towards Jehovah. The many established Synagogues wherein the Old Testament was read and God was worshipped; as well as the translation by the Seventy Scholars (Septuagint - Old Testament Greek, LXX) during the third century (280 BC) in Alexandria of Egypt must be considered as the indirect preparation of the nations in Christ

Question 179: What is the fullness of time?

Answer: This long period of preparation of mankind by Divine Providence ended in *"the fullness of time"*[1085] when the idol worshipping religions lost their credibility and instead of respect and piety they suffered the mockery and scorn of intellectuals. Syncretism replaced the old superstitious traditions at a time when the Oracles had almost closed their doors and their predictions had been silenced. Philosophy had declined, whereas Skepticism and Negativism progressed amongst the intellectuals. Hence the level of morality had fallen to its lowest degree. The worship of the flesh and the hardness of heart caused St Paul to correctly stress that " *it is shameful even to speak of those things which are done by them in secret."*[1086]

The pinnacle of this period of preparation was the political condition of the world. The political and ethnical obstacles which separated the different nations, were dissolved by the conquest of the known world by the Roman Empire. The use of the Greek language from the time of Alexander the Great contributed to the study of the Old Testament and the spreading of the new Message. Furthermore, Syncretism also created the proper religious tolerance, which greatly assisted the servants of the Gospel. Parallel to this was the desire for the Coming of the Messiah Who would be the Salvation of Israel, the restoration of the kingdom of David and the

---

[1084] Clement the Alexandrian, *Stromata,* book I, ch. 5, 7 and 15, in *B,* v. 7, pp. 245, 249 and 267.
[1085] Gal. 4:4.
[1086] Ephes. 5:12.

Light of all Nations. This was the *"fullness of the time"* when God sent His Son into the world.[1087]

Question 180: What is the *Economia* (Dispensation) in Christ?

Answer: The Salvation in our Lord and Saviour Jesus Christ, the Son of God, is the most important and central Christian Doctrine. According to this Doctrine, mankind was unable to find the means of Salvation on his own. Therefore, the Divine Love moved, restored and saved mankind. This occurred at the centre of man's history. Thus the relationship between Divine Providence and Salvation in Christ is obvious. The God of Love in His All-wise Providence intervened right from the beginning in mankind's history and guided everything towards Salvation in Christ[1088]

This Salvation is called Divine *Economia* [Dispensation]. Thus the Old and New Testament are the one unique Work of the same Divine Providence. The term *"Economia"* primarily refers to God the Father Who in His admirable Providence made Moses His faithful servant in all His Household, thereby establishing the old *Economia* while the Bearer of the new *Economia*, Jesus Christ, as His Son, sustains the Faithful in His Kingdom, the Church.

Because the Salvation in Christ gathers the Work of Divine Providence, which leads to *"the fullness of time"* when the Lord will manifest Himself, the term *Economia* therefore reveals two things: the Divine Incarnation of the Word, the Son of God, and the Salvation of man.

CHAPTER THREE
THE INCARNATION OF THE WORD

Question 181: What is Incarnation?

Answer: The *Incarnation,*[1089] *Epiphany* or *Theophany* is the Incarnation of the second Person of the Holy Trinity, the Son and Word of God, Who *"became flesh"* taking up human nature. Hence Divine Nature was united with human nature. This Work was the Work of the three Persons of the Holy Trinity. In the Incarnation, the Father having conceded to send His Son into the world, the Son came down and was Incarnated when the Holy

---

[1087] St John of Damascus, *Exposition. About the divine Economia,* III, 45, in Migne, *P.G.,* 94, 981.
[1088] Cf. Frangopoulos, *Christian Faith,* pp. 121-122.
[1089] Lossky, *Theology,* pp. 90-94.

Spirit Sanctified the Ever-Virgin Mary, giving her the Power to bring forth the Only Begotten Son of God.[1090]

Question 182: Why did the second Person of the Holy Trinity have to be Incarnated instead of one of the other two Divine Persons?

Answer: This subject remains an unapproachable and unsearchable Mystery to the human mind. The main explanation given by the Holy Fathers of the Orthodox Church is that the Word was Incarnated in order that the Hypostatic Attributes of the three Persons of the Holy Trinity would remain unmovable. It was not intended for the Father to become the *"Son of Man,"* rather than the Word Who has the Attribute of being *"the Son"* in the Trinity. Christ's Incarnation is already an Act of Salvation. By assuming our broken humanity into Himself, Christ restores it to its former condition.[1091]

The Word Who had formed man from the dust of the earth and Who is the living Image of the Father, was being shown in order to reform man for adoption, completely raising in him the wounded *"image"* since everything was made through the Son. In Him everything is renewed. He is the Light of the world Who knows the Father. He is the only One Who can manifest the Father to us and bring us into a new Creation.

The condescension of the Son in the Incarnation was not enforced on Him because of some need. Instead it was an absolutely free Act, which is described by Holy Scripture as the *"good pleasure of His Will."*[1092] It reveals not only the infinite Love of God towards fallen man, but the infinite Divine Wisdom and Power that worked out the Supernatural, Mysterious and effective Way through which the Justice and Holiness of God was satisfied and so that man, who was led by death, would rise and be restored into the Blessed Life. God became Man in order to deify humanity who in turn becomes *"..by Grace"* whatever God is *"by Nature."*[1093]

In addition, the union of the Unapproachable Divine Nature with the limited human nature was characterised as a Mystery of Divine Power, which shines upon all the other beneficial results for man. The importance and necessity of the Incarnation of the Word of God is manifested in the infinite Power of Salvation offered by Christ on the Cross - a Sacrifice without which mankind cannot be reconciled to God.

[1090] Plato of Moscow, *Orthodox Teaching,* pp. 112-115. Dositheus, *Confession,* ch. 7, p. 31. Mitsopoulos, *Themata,* p.74 Kefalas, *Catechesis,* pp.71-72
[1091] Ware, *Way,* p. 103.
[1092] Luke 2:14; 10:21. Matth. 11:26. Ephes. 1:5, 9. Phil. 2:13.
[1093] Evdokimov, *Orthodoxia,* p. 127.

Question 183: What is the definition of the Incarnation?

Answer: The Incarnation of the Word of God can be defined as an Act of the Holy Trinity. Through this Act, God the Word *"took up from the beginning our nature, not in that it existed by itself and became a person, but in that it existed in His own hypostasis."* From the Holy Spirit and in the Holy Virgin, God the Word was conceived and His human nature was formed from her blood. On the other hand, the Incarnation can be defined as the permanent and Eternal Union of God the Word with human nature, in which *"the hypostasis of God the Word became hypostasis in the flesh without any change"* whereas His human nature was not absorbed by His Divine Nature and each nature remained unchanged, preserving their own Attributes.[1094] In other words: the Incarnation is the unmixed and undivided union of human nature with Divine Nature in the *Hypostasis* of God the Word in one Person. Thus, because of the real and full union of the two natures in the God-Man Christ, He says: *"I and My Father are one."*[1095] He never said: *"I and the Word are one"* because it is the human revelation of the Word.[1096] The Incarnation, it was said, is an Act of identification and sharing. God saves us by identifying Himself with us, by knowing our human experience from within His own experience.[1097]

Similar terms of the meaning of the Incarnation used by the Holy Fathers are: *"manifestation,"*[1098] *"appearance,"*[1099] *"coming into the world,"*[1100] *"taking the form of a bond-servant,"*[1101] *"Epiphany"* and *"Theophany."*[1102] In the West, the term *"Incarnation"* prevailed according to the use of the terms *"flesh"*[1103] and *"flesh and blood"*[1104] to manifest the whole man. St John the Apostle, Evangelist and Theologian proclaimed *"And the Word became flesh"*[1105] and renounced all those who do not

---

[1094] St John of Damascus, *Exposition, About the difference between union and incarnation*, III, 55, in Migne, *P.G.,* 94, 1024.
[1095] John 10:30.
[1096] Martensen, *Dogmatique*, p. 408.
[1097] Ware, *Way,* p. 104.
[1098] 1 Tim. 3:16. 1 John 1:2, 8.
[1099] 2 Tim. 1:10. Titus 2:11; 3:4.
[1100] Heb. 10:5. Origen, *Against Celsus,* I, 43; II, 38; VI, 78, in Migne, *P.G.,* 11, 741, 860, 1417. St Basil the Great, *To Psalm 29(30),* in Migne, *P.G.,* 29, 305. Tertullian, *De carne Christi,* c. VI, in Migne, *P.G.,* 2, 809.
[1101] Phil. 2:7. St John of Damascus, *Exposition. About the divine Economia,* III, 45, in Migne, *P.G.,* 94, 981. St Athanasius the Great, *About the incarnation of the Word,* § 46, in Migne, *P.G.,* 25, 177.
[1102] St Athanasius the Great, *About the incarnation of the Word,* §§ 1, 46 and 47, in Migne, *P.G.,* 25, 97, 177 and 180. St Gregory of Nazianzus, *Homily* 38, § 3, in Migne, *P.G.,* 36, 313.
[1103] Luke 3:6. John 17:2. Acts 2:17. Joel 2:28. 1 Peter 1:24. 1 John 3:2-3.
[1104] Matth. 16:17. Gal. 1:16. Ephes. 6:12. 1 Corinth. 15:50.
[1105] John 1:14.

confess that *"Jesus Christ came in the flesh."*[1106] The term *"Incarnate"* was incorporated in the Nicene Creed but to avoid any misinterpretation that favoured the heresy of Apollinarius, (according to which Christ did not have a mind or intellectual soul), after the phrase *"And was Incarnate of the Holy Spirit and the Virgin Mary"* the phrase *"and was made man"* was added.

Question 184: Why was the Son incarnated?

Answer: In the Holy Trinity *"there is one Divine Brightness and Action, simple and undivided"* and the Son *"does not have a different Energy from the Father"* *"for in the Trinity there is one Essence, one Goodness, one Power, one Will, one Energy, not three similar to one another, but one and the same Movement of the three Hypostases."*[1107] Consequently, concerning the Incarnation of the Word, although *"under no circumstances the Father and the Holy Spirit participated in the Incarnation of God the Word,"*[1108] that Creation that the Virgin conceived and brought forth, although referring only to the Son, was made possible by all three Persons of the Holy Trinity since their Works are always united and inseparable.

Our Lord and Saviour Jesus Christ, the Son of God, proclaimed that He was sent into the world by the Father.[1109] St Paul referring to the fullness of the time, assured us that *"when the fullness of the time had come, God sent forth His Son, born of a woman, born under the Law."*[1110] St John the Evangelist observed that *"in this the Love of God was manifested towards us, that God has sent His Only Begotten Son into the world, that we might live through Him."*[1111] According to St Justin the Theophorus *"through and in accordance to the Will of God the Word was made man for the human race."* He emphasised also that *"the Father wanted and the Son acted."* The Father did not remain out of the Act and Will of Incarnation because *"everything is common to the Father and the Son."*[1112] Whatever applies to the Father concerning the Incarnation also applies to the Holy Spirit.[1113]

[1106] 1 John 4:3.

[1107] St John of Damascus, *Exposition. About the Holy Trinity,* book I, ch, 8, §§ 13, 14 and book III, ch. 6, in Migne, *P.G.,* 94, 828, 856, 860, 1005. Kefalas, *Christology,* pp. 256-261.

[1108] St Augustine, in migne, *P.L.,* 40, 252.

[1109] John 4:34; 5:23-24, 30, 37; 6:38, 44; 7:29, 33; 8:18; 11:42; 12:44-45, 49; 13:20; 17:8, 21, 23, 24.

[1110] Gal. 4:4.

[1111] 1 John 4:9.

[1112] St Justin, the philosopher and martyr, *1 Apology,* 63, §§ 10 and 16, in *B*, v. 3, p. 196.

[1113] St John of Damascus, *Exposition. About the way of the conception of the Word and His divine incarnation,* book III, ch. 46, §§ 1 and 2, in Migne, *P.G.,* 94, 984 and 985.

One must never forget that being the God-Man, in Christ *"dwells all the fullness of the Godhead bodily."*[1114] In other words, God dwells essentially within Jesus Christ.[1115] The actual Nature of God dwelled in the nature of man, as the soul dwells in the body, so that what was seen was united with the Only Begotten Son's Deity but it was not an Energy of God ruling over the body.[1116] We confess that God is *"one Principle, simple, without synthesis, one Essence, one Deity"* while the Son is *"perfect Hypostasis, inseparable from the Hypostasis of the Father"* as the Holy Spirit *"exists in its own Hypostasis, but is inseparable from the Father and the Son."*[1117] It is obvious that only the Word became man.[1118]

Question 185: Is the Incarnation of the Word an incomprehensible Mystery?

Answer: The Incarnation of Christ is a Mystery that surpasses all human understanding. It is not an enigma, but a Divine Mystery *"which from the beginning of ages has been hidden in God."*[1119] This Mystery is admired even by the Angelic Hosts and amongst men It is *"confidential, unutterable and beyond understanding."*[1120] The Incarnation of the Word is in reality the *"most new of all news, the only* [thing] *new under the sun"*[1121] and even before it occurred it was unknown, not only amongst men but also amongst Angels.

Question 186: Why did the Son became Man and not either of the other two Persons?

Answer: The Word became Man in order that the Hypostatic Attribute of each Person would remain immovable. With regard to the Deity, the Father is essentially *"the Father,"* not born of another father as it is among men, remaining forever Father. Likewise the Son is essentially *"the Son,"* never becoming a father as do the sons of men who, in their adulthood when

---

[1114] Col. 2:9.

[1115] St Isedorus of Pelusion, book IV, Epist. 166, in Migne, *P.G.,* 78, 1256.

[1116] St John Chrysostom, *To Colossians,* Homily 6, § 2, in Montfaucon, v. 11, p. 422.

[1117] Theodoretus of Cyrus, *To Colossians 2:9,* in Migne, *P.G.,* 82, 608-609.

[1118] St John of Damascus, *Exposition. About the Holy Trinity,* book I, ch. 8, in Migne, *P.G.,* 94, 809, 821; Ibid, *Exposition. That all the divine nature in one hypostases was united to all the human nature, and not part,* book III, ch. 50, § 6, in Migne, *P.G.,* 94, 1004-1005.

[1119] Eph. 3:9.

[1120] See decisions of the 3rd Ecumenical Synod.

[1121] St John of Damascus, *Exposition. About the way of the conception of the Word and His divine incarnation,* book III, ch. 46, § 1, in Migne, *P.G.,* 94, 984.

married, become fathers. Thus in respect of the three Persons of the Holy Trinity the Father is forever *"the Father"* while the Son is forever *"the Son"* although in the Incarnation only the Son of God becomes *"the Son of Man."* Thus the Hypostatic Attribute of the Son remains immovable and as Man, the Word remains forever Son. On the other hand, how could the Attribute remain immovable if it was moving and changing, since the Father from Father would have become the Son of Man?[1122]

Only through our Lord and Saviour Jesus Christ, the Son of God, Who came into the world, was it possible for the Image of God to be Restored. For it was impossible for men to accomplish this, although *"they were also made in the Image"* because they had defiled it through the Fall. Neither could this Restoration be accomplished by the Angels *"for they are not in the Image."*[1123] Therefore, He Who *"gave us His Image and we did not keep it, partakes in our weak nature, in order to make us once again partakers of His Divinity."*[1124] Through this Recreation, from deplorable servants, we become sons of God through adoption by Grace. But, who else could free us from such slavery, raising us to the rank of the sons of God besides Him Who is by Nature from the same Essence as the Father - the Son Who is born from all Eternity, assuring us: *"Therefore if the Son makes you free, you shall be free indeed."*[1125]

Since man was corrupted after his creation, *"he was in need of being recalled"* and Restored in order to manifest again *"God the WordWho had made in the beginning from nothingness all things"* and with them man.[1126] *"For in no one else our life should be founded"* except only in the Lord *"through Whom also He made the world,'*[1127] *in order that we might also inherit the Life, which exists only in Him."*[1128]

The Regeneration of mankind was taken up by the Son in order that He, through Whom *"all things were made"* *"and without* [Whom] *nothing was made that was made"*[1129] Who *"breathed upon his face the Breath of Life"*[1130] would restore to the first condition our fallen nature and would recreate whatever He had created. The Son of God as the Eternal Word, is

---

[1122] St Athanasius the Great, *Against Arians,* I, § 21, in Migne, *P.G.,* 26, 55. St John of Damascus, *Exposition. About the descent to Hades,* book IV, ch. 73, § 4, in Migne, *P.G.,* 94, 1108.

[1123] St Athanasius the Great, *About the incarnation of the Word,* § 13, in Migne, *P.G.,* 25, 120.

[1124] St John of Damascus, *Exposition. About the holy and precious mysteries of the Lord,* book IV, ch. 86, § 13, in Migne, *P.G.,* 94, 1137.

[1125] John 8:36.

[1126] St Athanasius the Great, *About the incarnation of the Word,* § 7, in Migne, *P.G.,* 25, 108.

[1127] Heb. 1:2.

[1128] St Athanasius the Great, *Against Arians,* II, 77, in Migne, *P.G.,* 26, 309.

[1129] John 1:3.

[1130] Gen. 2:7.

the presupposition of the Creation, through Whom all things were made; likewise in the Incarnation, in which He is manifested in time as the Christ, He is the Purpose of Creation, Who through all things, as the supreme Head, would unite all things and reconcile everything under His Command.[1131]

The Word of God *"was the true Light which gives Light to every man coming into the world."*[1132] If our Teacher, the Word, did not become Man, it would be impossible to learn those things of God.[1133] *"The Word of God vested Himself with human nature, in order that as Man* [he could] *speak to men, as the Word and Wisdom of God* [he could] *teach men to believe in the one and true God and to live according to the Law, which He gave."*[1134] No one else could make the Father known, except the Word Himself.[1135] It remained dependent only on the Word through Whom *"all things were made"*[1136] and Who is called *"the Wisdom"* by all the Prophets. He is the only *"Teacher of all men, the Advisor of God, Who foreknows everything."*[1137] He *"from the beginning of the world 'at various times and in various ways,'*[1138] *prepared and perfected everything."*[1139] He is the Light, which in the beginning shone in the darkness *"and the darkness did not comprehend it."*[1140]

All the seeds of Divine Truth, which are scattered throughout the entire world by the Hand of the Son of God, were spread in the souls of men. The Word had to appear in the restricted and approachable form of Man to reveal God Whose unapproachable Divine Splendour is impossible for mortal man to see. In Christ, the Incarnated Word of God, man could understand the fullness of the Deity within the limited ability of human nature and to see the Attributes of the Divine Nature, although not in their Infinite Power but according to man's capability. Thus in the Incarnated Christ, instead of the All-presence of God, we meet the Living, Acting and real Presence of God, which enabled Christ to proclaim: *"He Who has seen Me has seen the Father."*[1141] Instead of the Divine All-knowing God, we have in our midst the Wisdom of the God-Man Who explains the Mysteries of the Heavenly Kingdom to men who ignore them. The Creative

---

[1131] Martensen, *Dogmatique,* p. 407.
[1132] John 1:9.
[1133] St Irenaeus, *Heresies,* book V, ch. 1, § 1, in Migne, *P.G.,* 7, 1120. Cf. Ibid, in Hadjephraimides, p. 362.
[1134] Gennadius, in Karmeris, *The dogmatics,* v. I, p. 366.
[1135] John 14:6-7.
[1136] John 1:3
[1137] Clement the Alexandrian, VI, 7, in **B**, v. 8, p. 199.
[1138] Cf. Heb. 1:1.
[1139] Martensen, *Dogmatique,* pp. 368, 398 and 409.
[1140] John 1:5.
[1141] John 14:9. 12:45.

Almightiness becomes in Him the Supreme Power, which rules all the energies of nature and perfects them. The All-powerful Holy Love can proclaim that: *"All Authority has been given to Me in Heaven and on earth."*[1142] For all the Powers in Heaven and on earth, all the Powers of nature and man's history are in the Lord and Saviour Jesus Christ and cooperate with Him in the preparation of the Heavenly Kingdom, the Church of which He is the Head.[1143]

Question 187: What is the nature of the Incarnation?

Answer: The Incarnation of the Word of God is a free Act, an expression of Divine Pleasure, which did not occur because God had any need of it or because it was forced upon Him. It is the Divine Condescension that manifests the Divine Attributes of God's Goodness, Wisdom and Power. On the contrary, the Incarnation was necessary for humanity's sake because if Divine Justice demanded a ransom, man would have been unable to pay it and thus it would have been impossible for him to be Saved. The Incarnation was not forced as a necessity upon the Deity but as the Creation was a free Act of God's Goodness, Power and Wisdom, which can be characterised as *"fitting for God"* likewise the Incarnation was a free Act *"fitting for God."* Without any doubt it was an excellent Manifestation of the Divine Perfections. In other words, that of God's Goodness, Wisdom and Power, which responded to the needs and desires of human nature. Thus it appears as the most *"fitting for God."*

The fact that the Incarnation was a free Act of God is characterised by Holy Scripture as being His *"good Pleasure"* or *"Goodwill."* At the Birth of Christ in Bethlehem, the Angels sang: *"Glory to God in the Highest, and on earth peace, Goodwill towards men"*[1144] confirming that the Peace offered by our Saviour derives from the Goodwill of God.[1145] St Paul proclaimed the Revelation of the Mystery of the Divine *Economia* as being fulfilled by God because of His *"Goodwill," "for by Grace you have been Saved through Faith, and that not of yourselves; it is the Gift of God."*[1146]

According to the above, God conceived the Plan of our Salvation and realised it not because of any need. God showed Mercy to mankind because He wants and loves His Creation. Also the Will of God concerning the Salvation of man was a free Act. God had the Power to save man without

---

[1142] Matth. 28:18; 11:27.
[1143] Ephes. 5:23.
[1144] Luke 2:14.
[1145] Origen, *To Luke 2:14,* Homily 13.
[1146] Ephes. 2:8.

sending His Only Begotten Son into the world, for nothing is impossible for God. He could have Commanded and everything would have been restored.[1147] God the Word became Man, not because He could not have Saved man otherwise, but because He considered this way to be the most perfect.[1148]

Question 188: What is the glorification of Divine Attributes?

Answer: St Gregory of Nyssa commented on the manifestation of the Divine Attributes revealed at the Incarnation of the Word of God as follows: "*It has revealed the Goodness, the Wisdom, the Justice, the Power, the Immortality; everything was shown because of our Economia.*" And the Goodness is revealed "*in that God wanted*" to Save the lost. "*The Wisdom and the Justice were shown in the way of our Salvation*" while the Power was proved "*in the making*" of the Infinite Word "*in the image of man according to our humble natureand being made He worked*" the Salvation of men.[1149]

Concerning the Goodness, Kindness and Love of God, one must remember the words of St Paul: "*God demonstrates His own Love towards us, in that while we were still sinners, Christ died for us*"[1150] and "*when we were still without strength, in due time Christ died for the ungodly.*"[1151] St John remarked on this Love of God by pointing out that "*He first Loved us.*"[1152] "*In this the Love of God was manifested toward us, that God has sent His Only begotten Son into the world, that we might live through Him. In this is Love, not that we loved God, but that He Loved us and sent His Son to be the Propitiation for our sins.*"[1153] "*For God so Loved the world that He gave His Only Begotten Son, that whoever believes in Him should not perish but have Everlasting Life. For God did not send His Son into the world to condemn the world, but that the world through Him might be Saved.*"[1154] In addition, St Paul proclaimed once again that the Son of God

---

[1147] St Athanasius the Great, *About the incarnation of the Word*, § 6, in Migne, *P.G.*, 25, 105-108. Ibid, *Against Arians*, II, § 68, in Migne, *P.G.*, 26, 292. St Gregory of Nazianzus, *Homily* 19, § 13, in Migne, *P.G.*, 35, 1060. *Epist.* 101, in Migne, *P.G.*, 37, 183. Theodoretus of Cyrus, *Homily* IV, in Migne, *P.G.*, 83, (?).

[1148] Kritopoulods, ch. III, in Karmeris, *The dogmatics,* v. II, p. 518.

[1149] St Gregory of Nyssa, *Catechesis*, § 24, in Migne, *P.G.*, 45, 64.

[1150] Rom. 5:8.

[1151] Rom. 5:6.

[1152] 1 John 4:19.

[1153] 1 John 4:9-10.

[1154] John 3:16-17.

"humbled Himself and became obedient to the point of death, even the death of the cross."[1155]

Divine Wisdom is apparent in that God *"found the most beautiful solution for the poor"* man.[1156] For after the Fall of man, one of the following consequences had to occur: *"either God* [had] *to make everyone truthful"* by surrendering them to death according to the warning that accompanied the Law, *"or* [by] *showing love towards man"* to paralyze *"the Decision"* and to prove it inoperative by not realising the threat.[1157] *"But see God's Wisdom. For He kept the Truth of the decision and acted the Love towards man. Christ took upon the Cross the sins"* and suffered the consequences of man's Offence, in order that he might be Saved.[1158] *"Christ took up the punishments of the first Offence, in order to free us from the Curse." "He takes up the Way of our Restoration as Good and Wise."*[1159] God's Wisdom found the way to satisfy His Divine Justice and simultaneously to Save Fallen man.

The Incarnation of God the Word was an admirable and Supernatural Act of God. The Truth is that healthy human nature, born from the Ever Blessed Virgin Mary, the Theotokos, was able to be united with Divine Nature because *"neither the logic, or the intellect, or any other such thing of human nature is opposite to virtue"* nor did it present any obstacles that prevented God from touching *"human nature"* uncorrupted by sin. God the Word at the Incarnation did not become a rock or a plant or some kind of irrational being, but *"flesh"*- a man, a rational and moral being.[1160]

Man was not only made in the Image of God but was also created to be united with God, becoming His Temple, which is only achieved in the union of the two natures. The two special Attributes of Self-conscience and Freedom, which are found perfectly in God, are also found in man and made human nature receptive to the Divine Nature, for Divine Power is natural for the performance of Wonders. Nevertheless, for the unapproachable God to descend to the humble creature, proves unlimited Power.

[1155] Phil. 2:7-8.

[1156] St John of Damascus, *Exposition. About the way of the conception of the Word and His divine incarnation,* III, 46, 1, in Migne, *P.G.,* 94, 984.

[1157] St Cyril of Jerusalem, *Catechesis,* XIII, § 33, in Migne, *P.G.,* 33, 813.

[1158] St John of Damascus, *About the two wills,* 44, in Migne, *P.G.,* 94, 185.

[1159] St Gregory of Nyssa, *Catechesis,* ch. 22, in Migne, *P.G.,* 45, 60.

[1160] St Gregory of Nyssa, *Catechesis,* ch. 15 and 24, in Migne, *P.G.,* 45, 49 and 64. St Basil the Great, *To Psalm* 44, § 5, in Migne, *P.G.,* 29, 400; *About the Holy Spirit,* ch. 8, in Migne, *P.G.,* 32, 100.

Question 189: Was the Incarnation necessary?

Answer: From the human point of view the Incarnation was necessary, especially if Divine Justice demanded satisfaction from sinful man for the Offence. It is true that God could have only Commanded in order for man to be instantly restored and for Him not to have been Incarnated in order to remove the Curse. But in that case, if God had Commanded the Curse to be expunged, for it was certainly possible for Him to do so, then His Power would have been manifest, but mankind would have become the same as Adam before the Offence, receiving Grace from without and not united within the body.[1161] As a consequence, man would face the danger of falling again, but even into a condition far worse than before, having already experienced the first Fall. Thus, it would be necessary once again for God to loosen the Curse and no real progress would have been achieved.

The Holy Fathers of the Orthodox Church proclaimed that it was necessary for the Incarnate Word to die so as to Save mankind by paying a ransom equal in value to the price of all men. For what help could man have offered to his fellow men, since all needed the same Help? How could the Curse be loosened since everyone was held under the same bondage and all needed a Saviour? The Saviour had to be absolutely sinless and unrestricted by death. Which man had the ability to offer a Ransom to God even for his own sins? We were all enslaved and we all needed a Ransom to be paid for our freedom. Consequently none of us could have saved ourselves so how then was it possible to save others?

Not even the Angels could have saved mankind, because they receive their holiness from their Communion with the Holy Spirit. How then would it have been possible to free men from all guilt and to bestow Sanctification upon them since they are not the Source of Holiness? How could it be possible for a creature to loosen the Commandment of God and to forgive sins, since this is the Work of God alone?[1162]

[1161] St Athanasius the Great, *Against Arians,* II, § 68, in Migne, *P.G.,* 26, 292.
[1162] St Basil the Great, *To Psalm* 48 (49), §§ 3 and 4, in Migne, *P.G.,* 29, 440 and 441. St Athanasius the Great, *Against Arians,* II, § 69, in Migne, *P.G.,* 26, 289. St John of Damascus, *Exposition. About the divine economia,* book III, ch. 45, § 1, in Migne, *P.G.,* 94, 981.

CHAPTER FOUR
THE SAVIOUR
THE DIVINITY OF JESUS CHRIST

Question 190: What do we mean when we speak about the Divinity of Christ?

Answer: The fundamental Doctrine concerning the whole work of Salvation, which Christ achieved for man, is that He is God Incarnated.[1163] The Lord Jesus Christ was not only simply a perfect Man Who came to Save men, but the Son of God, perfect God and the Only Begotten Son of God Who was born before all Eternity from the Father.[1164] As God He surpasses all creatures in Heaven and on earth[1165] and His Appearance on earth consists of the greatest of all Miracles in human history. As the Messiah, Jesus Christ, the Son of David[1166] and Son of Man,[1167] is the preeminently anointed Prophet,[1168] King and High Priest[1169] Who was spoken of in the Old Testament by all the Prophets.[1170]

When God the Father addresses the Son, He calls Him "*Son*"[1171] being born from Him "*before the rising star*" and to Whom He will give as heritage all the nations.[1172] He invites Him to sit on His Right Hand[1173] until He makes His enemies His "*footstool.*"[1174] The Messiah, being the Eternal High Priest[1175] according to the Prophets, having the Priesthood without successor,[1176] appears to be Anointed by God Himself,[1177] being called "*God*" by King David and Whose Name "*.is called the Messenger of Great*

[1163] Cf. Frangopoulos, *Christian Faith*, pp. 125-126. Mitsopoulos, *Themata*, p. 75.

[1164] Acts 4:12; 13:23. Ephes. 5:23. Phil. 3:20. 1 Tim. 1:1; 2:3; 4:10. Tit. 1:3, 4; 2:10; 3:4, 6. 2 Peter 1:1, 11; 2:20; 3:18. 1 John 4:14. Jude 25.

[1165] Ephes. 1:21.

[1166] Matth. 12:23; 15:22; 20:30; 21:9. Mark 10:47, 48; 12:35. Luke 18:38; 20:41. Kefalas, *Christology,* pp. 292-294.

[1167] Matth. 13:37; 16:13, 27, 28; 17:9, 12, 22; 18:11; 19:28; 20:18, 28; 24:30, 44; 25:13, 31; 26:2, 24. Mark 2:10, 28; 8:31, 38; 9:9, 12; 10:33, 45; 13:26; 14:21, 41. Luke 5:24; 6:5, 22; 7:34; 9:22, 26, 44, 56, 58; 12:8, 10, 40; 19:10; 21:27, 36; 22:22, 48, 69; 24:7. John 1:52; 3:13, 14, 16; 4:27; 6:27, 62; 8:28; 12:23, 34.

[1168] Deut. 18:15, 18-19. Matth. 16:16. Mark 8:29. Luke 4:18.

[1169] Heb. 5:6, 10; 7:16-17, 21; 9:11. Psalm 109(110):4.

[1170] Deut. 18:15-22. Is. 42:1-4. Acts 3:22-24.

[1171] Heb. 5:5. Psalm 2:7

[1172] Psalm 2:8.

[1173] Mark 16:19.

[1174] Matth. 22:44. Psalm 109(110):1.

[1175] Heb. 2:17; 3:1

[1176] Heb. 4:14-15; 5:6, 10; 6:20; 7:17, 21. Psalm 109(110):4.

[1177] Is. 61:1-3.

Counsel" and "*His Peace* will have *no end;*"[1178] Who will be the Son of the Virgin as foreseen by the Prophet Isaiah who said: "*Behold, a virgin shall conceive in the womb, and shall bring forth a son, and thou shall call His Name Emmanuel.*"[1179] But generally all the Prophets emphasized the Messiah's Divine descent and important Work of the Salvation of all men, which He fulfilled as the Lord, the Angel of the New Testament and the Son of Man.

In the New Testament Jesus Christ is witnessed by the Father as His beloved Son,[1180] Who is above Moses and Elijah and all the Prophets[1181] and even above all the Angelic Hosts[1182] and Who has the Power to forgive sins[1183] and which Authority He passed down to His Holy Disciples.[1184] Similarly the Father assures us that the Son is not only a son, but the Son of God Who knows the Father and Who has only been known by the Father.[1185] He announced that He would come again, sitting on the Right Hand of God the Father[1186] and He gave instructions that all His Disciples were to be baptised[1187] "*in the Name of the Father and of the Son and of the Holy Spirit.*"[1188] He is the "*Only Begotten Son Who is in the Bosom of Father*"[1189] Who "*came down from Heaven to the earth*" although at the same time being in Heaven.[1190] Furthermore, "*before Abraham was born*" He was[1191] and He, together with the Father is one.[1192] St John the Apostle, Evangelist and Theologian stated, before the world was created, He existed together with the Father and is Co-eternal[1193] as the A and Ω (*Alpha* and *Omega*), "*the Beginning and the End*" of all.[1194]

St Paul characterised Christ as "*the God of all*"[1195] and as the "*First born*"[1196] Who was born of the Father before all Creation. Being in the

---

[1178] Is. 9:6, 7.
[1179] Is. 7:14.
[1180] Matth. 3:17; 12:18. Mark 1:11. Luke 3:22; 9:35. Ephes. 1:6.
[1181] Matth. 13:16-17.
[1182] Ephes. 1:21. Phil. 2:9-11.
[1183] Matth. 9:6. Mark 2:10.
[1184] Matth. 16:19; 18:18. John 20:22-23.
[1185] Matth. 11:27. John 10:15.
[1186] Matth. 25:31; 26:64. Mark 13:26. Acts 1:11; 7:55-56. Dan. 7:14.
[1187] Mark 16:16. Luke 24:47.
[1188] Matth. 28:19.
[1189] John 1:18.
[1190] John 3:13
[1191] John 8:58.
[1192] John 10:30.
[1193] John 1:1-2.
[1194] Rev. 1:8, 11, 17; 21:6; 22:13.
[1195] Rom. 9:5.
[1196] Rom. 8:29. Col. 1:15, 18. Rev. 1:5.

Form of God, the Son emptied Himself in order to take the form of a bondservant,[1197] thereby redeeming the Church with His own Blood,[1198] being the Blood of God[1199] through Whom all things were made.[1200] Even the Angels in the Heavenly Places and all things are sustained in Him. Christ is the Brightness of the Glory and the Character of the Hypostasis of the Father.[1201]

The Truth concerning Jesus Christ as the Only Begotten Son of God is based on His own Conscience, which was expressed by His own testimony[1202] and proclaimed by all the God-inspired authors of the New Testament. This Truth was inherited by the Orthodox Church since the first century and is continuously proclaimed by the Apostolic Fathers and all the Holy Fathers and Ecclesiastic Scholars to this very day.

One understands the importance and clarity of the Teachings of the Apostolic Fathers concerning Christ, when one considers that St Clement of Rome used the name *"Lord"* irrespective of whether referring to Christ or God the Father, calling Christ *"the Son and Brightness of the Majesty"* of God.

Question 191: Who is the Messiah?

Answer: The Person Who made the Promises to Abraham and the nation is referred to in Holy Scripture as *"Messiah"* or *"the Christ,"*[1203] being the most Anointed Prophet, High Priest and King[1204] Who shepherds Israel[1205] and Who contains within His Person the threefold Offices. These Offices are found separately in different people of the Old Testament who were anointed by special Blessed Oil and who were called *"the anointed of the Lord."*[1206] The Lord, however, was not anointed with material ointment made by the hands of men.[1207] He was anointed by God through the Holy Spirit Who was poured upon Him.[1208] He was anointed *"not as the rest of the high menand not by partial Anointment, as in the case of the spiritual*

[1197] Phil. 2:6-8.
[1198] Rom. 3:25; 5:9. Gal. 3:13; 4:5. Ephes. 1:7; 2:13. Col. 1:14, 20. Heb. 9:12, 14; 10:19-20. 1 Peter 1:19. 1 John 1:7. Rev. 1:5; 5:9; 7:14; 12:11.
[1199] Acts 20:28
[1200] John 1:3.
[1201] Heb. 1:3.
[1202] Matth. 26:64. John 4:26; 5:18; 9:35; 10:36.
[1203] John 1:41. Kefalas, *Christology*, pp. 294-298.
[1204] Zach. 9:9. Heb. 1:9.
[1205] Ez. 34:23-24. Is. 40:11. Mich. 5:4.
[1206] Deut. 18:15, 18. Psalm 109(110):4 and Psalms 2, 44(45), 109(110).
[1207] St Ecumenius, *To Hebrews*, in Migne, *P.G.*, 119, 288.
[1208] Psalm 2:2. Acts 4:26-27. Heb. 1:9.

men."[1209] Thus "*under the Name Christ is implied the One Who anoints and Who has been Anointed and the Ointment through which He was Anointed. And the Father Anoints, the Son is Anointed in the Holy Spirit, which is the Ointment.*"[1210]

In the Old Testament the Messiah appears to be the Son of God. This term is also referred to the Angels, the Just, the whole of Israel, the Kings and Judges. However, with regard to the Messiah Who is mentioned in the second Psalm,[1211] firstly His victory is described over the kings and rulers of the earth who had gathered "*against the Lord and against His Anointed*" and secondly, it refers to Him saying: "*Thou art My Son, today I have Begotten Thee.*"[1212] Thus the Messiah is presented not only as an invincible King Whose Kingdom is extended throughout the world but also as the Son of God Who is born of the Father. Under the scrutiny of the New Testament one sees in this verse the Son of God Who is born of the Father and Who has inherited "*the Name which is above every name, that at the name of Jesus every knee should bow, of those in Heaven, and of those on earth, and of those under the earth, and that every tongue should confess that Jesus Christ is Lord, to the Glory of God the Father.*"[1213] Furthermore, in Psalm 109(110) the Messiah is presented as being superior to King David who acknowledges Him as his "*Lord*" Who is vested with an Office that surpasses this world and Who is manifested by the invitation of God: "*Sit at My Right Hand, until I make Thine enemies Thy footstool*"[1214] and Who has Eternal Priesthood "*according to the Order of Melchizedek.*"[1215]

The mysterious figure of Melchizedek represents an entirely different kind of Priesthood. He appears in Genesis long before the establishment of the Levitical Priesthood. He is given no genealogy and nothing is said of his death. He received tithes from Abraham, implying his superiority to Abraham – and by extension - superiority to Abraham's descendants, the Levites as well. Melchizedek is not only a Priest but a King too. In this dual Office he is able to reconcile the Justice of God (the work of a King) with His Mercy (the work of a Priest). His name means "*King of Righteousness*" while his title "*King of Salem*" means "*King of Peace.*" He may be a *Theophany* – a pre-Incarnation Appearance of Christ. At the very least he is a type of Christ, as the author of the Hebrews explains in detail.

[1209] Theophylactus of Bulgaria, *To Hebrews,* in Migne, *P.G.,* 125, 200.
[1210] St Irenaeus, *Heresies,* book III, ch. 18, § 3, in Migne, *P.G.,* 7, 934.
[1211] Psalm 2:2.
[1212] Psalm 2:7.
[1213] Phil. 2:9-11. Matth. 22:43, 45. Mark 12:35, 37. Luke 20:44.
[1214] Psalm 109(110):1. Matth. 22:44. Mark 12:36. Luke 21:42-43.
[1215] Psalm 109(110):4. Heb. 5:6, 10.

The Priesthood of Melchizedek was without earthly genealogy, so is Christ by virtue of His virginal Birth. He is God Incarnate, Immortal and Sinless, therefore His Priesthood is able to transform humanity. The power given at Ordination is strong and effective. The power of Christ's Priesthood is perfect and draws us near to God. His Sacrifice is offered once for all. Since Christ is Immortal, the Priesthood of Melchizedek needs only one Eternal Priest. Jesus Christ is more than a mere man, He is the Son of God, the God-Man. All the Prophesies find their harmonious union in the God-Man, Jesus Christ, the Son of God and Saviour of all mankind.[1216]

Question 192: What are the teachings of the New Testament concerning the Divinity of Jesus Christ?

Answer: We distinguish the Testimonies of the New Testament concerning the Divinity of our Lord and Saviour Jesus Christ, the Son of God, into three categories:

  a) those of the Synoptics,
  b) those of St John the Apostle, Evangelist and Theologian and
  c) those of the rest of the Holy Apostles.[1217]

In the Synoptic Gospels, the Testimony of God the Father first appears during the Baptism of Christ by St John the Forerunner and Baptist, according to which our Lord Jesus is His *"Beloved Son, in Whom I Am well pleased."*[1218] This Testimony is repeated at the Transfiguration of our Lord on Mount Tabor[1219] where His superiority was evident when the two Prophets, Moses and Elijah, appeared as His honouring companions,[1220] but not having the same brightness as Him nor being witnessed to by the Father. He testified that His Teachings and Mission are superior to those of Solomon and Jonah.[1221] He also presented the Testimony of the Prophet and King David who spoke as a humble servant of the Supreme Lord by saying: *"The Lord said to my Lord."*[1222] Christ is superior even to the Angels who ignore His Second Coming[1223] and with regard to the General Judgement,

---

[1216] Kefalas, *Christology*, pp. 311-314, 326-329.
[1217] Ibid, *Catechesis*, pp. 258. Fragkopoulos, *Christian Faith*, pp. 126-127. Mitsopoulos, *Themata* p.76
[1218] Matth. 3:17. Mark 1:11. Luke 3:22.
[1219] Matth. 17:5. Mark 9:7. Luke 9:35.
[1220] Matth. 17:3. Mark 9:4. Luke 9:30.
[1221] Matth. 12:41-42. Luke. 11:31-32. Jonah 3:5.
[1222] Psalm 109(110):1.
[1223] Matth. 24:36. Mark 13:32. Acts 1:7. Zach. 14:7.

He explained that they would be sent as His servants to gather the Just from the four corners of the earth.[1224]

"*Being in the form of God, He did not consider it robbery to be equal with God.*"[1225] Therefore Christ sent "*Prophets, wise men, scribes*" and "*Apostles,*"[1226] promising to give them the necessary " *mouth and wisdom*"[1227] just as God had promised Moses that He would speak through the mouth of Aaron.[1228] As God, He appears to be the Law-giver Who fulfils the Law[1229] and proclaims to be the Master of the Law concerning the Sabbath[1230] as well as divorce.[1231] As the Heavenly Father made a Covenant with Abraham and his descendants, likewise Christ offerred His Blood as the Blood of the New Covenant[1232] and promised His Disciples that He would "*bestow upon them a Kingdom, just as His Father bestowed one upon Him, that they may eat and drink at His Table in His Kingdom, and sit on thrones judging the twelve Tribes of Israel.*"[1233]

Jesus Christ, as Lord and God, demands that the faith of His Disciples in Him must be the same as their faith in God, steadfast and faithful until the end, even if they have to offer their lives for His Name's sake.[1234] He also demands that the love of His faithful for Him must be greater than that of their most beloved ones.[1235] Furthermore, all those who confess Him before men, will also be confessed by Him before His Father and those who deny Him in this life, will be denied by Him before His Father.[1236]

Jesus Christ claimed the Authority of the forgiveness of sins, an Authority that belongs exclusively to God, [1237] and transmitted it to His Holy Apostles and Disciples.[1238]

Since Jesus Christ proclaims to be the new Law-giver equal to the Heavenly Father and has with the Authority to forgive sins, it is natural for Him to claim the Office of the Supreme Judge and to foretell that He will return with all His Glory to Judge the world and to reward or punish each

---

[1224] Matth. 13:49; 16:27; 24:31; 25:31. Mark 8:38; 13:32. Luke 9:26. Dan. 7:10.
[1225] Phil. 2:6.
[1226] Matth. 23:34. Luke 11:49.
[1227] Luke 21:15.
[1228] Ex. 4:10-17.
[1229] Matth. 5:17.
[1230] Matth. 12:8.
[1231] Matth. 5:32.
[1232] Matth. 26:28. Mark 14:24. Luke 22:20.
[1233] Luke 22:30.
[1234] Matth. 10:22. Mark 13:13. Luke 21:17.
[1235] Matth. 10:37. Luke 14:26.
[1236] Matth. 10:32-33. Luke 12:8-9.
[1237] Matth. 9:2, 6. Mark 2:10. Luke 5:20, 24; 7:47-49.
[1238] Matth. 16:19; 18:18. John 20:22-23.

man according to their deeds.[1239] For "*all Authority has been given to Me in Heaven and on earth.*"[1240]

In the texts of the Synoptic Gospels one finds verses in which the Lord reveals why He believes that He is the Son of God. When speaking of God the Father, our Lord Jesus always distinguishes His relationship as the Son of God by Nature from that of the rest of men. In the former, He always uses the term "***My** Father*," whereas in the latter He uses the term "***your** Father*." He also accepts the confession of faith by St Peter that was expressed at Caesarea Philippi: "*Thou art the Christ, the Son of the Living God.*"[1241] Through this confession Christ is placed in a superior position to that of St John the Baptist, St Elijah, St Jeremiah and all the Prophets. Consequently He is confessed as the Son of God, not in a moral meaning as the Prophets and all the Just were called. Our Lord Jesus also proclaimed that: "*All things have been delivered to Me by My Father. Nor does anyone know the Father except the Son, and the One to Whom the Son Wills to reveal Him.*"[1242] In this verse everything that the Father has delivered to the Son[1243] reveals the equality between the Father and the Son. It also reveals that He (the Son) is beyond any intellectual conception as is the Father Who is known only by the Son. The Infinite Father is known only by Christ, being His Son. No other creature can know the Son besides the Father. This Teaching is expressed in the Parable of the Wicked Vinedressers[1244] according to which Christ is the "*one Son, the Beloved*" Who is recognised as being "*the Heir*" and Who is killed by the Jews.

When Judged by the High Priests Annas and Caiaphas, Christ was asked and gave witness about Himself.[1245] If Christ is not by Nature and Essence the Son of God, was it possible for Him to declare that He would be "*sitting at the Right Hand of the Power, and coming on the clouds of Heaven?*" The reaction caused by His declaration and the denunciation that followed because they perceived Him to be a self-condemned blasphemer, proves that the Archpriests and members of the High Court understood the term "*Son of God*" according to the special, apocalyptic meaning. The Lord, unwilling to explain further, confirmed through His silence that they had very correctly understood the meaning of His Testimony.

[1239] Matth. 25:31-46. John 5:22, 30; 8:16, 26; 12:47-48. Daniel 12:2-3. Ez. 37:1-14.
[1240] Matth. 28:18. Kefalas, *Christology,* pp. 48-49.
[1241] Matth. 16:16.
[1242] Matth. 11:27.
[1243] John 16:15.
[1244] Matth. 21:33-46. Mark 12:1-9. Luke 20:9-19.
[1245] Matth. 26:57-68. Mark 14:53-65. Luke 22:54, 63-65. John 18:13-24.

After Christ's Resurrection He gave instructions to His Apostles and Disciples to *"go and make disciples of all the nations, baptising them in the Name of the Father and of the Son and of the Holy Spirit"*[1246] assuring them that *"thus it was written, and thus it was necessary for the Christ to suffer and to Rise from the dead on the third day."*[1247]

Question 193: What is the testimony of St John the Apostle and Evangelist?

Answer: The fourth Gospel was *"written that you may believe that Jesus is the Christ, the Son of God, and that believing you may have Life in His Name."*[1248] St John the Apostle and Evangelist established this belief by hearing the Lord's Teachings, witnessing Christ's innumerable Miracles, Divine Life and His Personal Testimonies.[1249] St John firmly believed that our Lord Jesus is the Eternal Word of God Who existed from the beginning with the Father, and that *"the Word was God"*[1250] through Whom *"all things were made"*[1251] Who *"was the True Light which gives Light to every man coming into the world."*[1252] When the time came, *"the Word became flesh"* and was Incarnated thereby manifesting *"His Glory, the Glory as of the Only Begotten of the Father, full of Grace and Truth"*[1253] as he stressed at the beginning of his Gospel, in order to convince his readers to believe that our Lord Jesus is the Christ, *"the Only Begotten Son Who is in the Bosom of the Father."*[1254]

In the Gospel of St John Christ refers more often to God as His Father and calls Himself *"Son of God."* The quotations are innumerable. To identify Himself Christ used the terms *"the Son of God"* stating *"that whoever believes in Him should not perish but have Everlasting Life."*[1255] If one is convinced, that Jesus is the Lord, the Son of God, then *"the Son will make him free, he shall be free indeed"*[1256].

The Lord uses the unique title of *"the Son"* that applies specifically to Him and to no other creature. His Sonship differs from that of mankind as

---

[1246] Matth. 28:19.
[1247] Luke 24:46.
[1248] John 20:31.
[1249] 1 John 1:1-3.
[1250] John 1:1.
[1251] John 1:3.
[1252] John 1:9.
[1253] John 1:14.
[1254] John 1:18.
[1255] John 3:16.
[1256] John 8:36.

evident from His words to St Mary Magdalene following His Resurrection: *"Do not cling to Me, for I have not yet ascended to **My Father**; but go to My brethren and say to them, 'I Am ascending to **My Father** and **your Father**, and to **My God** and **your God**.*"[1257] Furthermore, the Son has the Father by Nature and His Nature is exactly the same as that of the Divine Essence long since before He was Incarnated, having existed with the Father before all time.

God the Father bears witness to Him and has sent Him[1258] so *"that of all He has given Him, He should lose nothing, but should raise it up at the Last Day."*[1259] Coming *"from Above"* He *"is above all"*[1260] and grants to all who believe in Him *"Everlasting Life."*[1261] He is the *"Bread of Life,"*[1262] and *"If anyone eats of this Bread, he will live forever; and the Bread that He shall give is His Flesh, which He shall give for the Life of the world."*[1263] He came from the Father, being Loved by the Father *"before the foundation of the world."*[1264] Therefore, *"all should honour the Son just as they honour the Father. He who does not honour the Son does not honour the Father Who sent Him."*[1265]

When St John the Apostle and Evangelist, emphasised the eternal pre-existence of the Incarnated Word by writing: *"In the beginning was the Word, and the Word was with God, and the Word was God"*[1266] he based this testimony upon the assurance of the Lord Jesus Christ Who proclaimed that *"before Abraham was, I Am."*[1267] In addition to this, the proclamation that *"the Word was God"* is based upon the Testimonies through which Christ declared His equality with the Father.[1268] According to the Gospel of St John Christ stated: *"My Father is greater than I."*[1269] However, this refers to His human nature.

Clarifying the equality between Himself and His Father, Jesus Christ proclaimed: *"I and the Father are One."*[1270] *"The 'One' declares the sameness of their Divine Essence (Homoousion), while the verb 'are'*

[1257] John 20:17.
[1258] John 5:37.
[1259] John 6:39.
[1260] John 3:31.
[1261] John 3:36; 6:47.
[1262] John 6:48.
[1263] John 6:51.
[1264] John 17:24.
[1265] John 5:23.
[1266] John 1:1.
[1267] John 8:58.
[1268] John 5:18, 23, 26.
[1269] John 14:28.
[1270] John 10:30.

manifests the two Persons of the Trinity."[1271]   In His prayer before His Passions, Christ did not hesitate to declare that: *"I Am in the Father and the Father in Me"*[1272] and *"he who has seen Me has seen the Father."*[1273]   For this reason He prayed *"that they may be one as We are One"*[1274] so that the voluntary union of the Disciples becomes *"the image of the natural Union that applies to the Father and the Son."*[1275]

Jesus Christ also proclaimed to have the Authority to forgive the sins of men, which He passed down to His Disciples after His Glorious Resurrection.[1276] He demands faith in Him as one has in God the Father.[1277] He assured us that *"he who believes in Him has Everlasting Life"*[1278] and that He is *"the Light of the world"*[1279] *"the Way, the Truth and the Life."*[1280] Exalting His relationship with His Father, He promised to all who love Him and keep His Commandments that the Father *"will give them [another] Helper, that He may abide with [them] forever"*[1281] and *"if anyone loves Me, he will keep My Word; and My Father will love him, and We will come to him and make Our home with him."*[1282]

This Testimony of the fourth Evangelist is supported in the other works of St John: his three Catholic Epistles and the Book of Revelation. The Testimony of the latter is important not only because it includes the Evangelist's belief but it also contains the belief of the seven Churches of Asia Minor, which were under his spiritual guidance.

According to St John, the Lord *"was from the beginning"*[1283] the *"Eternal Life, which was with the Father and was manifested to us."*[1284]   He is *"His Only Begotten Son sent into the world, that we might Live through Him"*[1285] because *"He loved us and sent His Son to be the Propitiation for our sins"*[1286] and *"Saviour of the world."*[1287]   *"This is His Commandment:*

[1271] St Cyril of Alexandria, *To John,* Homily 1, in Migne, *P.G.,* 74, 24.

[1272] John 14:10-11; 17:21.

[1273] John 14:9.

[1274] John 17:11, 21.

[1275] St Cyril of Alexandria, *To John 17:11,* in Migne, *P.G.,* 74, 516.

[1276] John 20:22-23.

[1277] John 14:1.

[1278] John 5:24; 6:47; 8:52; 11:26.

[1279] John 8:12.

[1280] John 14:6.

[1281] John 14:15-16.

[1282] John 14:23.

[1283] 1 John 1:1.

[1284] 1 John 1:2.

[1285] 1 John 4:9.

[1286] 1 John 4:10.

[1287] 1 John 4:14.

that we should believe in the Name of His Son Jesus Christ and love one another."[1288]

According to the Book of Revelation, Christ is the *"Alpha and Omega"* (A and Ω), *"the beginning and the end of all"*[1289] Who has *"the keys of Hades and of Death."*[1290] He sits upon the Throne and is Blessed by *"every creature which is in Heaven and on the earth and under the earth and such as are in the sea."*[1291] He is the One Who is *"coming quickly"* to reward *"every one according to his work."*[1292]

Question 194: What are the testimonies of St Paul concerning the Divinity of Christ?

Answer: St Paul the Apostle persecuted Christ as a *"false-messiah"* before he believed in Him, however, after his conversion, he worshipped Him as the True and Perfect God Who existed before all ages and Who was sent in due time by His Father to die for us sinners. Henceforth, Jesus Christ is repeatedly called *"the Eternally Blessed God"*[1293] as His Throne is the Throne of God, which is for ever. He is *"the Firstborn over all Creation"*[1294] but not the First-**created**. *"He is before all things, and in Him all things consist."*[1295] Thus, St Paul ascribed to Him Divine Attributes, which are ascribed only to God.

St Paul proclaimed that *"by Him all things were created that are in Heaven and that are on earth, visible and invisible, whether Thrones or Dominions or Principalities or Powers. All things were created through Him and for Him."*[1296] He ascribed Almightiness to Christ, by which all things exist and *"all worlds were made."*[1297] Furthermore, St Paul ascribed Infinite Wisdom and Knowledge to Him *"in Whom are hidden all the Treasures of Wisdom and Knowledge."*[1298] By the expression *"all Treasures"* he manifests the Infinity of God and by the words *"are hidden all"* reveals all the things that Christ alone knows.[1299] Christ is *"Self-*

[1288] 1 John 3:23.
[1289] Rev. 1:8, 11, 17; 21:6; 22:13.
[1290] Rev. 1:18.
[1291] Rev. 6:13.
[1292] Rev. 22:12.
[1293] Rom. 9:5.
[1294] Col. 1:15.
[1295] Col. 1:17.
[1296] Col. 1:16.
[1297] Heb. 1:2.
[1298] Col. 2:3.
[1299] St John Chrysostom, *To Colosians,* Homily 5, § 2, in Monfaucon, v. 11, p. 416.

wisdom and Self-knowledge,"[1300] besides which He has the Sameness and the Eternity of God according to the statement: *"Thou art the same, and Thy years will not fail"*[1301] and *"Jesus Christ is the same yesterday, today, and forever."*[1302]

Christ is Perfect God *"Who, being in the Form of God, did not consider it robbery to be equal with God Therefore God also has highly exalted Him and given Him the Name which is above every name, that at the Name of Jesus every knee should bow and confess that Jesus Christ is Lord, to the Glory of God the Father."*[1303]

Through the Blood of Jesus Christ, which was shed on the Cross,[1304] He Sanctified the Church[1305] that is called *"the Church of God which He purchased with His own Blood"*[1306] and by His becoming our Saviour, we *"look for the Blessed Hope and Glorious Appearance of our great God and Saviour Jesus Christ."*[1307]

It is obvious that St Paul proclaimed Christ as the Great God Who has Divinity by Nature. When he referred to Him as *"Lord,"* he ascribed to Him the same Name by which God is addressed in the Old Testament such as *"Jehovah"* and *"Adonai"* - in other words, *"Lord."* In verses where the Name *"Lord"* refers to God, St Paul applied them to Jesus Christ such as in Romans 10:13 when he referred to Joel 2:32. Likewise in 1st Corinthians 1:31 where he referred to Jeremiah 9:23 and 1 Samuel (1 Kings) 2:10; as well as in 1 Corinthians 2:16 where he referred to Isaiah 40:13, and in his Epistle to the Hebrews 1:10 where he referred to Psalm 101(102):26. Also in numerous other verses Christ is called *"Son of God"* by St Paul.[1308]

Question 195: What are the teachings of the Apostolic Fathers concerning the Divinity of Jesus Christ?

Answer: The Apostolic Teachings concerning Christ as the Son and Word of God and God Himself, which were cherished in the Books of the New Testament, is also proclaimed in the writings of the successors of the Holy Apostles and Disciples of Christ who are known as *the Apostolic Fathers.*

[1300] Theophylactus of Bulgaria, *To Colosians,* in Migne, *P.G.,* 124, 1236.
[1301] Heb. 1:12.
[1302] Heb. 13:8.
[1303] Phil. 2:6-11. St John Chrysostom, *To Philippians 2:6,* Homily 7, § 1, in Montfaucon, v. 11, p. 282.
[1304] Col. 1:14, 20. Rom. 3:25; 5:9. Ephes. 1:7; 2:13. Heb. 9:14.
[1305] Heb. 13:12.
[1306] Acts 20:28.
[1307] Tit. 2:13.
[1308] Rom. 8:3, 32. Col. 1:13. Gal. 4:4-5. Heb. 1:3-4, 6.

What was believed and preached about Christ by His Holy Apostles was preached and worshipped by their disciples as well. The quotations referring to Jesus Christ as *"Lord," "God"* and *"Son of God,"* are innumerable.[1309]

St Clement the Bishop of Rome confirmed that *"through the Blood of the Lord Redemption will come to all who believe and hope in God."*[1310] In the Second Letter to the Corinthians St Clement of Rome commented: *"Brothers, we ought to think of Jesus Christ, as we do of God."*[1311]

St Ignatius the Theophorus and Bishop of Antioch, referred to Jesus Christ as *"God"* more than 15 times while in numerous other cases he addressed Him as *"Lord."* According to this Apostolic Father the expression: *"Jesus Christ our Lord"*[1312] or *"Jesus Christ our God"*[1313] means *"the Incarnated God" "Who before the ages was with the Father and appeared at the end of time."*[1314] *"For our God Jesus Christ is more visible now that He is in the Father."*[1315] He is *"God Who appeared in human form"*[1316] but as our God Who is in the Father. He is *"the Eternal, the Invisible, Who for our sake became visible, the Intangible, the Unsuffering, Who for our sake suffered, Who for our sake endured in every way."*[1317] He is *"the Son of Man and Son of God"*[1318] Who is united with the Father and *"as the Lord did nothing without the Father."*[1319] Dying for us, He shed His Blood for our Salvation. For this reason His Blood is the *"Blood of God"*[1320] through which we are Regenerated. He died because *"He suffered all these things for our sakes, in order that we might be Saved; and He truly suffered just as He truly Raised Himself."*[1321]

St Polycarp of Smyrna, in his letter to the Philippians, repeatedly called Jesus *"our Lord Jesus Christ"*[1322] *"Who endured for our sins, facing even death, 'Whom God raised up, having loosed the pangs of Hades."*[1323]

[1309] Frangopoulos, *Christian Faith*, pp. 127-129.

[1310] St Clement of Rome, *1st Corinthians*, 12, 7, in Lightfoot, *The Apostolic Fathers*, pp. 34-35.

[1311] St Clement of Rome, *2nd Corinthians*, 1, 1, in Lightfoot, *The Apostolic Fathers*, p. 68.

[1312] St Ignatius of Antioch, *To Ephesians*, 7, 2, in Lightfoot, *The Apostolic Fathers*, p. 88

[1313] Ibid, *To Romans, Introduction; To Polycarp*, 8, 3, in Lightfoot, *The Apostolic Fathers*, pp. 101, 102, 118. Ibid, *To Ephesians*, 20, 2, in Lightfoot, *The Apostolic Fathers*, p. 93.

[1314] Ibid, *To Magnesians*, 6, 1, in Lightfoot, *The Apostolic Fathers*, pp. 94-95.

[1315] Ibid, *To Romans*, 3, 3, in Lightfoot, *The Apostolic Fathers*, p. 103.

[1316] Ibid, *To Ephesians*, 19, 3, in Lightfoot, *The Apostolic Fathers*, p. 92

[1317] Ibid, *To Polycarp*, 3, 2, in Lightfoot, *The Apostolic Fathers*, p. 116.

[1318] Ibid, *To Ephesians*, 20, 3, in Lightfoot, *The Apostolic Fathers*, p. 93

[1319] Ibid, *To Magnesians*, 7, 1, in Lightfoot, *The Apostolic Fathers*, p. 95.

[1320] Ibid, *To Ephesians*, 1, 2; *To Smyrnaeans*, 1, 1; 6, 1; *To Philadelphians, Introduction*, in Lightfoot, *The Apostolic Fathers*, pp. 86, 110, 112, 106.

[1321] Ibid, *To Smyrnaeans*, 2, 1, in Lightfoot, *The Apostolic Fathers*, p. 110.

[1322] St Polycarp, *To Philippians*, 1, 2; 2, 1; 12, 2. *The Martyrdom of Polycarp*, 19, 2; 22,3, in Lightfoot, *The Apostolic Fathers*, pp. 123, 129, 143, 144.

[1323] St Polycarp, *To Philippians*, 1,2, in Lightfoot, *The Apostolic Fathers*, p. 123

In the *Epistle of Barnabas*, Jesus Christ is proclaimed to be the *"Lord of the whole world, to Whom God said at the foundation of the world, 'Let Us make according to Our Image and Likeness.'*[1324]"[1325] *"He revealed Himself to be God's Son."*[1326]

Finally, the *Epistle to Diognetus* provides us with a short but complete Christology. Truly, according to this Epistle, Jesus Christ is the Only *"Beloved Child,"*[1327] *"the Son of God alone"*[1328] *"for God loved men them He sent His one and only Son, to them He promised the Kingdom in Heaven, which He will give to those who have loved Him."*[1329] God has sent His Son *"in gentleness and meekness He sent Him as God; He sent Him as a Man to men.."*[1330]

Question 196: What are the teachings of the ecclesiastical Scholars concerning the Divinity of Jesus Christ?

Answer: The writings of the Apologists, although they are addressed to idol worshippers, in order to defend the false accusations against Christianity, are not full reports of the Christian Faith but their Faith in Christ's Divinity continues to be confessed as in the Apostolic and Post-Apostolic periods.

Aristides declared that *"the Christians are from the Lord Jesus Christ, Who is confessed to be the Son of the Most High God, Who in the Holy Spirit came down from Heaven for the Salvation of men; and was born of the Holy Virgin Immaculately and took up flesh."*[1331] Aristides proclaims Christ's Sonship and His pre-existence with the Father, as well as His Incarnation in time from the Holy Spirit and of the Virgin Mary.

St Justin the Philosopher and Martyr wrote: *"We confess God (the Father of Justice and Wisdom) and His Son Who is with Him and taught us"* *"Who was Crucified under Pontius Pilate as the Son of God."* He, *"the Son of God and Apostle Jesus Christ, Who is the Word and appeared in the form of Fireand in other cases in a bodiless Imageto Moses and other Prophetsnow born of the Virgin, becoming Man according to the Will of God, suffered for the Salvation of those who will believe."* Hence those who

---

[1324] Cf. Gen. 1:26.
[1325] *Barnabas,* 5, 5; 6, 12, in Lightfoot, *The Apostolic Fathers,* pp. 167, 169.
[1326] *Barnabas,* 5, 9-11, in Lightfoot, *The Apostolic Fathers,* pp. 167-168.
[1327] *Epist. to Diognetus,* 8, 11, in Lightfoot, *The Apostolic Fathers,* p. 301.
[1328] Ibid, 9, 4, in Lightfoot, *The Apostolic Fathers,* p. 302.
[1329] Ibid, 10, 2, in Lightfoot, *The Apostolic Fathers,* p. 303.
[1330] Ibid, 7, 4, in Lightfoot, *The Apostolic Fathers,* p. 301.
[1331] Aristides, in Trempelas, *Dogmatique,* v. II, p. 55.

believe in Him and are baptised *"are reborn in the Name of the Father and our Saviour Jesus Christ and the Holy Spirit."*[1332]

The *"Word became flesh"*[1333] specifically in order to Save mankind. This Salvation and Redemption was accomplished not only through Divine Knowledge to which the Incarnated Word led mankind through His Divine Teachings and the new moral Law but through the outpouring of the Gifts of the Holy Spirit that were derived as a consequence of His Death.

The first scholars, after the Apologists, were called to defend the Divinity of the Incarnated Son and Word of God against the heresies of the 2nd and 3rd centuries. Cerinthos who was a contemporary of St John the Apostle and Evangelist, the Ebionites and different Gnostics, are few of the heretics who are mentioned in their writings,[1334] specially those by St Irenaeus,[1335] the Church Historian Eusebius[1336] and those by St Epiphanius.[1337]

Origen referred to the Holy Trinity as the *"Holy Trinity,"* *"Eternal Trinity,"* *"Primary Trinity,"* and *"Worshipped Trinity."* He believed that the Son of God is *"the Word of God"* and *"God the Word."*[1338]

From the 2nd Century, the symbol of the fish prevailed because the Greek word for fish, *"Ι Χ Θ Υ Σ"* hid a full Confession of Faith concerning the Divinity and Humanity of the Lord. (Ι = *"Jesus,"* Χ = *"Christ,"* Θ = *"God's,"* Υ = *"Son,"* Σ = *"Saviour"*), in other words: *"Jesus Christ, God's Son, the Saviour."*

CHAPTER FIVE
THE HUMAN NATURE OF CHRIST

Question 197: What is the Human Nature of Christ?

Answer: The Word and Son of God *"became flesh"*[1339] partaking of *"flesh and blood"*[1340] and becoming similar in everything to us but *"without*

[1332] St Justin, the philosopher and martyr, *1 Apology,* 15, 1; 6, 1; 13, 3; 63, 10 and 16; 61, 3, in **B,** v. 3, pp. 147, 164, 167, 196, 194, 178, 187. Ibid, *1 Apology,* 32 and 50. Ibid, *Dialogue,* 40, 54, 111, 134.

[1333] John 1:14.

[1334] Theodoretus of Cyrus, *Heresies,* book II, chs. 1, 5, 24, in Migne, *P.G.,* 83, 388, 392. Tertullian, *Adversus Marcianem,* I, 11, 14; II, 27; III, 9; IV, 7, in migne, *P.L.,* 2, 259, 262, 326, 333 and 369.

[1335] St Irenaeus, *Heresies,* book I, ch. 25, § 1; ch. 26, § 2; ch. 27, 2; book III, ch. 11, § 9, in Migne, *P.G.,* 7, 686-687, 688, 890. Cf. Ibid, in Hadjephraimides, pp. 94, 97, 97-98, 213.

[1336] Eusebius, *Church History,* III, 27 and 38, in Migne, *P.G.,* 7, 273

[1337] St Epiphanius, *Heresy,* 27, 28, 41-42, 51, in Migne, *P.G.,* 41, 368, 377, 696, 888.

[1338] Origen, *About Principals,* Introduction I, 1-4, in Migne, *P.G.,* 11, 115-121. Ibid, *Fragments to John,* 36, *To John* book 10, 23, in Migne, *P.G.,* 14, 384. Ibid, *To Matthew,* book 15, 31, in Migne, *P.G.,* 13, 1345. Ibid, *To John,* books 2, 2; 6, 17, in Migne, *P.G.,* 14, 108, 257. Ibid, *Against Celsus,* III, 37; V, 39; VI, 61; VII, 17, in Migne, *P.G.,* 11, 968, 970, 1244, 1392, 1445.

sin."[1341]   He confirmed the reality of this by calling Himself *"the Son of Man"*[1342] manifesting in this way that He is a descendant of man. By adding the article *"the,"* He revealed that He is the perfect and pre-eminent Man. In addition, the title *"Son of David,"*[1343] which is used in the genealogies found in the Gospels,[1344] is not rejected by Christ During His last entrance into Jerusalem.[1345] He accepted this title when the people addressed Him as the descendant of King David and He used it as the basis of His argument that, although He is the Son of David, how then could David address Him *"Lord?"*[1346]

The human nature of Christ was rejected by the Docites as well as other Gnostics who believed that not having a real but an imaginary body, the Lord dwelled amongst men. They supported the opinion that the Saviour was unable to assume a human and material body since matter is the basis of evil and the work of *"an evil Creator."* St John the Apostle and Evangelist, St Irenaeus, Tertullian, St Hippolytus, St John Chrysostom and many other Holy Fathers defended the Truth against their heretical teachings

Question 198: What are the New Testament teachings concerning the Lord's Humanity?

Answer: According to the Holy Gospels, the title *"the Son of Man"* is used most often. In the Gospels of St Matthew it is found (32) thirty two times, St Mark (14) fourteen times, St Luke (25) twenty five times, St John (11) eleven times and (3) three times in the other Books of the New Testament.

In the Gospels and especially in the Synoptics, it is stressed that the Lord is the *"Son of David."*[1347] This title was used particularly by the people during Christ's childhood as well as by all the afflicted who sought His help. Although the Lord showed some reluctance towards this title because it epitomized the earthly and ethnic expectations of His

---

[1339] John 1:14.

[1340] Heb. 2:14.

[1341] Heb. 4:15. Cf. Frangopoulos, *Christian Faith,* pp. 129-131. Mitsopoulos, *Themata,* p. 77.

[1342] **Matth.** 8:20; 10:23; 11:19; 12:8, 32, 40; 13:37, 41; 16:13, 27, 28; 17:9, 12, 25; 18:11; 19:28; 20:18, 28; 24:44; 25:13, 31; 26:2, 24, 45, 63. **Mark** 2:10, 28; 8:31, 38; 9:9, 12, 31; 10:33, 45; 13:26; 14:21, 41, 62; **Luke** 5:24; 6:5, 22; 7:34; 9:22, 26, 44, 56, 58; 11:30; 12:8, 10, 40; 17:21, 24, 26, 30; 18:8, 31; 19:10; 21:36; 22:22, 48, 69; 24:7. **John** 1:52; 3:13, 14, 16; 4:27; 6:27, 53,62; 8:28; 12:23, 34; 13:31.

[1343] **Matth.** 12:23; 15:22; 20:30; 21:9. **Mark** 10:47, 48; 12:35. **Luke** 18:38; 20:41

[1344] Matth. 1:1-16 and Luke 3:23-38.

[1345] Matth. 21:8-11. Mark 11:1-10. Luke 19:28-44. John 12:12-19.

[1346] Matth. 22:41-46. Mark 12:35-37. Luke 20:41-44. Psalm 109(110):1.

[1347] **Matth.** 1:1, 6, 21; 3:31; 12:23; 15:22; 20:30; 21:9, 15; 22:42. **Mark** 10:47, 48; 11:47; 12:35. **Luke** 1:27, 32, 69; 2:4; 3:31; 18:38; 20:41. John 7:42.

contemporary Israelites, He did not refute it. During Christ's last triumphant entrance into Jerusalem,[1348] He appeared to accept the title and blessed the children who addressed Him as *"the Son of David."*[1349] He used this title as a basis of proving His Divine Origin by opening the minds of the Israelites so that they would *"remember the Promises which God promised to Abraham and to David that He will raise from their offspring the Christ."*[1350] The Jews awaited the Messiah as the descendant of King David, as a powerful King and conqueror who would restore the old glory of the Royal Throne of King David.[1351]

The Holy Apostles presented Christ as being relative to us in everything. St John the Apostle proclaimed that *"the Word became flesh and dwelled among us."*[1352] He also presented Him as having been tired from travelling, sitting at Jacob's Well to rest and asking for a drink of water from the Samaritan woman in order to quench His thirst.[1353] He presented Him not only as being *"troubled"*[1354] before He surrender to the arresting authorities but also as being *"thirsty"* during His Crucifixion.[1355] He presented Christ as enduring all human sensations and emotions. He *"groaned and was troubled"* as all men are at the death of a beloved friend, as in the case of St Lazarus.[1356] He drove out and overturned the tables of the money changers as well as the seats of those who sold doves in the Temple.[1357] He referred to Himself as *"a Man"* Who spoke *"the Truth"*[1358] and expressed His Love towards His Disciples.[1359]

Contrary to the fourth Holy Gospel, the three Synoptic Gospels portray the Humanity of Jesus Christ They speak clearly of His Conception within the Ever Virgin Mary,[1360] His Birth,[1361] His Circumcision,[1362] His Presentation at the Temple[1363] and His physical growth.[1364] At the age of

---

[1348] Matth. 21:9.
[1349] Matth. 21:16. Mark 11:10. Luke 19:38. John 12:13.
[1350] Zigabinos, *To Matthew 1:1,* in Migne, *P.G.,* 129, 117.
[1351] Acts 1:6.
[1352] John 1:14.
[1353] John 4:5-42.
[1354] John 12:27; 13:21.
[1355] John 19:28.
[1356] John 11:33
[1357] Matth. 21:12. Mark 11:15. Luke 19:45. John 2:15.
[1358] John 8:40.
[1359] John 13:1.
[1360] Luke 1:35.
[1361] Matth. 1:25. Luke 2:7.
[1362] Luke 2:21.
[1363] Luke 2:22-24.
[1364] Luke 2:40, 52.

twelve He appeared[1365] in the Temple, listening and questioning the teachers as a disciple,[1366] "*not teaching, but simply listening*" and "*giving the example to all youth not to be insolent.*"[1367] Appearing to be hungry,[1368] "*eating and drinking*" He was accused by the Pharisees of being a "*glutton and a winebibber.*"[1369] Being exhausted from the day's work,[1370] our Lord slept on the boat, completely unaware of the storm.[1371] In the Garden of Gethsemane He was extremely troubled by His approaching Death to such an extent that He literally sweated blood.[1372] Furthermore, on various occasions, He became indignant, He became angry, He wept, He was compassionate, He was merciful and He truly experienced every sensation and emotion to which any Holy Man would be subjected. He participated in the joy and sadness of His fellow men, never refusing their invitations to sit with them at dinners or wedding feasts. After Christ's Resurrection He allowed the Apostles to touch and feel His Wounds. Christ is perfect Man only because His Nature is in "*Communion*" with His Divine Nature - with Perfect God.[1373]

St Peter, addressing the Jews, referred to the Lord as the "*Man from God*" "*Who Himself bore our sins in His own Body on the tree*" so that by His "*stripes we were healed.*"[1374] St Paul assured us that "*One is the Mediator between God and men, the Man Christ Jesus*"[1375] Who "*is ready to Judge the living and the dead*"[1376] whom He shall raise from the dead. Teaching the Christians of his time, he affirmed that "*since by one man came death, by* [one] *Man also came the Resurrection of the dead*"[1377] and that the Gift of Grace[1378] came through one Man - Jesus Christ – as well. According to St Paul the Lord is the Son of God Who was Born from the offspring of David "*according to the flesh*"[1379]

[1365] Luke 2:42.
[1366] Luke 2:46.
[1367] Origen, *To Luke 2:46,* in Trempelas, *Dogmatique,* v. II, p. 64.
[1368] Matth. 4:2; 12:3; 21:18. Mark 2:25; 11:12. Luke 6:3.
[1369] Matth. 11:19.
[1370] John 4:6.
[1371] Matth. 8:24.
[1372] Matth. 26:38. John 12:27.
[1373] Evdokimov, *Orthodoxia,* p. 118.
[1374] 1 Peter 2:24. Heb. 9:28. Is. 53:4-5.
[1375] 1Tim. 2:5.
[1376] 1 Peter 4:5.
[1377] 1 Corinth. 15:21.
[1378] Ephes. 2:8.
[1379] Rom. 9:5.

Question 199: What does the Decree of the 4ᵗʰ Ecumenical Synod of Chalcedon declare?

Answer: *"Pursuantly therefore to the Divine Fathers we all consonantly join voices in teaching outright that we confess one and the same Son or Lord Jesus Christ, perfectly the same in Divinity, and perfectly the same in humanity. Truly a God, and truly a human being, the same (composed) of a soul and body and One Who is at the same time of like Essence with the Father in respect of Divinity, and of like Essence the same with us in respect of humanity, in all respects like us, apart from sinfulness. Though Begotten before the ages out of the Father in respect of Divinity, yet in latter days born out of Mary the Virgin and Theotokos, in respect of humanity, the same for us and for our Salvation. One and the same Christ, Son, Lord, Only-begotten (composed) of two Natures unconfusably, inconvertibly, inseparably identifiable, there being nowhere anything removed or annulled in the difference of the Natures on account of the union, but rather on the contrary the peculiarity of each Nature being preserved, and concurring in one Person and one Substance. Not being divided or parted into two Persons, but (forming) on the contrary one and the same Son and Only-Begotten God Logos, Lord Jesus Christ, precisely as the Prophets formerly had prophesied concerning Him and as He Himself, the Lord Jesus Christ, did explicitly teach us, and the Symbol (i.e. the Creed) of the Fathers has imparted the matter to us."*[1380]

Question 200: What do the holy Fathers teach on our Lord's Similarity to us?

Answer: According to Holy Scripture the Son of God *"consented to be in the form of a bondservant like His fellow servants"*[1381] *"having within Him the whole manbecoming everything which we have, without sin.*[1382] *In other words with body, soul, mind"* He *"united Himself to that which was condemnedin order to Sanctify man through Himself"* and to free human nature from the curse.[1383] Hence *"He took up all the natural motions of man."* In other words, Christ took on all the illnesses and weaknesses of human nature. However, because the human nature of Christ does not depend on human will, being completely natural, it is therefore free of guilt

---

[1380] Pedalion, pp. 241, 243. Kefalas, *Catechesis,* p. 259.
[1381] Cf. Phil. 2:7.
[1382] Cf. Frangopoulos, *Christian Faith,* pp. 132-134.
[1383] St Gregory of Nazianzus, *Homily* 30, § 6, in Migne, *P.G.,* 36, 109 and 132.

and sin.[1384]   These natural human weaknesses are called *"irreproachable passions"* being *"hunger, thirst, tiredness, pain, tears, mortality, fear, agony, which is the cause of sweat and drops of blood,[1385] the human weakness and the others, which by nature are found in men."*[1386]

Christ did not take up sin because His human nature was *"from the immaculate and spotless Virgin, pure and without the mixing with men."* Conceived by the Holy Spirit, absolutely sinless and Holy from its Conception since the Annunciation by the Archangel Gabriel.[1387]

Christ's sinlessness does not alienate Him from our relationship because, although He is sinless and was born Supernaturally by the Virgin Mary, He does not cease being true Man, our Brother, being the same in everything as us, bearing the same human nature but being completely without sin. This is understood when we consider that sin is unnatural, nor was it included in our nature by our Creator. Instead sin is the result of the devil's sowing because at the Offence and afterwards, he deceived the rational nature of man by implanting sinful thoughts and establishing *"the law of sin in the nature of man."*[1388]   Since the Lord was sent by His Father into the world in order to restore fallen human nature[1389] as another Forefather and as a new Adam, it was natural to assume the human nature that *"Adam had sinless from the first Creation"* and this, which Adam *"threw into mortality and death"* the Lord will raise *"according to His sinless Nature."*[1390]

So the Word and Son of God did not take up another type of human nature that was different from that which He had created and the same as we have, but a healthier nature, uncorrupted by sin, which presented Him as perfect Man, as Adam had been in Paradise before the Fall.

The first Adam was from the soil of the earth while the second Adam was from Heaven. The first Adam's creation was from Divine Grace that existed externally and which was not from himself. The second Adam, on the contrary, had Divine Grace within Himself because of the Hypostatic Union.   Life came to the human nature of the first man from a Source

---

[1384] St John Chrysostom, *To Romans,* Homily 13, § 5, in Migne, *P.G.,* 60, 514.

[1385] Luke 22:44.

[1386] St John of Damascus, *Exposition.   About the natural and incontestable passions*, III, 64, 20, in Migne, *P.G.,* 94, 1081.

[1387] Luke 1:35.

[1388] St Athanasius the Great, *About the incarnation of the Word,* § 8, in Migne, *P.G.,* 25, 109. St John of Damascus, *Exposition.   About the natural and incontestable passions*, III, 64, 20, in Migne, *P.G.,* 94, 1081.

[1389] St Symeon, *Euriskomena,* Homily XXXVIII, pp. 179-181.

[1390] St Athanasius the Great, *Against Apollinarius,* Homily II, § 6 and Homily I, § 7, in Migne, *P.G.,* 26, 1141 and 1104.

separate to him, whereas the human nature of the Lord was received from the Source of Life that was inseparably united with it, similar to members of a body receiving life from the head or branches receiving sustenance from the trunk of the vine to which they are naturally united. Since the human nature of Christ directly receives from the Source of His Divine Nature with which it is inseparably and Hypostatically united, the Grace that was received was superior to that which the first Adam partook of, such as the comparison of a great river to a small stream.[1391]

The Lord, as the second Forefather and as the new Adam through direct Divine Intervention and Creative Action, had to have a similar birth to that of the first Adam. It was appropriate for a new Creation to occur so that the regeneration as well as the new creation of mankind who has been recalled, would be sinless and perfectly healthy.[1392] Because this new beginning had to be created within the regenerated human race as well as that of the old Adam, *"God did not take dust, but made the formation from the Virgin Mary in order not to make a different formation, not different from the one being Saved"* and thereby restoring the fallen man.[1393] *"From a Virgin"* the Lord *"took upall which God from the beginning used for the creation of man and made without sin."*[1394]

Question 201: Did the Lord had His own Will and Authority?

Answer: Since the new Adam of Grace *"committed no sin, nor was deceit found in His mouth"*[1395] He had the right to enjoy the same life without any suffering or pain as that of Adam before the Fall. Born of the Virgin in a condition *"with the possibility of not dying"*, He did not face death as being unavoidable and necessary as we have to do and although the Divine Saviour *"was rich, yet for your sakes He became poor,* [so] *that you, through His poverty, might become rich."*[1396] Consequently, surrendering His rights that were offered because of His sinlessness, He became a *"partaker of our irreproachable passions,"* in order to achieve our restoration.[1397] Hence it is understandable how the Lord's Death was absolutely by His own Will, and it shines light upon the words that He Himself spoke: *"I lay down My Life that I may take it again. No one takes it*

[1391] Scheeben, *Les Mystères,* pp. 330-331.
[1392] St Symeon, *Euriskomena,* Homily XXXV, pp. 167-170.
[1393] St Irenaeus, *Heresies,* book III, ch. 21, § 10, in ***B,*** v. 5, p. 151.
[1394] St Athanasius the Great, *Against Apollinarius,* Homily 2, § 5, in Migne, *P.G.,* 26, 1140.
[1395] 1 Peter 2:22. Is. 53:9.
[1396] 2 Corinth. 8:9.
[1397] St Justin, the philosopher and martyr, *2 Apology,* 13, 4, in ***B,*** v. 3, p. 207. St Athanasius the Great, *Against Arians,* Homily III, § 33, in Migne, *P.G.,* 26, 393.

from Me, but I lay it down of Myself. I have power to lay it down, and I have power to take it again."[1398] These words are not addressed to us who, when we fall "*into the hands of those who wish to kill us, we do not have the power to lay down*" our life "*or notbut without our will they slay us*" whereas the God-man "*had the Power not to lay down His Life*" by abolishing every adversity and hostile power.[1399] These words were also spoken in reference to the "*possibility of not dying*" ("*posse non mori*"), which through sinlessness would be replaced with True Immortality.

Christ at His glorious Transfiguration had the Power, if He Willed it, to enter into the Glorious Immortality and Theosis (Deification) even without Sacrificing His own Life but then human nature would not have been Saved. Our Lord spoke of this Salvation with the two Prophets, St Moses and St Elijah "*who appeared in glory and spoke of His decease which He was about to accomplish at Jerusalem*"[1400] "*speaking among themselves about the Mystery of the Divine Economia of the Incarnation and the Redeeming Suffering on the Cross.*"[1401] "*The Lord being Immortal*" has the Power to make His "*mortal flesh*" Immortal and "*with authority as God*" as well as being the new, sinless Adam "*to depart from the body and again to take it back*" surrendered Himself to death by His own Will for our sake. Thus the Lord achieved the "*natural and essentialfamiliarities*" of our nature. He "*became experienced with our irreproachable passions*" and the "*personal and relative*" aspects of life. "*He took up our personality and, taking our place*" as our Guarantee, He sacrificed His Life willingly "*and became familiar with our curse and abandonment and the rest of these things which are not natural*" for although He was not accursed Himself He became so for us.[1402]

Question 202: Who renounced the Lord's Humanity?

Answer: At the end of the first century various heresies renouncing Christ's Humanity began to surface.[1403] Among these were:

[1398] John 10:17-18.

[1399] St John Chrysostom, *To Genesis,* in Migne, *P.G.,* 59, 330.

[1400] Luke 9:31.

[1401] St Cyril of Alexandria, in Migne, *P.G.,* 72, 653.

[1402] St John of Damascus, *Exposition. About familiarization,* III, 69, 25, in Migne, *P.G.,* 94, 1093.

[1403] St Ignatius, *To Ephesians,* 7, 1, in Lightfoot, *The Apostolic Fathers,* p. 88. St Gregory of Nazianzus, *Epist.* 101, in Migne, *P.G.,* 37, 177. St John Chrysostom, *To Matthew,* Homily 4, § 3, in Migne, *P.G.,* 57, 43. St Cyril of Jerusalem, *Catechesis,* XII, § 32, in Migne, *P.G.,* 33, 765. St Irenaeus, *Heresies,* book I, ch. 27, § 2, in Migne, *P.G.,* 7, 688. Ibid, in Hadjephraimides, p. 167. Tertullian, *Adversus Marcianem,* I, 19; IV, 6, in migne, *P.L.,* 2, 292 and 397.

a. **Docetism** about whom St John the Apostle, Evangelist and Theologian mentions in his 1st Epistle.[1404] According to them, Christ was simply a higher spirit who dwelled among men with an imaginary but not a real body. Hence they did not partake of Holy Eucharist because they did not accept that the Consecrated Bread is the Body of Christ.

b. Some of the **Gnostics** based their teachings on the belief that matter opposes the spirit because of the evil that exists in matter. Consequently they did not accept that the Redeemer was able to take up material flesh, which is the basis of evil. Thus they were led to Docetism and believed that the Body of Christ was a deceptive body and not real. (Marcion[1405] and Basilides[1406]) Others ascribed a celestial and Heavenly Body to Christ (Apelles and Ualentinus[1407]).

Our Lord and Saviour Jesus Christ, the Son of God, was *"conceived by the Virgin Mary"*[1408] and *"came from the Virgin's flesh"*[1409] according to the Testimonies of the Angel who assured the Virgin Mary that she would *" conceive in the womb and bring forth a Son"*[1410] and who appeared in St Joseph's dream declaring *"for that which is conceived in her is of the Holy Spirit."*[1411] St Paul also stated that Christ was *"born of a woman"*[1412] thus sealing the mouths of those who say that Christ passed through the Virgin as through a channel.

St Ignatius the Theophorus, opposing Docetism, proclaimed that *"our God, Jesus Christ, was conceived by Mary according to God's Plan, both from the seed of David and of the Holy Spirit. He was Born and Baptised"*[1413] by St John the Baptist in order *"to fulfill all Righteousness by Him."*[1414] Moreover *"He was truly nailed in the flesh for us under Pontius Pilate and Herod the Tetrarchand He truly Suffered as He truly Raised Himself - not as certain unbelievers say, that He suffered in appearance only."*[1415]

St Irenaeus correctly observed that if the Lord did not receive anything from the Ever Blessed Theotokos, then *"He did not receive from*

[1404] 1 John 4:3.

[1405] Cf. St Irenaeus, *Heresies,* book I, ch. 27, §§ 2-4, in Hadjephraimides, pp. 97-98.

[1406] Ibid, *Heresies,* book I, ch. 24, § 3, in Hadjephraimides, pp. 92-93

[1407] Ibid, *Heresies,* book I, ch. 1-10, in Hadjephraimides, pp. 44-66.

[1408] St Ignatius, *To Ephesians,* 18, 2, in Lightfoot, *The Apostolic Fathers,* p. 92.

[1409] St John Chrysostom, *To Matthew,* Homily 4, § 3, in Migne, *P.G.,* 57, 43.

[1410] Luke 1:31.

[1411] Matth. 1:20.

[1412] Gal. 4:4.

[1413] St Ignatius, *To the Ephesians,* 18, 2, in Lightfoot, *The Apostolic Fathers,* p. 92.

[1414] Cf. Matth. 3:15. St Ignatius, *To the Smyrnaeans,* 1, 1, in Lightfoot, *The Apostolic Fathers,* p. 110.

[1415] St Ignatius, *To Smyrnaeans,* 1, 2 and 2, 1, in Lightfoot, *The Apostolic Fathers,* p. 110.

the earth's food, from which the body is nourished" and neither would He have become hungry after forty days of fasting in the desert "since the body was demanding food" nor would the Apostle have written: "Jesus, tired from the journey, sat" besides Jacob's Well; nor would the Lord have shed tears "on Lazarus; neither would He have sweated blood; neither would He have said 'My soul is troubled'" and when His Side was pierced neither would blood and water have come out.[1416]

St Cyril of Jerusalem, criticising the followers of Docetism and referring to the events of the Lord's Conception and Birth commented: "Even if the heretics contradict the Truth, they are criticised by the Holy Spirit; the Power which overshadowed the Virgin will be angry; Gabriel will be replaced on the Day of Judgement; the place of the Manger, which received the Master, will disgrace them; the Shepherds who were then evangelized, bear witness and the army of Angels glorifying and singing."[1417]

St John of Damascus remarked: "if by appearance was achieved those things by Christ, then the Mystery of the Economia was a put-on and scheme; and in appearance and not in reality was the Lord Incarnated; and in appearance and not in reality we have been Saved."[1418] "Our faith then is false and an illusion of everything in which we hoped from Christ"[1419] "For, if the Incarnation was a fantasy, then a fantasy was the Salvation."

St John Chrysostom stated that if "Christ came as through a channel" from the Ever Blessed Virgin, receiving nothing from her, then His flesh "was another" and "not from our dough" and He then ceases carrying the lost sheep on His shoulders.[1420]

The Fathers of the Orthodox Church used Biblical verses against Docetism such as: "The first man was of the earth, made of dust; the second Man is the Lord from Heaven"[1421] and "God by sending His own Son in the likeness of sinful flesh, on account of sin condemned sin in the flesh."[1422] St John Chrysostom noted that: "the Lord from Heaven" does not mean "the nature, but the perfect Life." St Gregory of Nazianzus also stated that the human nature of Christ, being in fullness the same as that of the first Adam

---

[1416] St Irenaeus, *Heresies,* book III, ch. 22, §§ 1 and 2, in **B**, v. 5, p. 152. Cf. Ibid, in Hadjephraimides, pp. 252-253.

[1417] St Cyril of Jerusalem, *Catechesis,* XII, §§ 32 and 33 in Migne, *P.G.,* 33, 765 and 768.

[1418] St John of Damascus, *Exposition. About mortality and corruption*, III, 72, 28, in Migne, *P.G.,* 94, 1100.

[1419] Tertullian, *De cane Christi,* ch. V, § 3, in migne, *P.L.,* 2.

[1420] St John Chrysostom, *To Matthew,* Homily 4, § 3, in Migne, *P.G.,* 57, 43.

[1421] 1 Corinth. 15:47.

[1422] Rom. 8:3.

before he sinned, by saying *"from Heaven"* we must understand that this reveals the perfect union of the Human and Divine Natures of Christ[1423]

Didymus the Blind, referring to St Paul's words, *"do you not know that your bodies are members of Christ?"*[1424] also used another Biblical verse to oppose the teachings of Docetism by observing that *"from this Apostolic phrase are cast out"* as heretics *" those who criticize the Flesh of the Master from Heaven, proclaiming that It was not human"* because if the Master's Flesh was not human, how could we become Its members?[1425]

Question 203: Who renounced the integrity of the Lord's Human Nature?

Answer:

1. **Arius**, according to his heresy, supported the opinion that *"instead of the inner man, that is, the soul, the Word became in the flesh."*[1426] The Incarnated Word was deprived of a human soul since He replaced it and was the Source of the spiritual expressions and life. Arius believed that by introducing such teachings, he would prove that the Word was created.

2. **Apollinarius**, although agreeing to the Nicene Creed, he supported the opinion based on the Platonic Trilogy, (body, soul and spirit = man). He believed that when the Word was Incarnated He took up only body and irrational soul or spirit being unnecessary for Christ, since the Word was replacing the soul or the human mind. He believed that *"Nature"* and *"Person"* are inseparable and that consequently he who accepts two perfect Natures in Christ, must also accept two Persons in Christ. Furthermore, he also supported the belief that the Incarnated Word has *"one Hypostasis and one Person."* He taught that the Word of God has *"not two Natures, but one Incarnated Nature"* merely because *"two perfects cannot make one."*[1427] Apollinarius tried to find a basis for his heresy in the verse of St John's Holy Gospel: *"And the Word became Flesh and dwelt among us"*[1428] in which he explained that *"many times the whole is expressed through the part, and by the soul, the whole man is called, by the flesh, the whole animal is expressed."*[1429] Similarly in the following verses: *"As you gave Him Authority over all flesh."*[1430] *"For all souls are Mine; as the soul of the*

[1423] St Gregory of Nazianzus, *Epist. 101 to Cledonius*, in Migne, *P.G.*, 37, 176-189.
[1424] 1 Corinth. 6:15.
[1425] Didymus the Blind, *About the Trinity*, III, 8, in Migne, *P.G.*, 39, 849.
[1426] St Athanasius the Great, *Against Apollinarius*, II, § 3, in Migne, *P.G.*, 26, 1136, 1137.
[1427] Trempelas, *Dogmatique*, v. II, p. 74.
[1428] John 1:14.
[1429] St Cyril of Alexandria, *About the incarnation of the Word*, ch. XVIII, in Migne, *P.G.*, 75, 1448.
[1430] John 17:2.

father, so also the soul of the son, they are Mine: the soul that sins, it shall die."[1431] "*And the Glory of the Lord shall appear, and all flesh shall see the Salvation of God*"[1432] and "*..All flesh will bless His Holy Name.*"[1433] It is obvious from these verses the word "*flesh*" manifests the whole man.

St Athanasius the Great of Alexandria (*Against Apollinarius, books I and II*): and others such as St Gregory of Nyssa (*Homily objecting to the teachings of Apollinarius*) and St Gregory the Theologian of Nazianzus (*To Cledonius Epistle 101, and Homily 51*) through their various writings contested the heresy of Apollinarius, which was eventually condemned by the 2nd Ecumenical Synod (381).

To the quibble of the Apollinarians, according to which in Christ "*two Perfects cannot be contained*" in other words, the perfect God and the perfect Man, St Gregory of Nazianzus answered: "*Where is the perfect mind of man or Angel*" when compared to the Deity "*in order that the other can be cast out by the Supreme One?*" Our mind is perfect for ruling the soul and body but compared to God, it is "*a servant and a pawn but not co-princely nor equal.*" Moreover, the inseparability that applies to the material and physical, does not apply to the Bodiless and Intellectual.[1434]

St Gregory opposed another argument that the Apollianrians presented whereby "*our mind is condemned*" and was therefore not fit to be received by the Incarnated Word. Their belief that the flesh was condemned was far worse than their belief that the mind is condemned because if "*the worst was received*" by the Word "*in order to be Sanctified through the Incarnation*" would not the Supreme Mind be received so as to be Sanctified through the Incarnation? If the flesh which came from dust "*was mixed and a new dough was made*" which consists of the Image of God in us, would it not be mixed with God in order to be Deified through the Divinity? Moreover, because the mind in us is the Image of God, being closer to God and more susceptible than that of the body, it is easier to be united with the Word.

The Apollinarians ended up in madness by insisting on tying God to flesh, as they believed that the mind was the middle wall that prevented the true union of the two Natures of Christ On the contrary, "*the Mind*" (the Word) Who was Incarnated is closer and more relative "*to the mind*" of man. Furthermore, the mind that "*mediated*" between the "*Divinity*" and humanity is absolutely simple, spiritual and of the flesh. Accordingly the

---

[1431] Ezek. 18:4.
[1432] Is. 40:5. Luke 3:6. Is. 52:10.
[1433] Psalm 144(145):21.
[1434] St Gregory of Nazianzus, *Epist. 101 to Cledonius,* in Migne, *P.G.*, 37, 176-189.

Bodiless God is united in a perfect manner with the flesh-bearing human nature.

St Irenaeus clearly proclaimed that if the Incarnated Word did not become whatever we are, then Christ would not have accomplished anything important for which He suffered and endured.[1435] Neither would He truly have saved us by His own Blood, if He had not become truly human.[1436] Consequently, in order for the Lord to Save the human race He took "*upon His shoulders all the lost sheep, not only the sheep's skin.*" In reality, what makes man "*an intellectual sheep*" is his mind. Should this have been absent, we would not have had an intellectual existence but merely "*a skin*" of an intellectual sheep. However, Christ "*had not left anything of our nature which He did not take up*" and "*in order to make whole the Man of God, He mixed the soul and body with the Deity.*" If truthfully only "*half of Adam sinned*" He would have taken up that half because "*the half would have had need of Salvation.*" Since the whole of Adam sinned, "*all*" with the body and the mind "*in all He* [Christ] *is Born and United and thus Saves.*" It was so necessary for the Incarnated Word to take up our mind, as the mind "*not only sinned in Adam, but first suffered, as the doctors say about the ill.*" For the mind "*received the Commandment*" from God although it thought about and decided to commit the Offence "*and did not keep the Commandment.*" Since Adam dared to disobey the Commandment "*he also needed Salvation*" and exactly for this reason "*it was taken up*" by the Word Who, as He partook of flesh "*for the flesh which was condemned*" and a living soul "*for the soul*" likewise He partook of the mind "*for the mind.*"[1437]

Finally, St Gregory answered the argument of the Apollinarians that "*the Deity was enough, instead of the mind*" and that it was possible for God "*without the mind to Save man.*" He accepted the possibility of Christ Saving mankind even "*without flesh, and only through His Will, as everything He made* [was] *without body.*" He then added that since the Word was well pleased to be Incarnated, He also took up our mind. For "*the Deity only with the flesh is not a full man*" but neither with "*only the soul*" is He fully Man. In fact, neither with "*both,*" - in other words, flesh and soul - "*without mind,*" is He completely Man because the mind of man is more than the flesh and the living soul. He believed that to truly benefit from the Incarnation, it is necessary to "*keep the man*" whole "*and mix the*

[1435] St Irenaeus, *Heresies*, book III, ch. 22, § 1, in Migne, *P.G.*, 7, 956. Cf. Ibid, in Hadjephraimides, pp. 252-253.

[1436] St Irenaeus, *Heresies*, book V, ch. 2, § 1; ch. 7, in Migne, *P.G.*, 7, 1124. Cf. Ibid, in Hadjephraimides, pp. 363-364 and 371-372.

[1437] St Gregory of Nyssa, *Against Eunomius*, II, in Migne, *P.G.*, 45, 545.

Deity."[1438] St Cyril of Alexandria concluded that if "*the Nature which was taken up by the Word did not have a human mind*" then He Who fought against the devil was not a True Man, but God. However, in the event of God having gained the Victory, man would then not have benefitted at all from this Victory, resulting in the devil boasting that "*he was struggling with God and by God he was defeated.*"[1439]

CHAPTER SIX
THE HYPOSTATIC UNION OF THE TWO NATURES IN THE ONE PERSON OF JESUS CHRIST

Question 204: What is the Hypostatic Union of the two Natures of Christ?

Answer: According to the Teachings of Holy Scripture, the two Natures, the Divine and the human, were united in one Person in the Eternal Hypostasis of God the Word, Who, at His Incarnation, took up the human nature in the Holy womb of the Ever-Virgin Mary,[1440] the Ever Blessed Theotokos. The human nature did not pre-exist but became Hypostasis in the Incarnated Word.

Holy Scripture bears witness to this Hypostatic union of the two Natures in Christ, either indirectly or directly. Indirectly, it is evident when ascribed to the Son of Man Divine Attributes, which are not human, as well as to Christ as the Word and Son of God, by means of birth and human descent, a body that suffers in addition to suffering by the shedding of blood accompanied by death. Directly, Holy Scripture gives witness of this union when it proclaims that the Word became flesh, having emptied Himself and taking the form of a servant.

The early Holy Fathers, in order to express this union, used terms that were inaccurate although they explained these terms in an Orthodox way. St Ignatius the Theophorus used the expression "*clothed in flesh*"[1441] to describe the One Who was in the Virgin's Womb, Who was an offspring of King David and Who was Born of the Holy Spirit: our God, Jesus, the God Who became Flesh.

The Holy Fathers, during the 3rd Ecumenical Synod, used different terms such as: "*union,*" "*relevance,*" "*contract,*" "*union by synthesis,*"

[1438] St Gregory of Nazianzus, *Epist. 101 to Cledonius,* in Migne, *P.G.*, 37, 183.

[1439] St Cyril of Alexandria, *About the incarnation of the Word,* XV, in Migne, *P.G.,* 75, 1444.

[1440] Cf. Plato of Moscow, *Orthodox Teaching,* p. 115. Kefalas, *Catechesis,* pp. 74-75. Frangopoulos, *Christian Faith,* pp. 134-137. Mitsopoulos, *Themata,* pp. 78-79, 148.

[1441] St Ignatius, *To Smyrnaeans,* 5, 2, in Light foot, *The Apostolic Fathers*, p. 111.

"synthesis," "co-mixture," "mixture," "inhabitation" and many others, which were used in an orthodox understanding and manifested the union in the one Hypostasis or Person of the two Natures, not externally or morally connected, but naturally and essentially united, without any confusion or mixture, perfectly preserving their own Attributes.

This real and hypostatic union of the two Natures in Christ, was renounced by the heretic Nestorius, who, due to the influence of the theories of Aristotle, supported the opinion that true nature co-exists as a personality; hence the human nature in Christ consists of a personality. Consequently, the union of the two Natures in Christ is a union of two Personalities, which is achieved through the moral entrance of the one into the other, resulting in one moral Personality. It is a Moral union, and not a union of two Natures in one Hypostasis. In this Moral union the two personalities exist separately as two *"egos."* Henceforth, Nestorius concluded by not calling the Holy Virgin Mary *"Mother of God"* (*"Theotokos"*) but *"Mother of Christ"* (*"Christotokos"*) and used the terms *"well pleased," "inhabitation," "relevance,"* and *"relative union."*

The terms *"Nature"* and *"Essence"* on the one hand, and the *"Hypostasis"* and *"Person"* on the other hand, became synonymous. The union of the two Natures or Essences in the God-Man was determined as a *"union by Hypostasis"* and the Incarnated Word was proclaimed as being *"two in Natures, but not in Hypostases"* when the two Natures, the Divine and the human, united undividedly, unchangeably and without any mixture in the one Person of Jesus Christ.

The basis of the theoretical justification of the two Wills in Christ was the principle: *"What is different in essence, is different in will and in energy."* Since in Christ we have two Essences or Natures, we also confess that the two Wills and Energies are different. Furthermore, the expression concerning *"the new Godly Energy"* was accepted not as a synthetic energy that is composed of Divine and human Energy but for the exaltation of the unity of the Person of Christ Who is one and the same Who wants and acts in a Godly as well as a human way.

This union is an unapproachable and inconceivable Mystery, really new and unknown even to the Angels. It is a union of the two Natures in one Godly Person, united without confusion, undividedly and inseparably.

Question 205: What are the teachings of Holy Scripture concerning the Hypostatic Union of the two Natures in Christ?

Answer: The Hypostatic Union of the two Natures in Christ is testified to in Holy Scripture either indirectly or directly, especially in the New Testament. It is testified to indirectly when Christ, as the Son of God and as God, is ascribed with actions and sufferings that are completely alien to His Divine Nature although natural to the human nature, or vice versa, when Divine Attributes are ascribed to the Son of Man that are unnatural to the human nature, whereas it is directly testified to in a few verses that clearly proclaim that the Word became Man by emptying Himself and taking the form of a servant.

Beginning with the indirect Testimonies that assure us that *"concerning His Son Jesus Christ our Lord Who was born of the seed of David according to the flesh"*[1442] He *"the Eternally Blessed God"* descended *"according to the flesh"*[1443] from the *"Israelites"*[1444] and is the blessed *"seed of Abraham"*[1445] The Son of God Who, at the fullness of time, was sent by the Father and *"was born of a woman"*[1446] therefore was a descendant of Abraham. Hence, although He is *"the Word of Life"*[1447] He *"was manifested"*[1448] in the midst of men and the Holy Apostles *"have seen Him with their eyes and their hands handled Him"*[1449] *" being found in the appearance as a Man."*[1450] Thus to Christ, as the Word and Son of God and God, is ascribed birth and human descendant, life and a human body that suffered and faced death, which was capable of suffering and shedding of blood.

Jesus the Son of Man, as God Who existed *"before Adam was"*[1451] *"is the same yesterday, today, and for ever."*[1452] He pre-existed and came *"into this world to save sinners."*[1453] He *"gives Eternal Life"* to His sheep and no one can *"snatch them out of"* His Hands.[1454] In the Epistles of St Paul, Jesus Christ is called *"our Lord Jesus Christ"* fifty times. He was

---

[1442] Rom. 1:3.
[1443] Rom. 9:5.
[1444] Rom. 9:4.
[1445] Rom. 9:7.
[1446] Gal. 4:4.
[1447] 1 John 1:1.
[1448] 1 John 1:2.
[1449] 1 John 1:1.
[1450] Phil. 2:8.
[1451] John 8:58.
[1452] Heb. 13:8.
[1453] 1 Tim. 1:15.
[1454] John 10:27-28.

"highly exalted" after His Resurrection above *"those in Heaven, and those on earth and those under the earth"*[1455] as the Christ *"Who is over all, the Eternally Blessed God"*[1456] Who sits on the Right Hand of God[1457] and Who is *"far above all Principality and Power and Might and Dominion"*[1458] and is worshipped by all the Angels.[1459] He sent the Holy Spirit to His Disciples[1460] and through Him one sees the Father because He is in the Father and the Father in Him,[1461] for they are One.[1462] He is *"the Only Begotten Son Who is in the Bosom of the Father"*[1463] *"for in Him dwells all the fullness of the Godhead bodily."*[1464] He Who was touched by St Thomas and bears the prints of the nails on His Hands and Feet, is our Lord and God.[1465] By *"looking for the blessed hope and Glorious Appearing of our great God and Saviour Jesus Christ"*[1466] we await Him as *"our true God"*[1467] *"Who is the Eternally Blessed God."*[1468]

From the above Biblical verses and many others, it is obvious that the One Whom St Paul calls *"the Man Christ Jesus"*[1469] has Divine Attributes and Who not only as Man is perfect but as God is truly the One *"Who came down from Heaven"*[1470] and as the Son of Man, dwelt among men in the Flesh, simultaneously being in Heaven as *"the Only Begotten Son of God"*[1471] *"Who is in the Bosom of the Father."*[1472] Christ Himself, whenever He spoke of Himself, confirmed that the Only Begotten Son of God is the same as the Son of Man.

The Hypostatic Union of the Divine and human natures of Christ is evident in the Biblical verses of St John 1:14 and in St Paul's Epistle to the Philippians 2:6-7. St Paul proclaimed the eternal pre-existence of Jesus Christ as being in the form of God by Nature and not by robbery, stating that He emptied Himself by coming in the likeness of men. One must note

---

[1455] Phil. 2:9, 10.
[1456] Rom. 9:5.
[1457] Mark 16:19.
[1458] Ephes. 1:21.
[1459] Rev. 5:11-14.
[1460] John 15:26.
[1461] John 14:9-10.
[1462] John 10:30.
[1463] John 1:18.
[1464] Col. 2:9.
[1465] John 20:27-29.
[1466] Tit. 2:13.
[1467] 1 John 5:20.
[1468] Rom. 9:5.
[1469] 1 Tim. 2:5.
[1470] John 3:13.
[1471] John 1:14-15.
[1472] John1:18.

that in the first verse the words *"and the Word became flesh"* is equivalent to *"the Word became Man"* as Holy Scripture usually refers to *"flesh"* as being the whole *"man."*[1473] He became Flesh *"without changing His Essence into fleshfor the Divine Essence is beyond any changebut taking up"* human nature, *"that Essence remained untouched."*[1474] In other verses Christ is presented as *"coming in flesh"*[1475] and that *"He came forth from the Father and had come into the world"*[1476] by *"coming down from Heaven."*[1477]

Question 206: What are the teachings of the Apostolic Fathers & Apologists?

Answer: In the Teachings of the Apostolic Fathers one clearly finds the Doctrine concerning the hypostatic union of the two Natures in Christ, although they ignore the exact Doctrinal term that declares this union. Thus in the *Epistle of Barnabas* it is specified that *"the Lord"* Who *"submitted to suffer for our soulsis Lord of the whole world, to Whom God said at the foundation of the world, 'Let Us make man according to Our Image and Likeness'"* and *"the Son of God, Who is Lord and is destined to Judge the living and the dead."*[1478]

St Ignatius the Theophorus of Antioch used the term *"clothed in flesh"*[1479] signifying the Incarnation of the Lord. *"For our God Jesus the Christ was conceived by Mary according to God's Plan, both from the seed of David and of the Holy Spirit. He was born and was baptised"*[1480] and His suffering is *"the suffering of God"*[1481] as His Blood is *"the Blood of God."*[1482]

According to *The Epistle to Diognetus, "the omnipotent Creator of all, the invisible Godsent to menthe Designer and Creator of the Universe Himselfby Whom all things have been ordered and determined and placed in subjection"* God *"sent Him as a Man to menas a king might send his son who is a king, He sent Him as God."*[1483] Jesus Christ Who was crucified for

---

[1473] St Athanasius the Great, *To Serapion* II, § 7; *Against Arians,* IV, § 30, in Migne, *P.G.,* 26, 620 and 388.

[1474] St John Chrysostom, *To John 1:14,* in Monfaucon, v.8, p. 74.

[1475] 1 John 4:2.

[1476] John 16:28.

[1477] John 6:41.

[1478] *Barnabas,* 5, 5 and 7, 2, in Light foot, *The Apostolic Fathers,* pp. 167 and170.

[1479] St Ignatius, *To Smyrnaeans,* 5, 2, in Light foot, *The Apostolic Fathers,* p. 111.

[1480] St Ignatius, *To the Smyrnaeans,* 18, 2, in Light foot, *The Apostolic Fathers,* p. 92.

[1481] Ibid, *To the Romans,* 6, 3, in Light foot, *The Apostolic Fathers,* p. 104.

[1482] Ibid, *To the Ephesians,* 1, 1, in Light foot, *The Apostolic Fathers,* p. 86.

[1483] *The Epist. to Diognetus,* 7, 2 and 4, in Light foot, *The Apostolic Fathers,* pp. 300 and 301.

us and was sent as a Man, is one and the same with the Creator and Provider and Preserver of all things.

According to *The Shepherd of Hermas*, "*the Son of God is far older than all His Creation, with the result that He was the Father's Counsellor in His Creation*" and "*He was revealed in the last days of the consummation; that is why the door is new, in order that those who are going to be saved may enter the Kingdom of God through It.*"[1484]

According to the Apologists, "*the Lord Jesus Christ*" is "*the Son of the High God*" Who "*came down from Heaven for the Salvation of men*"[1485] Who "*was born from a Holy Virgin without seed and imperishably took up Flesh*" He is "*the Word of God*" Who "*..became Man for the human race*" "*Who was born according to the Will of God and Father*" "*and becoming partaker of our passions*" in order "*to heal them.*"[1486] "*He pre-existed*" as "*the Son of the Creator of all, being God and becoming Man through the Virgin*" "*suffering the same as us, having flesh as man born from men.*"[1487] Hence the Holy Gospel proclaims "*that God has become in the likeness of Man*" He Who "*is God and perfect Man, assured us that He has the two Essences of His Deity and His humanity.*"[1488]

Question 207: Which clarifications concerning the Union of the Two Natures and what accurate terms were used?

Answer: The heresy of Apollinarius[1489] made it necessary to completely clarify the manner of the union of the two Natures in Christ, thereby gradually establishing more accurate terms in order to explain this union.[1490] St Alexandrus the Great of Alexandria, in his letter to Alexandrus of Constantinople, spoke of the "*Unchangeability of the Word*" at the Incarnation and introduced the term "*Unchangeable,*" which subsequently the 4th Ecumenical Synod of Chalcedon accepted.

St Athanasius the Great of Alexandria, explaining the unchangeable union of the two Natures that are Hypostatically united in the God-Man, observed that "*neither is man the Son of God*" nor did God abolish "*the Divine Form; nor being God did He renounce the human form.*" In the God-Man "*two things were united; two in one. For neither God the Word is*"

[1484] *Shepherd of Hermas*, Parable 9, 12, 2 and 3, in Light foot, *The Apostolic Fathers*, p. 272.

[1485] Aristides, *Apology*, 15, in *B,* v. 3, p. 147.

[1486] St Justin, the philosopher and martyr, *1 Apology*, 63, §§ 4 and 10. Ibid, *2 Apology,* 6, § 5 and 13, § 4; Ibid, *Dialogue* 48, § 2-3, in *B,* v. 3, pp. 195-196, 203, 207 and 250-251.

[1487] Tatianus, *Homily to the Greeks*, § 21, in *B,* v. 4, 256.

[1488] Meliton Sardeis, Extract 7, in Migne, *P.G.,* 5, 1221.

[1489] Kefalas, *Synods*, pp.111-112

[1490] Lossky, *Theology,* pp. 95-100.

divided from the body, nor do we see two Sons and Christs, but the One Son of God Who is before all ages and in later times became perfect Man."

Didymus the Blind proclaimed in an orthodox manner that this union of the two Natures in Christ exist as *"other and other"* not *"another and another."* They are two different Natures in the God-Man, not two different Persons, although the different Natures exist in one and the same Person.[1491]

St Gregory of Nyssa and St Gregory the Theologian of Nazianzus, so as to explain the union of the two Natures, used the terms *"mixture,"* *"physique"* and *"commixture."* Nevertheless St Gregory of Nazianzus determined that *"this new mixture of God and man"* in order to be *"one from two and through one two"*[1492] although *"the natures are two, the sons are not two, nor are they two gods."* Henceforth, he who does not *"worship the Crucified, let him be anathema and let them be with those who killed God"* as he is condemned and the other, who *"does not take in consideration as the Theotokos the Holy Mary."* St Gregory clearly determined that by saying *"mixture,"* does not mean confusion and change, but union inseparable from the two Natures, the human never having received its own hypostasis, but from the beginning within the Virgin's Womb was united Hypostatically with the Incarnated Lord and remaining forever united. St Gregory renounced everyone who would deny *" the Holy flesh"* or say *"the Deity stripped from the body."*[1493]

St Gregory of Nyssa unmistakably distinguished the Attributes of each of the two Natures of Christ. *"The humanity* (of Jesus) *was raised after the Suffering and through the Lord, became the Christ"* when *"He was raised on the Right Hand of God and became, instead of the subject, Christ the King, instead of the humble the Highest, instead of the Man the God."* St Gregory emphasised the state of each Nature's Attributes which influenced one another before the Ascension and Deification.[1494]

St Epiphanius, stressing the wholeness and the immixture of the two Natures in their essential union observed that *"the Word becoming flesh"* did not change *"being God"* neither was *"the Divinity changed into humanity"* but *"the same Hypostasis of God the Word included man to be Hypostasis"* not *"dwelling in man as speaking, dwelling and in power and acting in the Prophets, but became flesh."* Likewise He did not *"suffer alteration"* but *"completely Incarnatedtook up the whole man"* and *"regenerated the flesh to Himself"* uniting the humanity and the Deity *"in one Holy union"* in such a way that *"the Lord Jesus Christ is one and not two, the same God, the*

[1491] Didymus the Blind, *About the Trinity,* III, 12; Ibid, *To Psalms,* in Migne, *P.G.,* 39, 860 and 1232.

[1492] St Gregory of Nazianzus, *Homily II Apology,* § 23, in Migne, *P.G.,* 35, 432.

[1493] Ibid, *Epist. 101 to Cledonius*, in Migne, *P.G.,* 37, 180.

[1494] St Gregory of Nyssa, *Against Eunomius,* Homily V, in Migne, *P.G.,* 45, 705 and 697.

same Lord, the same King." He suffered the Passion "*in reality, in the flesh and in the perfect Incarnation He united it to the Deity, but not changed* (so as) *to suffer, being without suffering and unchangeable.*" Thus Christ suffering in the flesh for us remained "*without suffering in the Deity*" without being "*separate man*" and separate Deity but instead the Deity being united with the man, without suffering due to the purity and incomparability of the Divine Essence.[1495]

St John Chrysostom spoke of "*connection,*" "*inhabitation,*" "*dwelling*" and "*vestment*" of the Divine Nature "*in the flesh*" and "*through the flesh*" but he clarified these terms so as to exclude any misinterpretation or misunderstanding. "*The Word became Flesh*" without diminishing "*His own Nature from this descent*" and without the Divine Essence falling into flesh, "*but remaining what It is, likewise He took up the likeness of a servant*" and "*became the Son of Man, being the pure Son of God.*" The Divine Essence remained "*untouched*" because It " *was beyond any change.*" And explaining the Biblical term "*and dwelt among us*"[1496] he deduced that through this, "*the change of that which is unchangeable*" is excluded. "*Remaining what He was, He took up what He was not, and becoming Flesh remained God, being the Word.*" Thus exalting the immixture and unchangeability of the two Natures, he stressed their real union by concluding: "*One God, one Christ, the Son of God. When I say, the One, I mean the union, not a mixture of this Nature in the other.*"[1497]

Question 208: Is the Union of the two Natures in Christ an inconceivable and illogical Mystery?

Answer: We must never forget that the Hypostatic Union consists of a great and beyond any conception Mystery and the manner of the Incarnation is not at all possible for our limited mind to understand. Nothing in nature is similar to the supernatural union that remains unique, being a Mystery to which no image of this world can relate. Only once in the supernatural order it met in the Incarnated Word.

Truly, the union of Divine Grace with the faith of the Faithful and the inhabitation of God within them, according to Christ's statement: "*And We shall come and make Our home in him*" is not essential and Hypostatical but moral, through which the Faithful become "*Theophorus*" (God-bearers)

[1495] St Epiphanius, *Ancyrotus,* 75 and 119, in Migne, *P.G.,* 43, 233 and 236; Ibid, *Short true homily about faith,* § 17, in Migne, *P.G.,* 42, 813.
[1496] John 1:14.
[1497] St John Chrysostom, *To John,* Homily 11, §§ 1 and 2, in Montfaucon, v. 8, pp. 73-75. Ibid, *To Philippians,* Homily 7, §§ 2-3, in Migne, *P.G.,* 62, 232.

but never "*God-men.*" The union of the soul with the body that was used by the Holy Fathers as an example to explain the Mystery of the Hypostatic Union, remains weak and under a thick cloud. In man, soul and body, which are our two elements, are united to make one nature, whereas in Christ two Natures are united in one Person.

Since one accepts this Mystery in good faith and with piety, then one will understand that it is beyond any word of explanation although it does not contradict logic. Thus:

a) The unchangeability of the Deity is preserved untouched by this Union. For the Word of God does not lose anything nor does it add anything to it in order to become more perfect. The Word became Man "*without changing the Nature of His Deity into the Essence of the Flesh, nor* [did] *the Essence of His Flesh change into the Nature of the Divinity.*"[1498]

b) The Incarnation is not contrary to God's simplicity, for the human nature does not enter into the Divine Nature as something that completes it but conversely the human nature, not having with this union its own Hypostasis, is completed by the Person of the Word, which becomes *en-hypostasis* in Christ. The Divine Nature of the Word by nature is simple and non-synthetic. It must be understood that the simple Person and the non-synthetic Hypostasis of the Word unite two Natures and only in relation to the two Natures is a Hypostasis synthetic. In other words the Hypostasis and the Person of the Word born from all Eternity from the Father is not the result of the unity of the two Natures but pre-exists from all Eternity and in time unchangeably took up human nature.

c) From the human aspect there was no obstacle preventing the realisation of this Supernatural Union. Certainly the human nature as mortal, is greatly distanced from the Divine Nature. Although this distance is humanly impassable and impenetrable, the Infinite God when He wants, can bridge this chasm in such a way that the spiritual nature of man has the possibility of being united with Him. Man was formed by God in His Image and his soul is spirit created by the Spirit of God. The union of the two Natures in Christ was accomplished "*by the soul which stands between the Deity and the Flesh.*" The fact that human nature, when it was taken up by the Word and Son of God, was deprived individually from its own hypostasis and became en-hypostasis in the Person of the Word, is not deprived of anything from its fullness or wholeness. On the contrary, through the union with the Word, it became a more perfect individual

---

[1498] St John of Damascus, *Exposition. About the two natures, against Monophysites,* III, 47, 2, in Migne, *P.G.,* 94, 988.

Person, taking up all human nature and consequently presented the perfect Man Who was made according to His Creator Who formed Him.

CHAPTER SEVEN
THE RESULTS OF THE HYPOSTATIC UNION

Question 209: What are the results of the Hypostatic Union?

Answer: Since the two Natures, the Divine and the human, were united inseparably and undividedly in the one Person of the Word, *"the differences of the Natures are not refuted because of the unity, but the Attributes of each Nature are leading to the one Person and Hypostasis"* and for this reason *"one and the same was He Who was performing the Divine and human in each form"* *"with the communion of both."* Consequently the Word, by taking human nature into His Hypostasis, *"became familiar to the human things"* that were part of His own Flesh and as a result, He transmitted His own Divinity to humanity according to the measure it is capable of receiving.[1499]

Thus, in the Person of the God-Man, the sharing or notification of the Attributes *"through the containing of each member in one another and the Union by Hypostasis"*[1500] is established whereby we sometimes refer to the Christ as being from on High while at other times being *"only from the lowly"* thus ascribing to His one Hypostasis the Attributes of both Natures without them being mixed. Hence we can speak of the Blood of God and of the Glorification of the Crucified Lord but we may not speak of an uncreated or suffering-free human nature of the Incarnated Word, nor of Divinity that suffered. Generally speaking, when the Incarnated Word is called *"Son of God"* and *"God"* because of His Divine Nature, He is ascribed with the Attributes that are united with His Divine Nature and when He is called *"Man"* and *"Son of Man"* because of His human nature, He is ascribed with the Attributes of His human nature. Subsequently we address Christ always according to both His Natures that are united undividedly, remaining unmixed, preserving their own individual Attributes while transmitting to one another because of unity of the Person or the one Hypostasis of the Word, in which both Natures are united naturally and inseparably. In order to manifest the inter-relationship of the two Natures of Christ, we may use the example of the colour change of a piece of iron that

---

[1499] Cf. Frangopoulos, *ChristianFaith,* p. 134.
[1500] St John of Damascus, *Exposition. About the two natures, against Monophysites,* III, 47, 3, in Migne, *P.G.,* 94, 993 and 996.

occurs when it becomes red hot from its union with fire. Simultaneously, although a visible change occurs, the iron is still distinguishable from the fire.

With reference to the inter-relationship of the two Natures of Christ, we must never forget that it is different from the inter-relationship of the three Persons of the Holy Trinity. For in the Trinity, the Essence of Nature is One and the same and Infinite. Furthermore, the three Persons are Co-eternal and without beginning. Hence the inter-relationship is perfect, common and united in Essence. In the Person of the God-Man, however, we have the inter-relationship of two Essences of Natures, of which only the Divine is Infinite. The human nature of Christ, although limited, is completely penetrated by the Divine Nature, whereas the human nature is unable to completely enter into the Divine Nature because of its limitations.

In the God-Man we have two Natures but one and the same Son. Consequently, since His human nature is inseparable and undivided from the Hypostasis of the Word, it is also inseparably honoured and worshipped with the Word of God because it is inseparable and undivided from Him. The acceptance of the taking up of human nature that was accomplished by the Word from the moment of His Conception in the Virgin's Womb, declares the Ever Blessed and Holy Mary as truly the Mother of God and Theotokos ("God-bearer").

Through this union of the two Natures, the human nature became a *"partaker of the Divine Nature"*[1501] as in no other Theophorus or God-inspired men ever before, participating in the perfection of human knowledge, will and power of the Divine Nature. The Knowledge of God and the Heavenly things are transmitted to His human nature by direct supervision, vision and enlightenment, not as with us human beings, externally through movement, error and ignorance but instead supernaturally, infallibly and completely free of errors, not being identified with the All-knowledge and All-wisdom ascribed only to the Divine Nature of the God-Man.

The Lord took up the sanctification according to the human aspect, as *"the Yeast"* for all humanity through which we too shall receive, thereby being consecrated from His fullness. As a negative aspect of the perfect Holiness of the Lord, we can characterise His absolute sinlessness. This sinlessness was assured from the beginning because of His complete purity from all sinful inheritance from Adam. It was an automatic turn towards good. The Divine Grace that was derived from the Hypostatic Union of the two Natures from the extreme Conception did not enslave the freedom of

---

[1501] 2 Peter 1:4.

227

the human Will of the Lord. Instead, it made sin morally impossible for Him to commit. However, we must not forget that the Deification of the Power in the God-Man did not become Almightiness. It was raised to a far more superior level than any of the Holy men because of the Wonders and Signs performed by Him, since He did not borrow any external Power to perform the Miracles as the Prophets or the Holy Saints had to do. He healed all and raised the dead by His own Divine Power and for that reason, the Mystery of Holy Communion, His Flesh and Blood, are characterised as being Life-giving.

Question 210: Can the Attributes of the two Natures be transmited?

Answer: The result of the Hypostatic Union of the two Natures is the transmission or communication in Christ of the Attributes of the two Natures.[1502] This consists of the transmission and the offering of the Attributes of each Nature, the Divine and human, *"for the Hypostasis' identity and their inter-communion"* to the one Person of Christ the Incarnated Word. All the Attributes of the human nature are ascribed to the Incarnated Word, as all those of the Divine Nature are ascribed to the human nature in man.[1503]

Truly, in Holy Scripture it is written that *"the Lord and Godpurchased the Church with His own Blood"*[1504] and that God, being without suffering and Immortal, did not suffer on the Cross. It is proclaimed that *"we were reconciled to God through the death of His Son"*[1505] Whom the rulers of this world crucified, not knowing that He is *"the Lord of Glory"*[1506] and *"the Son of God"*[1507] Who was sent into the world, Who *"was born of a woman"*[1508] *"and gave Himself up"*[1509] for our sake, being also *"the Son of Man Who came down from Heaven"* and *"Who is in Heaven"*[1510] while at the same time able to speak to Nicodemus.[1511]

The two Natures remain without confusion, transmitting and communicating their Attributes to one another in the one Person in which

---

[1502] Cf. Fragkopoulos, *Christian Faith*, pp.134-137. Mitsopoulos, *Themata*, pp.148-149
[1503] St John of Damascus, *Exposition. About the way of the antidosis,* III, 48, 4, in Migne, *P.G.,* 94, 997 and 1000.
[1504] Acts 20:28.
[1505] Rom. 5:10.
[1506] 1 Corinth. 2:8.
[1507] Gal. 2:20.
[1508] Gal. 4:4.
[1509] Gal. 2:20.
[1510] John 3:13.
[1511] John 3:1-21.

they are united naturally and undividedly. Although *"the Natures are inter-related to one another, each one unchangeably preserves its own Attributes."* For this reason we must never say of Christ's humanity is uncreated nor that the *Divinity suffers.* We believe that Christ is everywhere but never that His human nature is All-present.[1512]

Under this same concept we must understand the *"Theosis"* (Deification) of the human nature of the Lord from the time of Its Conception in the Holy Womb of the Ever Blessed Theotokos. This was accomplished not because of the change of human nature but, as it is Confessed, the Incarnation was accomplished *"without change or alteration"* of the Divine Nature of the Word. Thus we believe that His human nature was Deified without changing. His human nature was enriched by the Divine Energies because *"of the Hypostatic Union according to which it is united with the Word of God and because of the containing in each other of the two Natures"* without *"falling from their own natures"* but remaining in their own natural boundaries. It is literally witnessed and clearly stated by the 6th Ecumenical Synod that *"the Theotokos gave life Immaculately"* to Christ's *"Flesh* (which,) *although Deified, was not destroyed but remained in itsr own boundary and reason."*[1513]

The Theosis did not change His human nature into Divine Nature, neither does it result in the two Natures becoming a third synthetic nature as a consequence of confusion and change of the two Natures. Instead Theosis preserves His human nature with its own attributes, transmitting to it from its Divine richness, according to the measure of its capability so that the enriched nature remains human and is not transformed into Divine Nature.

It is obvious that this *"inter-containment"* of the two Natures of Christ is not the same in value or level as that of the three Persons of the Holy Trinity. The inter-containment of the Holy Trinity occurs among the three Co-eternal Persons Who are distinguished from each other, although being of one and the same Infinite Essence of the Deity. In the Person of the God-Man, the inter-containment takes place in the one Person of the God-Man, between the two Natures from which only the Divine is Infinite. The human nature remains limited and although completely permeated by the Divine Nature, it cannot not enter the Divine Nature to the same degree due to its human limitations. In the Holy Trinity, however, the three Persons' inter-containment of one another is perfect, mutual and unified by

---

[1512] St John of Damascus, *Exposition. That all the divine nature was united all to the human nature, and not in part,* III, 50, 5 and 4, in Migne, *P.G.,* 94, 1001 and 997.
[1513] St John of Damascus, *Exposition. About the deification of the nature of the flesh and the will of the Lord,* III, 61, 17, in Migne, *P.G.,* 94, 1068, 1069.

the one Essence, whereas in the two Natures of the God-Man, the inter-containment preserves the Divine Essence in its Infinity that cannot be penetrated by His limited human nature.

The basis of the inter-containment of the Holy Trinity is the Infinite, Unique, Undivided and simple Essence of the Deity, while in Christ this inter-containment occurs between two different Natures, having the one Person of Jesus Christ as its basis. Consequently in this inter-containment of the two Natures, the Infinite Nature of the Word does not partake of the limited human nature although it alone acts and transfers from its Infinite Perfection to His human nature, which accepts the *Charismata* (Gifts) from His Divine Nature, according to its limitations so that it is elevated by this union with His Divine Nature, without being changed from its restricted character and always remaining human and unmixed with His Divine Nature. Thus the *"Deity transmits its own"* (Attributes) to His human nature, *"sharing always in its own boundaries and reason"* as expressed by the Doctrine of the 6th Ecumenical Synod whereby His Divine Nature *"remains, not partaking of the suffering of the Fleshand penetrates through all as it Wills, but not contained." "For, if our sun gives us its energies yet remains without participating in ours, how much more the Creator of the sun and the Lord?"*[1514]

His human nature and Flesh *"is not extended to the Infinite Deity of the Word"* and the two Natures *"are united by Hypostasis, being contained in one another" "without confusion being united and each of them preserving their own natural differences."* As St Gregory of Nazianzus expressed it: *"they are mixed and are contained in one another because of the common growth."*[1515]

Question 211: Do we worship separately the Divine Nature and separately the Human Nature of Christ?

Answer: A direct consequence of the acceptance that the human nature is inseparable and indivisible from the Hypostasis of the Word, is that the one worship that is offered to the Word as God, must not be distinguished or differentiated from the worship that must be offered to His human nature. Already the 5th Ecumenical Synod in its 9th Canon had condemned anyone who said *"Christ should be worshipped in two Natures"* and from which is

---

[1514] Ibid, *Exposition. About the energies in our Lord Jesus Christ,* III, 59, 15 and 7, in Migne, *P.G.,* 94, 1057, 1060 and 1012.

[1515] St John of Damascus, *Exposition.,* III, 59, 7 and 8, in Migne, *P.G.,* 94, 1060. Ibid, *Exposition.* III, 52, in Migne, *P.G.,* 94, 1013. St Gregory of Nazianzus, *Epist. 101 to Cledonius,* in Migne, *P.G.,* 37, 176.

introduced "*two worships, separately to God the Word and separately to the Man.*" The Synod determined that we should worship by means of "*one worship* [of] *the God Word Incarnated with its own Flesh.*"

Christ our Lord and Saviour proclaimed that "*all*" should "*honour the Son just as they honour the Father. He who does not honour the Son does not honour the Father Who sent Him.*"[1516] St Paul reminded us that for the obedience Christ showed by humbling Himself "*to the point of death, even death on the Cross*" and the Father had "*highly exalted Him and given Him the Name which is above every name*" so that at the mention of His Sacred Name.[1517] St Stephen the Archdeacon and first Holy Martyr of Christ called upon the Name of "*Jesus Christ,*" which expresses the human nature of the Lord, saying "*Lord Jesus, receive my spirit.*"[1518] "*In the Name of the Lord Jesus*" St Paul exhorted the Colossians to do whatever they had to do "*in word or deed.*"[1519] In Revelation the "*Blessing and Honour and Glory and Power*" is addressed not only "*to Him Who sits on the Throne*" but also" *to the Lamb.*" In other words it was addressed to the Son Who bears the human nature and before Whom "*twenty-four Elders fell down and worshipped.*"[1520]

St Athanasius the Great of Alexandria typified as proper, ("*clear*") worship of "*the Lord Who became in Body and is called Jesus*" because "*worshipping the Lord in the Flesh, we do not worship a creature, but the Creator Who vested the created body.*" Truly, by worshipping the human nature of the Lord, we do not worship a creature because "*we do not worship such a Body, dividing it from the Word, nor*" when we worship the Word, do "*we distance Him from the Flesh.*"[1521]

St John Chrysostom expressed his admiration and surprise that "*the Flesh which is from us*" is set on High and is worshipped "*by Angels and Archangels and the Seraphim and the Cherubim.*"[1522]

St John of Damascus analysed this Truth in detail and concluded that if we separate His two Natures "*with weak thoughts, the one which has been seen from that which has been thought of*" surely then the Flesh of the Lord is "*unworshipped as being creative.*" Christ is "*one, perfect God and perfect Man.*" We worship Him with His Flesh that is worshipped "*in the one Hypostasis of the Word*" which has become Hypostasis in the Flesh, not

---

[1516] John 5:23.
[1517] Phil. 2:8, 9, 10-11.
[1518] Acts 7:59.
[1519] Col. 3:17.
[1520] Rev. 5:13, 14.
[1521] St Athanasius the Great, *Against Arians,* I, § 43; Ibid, *To Adelphius,* §§ 6, 5, 3, 7, in Migne, *P.G.,* 26, 100, 1080, 1076, 1081.
[1522] St John Chrysostom, *To Hebrews,* homily 5, § 1, in Monfaucon, v. 12, p. 73.

existing on its own but being inseparable and indivisible from the Deity and *"as the one Person and one Hypostasis of God the Word Who consists of His two Natures."* As wood is not *"unapproachable to the touch"* until it comes into contact with fire and becomes hot and unapproachable, similarly *" the flesh* (of Christ) *according to its Nature"* is not worshipped until it came into contact with *"the Incarnated God the Word"* not *"individually, but because of its unity by Hypostasis with God the Word."* We do not say that *"we worship 'the flesh,' but 'the Flesh of God."* In other words, we worship *"God Incarnated,"* believing that once *"from the Womb"* human nature was taken up by God the Word, continuing to remain united with Him for all Eternity and we do not say that it will ever *"..put asidethe Holy Flesh and the Deity, to be naked of the Body and not with that which has been taken up and is and will come again"* at the Second Coming.[1523]

Question 212: Is the Mother of the Lord truly Theotokos?

Answer: The acceptance of the taking up of the human nature by the Word *"from the womb"* appoints the Ever-Virgin Mary and Mother of the Lord to be truly THEOTOKOS.[1524] Since there was not a moment according to which the human nature was separated from the Word because He immediately existed with the Word's Flesh at the conception in the Virgin's Womb and as such grew within the Virgin,[1525] it is obvious that it was completely wrong to name her *"the Mother of Christ"* (*"Christotokos"*) as Nestorius proclaimed and not *"truly"* and *"mainly Theotokos"* (*"Mother of God"* or *"God-bearer"*).

In the New Testament the Virgin is addressed by St Elizabeth as the *"Mother of my Lord,"*[1526] and is greeted as such. Similarly St Paul declared that *"when the fullness of time had come, God sent forth His Son, born of a woman."*[1527]

The 4th Ecumenical Synod[1528] literally decreed Mary the Ever Virgin to be called *"Theotokos"* (*"and for our Salvation from Mary the Virgin and Theotokos according to the humanity"* born).[1529] The 5th

---

[1523] St John of Damascus, *Exposition,* III, 52, 8, in Migne, *P.G.,* 94, 1013. Ibid, *Exposition, IV,* 76, 3, in Migne, *P.G.,* 94, 1105. St Gregory of Nazianzus, *Epist.* 101 *yto Cledonius,* in Migne, *P.G.,* 37, 181.
[1524] Cf. Frangopoulos, *Christian Faith,* pp. 139-141.
[1525] St Symeon, *Euriskomena,* Homily XLV, pp. 210-211.
[1526] Luke 1:43.
[1527] Gal. 4:4.
[1528] Kefalas, *The Ecumenical Councils,* pp. 134-152.
[1529] 4th Ecumenical Synod.

Ecumenical Synod[1530] repeated the anathema against anyone who "*does not acknowledge truly Theotokos the Holy Glorious and Ever-virgin Maryor calls her 'Anthropotokos' or 'Christotokos'but not mainly and truly confesses her Theotokos.*"[1531]   In the Doctrine of the 6th Ecumenical Synod,[1532] the proclamation of the Birth of Christ is repeated that "*at the end of days for us and for our Salvation from the Holy Spirit and Mary the Virgin, the mainly and truly Theotokos.*"[1533]

St John of Damascus exhibited the meaning of this Doctrine by observing that "*we proclaim the Holy Virgin to be mainly and truly the Theotokos*" not because the Deity of the Word took up "*Its beginning from her*" but because God the Word was born without time, before all ages, from the Father Who inhabited "*her womb and from her unchangeably*" was Incarnated and Born. The Lord did not carry "*the Body from Heaven*" and did not pass through the Virgin "*as through a channel.*" Neither did He inhabit a "*pre-formed man as in a Prophet*" but from the Holy Virgin took up "*flesh substantial to ours*" and "*in His Hypostasis received an intellect and logical soul with the living Fleshbecoming Himself its Hypostasis.*" The aim of the Incarnation would be fulfilled since it "*took place for this, in order that the sinful and fallen and corrupted nature becomes victorious over the deceiver tyrant*" according to the Apostolic words "*since by man came death, by Man also came the Resurrection of the dead.*"[1534]   Under no circumstances do we call "*the Holy Virgin 'Christotokos',*" nor do we call "*He Who is born from the Virgin, 'Theophorus'*" ("*Carrier of God*"), "*as Nestorius the thief said in his madness*" because at the Incarnation of the Word there were "*three things togetherthe Engagement, the Existence and the Theosis by the Word*" of the human nature. As soon as the Conception occurred there was "*the Existence within the Word of the Flesh;, the Mother of God giving Supernaturally to the Creator to be formed and for God to become Man.*" On the other hand, He Deified that which He received, without confusion or change of the two united Natures. Truly then the Holy Virgin is Theotokos because "*from the first Existence*" of the Lord's human nature, He existed "*in both*" human and Divine Nature. Thus "*from extreme Conception*" His human nature existed "*in the Word.*"[1535]

[1530] Kefalas, *The Ecumenical Councils,* pp. 152-163.
[1531] 6th Canon of the 5th Ecumenical Synod. Pedalion, pp. 299; 2nd Canon of the same Synod, Cf. Pedalion, pp.294-296.
[1532] Kefalas, *The Ecumenical Councils,* pp. 164-190.
[1533] 6th Ecumenical Synod.
[1534] 1 Corinth. 15:21.
[1535] St John of Damascus, *Exposition, About the holy Theotokos; against Nestorians.* III, 12, in Migne, *P.G.,* 94, 1028, 1029 and 1032.

Question 213: Was the Human Nature of Christ deified?

Answer: Human nature was Deified because of the Hypostatic Union of the two Natures of Christ.[1536] When we take into consideration how much we benefit from the moral union of those who are sinners and yet are united with the Deity, becoming *"partakers of the Divine Nature,"*[1537] we get a vague idea of the Supernatural through the fullness and richness of the *Charismata* [Gifts] and Divine Exaltation that human nature receives by means of the Essential and Hypostatic Union in Christ with His Divine Nature. The measure, according to which Divine Nature is transmitted from Its infinite richness to human nature, was in this unique circumstance, determined by the infinite boundaries of the Divine Nature, through which the Divine *Charismata* and benefits are assigned. Even in the God-Man, the human nature did not cease to be a creature and a creation, and as such had to remain according to the Theosis and its perfection.

This measure was as Supernatural and unique as the union of the two Natures of Christ. Consequently our nature, besides its limited measure and transmission, was exalted in the God-Man as never before. It did not occur in the past in the Patriarchs or the Prophets, nor afterwards in the Saints. Neither will anything like it occur in the future, having made a New Creation in Christ and the God-bearing and God-inspired men becoming *"partakers of the Divine Nature."*[1538] The Perfection of Divine Nature can be differentiated into *perfection* and *Charismata* that refer to human knowledge, human will and human power.

Question 214: How was the supernatural Knowledge transmitted from the Divine to the Human Nature of Christ?

Answer: It must be noted that the Perfection that human knowledge received from the Divine Nature of the God-Man, was raised to the Knowledge of God. The Heavenly things were revealed through direct supervision and vision, not like other men who are gradually led from complete ignorance to the Knowledge of God and the Divine through participation in the Mysteries of the Supernatural Revelation. Man's worldly knowledge is always subject to errors.[1539]

[1536] Cf. Frangopoulos, *Christian Faith*, p. 137. Mitsopoulos, *Themata*, p. 150.
[1537] 2 Peter 1:4.
[1538] 2 Peter 1:4.
[1539] Cf. Mitsopoulos, *Themata*, pp. 150-151.

According to the fourth Gospel, the Lord verified that *"what He has seen and heard"*[1540] and that which He does *"which are shown to Him"* by the Father[1541] He is ready to do, even those things that are *"greater than"* the paradox, which was the healing of the Paralytic, when these were manifested to Him by the Father. *"Greater than these He will show Him"* says the Lord. Correctly speaking, the term *"show"* refers to the *"in time Action"* of the God-Man. He appears to be speaking *"of what He has seen from His Father."*[1542] In other words, what *"He saw through implanted Knowledge"* judging *"as He hears"* *"from the Father."* *"Commanding"* Him *"as Man; as from the form of a servant, not from the form of God, saying 'As I hear, I judge.'*[1543]*"* [1544] Additionally, in the Book of Acts, St Peter presents Him as being Predestined according to the Humanity of the Lord *"always on His Right Hand"*[1545] and always understanding His Presence. During His childhood, He was found in the Temple of Jerusalem, having forgotten His Mother and Joseph, His Righteous Guardian, where for three whole days He had not left the Temple but rather indulged in the events and discussions that took place there.[1546] According to these Evangelic and Apostolic Testimonies, the God-Man is in direct Communication with the Father. He sees Him and *"what He sees He testifies."*[1547] Christ continuously accepted revelations from the Father and *"as He hears"* He judges the new and greater Works of the Father accordingly. [1548]

This direct Vision and Communication of the Divine Knowledge and Wisdom was called *"implanted Knowledge"* by the Holy Fathers when they spoke of *"the brightness of the Wisdom of the Word of God growing gradually according to His Body's age"* and of the Divine Nature *"which revealed Its Wisdom according to the measure of the Body's age"* when they observed that the humanity of the God-Man *"increased in Wisdom and stature, and in favour with God and men."*[1549] The Wisdom of God and the Divine Things are not received from an external Source outside of the Deified human nature, nor was this graduation " *externally from the Word,*

[1540] John 3:32.
[1541] John 5:20.
[1542] John 8:38.
[1543] Cf. John 5:30.
[1544] St Cyril of Alexandrian, *To John 8:38,* in Migne, 73, 873.
[1545] Acts 2:33.
[1546] John 2:42-50.
[1547] John 3:11.
[1548] Zigabinos, *To John,* in Migne, *P.G.,* 129, 1225. St Augustine, *In Johannis evangelium, Tractatus XXIII,* 15, in migne, *P.L.,* 35, 1592.
[1549] Luke 2:52.

but 'the flesh which increased in Him'" and from God giving Wisdom to Him.[1550]

Besides this Supernatural Vision and internal transmission of the Divine Wisdom to the human nature of Christ, the God-Man received knowledge from experience as well, advancing according to the measure of His human nature. Hence, it is written in Holy Scripture that *"although He was the SonHe learned obedience"* from the things that *" He suffered"*[1551] and *"learned the obedience to God as a Man."*[1552] Furthermore, by means of His experience and the temptations that He resisted, He learnt *"to sympathize with our weaknesses."*[1553]

It is obvious that the Supernatural, the direct Divine Godly Vision and revealed Wisdom, as well as the knowledge that Christ gained from His experience of the material world, could not be compared to the Word's All-wisdom and Infinite Knowledge. No matter how Supernatural the direct Divine Enlightenment was, it remained a rich Treasure of Truth, Divine, uncontaminated by errors or lies and a Vessel for the limited human nature of the Word. Hence He was admired by the teachers of the Temple who *"were astonished at His understanding and answers."*[1554] Christ proclaimed Himself as being the *" Light of the worldwhich came into the world"*[1555] to free from darkness those who believe in Him. He declared that He is *"the Truth"*[1556] and that *"He came into the world, in order to witness the Truth."*[1557] He claimed the title of *"Teacher"* under a unique meaning, discouraging His Disciples from being referred to as *"Teachers," "for One is our Teacher, the Christ."*[1558] All these Divine Declarations testify that above every Holy Prophet or God-inspired man, Christ our Lord is the Teacher of the Truth[1559] Who Incarnated the Divine Truth within Him. For this reason He is the unique *"Light of the world"*[1560] Who gave mankind the supremely perfect Revelation and Divine Enlightenment.[1561] Whenever He reveals the unknown future to men, what is to happen to the Church and to

---

[1550] St Cyril of Alexandrian, *To John 8:38,* in Migne, 73, 873. Ibid, *To Luke,* in Migne, *P.G.,* 72, 508. St Athanasius the Great, *Against Arians,* III, § 53, in Migne, *P.G.,* 26, 433.
[1551] Heb. 5:8.
[1552] Zigabinos, *To John,* in Migne, *P.G.,* 129, 1225.
[1553] Heb. 4:15.
[1554] Luke 2:46-47.
[1555] John 12:46.
[1556] John 14:6.
[1557] John 18:37.
[1558] Matth. 23:8.
[1559] John 1:45.
[1560] John 8:12.
[1561] John 1:9.

the servants of the Gospel[1562] as well as what is to happen elsewhere, or by showing that He knows and *"searches the minds and hearts"* of men,[1563] He reveals His Supernatural Knowledge and pronounces that *"for the sameness of the Hypostasis, the Lord's Soul was enriched with the things of the future and unknown Knowledge."*[1564]

Although Christ, according to His human nature, is the fullness of the Saving Truth, He does not ignore anything concerning the means of Salvation and without any error, He interprets the perfect Revelation of God to us. He appears to ignore either details of human knowledge or elements of Divine Truth that God does not want to reveal. Although these remain unknown, they do not affect the perfection of Divine Revelation. Thus, for example, in Bethany He inquired where St Lazarus had been buried.[1565] Another example was when, after His Transfiguration, a demon-possessed youth was brought to Him whereupon He asked the boy's father.[1566]   At the time of His Second Coming, He verifies that *"of that day and hour no one knows, not even the Angels in Heaven, nor the Son, but only the Father."*[1567]

Question 215: How was the Holiness & Sinlessness transmitted from the Divine to the Human Nature of Christ?

Answer: The Divine Nature's perfection that was transmitted to the Lord's human nature, is the Lord's Holiness and absolute sinless condition.[1568] St Luke in his Holy Gospel, when speaking of the Annunciation of the Theotokos by Archangel Gabriel, characterised that which would be born from the Holy Spirit and the Virgin as the *"Holy One."*[1569] In St Joseph the Betrothed's dream, the Angel comforted him with the assurance that *"that which is conceived in her is of the Holy Spirit."*[1570] It is obvious that from the time of the Word's Incarnation in the Virgin's Womb, " *the Word became Flesh."* Christ's Flesh was anointed with Deity and *"with us it is Sanctified according to human capability."* Because of the conception by the Holy Spirit, the Anointing occurred. As a result *"the sanctification of*

[1562] Rev. 1:19.
[1563] Rev. 2:23.
[1564] St John of Damascus, *Exposition. About the natural and incontestable passions,* III, 64, 21, in Migne, *P.G.,* 94, 1084.
[1565] John 11:34.
[1566] Mark 9:21.
[1567] Mark 13:32.
[1568] Cf. Frangopoulos, *Christian Faith,* pp. 137-139. Mitsopoulos, *Themata,* p. 151.
[1569] Luke 1:35.
[1570] Matth. 1:20.

the Flesh, which is not by nature Holy" happened, due to being a *" participant with God."*[1571]

Jesus Christ is the absolute Anointed One, the CHRIST, because *"when He became flesh" "He was anointed with the Oil of Gladness; in other words, with the Holy Spirit by God the Father"* Who gave Him unrestricted *"Energy of the Holy Spirit" "for God does not give the Spirit by measure."*[1572] He was Anointed with *"the Oil of Gladness more than* (His) *companions"*[1573] or more than anyone who participated in this Anointing. Christ was not Anointed by the Holy Spirit as were other Holy men by their limited capacity. The Father did not give Him *"one or two Energies"* but bestowed upon Him *" all the Energy"* of the Holy Spirit so that the Christ *"has essentially the Spirit."* His Anointing was *"not by Energy which sanctified other anointed ones"* but was accomplished *"in the complete Presence of Him Who anointed."*[1574]

The Lord, through the anointing of His Flesh, did not receive the Sanctification for Himself only as it transpires with humanity. He received it so that *"it will become for all men as it is for Himself."* The Lord sanctifies *"through Himself the whole man, as becoming the yeast for the whole dough"*[1575] of mankind *"and uniting to Himself that which was once condemned, loosens all who were bound because of the Offence."*[1576] Thus *"we have the Grace of the Holy Spirit, receiving it from His fullness"*[1577] being *"full of Grace"*[1578] *"which we all receive."*[1579]

Many of the Holy Fathers accept that when our Lord Jesus was baptized in the River Jordan, *"the Holy Spirit came upon Him as in the form of a dove"*[1580] *"and the descent of the Holy Spirit was essential and He was Anointed with the spiritual Oil of Gladness"* and *"as a dove, appeared the Holy Spirit descending and resting upon Himand He received as a Man."* The same Holy Fathers who refer to the Anointing of Christ during His

---

[1571] St John of Damascus, *Exposition. About when was Christ called,* IV, 79, 6, in Migne, *P.G.,* 94, 1112. St Cyril of Alexandria, *To Psalm 44,* in Migne, *P.G.,* 69, 1040.

[1572] John 3:34.

[1573] Heb. 1:9. Psalm 44(45):7. Is. 61:1-3.

[1574] St John of Damascus, *Exposition. About when was Christ called,* IV, 79, 6, in Migne, *P.G.,* 94, 1112. St Cyril of Alexandria, *To Psalm 44,* in Migne, *P.G.,* 69, 1040. Zigabinos, *To John 3:34,* in Migne, *P.G.,* 129, 1181. St Ecumenius, *To Hebrews,* in Migne, *P.G.,* 119, 288. St John Chrysostom, *To John 3:34,* in Montfaucon, v. 8, 199. Theophylactus of Bulgaria, in Migne, *P.G.,* 123, 1221. St Gregory of Nazianzus, *Homily* 30, § 21, in Migne, *P.G.,* 36, 132.

[1575] St Athanasius the Great, *Against Arians* I, § 47, in Migne, *P.G.,* 26, 109.

[1576] St Gregory of Nazianzus, *Homily* 30, § 21, in Migne, *P.G.,* 36, 132.

[1577] St Athanasius the Great, *Against Arians* I, § 50, in Migne, *P.G.,* 26, 117.

[1578] John 1:14.

[1579] John 1:16.

[1580] Matth. 3:16. Mark 1:10. Luke 3:22. John 1:32.

Baptism in the Jordan River also refer to it occurring previously, during the pregnancy of the Blessed Ever-Virgin Mary and Theotokos. This manifests that the anointing took place in both cases. The Conception and Unity of the Word of God with the Flesh that He received, was simultaneously the anointing and sanctification of His flesh, according to which the Incarnated *"was He Who was Anointing and the Anointed; Anointing as God and being Anointed as Man." "Anointing as God the Body to His Deity, being Anointed as Man"* and *"the Deity Anointing the Humanity."* Our Lord's Holy baptism was exalted by the special Grace that was granted after He reached manhood in order to complete the Messianic Work for which He was called. The One Who was sanctified from His Immaculate Conception and Who pleased the Heavenly Father, was anointed *"by the Father as the Saviour of the whole world with the Holy Spirit."*[1581] This repeated anointment of the Lord according to His humanity, appears to be in agreement with the testimony of St Luke, according to which the Lord *"increased in wisdom and stature and in favour with God and men."*[1582] Hence the Holy Fathers, referring to the second anointment proclaimed that *"as a price of good achievements, we think that it was given"* to Christ and that *"the Son of sinlessness was Anointed with praises according to us as a Man, being worthy of the Anointment of the Holy Spirit"* in that He descended and remained upon Him forever. Thus the Lord, having the Hypostatic Union in Him as well as the full Grace of Sanctification, received an additional Anointment, by leading a Holy Life during His thirty years of earthly time, thereby pleasing the Father Whose Divine Words He heard at the Jordan River:[1583] *"This is My beloved Son, in Whom I Am pleased."*[1584]

As the negative side of the Lord's perfect human Holiness, one can characterise His sinlessness, which is guaranteed by the Hypostatic Union of the two Natures. Truly, if even a shadow of sin had ever entered in the God-Man, the contaminated human nature would have immediately separated from the absolute Holy Divine Nature and the God-Man would not exist.

[1581] St Cyril of Alexandria, *To Psalm 44,* in Migne, *P.G.,* 69, 1040. St Cyril of Jerusalem, *Catechesis,* III, 1-2, in Migne, *P.G.,* 33, 1088 and 1089. St Athanasius the Great, *About the incarnation epiphany of God the Word and against Arians,* § 9, in Migne, *P.G.,* 36, 997. St John of Damascus, *Exposition. About the genealogy of the Lord and about the holy Theotokos,* IV, 14, in Migne, *P.G.,* 94, 1161. Ibid, *Exposition. About the two natures, against Monophysites,* III, 47, 3, in Migne, *P.G.,* 94, 989. St Cyril of Jerusalem, *Catechesis,* III, 2, in Migne, *P.G.,* 33, 1089.
[1582] Luke 3:52.
[1583] St Basil the Great, *Homily to Psalm 44,* § 5, in Migne, *P.G.,* 29, 397. St Cyril of Alexandria, *About the incarnation of the only Begotten,* in Migne, *P.G.,* 75, 1369.
[1584] Matth. 3:17. Mark 1:17. Luke 3:22. 2 Peter 1:17.

Since our Lord, until the end, "*had conquered the world*"[1585] and "*the ruler of the world*" could not find anything with which to accuse Him,[1586] even at the last moments, He had the right to say to His Father: "*The Work I have completed, which Thou had given to Me to do*" and thus He requested to be glorified by the Father "*with the Glory which He had from Him before the world was made.*"[1587] We have complete assurance that throughout His entire life Christ remained sinless. This was verified by our Lord Himself Who confronted His opponents by saying to them: "*Which of you convicts Me of sin?*"[1588] and asserting that "*as My Father had Commanded Me, thus I do*"[1589] thereby distinguishing Himself from other men[1590] who were forced to seek the forgiveness of God by means of their repentance but which He never had to ask of the Father.

Furthermore, the hope of those Disciples who surrounded Him for three years, bears witness of His sinlessness. St John the Apostle convinces us that "*He was manifested, in order to take up our sins and sin was not found in Him.*"[1591] St Peter proclaimed that Christ "*committed no sin, nor was deceit found in His mouth.*"[1592] St Paul manifested the universal belief of the Church that is based on the evidence of all the eyewitnesses of our Lord that "*He knew no sin, but became for us sin*" and conquered sin in order that "*we become righteous of God in Him.*"[1593]

The Angelic words addressed to the Blessed Ever-Virgin Mary and St Joseph the Betrothed that our Lord Jesus was Conceived by the Holy Spirit and that from the moment of His Conception He was Holy, assure us that the Lord was completely free of the Original Sin as well as evil desire ("*concupiscentia*").

The 5th Ecumenical Synod condemned Theodorus of Mopsuestias and all those who said that Christ had sinful passions of the soul, desires of the flesh and that He progressed from the worst state towards a perfect and blameless Life.[1594] The 6th Ecumenical Synod proclaimed Christ to be "*consubstantial to us according to the humanity; in all the same with us without sin*" "*His human will not opposing, but submitting to His Divine Will.*"

[1585] John 16:33.
[1586] John 14:30
[1587] John 17:4, 5
[1588] John 8:46.
[1589] John 14:31.
[1590] Matth. 6:9; 7:11 etc.
[1591] 1 John 3:5.
[1592] 1 Peter 2:22.
[1593] 2 Corinth. 5:21.
[1594] Canon 12 of the 5th Ecumenical Synod, *Pedalion*, pp. 303-305.

Question 216: Could our Lord have committed sin?

Answer: Concerning the question of whether our Lord could have committed sin, being free of the tendency towards evil and being completely free of sinful desire, the second Adam (Christ), was in a more superior state than Adam before the Fall. The first Adam was called to progress within the union with God by means of the Grace that was granted to him externally, which assured his permanent adoption by Grace. The second Adam Who came from Heaven, was united with God the Word from His conception in the Ever Blessed Virgin's Holy Womb, having by Nature the Sonship as a result of the Hypostatic Union of His two Natures. In the first Adam, the Divine Life was externally transmitted like a fountain, whereas the human nature of the second Adam was received from the Divine Fountain of Life that was hypostatically united with it like members of one and the same body that receive the source of life from the head or as the branches of a tree are nourished directly from their source. It is obvious that the new Adam of Grace received the richness of Grace directly from the Source of the Deity that dwelt within Him. Indisputably, the Lord's human nature is not Infinite, for even after the Hypostatic Union the human nature continued to be restricted. In relation to us who are extracted from sin and who are struggling daily against sin, His human nature is incomparable, being *"the fullness of Grace and Truth."*[1595] Consequently the God-Man could never have sinned, being from the beginning, untouched by sinful heredity, having the purest moral conscience and the automatic tendency towards good since His conception in the Ever Blessed Virgin's Womb.[1596]

According to Holy Scripture the God-Man appears *"familiar in all"* to us.[1597] The Lord's temptations were neither a type of fantasy, delusion nor imagination. They transpired within the God-Man as much as *"the Deity which dwelt in Him allowed"*[1598] *"and in absentia, left the Flesh naked of its own Power, in order to reveal its weakness and thus to ascertain its nature."*[1599] The weak human nature struggled against the temptations while at the same time being assisted by the Deity that dwelt within Him, just as the first Adam would have been Divinely assisted had he resisted the Tempter. Thus the Lord *"had to put on the form of a servant in order to gain victory for the one who was once defeatedand gave Power to the (human) Nature"* in order that *"that which was once defeated by those*

[1595] John 1:14.
[1596] St Basil the Great, *To Psalm 44(45)*, § 8, in Migne, *P.G.,* 29, 405.
[1597] Heb. 4:15.
[1598] St Cyril of Alexandria, *About the Lord's incarnation,* in Migne, *P.G.,* 75, 1457.
[1599] St John Chrysostom, in Mansi, v. 11, p. 397.

temptations, through the same, to gain victory over the one who once became victorious."[1600]   Otherwise, if His human nature had not gained victory over Satan as it happened with the first Adam at the Fall and had the Divine Nature of the God-Man gained victory over him instead, then fallen man would have gained nothing and Satan would have boasted that he had "*.fought with God and was defeated by God.*" Death would not have been defeated if the human nature of our Lord had not been delivered unto death. Likewise, according to the opinion of the Holy Fathers, the Lord had to be tempted by each passion of the flesh so as to gain victory over them, thereby moving them to *apatheia* ("*without passions*") and causing the nature of the entire human race to benefit. If the Lord had not lost courage in the Garden of Gethsemane, "*human nature would not have been freed from this passion; if He had not been saddened, He would not have been freed of sadness*" and generally the irreproachable passions are changed for the better in Christ.[1601]

During the Lord's temptations "*the Tempter attacked Him externallynot through thoughts*" that are caused by sinful tendencies or desire, of which the Lord was completely free. We could never accept that "*in discrimination of thoughts*" and with wavering, the Lord renounced "*the corrupt*" and preferred "*the good.*" In spite of this, Satan took advantage of the circumstances that arose due to the Lord's irreproachable passions, attempting to enter His inner parts. After the forty days of fasting in the desert, the Lord was hungry and "*that of the Flesh prevailed, in order to gain experience and for the tempter to be ashamed; and the first man who had fallen because he partook from the Forbidden Fruit, through self-restraint to be raised.*"[1602]   The Tempter had found an opportunity in the inner need of hunger, which at that moment the God-Man suffered. Similarly in the Garden of Gethsemane "*the human nature of Christ was found weak*"[1603] because through the irreproachable passion of repugnance of death, He experienced "*the opposite to that of the Flesh*"[1604] whereupon

---

[1600] St Cyril of Alexandria, *Homily* II, ch. 36, in Migne, *P.G.,* 76, 1384.   Ibid, *About the Lord's incarnation,* in Migne, *P.G.,* 75, 1464.   St Athanasius the Great, *Against Apollinarius* II, § 9, in Migne, *P.G.,* 26, 1148.   St John of Damascus, *Exposition. About the natural and unslandered passions,* III, 64, 20, in Migne, *P.G.,* 94, 1081.

[1601] St Cyril of Alexandria, *About the Lord's incarnation,* in Migne, *P.G.,* 75, 1444. St Athanasius the Great, *To the Now My soul is troubled,* in Mansi, v. 11, p. 597. St Cyril of Alexandria, in Migne, 75, 397 and Mansi v. 11, p. 409.

[1602] St John of Damascus, *Exposition. About the natural and unslandered passions,* III, 64, 20, in Migne, *P.G.,* 94, 1081. St Cyril of Alexandria, *To John,* book IV, 20, 5, in Migne, *P.G.,* 73, 657.

[1603] St Cyril of Alexandria, *To John,* book IV, ch. 1, in Migne, *P.G.,* 73, 529. See also the 10th Act of the 6th Ecumenical Synod, in Mansi, v. 11, p. 420.

[1604] St Athanasius the Great, *To Now My soul is trouble,* in the 14th Act of the 6th Ecumenical Synod, in Mansi, v. 11, p. 597.

the Divine Nature *"immediately moved to assist"* the irreproachable passion of fear and cowardliness by transforming *"immediately to incomparable daring that which was defeated by cowardliness."*[1605] It appears clearly that in the Garden of Gethsemane *"death was not wanted by Christ because of the Flesh and the inglorious suffering of the Cross."*[1606] *"Although He was in agony"* He did not resign from His obedience to His Heavenly Father for the benefit of mankind[1607] and through Divine Assistance, the *"very weak of will was made into wanting."*[1608] Consequently in the God-Man the *"non potuit peccare"* presupposed the *"potuit non peccare."*

In the Hypostatic Union of the two Natures, the human freedom of the God-Man was not lost but was raised and Deified *"manifesting the sinlessness by Nature and by Power."* The Hypostatic Union of the two Natures contributed to the natural inability of sinning, whereas the direct Vision of God contributed to the moral determination not to sin.[1609] We can understand Christ's natural inability to sin when we refer to St John's words that *"whoever is born from God does not sin, for His seed remains in him; and he cannot sin, because he has been born of God."*[1610] From the beginning, before the Fall, Adam's nature *"was made not to sin."*[1611] We *"were led from the natural to the unnatural* (state) *because of the Offence."*[1612] Consequently, *"sinning became a necessity."*[1613] However, *"the condition of this necessity and the law of sin"*[1614] was smashed by the human nature of our Lord Jesus and, being united with the Word of God, *"brought us back from the unnatural to the natural"* state.[1615] Power was revealed when the God-Man *"captured the tyrant of captivity"*[1616] and *"changed the* (fallen human) *nature towards a greater and Divine condition"*[1617] so as not to be moved or overthrown due to weakness of virtuous effort. This absolute sinless condition of our Lord did not deprive

---

[1605] St Cyril of Alexandria, *To Matthew,* in Migne, *P.G.,* 72, 926, passage in the 10th Act of the 6th Ecumenical Synod, in Mansi, v. 11, p. 413.

[1606] St Cyril of Alexandria, *To John,* book IV, ch. 1, in Migne, *P.G.,* 73, 529. Passage in the 10th Act of the 6th Ecumenical Synod, in Mansi, v. 11, p. 420.

[1607] St John Chrysostom, *To John,* book II, homily 67, in Mansi, v. 11, p. 408.

[1608] St Cyril of Alexandria, in Migne, *P.G.,* 72, 456. Mansi, v. 11, p. 412.

[1609] Ott, *Precis,* p. 243.

[1610] 1 John 3:9.

[1611] St Athanasius the Great, *Against Apollinarius,* II, § 9, in Migne, *P.G.,* 36, 1145.

[1612] St John of Damascus, *Exposition. About the wills and free-wills of our Lord Jesus Christ,* III, 58, 14, in Migne, *P.G.,* 94, 1044.

[1613] St Athanasius the Great, *Against Apollinarius,* II, § 9, in Migne, *P.G.,* 36, 1145.

[1614] St John of Damascus, *Exposition. About the wills and free-wills of our Lord Jesus Christ,* III, 58, 14, in Migne, *P.G.,* 94, 1044.

[1615] St Athanasius the Great, *Against Apollinarius,* II, § 9, in Migne, *P.G.,* 36, 1145.

[1616] St Cyril of Alexandria, *To Matthew,* book VIII, in Migne, *P.G.,* 72, 921.

[1617] Fragment from the 10th Act of the 6th Ecumenical Synod, in Mansi, 11, 413.

Him of His freedom to choose between good and evil, nor did it decrease His freedom, since it is impossible for God to turn towards evil. Committing wickedness is not perfection but imperfection and weakness of will.

It is therefore evident that our Lord Jesus Christ became our moral Prototype in reality and not implausibly, in view of the fact that He became like us in everything except sin, being *"without sin."* He cultivated Virtue as Man and His moral perfection is projected to us in order to be imitated. His human nature fulfills the receptive capacity of our human nature. Although He was tempted as one of us, it was only externally because His inner world is free of all tendency to sin. The victory over the Tempter was achieved through the One Who was similar to him who was once deceived in the Garden of Eden, by projecting the form of the servant against the enemy. In Flesh, Christ fulfilled the Obedience as perfect Man within Himself. Through Himself He submitted human nature to God the Father, thereby offering us a perfect type and model to imitate. In His struggle against sin, He gained victory over the ruler of this generation and over his instruments, not by using the Power of His Deity nor by calling upon the Angels for assistance but by becoming one responsible Person Who was tempted and Who Anointed the Man Who was taught Virtue and Justice to the extreme.[1618]

In addition, the Lord's perfection in Virtue and Knowledge as Man increased as He grew and progressively became alienated from all *"evilness."* Although our Lord became like us, He advanced to a more superior level of Knowledge. He learnt *"obedience from what He had experienced, receiving the experience as His teacher not knowing* (the obedience) *before the experience" "taking the perfection in part" "continuing to be obedient to God and becoming perfect through all that He experienced."* Throughout His Life on earth there was not a moment when He was disobedient despite being imbued with the tendency from His birth. His obedience was manifested especially at the time of His Passions *"where He honoured the obedience to the Father by His action"* and *" which He experienced from the suffering."* Our Lord Jesus Christ was always sinless and Holy. In His growth of Virtue *"He is shaped in all according to the human capacity"*[1619] not progressing from weakness towards Power or from

---

[1618] St Athanasius the Great, *Against Apollinarius,* II, § 9, in Migne, *P.G.,* 26, 1148. St John of Damascus, *Exposition. About wills and free-wills,* III, 62, 18, in Migne, *P.G.,* 94, 1076. St Cyril of Alexandria, *About the Lord's incarnation,* in Migne, *P.G.,* 75, 1433. Ibid, *That one is the Christ,* in Migne, *P.G.,* 75, 1332.

[1619] St Cyril of Alexandria, *About the Lord's incarnation,* in Migne, *P.G.,* 75, 1457. St John Chrysostom, *To Hebrews,* Homily VIII, § 2, in Migne, *P.G.,* 63, 70. St Gregory of Nyssa, Homily 30, § 6, in Migne, *P.G.,* 36, 109. St Athanasius the Great, *To Psalm 15 (16),* in Migne, *P{.G.,* 27, 104.

defectiveness towards Perfection but instead always manifesting the Power and tendency towards Virtue that were within Him.

Question 217: What was the deification of the power in the God-Man?

Answer: The human nature of our Lord and Saviour Jesus Christ, as the Instrument of the Word of God, partook of the Power to perform Supernatural Works of the Divine Nature according to the natural world. This Deification of Power in the human nature of our Lord did not eliminate its limitations nor did it change into Almightiness ascribed only to the Infinite Divine Nature. The Lord acted Supernaturally on a level incomparably more superior than that of any other Holy men who performed Miracles in the past, present or future.

In the Holy Gospels, the Lord Jesus Christ healed everyone who was presented to Him including those who, by simply touching Him, received restoration of health.[1620] Christ did not borrow Power from anyone else like it had been necessary for the Prophets and other Holy men who did not possess Power by nature. Instead they received it from Above and only through God's Grace were they able to perform miracles.[1621] The Lord, on the contrary, *"being the Fountain of all Good* [things] *has all the Power coming out of Him"* and not only as Man but *"being by Nature God"* and *" although He became Flesh, He healed everyone by the outpouring His Power."*[1622] His human nature became *"the Instrument of the Divinity"* serving the Work of miracles, being *"the Body of God."*[1623]

The Supernatural Energy within the moral field of the Lord's Flesh is manifested particularly in the Mystery of the Divine Eucharist, where the Lord's Flesh is characterised as *"Life-giving"* and as *"the Bread of Life"* *"which nourishes us in the Eternal Life"* and *"uproots from the foundations the mortality and death which inhabited the human flesh."*[1624] For this Flesh is not *"the flesh of a high man, but that of the Son"* Who was Incarnated *"full of all the Deity"* and to it the Word *"was united to the extreme."* For this reason, *"it is Life-giving, although It remained what It was and did not change into the Word's Nature."*[1625] Although through the union with the Divine Nature *"It is not one Nature, but one of the Body, and another of the*

[1620] Matt. 4:23-24; 8:7, 16; 10:1; 12:22; 14:14; 17:18; 19:2. Mark 1:34; 3:10, 15; 6:13. Luke 6:18; 7:21; 8:43; 9:1, 6; 13:14.

[1621] Theophylactus of Bulgaria, *To Luke 6:19,* in Migne, *P.G.,*123, 772. Ibid, *To Luke 8:46,* in Migne, *P.G.,*123, 809

[1622] St Cyril of Alexandria, *To Luke 6, 19,* in Migne, *P.G., 72,* 588.

[1623] St Athanasius the Great, *Against Arians,* III, § 31, in Migne, *P.G., 26,* 389.

[1624] St Cyril of Alexandria, *To John 6:35 and 55,* in Migne, *P.G., 74,* 517 and 584.

[1625] Ammonius, *To John 6:55,* in Migne, *P.G., 85,* 1440.

Deity, which is united with It"[1626] "*the Lord's Flesh is spiritual Life-giving, for it was conceived by the Life-giving Spirit and thus it is Life-giving and Divine.*"[1627]

Question 218: What was the deification of the Lord's Human Nature after His Resurrection?

Answer: The Deification of the Lord's human nature, as previously mentioned, refers to the period of Christ's Life on earth when He emptied Himself so as to appear in the form of a servant and dwell amongst men. From the moment the Lord died on the Cross, His human nature was elevated after His Suffering, "*putting aside all the irreproachable passions*" such as "*the mortality, the hunger and the thirst, the need of sleep and weariness and all the similar*" sensations, having a "*Body*" that is Imperishable, Immortal and Glorious, as well as a soul that is " *intellectual and spiritual*" with which "*He was raised into the Heavens and thus*" is now " *sitting at the Right Hand of God*" "*His Flesh being Glorified.*" Furthermore, He was given all the Authority in Heaven and on earth. The transmission of the richness of the Divine Nature to His human nature was accomplished to an even greater degree, although His human nature preserved its restrictions and remained unaltered although being elevated to such level that even "*the Heavenly and invisible Powers*" give more "*honour*" to It. Thus before the Sufferings and the Resurrection "*the Nature of the Flesh was not Glorified, nor enjoyed Immortality, nor participated of the Royal Throne*" for He said to His Father: "*Father glorify Me, with the Glory which I had with Thee before the world was made.*"[1628] Immediately after His Glorious Resurrection He prevented St Mary Magdalene from touching Him, commanding her: "*Do not touch Me*" but at the same time assuring her that "*this Body is not the same as the one during His Life on earth, but the Heavenly from Above.*"[1629]

By the specific words "*from Above*" we must distinguish the Deification (Theosis) of the Lord's human nature during the period of His humble estate and emptiness (Incarnation), from that of the Theosis, in

---

[1626] St John of Damascus, *Exposition. About the holy and precious mysteries of the Lord,* IV, 86, 13, in Migne, *P.G.,* 94, 1149.

[1627] Ibid, *Exposition. About the holy and precious mysteries of the Lord,* IV, 86, in Migne, *P.G.,* 94, 1152.

[1628] John 17:5.

[1629] St John of Damascus, *Exposition. About the after the resurrection,* IV, 74, 1 and 2, in Migne, *P.G.,* 94, 1101 and 1104. Matt. 28:18. Heb. 2:9. St John of Damascus, *To 1 Corinth. 13:1* in Migne, *P.G.,* 95, 692. St John Chrysostom, *To John 17:5,* in Montfaucon, v. 8, p. 544. John 20:17. Theophylactus of Bulgaria, *To John,* in Migne, *P.G.,* 124, 296.

which His human nature participated after the Resurrection and the sitting at the Right Hand of God the Father that is connected to the Royal Office of Christ as King.

CHAPTER EIGHT
THE WORK OF THE LORD: THE SALVATION
THE THREEFOLD OFFICE OF THE LORD

Question 219: What is the threefold Office of Christ?

Answer: The Work which God the Father gave to His Incarnated Son *"to do,"* is undivided in its nature and frees us *" from the authority of darkness and transfers us to His Kingdom"* and *"from death to Life"* granting us *"Salvation and the forgiveness of our sins through His Blood."*   In this united Work of Salvation, the Lord *"fulfilled"* for us *" Wisdom from God, Justice and Sanctification and Deliverance."*[1630] He Enlightened the human mind, which was darkened by the sinful passions. He achieved through His Sacrifice, the expiation of man's justification by yielding all sinful power to man's will through the Grace of God, which supports, strengthens and Sanctifies man's will. The threefold Office of the Lord as Prophet, High Priest and King are manifested in Holy Scripture. In the New Testament especially, the Lord appears to consolidate these Offices within Himself, whereas in the Old Testament they appear under shadowy Prototypes, being allocated to different Holy People.

This threefold Office of our Lord and Saviour Jesus Christ, consists of three inseparable elements united into one. It manifests the Unique and Indivisible Work of our one Saviour. It would be erroneous to think that our Lord received them separately, one after another and not simultaneously. We can say that the Lord exercised the Offices of Prophet and High Priest during His humble Appearance and the Royal Office in His Glory as the Risen and Ascended Christ but He is forever the Eternal Archpriest Who intercedes for us.[1631]

We must also never forget that the separate examination of each Office is for practical purposes only because the Work of Salvation is always undivided. In reality and Truth, these three Offices of our Lord Jesus Christ are unbreakably integrated and perfect. It is impossible to exclude or to separate them without damaging the Holy Gospel and the entire Work of Salvation. Therefore, we can understand the impossibility of

---

[1630] John 1:4. Col. 1:13. 1 John 3:14. Ephes. 1:7. 1 Corinth. 1:30
[1631] Cf. Frangopoulos, *Christian Faith,* pp. 142-144. Mitsopoulos, *Themata,* pp. 156-157.

considering which of the three Offices is more important, since all are united in the one Person of the Saviour and His Work of Salvation. Under the presupposition of their undivided unity and their ultimate purpose of restoration of the relationship between mankind and God, as a necessity for the expiatory Sacrifice of the Lord, the Office of the High Priest appears as being central to the unification of the two other Offices.

Question 220: What are the teachings of the holy Fathers concerning the three Offices of Christ?

Answer: The discernment of the three Offices of Christ was literally made by Eusebius of Caesarea who observed that in the past none of the anointed Priests, Kings or Prophets received *"such power of virtue as the Saviour and Lord."* The Lord did not receive *"symbols and types of the Archpriesthood"* from another person. Neither was He from the line of *"Archpriests,"* promoted *"to King"* nor made *"Prophet as the ones in the past."* *"He was Anointed not by men but by the Father"* *"not with man-made myrrh but with the Father's Divine Intellect and Divinity."* Thus He surpassed all other anointed ones who had been anointed with material and symbolic myrrh. *"He was called Christ above all those being the only True Christ."* He is *"the only Archpriest of all and the only King of all Creation"* as well as being *"the only Arch-prophet of the Father amongst all Prophets."*[1632]

St John Chrysostom continuously distinguished the three Offices of the Lord. Concerning the Royal Office he said that the Lord *"was always a King"* referring to His Divine Person as the Word through Whom God made everything. Concerning the Office of Archpriest he observed that *"He became Priest when He took up flesh, when He offered the Sacrifice."* Exalting the Majesty of the Raised Lord, he remarked: *"If He is a Great God, He is a Great Lord, Great and as King. Great King upon all the earth Great Prophet, Great Priest, Great Light, in everything Great ; for when Jesus was performing the miracles, the crowds were saying that a Great Prophet is amongst us thus again a Great Priest Wherefrom this? St Paul says: We have an Archpriest Who surpassed the Heavens."* According to Jewish belief, these three Offices belonged not to one but to different Tribes and consequently it was impossible for all three Offices to be found in one and the same Person. The Christ was not raised according to the Leviticus

---

[1632] Eusebius, *Church History,* I, 3 and 11, in Migne, *P.G.,* 20, 72 and 73. Ibid, in Migne, *P.G.,* 22, 296.

Priesthood nor according to the Order of Aaron but according to the Order of Melchisedek.[1633]

Question 221: What are the teachings of Holy Scripture concerning the Lord's threefold Office?

Answer: One can observe from Holy Scripture's reference to the threefold Office of Christ that our Lord and Saviour spoke directly of Himself as a Prophet. He referred to the unfavourable welcome by His own countrymen in the village of Nazareth when He said that *"no Prophet is welcomed in his own country and home"*[1634] and in Jerusalem He remarked that *"no Prophet was killed outside of Jerusalem."*[1635] Likewise when Christ accepted the title of *"Teacher."* The Lord accepted being called *"Christ"* or *"Messiah"* as King, Whom the Prophets proclaimed to the people of Israel and to Whom the Lord God would give *"the throne of David His father"*[1636] to rule *"upon the house of Jacob."*[1637] The Archangel Gabriel announced this good news as well to the Ever-Virgin Mary, the Theotokos.[1638] The Office of Archpriest is exalted especially in the Epistle to the Hebrews, in which Christ is called *"great Archpriest"* *"Who has surpassed the heavens"* and as the *"eternal Priest"* He has His Priesthood *"according to the order of Melchisedek."*[1639] In addition to the above, the Holy Apostles called Christ *"Prophet,"* referring to the prophetic words of Moses according to which *"the Lord will raise a Prophet like me."*[1640]

In the Old Testament the three Offices are found under a shadowy meaning and as a type which prefigures the future reality in the Christ Although the three Offices, as types of the future event, were used in the old *Economia* (Old Testament), it was prohibited to gather them in one person, as in the case found in 2 Chronicles 26:18. Although King David is anointed as King and was at the same time a Prophet, he was not anointed as a Prophet. He was prohibited from building a temple to the Most High and thus he remained alienated to all Priestly services. King Ozias was punished with leprosy because he dared to claim the Priestly service.

[1633] St John Chrysostom, *To Hebrew*, 13, § 1, in Migne, *P.G.*, 63, 103. Ibid, *To the Lord's Ascencion,* § 16, in Migne, *P.G.,* 52, 790. Ibid, *That one is the lawgiver of the Old and New Testament,* § 5, in Migne, 56, 405. Cf. Trempelas, *The laymen in the Church. "The Royal priesthood",* Athens, 1976.
[1634] Matt. 13:57. Act 3:22; 7:37.
[1635] Luke 13:33.
[1636] Luke 1:32.
[1637] Heb. 7:17-25.
[1638] Luke
[1639] Heb. 5:6.
[1640] Deut. 18:15.

These three Offices are united inseparably and eternally in the one Person and were the ideal of the old *Economia*, according to which the people of Israel were awaiting the perfect Prophet (the Messiah) Who would bring back the glorious and eternal kingship of David and Who would have the spotless, eternal and without successor Priesthood according to the order of Melchisedek.[1641]

This ideal described in the Old Testament is realised only in the Person of our Lord and Saviour Jesus Christ, the Son of God, because He is the only God-Man Who, as the Word of God, took up human nature and was anointed by God the Father, not with material or manmade oil, but with the Holy Spirit,[1642] to be the High Prophet and Teacher, the only great and without successor Archpriest and the eternal King within His Church. These three Offices in the Christ exist simultaneously. It would be erroneous to believe that Christ received them separately, first as Prophet, then as Archpriest and finally as King.

Question 222: Is the threefold Offices inseparable and unbreakable?

Answer: As mentioned above, the threefold Offices of Christ are examined separately for practical reasons only, but in reality they are inseparably united. Our Lord and Saviour Jesus Christ, the Son of God, teaching as Prophet and giving His Laws, simultaneously manifested His Kingship by performing the miracles as He taught. While hanging on the Cross He offered as Archpriest the unique Sacrifice for the Salvation of the world. He even taught as He stood before Pontius Pilate that He *"bears witness to the truth"* as Prophet and accepted the title of King Whose *"Kingdom is not from this world."*[1643]

Our Lord and Saviour Jesus Christ, the Son of God, was anointed to the threefold Office from the time of His Incarnation. These three Offices are related to one another. In Orthodox Christology it is mentioned that they are two conditions, that of *"humility"* or *"emptiness"* (*"inanitio"*) and that of *"exaltation"* or *"glorification"* (*"exaltatio"* or *"glorificatio"*). The Offices of Christ, being Prophet and Archpriest, were mainly evident during the period of the Lord's humility, whereas the Office of King was manifested at the time of His Glory (Crucifixion-Resurrection-Ascension-Enthronement on the Right Hand of the Father). This differentiation is not exact, because of the unity of the three Offices. For even after the

---

[1641] 2 Chron. 26:21. Psalm 109 (110).
[1642] John 3:34.
[1643] Androutsos, *Dogmatique,* p. 196. John 18:36, 37.

Resurrection and the Enthronement on the Right Hand of the Father, which includes the condition of the Lord's Glory, He still intercedes for us. During the period of His humility, (the period from Bethlehem to Golgotha), the Lord exercised His Royal Authority by giving the New Law, choosing His Disciples and preparing them to continue His work. It is obvious that in the beginning He appeared as a Prophet teaching in the Synagogues and whenever He had the opportunity, whereas the performance of miracles were performed by His Authority and Power as King.

These three Offices are inseparably united in the God-man and fully express the range of the work of the Salvation. It is impossible that one of them could be omitted or extracted from the other two. Those who accept only one or two of the three Offices in Christ and exclude the other two, or even the third, are dividing the Gospel of Salvation. In other words, by stressing only the Office of Christ as a Prophet, putting aside the other two, one is led to Rationalism. Jesus, then, is nothing more than a great teacher and founder of a religion. If one emphasises the Office of High Priest, disregarding the other two, then one falls into an ill mysticism. If one puts aside the other two and stresses the Office of King, then one is led to heresy. Only in the unity of these three Offices can we confess Jesus Christ Who was born to us as *"Wisdom from God"* that He is the High Prophet, as the only *"Just."* He is the High Archpriest and as our *"Sanctification"* He is our High King Who crushes all adverse powers within us and assures us our *"deliverance"* through these three Offices.

Through the inseparable unity of the three Offices, the work of Salvation is fulfilled. They completely enter into the depths of human nature by freeing the human mind from all darkness through the Truth that is spoken by the Lord being the High Prophet. Through the expiation (*"catharsis"*) of the human heart in the bath of the precious Blood of the High Priest, the human will is encouraged to reach the royal heights by participating in the triumph of the Eternal King.

Question 223: Which of the three Offices of the Lord is the most important and essential in the work of Salvation?

Answer: It is obvious that these three are united to one another in such a way that if we emphasise one of them, disregarding the others, then we are misled. Jesus Christ is the One Lord and Saviour, the Son of God. He is the one true Sun of Righteousness, Who sends forth His boundless, and infinite Grace and Gifts to the world upon which the work of deliverance is based. We will not be wrong if we say that the centre that unites the other two Offices is that of the Archpriest, through which the friendship and restoration of man with God was accomplished. Through the Sacrifice on the Cross that was offered by the Archpriest Christ came forth the Grace that Enlightens and Sanctifies all faithful.

CHAPTER NINE
THE PROPHETIC OFFICE OF CHRIST

Question 224: What is the Prophetic Office of Christ?

Answer: Our Lord and Saviour Jesus Christ, the Son of God, came into the world to destroy the works of the Devil and to deliver men from his slavery. It was first necessary to destroy moral darkness caused by error and to bring the Light of True Knowledge to men who had been led astray by the lie. This Truth, according to the assurance of our Lord, will set man free.[1644]

The Redeemer, according to Holy Scripture, was the Most High Prophet and Teacher. As the unique God-Man and as the Incarnated Word of God the Father, not only in the condition of His eternal pre-existence but during His life on earth, He maintained a continuous communication with the Father. He is the fulfilment of all the Prophets and all Prophecies[1645] and not only did He authentically interpret the Revelation that was manifested by means of the Mosaic Law and the Prophets, such as no other man had ever spoken of before or shall speak of again, but he also fulfilled the Prophecies of the Old Testament by becoming the conveyor of the perfect and Divine Revelation. The Prophets of old had foretold the realisation of the Divine Plan concerning Salvation in Christ The Lord announced the establishment of this new condition of Salvation by revealing Himself as the One Who reveals and accomplishes all the ancient Prophecies. The Great Prophet appeared at the end of the Old Testament because the Prophets spoke only of Him, and after Him no one would be able to speak of any new Prophecies.

The Hypostatic Union of the two Natures in Christ explain the high Authority with which the Great Prophet spoke, that is *"with authority and not as the Scribes."*[1646] Since the Revelation of Jesus Christ surpasses all those revealed by men, He completely fulfilled the measure of the perfect and Divine Revelation, in that no other complete Revelation can ever possibly appear. Jesus Christ is God's Revelation and has become for us

---

[1644] 1 John 3:18. John 8:32. Cf. Kefalas, *Catechesis,* pp. 78-79. Damalas, *Catechesis,* p. 63. Frangopoulos, *Christian Faith,* pp. 144-146. MItsopoulos, *Themata,* pp. 157-158.
[1645] Matth. 3:15.
[1646] Matth. 7:29. Cf. Kefalas, *Catechesis,* p. 81.

"God's Power and God's Wisdom."[1647]   For this reason, He assures us that He is the *"Light of the world"*[1648] Who alone reveals the Father and forgives all sinners who return in repentance to Him.   He is the *"Way"*[1649] through which we are led to the Father and through faith in Him we achieve Salvation.

Question 225: What do Holy Scripture teach about the Prophetic Office?

Answer: According to the words of our Lord and Saviour Jesus Christ, Satan is the liar and the father of lies[1650] who rules over the world through deception and moral darkness, which he brought upon the minds of men through sinful passions that lead them away from the True God, towards idol worship and the lusts of the flesh.   The Redeemer Who came to free men from this slavery, as the Bearer of Truth that sets man free from all errors.   He is the One Who was announced by Moses as coming as a Prophet like himself and Who would intercede between God and men through direct communication with God, manifesting Him to whom He Wills, speaking to them and giving them the Law.[1651]   This Mosaic Prophecy was realised in the Person of Jesus Christ

The Lord indirectly proclaimed the title of Prophet[1652] for Himself whereas in other cases, He directly accepted the title,[1653] fulfilling the prophecy of Prophet Isaiah.[1654]   He assured His Mission of evangelising the Kingdom of God not only to Capernaum but to all other cities as well because He had been sent for that reason.[1655]   Before Pontius Pilot He manifested that *"to this He had come, to reveal the Truth."*[1656]

Being fully conscious that He is the Bearer of the complete and perfect Divine Revelation, He did not hesitate to assure His Disciples that He is *"the Truth"*[1657] and the *"Teacher."*[1658] He did not hesitate to proclaim Himself as the Law-giver Who with Authority interprets and fulfils the Law, placing His Authority above that of Moses, Elijah and all the Prophets

---

[1647] 1 Corinth. 1:24.
[1648] John 8:12.
[1649] John 14:6.
[1650] John 8:44.
[1651] Deut. 18:15, 18-19.
[1652] Matth. 13:57. Luke 4:18-19, 24; 13:33. John 1:46.
[1653] Matth. 5:17; 21:11; 23:8, 10. John 3:2; 4:19; 6:14; 9:17; 13:13. Acts 3:22.
[1654] Is. 61:1-3.
[1655] Luke 4:43-44.
[1656] John 18:37.
[1657] John 14:6.
[1658] Matth. 23:8.

because the Father proclaimed Him as His *"Only Begotten Son, in Whom I Am pleased listen to Him."*[1659]   He ascertained that His words have Eternal Authority and value.[1660]   The Holy Apostles and Disciples proclaimed our Lord Jesus to be the *"Prophet in Power and Word before God and all the people"*[1661] as had been proclaimed by Moses.[1662]

Question 226: What do the holy Fathers teach about the Prophetic Office?

Answer: St Ignatius the Theophorus proclaimed Christ to be *"the truthful Mouth by Whom the Father has spoken"*[1663] and *"our only Teacher."*[1664]

St Justine the Philosopher and Martyr proclaimed that *"greater of all human teachings are ours"* because the Word became *"for us the Christ"* and took up *"flesh and word and soul."* Those who dedicated themselves to the study of philosophy or made laws *"spoke well"* *"for they did not know everything about the Word."* The Word is the Christ Who *"is the Power of the unutterable Father and not the construction of the human logic."*[1665]

Clement the Alexandrian urged everyone to *"accept Christ, to accept to see, to accept the Light."* Characterising the sweetness of the Word that Enlightened us and which is more desirable than honey, he wondered: *"How can He (Christ) not be desirable Who Enlightened the mind, which was in darkness and cleansed the eyes of the soul?"* He assured us that if we had not known the Word and if we had not been Enlightened by Him, we would have been in darkness just as *"if the sun had not existed, everything would have been in darkness."* Addressing the Incarnated Word he exclaimed: *"I was misled until this day seeking God; because Thou hast Enlightened me, O Lord! I have found God through Thee and I enjoy the Father near Thee."*[1666]

St Athanasius the Great stressed the necessity of the Lord's Teachings and observed that True Knowledge was *"hidden"* because of the *"madness of idolatry and atheism"* which *"ruled over the whole world."* *"So who was to teach about the Father"*? Man was incapable of doing this, for everyone *"according to the soul"* had been wounded *"by the demonic deceit and the vanity of the idols."* How would it be possible for someone to change

---

[1659] Matth. 17:5. Mark 9:7. Luke 9:35.

[1660] Matth. 24:35. Mark 13:31. Luke 21:33.

[1661] Luke 24:19.

[1662] Acts 3:22-25.

[1663] St Ignatius, *To Romans*, 8, 2, in Lightfoot, *Apostolic Fathers,* p. 105.

[1664] Ibid, *To Magneseans*, 9, 2, in Lightfoot, *Apostolic Fathers,* p. 95.

[1665] St Justin, the philosopher and martyr, *2 Apology*, 10, § 8, in **B,** v. 4, p. 205.

[1666] Clement the Alexandrian, *Protrepticus*, XI, B, 7, 73.

"man's soul and man's mind" which no human being can see? *"That which no one can see, how can it be understood?"* It was necessary for the Word of God Who sees *"the soul and the mind"* and Who *"moves all in Creation through which we know the Father"* to come. He wanted to benefit men because *"He comes as a Man, taking up a body like theirs for Himself and as a Man lives amongst men, in order that through the works which the Lord will work through the body, they would understand the Truth and through Him will the Father be known."*[1667]

Question 227: What was the effect of the Hypostatic Union of the two Natures of Christ being the High Prophet?

Answer: Jesus Christ is the most unique and only Teacher and Prophet compared to all other Prophets. He is incomparably perfect and the only One Who is worthy to be called *"Teacher"* with the absolute meaning of the term and according to which no other man could ever be truly called *"Teacher"* or *"Prophet."* The incomparable perfection of the Office of our Lord Jesus is due to the Hypostatic Union of His human nature with the Divine Nature of the Word. He *"witnesses what He has seen"* not only due to the condition of His Eternal and beginninless pre-existence with the Father and the Holy Spirit but during His life on earth, by preserving His communion with the Father and as *"the Son of Man Who is in the Heavens"*[1668] judging *"as He hears"* *"for He does not seek His own Will, but the Will"* of the Father.[1669]

Christ's incomparable superiority having come as the Son of God[1670] is compared to all other Prophets who were sent throughout different periods as servants into the Divine Vineyard. Our Lord did not receive the Light as did the other Prophets because He is the Light. The Prophets received Divine Revelation in their daily lives throughout the different centuries. The Supernatural conditions they experienced was temporary and the miracles would pass by whereas Christ is *"the Prophet powerful in words and in deeds."*[1671] His Life is a continuous Miracle and Supernatural condition. Every deed and word is a manifestation of the Great Miracle of the Incarnation of the Word and Son of God. Christ is the Eternal Word of the Father Who Enlightened the Prophets. He is the Anointed Messiah about

---

[1667] St Athanasius the Great, *About the incarnation of the Word,* §§ 14 and 15, in Migne, *P.G.,* 25, 120 and 121.
[1668] John 3:13.
[1669] John 5:30.
[1670] Matth. 21:38-42.
[1671] Luke 24:19.

Whom the Prophets spoke and Who was the final goal of all their Prophecies. He is the Divine Revelation Himself.

The activities of the Prophets referred to the coming of the Great Prophet and His Activities. This was a preparation. The Prophets of old pre-announced the realisation of the Divine Plan of Salvation in Christ by prophesying the future *Economia* of Salvation. When the time was accomplished, the Great Prophet came announcing the establishment of this new *Economia*, of which He is the Leader and in Whom all Prophecies are fulfilled.

The Prophecy of Christ is the end of all Prophecies. All the Prophets who will follow after Him, will be His witnesses and will continue although they will be unable to announce any new Prophecies.[1672] Christ pre-announces the future similar to the Prophets of old except that an essential difference exists between them and Him. The Prophets did not prophesy about Christ and His Coming by means of their own abilities but through the Enlightenment of God whereas when Christ speaks of the future, He refers to Himself and reveals Himself as being the Centre of the Age to come. He appears as the One Who will come to Judge the living and the dead.[1673] Until the Second Appearance, the New World (His Church) will develop as a Supernatural structure built upon the ruins of the old world, which is the Kingdom of Heaven and of which He is the King.[1674] The Church is a God-built structure which is also His Body[1675] and over which He rules as its glorious Head.[1676]

Question 228: What was the Lord's authority as a Prophet?

Answer: The Hypostatic Union of His human nature with His Divine Nature, manifest Christ as the High Prophet and explains the high Authority with which He decides and speaks. He does not use the usual phrase: "*Thus said the Lord*" [1677] according to which the other Prophets prepare their Prophecies and announcements in the Name of God. Instead our Lord speaks "*as having Authority and not as the Scribes.*"[1678] Contrary to the old Law-givers of Israel and those who interpreted the Law, many times He repeated the phrase "*I say unto you.*"[1679]

[1672] Martensen, p. 451.
[1673] 2 Tim. 4:1.
[1674] Rev. 11:15; 22:5.
[1675] 1 Corinth. 12:27.
[1676] Ephes. 4:5. Col. 1:18.
[1677] Is. 45:1; 66:1. Jer. 2:1; 13:1; 22:1; 28:1; 29:1, 7; 32:1; 34:1; 40:2; 41:2; 45:2.
[1678] Matth. 7:29.
[1679] Matth. 5:22, 28, 32, 34, 39, 44.

The Lord appears as the High and the absolutely infallible Teacher Who reveals the Law in a completely new light, proclaiming that He " *has not come to destroy the Law or the Prophets, but to fulfil them.*"[1680] He fulfilled "*the Prophets*" who spoke about Him and He proved all the Prophecies to be truthful. He accomplished and clarified the Prophecies, shedding complete light upon them. He fulfilled the Law because He did not break any of the laws and because He granted this also to us.[1681]

The Lord's Attribute as the infallible and unique Teacher of the Truth does not use His Office as the High Prophet or the utmost Teacher of Divine Truth. The Teacher knows only to expose, to explain and to prove the contents of the Divine Word, whereas the Prophet carries a new word and His Appearance coincides with new times for the Divine *Economia' s* history.

Through His Prophetic Office, Christ guaranteed us that He is the "*Light of the world*" and he who follows Him "*will not walk in darkness, but will have the Light of Life.*"[1682] The beneficial influence of this Light, which originates from the Divine Teachings of the Great Prophet, was experienced by His Disciples as well as by St Peter who spoke on behalf of all the Apostles when the Teacher asked those who were scandalised and who departed from Him, "*do you also want to go?*"[1683] St Peter responded on behalf of all the Apostles by saying: "*Lord, where shall we go? Thou hast words of Eternal Life.*"[1684] The same experience and beneficial influence that His Apostles had, the Lord invited every man who thirsts to come to Him[1685] in order to drink and quench his spiritual thirst. He declared that from all those who believe in Him and accept His Teachings "*rivers of Living Water will come out of his belly*"[1686] for, "*he who drinks from the Water*" of His Teachings "*will not thirst forever*"[1687] and he who preserves His Word "*will not see death for ever.*"[1688]

[1680] Matth. 5:17.
[1681] St John Chrysostom, *To Matthew* 16, §§ 2 and 3, in Migne, *P.G.,* 57, 240 and 241.
[1682] John 8:12.
[1683] John 6:67.
[1684] John 6:68.
[1685] John 7:37.
[1686] John 7:38.
[1687] John 4:14.
[1688] John 8:51.

Question 229: What is the newness of the Revelation of the High Prophet?

Answer: The complete originality of the New Revelation that the High Prophet brought, is found in the sphere of the *Soteriology* (Teachings of Salvation). The Father appears forgiving, by having forbearance and love towards all those who turn to Him with repentance. Christ is the *"Way"* through which one finds the Father[1689] and achieves Salvation through faith in Him as the Son and Word of God Who was sent by the Father so that all who believe in Him shall have Eternal Life.[1690] The Prophets proclaimed the Will of God, the Incarnated Word and Son of God, our Lord and Saviour Jesus Christ, Who reveals within Himself the Father's Nature as love and the Eternal Plan of Salvation, which the Father conceived for the Redemption of the whole world. The Son comes to fulfil this Plan and *"to preach the Gospel to the poor; to proclaim liberty to the captives and recovery of sight to the blind, to set at liberty those who are oppressed; to proclaim the acceptable year of the Lord."*[1691] The Prophets were called by God *"those who restore the things of Israel"* whereas the Lord *"came to restore all the world."*[1692] As long as He lived on earth, Christ was sent to all the lost sheep of the House of Israel[1693] and when He accomplished the Work of Salvation, He sent His Holy Disciples to preach the Gospel *"into all the world"*[1694] and to make Disciples from *"all nations"*[1695] beginning in Jerusalem[1696] and becoming His witnesses *"to the end of the earth."*[1697] It is also characteristic that the only Prophet with whom the Lord compared Himself and from whose life He recalled examples and analogies for His Teachings, Sufferings and Resurrection, is the Prophet Jonas who preached to the pagans of Nineve.[1698]

All of these show the Newness of the Revelation through Jesus Christ and that which proved His incomparable perfection as Prophet was the perfect harmony of His Teachings with His Life. Jesus Christ, the Incarnated Word and Son of God, proved to be the High Teacher and Prophet Who practised the Prophetic Office in a perfect manner. He

---

[1689] John 14:6.
[1690] John 3:16-18.
[1691] Luke 4:18-19. Is. 61:1.
[1692] Origen, *Against Celsus,* IV, § 9, in *B*, v. 9, p. 238.
[1693] Matth. 10:6.
[1694] Mark 16:15.
[1695] Matth. 28:19.
[1696] Luke 24:47.
[1697] Acts 1:8.
[1698] Jonas 3:4

manifested the Light of Divine Revelation as the last and final word that would be heard from Heaven. His Teachings and Work left no place for another new Revelation. It had universal character and Eternal Power as He Himself assured us by saying: *"Heaven and earth will pass away, but My Words will by no means pass away."*[1699] He does not restrict Himself to certain nations but accepts all, regardless of culture, generation, nationality, tribe, language or complexion. Great and small, educated and uneducated, *"male or female,"*[1700] *"Greeks and barbarians, both wise and unwise"*[1701] are all called to become Disciples of this Divine Prophet. All are called as long as they desire and will to become *"taught by God."*[1702]

CHAPTER TEN
THE OFFICE OF CHRIST AS THE HIGH PRIEST

Question 230: What is the Office of Christ as a High Priest?

Answer: The Salvation of which our Lord and Saviour Jesus Christ, as the Great Prophet, foretold and His perfect Teachings, accompanied by His high moral standards, became our model and prototype. However, His Holy example would have remained meaningless for us without His Sacrifice on the Cross. He offered the Sacrifice that was required to satisfy Divine Justice and to restore the broken relationship between men and God. The Coming of the Word and Son of God to save the world was foretold in the Old Testament. He is the Eternal High Priest *"according to the Order of Melchizedek."*[1703] In the Epistle to the Hebrews His Priesthood appears to be incomparably higher than that of the Priesthood of the Levites. Continuing the Tradition of the New Testament, the Holy Apostolic Fathers as well as all the other Holy Fathers of the Orthodox Church proclaimed the Office of the High Priest of Christ.

The importance of the Office of Christ as High Priest is manifested by the necessity of man's reconciliation with God by means of offering blood sacrifices rather than his own life, as an expiatory way of appeasing the anger of God. These Sacrifices of the Old Testament were simple symbols and prototypes of the future Sacrifice of the Great High Priest. The precious

---

[1699] Matth. 24:35.
[1700] Gal. 3:28.
[1701] Rom. 1:14.
[1702] John 6:45. Is. 54:13.
[1703] Heb. 7:17. Cf. Plato of Moscow, *Orthodox Teaching,* pp. 237-244. Damalas, *Catechesis,* p. 63. Frangopoulos, *Christian Faith,* pp. 146-148. Mitsopoulos, *Themata,* pp. 159-160. Kefalas, *Christology,* pp. 238-240.

Blood of the God-Man, Who by His own Will as the spotless Lamb of God, offered Himself on the Cross and was thus able to raise and cleanse the world of sin. Our Lord Jesus Christ became the unique Mediator between God and man. He was able to speak with His Father while at the same time addressing mankind as one of their own and on behalf of all humanity. He became the most precious representative of the human race. His Sacrifice was invaluable because of the Hypostatic Union of His two Natures, the Divine and human, in one Great High Priest. No other man was able to offer this Sacrifice, for everyone was bound by and enslaved to sin.

This Sacrifice is not restricted to His Sufferings because it consists of His entire life, which was a Sacrifice of perfect obedience to His Father and which was sealed by His free, unconstrained and willing deliverance to death. Through this obedience, the greatness and supremacy of His humility and self-denial were manifested. Throughout His absolutely sinless life, He displayed perfect obedience and made His human nature the beginning of a new Holy and pure life for all mankind. He made man victorious against his opponent, the Devil, becoming Himself the Holy Yeast through which the whole dough is Sanctified and Deified. This incorporation was achieved through His Death on the Cross. He delivered Himself for our sins and became a curse for us, in order that we partake in His Death and become one Nature and one Body. With Christ we become Just before God in Him. The Death of our Lord Jesus Christ became an atonement and representative Sacrifice, in which He gave *"His life a ransom for many"*[1704] for all those who believe in Him.

The Death of our Lord and Saviour is proclaimed by Holy Scripture and the Holy Fathers of the Orthodox Church to be an expiatory and representative Sacrifice for all. This Ransom, which was offered by our sinless Lord for all mankind, was not offered to Satan as some Fathers stated. It was simply offered in indescribable Love for the Sanctification of man. The term *"ransom"* was used to stress the satisfaction of the Divine Justice through the Blood of Jesus Christ. The Sacrifice of the Great High Priest was a Sacrifice of an absolutely sinless and perfect Man. Furthermore, the Sacrifice of the God-Man, a Man Who was Hypostatically United with the Son of God, was enough not only to reconcile the entire world with God but also for the abundant outpouring of Divine Grace and *Charismata*, which enabled mankind to become sons of God by adoption and co-heirs of His Only Begotten Son.

The Work of Christ as High Priest continues in Heaven, mediating with the Father for each and everyone separately, as well as for the whole

---

[1704] Matth. 20:28.

world, by way of the outpouring of the results of His Sacrifice from the Heavenly Altar. Under no circumstances should the Heavenly Intervention and Mediation of the High Priest be understood as some supplement of His Offering on earth, for it would be considered imperfect. Both earthly and Heavenly Mediation are the Work of the High Priest and are united inseparably as one unique, indispensable perfection, which offers Life and Sanctification to all Faithful including the whole Orthodox Church.

Question 231: What is the relationship between the Prophetic Office and that of High Priest of Jesus Christ?

Answer: The relationship which exists between the two Offices of Christ as Prophet and High Priest is that as a Prophet of the New Testament, the Lord repeatedly foretold His Death and Work, which He, as the unique High Priest would accomplish, confirming the New Testament of which He became the bearer and servant. To achieve Salvation of which He prophesied, He fulfills all necessary requirements as High Priest through His Sacrifice,[1705] without which His entire Teaching would remain merely an ideal and unaccomplished.

The Teachings and the Holy Life of the High Prophet without the Sacrifice on the Cross would not have been enough to save mankind. Christ did not come to reveal God the Father to humanity but instead He had to reconcile us to Him, otherwise, although He would have fulfilled the Law and the Prophets, mankind would have remained separated for all Eternity from the Mercy and the Love of God. Consequently, the Work of our Lord, as the High Prophet, leads directly to His Work as the High Priest, only through which the reconciliation of the world with God was achieved.

Question 232: What are the teachings of the New Testament concerning Christ's Office as a High Priest?

Answer: The Old Testament speaks of Christ as High Priest. God the Father speaks through the mouth of King David, addressing the Messiah: *"Thou art a Priest forever according to the Order of Melchizedek."*[1706]

The Epistle to the Hebrews characterised the Lord as the High Priest Who received the Office, not by Himself but by being Called by God Who said to Him: *"Thou art a Priest forever according to the Order of*

[1705] Mitsopoulos, *Themata,* pp. 162-166.
[1706] Psalm 109(110):4.

Melchizedek."[1707]   The God-inspired author explained this phrase by reminding us that Melchizedek was a Priest and a King of Salem. In other words He was a *"King of Righteousness"* and a *"King of Peace."*[1708] Holy Scripture remains silent concerning the genealogy and death of Melchizedek by stating *"without father, without mother, without genealogy, having neither beginning of days nor end of life, but made like the Son of God, remains a Priest continually."*[1709] As a result, Melchizedek appears to pre-announce the Eternal High Priesthood of Christ, which is higher than the Priesthood of the Levites, just as that of Melchizedek was higher than that of the Patriarch and ancestor of the Levites, Abraham, who offered Melchizedek *"the tenth of all"* the loot and who was consequently blessed by Him.[1710]

The supremacy of Christ the Great High Priest is manifested by the fact that He became Eternal High Priest *"with an Oath"* by the Lord, *"Who said to Him: 'The Lord has sworn and will not relent, 'Thou art a Priest forever according to the Order of Melchizedek."*[1711]   In addition to that, Christ is the High Priest *"Who is Holy, harmless, undefiled, separate from sinners, and has become higher than the Heavens; Who does not need daily, as those High Priests, to offer up Sacrifices, first for His own sins and then for the people's, for this He did once for all when He offered up Himself."*[1712] Christ Who *"through the Eternal Spirit offered Himself without spot to God"* cleanses our *"conscience from dead works to serve the Living God."*[1713]   For *"He had offered one Sacrifice for sins forever, sat down at the Right Hand of God."*[1714] *"Therefore, having boldness to enter the Holiest by the Blood of Jesus, by a new and living Way which He Consecrated for us, through the Veil, that is, His Flesh."*[1715]

According to the above, St Peter proclaimed that *"Christ also suffered once for sins, the Just for the unjust, that He might bring us to God, being put to death in the flesh but made alive by the Spirit"*[1716] and He *"Himself bore our sins in His own body on the tree, that we, having died to sins, might live for Righteousness – by Whose stripes"* we *"were healed."*[1717]

[1707] Psalm 109(110):4.
[1708] Heb. 7:2. Kefalas, *Christology*, p. 239.
[1709] Heb. 7:3.
[1710] Heb. 7:2,1. Cf. Plato of Moscow, *Orthodox Teaching*, p. 242-243. Kefalas, *Catechesis*, p. 82.
[1711] Heb. 7:20-21.
[1712] Heb. 7:26-27.
[1713] Heb. 9:14.
[1714] Heb. 10:12.
[1715] Heb. 10:19-20.
[1716] 1 Peter 3:18.
[1717] 1 Peter 2:24.

Question 233: What are the teachings of the holy Fathers concerning Christ's Office as a High Priest?

Answer: Jesus Christ is proclaimed as *"the High Priest of our offerings, the Guardian and Helper of our weakness."*[1718] St Clement of Rome said that we *"look steadily into the heights of Heaven"*[1719] as He is the *"greater"* of the Priests of the Old Testament. *"He is the excellent Priest and Eternal King"* for Whom *"was foresaid"* that *"the Lord gave an Oath according the Order of Melchizedek."*[1720]

Origen was the first to point out the Attribute of Christ as Priest and the Sacrificial Victim. He based his conclusion that Christ is Priest on the Books of Psalms and the Epistle to the Hebrews. Furthermore, based upon the witness of St John the Baptist who exclaimed: *"Behold! The Lamb of God Who takes away the sin of the world."*[1721] Origen, stressed the fact that He is also the Victim! He concluded that Christ *"is the Lamb which was slaughtered and cleansed the whole world."*[1722]

St Epiphanius, according to the Epistle to the Hebrews, presented Christ as offering *"the Priesthood to the Father since He received the dough of humanity, in order that He becomes for us a Priest according to the Order of Melchizedek, which has no succession"* *"presenting Himself on the Cross"* and *"offering the most perfect and living Sacrifice for all the world."* Thus *"He is the Victim, He is the Priest, He is the Altar, He is God, He is Man, He is the King, He is the High Priest, He is the Lamb, He has become all in all for us"* *"serving as High Priest above all Creation. Ascending spiritually and gloriously with His own Body He sat on the Right Hand of the Father becoming a High Priest forever and passing through the Heavenly places."*[1723]

St John Chrysostom proclaimed that *"the Son is the only faithful High Priest, Who is able to free men from sin, to whom He is the High Priest"* and seeing that we were sad and defeated *"showed Mercy, not only rendering for us a High Priest but becoming Himself a faithful High Priest."* In order to offer *"a Sacrifice which was able to cleanse us, He became Man."* *"He Himself* (became) *an Altar and a Priest"* and presented *"by Himself"* in such

---

[1718] St Clement of Rome, *1st Corinthians* 36, 1, in Lightfoot, *Apostolic Fathers,* p. 48.
[1719] Ibid.
[1720] St Justin, the philosopher and martyr, *Dialogue,* 118, 2, 1, in *B*, v. 3, p. 317.
[1721] John 1:29.
[1722] Origen, *To Romans,* 3, 8, in Migne, *P.G.,* 14, 946-951.
[1723] St Epiphanius, *Heresies,* 55, 4, in Migne, *P.G.,* 41, 980. Ibid, *Heresies,* 69, 39, in Migne, *P.G.,* 42, 261.

a way that Holy Scripture shows *"Him not only as a Priest, but as Victim and Altar."*[1724]

Mogilas[1725] observed that according to the Order of Melchizedek Christ was superior to the others because of His Priesthood. He was called as High Priest by God, according to the Order of Melchizedek. He also referred to Christ as Priest because He offered Himself to God the Father. The Death of Christ was different to that of other men due to the following reasons:

1. Firstly, because of our many sins, as the Prophet said: *"He bears our sins, and is pained for us: yet we accounted Him to be in trouble, and in suffering, and in affliction. But He was wounded on account of our sins, and was bruised because of our iniquities."*[1726]

2. Secondly, He fulfilled the Priesthood on the Cross by presenting Himself to God the Father for the Salvation of the human race as the Holy Apostle Paul said: Christ *" gave Himself* [as] *a Ransom for all."*[1727] *"Christ also has loved us and given Himself for us,* [as] *an Offering and a Sacrifice to God for a sweet-smelling aroma."*[1728] In addition, *"God demonstrates His own love towards us, in that while we were still sinners, Christ died for us."*[1729] On the Cross our Lord completed the Mediation between God and men, as stated by the same Holy Apostle who wrote: *"that He might reconcile them both to God in one Body through the Cross, thereby putting to death the enmity"*[1730] and *" having wiped out the hand-writing of requirements that was against us, which was contrary to us. And He has taken it out of the way, having nailed it to the Cross."*[1731]

Question 234: Was the work of Christ as a High Priest necessary?

Answer: The necessity of Christ's Office and Work as High Priest is obvious when one takes into consideration that mankind, due to its sinful state, was separated by enmity with God.[1732] No other matter was of such importance as the necessity of reconciling mankind with the Divine. Since he was created under an unbreakable Communion with God with which he

---

[1724] St John Chrysostom, *To Hebrews,* Homily 5, § 1, and Homily 17, §§ 1-2, in Migne, *P.G.,* 63, 47 and 129.

[1725] Mogilas, in Karmires, *The dogmatics,* v. II, pp. 610 and 615.

[1726] Is. 53:4-5.

[1727] 1 Tim. 2:6.

[1728] Ephes. 5:2.

[1729] Rom. 5:8.

[1730] Ephes. 2:16.

[1731] Col. 2:14.

[1732] James 4:4.

was Blessed and thereby able to fulfill his destiny, it is obvious that when man was separated from God due to sin, he fell away from his objective and became unable to enjoy the supreme Good. Consequently, in order to be free of the misery in which he had fallen, it was crucial for his reconciliation with God. Christ freely took our place and became accursed. The abandonment of Christ on the Cross was therefore necessary, for God departs from the accursed.[1733]

The need of Atonement was required because sin entered the world and atonement is achieved through a sacrifice. Consequently, it was necessary that an ultimate Sacrifice be offered for sin and that was the one of the Lamb Who carried the sin of the entire world[1734] as witnessed by St John the Baptist who exclaimed: *"Behold! The Lamb of God Who takes away the sin of the world!"*[1735]

Question 235: Was Christ's Sacrifice predestined by God?

Answer: When St Peter referred to the precious Blood of this Sacrifice, he proclaimed Christ as being *"foreordained before the foundation of the world"* but who was revealed *" in these last times."*[1736] Truly God, Who from the beginning of time, foresaw the events that would occur in man's life, and *"from Above and before the creation of the world prepared the Mystery in Christ."*[1737] Before all time, God had prepared the Reconciliation through the Sacrifice of Christ Whom He would offer on the Cross, as High Priest. It was up to God, Who had been insulted by man's Fall, to determine the means by which Divine Justice and Holiness would be satisfied and thereby fallen man would be reconciled with the infinite Lord. Under the guilt of his conscience and unable to set himself free, sinful man made it essential for God's Grace that offered him the Knowledge and means of obtaining the desired Reconciliation, which is achieved and secured only through Jesus Christ our Lord and Saviour.

The manifestation of this Sign of Grace was the fact that the Father sent the High Priest, Who, as Mediator, brought both God and man to Communion. The Mediator had to be both God and Man because through His familiarity with God and men, He was able to restore their Fellowship and Peace. He had to present man to God and to make God known to man.

[1733] Lossky, *Theology*, p. 112.
[1734] Origen, *In Numerum*, XXIV, 1, in Migne, *P.G.*, 12, 757. Plato of Moscow, *Orthodox Teaching*, pp. 77-79.
[1735] John 1:29.
[1736] 1 Peter 1:20.
[1737] St Ecumenius, *To 1 Peter,* in Migne, *P.G.*, 119, 525.

If the Mediator was only God or merely man, it would not have been possible for Him to accomplish His Work as Mediator. If He was simply a man, He could not have been a Mediator because He had to meditate with God and on the contrary, had He been only God, He could not have been a Mediator since human beings would not have had the courage to accept or to approach Him. Because the Word and Son of God consisted of two Natures, He had to be close to both Natures. He has His Divinity for all Eternity because He came from God being by Nature the Son of God and God. He had to take up human nature because He came to mankind in order to reveal, to speak of and to present them to God.[1738] Through His Sacrifice on the Cross, He convinced and informed humanity that they have peace with God. This *"exchange"* that was offered by our Lord and Saviour Jesus Christ, no other man could *"give in exchange for his soul."*[1739]

It is unquestionable that God the Father sent His Only Begotten Son, our Lord and Saviour Jesus Christ, as Mediator[1740] and High Priest[1741] of the New Testament into the world out of love towards man.[1742] The Reconciliation with Him was the Work of Divine Love, Goodness and Wisdom in perfect harmony with Divine Holiness and Justice. For God *"can perform all that He wants, but He does not want all that He can."*[1743] In other words, God was able to achieve the Salvation and Restoration of man directly and without any other measure, but under no circumstances did He want to achieve this by renouncing Himself and opposing His Holy Nature. It was always possible to please His Good Will without violating or abolishing His Divine Justice. If the Grace of Salvation was granted without satisfying Divine Justice, then the moral order would have been shaken and sin would have no longer been sin, since there would have been no need for expiation. Sin would have become something indifferent before the eyes of Holy God if Divine Justice ceased to demand its punishment. It was required by Divine Holiness and Justice to present and offer a True Sacrifice, not from the blood of irrational animals or lifeless things but a Sacrifice of the root of evil that was hidden in man and which again consists of putting to death the sinful ego of man, so as to be regenerated and reconciled to God in perfect obedience. By perfect obedience to God it was required for man, through his free action, to cut off the development of sin

---

[1738] St Irenaeus, *Heresies*, book III, ch. 18, § 7, in Migne, *P.G.*, 937. Cf. Ibid, in Hadjephraimides, p. 242-243. St John Chrysostom, *To 1 Timothy*, Homily 7, § 2, in Migne, *P.G.*, 62, 536.
[1739] Mark 8:37. Cf. Plato of Moscow, *Orthodox Teaching*, pp. 119-124.
[1740] Heb. 8:6.
[1741] Heb. 9:11
[1742] John 3:16-17.
[1743] St John of Damascus, *Catechesis*, I, 15, in Migne, *P.G.*, 94, 860-861. St Symeon, *Euriskomena*, Homily XXVIII, pp. 143-144.

within himself, in order to mollify God for his previous actions and to begin a new life in goodness and Virtue.

The question of whether man was able to offer such a Sacrifice is answered by the fact that everyone was *"under sin"*[1744] and consequently deprived of Divine Grace that enabled them to perform good things and to deliver themselves and their free-will to God. Again, how was it possible for man to please the infinite God?

The Expiation and Salvation of fallen man was acknowledged by God through the Incarnation of His Word and Son Who took up the form of a servant. At the time *"it was necessary for mankind to suffer death for the Offence of Adam and sin the Word of God the Father Who was plentiful in calmness and love towards man, became flesh - in other words, Man - and took up our lot"* *"and realized the exchange of the life of all with His Soul."* *"As Priest and Sacrificial Victim for all,* [being] *spotless, He took up the Body which He presented to death and immediately vanquished death from those of the same* [nature] *through the offering of His Righteousness."*. For He was not *"a High Man, but the Only Begotten Son of God Who died for all."* *"The Man-God Jesus Christ.."* Who *"does not have need of Expiation but is the Expiation"* *" is the only One Who is able to give Expiation to God for all."*[1745]

Question 236: Was the Sacrifice of Christ extended throughout His life?

Answer: The Sacrifice of the God-Man is not restricted to His Sufferings and Death. It includes His entire Life, which is a Sacrifice of perfect obedience to the Father. This obedience was sealed through His Sufferings as St Paul exphasised: *"Let this mind be in you which was also in Christ Jesus, Who, being found in appearance as a Man, He humbled Himself and became obedient to the point of death, even the death of the cross."*[1746]

The history of Christ's Suffering did not begin at the Garden of Gethsemane but extended throughout His whole Life. It began at Bethlehem and ended at Golgotha.[1747] In order that the High Priest offered a perfect Sacrifice acceptable to God, it had to be a rational, moral and spiritual Sacrifice - a Sacrifice of utmost obedience - and for this reason the

---

[1744] Gal. 3:22.

[1745] St Cyril of Alexandria, *Epist.* 41, in Migne, *P.G.*, 77, 209. Ibid, *To Leviticus,* in Migne, *P.G.*, 69, 548. St Athanasius the Great, *Homily about the incarnation of the Word,* § 9, in Migne, *P.G.*, 25, 112. St Cyril of Jerusalem, *Catechesis,* 13, § 1-2, in Migne, *P.G.*, 33. St Basil the Great, *To Psalm 48,* § 4, in Migne, *P.G.*, 29, 440.

[1746] Phil. 2:5-8.

[1747] Martensen, *Dogmatique,* p. 470.

Lord's Death and the shedding of His Blood on the Cross is the most perfect Sacrifice, the like of which has never been offered before or since and which was extremely pleasing to God, not that God is pleased with human sacrifices or the shedding of human blood, but because, on the Cross, the obedience of the Son towards His Father was shown to its extreme level. Hence the Sacrifice of the Saviour began from the moment He entered into the world and His Death was the fulfillment of His obedience, which was sealed through the Sufferings of the Cross.

One can distinguish Christ's obedience by two Acts. First, the *"active obedience"* which is expressed by the Acts of His Life through which He fulfilled the Law as well as through His absolutely sinless and virtuous Life that presented Him as everything pleasing to the Father. Secondly, the *"passive obedience"*, which was expressed by His Suffering *"as the Lamb led to the slaughter"*[1748] and which He faced through His own Free-will.[1749] This is impossible for any other human being to accomplish.

According to the proclamation of our Lord, His Suffering on the Cross was *"a Command"* that He received from His Father. However this does not mean that the Son was forced to fulfill it in a passive manner but that our Lord faced Death by His own Free-will. For this reason He declared: *"I Am the Good Shepherd. The Good Shepherd gives His Life for the sheep."*[1750] By His own Free-will our Lord accepted the bitter cup of death, pleasing His Father and being perfected in obedience. All this was the Fruit of the Son's Love towards man. He did not come down to the level of our humility, although He was in the form of and equal to God the Father. He did not became poor, although He was rich, nor did He suffer the bitter death of the flesh for any other reason than because He loved us more than He loved Himself. Although He had the authority as Man to enjoy life, He left it aside for our sake.[1751] Out of love towards mankind the High Priest suffered and carried the weight of the sins of the world upon Himself. Consequently, His whole life was a continuous Sacrifice, a silent Suffering, an expression of free obedience in the midst of an evil world, which made His final Suffering present throughout His entire Life.

[1748] Is. 53:7.

[1749] John 10:18.

[1750] John 10:11.

[1751] St John Chrysostom, *To John,* Homily 60, § 3, in Montfaucon, v. 8, p. 407. St Cyril of Alexandria, *To John,* book IX, *To John 13:34,* in Migne, *P.G.,* 74, 161 and 162.

Question 237: Did the obedience of Christ as the second Adam healed the disobedience of all mankind?

Answer: The obedience of our Lord Jesus Christ that He displayed throughout His Life regenerated and restored human nature. Christ was the perfect Man Who, through His sinless Life, became the Elect and Representative of the entire human race, the second Adam of Grace and the new Yeast, which regenerates the whole dough of the human race through its union with Him. This High Priest, taking human nature like a Lamb in His Divinity, manifested it as the beginning of the human race, justifying it in His Sufferings and presenting it with all the Virtues, thereby showing man to be an unbeatable victor against his opponent, Satan. If Satan had not been defeated by Man, then the enemy had not been defeated justly. As in the first Adam, we moved God to anger by not preserving His Commandment, likewise in the second Adam we are reconciled with Him through the obedience to the point of death, since our disobedience was healed through His perfect obedience.[1752] Through the struggle against the wickedness of the world human nature was raised to a higher condition in Christ.[1753]

Christ did not carry the whole human race within Himself except only His personal human nature that was united within the Divine Hypostasis. The human race consists of one whole union. All members have a common nature, having received it from the same forefather, thus uniting them to one another as one family and one body, like the branches of one tree. The first Adam, from whom all human race derived, and who is the root from which the whole tree grew, is the natural or biological leader of the human race. The second Adam, Who was united with the whole body of the human race, having taking up human nature supernaturally through the Action of the Holy Spirit and from the pure blood of the Ever-Virgin Mary, the Theotokos, is the noblest member of the human family. He is the perfect Man Who is able to represent all mankind. He is the new worthy Leader, since the first Adam had fallen and was corrupt. The first Adam was responsible for sin and although he was made first, he was not presented as the beginning of our nature to God because the beginning of our nature was presented by Christ.[1754]

[1752] St Irenaeus, *Heresies,* book V, ch. 16, § 3 and ch. 17, § 1, in Migne, *P.G.,* 7, 1168. Cf. Ibid, in Hadjephraimides, pp. 388-389 and 389. 1 Corinth. 15:45-49. Rom. 5:16-19.
[1753] St Cyril of Alexandria, *To Matthew, book VIII, in Migne, P.G.,* 72, 921. See also the 10th Act of the 6th Ecumenical Council, in Mansi, v. 11, p. 413.
[1754] St John Chrysostom, *To the Ascension of our Lord Jesus Christ,* § 2-3, in Migne, *P.G.,* 50, 446.

The Holy Fathers of the Orthodox Church stressed this mystical aspect of the Work of Salvation of our Lord, proclaiming that the Incarnated Son of God took up human nature in order to Sanctify the whole human race through Himself. He became the Yeast for the whole dough, uniting to Himself that which was previously condemned. He completely freed us from the first Curse. Hence, man participated with Divine Nature due to the union of the two Natures in Christ When the Word of God became Man, He became familiar with all the things of the flesh and by His taking up of the completely human nature, men are no longer sinners and dead, considering that through the Word of God Who became flesh for us, sinful mankind has Communion with God and our nature thereby becomes Divine due to its union with the Divine, since in the human Body that the Son of God assumed, there now flows Immortality and Resurrection.[1755]

Question 238: What was the Nature of Christ's Sacrifice?

Answer: Through the perfect obedience of Jesus Christ human nature was perfected and through union and communion with the Incarnated Divine Nature, it was raised and Deified. All these were achieved because of the representative Sacrifice offered on the Cross by the God-Man Who became the Expiatory Victim and Who reconciled man with God. As the High Priest and Mediator, He mediates with the Divinity for human nature. Through Christ our whole human nature is blessed.[1756] The Salvation and Glorification of human nature, which was achieved through the Mystical Union of human nature with Christ, cannot be separated from the Death of our Lord, nor can the Sacrifice on the Cross be considered as of secondary importance. Our incorporation and union with the Glorified and Deified human nature of Christ, which makes us partakers of His Body and Nature, was realised only through His Death on the Cross and our participation in that Death through faith in Him.

From the beginning of His Ministry, our Lord Jesus, the Incarnated Son of God the Father, was proclaimed by St John the Forerunner and Baptist as the *"Lamb of God Who takes away the sin of the world."*[1757] Holy Scripture proclaims that He was delivered to death *"because of our offences*

[1755] St Gregory of Nazianzus, *Homily* 30, §§ 6 and 21, in Migne, *P.G.,* 36, 109 and 132. St Athanasius the Great, *Against Arians,* III, § 33, in Migne, *P.G., 26, 393.* St Cyril of Jerusalem, *Catechesis,* 12, § 15, in Migne, *P.G.,* 33, 741. St Gregory of Nyssa, *Catechesis,* ch.25, 16, 32, in Migne, *P.G.,* 45, 65, 52 and 80.
[1756] St John Chrysostom, *Homily to the Ascension of our Lord Jesus Christ,* § 3, in Migne, *P.G.,* 50, 446.
[1757] John 1:29. Is. 53: 7-12.

and was raised because of our Justification"[1758] in order that He could *"wipe out the hand-writing of requirements that was against us, which was contrary to us. And He has taken it out of the way, having nailed it to the Cross."*[1759] Christ took away our debt and His Resurrection accomplishes the General Resurrection of all. *"For as in Adam all die, even so in Christ all shall be made alive."*[1760] He assured us that He came *"to serve, and to give His Life* [as] *a Ransom for many."*[1761] Delivering the Mystery of the Divine Eucharist to His Holy Disciples and Apostles He declared that *"this is My Blood of the new Covenant, which is shed for many for the remission of sins."*[1762] He spoke of the New Covenant by remembering the Old Covenant that was also consecrated with sacrifices of blood whereas the Blood of the New Testament is shed *"for the remission of sins"* of all mankind.

St Paul proclaiming Christ as the Sacrificial Lamb of the Passover, assured us that Christ has *"given Himself for us, an Offering and a Sacrifice to God for a sweet-smelling aroma"*[1763] according to God's Plan of Salvation.[1764] Christ's Sacrifice was His destiny that had been predestined before all ages for the High Priest, to offer His Blood as a way of Expiation of all those who believe in Him.[1765]

The terms used in Holy Scripture such as *"for our offences,"* *"which is shed for many,"* *"an Offering for us,"* *"Expiation in His Blood"* and other expressions, clearly reveal that the High Priest had come to die for our sins and that His Blood, which was shed on the Cross, bears the nature of a Expiatory Sacrifice. Undoubtedly, our Lord and Saviour Jesus Christ suffered under Pontius Pilate and gave witness to the Truth, in order to leave *"us an example, that we should follow His steps."*[1766] He *"bore our sins in His own Body on the Tree, that we, having died to sins, might live for Righteousness."*[1767]

The primary Goal and Nature of Christ's Suffering is that it is an Expiatory Sacrifice for the Salvation of the whole world. Christ, being sinless, nor had any experience of it. He became a *"sin for us"* by God so

---

[1758] Rom. 4:25.
[1759] Col. 2:14.
[1760] 1 Corinth. 15:22.
[1761] Matth. 20:28.
[1762] Matth. 26:28.
[1763] Ephes. 5:2.
[1764] Rom. 3:24-25.
[1765] Heb. 10:12-14.
[1766] 1 Peter 2:21.
[1767] 1 Peter 2:24.

"that we might become the Righteousness of God in Him."[1768] Christ took up our punishment and suffered pain for all humanity. The Father *"loved us and sent His Son to be the Propitiation for our sins."*[1769] Christ became a *"sin"* for the world although He Himself did not become a sinner, being the only True Just One Who, by His own Free-will became the Sacrificial Victim for the sins of the entire world. Although He was the One suffering as Man, He was above all Creation as God.[1770] As in the Old Testament, the Sacrificial animal, symbolically and unconsciously carried the sins and guilt of the one who offered it on the Altar, likewise the High Priest, simultaneously being the One Who made the Offering and the Victim, Altar and Lamb, by His own free-will consciously took up our sins and *"by His Wounds"*[1771] He vanquished *"the hand-writing that was against us."* He *" took it out of the way, having nailed it to the Cross."*[1772] He was punished so as to free us from sin. He presented Himself as a Holy Sacrifice to God the Father Who reconciled *"us to Himself through Jesus Christ"* having *"committed to us the Word of Reconciliation."*[1773]

Truly the sinless Lord was punished and experienced extreme humiliation because of sin that we committed. When the religious leaders of the Jews and the civil authorities of Rome co-operated and thereby committed the worst, cruelest crime of all centuries, the sinless Lord on the Cross, although having no need of repentance, experienced the fullness of mankind's corruption of sin and He suffered as though He was a sinner. The new Adam, as true and healthy human nature, during His Suffering cried out with tears for the fallen human race. At those extremely painful moments He confessed the sin of the world that He carried because of His love towards man, although He Himself is alien to sin.[1774]

Question 239: What are the teachings of the holy Fathers concerning the representative Nature of Christ's Sacrifice?

Answer: The Apostolic Fathers proclaimed that *" in love the Master received us. Because of the love He had for us, Jesus Christ our Lord, in*

[1768] 2 Corinth. 5:21.

[1769] 1 John 4:10.

[1770] St John Chrysostom, in Migne, *P.G.,* 61, 478. Ibid, *To the Ascension,* Homily 2, in Migne, *P.G.,* 50, 445. St Cyril of Alexandria, *Epist.* 41, in Migne, *P.G.,* 77, 209. Ibid, *To John,* book XII *To John 19:19,* in Migne, *P.G.,* 74, 656.

[1771] Is. 53:5.

[1772] Col. 2:14.

[1773] 2 Corinth. 5:18-19.

[1774] Heb. 5:7-10.

accordance with God's Will, gave His Blood for us, and His Flesh for our flesh, and His Life for our lives."[1775]

Barnabas wrote that Christ suffered "*for our souls, even though He is Lord of the whole world*"[1776] in order that "*by His Wounds*" we shall be healed.[1777]

St Ignatius the Theophorus urged all Christians to "*be more diligent than you are. Understand the times. Wait expectantly for Him Who is above time: the Eternal, the Invisible, Who for our sake became visible; the Intangible, the Unsuffering, Who for our sake Suffered, Who for our sake endured in every way.*"[1778]

Origen presented the Lord according to His Humanity, being "*the most pure creature, Who took up our sins and our weaknesses, which*" as absolutely sinless, "*is able to take up to Himself and to loosen, to forgive and to vanquish the sin of the whole world.*"

St Athanasius the Great of Alexandria portrayed our Lord as " *the One Who is from our own Who took up Death instead of all*" and He Suffered "*the blasphemy from men, in order that we might inherit Immortality.*" Because everyone was guilty of death, He gave up His own Life, delivering His own Temple to Death, in order to make all free from the responsibility of the ancient Offence.[1779]

St John Chrysostom stated that He "*Who knew no sin, the Self-righteous, was left to die as a sinner*" "*in order to make sinners Righteous.*" Being sinless and not bound under the Curse due to the Offence, He took upon Himself the Curse in order to loosen the Curse of those who were under the Law.[1780]

St Cyril of Jerusalem emphasised that "*we were enemies of God through sins and God appointed the sinner to die.*" The Wisdom of God preserved the Truth in its decision that required the death of the sinner and He acted through His love of mankind. Christ took up the sins in His Body on the Cross. "*Therefore, do not be ashamed of the One Who was Crucified, but be proud saying: 'He bears our sins, and is pained for us: yet we accounted Him to be in trouble, and in suffering, and in affliction. But He*

[1775] St Clement of Rome, *1st Corinthians,* 49, 6, in Lightfoot, *The Apostolic Fathers*, p. 56.
[1776] *Barnabas,* 5, 5, in Lightfoot, *Apostolic Fathers*, p. 167.
[1777] Is. 53:5.
[1778] St Ignatius, *To Polycarp,* 3, 2, in Lightfoot, *Apostolic Fathers*, p. 116.
[1779] St Athanasius the Great, *About the incarnation of the Word,* §§ 8, 20 and 54, in Migne, *P.G.,* 25, 109, 129 and 192.
[1780] St John Chrysostom, *To 2 Corinthians,* Homily 11, § 3, in Migne, *P.G.,* 61, 478. Ibid, *To Galatians,* III, § 3, in Migne, *P.G.,* 61, 655.

was bruised because of our iniquities: the chastisement of our peace was upon Him; and by His Bruises we were healed.[1781]"[1782]

St Cyprian proclaimed that *"He is the only One Who can achieve the forgiveness of our sins, He Who carried our sins and Suffered for us and Whom God gave for our sins."* He is the Christ Who intervened *" for us, for He, being sinless, carried our sins"* and *"through Him we must please the Father."[1783]*

Question 240: What is the true meaning of the offered Ransom?

Answer: The Holy Fathers and Ecclesiastical Writers of the Eastern Orthodox Church based their Teachings of Christ having bought us with His Blood, upon the Teachings of Holy Scripture according to which the precious Blood of our Lord and Saviour was offered as a *"Ransom for many"[1784]* and by means of which our Lord *"bought (us) at a price"[1785]* *"by His Blood"[1786]* for *"in Him we have Redemption through His Blood"* and *" the forgiveness of sins, according to the riches of His Grace."[1787]* Christ *"bought us"* so consequently, we do not belong to ourselves but to Him Who has bought us, Redeeming us *"from the curse of the Law, having become a curse for us."[1788]* Our Lord Jesus *"gave Himself for us, that He might redeem us from every lawless deed and purify for Himself His own special people, zealous for good works."[1789]*

Because sin entered the world, Satan received authority over it and as a result, he is referred to by Christ as the *"strong man"[1790]* and by the Holy Apostles as *"the god of this age"* who *"has blinded"* those *"who do not believe."[1791]* This authority of Satan does not give him infinite rights upon God's Creation nor does it make him *"lord"[1792]* over them either. Satan is not of an equivalent stature to negotiate with the Saviour about the freedom of men as though they belonged to him. Satan ruled only because God allowed it and consented to it for His own specific Purpose.

[1781] Is. 53:4-5.
[1782] St Cyril of Jerusalem, *Catechesis,* XIII, §§ 32 and 33, in Migne, *P.G.,* 33, 813.
[1783] St Cyprian, *De lapsis,* 17 and *Epist.* 40, § 5, in migne, *P.L.,* (?), 494 and 345.
[1784] Matth. 20:28. Mark 10:45. 1 Tim. 2:6.
[1785] 1 Corinth. 6:20.
[1786] Rom. 3:25; 5:9. Ephes. 2:13. Col. 1:14, 20. Heb. 9:12, 14, 20; 10:19; 13:12. 1 Peter 1:19. 1 John 1:7. Rev. 1:5; 5:9; 7:14; 12:11.
[1787] Eph. 1:7.
[1788] Gal. 3:13.
[1789] Tit. 2:14.
[1790] Matth. 12:29.
[1791] 2 Corinth. 4:4.
[1792] St Cyril of Alexandria, *To John,* book X, ch. 1, *To John 14:30,* in Migne, *P.G.,* 74, 329.

Question 241: Does the Hypostatic Union give a priceless value and power to the representative Sacrifice?

Answer: The fact that the Sacrifice of Christ was able to lift up the sin of the whole human race, from Adam to the last man to be born before the Second Coming, was the result of the Son of God, as the second Adam and the absolutely sinless, most precious and perfect Man, consenting, by His own Will, to represent the human race and by offering Himself as an Expiatory Sacrifice to God the Father for all of us. This second Adam is not merely man. What could any man find to offer for his life? Christ is True Man and He is True God the Word Who became Man. He is not a fine Man but the Only Begotten Son of God Who takes up a body in order to change all people and through His Death to end their mortality through the Grace of Resurrection. The Sacrifice on the Cross was not a Sacrifice of a fine Man but that of the Word of God. As High Priest He offered and as Sacrificial Victim He was offered for all humanity's freedom from guilt and by His Death He defeated Satan through His Most Proper Offering.[1793]

According to the above, the Sacrifice offered by the God-Man was a representative Sacrifice that the Son of God offered not only for the sake of sin but also for the sake of all sinners. He took the place of all sinners by suffering that which they had to endure and completed whatever was required of them. This Sacrifice was the Ransom that was paid for all mankind. The Death of the One Who "*died for all*" and who "*all died*" in Him[1794] "*redeemed us from the curse of the Law*" by "*becoming for us a curse.*"[1795] He carried the heavy weight of the guilt of all sinners. His obedience and love with which He suffered so patiently for others, was beyond price because He Who died for all is more valuable than all humanity, for He is by Nature God, the Word of God Who presented His own Body as a "*sweet-smelling aroma*"[1796] and Who became the starting point of all Virtue.[1797] The Heavenly Father admired this New Beginning, the worthiness of Him Who offered the Sacrifice and the purity of Him Who presented Himself as the Offering.

[1793] St Basil the Great, *To Psalm* 48 (49), § 4, in Migne, *P.G.,* 29, 440. St Epiphanius, in Migne, *P.G.,* 43, 185. St Cyril of Jerusalem, *Catechesis,* XIII, § 1-2, in Migne, *P.G.,* 33, 773. St Athanasius the Great, *About the incarnation of the Word,* § 9, in Migne, *P.G.,* 25, 112. St Cyril of Alexandria, *That one is the Christ,* in Migne, *P.G.,* 75, 1337.
[1794] 2 Corinth. 5:14-15.
[1795] Gal. 3:13.
[1796] Ephes. 5:2.
[1797] St Cyril of Alexandria, in Migne, *P.G.,* 76, 1208 and 1436. Ibid, *To John,* book IV, ch. II, in Migne, *P.G.,* 73, 569.

This Sacrifice, which was so elect and spotless, became acceptable to the Heavenly Father as though it had been offered by the sinful human race. Through faith in Jesus Christ all those who believe are incorporated into Him, the Deified Beginning, being at the same time united with Him Who pleases God.[1798] For the Son of God became Man so that He may deify us in Himself and so that He may make us *".a chosen generation, a Royal Priesthood, a Holy Nation*"[1799] and *"partakers of the Divine Nature."*[1800]

Question 242: What are the benefits of the Expiatory Sacrifice?

Answer: It is obvious that this Sacrifice of the Only Begotten Son of God was considered as being offered by all mankind, which He, as the High Priest, represented and which consists of an Expiatory Sacrifice for the whole world. *"For God so loved the world that He gave His Only Begotten Son, that whoever believes in Him should not perish but have Everlasting Life."*[1801] Christ is not only the Expiatory of the sins of the Faithful and the Elect but also of the whole world. According to St Paul, *"Christ died for the ungodly"*[1802] *"while we were still sinners."*[1803] He did not die for the elect alone but to take away the sin of the entire world and so *"that the world, through Him, might be Saved."*[1804] Although the Sacrifice was offered for the whole world, only those who believe will benefit from it. St John Chrysostom emphasied that *"the Lord died for all to save all"* as it was fitting for Him to do so, *"He did not take up the sins of those who did not want"* His Redemption.[1805] The Lord assured us that *"he who believes in Him is not condemned; but he who does not believe is condemned already, because he has not believed in the Name of the Only Begotten Son of God."*[1806]

Christ offered the Sacrifice for the sin of the world, which enabled the reconciliation of the entire world with God the Heavenly Father. Those who do not believe in the Son alienate themselves from this Reconciliation and

---

[1798] St Gregory of Nyssa, *Against Eunomius,* Homily 12, in Migne, *P.G.,* 45, 889. St Athanasius the Great, *To Adelphius,* § 4, in Migne, *P.G.,* 26, 1077. St Cyril of Alexandria, *Homily* IV, *That the Son is not a creation,* in Migne, *P.G.,* 75, 905. Ibid, *To John,* book XI, ch. X, in Migne, *P.G.,* 74, 545. Ibid, *To Isaiah,* book IV, Homily II, in Migne, *P.G.,* 70, 965. Ibid, *To 1 Corinthians,* in Migne, *P.G.,* 74, 913.

[1799] 1 Peter 2:9.

[1800] 2 Peter 1:4.

[1801] John3:16.

[1802] Rom. 5:6.

[1803] Rom. 5:8.

[1804] John 3:17.

[1805] St John Chrysostom, *To Galatians 2:8,* in Migne, *P.G.,* 61, 647.

[1806] John 3:18.

all its Divine Gifts. Consequently they are condemned for their lack of faith. The Blood of the New Testament was shed for their Salvation and it is for them, as for the whole human race, more than sufficient to cleanse their sins. The Sacrifice of Christ was sufficient to save all people. Therefore even the lawless of sinners are not greater than the Justice of Him Who died. Neither have we sinned more than His Justice – the One Who offered His Life up for us. He gave more than we owned:*"just like the drop of water which falls into the infinite ocean."*[1807]

Henceforth, we can say that the Sacrifice of the Lord abundantly satisfied God in that it was not restricting to only appeasing the anger of God and to reconcile us to Him, but it furthermore became the Fountain of many Gifts and Graces that the human nature of the Incarnated Son first enjoyed, being Deified and Glorified and from Whom these riches poured forth to us.

In the outpouring of the riches of Gifts and Graces, one must recall St Paul who wrote: *"The Grace of God and the Gift by the Grace of the Man, Jesus Christ, abounded to many"*[1808] and *"where sin abounded, Grace abounded much more."*[1809] According to St John Chrysostom, we received an abundance *" of Grace"* because *"we were freed from the punishment of Hell and had put aside all evilness and we were regenerated from above and saved and sanctified and led to be sons by adoption and became brothers of the Only Begotten and co-heirs and of His same Body and perfected in His Flesh and are united with Him in one Body, having Him as the Head."*[1810]

Question 243: Does the work of Christ as a High Priest continue in Heaven?

Answer: The Work of our Lord and Saviour Jesus Christ, the Son of God, as High Priest, which was achieved on earth, continues in Heaven[1811] where He *"lives in God"* and, according to His Humanity, being dedicated completely to God in prayer and Communion with Him. On the last night of His earthly life He Himself assured His Holy Apostles that He would ask the Father to send *"another Helper."*[1812] After His glorious Resurrection and Ascension Christ, sitting at the Right Hand of the Father *"continues*

[1807] St John Chrysostom, *To Romans,* Homily 10, in Migne, *P.G.,* 60, 447.
[1808] Rom. 5:15.
[1809] Rom. 5:20.
[1810] St John Chrysostom, *To Romans,* Homily 10, § 2, in Migne, *P.G.,* 60, 446-447.
[1811] Heb. 9:24.
[1812] John 14:16.

forever[1813] *"to make intercession for them"*[1814] by appearing *"in the Presence of God for us."*[1815] Not like the High Priest of the Old Testament who entered in *"the most holy place every year with blood of another"*[1816] our High Priest *"Christ, has not entered the holy places made with hands, which are copies of the True, but into Heaven itself."*[1817] In Heaven our Lord remains *"an Advocate to the Father,"*[1818] Mediator and High Priest Who prays for us and assures *" our forgiveness and the riches of Grace."*[1819]

The exaltation of the High Priest on the Throne of God was the result and direct consequence of the Sacrifice offered by Jesus Christ on the Cross, which completely satisfied God and being perfected, opened the Way to Heaven, *"where the Forerunner has entered for us, even Jesus."*[1820] Christ's Work of intervention and prayer to the Father is necessary, not because His Sacrifice was imperfect, but because those faithful on earth who struggle against sin are imperfect. They fall and are wounded, and continuously need the Divine Mercy and Grace of Christ Who continues to intercede for our Salvation. All our weaknesses, all our discouragements, all our daily falls, all our requests and prayers to God are covered by our Holy High Priest Who presents them to Him. Our High Priest is our *"Helper"* Who intercedes with the Father, not as a servant, but as Man and as His Word and Son.[1821]

Exactly how the intervention of our Lord takes place in Heaven is beyond our knowledge, for it is impossible for any man to conceive those things that take place in Heaven, unless revealed by the Holy Spirit. Nevertheless, according to Holy Scripture, our Lord, after His Resurrection, *"makes intercession for the Saints"*[1822] and like *"a Lamb as though it had been slain"*[1823] for *"it is Christ Who died, and furthermore is also Risen, Who is even at the Right Hand of God, Who also makes intercession for us."*[1824]

The prayer and communion with the Father by the High Priest Christ and His Sacrifice on the Cross continues without end in Heaven and consists

---

[1813] Heb. 7:24.
[1814] Heb. 7:25.
[1815] Heb. 9:24.
[1816] Heb. 9:25.
[1817] Heb. 9:24.
[1818] 1 John 2:1
[1819] St Cyril of Alexandria, *To John* IX, ch. 9 *to John 17:16,* in Migne *P.G.,* 74, 553.
[1820] Heb. 6:20.
[1821] St Gregory of Nazianzus, *Homily* 30, § 14, in Migne, *P.G.,* 36, 121.
[1822] Rom. 8:27.
[1823] Rev. 5:6.
[1824] Rom. 8:34.

of a unique and undivided Work, which was offered once for the entire world. St Augustine emphasised that Christ intercedes for us as High Priest. He intercedes in us as our Head and He accepts prayers from us as our God. Let us realise that in Him are our voices and in us is His Voice.[1825]

Concerning the words addressed to Christ by King David: *"Thou art a Priest forever"*[1826] and that He *"has an unchangeable Priesthood"*[1827] it is important to know that Christ received His Priesthood from the moment of the Incarnation of God the Word. Through the Hypostatic Union of Christ's Humanity with His Divinity, His Priesthood remains forever because His Divinity is forever. The results of the Lord's Priesthood furthermore, remain forever unchangeable since He, as High Priest, became the reason for their Eternal Salvation to those who believe.

Christ's Heavenly intervention for the faithful will come to an end when His Second Coming and Last Judgement takes place. For it will no longer be necessary since all those who will be Saved will enjoy the Fruits of Christ's Sacrifice.[1828]

CHAPTER ELEVEN
THE OFFICE OF CHRIST AS KING

Question 244: What is the Office of Christ as King?

Answer: As Orthodox Christians we confess that Christ is our Eternal King,[1829] Who was raised on His Eternal Throne through His Sufferings on the Cross and His victory over Death and Satan. This Confession and recognition of the Lord Jesus Christ as our King is based on Holy Scripture and Apostolic Tradition from the time of the Apostolic Fathers throughout the entire life of the Orthodox Church.

The first actions of our Lord as King are found:

1) In the fulfillment of the Law and the new Institutions and Mysteries, which as the Law-giver He instituted in order to be accomplished within His One, Holy, Catholic and Apostolic Church.

2) In the choosing of His Holy Apostles to whom He gave equivalent authority as that of His own.

[1825] St Augustine, in Oosterzee, *Dogmatics*, p. 619.
[1826] Psalm 109(110):4. Heb. 5:6.
[1827] Heb. 7:24.
[1828] 1 Corinth. 15:28.
[1829] Cf. Frangopoulos, *Christian Faith,* pp. 149-150. Mitsopoulos, *Themata,* pp. 160.

3) Our Lord and Saviour Jesus Christ appeared as the Great and High King after His victory on the Cross. With His Soul He went down to Hades and became the Lord of all. Through His Resurrection He conquered and defeated Death and consequently He proclaimed that *"all authority has been given to"* Him *"in Heaven and on earth."*[1830]

4) And finally, He ascended into Heaven and sat at the Right Hand of the Father.

Our Lord Jesus Christ will reign within His Church for all ages, leading His Faithful to victory over Satan and all His malicious foes, by protecting and guiding them to their Salvation and leading His Church to perfection. As the Eternal King, Christ takes care of each and everyone separately. He regenerates, sanctifies, nourishes and gives Life to each one. The Royal Authority of Christ aims for the final victory and conquest over the world, in order that it might be incorporated into His Heavenly Kingdom as well as for the Will of God the Father to be *"on earth as it is in Heaven."*[1831]

Thus Christ as King, as Head, as Leader and as Shepherd of His people becomes to all Sanctification from God, perfecting through Himself the Work of Salvation. Finally, the action of Christ as King will be manifested at His Second and glorious Coming and Final Judgement, after which He will submit everything to God the Father with Whom, together with the Holy Spirit, He will reign for all Eternity.

Question 245: What is the relationship of Christ's Office as King to the two other Offices?

Answer: As a direct and mutual relationship exists between Christ's Offices of Prophet and High Priest, likewise is the relationship between His Office of King and High Priest. Our Lord and Saviour Jesus Christ, the Son of God, was elevated to His Throne as the Eternal King not simply *after* His Suffering on the Cross, but *because* of His Suffering. Due to His perfect obedience that was *" to the point of death, even the death of the Cross"* God *"highly exalted Him and* (gave) *Him the Name which is above every name."*[1832]

It is also obvious that whatever Enlightenment we may enjoy from the Office of Christ as Prophet and no matter what we owe for His Sacrifice,

---

[1830] Matth. 28:18.
[1831] Matth. 6:10.
[1832] Phil. 2:8, 9.

which was offered by Him as High Priest on the Cross, our Salvation, Exaltation in Heaven and Restoration is perfected through the Action of Jesus Christ as King and Lord. Together with the Enlightenment from the Teachings of the Great Teacher and the Knowledge of the Truth that has set us free from the slavery of sin and death, and which gave peace to our conscious through the Atonement Sacrifice of the High Priest that vanquished the curse and enmity between man and God, it is essential and necessary that our whole inner existence be Regenerated and purified. It is also vital that the evil that exists within us be conquered and crushed. This is achieved through the Work of Christ as King. Truly, Christ in His extreme humbleness *"was delivered up because of our offences, and was raised because of our Justification"*[1833] as the High King Who conquered Death.

Question 246: What are the teachings of Holy Scripture concerning the Office of Christ as King?

Answer: Our confession and recognition of Christ as our King and Lord is based on Holy Scripture. The Jews in the Old Testament awaited the Messiah as a powerful wordly Ruler and King, Who would restore the ancient and glorious throne of His forefather, King David. However they misinterpreted the Messianic Prophecies, according to which the Messiah would be set as King on *"the Holy Hill of Zion"* proclaiming *"the Decree of the Lord"*[1834] and Whose *"Throne is forever and ever."*[1835] He would be sitting at the Right Hand of God until His enemies became His *"footstool."* He would rule over them with *"the rod"* of His *"strength"* and *".in the midst"* of His *"enemies."*[1836] He would enter Jerusalem[1837] according to the Prophet Zacharias.[1838] The Prophet Daniel declared: *"And to Him was given the Dominion, and the Honour, and the Kingdom; and all nations, tribes, and languages, shall serve Him: His Dominion is an Everlasting Dominion, which shall not pass away, and His Kingdom shall not be destroyed."*[1839]

In the New Testament at the Annunciation of the Ever-Virgin Mary, the Theotokos, the Archangel Gabriel foretold that *"the Lord God will give Him the Throne of His father David. And He will reign over the House of*

[1833] Rom. 4:25.
[1834] Psalm 2:6-7.
[1835] Psalm 44(45):6.
[1836] Psalm 109(110):1-2.
[1837] Matth. 21:1-11. Mark 11:1-10. Luke 19:28-44. John 12:12-19. Is. 62:11.
[1838] Zach. 9:9-10.
[1839] Daniel 7:14.

Jacob forever, and of His Kingdom there will be no end."[1840]   When the Messiah was born, the three kings *"from the East came to Jerusalem"* and worshipped Him as King and said: *"Where is He Who has been born King of the Jews?"*[1841]

It is true that Christ, during His life on earth, refused to accept the title of *"King"*[1842] and rebuked His Holy Disciples when they sought earthly glory and when they requested to be seated at His right and left hand in His Kingdom.[1843] He acknowledged the civil authorities of His time.[1844] Our Lord's reluctance of earthly status can be understood when one considers that the Jews were awaiting an earthly Messiah who would deliver them from the humiliation of subjection to the Romans and who would restore the worldly Kingdom of King David.[1845] It was natural, however, during the four last days of His life on the earth that our Lord permitted the crowd to welcome Him to Jerusalem with accolades of *"the King of Israel!"*[1846] Neither did He reject the title of King before Pontius Pilate but He tried to explain that His *"Kingdom is not of this world."*[1847] He assured us on numerous occasions that His Kingdom would not be established on earth as a visible Institution and that it does not have its foundation in this world. Neither is it based on violence. Instead it is the Kingdom of Truth, Justice and Sanctification, founded on the hearts of those who freely accept it.

The sign that Pontius Pilate had placed on the Cross is important and significant for it declares: *"JESUS OF NAZARETH, THE KING OF THE JEWS."*[1848] It was written in three languages - Hebrew, Greek and Roman - in order that many Jews could read it. In the Book of Revelation St John saw that Christ had *"on His robe and on His thigh a Name written: 'KING OF KINGS AND LORD OF LORDS.'"*[1849] The rest of the Holy Apostles call Christ *"Lord"* which expresses the meaning of Ruler and King. St Paul called Christ *"Lord"* proclaiming that *"He must reign until He has put all enemies under His Feet."*[1850]

[1840] Luke 1:32-33.
[1841] Matth. 2:1-2, 11.
[1842] John 6:15.
[1843] Matth. 20:20-28. Mark 10:35-40.
[1844] Matth. 17:25-27; 22:21. Rom. 13:1-7. 1 Peter 2:13-14.
[1845] Acts 1:6.
[1846] John 12:13.
[1847] John 18:36.
[1848] John 19:19. Matth. 27:37.
[1849] Rev. 19:16.
[1850] 1 Corinth. 15:25.

Question 247: What are the teachings of the holy Fathers concerning the Office of Christ as King?

Answer: In the *Epistle of Barnabas* one reads: *"the Kingdom of Jesus is on the Tree, and that those who hope in Him will live forever."*[1851] The phrase *"the Kingdom of Jesus is on the tree"* signifies that the Sacrifice offered by Christ on the Cross depended directly on His Office as King.

St John Chrysostom emphasised the Kingship of Christ as God, simultaneously exalting His Kingship as the God-Man, when he proclaimed that *"He is truly a Great King Who cleansed the world from error and brought back the Truth very quickly and destroyed the tyranny of the devil."* Furthermore he saw Him sitting at the Right Hand of God as King, until His enemies are set before His Feet by the Father. *"Christ was dominating"* through the Apostles and not only *"ruling"* in the midst of His enemies. Although it is said that the Heavenly Father placed His enemies at His Feet, it is the Work of the Only Begotten Son Who achieved everything.[1852]

Question 248: What are the manifestations of Christ's Office as King?

Answer: The first manifestations of the Office of Christ as King[1853] are manifested during the period of His humbleness. At first it was the giving of the Law that He realized by fulfilling the Mosaic Law[1854] and giving the new Law of Love,[1855] then establishing Institutions and Mysteries, vested by Eternal Authority and which are to be used within His Orthodox Church. The choosing of His Apostles,[1856] as well as the assurance that He would give them all the Spiritual Authority to forgive or to bind the sins of the people[1857] in order to continue His Work as He was sent to do by His Father,[1858] manifests His Office as King. After the Sacrifice on the Cross He ascended with glory to His Royal Throne; at His Resurrection, He accomplished His Eternal Victory and glorious Triumph; at His Ascension, He was crowned at the Right Hand of the Father as the Eternal King.

From the time that He *"cried out with a loud voice"*[1859] *" 'it is finished!' And bowing His Head, He gave up His Spirit"*[1860] His

---

[1851] *Barnabas,* 8, 5-6, in Lightfoot, *Apostolic Fathers,* p. 172.
[1852] St John Chrysostom, *To Psalm* 46(47), § 3, and *To Psalm* 109(110), § 4, in Migne, *P.G.,* 55, 271.
[1853] Cf. Damalas, *Catechesis,* pp. 63-64.
[1854] Matth. 5:17.
[1855] John 13:34.
[1856] Matth. 10:1-4. Mark 3:13-19. Luke 6:12-16.
[1857] Matth. 16:19; 18:18. John 20:23.
[1858] John 20:21.
[1859] Matth. 27:50.

Glorification and Exaltation began. The *"Blood and the Water"*[1861] that came out of the Lord's Side when He was pierced by the soldier, proved that He was above man because the blood of others would have been thick and clear water would not have flowed from their wounds, whereas the marvellous thing about Christ's dead Body was that Blood and Water issued forth from His Side. The laws of nature with regard to Christ's Body diverted from their usual course. While bodies of dead men always begin to decompose immediately after death occurs, Christ's Body entered the Path of Glory and immediately began to fulfil King David's Prophecy: *"For Thou will not leave My Soul in Sheol, nor will Thou allow Thy Holy One to see corruption."*[1862]

Our Lord and Saviour, practised His Office as King with *"His Soul stripped from its Body, (He) preached to the souls which were stripped from their bodies"* thereby achieving His first conquest of those who were in the infernal Hades.[1863] This triumphal Descent of our Lord into Hades was mentioned by Him.[1864] *"And other sheep I have which are not of this fold; them also I must bring, and they will hear My voice; and there will be one flock and one Shepherd."*[1865]

The event of Christ's Descent into Hades was clarified by the Holy Fathers and Ecclesiastic Writers[1866] such as St Ignatius the Theophorus who referred to *"the Prophets, who were His Disciples in the Spirit, were expecting as their Teacher"* and *"because of this He for Whom they rightly waite,d raised them from the dead when He came."*[1867]

The 9th Canon of the 5th Ecumenical Council stated that *"the Word of God was Incarnated in Flesh with a Soul, with His intellectual Soul He descended into Hades and again the same ascended into Heaven."*[1868] Also the 7th Ecumenical Council proclaimed that *"this (Christ) we confess the One Who conquered Hades and freed those who were bound from old times."*[1869]

Finally, St John of Damascus observed that *"into Hades descended the Deified Soul; in order that the Sun of Righteousness rise to those who*

[1860] John 19:30.

[1861] John 19:34.

[1862] Psalm 15(16):10. Acts 2:31.

[1863] Origen, *Against Celsus,* II, 42, in **B,** v. 9, p. 154.

[1864] Matth. 12:40.

[1865] John 10:16.

[1866] Karmeris, *The descent of Christ into Hades from an Orthodox view,* Athens, 1939. See also: Mogilas, in Karmeris, *The dogmatics,* v. II, pp. 617, 519-520. St Symeon, *Euriskomena,* Homily XLV, p. 211.

[1867] St Ignatius, *To Magnesians,* 9, 2, in Lightfoot, *Apostolic Fathers,* p. 95.

[1868] Mansi, IX, p. 397.

[1869] Mansi, XII, p. 1138.

were in the earth, likewise for those who were under the earth in darkness and the shadow Light shined and thus freeing those who were bounded from old times, immediately raised from the dead, making the path to the Resurrection."[1870]

The importance of the descent of Christ into Hades is that our Lord Jesus is revealed as the Saviour of all souls, proving that He is indeed King and that His Kingdom differs from any other earthly kingdom. No power of nature or other force in the universe could prevent the Saviour from finding the way for the souls.[1871] He is the Redeemer of all human generations, even those who were before His Epiphany, and there is no " S*alvation in any other, for there is no other name under Heaven given among men by which we must be Saved*"[1872] except in Him alone Who has no need *"to suffer often since the foundation of the world; but now, once at the end of the ages, He has appeared to put away sin by the Sacrifice of Himself."*[1873]

Question 249: What was Christ's triumph after His glorious Resurrection and Ascension?

Answer: The Resurrection of our Lord Jesus Christ was revealed as was His triumphant Entrance into His Glory. Conquering Death, He took up in His own Authority *"the keys of Hades and of Death."*[1874]

Christ's Resurrection proved that His Sacrifice on the Cross was accepted by the Heavenly Father. Our Redemption was accomplished by the destruction of Death and mortality, which was enforced because of the Fall of Adam was corrected. *"Christ through His Resurrection assured us fully that He conquered Death, that He is the True Saviour sent by God to us and that the hope in Him is not in vain but secure and undoubted."*[1875]

In the Lord's Resurrection we greet the Glory of His Kingdom. His Resurrection is a Vision of the Glory in which the present world will end at its final stage when, at the General Resurrection, the whole world will be Regenerated.[1876] This is understandable when one takes into consideration that the Lord's Resurrection is not simply the point and fore-announcer of this *"Regeneration"* but is itself the Regeneration in its living principal whereby Death was triumphantly conquered in God's Creation. From the

---

[1870] St John of Damascus, *Exposition. About the after the resurrection,* IV, 74, 29, in Migne, *P.G.,* 94, 1101.
[1871] Martensen, *Dogmatique,* p. 483.
[1872] Acts 4:12.
[1873] Heb. 9:26.
[1874] Rev. 1:18.
[1875] Plato of Moscow, *Orthodox Teaching,* p. 125.
[1876] Martensen, *Dogmatique,* p. 485.

moment that Christ was Raised, our spiritual resurrection began in order that the resurrection of the bodies of all men would follow at the appointed time.[1877] He Who was delivered to Death *"because of our offences" ".was Raised because of our Justification."*[1878] The General Resurrection of all is made possible through our Justification and will be accomplished and assured by our Saviour and Redeemer Who is the Leader, Lord and Head of His Orthodox Church.

Between the Lord's Resurrection and our Justification as well as between the resurrection of each individual who believes in Him, there exists an unbreakable relationship. The same relationship exists between the Resurrection of the Head of the Church and the final triumph of His Church, which is His Mystical Body consisting of all those who are Regenerated. The future of the Church, its final Glorious Destination towards which it is guided and the Faithful can be seen in the Resurrection of our Lord.[1879] With His Mystical Body, His Orthodox Church, Christ sat in the Heavenly Places at His Ascension, which was the result of His Resurrection, being the manner through which the human nature of the Lord was Raised to the utmost height of its Deification and Glorification.

In the Communion of human nature with Divine Nature, the Lord's human nature and its Attributes were not rejected but raised to become the Living Holy Temple of the Deity and to be the King seated on the Throne of the Heavenly Father. These results are extended to all generations submitting His enemies and those who resist His Work of Salvation.

This Heavenly Glory of Christ is described by Holy Scripture as His Enthronement *"at the Right Hand of the Majesty on High."*[1880] The expression *"at the Right Hand"* is not a specific place *"for the Divine is indescribable"* although it is expressed as *"Deified Glory."*[1881] In the Person of the God-Man all human nature was raised to Himself as its Head.

Question 250: What is the manifestation of the Royal Power of Christ within the Church?

Answer: The God-Man was vested with Royal Power. This Power is distinguished from His Creative Almightiness, which as Co-eternal to the Father, He always had. He perfects the first Creation in all spiritual and natural spheres, in which fallen man moves and thus established the *"New*

[1877] St Symeon, *Euriskomena,* Homily XLII, pp. 193-195.
[1878] Rom. 4:25.
[1879] St Symeon, *Euriskomena,* Homily XXIX, p. 148.
[1880] Heb. 1:3.
[1881] St John of Damascus, *To Hebrews 1:3,* in Migne, *P.G.,* 95, 932.

Creation"[1882] in Christ. On His Royal Throne the Most High King and Eternal High Priest does not rest but continues to work.[1883]

The Church is the sphere in which Christ's Royal Power and Authority is manifested. He continues even in Heaven to practice this Authority. All those who are called[1884] and who believe in the Son, are transmitted from the authority of darkness to the Kingdom of the Son, making them citizens of His Heavenly Kingdom. The Work of Christ as King is to gather His Flock throughout all generations - those who have accepted and believe in Him - awaking them through the Divine Grace of the Holy Spirit, the outpouring of which is from the Heavenly Throne and which unites them to Himself and to one another. The High King rules the Church, which is His Mystical Body, through His Word and His Spirit, being Himself the Head from which Life issues forth to each member according to their needs and ability to receive.

Christ being the Head of the whole Body of the Church in which each member has its position and is familiar with how it is joined to the other members, being at peace with God, they grow. They receive the Holy Spirit Who is richly bestowed upon them from Above, touching all and being given to all. Christ excludes anyone from entering as Co-ruler or from be called *"Rabbi"* or *"Teachers"* for only One is the *"Teacher, the Christ."*[1885] The Holy Apostles presented Him as *"purchasing the Church through His own Blood"*[1886] as *"Chief Shepherd"* [1887] and Bridegroom, Who loved and gave Himself for the Church.[1888]

Ruling the Church as One Lord and King, He protects Her against any enemy, according to His Promise that " *the gates of Hades shall not prevail against it."*[1889] Finally, Christ leads His Church to perfection, cleansing the whole Body and each member individually from any *"spot or wrinkle or any such thing"* in order that they *"should be Holy."*[1890]

That the Work of Christ as King is extended and achieved within the Church, does not mean that each member of the Church is not in a direct relationship with the Great King. Since the Church consists of each and every individual member and in order for them to be united as one, they need to be overseen and taught by the Lord. The assurance was given by

---

[1882] Gal. 6:15.
[1883] John 5:17.
[1884] John 6:44.
[1885] Matth. 23:8.
[1886] Acts 20:28.
[1887] 1 Peter 5:4.
[1888] Ephes. 5:27.
[1889] Matth. 16:18.
[1890] Ephes. 5:27.

our Risen Lord to His Holy Apostles that He would be with them " *always, even to the end of the age*"[1891] and this is accomplished by all Faithful according to His Promise that He and His Father "*will come and make*" their "*.home with* "[1892] all who love Him.

In the internal Regeneration of each individual member of the Church, it is the Holy Spirit Who acts. Christ requested the Heavenly Father to give us "*the Helper*"[1893] and not only was the Holy Spirit sent by the Father into the world in His Name[1894] but He also sent Him to His Holy Disciples who bear witness to the Christ[1895] and glorify Him.[1896] He promised that whatever they asked of the Father in His Name, they would receive.[1897] Furthermore, He would "*manifest*" Himself to all those who love Him.[1898] He is the "*Source of Life*" to Whom the Father "*granted to have Life in Himself*"[1899] in order "*to give Life to whom He Wills*"[1900] and that whoever "*believes in Him may have Eternal Life*" and " *raise him up at the Last Day.*"[1901] Christ possesses and bestows this Source of Life upon all Faithful whom He protects and nourishes as His own sheep and by granting "*them Eternal Life.* "[1902] Christ does not simply live in the memories of each Faithful but also in the heart and will of each individual who has Christ "*formed*" in him[1903] and no longer do the Faithful live for themselves but instead "*Christ lives in*" them.[1904]

Question 251: Is Christ the King of the world?

Answer: The Authority of Christ has an individual and universal meaning. The Work of King Christ does not aim to gain victory only over sin within either one person or many, but to completely destroy evil in such a way that the Will of God is "*on earth as it is in Heaven.*"[1905]

[1891] Matth. 28:20.
[1892] John 14:23.
[1893] John 14:16.
[1894] John 14:26.
[1895] John 15:26-27.
[1896] John 16:14
[1897] John 14:13-14; 16:23.
[1898] John 14:21.
[1899] John 5:26.
[1900] John 5:21.
[1901] John 6:39, 40.
[1902] John 10:28.
[1903] Gal. 4:19.
[1904] Gal. 2:20.
[1905] Cf. Kefalas, *Catechesis,* pp. 83-84.

The word of God's Kingdom has influenced the moral world. As a rock falls into a lake and creates ripples that spread across the water, likewise is the Holy Gospel of Christ spread throughout the world. The fact that the world hates[1906] the Message of the Gospel proves its Life-giving Power. Victory over the adverse reactions of the sinful world will end with God's Kingdom prevailing: "*And this is the Victory that has overcome the world – our Faith.*"[1907]

This type of Triumph will be the end of the struggle of the Church and is assured by the character of Christ the King as the Head of His Church and as Leader and Chief Shepherd of His people.[1908] Christ, as the Head of the Church, is not just her Lord and Ruler but also the Fountain of Life and the Centre of her unity. Consequently, anyone who is in Communion with Him through the Living Faith, receives from Him Eternal Life and Power of Sanctification through which every worldly force is conquered. As "*the Author and Finisher of our Faith*"[1909] He appears to the people as the Leader of the utmost Moral Perfection. The Holy Apostles invite everyone to become imitators of Christ and "*to walk just as He walked*"[1910] "*because Christ also suffered for us, leaving us an example, that you should follow His steps.*"[1911] Faith and Love in Christ keeps our minds and hearts with Him.[1912] As High Priest and Chief Shepherd of His people, He perfects His Work that He began in the Church by leading us to Perfection and Sanctification and by pursuing "*peace with all people, and Holiness, without which no one will see the Lord.*"[1913]

Question 252: What is the last act of Christ as King?

Answer: The last Act of Christ as King will be His Second Glorious Coming and the Judgement of the world.[1914] Our Lord foretold that He would return with Glory and Power to Judge the living and the dead. After this Judgement each man will receive his Eternal Condition and will enter either "*into Everlasting Punishment*" or "*into Eternal Life.*"[1915]

[1906] John 15:18-20.
[1907] 1 John 5:4.
[1908] Rev. 6:2.
[1909] Heb. 12:2.
[1910] 1 John 2:6.
[1911] 1 Peter 2:21.
[1912] 2 Corinth. 3:18.
[1913] Heb. 12:14.
[1914] Matth. 24:29-31; 25:31-46. Mark 13:24-27. Luke 21:25-28. 1 Thess. 4:15-17.
[1915] Matth. 25:46.

Christ will return, accompanied by all His Angels, not to add anything to the Work of Salvation but to Judge each and every man according to his deeds. He will demand an account from every human being on how His Grace that He offered on the Cross was used. After this, He will present all those who followed Him to His Father and "*then comes the end, when He delivers the Kingdom to God the Father, when He puts an end to all rule and all authority and power*"[1916] being subject to God the Father "*that God may be all in all.*"[1917]

Christ as the King of the Church, will reign forever as the Head of the Church, "*as Firstborn among many brethren*"[1918] transforming "*our lowly body that it may be conformed to His Glorious Body.*"[1919] Consequently, "*He will reign over the House of Jacob forever, and of His Kingdom there will be no end*"[1920] for His "*Throne, O God, is forever and ever.*"[1921]

CHAPTER TWELVE
THE MOTHER OF GOD

Question 253: Who is the Mother of God?

Answer: Since the Hypostatic Union of the two Natures in Christ was accomplished from the moment of Conception, the Mother of the Saviour, Mary is truly honoured to be called "*the Mother of God*," "*Ever-Blessed*", "*Ever-Virgin*" and "*Theotokos*," for she did not give birth merely to a fine Man but to the Incarnated Word and Son of God Who is the unique and only True God-Man.[1922] This Truth was proclaimed by the four Ecumenical Councils who interpreted the Teachings of the New Testament and the Sacred Tradition of the Orthodox Church. They acknowledged the real Motherhood of the Ever Virgin Mary in relation to Christ and the Conception by her of the Incarnated Son and Word of God. Conceiving the God-Man in her Womb from the Holy Spirit, she remained Ever-Virgin. She is the only woman to ever be simultaneously a Mother and a Virgin, a Virgin and a Mother. Her Supernatural and Immaculate Conception and Birth-giving of the God-Man did not damage her virginity at all, neither

---

[1916] 1 Corinth. 15:24.
[1917] 1 Corinth. 15:28.
[1918] Rom. 8:29. Psalm 44(45):6.
[1919] Phil. 3:21.
[1920] Luke 1:33.
[1921] Heb. 1:8.
[1922] Cf. Evdokimov, *Orthodoxia*, pp. 202-209.

before the Birth nor during the Birth of her Child because even after the Birth she remained a Virgin. Mary, the Mother of the Messiah, Jesus Christ, the Son of God, never had any sexual relationship with St Joseph the Betrothed before or after the Birth of the Incarnated Son of God. The "*brothers*" of Christ who are mentioned in Holy Scripture are not the children of the Ever Blessed Mary but of St Joseph's first marriage.

From the beginning the Orthodox Church proclaimed Mary to be Ever-Virgin and Theotokos. Her virtuous and spotless life made her higher in Holiness than the Cherubim and more honorable than the Seraphim, for she gave Birth to the God-Man. Although we confess her as Ever-Virgin, spotless, stainless and undefiled from any personal sins, she was not free of Original Sin. We believe that she was cleansed from Ancestral Sin at the Annunciation when the Holy Spirit descended upon her and she conceived the Incarnated Word of God Supernaturally. Addressing her as "*Panagia,*" meaning "*Above all Saints,*" we proclaim and confess that she surpassed all righteous men and women of all times in Holiness. However, she was not completely sinless as having been born of Adam, she was guilty of Original Sin, although her Son, the God-Man, is the only sinless One.

Question 254: What does the term "THEOTOKOS" mean?

Answer: The 4th Ecumenical Council in Ephesus, using the first Anathema of St Cyril of Alexandria, condemned Nestorius who insisted that the Ever-Virgin Mary gave Birth to the Man Christ and consequently she should be referred to as "*Man-bearer*" (i.e. Mother of the Man Who was never united with the Word) or "*Christotokos*" (i.e. Mother of Christ but not Mother of the God-Man). This Council proclaimed the Ever-Virgin to be Truly "*THEOTOKOS*" ("*God-Bearer*") for she had indeed given Birth to the Word of God Who became Flesh. This term was repeated by the 4th Ecumenical Council in Chalcedon, which proclaimed that Christ "*during these last days for us and our Salvation*" was Born "*from Mary the Virgin and Theotokos according to His Humanity.*"

The 6th Ecumenical Council also proclaimed "*Mary to be Virgin*" "*mainly and Truly Theotokos.*" Obviously by calling her "*Above all Saints Virgin*" ("*Panagia*"), it is proclaimed that she is "*Mother*" for she gave real birth to the human nature of the God-Man, whereas she is certainly the "*Mother of God*" because she conceived, carried and gave birth to the Incarnated Word and Son of God, the Second Person of the Holy Trinity Who is true God. She did not give birth to His Divine Nature but only to His human nature, which He took up Hypostatically.

The Ever Blessed and Ever Virgin Mary was Truly, not falsely, the Mother of the Lord Jesus Christ, the Son of God. This fact is witnessed by Holy Scripture that refers to her as *"the Mother of Jesus"* or *"His Mother"*[1923] and by the Archangel Gabriel when he announced that she would conceive in her *"womb and bring forth a Son."*[1924] To St Joseph the Betrothed the same Archangel announced that *"that which is conceived in her is of the Holy Spirit."*[1925] The Ever Blessed Virgin Mary was first addressed as *"the Mother of the Lord"* by St Elizabeth, the mother of St John the Baptist.[1926]

The real motherhood of the Ever Virgin Mary in relation to the Lord was defended by the Holy Fathers and Ecclesiastic Writers of the Orthodox Church, such as St Ignatius the Theophorus who declared that our Lord *"is truly of the family of David with respect to human descent"* and that He was *"truly born of a Virgin."*[1927] Elsewhere the Apostolic Father said: *"For our God, Jesus the Christ was conceived by Mary."*[1928]

The term *"Theotokos"* was first used by Origen and then by the Holy Fathers. St Athanasius the Great of Alexandria believed that the Son of God became Man by taking flesh *"from the Virgin Theotokos."*[1929]

St Cyril of Alexandria emphasised that: *"Truly and Theotokos and Virgin-Mother the rightly Blessed should be called. For Jesus Who was Born from her was not merely a fine Man."*[1930]

St John of Damascus, rejecting the title *"Christotokos"* observed that *"rightfully and truthfully we should call the Holy Mary Theotokos"* *"for He Who was Born from her is Truly God."*[1931]

Question 255: What are the teachings of Holy Scripture and the holy Fathers?

Answer: Holy Scripture clearly bears witness to the Virginity of the Theotokos in relation to the time of the Conception and Nourishment, primarily in the question of the Ever Blessed Virgin Mary who said: *"how*

[1923] Matth. 1:18; 13:55. Mark 3:31, 32; 6:3. Luke 2:33, 43, 48. John 2:1; 19:26. Acts 1:14.
[1924] Luke 1:31.
[1925] Matth. 1:20.
[1926] Luke 1:43.
[1927] St Ignatius, *To Smyrnaeans,* 1, 1, in Lightfoot, *Apostolic Fathers,* p. 110.
[1928] Ibid, *To Ephesians,* 18, 2, in Lightfoot, *Apostolic Fathers,* p. 92.
[1929] St Athanasius the Great, *Against Arians,* III, § 29, in Migne, *P.G.,* 26, 385.
[1930] St Cyril of Alexandria, *Homily against those who do not confess the holy Virgin to be Theotokos,* § 4, in Migne, *P.G.,* 76, 260.
[1931] St John of Damascus, *Exposition. That the holy Virgin is Theotokos,* III, 56, 12, in Migne, *P.G.,* 94, 1028.

can this be, since I do not know a man?"[1932]   St Matthew the Evangelist bore witness to this by proclaiming that *"the Virgin shall be with child"*[1933] and *"that which is Conceived in her is of the Holy Spirit."*[1934]

The Son of God was born *"truly from the Virgin"*[1935] and that *"the Power of God came down upon the Virgin and overshadowed her and made her to be with child, being a virgin"*[1936] according to the Prophecy of the Prophet Isaiah: *"Behold, the Virgin shall be with child, and bear a Son, and they shall call His Name Emmanuel."*[1937]

St Irenaeus referred to the above Prophecy by underlining the part that speaks about Mary being a *"virgin"* and stressed that this was given to her through the Incarnation of God.   Comparing the Virgin Mary to Eve he observed that *"as Eve had a husband, but still being a virgin, she disobeyed and through this disobedience she became the cause of death to herself and for all the human race, likewise Mary being betrothed but being a virgin showed obedience and became the reason for Salvation to herself and to all the human race."*[1938]

Tertullian[1939] repeatedly spoke of the Virgin's Supernatural Conception, which preserved her virginity.   With one voice, all the Fathers and Ecclesiastic Writers of the Orthodox Church proclaimed that Mary was **"a virgin before the Birth, during the Birth and after the Birth."**   No one renounced this great honour of the Ever-Virgin Mary, the Theotokos, except the heretic Ebionites, Celsus,[1940] Julian the Offender, Jehova Witnesses, some contemporary Protestants and Pentecostals heretics who have renounced Apostolic Tradition.[1941]

During the Birth of Jesus Christ, the Ever-Virgin Mary the Theotokos, remained a Virgin. We must take note that her purity and spotlessness as a virgin consisted of the purity of her heart and the preservation of her mind as well as her complete inner and external existence, which was far from any corruption of the flesh, thought, desire or will.   This purity and chastity of her heart was preserved during the time that she gave Birth as *"virginity*

[1932] Luke 1:34.

[1933] Matth. 1:23. Is. 7:14.

[1934] Matth. 1:20.

[1935] St Ignatius, *To Smyrnaeans,* 1, 1, in Lightfoot, *Apostolic Fathers,* p. 110.

[1936] St Justin, the philosopher and martyr, *Apology* 1, 33, § 4, in **B,** v. 3, p. 178. Ibid, *Dialogue,* 76-78, in **B,** v. 3, pp. 280-282.

[1937] Is. 7:14.

[1938] St Irenaeus, *Heresies,* book III, ch. 21, § 1 and 22, 4, in Migne, *P.G.,* 7, 946 and 951. Cf. Ibid, in Hadjephraimides, pp. 247-248 and 2553-254.

[1939] Tertullian, *Apologeticus,* 21, in migne, *P.L.,* 1, 453. Ibid, *De virg. vel.* 6, in migne, *P.L.,* 1, 2946. Ibid, *De carne Christi,* 17, in migne, *P.L.,* 2, 827. Ibid, *De monogamia,* 8, in migne, *P.L.,* 2, 989.

[1940] Origen, *Against Celsus,* I, 32, in **B,** v. 9, p. 92.

[1941] Trempelas, *Dogmatique,* v. II, p. 208.

of mind" (*"virginitas mentis"*), *"virginity of senses"* (*"virginitas sensus"*) and *"virginity of body"* (*"virginitas corporis"*).[1942]

St John of Damascus, proclaiming the above Truth, observed: *"As Christ was Conceived He preserved the Virgin, and thus when He was Born, He preserved her virginity unharmed, for He alone passed through her and it remained shut." " for it was not impossible for Him to pass through this Gate and not to harm her virginity."*[1943]

To the above we can add that the spotless and Most-Holy Birth of our Lord from the Ever-Virgin Mary and Theotokos not only preserved the purity of her virginity but also exalted it and raised it to a higher Glory.

Question 256: Did the Theotokos after the Birth of Christ remained a Virgin?

Answer: It is a real and natural result that *"the office of Mary* (as a Virgin) *be preserved in virginity till the end, in order that her body"* before the descent of the Holy Spirit, was found worthy to serve the Mystery of the Incarnation.[1944] It was therefore impossible for her, being *"the beginning of purity"* among all women, to have a relationship with a man having been the one who *"gave birth to God and learned the Miracle from experience."*[1945]

Many Holy Fathers besides Origen, such as St Ambrosius of Mediolan,[1946] St Jeronimus,[1947] St Augustine[1948] and St Epiphanius,[1949] defended the Truth of this Doctrine against all the heretics who opposed the Ever-Virginity of the Theotokos. St Augustine's words became the classic testimony: *"As a Virgin she conceived, as a Virgin she gave birth and as a Virgin she remained."*[1950]

[1942] Ibid, *Dogmatique,* v. II, p. 208-209.

[1943] St John of Damascus, *Exposition. About the geneology of the Lord, and about the holy Theotokos,* IV, 87, 14, in Migne, *P.G.,* 94, 1161.

[1944] Origen, *To Matthew,* 13, 55, in *B,* v. 13, p. 29.

[1945] St John of Damascus, *Exposition. About the geneology of the Lord, and about the holy Theotokos,* IV, 87, 14, in Migne, *P.G.,* 94, 1161.

[1946] St Ambrosius, *De inSt Virgin et S. Mariae virginitate perpetus,* in migne, *P.L.,* 16, 319-348..

[1947] St Jeronymus, *De perpetua virginitate B. Marie Adversus Helvidium,* in migne, *P.L.,* 23.

[1948] St Augustine, *De haereasibus* 56 and 84, in migne, *P.L.,* 42, 40 and 46.

[1949] St Epiphanius, *Panarion, Herecy* LXXVII, book III, § 1, *P.G.,* 43, 641-699.

[1950] St Augustine, *"Virgo concepit, virgo peperit, virgo permansit",* Sermo 51, 11, 18, in migne, *P.L.,* 38, 343.

Question 257: Was the Theotokos relative sinless?

Answer: The Orthodox Church teaches that the sinless condition of the Ever-Virgin Theotokos[1951] was a *"relative condition and by Grace"* not by nature, *"for only God is absolutely sinless by Nature."*[1952] The Mother of God was born a human being and thus a descendant of Adam. She participated in Original Sin as do all human beings. She achieved a state of relative sinlessness due to her virtuous life and the Grace of God that overshadowed her at the Annunciation when she humbly and obediently accepted Motherhood of the Son of the Most High. She became *"blameless"* as St Paul said of himself when he became *"blameless"* according to *"the Righteousness which is in the Law."*[1953]

Amongst all the ancient Fathers and scholars of the Church only St Augustine accepted the Ever-Virgin Mary and Theotokos as being completely sinless and free from any personal sin. All men should consider themselves as sinners *"except the Holy Virgin Mary, about her, for the honour of the Lord, when it comes to refer about sin, I do not want to place the matter."*[1954] These words referred to the sinless condition of the Ever-Virgin Mary and did not imply that she was free from the Original Sin.[1955]

St John of Damascus proclaimed that the Theotokos *"became the Source of all Virtues, of all Life and rebuked the sexual desire from the mind thus she preserved her soul and body in virginity, as should the one who was to receive within her bosom the Son of God."* For this reason, we the Orthodox, confess her to be above all Saints (*"Panagia"*).[1956]

[1951] Mitsopoulos, *Themata,* pp. 151-154.

[1952] Karmeris, *Synopsis,* p. 50.

[1953] Phil. 3:6.

[1954] St Augustine, *De natura et gratia,* XXXVI, 42, in migne, *P.L.,* 44, 267.

[1955] Ott, *Precis,* p. 288.

[1956] St John of Damascus, *Exposition. About the genealogy of the Lord, and about the holy Theotokos,* IV, 87, 14, in Migne, *P.G.,* 94, 1160.

PART FOUR

MAN IN GOD'S KINGDOM
THE WORK OF GRACE

CHAPTER ONE
DEFINITION AND NECESSITY OF THE DIVINE GRACE

Question 258: What is the definition of "Grace"?

Answer: The word *"grace"* has the general meaning of *favour, mercy, condescension, kindness* from the superior to the inferior and especially from God to man[1957]. The objective meaning of the word signifies the Gift of God that is granted to man for his Salvation and their establishment in the condition of Holiness.[1958] It also means the Gift that refers to the Salvation or a specific charisma related to Salvation. Another meaning is the condition of the faithful after the Coming of Jesus Christ in opposition to the ruling of the Law.[1959] Grace presupposes real and essential transformation in man. It is the close relationship between God and man, which transforms not only man's thoughts, but his whole being. The familiar relationship between God and man is not merely some kind of change in God's attitude towards man, but the complete change within man himself. It is the Sanctification and the Regeneration of the inner man through the willing acceptance of God's Gifts derived from the Death of Christ on the Cross.[1960] The word *"grace"* furthermore has the meaning of one's Attribute which makes one attractive and loving to others,[1961] as well as thankfulness for the received beneficence or Grace.[1962]

In Theology the word is used with the objective meaning of Favour, Gift and abundant Mercy of God that is granted to man who is too unworthy to even to ask for such a Gift. Thus St Paul uses the term *"Grace"* concerning the choosing of those Jews who believed in Christ.[1963] One may speak of *"natural Grace"* and *"supernatural Grace."*

[1957] Luke 1:30; 2:40. Rom. 5:15. Cf. Frangopoulos, *Chrisrtian Faith,* p. 160.
[1958] 2 Corinth. 6:1. Rom. 5:2. 1 Peter 5:12.
[1959] Rom. 6:15. John 1:17.
[1960] Leeming, *Principles*, p. 3.
[1961] Ephes. 4:29. 1 Peter 2:20. Psalm 44(45):3.
[1962] Luke 17:9. 1 Corinth. 10:30.
[1963] Rom. 11:6.

Natural Grace includes all good things in Creation - preservation of life, health of body and soul, and many more that are God's natural Gifts to His Creation.

Supernatural Grace is granted by the Divine Mercy and Kindness to all intellectual beings, especially to fallen man in order to Regenerate him and to make him worthy of Eternal Salvation.

Consequently, Grace is the Action of the Holy Spirit that forgives the past and secures the future of those who struggle, working out the new Creation within them. Divine Grace is the Power and Act of God, through which the work of Salvation of Christ is realized and which is always related to man's free-will and action. It is expressed through man's return, Regeneration, Justification and Sanctification.[1964] It is also the internal power that brings forth and nourishes the spiritual life in man.[1965]

Question 259: What is the supernatural nature of Divine Grace?

Answer: Divine Grace is a supernatural Gift, without which the weak human will is unable to familiarize itself with the Salvation Work of our Lord and Saviour Jesus Christ, the Son of God. No man, being under the slavery of sin, was able to come to the Knowledge of God and the religious and moral Truths. With regard to the healing of man's heart from the contagious illness of sin and his Regeneration, Holy Scripture and the experience of all Holy men teach that under no circumstance can the Divine Grace be the natural fruit of man's struggle. On the contrary, it is the Fruit of Grace that makes man's corrupted heart become the temple of God, whereas man, accepting this Divine Work and cooperating with God's Grace, abolishes the power of sin, is Regenerated completely and restored in all glory and perfection to the *"image and likeness."*[1966] The change of man through God's Divine Grace is not the work of human power. It is the new Creation that is made possible through the Divine and creative Power of God.

Our Lord proclaimed that our Birth from Above is essential and necessary.[1967] St Paul characterized our body as *"the temple of the Holy Spirit Who is in"* us.[1968] He speaks of the Love of God, which is demonstrated *"in that while we were still sinners, Christ died for us;"*[1969] and

---

[1964] Mesoloras, in Karmeris, *Symbolique,* v. II, 1, pp. 244 and 267.
[1965] Androutsos, *Dogmatique,* p. 219.
[1966] Gen. 1:26.
[1967] John. 3:5.
[1968] 1 Corinth. 6:19.
[1969] Rom. 5:8.

that *"He saved us, through the washing of Regeneration and renewing of the Holy Spirit."*[1970]

The Apostolic Fathers assure us that: *"Before we believed in God, our heart's dwelling-place was corrupt and weak, truly a temple built by human hands, because it was full of idolatry and was the home of demons, for we did whatever was contrary to God. But it will be built in the Name of the Lord,"* *"by receiving the forgiveness of sins and setting our hope on"* His *"Name, we became new, created again from the beginning. Consequently God truly dwells in our dwelling-place – that is, in us."*[1971] For the Lord *"renewed us by the forgiveness of sins, He made us men of another type, so that we should have the soul of children, as if He were creating us all over again."*[1972]

St John Chrysostom calls this cleanness *"Mystical"* observing that: *"God does not only forgive our sins, nor simply cleanses the sins,"* but *"creates and makes us from Above,"* *"not simply cleaning the vessel, but refining it completely"* *"through the Grace of the Holy Spirit instead of fire"* and *"the old man who was crushed, He makes new and more glorious."*[1973]

St Cyril of Alexandria, assuring the direct supernatural Action of Divine Grace, proclaimed that *"through the Spirit we ascend into the shape of the image of the Prototype"* and *"to the level of above the nature,"* *"the old beauty being regenerated and transformed to the Divine Nature."*[1974]

Question 260: What is the main source of the Divine Grace?

Answer: It is necessary to note that Holy Scripture generally refers to God as the principal and main Source from which Divine Grace comes. God increases the word of Truth that was spread by the Holy Apostles. Sometimes it refers to God the Father Who makes us strong so that we remain *"qualified to be partakers of the inheritance of the Saints in the Light"*[1975] while at other times it refers to the Son and our Lord Jesus Christ Who adds *"to the Church daily those who were being saved."*[1976] The Source of Grace in Salvation is proclaimed in the Old and New Testament to be the Holy Spirit, the outpouring of Whom was foretold in the Old Testament[1977] and realised in the New Testament.[1978] Our Lord and Saviour

---

[1970] Tit. 3:5.
[1971] *Barnabas,* 16, 7 and 8, in Lightfoot, *Apostolic Fathers,* p. 184.
[1972] Ibid, 6, 11, in Lightfoot, *Apostolic Fathers,* p. 169.
[1973] St John Chrysostom, *Catechesis,* 1, §§ 4 and 3, in Migne, *P.G.,* 49, 227.
[1974] St Cyril of Alexandria, *To John,* book I, ch. IX, *to John 1:12,* in Migne, *P.G.,* 73, 133.
[1975] Col. 1:12.
[1976] Acts 2:47.
[1977] Joel 2:28-32.

Jesus Christ, the Son of God, proclaimed the abundant outpouring of the Holy Spirit on the souls of the faithful who are Regenerated, with the assurance that the Holy Spirit is He Who Regenerates those who will inherit the Heavenly Kingdom[1979] and that His Grace, as *"rivers of Living Water"* will spring out from the hearts of the faithful.[1980] Elsewhere, the Lord calls the Holy Spirit *"Helper"*[1981] *"for He helps and gives courage and assists our weaknesses."*[1982] St Paul assures us that *"no one can say Jesus is the Lord except by the Holy Spirit."*[1983] This Holy Spirit is the One Who divides the various Charismata or Gifts[1984] *"in the inner man"*[1985] and through their participation and communion[1986] with Him, *"everyone is Sanctified."*[1987]

According to the above, we are in full agreement with Holy Scripture when we say that the Holy Spirit is not the only Source but the main Source of Divine Grace which Enlightens, Strengthens and Sanctifies the sinful man. The Son of God and our Lord and Saviour Jesus Christ is the true Sun of Righteousness and the main Source of Divine Revelation; He, as the Incarnated Word and Son of God Who offered the Sacrifice on the Cross and became the cause of our Redemption. Likewise, the Holy Spirit, granting mankind the Fruits of Salvation and working the approach to this Gift as well as familiarizing them to it in the hearts of the faithful, is *"the Treasurer of all good things and the Giver of Life."* He is the Fountain of the Life-giving Power which raises up the sinner from his sinful dead works. In the Old Testament it was foretold of the outpouring of the Holy Spirit.[1988] The Lord also said that *"it is the Spirit Who gives Life"*[1989] and promised His Apostles that He would send them *"another Helper"*[1990] Who will teach them *"all things, and bring to"* their *"remembrance all things."*[1991] He would guide them *"into all Truth."*[1992] St Paul stated: *"But you were washed, but you were Sanctified, but you were Justified in the Name of the Lord Jesus and by the Spirit of our God."*[1993]

[1978] Acts 2:1-4.
[1979] John 3:5.
[1980] John 7:38.
[1981] John 14:16.
[1982] St Cyril of Jerusalem, *Catechesis,* XVI, 20, in Migne, *P.G.,* 33, 948.
[1983] 1 Corinth. 12:3.
[1984] 1 Corinth. 12:4-11.
[1985] Ephes. 3:16.
[1986] 2 Corinth. 13:14.
[1987] St Ecumenius, *To Galatians,* in Migne, *P.G.,* 118, 1088.
[1988] Joel 2:28-32.
[1989] John 6:63.
[1990] John 14:16.
[1991] John 14:26.
[1992] John 16:13.
[1993] 1 Corinth. 6:11.

In the Work of our Regeneration and Salvation, the different Charismata of the Holy Spirit are distributed *"to each one individually as He Wills"*[1994] and at different stages. At first He prepares the faithful to accept the Work of Salvation. Then He increases it to its fullness of perfection. Nevertheless, it is the *"One and the same Spirit"*[1995] Who acts and consequently is the Grace that distributes these Gifts, remaining always One, Active and Powerful, but different only in the needs of each member accordingly.

Question 261: Is the Divine Grace necessary?

Answer: It is understandable that Divine Grace is absolutely necessary in order to create within man the Newness of Life in Christ, when we take into consideration that because of man's Offence, corruption entered his nature. Man, who lives in the darkness and bondage of sin, is deprived of the True Light and Moral Might necessary for the learning of Divine Truth and living according to this Truth. For how can the light of the sun benefit the blind? Or of what benefit will it have for those who are neither willing nor have the strength to enter the Heavenly Gates? Or how will it benefit one's good will if it is weak and deprived of the encouragement and help that enables it to become strong and capable for Eternal Life?

Our Lord and Saviour Jesus Christ, the Son of God, proclaimed that: *"Most assuredly, I say to you, unless one is born of water and the Spirit, he cannot enter the Kingdom of God,*[1996] whereas *"without Me you can do nothing"*[1997] and *"no one can come to Me unless the Father Who sent Me draws him."*[1998] St Paul assured us that God is the one *"Who works in you both to will and to do for His good pleasure"*[1999] and increases the Word of Salvation. *"So then neither he who plants is anything, nor he who waters, but God Who gives the increase."*[2000] In addition, *"no one can say Jesus is the Lord except by the Holy Spirit"*[2001] because we *"were dead in trespasses"* and God *"made us alive together with Christ"* Who saved us by Grace *"through faith"* and *"not of works, lest anyone should boast."*[2002] *"The Spirit helps in our weaknesses. For we do not know what we should pray for as we*

1994 1 Corinth. 12:11.
1995 1 Corinth. 12:4, 8, 9, 11.
1996 John 3:5.
1997 John 15:5.
1998 John 6:44.
1999 Phil. 2:13.
2000 1 Corinth. 3:7.
2001 1 Corinth. 12:3.
2002 Ephes. 2:5, 8, 9.

ought, but the Holy Spirit Himself makes intercession for us."[2003]   St Paul, concerning Salvation, comes to the conclusion that "*it is not of him, who wills, nor of him who runs, but of God Who shows Mercy.*"[2004]

The Orthodox Church emphasized the absolute necessity of Divine Grace.[2005]

St John Chrysostom proclaimed that "*we cannot achieve anything good without enjoying the inclination from Above*" "*and not with our power, but by the Help of the Grace from Above, he who confesses bears witness*" of the faith in Christ because "*the faith in Christ is not a simple thing, but needs the inclination from Above.*"   Referring to 1 Corinthians 4:7, he observed: "*You do not have this from your own, but you have received it from God.*"   "*So then, since you have received this or that, or whatever you may have.   For, it is not your achievements, but the Grace of God.   Even if you say about the faith, it became from the Calling; even the forgiveness of sins, even the Charismata, even the word of Teaching, even the Powers, you received them all from Him.*"   The Holy Fathers confess that in order to become worthy of the help and "*inclination from Above,*" it is necessary to "*bring forth our own.*"   He also said, that "*even if we struggle a thousand times, we cannot achieve anything, if we do not enjoy and the inclination from Above.*"[2006]

St Augustine repeatedly referred to the necessity of Divine Grace and stressed that the Lord prepares the will and brings to completion whatever He began through His Action.   He acts without us, in order for us to want and when we want, He cooperates with us, in order to perfect with our will, the work that has begun.   As the physical eye, even when completely healthy, cannot see unless assisted by light, likewise he who is Justified, cannot live justly, if he is not assisted by the Eternal Light of Justice.[2007]   It is necessary, not only for the ill to be Justified by God's Grace, but even those who have been Justified through faith: to walk with them and to overshadow them in order to prevent them from falling.[2008]   Referring to John 15:4-5, he observed that the Lord, in order for no one to think that the vine could bring forth fruit on its own, even the smallest fruit, He added: "*Without Me you can do nothing,*" not even the smallest thing. Mankind cannot do anything.

[2003] Rom. 8:26.

[2004] Rom. 9:16.

[2005] Cf. Frangopoulos, *Chrisrtian Faith,* p. 160.

[2006] St John Chrysostom, *To Genesis,* Homily 25, § 7, in Migne, *P.G.,* 53, 228. Ibid, *To Matthew,* Homily 34, § 3, in Migne, *P.G.,* 57, 401. Ibid, *To John,* Homily 45, § 3, in Migne, *P.G.,* 59, 254. Ibid, *To 1 Corinthians,* Homily 12, § 1-2, in Migne, *P.G.,* 61, 97-98. Ibid, *To Genesis,* Homily 58, § 5, in Migne, *P.G.,* 54, 513.

[2007] St Augustine, *De gratia,* VI, 13, in migne, *P.L.,* 44, 901. Ibid, *De natura et gratia,* XXVI, 29, in migne, *P.L.,* 44, 261.

[2008] Ibid, *De gratia,* VI, 13, in migne, *P.L.,* 44, 889.

Absolutely nothing great nor small can be done without Christ.[2009] Consequently, Divine Grace as the supernatural Action of the Holy Spirit is absolutely necessary, not only for the return of man, but for his Regeneration, as well as his remaining in virtue,his Perfection, Sanctification, Salvation and Glorification.

CHAPTER TWO
THE UNIVERSALITY OF GOD'S GRACE
AND IT'S RELATIONSHIP TO MAN'S FREEDOM

Question 262: What are the teachings of Holy Scripture concerning the Universality of Salvation?

Answer: In the Old Testament it is proclaimed that the universality of Salvation by the Prophets presupposes the Grace of Salvation offered by God not only to the Jews but to all nations. The Prophet Isaiah foretold that, through Israel, all nations would participate in the Salvation of God.[2010]

The Prophet Jeremiah foretold the Salvation of Christ by prounouncing the words: *"I will cleanse them from all their iniquities, whereby they shall have sinned against Me, and will not remember their sins, whereby they have sinned against Me and revolted against Me. And it shall be for joy and praise, and for glory to all the people of the earth, who shall hear all the good that I will do: and they shall fear and be provoked for all the good things and for all the peace which I will bring upon them."*[2011]

The Prophet Ezekiel declared: *" Therefore say to the House of Israel: Thus said the Lord; I do not this, O House of Israel, for your sakes, but because of My Holy Name, which you have profaned among the nations, among whom you went. And I will Sanctify My Great Name, which was profaned among the nations, which you profaned in the midst of them; and the nations shall know that I Am the Lord, when I Am Sanctified among you before their eyes I, the Lord, have spoken and will do it."*[2012] *"And the nations shall know that I Am the Lord that Sanctifies them, when My Sanctuary is in the midst of them for ever."*[2013]

The Books of Psalms proclaim that *"all nations whom Thou hast made shall come and worship before Thee, O Lord, and shall glorify Thy*

[2009] St Augustine, *In Johannis evangelium. Tractatus,* CXXXI, 3, in migne, *P.L.,* 35, 1841.
[2010] Is. 2:2-4. Is. 55:4-5.
[2011] Jer. 40:8-9.
[2012] Ez. 36:22-36.
[2013] Ez. 37:28.

Name."[2014] "The nations shall fear the Name of the Lord, and all kings of the earth Thy glory when the peoples are gathered together, and the kingdoms, to serve the Lord."[2015]

These words were preached among the people of Israel who believed that the true "*Good Will*" of God and His Salvation was their exclusive inheritance. They supposed it to be a Prophetic Promise whereby, at the appropriate time, the Lord would manifest His Grace of Salvation among them. Then it would be offered to "*all men*" and "*for this reasonthe Only Begotten Son of God*" became Man "*in order to make all men and rulers and servants worthy of the Salvation.*"[2016]

Truthfully, although it appears at first that our Lord Himself "*was sent to the lost sheep of the House of Israel*" [2017] He did emphasise the fact that He had "*other sheep*" who were outside Judaism but who were also exhorted to hear His Voice so that He could gather them as " *one flock and one Shepherd.*"[2018] Hence after His glorious Resurrection, He sent the Apostles out to their God-given Mission by instructing them to "*make Disciples of all nations*"[2019] by preaching the Gospel "*to every creature*"[2020] even to the ends of the earth. In the midst of Israel Christ preached the Gospel of Salvation despite His foreknowledge of His Suffering and Death in Jerusalem as had the Holy Prophets before Him.[2021] Nevertheless, He continued to seek the Salvation of the ungrateful.[2022] At the last moment when He was entering the city of Jerusalem.[2023]

Our Lord Jesus' words and behaviour, in conjunction with His proclamation to St Nicodemus that "*God did not send His Son into the world to condemn the world, but that the world through Him might be Saved,*"[2024] clearly highlights the Teachings of the Holy Apostles. "*For, this is good and acceptable in the Sight of God our Saviour Who desires all men to be Saved and to come to the Knowledge of the Truth*"[2025] for God is not "*the God of the Jews only*" but He is also "*the God of the Gentiles*"[2026] and the Master of both. For One is the Creator of all Who provides for and Who

---

[2014] Psalm 85(86):9.
[2015] Psalm 101(102):15, 22.
[2016] Theodoretus of Cyrus, *To Titus* 2, 11, in Migne, *P.G., 82*, 865.
[2017] Matth. 15:24.
[2018] John 10:16.
[2019] Matth. 28:19.
[2020] Mark 16:15.
[2021] Matth. 23:37. Luke 13:34.
[2022] St John Chrysostom, *To Matthew 23:37,* in Migne, *P.G., 58*, 682.
[2023] Zigabinos, *To Luke 19:41,* in Migne, *P.G., 129*, 1065.
[2024] John3:17.
[2025] 1 Tim. 2:3-4.
[2026] Rom. 4:29.

saves all through faith in Him[2027] *"for 'whoever calls on the Name of the Lord shall be Saved."*[2028] Proclaiming the commonality of Divine Grace, St Paul concluded: *"for there is no distinction between Jew and Greek, for the same Lord over all is rich to all who call upon Him."*[2029] St Peter presented God as taking up His fearful Coming because He is *"longsuffering towards us"* and *" not willing that any should perish, but that all should come to Repentance."*[2030] This indicates that God provides the means of Salvation to the ungodly since He desires their Salvation. It is a fundamental Teaching of the Holy Gospel that Christ *"died for all"*[2031] and that *"He Himself is the Propitiation for our sins, and not for ours only but also for the whole world."*[2032]

Question 263: What are the teachings of the holy Fathers concerning the universality of Salvation?

Answer: The Holy Fathers of the Orthodox Church proclaimed that because*"the Blood of Christ.."* was *"poured out for our Salvation, it won for the whole world the Grace of Repentance"* for *"from generation to generation the Master has given an opportunity for Repentance to those who desire to turn to Him"* and by *".repenting of their sins, made atonement to God by their prayers and received Salvation, even though they were alienated from God."*[2033]

  St Irenaeus compared *"the preaching of the Truth"* to the sun and commented that *"as the sun in the entire world is one and the same, likewise and the preaching of the Truth shines everywhere and Enlightens all men who will to come to the Knowledge of the Truth."* The Lord assured us that He, by *"becoming Man for us, sent to the whole world the Grace of the Holy Spirit."* Elsewhere he observed that when the Son of Man came to earth, eating and drinking and dwelling with men, the Life-giving Seed - in other words the Spirit of Forgiveness of sins through Whom we become alive - was bestowed upon the human race.[2034]

[2027] St John Chrysostom, *To Romans* 3, 30, and 7, § 4, in Migne, *P.G.*, 60, 446.

[2028] Rom. 10:13.

[2029] Rom. 10:12.

[2030] 2 Peter 3:9.

[2031] 2 Corinth. 5:15.

[2032] 1 John 2:2.

[2033] St Clement of Rome, *1st Corinthians,* 7, 4, 5 and 7, in Lightfoot, *Apostolic Fathers,* p. 32.

[2034] St Irenaeus, *Heresies,* book I, ch. 10, § 2 and book III, ch. 11, § 8, in *B,* v. 7, pp. 116 and 146. Ibid, book IV, ch. 31, § 2, in Migne, *P.G.,* 7, 1069. Cf. Ibid, in Hadjephraimides, pp. 65, 211-213, 328.

St John Chrysostom, interpreting John 1:9 asked: *"If He Enlightens all men by coming to the world, how can so many remain in darkness?"* He continued: *"He Enlightens all men who come to Him"* because the redeeming and enlightening radiance of the Sun of Righteousness falls upon all and if some *"by their own will keep their eyes ill"* they cannot receive *"the radiance of this Light"* for blindness and darkness comes upon them *"not because of the Light's Nature, but because of the evilness of those who, by their own will, deprive themselves of the Grace. The Grace is outpoured to all"* without *".depriving"* anyone at all, *"not Jew, nor Greek, not Barbarian, nor Scythes, nor free, nor slave, nor man, nor woman, nor elder, nor young; it comes to all equally and with the same honour invites everyone."* If there are some who do not wish *"to enjoy this Grace"* they should argue with themselves for causing their own *"hardness."*[2035]

St John of Damascus used the differentiation between the *"former Will"* and *"later Will"* of God. The *"first"* or *"former Will,"* is called *"Goodwill"* (*"ευδοκία"*) for through it God wants all men to be Saved because He did not create us to be Condemned but to partake of His Kindness. However, man too must desire his own Salvation. The *"later will"* is that through which those who accept the Work of Grace are guided to Salvation while God consents to the Condemnation of those who oppose or refuse His Grace.[2036]

St Augustine, although at first having accepted the universality of Salvation of God's Will, in his later writings he restricted the Will of God concerning Salvation only to those who are absolutely Predestined.[2037] His teachings of Predestination at the time of choosing the elect are unacceptable because he supported the idea that Predestination occurs, in other words, before God Foresees the things that make those who are Predestined, worthy.[2038]

Question 264: Is predestination based on God's Divine Foreknowledge?

Answer: The universal nature of Divine Grace concerning Predestination, does not contradict the Teachings of Holy Scripture and the Holy Fathers of

---

[2035] Ex. 4:21; 7:3; 8:15, 19, 32; 9:12, 35; 10:20; 11:10; 14:4, 8, 17.

[2036] St John of Damascus, *Exposition. About foreknowledge and destination,* II, 44, 29, in Migne, *P.G.,* 94, 969.

[2037] St Augustine, *De spiritu et litt.,* XXXIII, 58, in migne, *P.L.,* 44, 238. Ibid, *De dono perserentiae* VIII, 16, in migne, *P.L.,* 45, 1002. Ibid, *De anima et ejus origine,* IV, 11, 16, in migne, *P.L., 44, 533.* Ibid, *In Johannis evangelium. Tractatus* XLVII, 4, 6; CVII, 7; CXI, 5, in migne, *P.L.,* 35, 1742, 1743, 1914, 1929. Ibid, *Enchiridion,* 103, in migne. *P.L.,* 40, 230. Ibid, *Contra Julianum,* IV, 8, 44, in migne, *P.L.,* 44, 766. Ibid, *Epist.* 217, 6, 9, in migne, *P.L.,* 33, 936.

[2038] Tixéront, *Histoire,* v. II, p. 501.

the Orthodox Church. One must not forget that the Grace of God, which is offered to us, has an unconditional prerequisite of either accepting or renouncing it. Consequently, God predestined Salvation or Condemnation according to His Foreknowledge that He has of each and every human being.[2039] St Paul stressed that God *"foreknew"* and *"predestined"* them accordingly.[2040] Predestination is not restricted only to the Foreknowledge and preparation of God's Beneficences through which we have the assurance of Salvation of those who would be Saved[2041] but it also includes the will of those who are being Saved, who are predestinated for Salvation based on the Foreknowledge of God and whether they would accept the Grace offered to them and remain in it with their free-will.

The Predestination of those who would be Saved or the stubborn disobedience of those who shall perish is not the absolute decision or Will of God. This discrimination is found not only in the Will of God but also in the goodwill of those who were predestined by the Foreknowledge of God.

God foresaw their goodwill and their ability to accept His Grace of Salvation and according to His Foreknowledge, He predestined them. If Divine Providence has pre-determined whatever concerns this life on earth in such a way that every one of our hairs is numbered, it would be inconceivable that man's eternal condition would be of secondary importance. He who accepts the Providence of God contradicts himself if he refuses to accept the Predestinated Salvation of mankind. [2042]

Question 265: What are the teachings of Holy Scripture and the Holy Fathers concerning Predestination?

Answer: Holy Scripture speaks of the choosing *"before the foundation of the world"* and of Predestination *"of adoption as sons"* of all those who are Saved in Christ. They proclaim that those whom God *"Predestined, He also Called; whom He Called, these He also Justified; and whom He Justified, these He also Glorified."*[2043] In addition, the Orthodox Church proclaims, interprets and clarifies the Truth that the Scriptures proclaim, through the Teachings of the Holy Fathers.

St Irenaeus based Predestination on the Foreknowledge of God, commenting that He Who foreknows everything, prepared both proper dwellings. For those who seek the Light of imperishability He grants with

---

[2039] St Symeon, *Euriskomena,* Homily XXVI, pp. 137-141.
[2040] Rom. 8:29.
[2041] St Augustine, *De dono perserentiae,* XIV, 35, in migne, *P.L.,* 45, 1014.
[2042] Theophilactus of Bulgaria, *To Romans 8:27-30,* in Migne, *P.G.,* 124, 454. Ephes. 1:4-5.
[2043] Rom. 8:30.

favour the Light that they desire while to others who scorn and flee from it, He has prepared the Darkness. So to all those who avoid submission to Him, He delivers a fitting sentence.[2044]

St Gregory of Nazianzus proclaimed that it is *"good for everything to be ruled and to be brought to an end"* by God. Elsewhere he stated that *"His extreme Kindness"* is expressed in that *"the good was made possible for us, not only spreading to our nature, but cultivated by our free-will in both"* good and evil according to the inclination and action of *"our free-will."* Finally, the Holy Father, addressing the baptised, gave them the following advice: *"The forgiveness which you received, preserve it well, in order that the 'to be forgiven' is from God, but the '.to be preserved' is from you."*[2045]

St John Chrysostom, referring to the words of Christ: *"Come, you blessed of My Father, inherit the Kingdom prepared for you from the foundation of the world"*[2046] St John Chrysostom commented that *"come and inherit"* means it is *" our own from our Father "* having been provided for us from Above. *"For even before they are realised, it is said, that these were prepared beforehand for you because He knew that you would become."* blessed. Interpreting the words of St Paul in Ephesians he remarked: *"He chose us in Him before the foundation of the world, that we should be Holy and without blame before Him in Love, having predestined us for adoption as sons by Jesus Christ Himself, according to the good pleasure of His Will."*[2047] He emphasised that Christ predestined us *"in Love."* and *"not because of our struggle or achievements."* We were predestined to become the blessed of God *" because of Love"* and *"because of kindness alone; for the Grace is kindness."* Furthermore, *"not because of Love alone, but because of our virtue"* as well because if our predestination depended only on the Love of God *"everyone should have been Saved"* for Grace and Salvation is offered by God to all mankind, whereas if it depended only upon our virtue, Christ's presence would have been unnecessary as would have *" all that which He achieved."*[2048]

Distinguishing the two Wills of God in relation to the predestination of men, he stressed our predestined Adoption *"according to His Good Will, which is through the fervent desire."* He calls the *"Good Will"* of God *"the*

[2044] St Irenaeus, *Heresies,* book IV, ch. 39, § 4, in Hadjephraimides, pp. 355.

[2045] St Gregory of Nazianzus, in Migne, *P.G.,* 35, 737 and 428. Ibid, *To Matthew 19:1-12,* §§ 13 and 15, in Migne, *P.G.,* 36, 297 and 300. Ibid, *Homily* 40 *to holy Baptism,* § 34, in Migne, *P.G.,* 36, 408.

[2046] Matth. 25:34.

[2047] Ephes. 1:4-5.

[2048] St John Chrysostom, *To Matthew,* Homily 79, § 2; 69, § 2, in Migne, *P.G.,* 58, 719, 650. Ibid, *To Ephesians*, Homily 1, § 2, in Migne, *P.G.,* 62, 12.

former Will" "*the first Will, the strong Will, the obstinacy*" which is His need or wish "*not to lose the sinners.*" In other words God "*strongly desires our Salvation.*" Besides this first Will there is in God "*a second Will*" which is "*to condemn the evil ones. For it is not necessary to punish the bad, although it is the Will*" of God. Therefore God, according to "*His admirable Foreknowledge, knows all before they take place*"and by "*choosing us, He dedicated us to Himself*" before all ages. Moreover "*He dedicated us to believe and He Sealed us to inherit the future things to come*" and "*He saw us having inherited before it happened.*" Once He had chosen and dedicated us "*not acting anything after these, for He has formulated everything from above.*"[2049]

Finally, St John of Damascus emphasised the Foreknowledge of God according to which He "*justly works together with those who will the good according to His Foreknowledge*" while "*He justly abandons the evil, again according to His Foreknowledge.*" He also makes the same differentiation as St John Chrysostom concerning the two Wills of God. In other words His "*first*" or "*former Will,*" which is called His "*Good Will,*" wants all men to be Saved and to partake of His Heavenly Kingdom, while His "*following Will,*" being Just, consents to the condemnation of those who sin and oppose His Grace. God "*beforehand wants and has Good Will*" towards our good deeds and virtuous life, while "*for the evil and really bad,* [He] *neither wanted before nor will He ever want*" although " *He consents because of the free-will of man.*" For God does not want the evil that is done by man's own free-will and neither does He force goodness and virtue upon mankind. Consequently, St John of Damascus accepted the term "*Predestination*" but excluded the choice of Salvation of man because absolute Predestination restricts and removes man's free-will.

Question 266: Are those who would be condemned Predestined?

Answer: It is obvious that as God foreknows the capability of acceptance and good intention of men, He predestines them for Salvation and inheritance of the Heavenly Kingdom. Likewise, foreknowing the hardness of heart and the unrepentance of those who spitefully reject Divine Grace that is offered to them, God condemns them to Eternal Death. Between the Predestination of those who will be Saved and those who will be Condemned, there exists a great difference. For those who are predestined for Eternal Life, God "*works together*" with them through His Grace for

---

[2049] St John Chrysostom, *To Ephesians*, Homily 1, § 2, in Migne, *P.G.,* 62, 12. Ibid, *To Ephesians*, Homily 1, § 2, in Montfaucon, v. 11, p. 12.

their progress and perfection in the Life of Virtue, whereas those who will be Condemned, He simply permits them to continue according to their corrupted hearts and wills. He disapproves of and turns away from their evil deeds. God foresees their consequent Eternal Punishment and Condemnation but He certainly never Predestinated them to commit wickedness and sin. Undoubtedly, God wants their Salvation as well and for this reason He patiently tolerates them, *"not willing that any should perish, but that all should come to repentance."*[2050] Since the *"ungodly men"* alone and by their own stubborn free-wills alienate themselves from the Grace of Salvation by remaining in wickedness, their punishment was *"long ago"* *"marked out for this Condemnation."*[2051] It is understandable why Holy Scripture does not often refer to the Predestination of sinners as this term is used for the Just.[2052] Our Lord Jesus Christ, the Son of God, calls the Just to *"inherit the Kingdom prepared for them from the foundation of the world"*[2053] whereas sinners are admonished to *"depart from Him, you cursed, into the Everlasting Fire prepared for the devil and his angels."*[2054]

Question 267: Can man's free-will remain uncommitted?

Answer: Under the influence of Divine Grace, the human will remains free, even when man either submits to the Holy Spirit or when he rejects this Grace. The sinner who becomes hardhearted is completely responsible for the destruction caused within him, for this is due to his own corrupted free-will. Instead of being softened and healed as a result of the outpouring of Divine Grace upon him, the unrepentant sinner's spiritual state becomes more cynical and more degraded. This is evident from our Lord's words when He criticised the hardness of Jerusalem.[2055] It is also confirmed by St Stephen the Archdeacon and Protomartyr (First Martyr) when he addressed the members of the Sanhedrin (the High Court of the Temple). He accused them of being *"stiff-necked and uncircumcised in heart and ears"*[2056] If God, before all ages, foreseeing their stubborn disobedience, allowed them to be Condemned, it occurred for no other reason except due to their own free-will because God's Foreknowledge did not create them as sinners. Just

---

[2050] 2 Peter 3:9.

[2051] Jude 4.

[2052] St John of Damascus, *Exposition. About foreknowledge and destination,* II, 29 and 30, in Migne, *P.G.,* 94, 968-969 and 972. Ibid, *Dialogue against Manichaeans,* §§ 78 and 79, in Migne, *P.G.,* 94, 1577.

[2053] Matth. 25:34.

[2054] Matth. 25:41.

[2055] Matth. 23:37.

[2056] Acts 7:51.

as a doctor foreknows the resulting mortality of serious illness but his knowledge is not the cause of death, likewise Divine Foreknowledge is not the cause of man's Condemnation or Salvation. God foreknows because He is Almighty and time (past, present and future) is always present before Him.[2057]

God not only shows His Mercy and Kindness even to the *"vessels of wrath prepared for destruction"* but also by the outpouring of His Enlightening Grace in His good pleasure, which attracts man to Salvation. This Divine Grace, if it is not refused, works out the Life-giving Act while those who reject it suffer the consequences according to the examples of Judas and Demas. Judas Iscariot was Chosen by Christ Himself and was included among the Twelve Disciples. He enjoyed not only all the Divine Grace that the others received but also the special favour of our Lord when, at the last moment, Christ tried to prevent him from falling off the catastrophic precipice that he, by his own will, had prepared for himself. When Judas rejected the opportunity to repent, he became a *"vessel of wrath prepared for destruction."* Besides the corruption of a *"vessel of wrath"* God also used these people for the achievement of the Salvation of the world and the fulfillment of His Eternal Plan such as in the case of Demas, who was co-worker of St Paul during the Apostle's first imprisonment in Rome. Later, during St Paul's second imprisonment when the situation had become far more dangerous and the threats against the Apostle's life increased, Demas renounced the Saint, thereby revealing that he *"loved this present world"*[2058] rather than the Eternal Kingdom of God. In both circumstances, the Work of God's Grace at first appears to have been accepted by these men who progressed in their faith until they willingly renounced it for their own selfish reasons. Their downfall was caused by their own free-will and certainly not because of God.

It is therefore obvious that those who are chosen and predestined for Salvation do not have the Grace of God forced upon them because all the Work of Salvation is only possible through the Action of Divine Grace, *"to will and to do for His good pleasure"*[2059] but never without their consent and co-operation. The desire for Salvation and the Power to achieve it is the Work of Divine Grace, which is prepared and perfected in man in such a spiritual way that he does not become passive, participating or offering anything. Faith and man's return to God's Grace are Divine Gifts of Grace, which compel man to move by his own free-will towards Repentance and

---

[2057] Rom. 8:30.
[2058] 2 Tim. 4:10.
[2059] Phil. 2:13.

the acceptance of our Lord Jesus Christ as his Saviour and King. The Justification, the growth and the Perfection in the Newness of Life is the Work of Grace and through the Power and Strength of this Grace, man is cleansed and perfected in Moral and Spiritual Life.

The flesh and the *"carnally minded"*[2060] resist God's action of Regeneration. Man often expresses rebellious and wild intentions, which make the *"calling"* more difficult. Therefore Divine Grace (according to the Parable of the Great Supper)[2061] to *"compel them to come in, that My House may be filled"*[2062] is necessary to co-ordinate and to strengthen man in order for him to look up to God and to distance himself from the sinful path of the ancient deceit. Hence *"although it is optional to all to believe and this is acceptable to God"* concerning the Gentiles who were *"bonded under an unbearable greed and the devil's yoke"* it was essential for this co-ordinated calling.[2063] Again, through trials, other pedagogic measures or redeeming obstacles that are used by Divine Grace to *"compel"* us, it aims at convincing those who are compelled, to accept the Work of Divine Grace by their own Free-will, co-operating with it and developing the hidden seeds of their good intentions which God, Who *"searches the minds and hearts"*[2064]of everyone, discerned. Those who are compelled but who for a brief moment resist the Work of Grace, when the elements of acceptance and goodwill within them develop, will glorify the All-merciful God for the Victory that they gained over the resistance that they themselves had developed against the Saving Work of Grace.

From the beginning to the end, in the Work of the Return and Sanctification of man, Divine Grace and human will are continuously joined and connected to one another. Although they coincide to perfect the Work of Salvation of Predestined man, under no circumstances does this Work of Divine Grace ever abolish human will or vice versa. When this Work reaches completion, God is the One Who Regenerates man. Subsequently Regenerated man is glorified because he also willingly struggled and cooperated with Divine Grace to put the old man within him to death as well as to reform him *"in the image"* of God Who created him.

[2060] Rom. 8:6. See also: Rom. 7:14-24
[2061] Luke 14:16-24.
[2062] Luke 14:23.
[2063] St Cyril of Alexandria, *To Luke 14:23*, in Migne, *P.G.*, 72, 792.
[2064] Rev. 2:23. Jer. 11:20; 17:10.

Question 268: Can anyone fall from Grace?

Answer: Predestination according to the above is relative and the Salvation of man depends upon two factors: the synergy of man's weak will and Divine Grace. Holy Scripture addresses many admonitions to man in order that he may be attentive and not to fall from God's Grace. The examples of Judas Iscariot and Demas convince us that no matter how much the Work of Salvation is able to progress within us, there is always the danger of completely falling from Grace.[2065] St Paul the Apostle urged all Christians to *"work out their own Salvation with fear and trembling"* being constantly watchful of all the traps of the enemies and the threats of the devil, for he who thinks that he stands must *"take heed lest he fall."*[2066]

CHAPTER THREE
THE UNITED WORK OF GRACE

Question 269: What is the united work of Grace?

Answer: Divine Grace creates the Gladsome Radiance of Christian Life in man, which is none other than the Life of Christ within his life. The Regeneration and the Newness of Life in Christ depends upon this action because the human will is too weak to even begin putting to death its own sinful passions by itself.[2067] It is impossible for man alone to progress or gain knowledge of the Salvation in Christ through his own justification and sanctification. Divine Grace, although consisting of many *"diversities of Giftsdifferences of Ministries"* and *"diversities of Activities is the same."*[2068] Thus Divine Grace is one and its Works are united, undivided and inseparable. If we distinguish the Action of Divine Grace by means of its different stages through which the called enter and progress in the Newness of Life, we do this in order to clarify the various manifestations of the one action, not because it is possible to separate one from another or that they clash. The unapproachable and dazzling Light of the absolutely infinite Perfection of God falls upon our limited sight as different but distinguishable colours, while Divine Perfection is undivided and simple. He Who sends His Radiance to us is the Eternal Sun of the Divine Essence, which is absolutely simple. Divine Grace that is constantly working in man, remains one and the same although it manifests itself at various levels and

---

[2065] Heb. 6:4-6.
[2066] 1 Corinth. 10:12.
[2067] Cf. Dositheus of Jerusalem, *Confession,* ch. 3, p. 29.
[2068] 1 Corinth. 12:4, 5, 6.

stages of human and Christian Life. The different manifestations of Divine Grace necessitate the separate examination of the riches of these Divine and Life-giving Gifts.

Question 270: What was the work of Preparation?

Answer: The awakening of man from the lethargic sleep of sin, which is the beginning of Spiritual Life, is due to the Grace of the Holy Spirit, which cannot be explained other than as being the direct and Saving Action of God. Man became so slothful and even spiritually dead because of sin that it is impossible for him to wake up, to turn to God and to ask Him for Redemption and Justification. To begin with, God, through the Grace of the Holy Spirit, moves towards sinful man. From this Divine Grace, after the proper preparation, the calling is heard from within the depths of the sinner who is Predestined to be Saved: *"Awake, you who sleep, arise from the dead, and Christ will give you Light."*[2069] Furthermore in the Book of Revelation we read: *"Behold, I stand at the door and knock. If anyone hears My Voice and opens the door, I will come in to him and dine with him, and he with Me."*[2070]

The Work of Grace is extended right from the first blow, which is for the awakening of the one who is Predestined for Salvation until his final calling. It appears to consist of many stages like many links of a chain, whereby the first link is the awakening and the last is the final calling. This is the Work of the *"preparation Grace."* It consists of everything and whatever awakens the sinner, bringing him onto the Path of the Newness of Life in Christ, for our Lord assured us that *"no one can come to Me unless the Father Who sent Me draws him."*[2071]

The Work of Preparation Grace is the final calling of those who are Predestined for Salvation. It is different to the general and external calling addressed to all mankind.[2072] Justly Holy Scripture projects it as one of the greatest Gifts that aims for *the Fellowship of His Son, Jesus Christ our Lord"*[2073] being called *"by glory and virtue"* and making it possible to be accepted by those who *"become partakers of Divine Nature."*[2074] This Work can be described as a transmission from the stage of Preparation to the stage of the Grace of Sanctification and Salvation. Man's heart has been

---

[2069] Ephes. 5:14.

[2070] Rev. 3:20.

[2071] John 6:44.

[2072] Damalas, *Catechesis*, pp. 52-54. Mitsopoulos, *Themata*, pp. 292-293.

[2073] 1 Corinth. 1:9. 2 Corinth. 13:13. 1 John 1:7.

[2074] 2 Peter 3:3-4.

properly prepared and becomes able to accept the Divine Seed from Above. The Heavenly Lord, through His calling, begins to spread His saving seed so that when it springs up in the soul of mankind, it may bring forth Fruit "*a hundredfold and inherit Eternal Life.*"[2075] He who accepts the inner calling and the influence of Preparation Grace is Enlightened by it. He has complete trust in the Truth of the Holy Gospel and is led to the realisation of his sinful condition. He seeks to be freed from sin and turns to Jesus Christ, as his Saviour and Redeemer from Whom alone he awaits his Salvation. God has called them not only through the external calling of the Gospel but internally as well through the Enlightenment of Divine Grace that is sent upon the hearts of those who are called. In the case of Lydia, "*the Lord opened her heart to heed the things spoken by Paul.*"[2076] This was the Work of Preparation Grace acting in her heart and through which she accepted the Word of Truth, recognised her Saviour and turned to Him.

Question 271: What is the meaning of Justification?

Answer: Justification is in full agreement with God's Holiness, Kindness and Almightiness. The judges of men cannot influence their inner world and can only justify them externally as being innocent. However, Holy God cannot proclaim anyone innocent who has not become such within his heart, neither can He communicate with or have a close relationship with him who is unclean in his heart, since Divine Holiness despises sin and nothing can escape His Sight. God has the Power to wipe out the old man of sin and recreate him, making him a new creation. Even those who depart from the right of Sanctification confess that God has wiped out the sins of the Regenerated man. Since we accept that God has the Power to forgive the sins of those who are justified by Him, it is obvious that if He has not forgiven them, it is not because He does not want to forgive but because the unrepentant sinner does not want to be forgiven.

Justification is that which is inseparable from Sanctification. Justification and Sanctification are two inseparable aspects of one and same meaning and condition. Justification is not simply a covering over of previous sins. It is God Who justifies us.[2077] Thus Justification in its negative perspective is the true and real forgiveness of our sins and not just a covering over of them, whereas from a positive aspect, it is the Renewal and the Regeneration of mankind in this condition whereby he progresses

---

[2075] Matth. 19:29.
[2076] Acts 16:14.
[2077] Col. 1:13-14.

"to the unity of the Faith and of the Knowledge of the Son of God, to a perfect man, to the measure of the stature of the fullness of Christ"[2078]

Only this opinion corresponds completely with the Teachings of St Paul who emphasised the parallel between Adam and Christ. *"For as by one man's disobedience many were made sinners, so also by one Man's Obedience many will be made Righteous."*[2079] Whereas, if one accepts that sins are simply covered over and not completely forgiven, then the above parallel collapses, especially at the expense of Jesus Christ because, although through the first Adam we became sinners, through the Second Adam of Grace we become righteous even though only externally and not in reality or depth. However, our sins are completely forgiven through the Blood of our Lord and Saviour, especially by means of our regular participation in the Holy Sacraments of Repentance-Confession and Communion.

Question 272: What is the condition of Glory?

Answer: St Paul the Apostle teaches us that *"whom He justified, these He also glorified"*[2080] This refers, on the one hand, to the future glory that is accomplished according to the Will and Predestination of God, while on the other hand, the Head of the Church having already been glorified, the members of His Church are called and justified.[2081]

Glorification is the Justification and Perfection within the Blessedness of God, which the justified experience during this life but will enjoy in its fullness in the life to come.

In conclusion, the metastasis from the condition of sin to that of regeneration and Newness of Life in Christ occurs in two stages. First, the *"Preparation of Justification"* which also includes the stages of *"Calling"* and *"Return."*[2082] Second is the exact *"Justification"* that also includes *"regeneration"* and *"sanctification."*[2083]

[2078] Ephes. 4:13.
[2079] Rom. 5:12, 14-19.
[2080] Rom. 8:30.
[2081] Ephes. 2:4-7.
[2082] Androutsos, *Dogmatique,* p. 229. Frangopoulos, *Christian Faith,* pp. 170-171.
[2083] Mitsopoulos, *Themata,* pp. 295-296.

CHAPTER FOUR
THE PREPARATION OF JUSTIFICATION

Question 273: What is the universality of the calling by God?

Answer: Since God *"desires all men to be Saved and to come to the Knowledge of the Truth,"*[2084] He addresses the saving calling to all. According to the Parable of the Great Supper,[2085] those who were first honoured to participate in the festival, refused the invitation and *"all with one accord began to make excuses."*[2086] Although the invitation was general, many did not wish to accept, even after the second calling.[2087] Then, among those who were seated at the dinner, *"a man"* was found *"who did not have on a wedding garment"*[2088] and he was immediately excluded from the Wedding Feast. This is the reason for Christ to proclaimed *" many are called, but few are chosen."*[2089]

Truly, in many Christian countries where the Holy Gospel is spread, countless numbers of people, although entitled *"Christian,"* do not show any interest in listening to or practising the Commandments of God and therefore, even from those who are Baptized, only a *"few"* are *"chosen."* Those who are Baptized during their infancy become participants in the Newness of Life in Christ and are incorporated into the Kingdom of God as members of His Church. The Grace of the Holy Spirit acts upon them, fully Regenerating them, not only externally but also internally granting them all the Gifts. Nevertheless, they are not fully active members of Christ in awareness and conscience. Even more importantly, they are not perfected in Christ.[2090] Divine Grace holds these souls by accepting them and numbering them among the people of God, preserving within them the seed of the Newness of Life in Christ in a dormant condition, powerful and waiting to be awakened at an appropriate moment.

Thus Preparation Grace can be distinguished:

1. In the **"*general Grace*"**, which acts even upon those who are outside the Church, to those who completely ignore the Holy Gospel and

---

[2084] 1 Tim. 2:4.
[2085] Luke 14:16-24. Matth. 22:1-14.
[2086] Luke 14:18.
[2087] Luke 14:23.
[2088] Matth. 22:11.
[2089] Matth. 22:14. Matth.19:30; 20:16. Mark 10:31. Luke 13:30.
[2090] Ephes. 4:13.

for the first time hear of it; and even to those who are within the Church through Holy Baptism; and

2.   in the **"*special Grace*"**, which acts powerfully upon those who accept the calling in their hearts.

One may distinguish the *"Calling"* as being either *"external"* or *"internal."* Both are included in the Work of the Preparation Grace. The activity of Grace does not cease, as it uses the means of the external calling to influence the interior Calling of the one who is being prepared. By using the term *"external calling,"* we usually mean that which is done through the Holy Gospel.[2091]

It is also a fact that, among those who have been proven to be elect, at first and before the inner calling which awakened them, they were listening to the Word of God but did not show any interest and remained indifferent to its calling. Also, other people who were against the principal of hearing the Word of God, being disobedient and spiteful, were changed and freed, as prophesised by the Righteous Isaiah.[2092]

Trials, illnesses, deaths, financial difficulties, deliverance from bodily dangers, meetings, friendships with various persons: the experiences of which Divine Providence uses to prepare one for the acceptance of the calling and to soften the soul of those who are being called by Divine Grace. But, this upliftment is not done by force or without the participation of man's free-will. The pedagogic methods used by God aim to make man agree willingly and freely. Consequently, the means of Preparation for those who are called differ according to their characters and idiosyncrasies, which everyone has. Hence, the Path that each one who is called to follow, can be shorter for one but longer for others; more difficult[2093] for one while easier for others; narrower[2094] for one but wider for another.

It is possible that before the final calling of a person, one may go through many clashes with Divine Grace in order to be Awakened. Eventually one acknowledges one's sinful way of life and turns to Christ, receiving a Newness of Life in Him. However, one will never be able to pinpoint the exact moment when the Preparation Grace began one's final calling to Salvation. This final stage, when the seed of the new and immortal Life has been sown in man's heart, will always remain a Mystery.[2095]

[2091] Rom. 10:14-15.
[2092] Is. 50:5.
[2093] James 1:2-3, 12. 1 Peter 1:6-7. Rom. 5:3-4. Job.
[2094] Matth. 7:13-14.
[2095] Ephes. 2:5.

Question 274: Is the moment of Grace unforeseen?

Answer: It is obvious from the above, that the time of Grace for each man, as well as who the elect may be, is unforeseen. What we can say about the time when the Preparation Grace begins its Work of awakening and returning this or that soul, is that, as seen from the Parable of the Workers of the Vineyard,[2096] the Work of Grace, which ends in the final calling, has its own time for each and every one who is called. Some are called from *"their infancy and first age, others after their childhood are coming to the good faith in God"* others are led to it in their old age, and others *"at the time of their departure at the eleventh hour are Called."*[2097] We cannot say anything concerning the determination of this time, for the Work of Grace acts where we do not hope and at a time when we do not expect, proving *"the last will be first and the first last."*[2098]

It is not a rare phenomenon for those who appear to us as being closer to the Kingdom of Heaven to be overtaken and replaced by people who have been crushed and defeated by sin.[2099] The Grace of God presents so many wonderful and inexplicable phenomena when calling men, that anyone who follows up on the methods and the manifestations of God's Grace can only cry out: *"Oh, the depth of the riches both of the Wisdom and Knowledge of God! How unsearchable are His Judgements and His Ways past finding out. 'For who has known the Mind of the Lord? Or who has become His counselor?"*[2100] Thus, according to the judgment of men, those who are of high moral standards, because they seek by their own struggles to reach a higher level of life, are abandoned by Grace, while men of low moral standards, are preferred by God as Christ warned us: *"Assuredly, I say to you that tax collectors and harlots enter the Kingdom of God before you."*[2101]

Extraordinary natural talents or exceptional gifts do not secure the saving Preparation of Grace. Although these gifts are not obstacles to the saving Grace of God, nevertheless many gifted people are pushed aside by God's Grace because of their pride, whereas many unknown and insignificant, illiterate and completely uneducated, and even slow minded, are raised by Grace as teachers and leaders in the Heavenly Kingdom. The

---

[2096] Matth. 20:1-16.
[2097] Origen, *To Matthew* 20:1, in *B*, v. 13, p. 416.
[2098] Matth. 20:16; 19:30. Mark 10:31. Luke 13:30.
[2099] 1 Corinth. 1:27-28.
[2100] Rom. 11:33-35.
[2101] Matth. 21:31. Luke 7:29, 36-50.

Preparation Grace is being drawn by some kind of intention and Attribute, which can exist in the unwise as well as in the wise, in the rude and in the noble, in the educated and in the illiterate, and generally, speaking in all men regardless of their age, gender, ethnicity, language or skin tone. Thus, according to St John Chrysostom, St Paul *"was not presented only by his calling, but by his good intention,"*[2102] *"which became his medicine to see again"* and to acknowledge his Saviour, whereas *"Elymas the sorcerer"*[2103] did not have any good intentions and remained in his blindness.

What is this *"good intention"*? It is the intention to acknowledge the Truth and to submit to it. It is the desire of the heart for Justice and ill will towards injustice. It is acknowledgement of our sinfulness and the desire for Salvation. This *"good intention"* draws the Preparation Grace near and makes the human soul *"worthy to receive the enlightenment"* of it. This *"good intention"* is like a spark, unquenchable and unlimited. It remains covered by a thick layer of dust because of man's weaknesses and faults, being unable on his own to free himself from the filthiness of sin and to develop the cleansing fire that burns sinful passions and Regenerates the human soul.

St John Chrysostom observed that this *"good intention"* is neutral and *"to be called is not from our worthiness, but from the Grace."* This *"good intention"* attracts Divine Grace because Divine Kindness is unlimited. Without the Divine Visitation, however, this *"good intention"* would have disappeared due to the inheritance of the old man and not being known even by him who possessed it. Nevertheless, *"if the Father draws and the Son guides and the Holy Spirit enlightens, those who are not drawn nor guided, nor enlightened"* are deprived of this unseen Spiritual Attribute and for this reason *"do not offer themselves worthy to receive this enlightenment."*[2104]

Question 275: Is the *"Good Intention"* of man necessary?

Answer: How weak this *"good intention"* is to create the Newness of the new Creation in Christ, is manifested in the words of St Paul the Apostle, who characterizes the faithful in Ephesus as being before their return, *"dead in trespasses and sins,"*[2105] and presenting *"the exceeding greatness of God's Power toward us who believe, according to the working of His*

[2102] St John Chrysostom, in Migne, *P.G.,* 51, 143.
[2103] Acts 13:8.
[2104] St John Chrysostom, *To Matthew,* Homily 69, § 2, in Migne, *P.G.,* 58, 650. Ibid, *To Psalm 115(116),* § 2, in Migne, *P.G.,* 55, 322.
[2105] Ephes. 2:1.

mighty Power which He worked in Christ when He raised Him from the dead and seated Him at His Right Hand in the Heavenly places."[2106]

Man does not remain completely inactive at the first moments of his "*calling*" by Divine Grace. He has within him a spark that is lit at the time of God's visit, as St Justin the Philosopher and Martyr said: "*to make the beginning is not ours.*"[2107] This is clearly manifested from the Divine Invitation to "*awake, you who sleep, arise from the dead, and Christ will give you Light,*"[2108] as well as from the Book of Revelation, according to which our Lord stands at the door and knocks.[2109] God is the first to move towards the sinful man who is called to be awakened. The Lord our God knocks on the hearts of those who are able to hear and who open the doors of their soul. Hence, Divine Grace first acts, whereupon man should respond, regardless of how weak his intentions may be. For this reason Holy Scriptures state: "*Turn to Me, said the Lord of Hosts, and I will turn to you.*"[2110]

Hence, the Holy Fathers of the Orthodox Church stress the cooperation of man and his duty to do his best during the different stages of the preparation of Grace. For "*those who do not want, God does not force them, but those who want He draws them.*"[2111] "*God, when you want, you will have; for and even before you wanted, He came to you, and when you had your will turned away from Him, He was calling you, and when you turned to Him, He placed within you fear, and when you were afraid to confess, He comforted you.*" "*He, Who had created you without you, does not justify you without you wanting. He made you ignorant, but He justifies you wanting.*"[2112]

In other words, like one who falls into the water but does not know how to swim and who is saved from certain death by the skills of a sailor who rushes to assistant him, he then learns to swim through the continuous support of his teacher. Similarly, he who is in the depths of the waves of sin, is saved from spiritual death by the assistance of Divine Grace. He is subsequently exercised and prepared for the victory and submission of death through the continuous cooperation with Divine Grace, which pours out its

---

[2106] Ephes. 1:19-20.

[2107] St Justin, the philosopher and martyr, *Apology 1,* 10, § 4, **B**, v. 3, p. 166.

[2108] Ephes. 5:14. Is. 26:19 and 60:1-3.

[2109] Rev. 3:20.

[2110] Zach. 1:3.

[2111] St John Chrysostom, *To John,* Homily 10, § 2 and Homily 46, § 1, in Migne, *P.G.,* 59, 76 and 257-258.

[2112] St Augustine, *In Psalm* XXXII, 12; and *Sermo* 169, 13, in Trempelas, *Dogmatique,* v. II, p. 273, note 12.

new Gifts through new manifestations and the efforts of the free-will of the responsive man.

Question 276: What are the stages of the Preparation Grace?

Answer: The various stages that the Work of the Preparation Grace goes through till it brings the one who receives its benefit into the new Creation in Christ and Regeneration, can easily be pointed out by some indications of Holy Scripture. From the: *"Awake, you who sleep,"*[2113] one can conclude that the first stage of the Preparation Grace is the awakening of the one who is being called. This is not man's Regeneration. The sinful man who is alienated from the Spiritual Life, is distracted from the sins of the flesh and all worldly things, which absorb all his attention. He begins to realise that besides the material world and himself, there is also God's Kingdom and this draws his attention.

"Christ will give you Light" indicates the Divine Invitation. In other words, *"Christ will enlighten you."*[2114] Simultaneously with the awakening of the sinner, the first gladsome Radiance of Divine Light fall upon him. This supernatural Light will spread and enlighten the sinful man. This period is critical and dangerous in the history of man's return.[2115] At this time man faces critical moments when he can reject Divine Grace, although he might have wanted *"for a time to rejoice in its Light."*[2116] Because of moral relaxation he can let the time of Grace pass by and the period of awakening to remain inactive. Consequently the Work of Grace is interrupted and so he is counted among the *"many who are called"* but not amongst *"the elect."*[2117] The example given in the Book of Acts, according to which St Lydia showed interest in following St Paul to the place of *"worship"* to hear the word which was preached and that *"the Lord opened her heart to heed the things spoken by Paul,"*[2118] presents to us an advanced stage of awakening and a higher level of enlightenment.

The fruit of this enlightenment appears to be general faith, which consists of the full acceptance of the Truth of Divine Revelation that is preached and which, through the enlightenment of the mind, takes over the whole inner man. He then becomes conscious of his sinful condition. Moved by Divine Grace, and in fear of sin he seeks the Way of Salvation,

---

[2113] Ephes. 5:14.
[2114] St Photius, *To Ephesians 1:19,* in Migne, *P.G.,* 118, 1240.
[2115] Martensen, *Dogmatique,* p. 598.
[2116] John 5:35.
[2117] Matth. 20:16; 22:14.
[2118] Acts 16:14.

acknowledging Jesus Christ as his Lord and Saviour and returning through true repentance to Him.[2119]

The awakening is the inner enlightenment that arises the interest in hearing the saving Truth that opens the hearts of men with understanding. The acceptance of this enlightenment and general faith, which is not restricted to the mind but influences the whole inner man, is the acknowledgement of one's sinful condition and a broken heart, fear of the Divine Justice for one's crimes, the seeking and recognition of Jesus Christ, the Son of God, as one's Saviour and Redeemer and the return to Him in repentance, is the work of the Preparation Grace, from whence it begins and where it ends.

The *"return"* is an essential expression meaning that the Work of the Preparation Grace comes to a good conclusion. It is the starting point for the creation of the new Creation in the sinner. It is obvious that this is the Work of Grace that the sinner is unable to achieve by his own efforts. It is only attained when his will submits willingly and freely to the Grace that has awakened him. The *"return"* is conjoined to repentance and consists of a duty and an obligation even for those who are already baptised, but who have not experienced it, although they are incorporated into the Body of the Orthodox Church. They must also come to full awareness, to realize their sinfulness and with humble heart turn with complete faith to the Saviour, placing their lives under His Leadership and Providence. All those who are saved in Christ cannot do it of their own accord. They have to pass through the stages of awakening and return, as well as the whole Work of the Preparation Grace, regardless whether this period is short or lengthy.

CHAPTER FIVE
THE ESSENCE OF THE JUSTIFICATION

Question 277: What is the essence of Justification?

Answer: Justification dissolves the condition that sin created in man, which made him the *"old man."*[2120] It inaugurates in him the Newness of the Life of holiness, manifesting the Justified into a new Creation. These two aspects of Justification, the forgiveness of sins and the creation of the Newness of Life in Christ, is witnessed by Holy Scripture, especially in the Epistles of St Paul. One may find verses in which the negative side of Justification is emphasised, but the double aspects of Justification is also underscored by

---

[2119] Is. 1:16-20.
[2120] Rom. 6:6. Ephes. 4:22. Col. 3:9.

322

the Holy Fathers of the Orthodox Church. The accentuation of the positive side of Justification does not contradict the fact that, even after the entrance into the Newness of Life and the condition of Sanctification, the "*carnally minded*"[2121] are not wiped away completely as some fragments remain within the Justified as the "*desire to sin*" ("*concupiscentia*"). This one understands when one takes into consideration that the "*desire to sin*" is not a mortal illness within man, but the last recovering part of one who has only just regained good health after a long period of illness. This "*desire to sin*" does not have the same nature of guilt as it did before. It is changed into a centre of maturity, growth and perfection. On the contrary, however, one must never forget that the inauguration of the Sanctification of the inner man must not be understood as transmission into a higher level of perfection within Sanctification, but as a Regeneration in the condition of infancy in Christ from which the Justified man is Called, through continuous and ceaseless struggles, to increase and perfect himself within the Justification.

Consequently, Justification that occurs in one moment, does not exclude the successive development of Sanctification and the increase of the Newness of Life in Christ Hence, the Holy Fathers of the Orthodox Church speak of the forgiveness of sins as being given equally to all and of the communion of the Holy Spirit as giving Gifts according to the faith of each person. The increase and progress in the Newness of Holy Life depends on the struggle of each individual.[2122] The natural example of being "*grafted in,*"[2123] offers some analogies through which the meaning of Justification and the growth of Holiness is clarified. In the "*grafting in*" of the new Life in all Justified men, it is necessary for the development of unsleeping, ceaseless struggle in order to increase and develop the seed of new Life, through which its natural qualities will not be demolished, but will become noble and Holy. Accordingly, everyone who is Justified is called. Therefore, following Justification one has to struggle against the residue of the "*carnal minded*"[2124] and cultivate the seed of the new Life in Christ In this struggle those who rush towards Perfection, do not cease to work for their Salvation. Inspired and being strengthened by the Holy Spirit in the hope that they have already been Justified, they can look up to the Heavenly Father as being "*sons by adoption.*"[2125] It is true that, according to the assurance of St John the Apostle and Evangelist, those who have reached a

---

[2121] Rom. 8:6, 7.
[2122] Cf. Plato of Moscow, *Orthodox Teaching*, p. 94.
[2123] Rom. 11:16-24.
[2124] Rom. 8:6, 7.
[2125] Ephes. 1:5. Gal. 4:5. Rom. 8:23.

higher level of Holiness, *"cannot sin"*[2126] anymore. Since they are travelling the path of higher Virtue, not only are they required not to commit *"sin which does not lead to death"*[2127] but also to avoid falling away irreparably into sin, making *".it impossibleto renew them again to repentance."*[2128] There is double assurance for all the Justified: first of all that God *".is faithful and just to forgive"*[2129] them; and secondly that they must always be watchful[2130] not to fall from God's Grace and Salvation.

Question 278: What are the two aspects of Justification?

Answer: Through the return and Justification, the new birth or Regeneration of the new personality is accomplished.[2131] This is the beginning of Sanctification. It creates within us a new nature and develops our true personality, establishing us as temples of the Holy Spirit.[2132] It is the true Redemption of Christianity as well as the new Creation in Christ Regeneration and Sanctification must have the double nature and even after the forgiveness of sins, they must assure the appearance of new Life. Justification, Regeneration and Sanctification are inseparable from one another. They are not divided in time. They coincide in such a way, that the Newness of Life in Christ is implanted with forgiveness and the beginning of Sanctification. Therefore, no one should consider Justification as the absolution of the sinful deeds of the Justified man[2133] because, since they were done, they cannot be undone, for that which has occurred cannot be changed into that which has not occurred. Justification wipes out whatever has been caused by sin. Sinful deeds cause guilt and conditions that intensify the pre-existing condition of the ancestral guilt of the *"old man."* Although on one hand Justification wipes out the guilt, on the other it wipes out the condition. Thus Justification consists of two elements: the forgiveness of guilt, being the negative side and the abolition and removal of the old condition, which is the beginning of the Newness of Life in Christ through the restoration of the supernatural union between the justified man and God. This is the positive side. The first element is external. God covers the sinful deeds and by forgiving them, He no longer considers them. The second element, which is inseparable from the first, is the recreation of the

---

[2126] 1 John 3:9.
[2127] 1 John 5:16.
[2128] Heb. 6:4-6.
[2129] 1 John 1:9.
[2130] Matth. 26:41. Mark 14:38. Luke 12:37. 1 Thess. 5:6-8. 1 Peter 5:8. Rev. 3:2-3; 16:15.
[2131] Martensen, *Dogmatique*, p. 613.
[2132] 2 Corinth. 6:16.
[2133] Martensen, *Dogmatique*, p. 617.

sinner and his entrance into the sphere of Sanctification. The Grace of God, which is granted in Justification, creates not only simple psychological but real ontological change in man. We are not only considered simply Just by God, we become Just and receive Power to live according to Christ.[2134]

This Truth is based on the Teachings of Holy Scripture, which speak of the wiping out[2135] and of the washing away of sins, Sanctification and Justification,[2136] of Regeneration, through which we are born of God,[2137] of the Newness of Life that is offered to us,[2138] of the new Creation,[2139] of Transfiguration of the Image of God which is in us,[2140] of our condition as co-heirs of Christ,[2141] as sons of God,[2142] as temples of the Holy Spirit,[2143] as members of Christ's Body[2144] and as *partakers of the Divine Nature.*"[2145]

Regeneration is the element that makes Justification a distinguished moral Miracle. Through it the *"old man"* is put to death and the seed of the Newness of Life in Christ is planted upon his relics and developed in cooperation with the Grace of God, thereby making the Justified man a new Creation. The greatness of this new Creation can be understood when one takes into consideration that the first Creation was brought into being from nothingness, whereas with the new Creation it is essential to wipe out the old Creation, defeating corrupted nature, in order to build the glorious and eternal new Creation upon its ruins. Obviously for this reason, St John the Forerunner and Baptist of the Lord, characterised the Baptism of the New Testament as being performed by *"the Holy Spirit and Fire."*[2146] In reality, the Grace of the Holy Spirit, which overshadows the inner man through the effectiveness of His Fire, burns up the rottenness of sin and breathes the Life-giving Breath through which man is able to stand up in the Newness of Life, becoming a *"partaker of the Divine Nature."*[2147] Precisely this fact gives a supernatural nature to Justification.

[2134] Leeming, *Principles,* p. 4.
[2135] Acts 3:19.
[2136] 1 Corinth. 6:11.
[2137] John 1:13; 3:3-9. 1 Peter 1:23.
[2138] John 6:57; 10:28, 29. Gal. 2:20.
[2139] Ephes. 2:8-10; 4:24.
[2140] 2 Corinth. 3:18. Rom. 8:29.
[2141] Rom. 8:17. Tit. 3:7.
[2142] John 1:12. Gal. 4:6-7. Rom. 8:17.
[2143] 1 Corinth. 3:16-17; 6:19. 2 Corinth. 6:16.
[2144] 1 Corinth.6:15; 10:17; 12:27. Rom. 12:4, 5.
[2145] 2 Peter 1:4.
[2146] Matth. 3:11. Luke 3:16. Acts 2:3-4.
[2147] 2 Peter 1:4.

If we compare Justification in Christ to primitive justification, which the first Adam lost because of the offence, we find the former to be more superior than the latter. This new Justification begins, moves and is perfected by the incorporation of the Justified man within Christ, with Whose Death and Resurrection[2148] he is *"united together."*[2149] He is also a living member receiving Life through the Grace of God, which Justifies and Sanctifies him. As a living member of Christ's Body, he is raised to an honour and holiness that is obviously higher than and superior to those which the first Adam enjoyed in Paradise. For those who are Justified in Christ grow *"to a perfect man, to the measure of the stature of the fullness of Christ.."*[2150] and *"beholding as in a mirror the glory of the Lord, are being transformed into the same image from glory to glory, just as by the Spirit of the Lord."*[2151] It is true that in this present life Justification, which hides our Life in Christ and keeps us so that at His Appearance we *"also will appear with Him in glory"*[2152] does not render us the full harmony of our spiritual and bodily powers from the first moment, nor the possibility of avoiding death, general mortality, the illnesses of the body, nor *"carnal minded"*[2153] or the putting to death of sinful desires.[2154] Our incorporation in Jesus Christ, the Son of God, obviously presents us closer to God, the results of which will be revealed at the glorious Manifestation of Christ, proving us to be as Christ shinning *".as the sun in the Kingdom"* of our Father.[2155]

Question 279: What do Holy Scripture teach concerning Justification?

Answer: We must never forget, that in the Teachings of Holy Scripture, some terms are used regarding the forgiveness of sins, which consists of the negative side of Justification, and meaning the real wiping out of the sins. Thus the verbs *"to blot out"*[2156] the iniquities or sins, as well as the verbs *"to forgive,"*[2157] *"to cancel,"*[2158] *"to take away,"*[2159] *"to remove,"*[2160] *"to wash,"*[2161] *"to cease"* and *"to clean"*[2162] are used.

[2148] Rom. 6:3-11.
[2149] Rom. 6:5.
[2150] Ephes. 4:13.
[2151] 2 Corinth. 3:18.
[2152] Col. 3:4.
[2153] Rom. 8:6, 7.
[2154] Col. 3:5.
[2155] Matth. 13:43.
[2156] Psalm 50(51):1. Is. 43:25; 44:22. Acts 3:19.
[2157] **Matth.** 6:12, 14; 9:2, 6; 18:27, 35. **Mark** 2:5, 7, 10; 3:48; 4:12; 11:25-26. **Luke** 5:20-21, 23-24; 7:47-49; 11:4; 17:3; 23:34. **John** 20:23. **Col.** 2:13. **James** 5:15. **1 John** 1:9; 2:12.
[2158] Mich. 7:18.

Some verses manifest the forgiveness of sins as being *"covered"*[2163] or as not being *"remembered"*[2164] or not being *"imputed."*[2165] However, it is obvious that the above must be taken into consideration as the same meaning as in Acts 3:19, where it is clearly stated that repentance and return are before Justification and that the forgiveness of sins is their direct consequence. In other parts of Holy Scripture the positive side of Justification is stressed. Thus our Lord and Saviour Jesus Christ, the Son of God, speaks of the Regeneration of man: *"Most assuredly, I say to you, unless one is born of water and the Spirit, he cannot enter the Kingdom of God,"*[2166] conjoining it to the Mystery of Holy Baptism. Hence, St Paul the Apostle calls the Mystery of Baptism: *"the Washing of Regeneration and Renewing of the Holy Spirit, Whom He poured out on us abundantly through Jesus Christ our Saviour, that having been Justified by His Grace we should become heirs according to the hope of Eternal Life."*[2167]

From the above we are convinced by St Paul's teaching that during the Mystery of Holy Baptism on the one hand, the putting to death of the *"old man"* takes place, while on the other, our Regeneration and the Newness of Life occurs. This is clearly manifested, as the Holy Apostle assures us, when we were *"made alive together with Christ,"*[2168] being *"crucified with Him,"*[2169] having been *"united together in the likeness of His Death"*[2170] and when he proclaims that God *"has delivered us from the power of darkness and conveyed us into the Kingdom of the Son of His Love."*[2171] However, Redemption and exit from darkness is obviously inseparable from entrance into the Light. As correctly pointed out, with the rising of the Light, the darkness dissolves. Likewise and within man, as long as the Light of Divine Grace shines upon him, the darkness of sinful passions is dissolved and consequently the Newness of Life is introduced to him.[2172] This Teaching is also stressed by St John the Apostle, Evangelist and Theologian, who

---

[2159] John 1:29.
[2160] Psalm 102(103):12.
[2161] Is. 1:16. Psalm 50(51). Acts 22:16.
[2162] Psalm 50(51):2. Jek. 36:25. 1 John 1:7, 9.
[2163] Psalm 31(32):1.
[2164] Jer. 38:34. Heb. 10:17.
[2165] 2 Corinth. 5:19.
[2166] John 3:5.
[2167] Tit. 3:5-7.
[2168] Ephes. 2:5.
[2169] Rom. 6:6.
[2170] Rom. 6:5.
[2171] Col. 1:13.
[2172] Androutsos, *Dogmatique,* p. 232.

presents a supernatural change, being *"passed from death to Life,"*[2173] in every one who believes. The Newness of Life in Christ cannot be established within us except and only when death, which was caused because of sin, is put to death.

Justification in Christ is inseparably joined to Sanctification, as manifested by St Paul when he teaches us: *"But you were Washed, but you were Sanctified, but you were Justified in the Name of the Lord Jesus and by the Spirit of our God."*[2174] This reveals that not only has God forgiven our sins, but that He has Sanctified and Justified us. In other words, He has made us Just.[2175]

Question 280: What do the holy Fathers teach concerning Justification?

Answer: The Holy Fathers of the Orthodox Church, in agreement with Holy Scripture, proclaim that man *"descends in the water dressed with his sins"* and being *"dead in sins, he then rises, being made alive in justice."* As the Holy Apostles on the Day of Pentecost *"participated in fire not catastrophic but saving, which vanishes the thorns of sins, and makes the soul bright,"* likewise *"it comes now"* upon those who are to be baptised and *"the thorns of their sins to take away, their souls to make precious field and even to brighten,"* because *"the baptism is not only for the forgiveness of sins, but for Grace of adoption."*[2176]

St Basil the Great determined the Mystery of Holy Baptism as *"the freedom of those in captivity, forgiveness of wages, death of sin, regeneration of soul, bright vestment, seal, charisma of adoption,"* wherein man *"without mother is reborn and being old and mortal, according to the desires of the deceit, he becomes young again and relives and turns into a true flower of youth."* He is *"regenerated"* without being consumed. He is *"reformed"* without being crushed. He is *"healed"* without feeling pain.[2177]

St John Chrysostom asks: *"How and in which way were they born from God?"* And he answers: *"Through the Washing of Regeneration and Renewal of the Holy Spirit."* *"We were called sons, being born from Above and as one may say, Regenerated."* Addressing the Catechumen he describes the Mysterious Action of Baptism.[2178]

[2173] 1 John 3:14.

[2174] 1 Corinth. 6:11.

[2175] St John of Damascus, *To 1 Corinthians 6:11,* in Migne, *P.G.,* 95, 616.

[2176] St Cyril of Jerusalem, *Catechesis,* III, § 16; XVII, § 15; XX, § 62, in Migne, *P.G.,* 33, 441-443, 988, 1081.

[2177] St Basil, the Great, *To holy Baptism,* Homily 13, §§ 5 and 3, in Migne, *P.G.,* 31, 433 and 429.

[2178] St John Chrysostom, *To John,* Homily 14, § 2, in Migne, *P.G.,* 59, 94. Ibid, *Catechesis,* I, § 3, in Migne, *P.G.,* 49, 227.

St Cyril of Alexandria teaches that Baptism cleanses us from all stain. It works us into Holy temples of God and makes us *"partakers of His Divine Nature through the participation of the Holy Spirit."*[2179]

St John of Damascus observed that *"because man is of two (elements) of soul and of body, God gave him double the purification, through water and the Spirit, and by the Spirit He renews in us the 'in the image and likeness,' by the water through the Grace of the Holy Spirit He cleans the body of sin and frees us from mortality."* He also adds that *"through Baptism we receive the beginning of the Holy Spirit and the start of a new Life of Regeneration begins and a Seal and a Protection and an Enlightenment."*[2180]

Question 281: What is the remaining desire after Justification?

Answer: We must not forget that the desire (*"concupiscentiam"*), which, after receiving Holy Baptism, appears to remain within the Regenerated man, was not something evil[2181] from the beginning, for its *"..root is from nature; to desire is natural."* *"Greed, if not controlled"* changes into sin, whereas desire by nature *"is not a sin, but when it falls into greed, and abandons the laws of the lawful wedding, and turns to alien women, then it becomes adultery, not because of the desire, but because of the greed within it."*[2182]

Theodoretus of Cyrus, interpreting Romans 6:12, observed that: *"He orders us not to obey the desire which greedily enlightens the desires of the body for the movement and the annoyance of the passions are natural for us, but the act of those which are disapproved, depends on one's will."* Since desire is natural, whatever made it sinful is the unrestrained, which came from the first Offence.[2183]

According to the above the first-created, before the Offence *"were not flamed by the desire, not being besieged by other passions, neither had any need of clothing."* After the Offence, *"the flesh lusts against the spirit, and the spirit against the flesh; these are contrary to one another."*[2184] *"He now calls flesh the mind, because it deals with the things of the flesh"* and

---

[2179] St Cyril of Alexandria, *To Luke 22:8,* in Migne, *P.G.,* 72, 904. Ibid, *Against Julianus,* VII, in Migne, *P.G.,* 76, 880. Ibid, *To Psalm 50(51):12,* in Migne, *P.G.,* 76, 1096. Ibid, *To Isaiah,* VI, 2, in Migne, *P.G.,* 70, 936.

[2180] St John of Damascus, *Catechesis,* IV, 9, in Migne, *P.G.,* 94, 1121.

[2181] Dositheus of Jerusalem, *Confession,* ch. 6, p. 31.

[2182] St John Chrysostom, *To Statues,* Homily 19, § 4, in Migne, *P.G.,* 49, 195. Ibid, *To Romans,* Homily 13, § 1, in Migne, *P.G.,* 60, 507-508.

[2183] Theodoretus of Cyrus, *To Romans,* in Migne, *P.G.,* 82, 168.

[2184] Gal. 5:17.

"*struggles against the higher thoughts of the soul, and divides her*" through the "*lust of the flesh, and the lust of the eyes and the pride of life*" which "*are not from the Father, but from the world.*"[2185] This desire radiates in all directions through sin, which is within us and expands the division in the inner man, pushing him "*not to do the things* (he) *wishes*" but towards the evil that he does not want and to conduct "*in the lusts of our flesh, fulfilling the desires of the flesh.*"[2186]

Thus the terms "*desire*" and "*desire of the flesh*" and "*concupiscentiam*" took on the bad meaning of the unstoppable sinful desire of the old man, "*who follows behind the flesh in desire to soil him*" and to enslave the soul to "*the lust of uncleanness*"[2187] of the flesh. This sinful desire, since it enslaved man's mind to "*carnal minded*,"[2188] is in "*enmity against God*[2189] *and leads to death, because it made the mind thick*" and the "*earthly urge*" drags the will into the slavery of sin because "*of the desire of unlawful deeds.*"[2190]

The term "*desire*" also has a good meaning, signifying the Sanctified desire for good things and virtues of the soul. Thus our Lord and Saviour Jesus Christ, the Son of God, "*with fervent desire*" had wanted to eat the Passover meal with His disciples before He Suffered.[2191] It is obvious that in the Holy Mystery of Baptism and in the Regenerated man one might expect not the uprooting and vanishing of desire, but its relaxation and Sanctification. In the Regeneration of the baptised, one enters into the condition of Sanctification as an infant in Christ and as one recovering from a long and mortal illness. It is natural for one to bear the scars of a cured illness, which in good time and through spiritual struggle will be healed completely, growing in all holiness and being perfected in Christ It is also natural that the old desire, although at the time of Baptism casting aside its sinful nature, has some remaining tendency that is a healthy sensitivity rather than a sinful condition and a sign of guilt.

Desire in the Regenerated man is not an illness of the soul, but some kind of simple sensitivity, which has been cured. According to St Paul the Apostle, "*because through Baptism*" we are "*Crucified with*" Christ,[2192]

[2185] 1 John 2:16.
[2186] Ephes. 2:3. Gal. 5:17.
[2187] 2 Peter 2:10.
[2188] Rom. 8:6, 7.
[2189] Rom. 8:7. James 4:4.
[2190] St John Chrysostom, *To Genesis,* Homily 15, § 4, in Migne, *P.G.,* 53, 123. Ibid, *To Romans,* Homily 13, in Migne, *P.G.,* 60, 516. St Ecumenius, *To Romans,* in Migne, *P.G.,* 118, 473.
[2191] Luke 22:15.
[2192] Rom. 6:3-6.

buried with Him and Regenerated in Him,[2193] the Mystery of Holy Baptism is called *"the Washing of Regeneration"* and *"the Renewing of the Holy Spirit."*[2194] For this reason we must never forget that the nature of the *"carnal minded"* person who is still under sin and not yet baptised, differs from that of the baptised and Regenerated. For the one who is not Regenerated and not Justified, the carnal mindedness and the desire are symptoms of illness that still exists. The *"carnal minded"* desire of the non-baptised, in quantity and in quality, differs from that which exists in the Justified man in whom it remains as a remnant of a cured illness. The desire or carnal mindedness has expelled its miasmatic power.

The cured will of the Justified does not have absolute authority over all the movements of the body and soul, but in vain the *"old man"* conspires against the new man in Christ Man's new will, which is strengthened, can gain victory over the rebellious activities and is not polluted or enslaved by the *"old man."* The desire of the flesh lost its miasmatic and poisonous Attributes, which were moved from the inner to the external man.[2195] However, it is possible in times of weakness to fall into various sins. These occur daily but are weak and unable to drive us away from God or to wipe away the Newness of Life. The Justified will always turn to Repentance and, through the Mystery of Holy Repentance and Confession, will cleanse their souls from any stain of sin committed after Regeneration and Justification.

The desire of the flesh has limited sphere and influence. Through the restriction exercised upon the Justified, it offers opportunities for glory, humbleness or repentance. It offers opportunities for glory, because through necessity, as one resists sin, one achieves new triumphs against evil, making one stronger in virtue and becoming more loving to God. It also offers reasons for humility, because through daily sins it creates within us feelings of repentance leading to watchfulness, and instilling a fear of not repeating the same sins and thereby returning to our *"own vomit."*[2196] Consequently, the desire of the flesh that remains within the Justified man, since he does not relax his guard, is unable to pollute him, and even becomes the reason for him to cultivate virtues, gaining victory over sinful passions and desires of the flesh.[2197]

[2193] Col. 2:12.
[2194] Tit. 3:5.
[2195] Moehler, "Symbolique", v. I, p. 157.
[2196] 2 Peter 2:20-22.
[2197] Moehler, "Symbolique", v. I, p. 157. Damalas, *About Principles*, pp. 151 and 188.

Question 282: What is the starting condition of Justification?

Answer: It is necessary to single out another aspect of the positive side of Justification. Just as the abolishment of the sinful condition in the Work of Justification, does not at once bring the *"perfect man, to the measure of the stature of the fullness of Christ"*[2198] neither does Regeneration and the beginning of the Newness of Life in Christ Man's Regeneration, which takes place at his Justification, is at first *"as to babes in Christ."*[2199] He is called, through his persistence in faith and through his struggles, to put the last remnants of carnal mindedness to death, to exercise love and all virtues, increased through many trials and tribulations,[2200] and become a perfect man in the Lord Jesus.

The newly born in Christ bears within him the seed of the Newness of Life and the new Creation, as the seed of a tree bears within it the whole tree, or a new born baby bears the strength of the mature man. The newborn in Christ is required to continue increasing and progressing in the condition of Justification because, although from the first moments of Justification the immortal seed of Sanctification and the Newness of Life in Christ was sown within him, he is called to cooperate with Divine Grace in order to become perfect in Holiness.

Since the faithful was *"buried with Christ in Baptism"*[2201] and *"united together in the likeness of His death"*[2202] *"he was united with Him through faith"* and consequently, because of his Communion with Christ Whom at his Baptism he had *"put on"*[2203] he becomes one with Him and is Sanctified. But this new condition of Sanctification must be shown in the life of continuous Holiness, which cannot be understood without continuous struggle by the one who is Justified. He must struggle to become completely free from carnal mindedness and to submit himself day by day to Justice. As before his Justification he submitted to evil, which brought him to the slavery of sin, likewise having been freed completely from the bondage of sin, he is called to increase in justice and goodness, in order that he will do so as though he is enslaved to Justice. In other words, he will do so naturally, without any effort and automatically, as breathing and living within the atmosphere of virtue. The essence of Sanctification consists of continuous Regeneration and the complete reformation of the whole man.

[2198] Ephes. 4:13.
[2199] 1 Corinth. 3:1.
[2200] James 1:2, 12. 2 Tim. 3:12.
[2201] Col. 2:12.
[2202] Rom. 6:5.
[2203] Gal. 3:27.

According to this, Divine Grace, dwelling in man, makes *"the spiritual mind"*[2204] of the Holy Spirit permanent within him and replaces the *"carnal mind"* of the flesh, establishing within him faith and love, creating an aversion to evil as well as a repugnance and hatred of sin.

The Holy Fathers of the Orthodox Church stress that *"the forgiveness of sins is given to all equally, the communion of the Holy Spirit is granted according to one's faith. If you do little, little you will receive; if you work hard, your reward will be great."* The Work of Divine Grace in Justification is equal within all men. The further increase and progress within the new condition, in which the Justified entered, depends on and results from his own efforts and struggles.[2205]

Question 283: What is the *"grafting in"* of the Newness of Life?

Answer: The phenomenon of the *"grafting in,"* which St Paul uses in his Epistle to the Romans,[2206] in relation to the calling of the nations and the replacement of Israel by them, offers similarities and analogies that clarify the meaning of Justification and Regeneration. The *"grafting in"* refers to when the node of a cultivated tree is grafted onto a wild tree and grows into a strong new plant. However, if the grafted node is not carefully nurtured, the branches of the original, natural plant will regenerate and cause the graft to become weak and withered. Nevertheless, the node is not expelled and as soon as the wild branches are pruned back, it recovers and grows without necessity of re-grafting.

In a similar way this occurs in Justification. The seed of the Newness of Life is grafted in the faithful by Divine Grace. It is necessary for the faithful to remain alert, in order to avoid the influence of the *"old man"* who hides within his soul. But even if the Justified neglects the Work of his Salvation, the node of new Life in Christ is not removed nor dies, but remains. In the event of the recovery of the indolent faithful, it is unnecessary for him to be re-Baptised, because the neglected nodule of the Newness of Life in Christ recovers its Life-giving powers of Perfecting and Sanctifying him. Although in Justification the carnal mindedness remains without guilt and different in its nature, at the end it is also put to death while the Justified is Sanctified from his roots. Hence St Paul using the example of the *"grafting in"* presents it as working *"contrary to nature."* According to St Paul, the *"wild olive tree"* is grafted *"into a cultivated olive*

[2204] Rom. 8:6.
[2205] St Cyril of Jerusalem, *Catechesis,* I, § 5, in Migne, *P.G.,* 33, 377. Frangopoulos, *Christian Faith,* pp. 171-174.
[2206] Rom 11:16-24.

tree" the root of which "*is Holy*" and in it the "*wild olive tree*" becomes a "*partaker of the root and the fatness of the olive tree.*"[2207]

In Regeneration and Sanctification, the natural character of the Justified, man is freed from his bad nature while his personality remains within its natural Attributes even after his Sanctification. The Grace of God does not remove but restores nature. The wild fig tree, which was previously without fruit, becomes fruitful but never changes into an olive tree or a vine. Nature is Sanctified but never falsified. The natural character of each man remains, even though Sanctified by the operational Grace of the Holy Spirit. Through the mystical pains of Regeneration "*Christ is formed in us.*"[2208] Christ takes a specific form in each and every individual separately.[2209]

Question 284: What dangers and struggles one faces efter Justification?

Answer: According to the above, it is obvious that even after man's Justification and the Regeneration in Baptism, all who are baptised are called to struggle against the remnants of carnal mindedness, being alert and awake, so as not to be deceived by the "*old man.*" They must cultivate the seed of the Newness of Life in Christ that the Holy Spirit implanted in their souls in order to progress in holiness and virtue. Seeing that the faithful are confronted by temptations from the vanity and desires of this world in their struggles to grow in Justification, "*for the flesh lusts against the Spirit, and the Spirit against the flesh*"[2210] they must remain steadfast and watchful so as not to fall away from Salvation, working out their "*own Salvation with fear and trembling*"[2211] They must have unshakeable faith that in Baptism the "*old man*" was put to death while the new Life of Holiness was renewed and they must never doubt the Kindness and Love of the Heavenly Father and the sufficiency of the Sacrifice of Christ for the Salvation of the whole world. Man's free-will must also offer its part in achieving the Salvation in Christ.

Thus, all who have been Justified, those who struggle, have a certain sense of security or insecurity - the sense of security being strengthened as they realise that God, Who Justifies and Sanctifies them, is faithful, whereas the sense of insecurity is created by the realization of the weakness of man's nature and the possibility of falling from Salvation. However, no one

---

[2207] Rom. 11:16-17
[2208] Gal. 4:19.
[2209] Col. 2:11-12.
[2210] Gal. 5:17.
[2211] Phil. 2:12.

should consider this insecurity as troubling enough to cast the peace of Christ away from the soul of the faithful, plunging it into a deep, desperate anxiety. On the contrary, it secures the Justified by preserving them in continuous communion with God, from Whom they receive help and Grace, protecting them from any kind of fall, and in addition, it becomes the centre of spiritual work.[2212] Thus any anxiety is cast away from the soul of the Justified by the secure hope that the Mercy and Love of God will never abandon them. Because of this insecurity, one is always compelled to wakefulness and alertness, pushing aside laziness, unconcern and indifference that can lead one to mortal sleep.[2213]

This insecurity is reduced when the faithful progress in holiness and are raised to higher levels of virtue, where the remnants of carnal mindedness are completely put to death and wiped out within. The temptations, too, are put aside and one does not waver between good and evil, as in the beginning of one's new life. The efforts to achieve greater progress in holiness never ends.[2214] We must never, however, forget that the Holiness of God is infinite, and no matter how much the faithful struggle to *"become Holy, according to Him Who called him to 'be Holy"*[2215] they will always lack in holiness, since they are far more limited and having flesh in this life, it becomes naturally impossible to vest themselves completely with Divine Holiness. Hence, even those who reached higher levels of holiness, preserve within them the understanding of their imperfection.[2216]

Question 285: Can those who are reborn from God fall from Grace?

Answer: The answer is given by St Paul in his Epistle to the Hebrews: *"It is impossible for those who were once Enlightened, and have tasted the Heavenly Gift, and have become partakers of the Holy Spirit, and have tasted the good Word of God and the Powers of the age to come, if they fall away, to renew them again to repentance, since they crucify again for themselves the Son of God, and put Him to an open shame."*[2217] When one recalls that even the Angels who were created Holy, fell, how can it be possible to exclude the fall of any Justified man?

St Basil the Great considers the prayers for the Just as being of great importance so that his will and intention may remain straight and steadfast,

---

[2212] Damalas, *About Principals,* p. 188.
[2213] Matth. 26:41.
[2214] Oosterzee, *Dogmatics,* p. 661.
[2215] 1 Peter 1:16.
[2216] Phil. 2:12.
[2217] Heb. 6:4-6.

being assisted by God's Guidance and in order that he will not flee from the Truth, nor be harmed by the enemy of the Truth who twists the Doctrines.[2218]

St John the Apostle, Evangelist and Theologian, assures us that *"whoever has been born of God does not sin, for His seed remains in him; and he cannot sin, because he has been born of God."*[2219] Firstly, the Justified manifests measures of the condition of Regeneration and Sanctification that are permanently within the Justified man. Secondly, the terms *"he does not"* and *"he cannot"* must not be taken as an absolute meaning, but in a relative way, in that *"he does not"* manifest *"that which does not exist from the intention"* whereas the term *"he cannot"* signifies not *"the natural weakness"* nor *"that the nature is unable to sin, but that since he who is born from God, keeps the Grace of birth through a clean life, he cannot sin."* It is true that those who have moved to a higher level of Sanctification do not feel the impulse or pressure of carnal mindedness. Within them there is established a strong and stable habit of good and aversion towards evil, so that one may say they are morally unable to fall. Nevertheless, since one carries weak flesh, it is not possible to exclude any fall or to be alienated from Salvation.

CHAPTER SIX
THE CONDITIONS OF JUSTIFICATION

Question 286: What are the conditions of Justification?

Answer: The only condition requested by the New Testament in order to familiarise the work of Salvation of our Lord and Saviour Jesus Christ, the Son of God, is Faith. This Faith must not be only at the beginning but even during the growth and progress of Justification. It must not be the work of the mind but the possession of moral Attributes, influencing all the inner man, hiding the inner power of all those virtues which, when they bear fruit, will comprise the treasure of love. Thus man has the right through Faith which is *"working through love."*[2220] Faith, without works that are achieved through the Grace of Christ, are *"dead."*[2221] This is the opinion of all Holy Fathers of the Orthodox Church. Salvation is offered to us through *"Grace"*[2222] and *"not by works of righteousness which we have done."*[2223]

[2218] St Basil, the Great, *To Psalm 7*, § 6, in Migne, *P.G.*, 29, 241.
[2219] 1 John 3:9.
[2220] Gal. 5:6.
[2221] James 2:17, 20, 26.
[2222] Tit. 3:7. Rom. 11:6. Ephes. 2:5, 8.

One is convinced when he recalls that our Lord Jesus Christ, the Son of God, is the only sinless One Who became the Ideal and Perfect moral Example, compared to Whom we fall short. Consequently we are always guilty. Even these moral good works, which prove to be active and justify the Faith, are the *"fruit of the Spirit."*[2224] It was correctly stressed that God, rewarding these good deeds in each Christian, crowns the Gifts themselves.

The reward of good deeds and virtues in Christ is relative but not absolute. Hence, under no circumstances can we speak of abundance of reward, especially in regard to the extraordinary works of the Holy Saints. Extraordinary good works which make Justice much more abundant, do not exist, for even if we " *have done all those things which you are commanded"* We must believe that we *"are unprofitable servants"* and we must say: *"We have done what was our duty to do."*[2225] Again it is written *"there is none righteous, no, not one."*[2226]

Since the good deeds are inseparable from the Faith and are the fruit of it, they are necessary for Salvation.[2227] It is understandable that offences of Evangelical Law may disqualify one from Salvation. Henceforth St John the Evangelist, Apostle and Theologian assured us that *"there is sin leading to death"* and *"there is sin not leading to death."*[2228] The first sin that *"leads to death"* infests the Justification in Christ. This develops into *"the blasphemy against the Spirit"* which *"will not be forgiven, either in this age or in the age to come."*[2229] The second sin *"not leading to death"* occurs either because one was carried away in the moment or because of one's daily weaknesses. If the one who has fallen runs to correct his errors through the Holy Mystery of Repentance and Confession, he will be forgiven.

Question 287: What is the true meaning of Justifying Faith?

Answer: *"We conclude that a man is justified by Faith."*[2230] However, this Faith that justifies is not simply some kind of mental consent or fruitless knowledge. It is right from the beginning connected to Repentance according to the words of our Lord and Saviour Jesus Christ, the Son of God, Who said: *"The time is fulfilled, and the Kingdom of God is at hand.*

[2223] Tit. 3:5.

[2224] Gal. 5:22. Ephes. 5:9.

[2225] Luke 17:10.

[2226] Rom. 3:10. Psalm 14(15):1-3.

[2227] Dositheus of Jerusalem, *Confession,* ch. 9 and 13, pp. 32, 36.

[2228] 1 John 5:16-17.

[2229] Matth. 12:31, 32.

[2230] Rom. 3:28.

Repent and believe in the gospel.[2231] For this reason it becomes the focus and source of Light which enlightens all the spiritual powers of man, moving his whole inner world and shining its Life-giving radiance within the depths of his soul. This Faith is not a work of the mind but takes up the nature of moral work from which the *diakonia* (ministry) of the Word aims towards *"the obedience of Faith."*[2232]

At the beginning Faith appears to be a Heavenly Enlightenment of the mind. But since all the spiritual powers are connected very closely and inseparably, it is natural that this Enlightenment, if it is real and not a spark of the moment that shines in the darkness of the night, will not leave the heart unmoved and will not allow the will to fall into inactivity or lethargy. The Faith, even at its beginning, being united to the return and repentance, and generally to the work of Preparation Grace, has moral Attributes, which, when perfected by Divine Grace proves Faith to be active in Love. Consequently pure Faith only intellectually, not in reality, is different to Love.[2233]

True Faith and sincere Love influence one another in a very close relationship such as in that between the heart and the rest of the body. The former nourishes and gives life to the body while the latter supports and gives life to the heart. Likewise is the relationship between Faith and Love. Faith is the Life-giving Power that nourishes and strengthens Love and vice versa. Sinful life weakens the Light of Faith and can even completely extinguish it. On the contrary, the warmer and greater Love is in deeds, the stronger Faith becomes. As the mind becomes cleaner and purer through Love, being the eye of the soul, the more it is Enlightened by the Light of Faith. It becomes stronger and more skilful towards perfecting the understanding of its essence, according to the words of our Lord and Saviour: *"Blessed are the pure in heart, for they shall see God."*[2234] The conformity to the Commandments of the Great Shepherd and Physician of our souls[2235] make our Faith and trust in Him stronger.

Question 288: What is unformed, formed, abridged and dead Faith?

Answer: From the above it is very clear that the Orthodox Church calls the first Faith *"unformed Faith"* (*"fidem informem"*) which leads one to the Saviour and introduces one to the Justification in Christ This is different to

---

[2231] Mark 1:15. Matth. 4:17; 10:7.
[2232] Rom. 1:5.
[2233] Androutsos, *Dogmatique,* p. 242.
[2234] Matth. 5:8.
[2235] 1 Peter 2:25.

that of the fullness of understanding and fruitful works of Love that is referred to as *"formed Faith"* (*"fides formatem"*). One can accept this if he is not alienated from Love and good deeds. We call the first Faith *"unformed"* firstly because it has not yet produced its fruits which are the works of Love and secondly, because it has not become knowledge and understanding. It has nevertheless a form because it is not simply mental acceptance but has already borne its fruits. Repentance is the avoidance of sinful life, which is the first step towards our Saviour, consisting of good deeds and fruits of Faith.

It is possible that the justified man has not received the full knowledge of the essence of this Faith but has accepted the main guidelines of this Faith and its Doctrines with all his heart. This Faith being *"abridged Faith"* (*"fides implicita"*), represents the passive nature of Faith without being completely alien from its active part, which represents mostly the *"formed Faith"* (*"fides formata"*) that produces the full fruit of Love. He who is justified through Faith, in his first steps, accepts more and acts less. However, as he progresses in Justification and grows in Sanctification, his faith becomes more active through Love and becomes more energetic.

The *"unformed Faith"* is different to that of *"dead faith,"* which is simple and indefinite knowledge that cannot cleanse man's will nor can it influence his heart. Nevertheless, we must not forget that it is easier for *"unformed Faith"* to fall and become *"dead and lifeless faith."* If he who has returned and has been Justified does not persist in his struggle for virtue and cultivation of Love, he will lose his initial enthusiasm and the first radiance of Enlightenment. Consequently he will become *"shortsighted, even to blindness"*[2236] and will forget *"that he was cleansed from his old sins"* and he will eventually *"return to his own vomit."*[2237]

Question 289: What do we teach about Justifying Faith?

Answer: The Teaching of the Justifying and Sanctifying Faith, which is combined with good works as its fruits, is based upon Holy Scripture. It is proclaimed very clearly by St Paul the Apostle that *"in Christ Jesus"* nothing *"avails anything, but Faith working through Love"*[2238] and if someone has *"all the Faith"* making it possible to *" remove mountains, but has not Love"* he has *"nothing."*[2239] St John the Apostle, Evangelist and Theologian assured us that *"this is the Commandment of God"* *"that we*

[2236] 2 Peter 1:9.
[2237] 2 Peter 1:22. Prov. 26:11.
[2238] Gal. 5:6.
[2239] 1 Corinth. 13:2.

should believe on the Name of His Son Jesus Christ and love one another."[2240] St James the Adelphotheus ("*Brother of Christ*"), stressed that "*the testing of your Faith produces patience. But let patience have its perfect work, that you may be perfect and complete, lacking nothing.*"[2241]

Because of the close relationship between Faith and good works, Salvation appears as fruit of the Faith, through which only "*we having been justified by Faith, we have peace with God through our Lord Jesus Christ, through Whom also we have access by Faith into this Grace in which we stand, and rejoice in hope of the glory of God.*"[2242] "*For by Grace you have been saved through Faith, and that not of yourselves; it is the gift of God, not of works, lest anyone should boast.*"[2243] For this reason our Lord and Saviour Jesus Christ, the Son of God, assures us that "*he who believes and is baptised will be saved; but he who does not believe will be condemned.*"[2244] In other cases Justification and Salvation depend upon the good works and appear as fruits of Love. Thus our Lord assured us that when He returns to Judge the living and the dead, He "*will reward each according to his works*"[2245] calling those who practiced good to inherit "*the kingdom prepared for them from the foundation of the world.*"[2246] St John also taught that "*he who does not love his brother abides in death*"[2247] and that "*everyone who loves is born of God and knows God*"[2248] and that "*he who does not love does not know God, for God is love. In this the love of God was manifested toward us, that God has sent His only begotten Son into the world, that we might live through Him.*"[2249] St James again emphasised that "*a man is justified by works, and not by Faith only.*"[2250] Finally, St Paul excluded the fornicators, the idolaters, the adulterers, the homosexuals, the sodomites, the thieves, the covetous, the drunkards, the revilers and the extortioners from God's Kingdom as they would not "*inherit the Kingdom of God.*"[2251]

St Paul repeatedly taught "*that a man is justified by Faith apart from the deeds of the law*"[2252] and that "*a man is not justified by the works of the*

[2240] 1 John 3:23.
[2241] James 1:3-4.
[2242] Rom. 5:1-2.
[2243] Ephes. 2:8-9.
[2244] Mark 16:16.
[2245] Matth. 16:27.
[2246] Matth. 25:34.
[2247] 1 John 3:14.
[2248] 1 John 4:7.
[2249] 1 John 4:7
[2250] James 2:24.
[2251] 1 Corinth. 6:10.
[2252] Rom. 4:28.

law but by Faith in Jesus Christ, even we have believed in Christ Jesus, that we might be justified by Faith in Christ and not by the works of the law; for by the works of the law no flesh shall be justified.[2253] By means of these statements St Paul had in mind on the one hand the ceremonial orders of the Law[2254] whereas on the other hand, he referred to *"their own righteousness"* which they (the Jews) *"being ignorant of God's righteousness, have not submitted to the righteousness of God."*[2255] The Jews were seeking, as St Paul did before his return to Christ, their Justification through their own works and the practice of the Mosaic Law. *"So you shall keep all My ordinances, and all My judgments, and do them; which if a man do, he shall live in them."*[2256] They did not consider the words of the Lord *"cursed is every man that continues not in all the words of this law to do them"*[2257] and consequently *"every man who becomes circumcised is a debtor to keep the whole law."*[2258] Therefore, no one who remains in the Law is Justified by God because no one can observe all the Law perfectly and not fall into fault. Hence, St Paul advised us to avoid circumcision for *"if you become circumcised, Christ will profit you nothing"*[2259] as *"you have become estranged from Christ, you who attempt to be justified by law have fallen from Grace."*[2260] According to this opinion St Paul proclaimed that *"a man is not justified by the works of the law"*[2261] not because he does not consider the works of Love as being important for Salvation but because without the Grace of Christ, the works remain fruitless. In Galatians he stressed[2262] on the one hand, the Grace of Justification and Salvation through Faith and not by the works of the Law, while on the other hand he assured us that those who practice the works of the flesh *"shall not inherit the Kingdom of God."*[2263] For *"the fruit of the Spirit is love, joy, peace, longsuffering, kindness, goodness, faithfulness, gentleness, self-control"*[2264] *"for whatever a man sows he will also reap. For he who sows to his flesh will of the flesh reap corruption, but he who sows to the Spirit will of the Spirit reap everlasting life. And let us not grow weary while doing well, for in due season we shall reap if we do not lose heart. Therefore, as we have*

[2253] Gal. 2:16.
[2254] Rom. 3:28. Gal. 2:16; 3:11; 5:6. Col. 2:16 and Gal. 5:2.
[2255] Rom. 10:3.
[2256] Lev. 18:5. Rom. 10:5.
[2257] Deut. 27:26.
[2258] Gal. 5:3.
[2259] Gal. 5:2.
[2260] Gal. 5:4.
[2261] Gal. 2:16.
[2262] Gal. 5:19-24.
[2263] Gal. 5:21.
[2264] Gal. 5:22.

opportunity, let us do well to all, especially to those who are of the household of Faith."[2265]

St Paul emphasised Justification *"by Faith."*[2266] St James assured us that *"man is justified through works and not only by works alone"*[2267] and that *"faith by itself, if it does not have works, is dead."*[2268] These two Apostles seem to differ on their basic opinions. There are some works without which Faith is dead but again they are the works of the Law that are not required in order to be justified in Christ, as for example circumcision and the ceremonial orders.[2269] So when St James asked: *"Can Faith save you?"*[2270] he had in mind that Faith which even the demons have and which makes them *"tremble"*[2271] because their faith lacks love that proves the living Faith.

However, the works that will proclaim us finally Justified at the Second Coming of our Lord will be due to the fruits of the Faith performed in this life and which cannot be separated from the Justification of the Faith in Baptism. We must also never forget that in relation to future Life, we can only speak of the perfection of Justification and the Glorification of those who, in this life, have been Justified. St Paul said that *"who He justified, these He also glorified."*[2272] Under no circumstances can we speak of a second Justification. Our Lord and Saviour Jesus Christ, the Son of God, promised us that *"whoever believes in Him should not perish but have eternal life"*[2273] and *"shall not come into judgment, but has passed from death into life."*[2274] This Life, according to St Paul, *"is hidden with Christ in God"* for *" when Christ Who is our life appears, then you also will appear with Him in glory."*[2275] For this reason St Paul considered that Salvation through Justification has taken place *"for we were saved in this hope."*[2276] Furthermore in Jesus Christ *"by Grace (we) have been saved through Faith"*[2277] *"and raised up together, and sit together in the heavenly places."*[2278]

[2265] Gal. 6:7-10.
[2266] Gal. 2:20.
[2267] James 2:24.
[2268] James 2:17.
[2269] St Ecumenius, *To James 2:14,* in Migne, *P.G.,* 119, 480.
[2270] James 2:14.
[2271] James 2:19.
[2272] Rom. 8:30.
[2273] John 3:15, 36.
[2274] John 5:24.
[2275] Col. 3:3-4.
[2276] Rom. 8:24.
[2277] Ephes. 2:8.
[2278] Ephes. 2:6.

Question 290: What do the holy Fathers teach concerning Justifying Faith?

Answer: The close and inseparable relationship between Faith and works is clearly proclaimed by the Holy Fathers of the Orthodox Church since the time of the Apostolic Fathers. Thus St Clement of Rome, although on the one hand stressing that we *"are not justified through ourselves or through our own wisdom or understanding or piety or works which we have done in holiness of heart, but through Faith."*[2279] Further on he concluded: *"The good worker receives the bread of his labour confidently, but the lazy and careless dares not look his employer in the face For He forewarns us: 'Behold, the Lord comes, and His reward is with Him, to pay each one according to his work.'* [2280] *He exhorts us, therefore, who believe in Him with our whole heart, not to be idle or careless about any good work."*[2281] The same Apostolic Father wrote in his Second Letter to the Corinthians: *"Indeed, He Himself says, 'whoever acknowledges Me before men, I will acknowledge before My Father.'*[2282]

St Cyril of Jerusalem stressed that *"God-fearing consists of two ways:, the accurate pious Doctrines and the good works; and neither the Doctrines without the good works nor the works without the pious Doctrines are acceptable to God. What then is the benefit of knowing the things of God very well but practicing adultery? "*[2283]

St John Chrysostom declared that one must *" stand upon the true Faith and show a perfect way of Life. For if we do not add a worthy life to our Faith, we will be held accountable at the Last Judgment."*[2284]

St John of Damascus believed that Faith *"is perfected in all by the Commandments of Christ in works, being pious and practising His Commandments for he who does not believe according the catholic Church or is in communion with the devil through inappropriate works, is an unbeliever."*[2285]

St Cyril of Alexandria stated that *" Faith is to know the one God Who is by nature Holy and to confess Him without any deceit and truthfully. However, even this is lifeless if it is not followed by the brightness of good works."*[2286] Elsewhere he observed that *"for those who wish to*

[2279] St Clement of Rome, *1ˢᵗ Corinthians,* 32, 4 – 33, 1, in Lightfoot, *Apostolic Fathers,* pp. 45-46.
[2280] Cf. Is. 40:10; 62:11. Prov. 24:12. Rev. 22:12.
[2281] St Clement of Rome, *1ˢᵗ Corinthians,* 34, 1-4, in Lightfoot, *Apostolic Fathers,* pp. 46-47.
[2282] Cf. Matth. 10:32.
[2283] St Cyril of Jerusalem, *Catechesis,* IV, § 2, in Migne, *P.G.,* 33, 456.
[2284] Ibid, *To Matthew,* Homily 64, § 4, in Migne, *P.G.,* 58, 614.
[2285] St John of Damascus, *Exposition. About faith,* IV, 83, 10, in Migne, *P.G.,* 94, 1128.
[2286] St Cyril of Alexandria, *To John,* book IX, in Migne, *P.G.,* 74, 125.

approach God, they must have the True Faith followed by a clean life according to the measure of human capabilities."[2287]

Question 291: What is the worthiness of Good Works?

Answer: Thus good works appear to be necessary in order to achieve Salvation. Hence they are proclaimed by Holy Scripture as being worthy of reward. Our Lord and Saviour Jesus Christ, the Son of God, Commanded us to practise the giving of alms so as to "*lay up for yourselves treasure in Heaven*"[2288] and to "*provide yourselves with a treasure in Heaven that does not fail, where no thief approaches nor moth destroys.*"[2289] The promised inheritance of the Heavenly Kingdom has been prepared since the foundation of the world for those who practise good works of Love and who are generous to Christ's poor brethren of this world.[2290]

In the New Testament it is stressed that "*each one will receive his own reward according to his own labour*"[2291] and according to their work. At the Second Coming "*each one's work will become clear, for the Day will declare it, because it will be revealed by fire; and the fire will test each one's work, of what sort it is. If anyone's work which he has built on it endures, he will receive a reward. If anyone's work is burned, he will suffer loss; but he himself will be saved, yet so as through fire.*"[2292] Christ will "*render to each one according to his deeds: eternal life to those who by patient continuance in doing good seek for glory, honour, and immortality; but to those who are self-seeking and do not obey the truth, but obey unrighteousness – indignation and wrath, tribulation and anguish, on every soul of man who does evil, of the Jew first and also of the Greek; but glory, honour and peace to everyone who works what is good.*"[2293] "*Therefore do not cast away your confidence, which has great reward. For you have need of endurance, so that after you have done the Will of God, you may receive the promises.*"[2294] At the end of St Paul's life he wrote: "*I have fought the good fight, I have finished the race, I have kept the Faith. Finally, there is laid up for me the crown of righteousness, which the Lord, the righteous*

[2287] Ibid, *To Luke 13:23*, in Migne, *P.G.*, 72, 776.
[2288] Matth. 6:20.
[2289] Luke 12:33.
[2290] Matth. 25: 34, 40.
[2291] 1 Corinth. 3:8.
[2292] 1 Corinth. 3:13-15.
[2293] Rom. 2:6-10.
[2294] Heb. 10:35-36.

Judge, will give to me on that Day, and not to me only but also to all who have loved His appearing."[2295]

It is true that our good deeds are not free of imperfection or that even our most perfect good deed, when compared to God's Work, is vastly different. Nevertheless, good works do not lose their good nature, regardless of man's weakness and egoistic nature. Not all Orthodox Christians achieve the highest level of their perfection. This does not mean that they are not virtuous according to their ability or as in the Parable of the Sower [2296] like those seeds that *"fell on good ground and yielded a crop: some a hundredfold, some sixty, some thirty."*[2297]

The reward of good works is not absolute but relative. It is relative not only because of their imperfection but because they comprise the fruits that the Lord presents through the Grace of the Holy Spirit, as He declared: *"for without Me you can do nothing."*[2298] And it is true that Christ produces them with the cooperation of man but even this cooperation, although essential for the Action of Divine Grace, is not a serious prerequisite for the bearing of the fruit of virtue. Without the fire of Divine Grace, the good intention of man would not have been alive and thus it would not have developed into a genuine cooperation between man and the Grace of God. *"For, it is God Who works in you both to will and to do for His good pleasure."*[2299]

It is the Love of God and His *Philanthropia* (*"Love of mankind"*) which are the sources and reasons for the reward of good works. Only in absolute humility can man request, as son by adoption, to receive his reward. We must never forget that when we ask for anything of God it is very different to when we ask for anything from our fellow man. Furthermore, we must never forget that whatever good we have is from God and only with sincere humility may we ask God to give us what He promised.[2300] Thus Salvation is granted by Grace and as a Gift. It is God's Love that combines human virtue with Heavenly Blessedness, as manifested in the Parable of the Great Banquet.[2301]

[2295] 2 Tim. 4:7-8.
[2296] Matth. 13:3-9. Mark 4:1-9. Luke 8:4-8.
[2297] Matth. 13:8.
[2298] John 15:5.
[2299] Phil. 2:13.
[2300] St Augustine, *Sermo* 158, c. 2, in migne, *P.L.,* 38, 863.
[2301] Matth. 22:2-14. Luke 14:15-24.

PART FIVE

THE ORTHODOX CHURCH AS THE KINGDOM OF GOD ON EARTH

CHAPTER ONE
MEANING, DIVINE INSTITUTION AND THE NECESSITY OF THE CHURCH

Question 292: What is the meaning of the *"Church"*?

Answer: The etymology of the word *"Ecclesia"* (*"Church"*)[2302] originates from the Greek verb *"εκκαλέω"* (*"to call"*). It was used by the Greeks before Christ to signify the gathering of the citizens by the rulers for a public discussion. Under this same meaning, we find the word in the Old Testament[2303] and in the New Testament,[2304] where the term is used in conjunction with the words: *"the Lord's," "the Saints"* or *"the faithful."* In the Old Testament, however, it signifies the Israelites as the elect people of God who were called for a special Mission and were ruled by God as a Community from which the pagans were excluded as well as some of the disabled.[2305] The word was especially used to signify the gathering of God's people, as the *"Ecclesia"* ("the Church") of the Saints or Faithful, either to glorify God or to worship Him inside or outside the Temple.[2306]

In the New Testament the word *"Ecclesia"* signifies the gathering of the faithful: those who accepted and confessed the Christian Faith.[2307] It also signifies the gathering of the faithful to worship and the building up of their faith in private houses.[2308] It denotes all of the faithful of one city or providence, (i.e. the Ecclesia (Church) of Jerusalem, the Ecclesia of Antioch, the Ecclesia of Ephesus, the Ecclesia of Corinth, the Ecclesia of Galatia, Judea, Asia, Macedonia, e.t.c.[2309]). Most commonly, the word *"Ecclesia"* is used in the New Testament to indicate the Church of God that is spread throughout the entire world and which is founded upon the True

---

[2302] Cf. Kefalas, *Catechesis,* pp. 217-219. Frangopoulos, *Christian Faith,* pp. 175-178. Mitsopoulos, *Themata,* pp. 84, 228-229.
[2303] Psalm 25(26):5. Wisdom of Sirah 26:5.
[2304] Acts 19:32, 39 and 40.
[2305] Deut. 23:2-4, 9.
[2306] Psalms 88(89):6. 149(150):1. 21(22):23, 26. 39(40): 10. 106(107):32. I Macc. 3:10. Joel 2:16. Wisdom of Sirach 15:5; 44:15.
[2307] 1 Corinth. 4:17; 11:18. Cf. Damalas, *Catechesis,* pp. 56-60.
[2308] Rom. 16:5 and Col. 4:15. Cf. Mitsopoulos, *Themata,* pp. 229-230.
[2309] Acts 8:1; 13:1; 14:27; 15:3. 1 Corinth. 1:2; 16:19. 2 Corinth. 8:1. Rom. 16:1. Gal. 1:2, 22.

Faith and initiated by the Lord,[2310] *"which He purchased with His own Blood."*[2311]

The universal Ecclesia (Church) is composed of the local *"churches of God."*[2312] Christ is the Head of the Church,[2313] being the Saviour of the Body, for He *"nourishes and cherishes"*[2314] the faithful as being *"members of His Body,"*[2315] His Church, which is the *"pillar and ground of the Truth"*[2316] and which *"the whole building, being fitted together, grows into a Holy Temple in the Lord."*[2317]

Synonymous terms of the word *"Ecclesia"* are used in the New Testament, such as *"the Kingdom of God"* and *"the Heavenly Kingdom,"* by which the Ecclesia of God is characterized as being from Heaven and where her members find their Justification, Perfection, Sanctification, Salvation and Glorification in Christ Through the Church, within the Church and for the Church, man is united through Christ He is Regenerated within Christ and he lives for Christ achieving his *"Theosis"* (Deification). In addition, the term *"Kingdom"* signifies the Community in which the Lord is the supreme Ruler and King to whom all the faithful submit themselves. St John the Forerunner and Baptist presents this Kingdom as being *"at hand"*[2318] while the Lord refers to it as being already established upon the earth *"and the violent take it by force,"*[2319] or as the future to come *"in power"* before His Apostles die, or as an inheritance that the Father was well pleased *"to give"* to *"the little flock"*[2320] and which is bestowed by the Father to His Son and thereafter, at the last moments, by the Son to His Holy Apostles and Disciples.[2321]

The *"Ecclesia"* (Church) is also called *"the House of God,"*[2322] which is built *"on the foundation of the Apostles and Prophets"*[2323] *"into a Holy Temple in the Lord"*[2324] by the *"living stones"* of the faithful, *"to offer up spiritual sacrifices acceptable to God through Jesus Christ,"*[2325] so *"that*

[2310] Matth. 16:18.
[2311] Acts 20:28.
[2312] 1 Corinth. 11:16.
[2313] Ephes. 5:23. Cf. Mitsopoulos, *Themata,* pp. 234-236.
[2314] Ephes. 5:29.
[2315] Ephes. 5:30
[2316] 1 Tim. 3:15.
[2317] Ephes. 2:21.
[2318] Matth. 3:2. Cf. Daniel 2:44.
[2319] Matth. 11:12.
[2320] Luke 12:32.
[2321] Luke 22:29.
[2322] Heb. 10:21.
[2323] Ephes. 2:20.
[2324] Ephes. 2:21.
[2325] 1 Peter 2:5.

Christ may dwell" in the *"hearts through faith."*[2326] It is referred to as *"a chaste virgin"* presented to Christ.[2327] Who loves her *"and gave Himself for her, that He might Sanctify and cleanse her with the washing of water by the Word, that He might present her to Himself a glorious Church, not having spot or wrinkle or any such thing, but that she should be Holy and without blemish."*[2328]

The *"Ecclesia"* being characterized as *"the Body of Christ,"*[2329] reveals the close relationship of Christ with the faithful, of whom the Church consists. St John Chrysostom observedd: *"Can anything be a head without a body?" "Where the head is, there is the body; for if not, it would not be a body, neither a head."*[2330]

The term *"Bride of Christ"*[2331] manifests the unmixed and independence of each member and although the Church consists of the faithful who are closely united with the Bridegroom, they are distinguished from Him. Each individual soul has Christ as its Bridegroom and is not absorbed by the Church. Although all are one, united to one another and to Christ as the Head and Bridegroom, the personality of each individual is preserved.[2332]

Question 293: What is *"Ecclesia"* according to the holy Fathers?

Answer: St Ignatius the Theophorus of Antioch addressed the local communities of the faithful in Ephesus, Magnesia, Tralles, Rome, Philadelphia and Smyrna as *"Churches"* and he described them variously as being *"predestined before the ages for lasting and unchangeable glory,"*[2333] as having *"been blessed through the Grace of God the Father,"*[2334] as *"dearly loved by God,"*[2335] as having *"found mercy in the Majesty of the Father Most High,"* as *"beloved and enlightened through the Will"* of God,[2336] as having *"found mercy and is firmly established in godly harmony and unwaveringly rejoices in the Suffering of our Lord, fully convinced of*

[2326] Ephes. 3:17. Cf. Kefalas, *Catechesis,* p. 24.

[2327] 2 Corinth. 11:2.

[2328] Ephes. 5:25-27.

[2329] Rom. 12:5. 1 Corinth. 6:15. Ephes. 1:22-23; 5:30. Col. 1:18, 24. Evdokimov, *Orthodoxia,* pp. 193-195.

[2330] St John Chrysostom, *To 1 Corinthians,* Homily 8, § 4, in Migne, *P.G.,* 61, 72. Ibid, *To Ephesians,* Homily 3, § 2, in Migne, *P.G.,* 62, 26

[2331] John 3:29. Rev. 21:2, 9; 22:17.

[2332] Mouratides, *The essence,* p. 107.

[2333] St Ignatius, *To Ephesians,* Introduction, in Lightfoot, *Apostolic Fathers,* p. 86.

[2334] Ibid, *To Magnesians,* Introduction, in Lightfoot, *Apostolic Fathers,* p. 93.

[2335] Ibid, *To Trallians,* Introduction, in Lightfoot, *Apostolic Fathers,* p. 97.

[2336] Ibid, *To Romans,* Introduction, in Lightfoot, *Apostolic Fathers,* p. 101.

His Resurrection in all Mercy"[2337] and as having been "*endowed with every spiritual Gift, filled with faith and love, not lacking in any spiritual Gift, most worthy of God.*"[2338]

It is furthermore emphasized that all who believe are "*members of one another*" and thus rebellions and divisions in the Church are not allowed to "*split the members of Christ and to rebel against our own body.*" [2339]

This unity of the Church as one Body is stressed by St Irenaeus, who observed that "*the Church, although spread throughout the whole world to the edges of the earth,*" has one faith "*which she received from the Apostles and their disciples.*" She "*preserves this as living in one house, as having one soul and heart, and as having one mouth.*" St Irenaeus acknowledged that "*the dialects of the world are different tongues, through which the Word is preached*" but he stressed that "*neither those churches in Germany,*" nor those in Iberia, "*nor in the east, nor in Egypt, nor in Libya, nor those that were established in the midst of the world*" believe or preach differently. But, as the sun is "*one and the same*" for the whole world, likewise the Word of the Truth that is preached by the one Church shines upon and Enlightens all men who want "*to come to the Knowledge of the Truth.*"[2340]

St John Chrysostom observed that "*the faithful around the world and those who are and those who will be, are one body and this one body is composed of the many members and is in the many*" in such a way that the local Church "*is part of the all-present Church and the body which consists of the Churches*"[2341] and "*people, are all those who hope in Christ and one Church, are those of Christ, although they are from different places*" according to the assurance of St Basil the Great.[2342]

St Augustine characterises the Church as being a Communion of men, gathered together from all nations in one flock, in the hearts of which God rules, and as His Kingdom founded upon the earth but perfected in Heaven. He calls her "*the City of God*" in which her members, who have passed away and who will be born, are moving ahead through time, and are identified as being in the Kingdom of Heaven.[2343] He also proclaims that the Temple of God is the Holy Church, which is Catholic, in Heaven and on

---

[2337] Ibid, *To Philadelphians,* Introduction, in Lightfoot, *Apostolic Fathers,* p. 106.

[2338] Ibid, *To Smyrnaeans,* Introduction, in Lightfoot, *Apostolic Fathers,* p. 110.

[2339] St Clement of Rome, *1st Corinthians,* in *B,* v. 1, pp, 31, 46 and 7.

[2340] St Irenaeus, *Heresies,* book I, ch. 10, §§ 1, 2, in Migne, *P.G.,* 7, 552, 553. Cf. Ibid, in Hadjephraimides, pp. 64-65.

[2341] St John Chrysostom, *To Ephesians,* Homily 10, § 1, in Montfaucon, v. 9, p. 86. Ibid, *To 1 Corinthians,* Homily 32, § 1, in Migne, *P.G.,* 61, 264.

[2342] St Basil, the Great, *Epist.* 161, in Migne, *P.G.,* 32, 629.

[2343] St Augustine, *De civitate Dei,* XVII, c. 1, in migne, *P.L.,* 41, 523.

earth.[2344] Elsewhere he teaches that the Church is all the people of God, from Abel to those who will be born in the last days and who will believe in Christ

St Epiphanius observed that this Communion is composed by the Holy Spirit through the members who are born in her and that *"the Church is born of one faith, born through the Holy Spirit."*[2345]

St John Chrysostom asks: *"How can the bride be His daughter? How can the daughter be His bride?"* He noted that according to the flesh this cannot be, for the bride is different to the daughter, but, he adds, *"for God both are one."* Consequently the Church is simultaneously daughter and bride of Christ, for *"He Regenerated her through Baptism, and He united her."* In addition, *" the Lord and Master and Father wanted to become her Bridegroom."* This birth of the Church is compared to the origin of Eve as follows: *"As the woman was made from the part of Adam received from his bones and his flesh, likewise we are members of the Master's Body, made from His Flesh and from His Bones."* Clarifying this opinion, he adds that when Christ died on the Cross, *"one of the soldiers came and pierced His Side with a spear, and immediately Blood and Water came out.[2346] And from that Blood and Water the whole Church was born."* For all those faithful of whom the Church consists, *"are born through the Water of Baptism and are nourished through His Blood."* As from Adam when he was asleep, *"the woman was made; likewise when Christ died, the Church was formed from His Side."*[2347]

Describing the moral qualifications of the Church as the Bride of Christ, he observed the Truth of Him finding her to be *"unclean and unformed and worthless, with spot, enslaved, naked, dragged in blood"*[2348] before Baptism but *"He washes her from her uncleanness"* and He *"not only decorated her, but He made her glorious"*[2349] in Baptism. Thus *"He presented the Church to Himself, not having spot or wrinkle",*[2350] as a *"chaste virgin."*[2351] He *"called her a bride, being a chaste virgin through the Doctrines and true morals."* And with this new and strange phenonomen it was noted that although *"in the world the virgins remain before the wedding, after the wedding they are not anymore, but here"* those who are

---

[2344] Ibid, *Enchiridion,* 56, in migne, *P.L.,* 40, 259.

[2345] St Epiphanius, in Migne, 42, 781.

[2346] Cf. John 19:34.

[2347] St John Chrysostom, *Praise to Maximus,* § 3, in Migne, *P.G.,* 55, 200. Ibid, Migne, *P.G.,* 51, 229.

[2348] Ibid, *To Psalm 5,* § 2, in Migne, *P.G.,* 55, 63.

[2349] Cf. Ephes. 5:26.

[2350] Cf. Ephes. 5:27.

[2351] 2 Corinth. 11:2.

incorporated in the Church, *"even if they are not virgins before this Wedding, after this Wedding, they become virgins"* through this spiritual rebirth. *"For all the births from a father and a mother have the rebirth externally, but are Buried with Christ[2352] in an unutterable way."[2353]* *"The Church being a harlot, became a virgin."[2354]*

Question 294: Is the Church foretold by the Old Testament?

Answer: According to Holy Scripture and the Teachings of the Holy Fathers of the Orthodox Church, the Ecclesia appears to us to be a community of men who are united to one another through True Faith and Hope according to the calling of God by the Holy Spirit.[2355] It is not a social unity and a living together. It is a Divine Institute, which is the result of the supernatural Saving Action of the Holy Spirit. Surpassing the boundaries of the natural life of man, the Church opposes the society of evil men or the kingdom of darkness and the power of *"the ruler of this age."* It is distinguished clearly from other communities (marriage, family, state, tribe, e.t.c.), of which she does not doubt their rights and authority, seeking only to Sanctify them, being superior to them and as a matter of Faith consisting of the new Creation in Christ.

The day of the birth of the Church can be said to be the Day of Pentecost when the Holy Spirit descended upon the Holy Apostles and the first Disciples as the other *"Helper,"[2356]* *"the Holy Spirit Whom the Father will send"[2357]* and Who *"may abide with you forever,"[2358]* thus proving that the Church is the Teacher of the Truth and Treasury of Divine Grace.

The first appearance of the Church was in Jesus Christ, the Son of God, when, through His first preaching, He spoke of the coming of *"the Kingdom of Heaven,"[2359]* which was to be established on earth through His Church. Consequently the first disciples were gathered around Him and were then taught by Him so that they would be not only the first foundation stones of His Church but also the successors to His Work, continuing the

---

[2352] Cf. Rom. 6:4. Col. 2:12.

[2353] Origen, *Fragment 45, to John,* in **B,** v. 12, p. 363. St John Chrysostom, *To 2 Corinthians,* Homily 23, § 1, in Montfaucon, v. 10, p. 704. Theodoretus, *To Ephesians 5:30,* in Migne, *P.G.,* 66, 920. Kritopoulos, ch. VII, in Karmeris, *The dogmatics*, v. II, p. 528.

[2354] St John Chrysostom, *When Eutropius was found out of the Church,* §§ 6-7, in Migne, *P.G.,* 52, 402.

[2355] Cf. Evdokimov, *Orthodoxia,* pp. 171-172.

[2356] John 14:16.

[2357] John 14:26.

[2358] John 14:16.

[2359] Matth. 4:17.

spreading and establishing of the Divine Structure of God: the Ecclesia. In His prayer to His Father, Christ our Lord witnesses that they were given to Him by God the Father[2360] and He preserved them so that *"none of them were lost, except the son of perdition* (Judas Iscariot)."[2361] Although for a moment the Shepherd was stricken and the sheep were scattered,[2362] they were gathered once again in His Name and tarried *"in the city of Jerusalem until they were endued with the Power from on High."*[2363]

Thus, the Ecclesia being seen in the light of history, appears as the Fruit of Christ's Appearance and, simultaneously, the undoubtable proof of His Work throughout the centuries, which He continues through His Disciples. Without any argument, Jesus Christ is not only the Lord of the Church Who owns her having bought her, He is also her Founder, having foretold of the Rock of True Faith upon which He would build His Church and against which *"the gates of Hades shall not prevail."*[2364] For this reason He prayed to His Father *"that all may be one,"*[2365] those who would believe in Him and of whom His Church would consist, preserving *"them from the evil one"*[2366] and making them all as *"one."*[2367] In addition, He gave them Laws and Commandments, according to which the Church is administered. He elected His successors to continue His Work and instituted the Holy Mysteries as a means of receiving the Saving Grace. Finally, He sent *"the Holy Spirit Who proceeds from the Father"*[2368] and Who created the Birthday of the Church, giving Life to her members through the *"rivers of Living Water,"*[2369] which inexhaustibly pour forth from her.

Thus, the Ecclesia appears as a God-established Institution and Community. Existing as a model in the Old Testament[2370] and as forerunner of the God-ruled people of Israel, she appears to be from the beginning, proclaimed by the Prophets as a Kingdom, which *"the God of the Heaven shall set up, which shall never be destroyed." "It shall stand for ever"*[2371] and as *"the House of God shall be on the top of the mountains, it shall be exalted above the hills; and all nations shall come to it."*[2372] The Church

---

[2360] John 17:6.
[2361] John 17:12.
[2362] Mark 14:27.
[2363] Luke 24:49.
[2364] Matth. 16:18.
[2365] John 17:21.
[2366] John 17:15.
[2367] John 17:22.
[2368] John 16:26.
[2369] John 7:38.
[2370] St Cyril of Alexandria, *To Leviticus,* in Migne, *P.G.,* 69, 552.
[2371] Daniel 2:44.
[2372] Is. 2:2.

will "*rejoice*" when compared to the Old Testament Synagogue that was "*barren*" because, through the fulfillment of all the Prophecies and the Old Testament types of Jesus Christ her Founder, she will appear under a different form bearing Fruit, "*for more are the children of the desolate than of her that has a husband.*"[2373]

We must never forget the essential differences between the Ecclesia of the New Testament (the Orthodox Church) and those of the Old Testament (the Synagogue). The Old Testament Church was aiming, as God-ruled, to achieve political goals, being mixed with civil authorities while the Church of the New Testament, which "*is not of this world, but*"[2374]which is a Heavenly Kingdom[2375]although it acts in the world, looks forward to supernatural Goals (the Deification of man) by the use of supernatural means (Holy Mysteries). Also the Church of the Old Testament was purely Judaic, in which the boundaries of religion and nationality were mixed, in contrast to the Catholicity (Universal nature) of the New Testament Church. In the Old Testament Church the members were incorporated by birth and origin, whereas in the New Testament Church of Christ, those who believe and are baptised, are incorporated through Faith and Baptism, becoming the new Creation by the Operation of the Holy Spirit from Above. In the Judaic Church, inner cleanness and Sanctification were not achieved, as within the Orthodox Church of Christ, being the only Treasury of Divine Grace. The Judaic Church used symbols, types and shadowy pre-images of the future Reality and Truth, which is the Divine Revelation of Christ within his Orthodox Church. Thus, although the Ecclesia of the Old Testament is closely related to the Ecclesia of the New Testament, the two differ from one another.

Question 295: Is the Church a God-provided community?

Answer: The Orthodox Church is not only God-instituted, but also God-provided. Truly, in this God-instituted Community God is the One Who calls "*into the Fellowship of His Son.*"[2376] He "*chose for Himself*" those who will be the members of His Church. According to the assurance which He gave us that "*no one can come to Me unless the Father Who sent Me draws him,*"[2377] only he who will be "*guided by Him, reaches*" Christ and

---

[2373] Is. 54:1.
[2374] John 18:36.
[2375] Matth. 3:2; 5:3, 19, 20; 6:33; 7:21; 10:7; 11:11, 12; 13:11, 24, 31, 44, 47; 16:19; 18:1, 3, 4; 13:12; 20:1; 22:2; 23:13; 25:1.
[2376] 1 Corinth. 1:9.
[2377] John 6:44.

"believes in Him and not just anybody."[2378] Thus, regarding St Lydia, the seller of purple, *"the Lord opened her heart to heed the things spoken by Paul."*[2379] The new Creation and Spiritual Community consists of those who *"were called into the fellowship of the Son"*[2380] by the Father, and which is also fellowship with the Son of God, our Lord and Saviour Jesus Christ, for through faith in Christ and participation in the Holy Mysteries, we become partakers of the Sufferings, Life and Gifts of Christ.

Thus, in Baptism those who are incorporated in the Church *"have been united together in the likeness of Christ"* and certainly they *"also shall be in the likeness of His Resurrection."*[2381] And as Christ was raised from the dead and became a new Life, likewise the faithful enter a new kind of Life after Baptism, by which *"the sin has been put to death, justice has been raised, and the old way of life has been vanquished, living this new Angelic Life."*[2382] According to this, Christ becomes the Head of those who through faith and the Holy Mysteries are in Communion with Him, and are united to Him as one Body. For He is, on the one hand the centre of Life from whom the new Life *"descends as Spiritual Power touching every memberand the Spirit, being given to the members from the Head, acts from Above, being outpoured abundantly and touching all the members,"* while on the other hand, Christ is the centre of Guidance and Ruling, which holds all the members together.[2383] And from this, one understand the words of St Paul by which Christ is proclaimed as the *"Head of the Church"* [2384] Who gives accordingly to each member growth within Him *"in love,"* for *"from Him the whole body, joined and knit together by what every joint supplies, according to the effective working by which every part does its share, causes growth of the body for the edifying of itself in love."*[2385] As the Centre of unity, Christ is characterized as being *"the Cornerstone."*[2386] By this, Holy Scripture manifests that *"Christ is the One Who unites all"* in Him and by Whom the structure is upheld. *"And if you speak about the*

[2378] St John Chrysostom, *To Ephesians,* Homily 2, § 1, in Migne, *P.G.,* 62, 17. Zigabinos, *To John 6:37,* in Migne, *P.G.,* 129, 1248.

[2379] Acts 16:14.

[2380] 1 Corinth. 1:9.

[2381] Rom. 6:5.

[2382] St Photius, in Migne, *P.G.,* 118, 432. Diodorus, in Catenae Cramer. St John Chrysostom, *To Romans,* Homily 10, § 4, in Migne, *P.G.,* 60, 480. Theodorus Mopsuestias, in Migne, *P.G.,* 66, 800.

[2383] St Ecumenius, *To Ephesians 4:16,* in Migne, *P.G.,* 118, 1221. St John Chrysostom, *To Ephesians,* Homily 11, § 3, in Migne, *P.G.,* 62, 84. St Gregory of Nyssa, *About perfection,* § 10, in Migne, *P.G.,* 46, 273.

[2384] Ephes. 5:23.

[2385] Ephes. 4:15-16.

[2386] Ephes. 2:20. 1 Peter 2:6.

floor, and if you speak about the walls, and if speak about whatever else, He is the One Who upholds everything."[2387]

This Newness of Life is granted to the members of the Church "*from God through Christ in the Holy Spirit.*"[2388] Hence, St John Chrysostom proclaims, "*if the Spirit was not present, the Church would not exist; if the Church exists, it is obvious, that the Spirit is present.*" "*Before the Cross the Spirit was not given, because the world was in sin and there was no reconciliation*" but immediately after the Lord's Ascension, the Spirit was sent, Who is the Life-giving Power and Soul of the Church as well as the Creator of the Relationship within her. Thus, a greater Relationship than that of the flesh is created, by which the different nations become one Body, united "*into one Christ being joined by the Spirit.*"[2389]

Question 296: Do the "c*alled to be Saints*" composes the Church?

Answer: The faithful of whom the Church consists, are according to St Paul, "*called to be Saints.*"[2390] They are Saints because of their Calling by God, and by which they were separated from the rest of the people. Having received the Communion of the Holy Spirit, they were dedicated to God. Others, too, are called "*Saints by Faith and Life*" or "*by Faith alone, as dedicated to God only by Faith.*"[2391] Obviously there are also sinners within the Church, because our Lord and Saviour Jesus Christ, the Son of God, compared the Kingdom of Heaven to the Parable of the Dragnet[2392] that was "*cast into the sea and gathered some of every kind,*"[2393] in order to expose the various human intentions and differences.[2394] Hence St John Chrysostom observed that St Paul called us "*Saints and spotless before Him,*" distinguishing between the Holy and spotless in order to teach that "*the Saint is he who participates in the faith, spotless is he who leads a clean life.*"[2395] Likewise Origen correctly perceived that "*many of the*

[2387] St John Chrysostom, *To Ephesians,* Homily 6, § 1, in Migne, *P.G.,* 62, 44.

[2388] St Basil the Great, *Against Eunomius,* book III, 4, in Migne, *P.G.,* 29, 664. St John Chrysostom, *To 1 Corinthians,* Homily 30, § 1, in Migne, *P.G.,* 61, 650. St Basil the Great, *Epist.* 133, in Migne, *P.G.,*32, 569.

[2389] St John Chrysostom, *To the holy Pentecost,* Homily 1, § 4, in Migne, *P.G.,* 50, 457,458, 459, 463. Ibid, *To Ephesians,* Homily 9, § 3; Homily 1, § 4 in Migne, *P.G.,* 62, 72 and 15.

[2390] Rom. 1:7. 1 Corinth. 1:2, 24.

[2391] Zigabinos, *To John 6:37,* in Migne, *P.G.,* 129, 1248. Kalogeras, *Maria,* I, p. 9.

[2392] Matth. 13:47-50.

[2393] Matth. 13:47.

[2394] Origen, in *B,* v. 13, p. 21.

[2395] St John Chrysostom, *To John 28:13*, in Migne, *P.G.,* 14, 712.

sinners relate to Jesus as their Lord and in them there is the Holy Spirit."[2396]

It is the general belief of all Churches that in the Community of Saints, there are also unworthy Priests who act for the benefit of the members of Christ, since through them the Holy Mysteries are celebrated and the faithful are Sanctified. Likewise, sinful preachers can use the Word of God to draw new members. Although the Scribes and Pharisees "*were corrupted,*" our Lord did "*not remove them from their honourbut gave them the authority, although evil,*" urging the Jews "*to observe and to do whatever they tell to observe, that they should observe and do.*"[2397]

Question 297: Can the incorrigible members be cut off from the Church?

Answer: Although the Church, as the Body of Christ, is the extreme expression of God's Love for man, there are some limits that, when exceeded, cause a sinner to be cut off from the Community of the Church, alienating himself from the Life and Salvation, which is poured forth from her. Thus, the rebellious and the defectors, who through their own renouncement, "*have trampled the Son of God underfoot, countered the Blood of the Covenant,*" the Blood of Christ, by which they were "*Sanctified,*" considering it "*a common thing*" and thus insulting "*the Spirit of Grace,*"[2398] which secures Salvation within the Church, outside of which there is no Salvation. They alienate themselves from Christ, His Community, the Church and as a result, break all connection with her.

On the other hand, the heretics who misinterpret the Doctrines of Christ and His Holy Apostles, although they may Teach from the True Gospel, are "*anathema*" ("*accursed*") and separated from our Lord and Saviour Jesus Christ, the Son of God. For St Paul teaches: "*even if we, or an Angel from Heaven, preach any other gospel to you than what we have preached to you, let him be accursed. As we have said before, so now I say again, if anyone preaches any other gospel to you than what you have received, let him be accursed.*"[2399] St John the Apostle, Evangelist and Theologian, forbade receiving anyone who comes "*and does not bring*" with them the True Doctrines. They must not be received in homes nor

---

[2396] Origen, in Trempelas, *Dogmatique,* v. II, p.329.
[2397] Matth. 23:3. St John Chrysostom, *To Matthew 23:2,* in Migne, *P.G.,* 28, 667. Cf. Karmeris, *The dogmatics,* v. II, pp. 755, 527, 566, 579 and 633.
[2398] Heb. 10:29. Zigabinos, *To John 6:37,* in Migne, *P.G.,* 129, 1248. Kalogeras, *Maria,* II, p. 422.
[2399] Gal. 1:8-9.

even greeted.[2400] St Paul actually commanded us, to *"reject a divisive man after the first and second admonition, knowing that such a person is warped and sinning, being self-condemned."*[2401]

The heretics, according to their error of faith and egoistic insistence on their false teachings, alienate themselves from *"the Life-giving Root, the Faith in Christ, and becoming dry, they are cast out. For, if we do not stay firm upon the foundation of the Apostles, we are like not having any foundation and will collapse."*[2402] Their plight could be like that which had threatened the Galatians who, wanting to return to circumcision, almost became *"estranged from Christ"* by attempting *"to be Justified by Law"* which would have caused them to have *"fallen from Grace."*[2403]

St Cyril of Alexandria proclaimed *"those who join together with the unholy heretics and participate in their ungodly sacrifices (prayers), have multiplied for themselves their sins, for they have sacrificed the lamb outside the Holy and Divine yard, which is the Church."*[2404]

The Holy Fathers place the schismatics parallel to the heretics. St Basil the Great excellently distinguishes the difference between heretics and schismatics by observing that *"heresies are those that threw away and changed the Faith; schisms are those which for ecclesiastical reasons and matters which are curable, divided themselves."*[2405] Or according to St Jeronymos, *"the heresy consists of the changing of the Doctrine, whereas the schism divides him (the schismatic) from the Church because of estrangement to the Bishop."*[2406]

St Ignatius the Theophorus of Antioch, actually warns us: *"Do not be misled, my brothers: if anyone follows a schismatic, he will not inherit the Kingdom of God.[2407] If anyone holds to alien views, he disassociates himself from the Passion."*[2408]

Finally, one falls into the division of the ecclesiastic body *"when he dares to perform unworthily to that body."* When someone falls into disgraceful offence and, regardless of public scandal, does not express any repentance, it is advisable that those who alienate themselves from the Christian way of Life, should be cut off from the Church. On one hand this

---

[2400] 2 John 10.

[2401] Tit. 3:10-11.

[2402] St Basil, the Great, *To Isaiah*, ch. I, § 19, in Migne, *P.G.,* 30, 149.

[2403] Gal. 5:4.

[2404] St Cyril of Alexandria, *To Hosea*, v. V, ch. 8, 12, in Migne, *P.G.,* 71, 209.

[2405] St Basil the Great, Canon I, in Trempelas, *Dogmatique,* v. II, p.333.

[2406] St Jeronymus, *In cap. III, Epist.ola ad Titum*, in migne, *P.L.,* 26, 633.

[2407] Cf. 1 Corinth. 6:9.

[2408] St Ignatius, *To Philadelphians*, 3, 3, in Lightfoot, *Apostolic Fathers,* p. 107.

is for pedagogic reasons, whereas on the other hand, it is in order for a small amount of yeast not to harm the whole dough.

Question 298: Are all the Saints of all time members of the Church?

Answer: Coming back to those Saints who were Called by Divine Grace, we observe that they are not restricted to a specific time period or generation. They are primarily *"fellow citizens with the Saints."*[2409] The Apostle uses the word *"Saints"* meaning *"not only those who through Grace, but those who* [were] *in the Law and before the Law."* He also refers to *"those around Abraham and those around Moses and those around Samuel."*[2410] The members of the Church are *"all those faithful who were and are and will be,"* not only those who live, but those who lived in the past and *"those before the Coming of Christ* [who] *pleased God"* and who, with all those in any generation, believed in Christ and placed their hopes on Him. *"They are one body, for they also loved Christ."*[2411] This is obvious when the Lord said: *"Abraham rejoiced to see My day; and he saw it and was glad"*[2412] and that Moses *"wrote about Me."*[2413]

The Militant Church consists of those members who are alive and who are called to *"endure hardship as good soldiers of Jesus Christ,"*[2414] and to *"run with endurance the race that is set before them, looking unto Jesus, the Author and Finisher of our faith,"*[2415] not forgetting that *"this Life is a struggle; a struggle against the sins and the desires and the thoughts which fight one another in us."*[2416] The Church Triumphant in Heaven consists of those who have passed away, being part of the same Church and having come from the Church Militant, which is mostly visible.

Thus, the Orthodox Church is a matter of pure and undefiled Faith (*Orthodoxia*), not only according to her nature and her invisible Head, but including the Life-giving Divine Principal. Each member of the Orthodox Church on earth must consider himself a member of the New Testament Church, which is the only Christian Body that has kept the Doctrines of Christ undefiled till this day. These members are also part of the Heavenly

---

[2409] Eph. 2:19. Cf. Mitsopoulos, *Themata,* pp. 239-241.
[2410] Zigabinos, *To John 6:37,* in Migne, *P.G.,* 129, 1248. Kalogeras, *Maria,* II, p. 21.
[2411] St John Chrysostom, *To Ephesians,* Homily 10, § 1, in Migne, *P.G.,* 62, 75. Dositheus of Jerusalem, *Confession,* ch. 11, p. 35.
[2412] John 8:56.
[2413] John 5:46.
[2414] 2 Tim. 2:3.
[2415] Heb. 12:1-2.
[2416] St Ecumenius, *To Hebrews,* in Migne, *P.G.,* 119, 424.

and Triumphant Church as well as *"fellow citizens with the Saints,"*[2417] the Patriarchs, the Prophets, the Apostles, the Teachers, the Hierarchs, the Martyrs, the Ascetics, and all the Just who, through their lives, pleased God throughout all generations.

Question 299: What are the visible and invisible aspects of the Church?

Answer: This Communion of the Faithful, the Church Militant, was distinguished by the Elders and faithful right from the beginning. Our Lord and Saviour Jesus Christ, the Son of God, chose His Apostles and Disciples not only to comprise the first members of the Church around Him, but that *"as the Father has sent Him, He also sends them."*[2418]

The faithful are united together mystically and internally with Christ. They are born together and grow together with the tares, not in a special or separate field, according to the Parable of the Wheat and the Tares[2419] and according to which our Lord and Saviour Jesus Christ, the Son of God, compared His Kingdom. They are the healthy members of the Mystical Body of the Church, not known by the world but by God, for *"the Lord knows those who are His."*[2420]

The Saints do not comprise a special and invisible Church, but act within the visible Church, being detached from their old way of life and knowing Christ from within the Church. By means of the Holy Mysteries they receive Life and remain inseparable with her forever. In addition to this, these Elect and spotless, as long as they live here on earth, are visible members of the Church. The Mystical Communion with Christ and the other members is manifested visibly, as they come to personal Communion with one another, encouraging each other in the faith, nourished by the Divine Word of the Readings, hearing the Preaching, and generally displaying the Life of Christ through their own lives and actions within the Church. Nevertheless, they remain unknown to the world and even to the members of the Church. Only God, Who knows *"those who are His,"* knows who and how many they are.

We must never forget that the Church is not only visible, but also invisible. In the visible aspect human nature prevails while the invisible aspect consists of her Divine establishment and Life. In the inseparable union of the invisible and visible nature of the Church one can observe her God-Man nature that reminds us of the supernatural Union of the two

---

[2417] Ephes. 2:19.
[2418] John 20:21.
[2419] Matth. 13:24-30.
[2420] 2 Tim. 2:19.

Natures - Divine and human - in the one Person of Jesus Christ, Who is the unique God-Man, the invisible Head of the Church.

Consequently, no one can deny that within the Church there is the invisible aspect that gives Life without which she cannot exist, nor can her humanity receive Life and reach Deification (*Theosis*). This invisible Source is the Head of the Church, our Lord and Saviour Jesus Christ, the Son of God, and the Divine Grace which gives Life to her, as well as her invisible part that is in Heaven. We look up to our Head in Heaven and His Life-giving Grace, to His Eternal Plan of Salvation, which existed as the invisible part of the Church in Heaven before the creation of this visible world.

Visible and invisible, Divine and human nature are indivisibly united in the Church, just as the soul is united with its flesh, giving life to the human body, whereas the separation of the soul brings death. The invisible or internal aspect of the Church is the Mystical Body of our Saviour, by which, although He is in Heaven, the Incarnation and His dwelling on earth is extended, continuing His Work of Salvation amongst all human generations through the Holy Spirit and outpouring of the Gifts from His Sacrifice on the Cross. The visible or external side of the Church is the Community of men who confess Jesus Christ as their Lord and Saviour, having His Teachings that consist of the Divine Institution as their life style, which the Lord made as the unique Treasury of Grace and infallible Guardian, Interpreter and Teacher of the Truth revealed by Him.

Question 300: What is the definition of the Church?

Answer: According to the above, the definition of the Church must stress both the external and visible as well as the internal and invisible aspects. The Church is not simply a human institution, but is Divine in origin. Neither is she an unorganized society, having appointed administrators who, through the laying on of hands, continue the Work of Salvation of our Lord. As the Body of Christ she is governed by her Divine Head and receives Life from the Life-giving Holy Spirit, uniting within her those who believe and accept the Truth, the Newness of Life in Christ and leading the whole world to Salvation.

"The Church is the Body of Christ, she is the continuous Pentecost, she is the form of the Holy Trinity, the absolute Church of the three Divine Persons."[2421]

[2421] Evdokimov, *Orthodoxia*, p. 165.

"The Church is within the present world, but she is not of the present world. She is a Divine Community, the living from now of 'the future age.' For this reason the Life within the Church bears a completely new dimension and a new character, 'repentance,' the new valuation of the principals. The Mystery of the Church relies on being the 'Church of those who repent and the Church of those who where lost,' but simultaneously it is a Communion of Saints and a Communion of sinners with the 'Holy,' deified participation with the only 'Holy One.'"[2422]

Therefore we can define the Church as the Divine Community of all generations, from Adam till the end of this age, the God-called men who are united by the same True Faith and through the Communion of the same Divine Mysteries, under the one Head of our Lord and Saviour Jesus Christ, the Incarnated Son and Word of God, in one moral Body, visible and invisible, who are administrated and ruled by Clergymen of Apostolic Succession established by the Lord, and continuing the Work of Salvation of our Lord, under the Guidance of the Holy Spirit, until His Second glorious Coming.[2423]

Question 301: Is the Church an institution of Salvation?

Answer: The Orthodox Church is not simply a Community of God-called Faithful who are Baptised, but also a God-established Institution of Salvation.[2424]. As the Institution of Salvation she transmits the Light of the Holy Gospel; she is the pillar and ground of the Truth remaining always indestructible and infallible; she pours the Gifts forth from the Cross to the world, being the Treasury of Divine Grace. Since the Church is the Mystical Body of our Lord and Saviour Jesus Christ, the Son of God, He continues the Work of Salvation after His Ascension into Heaven through her in the entire world, uniting His Church and being in the midst of her *"always, even to the end of the age."*[2425] It is natural to accept that the Church lives and seeks the same goals as her Founder.[2426] This stems from the authority with which the Resurrected Lord authorized His Holy Apostles, sending them into the world as He was sent by His Father[2427] and giving them the same Work, establishing them as His successors. He

---

[2422] Evdokimov, *Orthodoxia,* p. 195.
[2423] Trempelas, *Dogmatique,* v. II, p. 340.
[2424] Cf. Damalas, *Catechesis,* p. 65. Dositheus, *Confession,* ch. 9, p. 32. Mitsopoulos, *Themata,* pp. 281-282.
[2425] Matth. 28:20.
[2426] Androutsos, *Symbolique*, p. 75. Karmeris, *Synopsis,* p. 79-80, 83.
[2427] Cf. John 17:18, 20.

clearly stated that *"he who hears you hears Me, he who rejects you rejects Me, and he who rejects Me rejects Him Who sent Me."*[2428] In addition to this, He gave them the Authority to forgive and bind sins[2429] but to those who refuse to hear the Church, they must be regarded *"like a heathen and a tax collector."*[2430] Even the Holy Apostles were conscious of their Mission, that they were *"servants of Christ and stewards of the Mysteries of God,"*[2431] *"ambassadors for Christ,"*[2432] *"interceding as though pleading to God through them"*[2433] and calling all men to reconcile with Him.

It is obvious that, if the internal and external aspects of the Church are united together inseparably, the terms *"Institution of Salvation"* and *"Community of Faithful in the Church"* are identical. But, as the Head of the Church was first, before the Church, afterwards coming into existence and her Body being completed throughout the ages, likewise the whole Body of the Church is first the Institution of Salvation and then the Community of Faithful. As the Institution of Salvation, she precedes the Community that is founded, strengthened and spread through Preaching and the Holy Mysteries, which are the Actions of the Holy Spirit celebrated in the Orthodox Church and by her being the Divine Institution.

The God-given Authority of the Church is because *"God gave to the Church Apostles, Prophets, Teachers and the Catholic Action of the Holy Spirit. Therefore, wherever the Church is, there the Spirit of God is and wherever the Spirit of God, there the Church and all the Grace. The Spirit is the Truth."*[2434] Precisely because the Holy Spirit dwells within the Church, she shows the only way to Salvation since she was entrusted with the Light and Wisdom of God, by which she saves all men.[2435]

Consequently, in order for man to achieve Salvation in Christ, he must belong to the Canonical Church that Jesus Christ established and which maintains the fullness of His Truth and the Apostolic Tradition undefiled throughout the centuries. This Church of the New Testament is only the Orthodox Church. All other Christian denominations have alienated themselves from the Truth, twisted the Teachings of the Holy Gospel to fit their own heretical teachings, and, by renouncing Apostolic Tradition, they

---

[2428] Luke 10:16.

[2429] Cf. Matth. 16:19; 18:18. John 20:23.

[2430] Matth. 18:17.

[2431] 1 Corinth. 4:1.

[2432] 2 Corinth. 5:20.

[2433] St John Chrysostom, *To 2 Corinthians,* Homily 11, § 3, in Montfaucon, v. 10, p. 607.

[2434] St Irenaeus, *Heresies,* book III, ch. 24, § 1, in Migne, *P.G.,* 7, 966. Cf. Ibid, in Hadjephraimides, p. 258.

[2435] St Irenaeus, *Heresies,* book V, ch. 20, in Migne, *P.G.,* 7, 1177. Cf. Ibid, in Hadjephraimides, pp. 394-395.

restrict the Divine Revelation only to the written word of Holy Scripture. Thus, they cannot be the Church of the New Testament, but rather man-made institutions where there can be neither Salvation nor Sanctification, as a result of being alienated from the Truth.

Only in the All-Wisdom of God Who knows the secrets of the hearts of all men and Who searches all minds and souls, can find ways, indescribable to our knowledge, to save a heretic or schismatic or anyone who is outside the Church but who out of good will, followed His Commandments as they were taught to them. Yet again we cannot say anything more on this matter for we have nothing in Holy Scripture pertaining to it and we cannot take the responsibility of expressing any opinion concerning the condemnation of others. God wants everyone to be Saved and to come to the Knowledge of Truth. However, if heresy and schism or unbelief separates man from the True God, then who are we to say what God should do or should not to do? Everyone must consider being able to stand on that Day of Judgement before Christ and give an account of his deeds, whether good or evil. We must be active Orthodox Christians, in all Holiness giving the good example to unbelievers so that they too come to the True Faith. In this way we will please God.

CHAPTER TWO
THE ATTRIBUTES OF THE CHURCH

Question 302: What do we mean that the Church is One?

Answer: The Eastern Orthodox Church is One because of her unity to her Head and to the Holy Spirit Who gives Life and unites her, as well as being One in the Faith and Hope of those members of whom she is composed in the unity of Peace and Love. These are inseparable and unique, One Moral Body, One Spiritual House, One Undivided Kingdom.[2436]

This unity of the Orthodox Church is stressed by our Lord and Saviour Jesus Christ, the Son of God Who proclaimed, *"and other sheep I have which are not of this fold; them also I must bring, and they will hear My Voice; and there will be one Flock and one Shepherd."*[2437] He assures us that He is *"the True Vine"*[2438] with which every faithful is united inseparably as branches that receive Life from Him. In addition to this, He beseeches

---

[2436] Cf. Plato of Moscow, *Orthodox Teaching*, pp. 134-137. Evdokimov, *Orthodoxia*, pp. 175-179. Frangopoulos, *Christian Faith*, pp. 181-182. Mitsopoulos, *Themata*, pp. 246-248. Kefalas, *Catechesis*, p. 104.
[2437] John 10:16.
[2438] John 15:1.

the Heavenly Father in His prayer not only for His Apostles, *"but also for those who will believe in Him through their word; that they all may be one, as Thou, Father, art in Me, and I in Thee; that they also may be one in Us."*[2439]

St Paul presents this unity of the Church by using three images. Firstly, by referring to the Church as the *"Body of Christ,"*[2440] he manifests the inseparable unity between the members to one another and to the Lord Who is the Spiritual Head of the Church.[2441] Finally, St Paul calls the Church *"the House of God"*[2442] and *"the Temple of God"*[2443] in which God dwells. St Peter refers to Christ as being *"a Living Stone"* and the faithful as *"living stones"* that *"are being built up"* into *"a Spiritual House."*[2444]

This unity of the Orthodox Church,[2445] which presents her as being *"One,"* regardless of her numerous members and the various local churches, is her essential Attribute that distinguishes her from all other religious communities. The Lord had precisely this Power in mind when praying to His Father *"that they all may be one in Us, that the world may believe that Thou sent Me."*[2446] In reality, the unity in One of the many is a Miracle that no man can perform. Only God can do so. Hence the Church is for the entire world even though she is separated in many places. She remains One for our Lord unites all the faithful. Thus the Church in a distant area is still part of the all-present Church and Body of Him Who unites all.[2447] As we mentioned before, the Lord is the one Head of the Body of the Church, whereas each individual is separate. He is the One Who gives Life and unites all the members, creating one God-bearing Organism, living harmoniously together and progressing with one Mind.

But the Holy Spirit Who Regenerates each faithful, is one and for this reason He was given to them, to unite their different ways.[2448] Additionally there is one Hope to which we have been called and one God the Father of all Who called us. There is also one Faith that unites in one way of thinking and in one Confession for all faithful as well as one Baptism that all members of Christ receive; one Bread of Eucharist, by

---

[2439] John 17:20-21.
[2440] Ephes. 1:22-23; 5:23. Col. 1:18; 2:19. 1 Corinth. 12:27.
[2441] 2 Corinth. 11:2. Ephes. 5:30-32.
[2442] 1 Tim. 3:15.
[2443] 1 Corinth. 3:16.
[2444] 1 Peter 2:4, 5.
[2445] Cf. Evdokimov, *Orthodoxia*, pp. 211-212.
[2446] John 17:21.
[2447] St John Chrysostom, *To 1 Corinthians*, Homily 1,§ 1; and Homily 32, § 1, in Migne, *P.G.*, 61, 3 and 264.
[2448] Ibid, *To Ephesians*, Homily 9,§ 3, in Migne, *P.G.*, 62, 72.

which everyone is nourished and incorporated in the one Redeemer.[2449] All *"though many, are one Bread and one Body; for we all partake of that one Bread"*[2450] and for this reason we become the Body of Christ; not many bodies, but one Body. For as the Bread is composed of many smaller elements but united as one, in a similar manner the many are united in one Body in Christ[2451]

The unity that is created by the one Head and the one Holy Spirit differentiates the unity of faith, and the unity of worship and participation in the same Mysteries, as well as the unity of the ecclesiastic communion and administration. Unity in the faith is expressed in the common Confession and Teachings of the Christian Truth. This is exalted by St Paul as the Fruit of the growth in Christ by which all Faithful.[2452]

The Orthodox Christian Faith is a unique, one and total organic Teaching, in which all the True Doctrines are united and based on one another so closely that the detachment of one places in danger the entire structure. Even Ecclesiastic History witnesses that the chief-heretics began their false-teachings from small things that they considered insignificant. As a result they fell into major errors that troubled the Church for many years or even centuries.

The unity in worship and participation in the Divine Mysteries refers mainly to the basis of the Doctrines within worship, which makes Baptism one[2453] and the Bread of the Eucharist one.[2454] Everyone is watered in the one Holy Spirit though these Mysteries. [2455] Since the basics are the same in worship, the small differences do not contradict one another.

Finally, the unity in the ecclesiastic community and administration is disturbed within the Church by men with their selfish egoism and personal interests. From these unbelievers begin the schisms and the catastrophic and disastrous divisions, which *"grow cold the love of many."*[2456] Those who are in error or heresy hold part of the Christian Truth but cannot proclaim that they are the incarnation of the One, Holy and Apostolic Church. The Orthodox Church is the true New Testament Church, which upholds the original Teachings and Apostolic Tradition undefiled and unchanged from the Day of Pentecost until this very momen

---

[2449] St John Chrysostom, *To Ephesians,* Homily 11, § 1, in Migne, *P.G.,* 62, 81.
[2450] 1 Corinth. 10:17.
[2451] St John Chrysostom, *To 1 Corinthians,* Homily 24, § 2, in Migne, *P.G.,* 61, 200.
[2452] Ephes. 4:14-16.
[2453] Ephes. 4:5.
[2454] 1 Corinth. 10:17.
[2455] 1 Corinth. 12:13.
[2456] Matth. 24:12. St John Chrysostom, *To Ephesians,* Homily 11, § 4, in Migne, *P.G.,* 62, 85.

Question 303: What do we mean that the Church is Holy?

Answer: If the unity of the Church is her essential Attribute, Holiness is her most precious Attribute, according to which she is the inexhaustible Source of Sanctification. The Church cleans and regenerates the polluted world and fulfils her Divine Destination. The Church is Holy first, because her invisible Head is by Nature Holy, pouring forth an unlimited Sanctification within Himself.[2457] God Who dwells in the Church is Holy and invites the faithful to come out from the sinful world and to become Holy[2458] as it is written: *"Be Holy for I Am Holy."*[2459] The Founder of the Church Who is her invisible Head, is He *"Whom the Father Sanctified"*[2460] and *"anointed with the Holy Spirit,"*[2461] *"the Holy Servant Jesus"*[2462] *"Who loved us and washed us from our sins in His own Blood,"*[2463] which He shed on the Cross *"that He might Sanctify and cleanse the Church with the washing of water by the Word, that He might present her to Himself a glorious Church, not having spot or wrinkle or any such thing, but that she should be Holy and without blemish."*[2464] In addition, the Holy Spirit Who gives Life to the Church, is Holy. The Gospel, too, is Holy and as such it should not be given to the *"dogs,"*[2465] because it contains the Word of God, which is *"Truth"*[2466] and Sanctifies those who hear and accept it.[2467] Holy is the prayer that Sanctifies and transmits Sanctification through the Holy Mysteries and through worship, especially through the Holy Mystery of Eucharist[2468]

The Orthodox Church is Holy because her members are *"partakers of the Heavenly calling"*[2469] by God for Heavenly things *"with a Holy Calling,"*[2470] which purifies and Sanctifies those who accept it and who separate themselves from the corrupted world, dedicating themselves to God. They are *"called to be Saints."*[2471] Through the Holy Mystery of

---

[2457] Mitsopoulos, *Themata,* pp. 248-250.

[2458] 2 Corinth. 6:16-18.

[2459] 1 Peter 1:16. Lev. 11:44, 45; 19:2; 20:7. Evdokimov, *Orthodoxia,* pp. 212-213.

[2460] John 11:36.

[2461] Acts 10:38.

[2462] Acts 4:27.

[2463] Rev. 1:5.

[2464] Ephes. 5:26-27.

[2465] Matth. 7:6.

[2466] John 17:17.

[2467] 1 Tim. 4:4-5.

[2468] Cf. Plato of Moscow, *Orthodox Teaching,* pp. 138-139. Kefalas, *Catechesis,* p. 105. Frangopoulos, *Christian Faith,* pp. 182-183. Mitsopoulos, *Themata,* p. 87.

[2469] Heb. 3:1.

[2470] 2 Tim. 1:9.

[2471] 1 Corinth. 1:2.

Baptism they *"are Sanctified in Christ Jesus,"*[2472] called to progress in Holiness and become unchangeably Holy. Hence our Lord and Saviour Jesus Christ compares His Church to *"dough,"*[2473] which changes everything slowly, signifying that the Sanctifying Power of the Church and her Teachings influence the sinful world *"uniting all in one Body and transferring it into a different kind of Life."*[2474] Christ generally calls His disciples *"light of the world"*[2475] and *"salt of the earth"*[2476] as *"receiving from Him the logical Power"* to correct *"the human nature which has fallen and to free those who are rotting."*[2477]

It is true that many members of the Church are also those who are not alive and active Orthodox Christians caught by the hearing of the Word,[2478] but, regardless of how many they are in number, they cannot pollute the Holiness of the Church. Also, through God's Divine Grace many of them have changed and turned from their evil ways, living a very Holy Life in Christ On the other hand, we have countless Holy men and women of all ages who became heroes of our Orthodox Christian Faith by upholding the True Faith in God or living a virtuous Life in Christ They are also those who lived with the fear of God, struggling against sin and ending their lives as unseen Saints. All generations have produced Saints and Holy men, Martyrs and Virgins. These are the Fruits of the Tree, which our Lord and Saviour Jesus Christ, the Son of God, has mentioned: *"You will know them by their fruits."*[2479]

In accordance to Holy Scripture, the Holy Fathers of the Orthodox Church proclaim the Holiness of the Church. St Ignatius the Theophorus of Antioch spoke of the Church of Smyrna in Asia as being *".most worthy of God, bearing Holy things."*[2480]

Question 304: What do we mean that the Church is Catholic?

Answer: The internal and external Attributes of the Church, which is inseparably joined to her unity, is her catholicity.[2481] Characterizing the

---

[2472] 1 Corinth. 1:2.

[2473] Matth. 13:33.

[2474] St John Chrysostom, *To Matthew,* Homily 46, § 2, in Montfaucon, v. 7, p. 544. Zigabinos, *To Matthew,* in Migne, *P.G.,* 129, 412.

[2475] Matth. 5:14

[2476] Matth. 5:13.

[2477] St John Chrysostom, *To Matthew,* Homily 46, § 2, in Montfaucon, v. 7, p. 544.

[2478] Matth. 13:47.

[2479] Matth. 7:17, 20..

[2480] St Ignatius, *To Smyrnaeans,* Introduction, in Lightfoot, *Apostolic Fathers,* p. 110.

[2481] Cf. Evdokimov, *Orthodoxia,* pp. 213-215.

Church as "*catholic*" (not the schismatic Roman Catholic Church) we mean that she is able to spread throughout the entire world, to be accepted by all nations and tribes, regardless of their spoken tongue or colour of skin.[2482] The Church is expanding in time and place, so the word "*catholic*" manifests the Church as Eternal. Therefore this Attribute is external. Subsequently the term requires the inseparability of her unity because, if the churches in different places and nations do not consist of the One Church, it would be impossible for the Church to be "*catholic.*" So this Attribute is internal.[2483]

In Holy Scripture we do not find the term "*catholic*" although they proclaim its meaning. In the Old Testament it is foretold of the universal ("*catholic*") ruling of the Messiah Who will include all nations in His Kingdom. Although the God-governing Community was restricted only to the Israelites, the future Kingdom to come of the Messiah was to include all the nations of the world. The Promise given to the Patriarch Abraham determined very clearly that in his seed "*shall all the nations of the earth be blessed.*"[2484] This Promise was repeated to the Patriarchs Isaac[2485] and Jacob.[2486] King David and the Prophets projected the Kingdom of the Messiah expanding to "*the ends of the earth*"[2487] in order that He may "*rule over the nations*"[2488] and "*have dominion also from sea to sea, and from the river to the ends of the earth*"[2489] and that "*all men shall be blessed in Him; all nations shall call Him blessed.*"[2490] The Prophet Isaiah spoke of the "*mountain of the Lord,*" which "*shall be exalted above the hills*"[2491] and "*in Him shall the Gentiles trust,*"[2492] for He shall be "*a Light of the Gentiles*" and "*Salvation to the end of the earth.*"[2493] Nations that did not know Him "*shall call upon*" Him "*and people who are not acquainted with*" Him "*shall flee to Him for refuge.*"[2494] His Kingdom, "*from the rising of the sun even to the going down,*" shall be "*glorified among the Gentiles; and in*

[2482] Cf. Plato of Moscow, *Orthodox Teaching,* p. 139. Kefalas, *Catechesis,* p. 105. Fragkopoulos, *Christian Faith*, pp.183-185. Mitsopoulos, *Themata,* pp.87,250-252.
[2483] Androutsos, *Symbolique,* p. 73.
[2484] Gen. 22:18; 12:3; 18:18.
[2485] Gen. 26:4.
[2486] Gen. 28:14.
[2487] Psalm 2:8.
[2488] Psalm 21(22):28.
[2489] Psalm 71(72):8.
[2490] Psalm 71(72):17.
[2491] Is. 2:2.
[2492] Is. 11:10. Dan. 48:35.
[2493] Is. 49:6.
[2494] Is. 55:4, 5.

every place incense is offered to" His *"Name, and a pure offering"*: for His *"Name is great among the Gentiles."*[2495]

In the New Testament, before the Lord's Suffering, He foretold that the *"Gospel of the Kingdom will be preached in all the world as a witness to all the nations."*[2496] After His glorious Resurrection He commanded His Apostles to *"go therefore and make disciples of all the nations,"*[2497] *"beginning at Jerusalem."* They were to be His *"witnesses"* *"in Jerusalem, in all Judea and Samaria, and to the ends of the earth."*[2498] St Paul stated that the Holy Apostles literally *"received Grace and Apostleship for obedience to the faith among all nations"*[2499] and that 25 years after Christ's Resurrection their word *"has gone out to all the earth, and their words to the ends of the world."*[2500] He also guaranteed that when *"the fullness of the Gentiles has come in"* the Church, then *"all Israel will be saved."*[2501]

Thus the term *"catholic"* was used by Tertullian, and even by heretics, being adopted as the title of the members of the Church.[2502] However, according to St Cyprian it generally referred to all Christians who believe in the Orthodox Way.[2503] The term was used in ancient Confessions such as that which known as the *"Apostolic"* Creed, as well as in the *Catecheses* of St Cyril and the Creed of St Epiphanius, until it was adopted by the 1st Ecumenical Synod in Constantinople and incorporated into the Nicene Creed.

The meaning of the term is explained by St Cyril of Jerusalem who observed that the Church is called *"catholic because she is in all the world, from one end to the other,"* *"because she teaches universally and unfailingly all the Doctrines which are beneficial to men, about the visible and invisible things, Heavenly and earthly,"* and even more *"because all mankind submits to piety, rulers and those who being ruled, learned and citizens."* In other words the Church is called *"catholic"* mainly *"because of the length"* and *"the width of the world,"* in which she has expanded and also because *"of the mass of the nations which have submitted"* to her. The fullness of the necessary Truth of Salvation is preserved and proclaimed honestly and securely by the Church. The catholocity of the Church also means that she *"will not only, be spread throughout the world but also throughout all*

[2495] Mal. 1:11.

[2496] Matth. 24:14.

[2497] Matth. 28:19. Mark 16:15.

[2498] Acts. 1:8.

[2499] Rom. 1:5.

[2500] Rom. 10:18.

[2501] Rom. 11:25, 26.

[2502] Tertullian, *Praescr.*, 30, in migne, *P.L.*, 2, 48.

[2503] St Cyprian, *Epist.ola* 73, 2.

ages."[2504] In other words, the Church will remain forever, until the end of this age, as a Militant Church, continuously proclaiming, without interruption, the Holy Gospel of the Kingdom and expanding the Power of the Lord throughout the entire world. In the future then, she will be the Bride of the Heavenly Bridegroom, the Holy Jerusalem *"which will descend from Heaven from God"* to rule with her Bridegroom to the ages of ages.[2505]

This Eternal Might and Power of the Church was foretold by the Prophets who spoke of an *"everlasting Covenant"*[2506] between God and His people, as well as the Kingdom of the Messiah[2507] and His *"Kingdom shall never be destroyed"* and *"shall stand for ever."*[2508]

Our Lord and Saviour Jesus Christ, the Son of God, very clearly proclaimed that *"the gates of Hades shall not prevail against"*[2509] His Church, promising at the same time that He will send the *"Helper,"* *"the Spirit of Truth"*[2510] to them Who will remain with them *"always, even to the end of the age."*[2511] These Promises of the Lord reveal that the Militant Church will be Eternal and indestructible since the Lord and the Holy Spirit will remain forever with the faithful. This is also revealed by the Parables of the Wheat and Tares[2512] and the Dragnet.[2513] At the time of the Harvest, which is *"the end of this agethe tares will be gathered,"*[2514] and they will be separated from *"the good seeds."*[2515] Then *"the Son of Man will send out His Angels, and they will gather out of His Kingdom all things that offend, and those who practice lawlessness."*[2516] In the second Parable it is emphasized that *"at the end of the age the Angels will come forth, [and] separate the wicked from among the just."*[2517]

St John Chrysostom repeatedly referred to this subject and maintained that *"nothing is stronger than the Church,"* which is *"higher than Heaven and wider than the earth"* and *"she never ages but always flourishes."* Elsewhere the Holy Father proclaimed that the Church *"alone knows to*

[2504] St Cyril of Jerusalem, *Catechesis,* XVIII, § 23, in Migne, *P.G.,* 33, 1044. St John Chrysostom, *To Psalm 44(45),* § 13, in Migne, *P.G.,* 55, 203.
[2505] Rev. 21: 9-10.
[2506] Is. 55:3; 61:8. Jer. 39:40.
[2507] Is. 9:7
[2508] Daniel 2:44.
[2509] Matth. 16:18.
[2510] John 14:16, 17.
[2511] Matth. 28:20.
[2512] Matth. 13:37-43.
[2513] Matth. 13:47-50.
[2514] Matth. 13:40.
[2515] Matth. 13:37.
[2516] Matth. 13:41.
[2517] Matth. 13:49.

remain for ever" and "*she shall remain for ever.*" At other times he observed that the Church "*will spread throughout the ages, for her memory is immortal.*"[2518] Elsewhere he asked: "*By how many the Church was fought, but never defeated? How many tyrants? How many generals? How many kings*"? "*Learned men, powerful, fought in so many ways the new born Church, but they did not uproot her. But some who fought her were delivered up to silence and forgetfulness, she being fought, surpassed Heaven.*" "*For Heaven was established*" and "*it is easier to wipe out the sun rather than to vanquish the Church.*"[2519]

The internal reason for the Church's eternity and indestructibility is because she is the Body of Christ, for "*Jesus Christ is the same yesterday, today, and forever.*"[2520] The Church has our Lord Jesus as her Head and Founder[2521] and the Holy Spirit dwells within her, giving her Life and Sanctifying all her members. The Holy Spirit gives her the "*Power of indestructible Life.*" However, this does not mean that the faithful do not participate. By being made alive by the Head of the Church and watered by the Power of the Holy Spirit, they become cooperators with God in order to realise what He has Promised concerning the Church. Hence it is understandable how many facets of the Church consisting of the seven churches in Asia Minor, the Churches of Revelation or the Church in North Africa and so many other examples, were wiped out by unbelievers. Nevertheless, these enemies of Christ's Church did not prevail but instead they enriched the Triumphant Church in Heaven with Confessors of our Orthodox Christian Faith, glorifying her with the blood of new Martyrs.

Question 305: What do we mean that the Church is Apostolic?

Answer: Finally, the Orthodox Church is Apostolic.[2522] She is referred to as "*Apostolic*" because she remained throughout all centuries, until this very moment, just as the Holy Apostles founded her. She preserved undefiled and unchanged the Holy Apostles' Teachings of the Christian Faith, exactly as taught by them.[2523] The Orthodox Church has not broken the Apostolic Succession in the line of the Canonical Ordination of Bishops who were

---

[2518] St John Chrysostom, *When Eutropius was found outside the Church*, § 6, in Migne, *P.G.*, 52, 397. Ibid, *To Ephesians*, Homily 7, § 2; and *To Psalm 44(45)*, § 13, in Migne, *P.G.*, 55, 203.
[2519] St John Chrysostom, *To Isaiah*, Homily 4, § 2, in Migne, *P.G.*, 56, 121.
[2520] Heb. 13:8; 7:16.
[2521] 1 Corinth. 3:11. Heb. 13:8; 17:16. St Cyril of Alexandria, *To Isaiah*, book IV, II, in Migne, *P.G.*, 70, 968.
[2522] Cf. Evdokimov, *Orthodoxia*, pp. 219-223. Kefalas, *Catechesis*, p. 105. Mitsopoulos, *Themata*, pp. 87-88, 252-254. Frangopoulos, *Christian Faith*, pp. 185-186.
[2523] Plato of Moscow, *Orthodox Teaching*, p. 140.

Ordained and placed in the Church with the authority of the Holy Apostles, in order to administer the Holy Mysteries of God. In other words the Apostolic Succession of the Church is notable for the Apostolic Teachings that make the Church throughout the centuries the Voice of Christ and His Apostles, and through which today's Bishops and Priests in the One, Holy, Apostolic Orthodox Church descend in an unbroken line from the Holy Apostles.

This differentiation is only imaginary and not real because the Apostolic Succession can be disrupted or abolished, not only through non-canonical ordinations, as in the West when the Protestants renounced either the Priesthood itself or just the rank of the Bishop. By doing this they disrupted and broke the line of Apostolic Succession but also by drifting away from the original Apostolic Teachings, as it occurs with heretics.

St Basil the Great assures us that those who detach themselves from the Church because of heresy, do not have the Grace of the Holy Spirit with them anymore and therefore they can no longer serve her. Although the first heretics had been Ordained and thereby had received the Spiritual Gift according to Apostolic Succession, by breaking away from the One, Holy and Catholic Church *"they became laymen who do not have authority to Baptise, nor to Ordain, neither could they give the Grace of Holy Spirit from Whom they had fallen away."*[2524]

To preserve the Apostolic Succession truthfully, it is not sufficient to merely pass it down through Canonical Ordination of Priesthood by Canonical Successors of the Holy Apostles. It must co-exist with the Apostolic Teachings. Consequently, even if one of the Bishops or any of the Presbyters has Canonical Apostolic Succession, he falls away from it as soon as he deviates from the pure Apostolic Teachings. Both the preservation of Apostolic Teachings and Canonical Ordination are united internally and inseparably as they compose the Apostolic Succession. Apostolic Teaching is the basis of Apostolic Succession, whereas Canonical Ordination in the Church is the external characteristic, which assures that a local Orthodox church is part of the firstborn Church established by the Holy Apostles.

Question 306: What do we mean that the Church is the Infallible Keeper and Teacher of the Truth?

Answer: The Attribute of the Church as Apostolic is combined with the unity and the infallibility of the Church. Frankly, if the different Orthodox

---

[2524] St Basil the Great, *To Amphilochius,* Epist. 1,canon I, in Rallis-Potlis, *Syntagma,* v. 4, p. 90.

churches around the world are united to one another, consisting of the one Church of Christ, it is because *"the Church, although in all the world until the ends of the earth, received the True Faith from the Apostles and their disciples, carefully preserves the preaching of truth as though having one mouth."* *"The dialects of the world are different, but the power of the Tradition is one and the same."*[2525]   Thus the Orthodox Church remained from the beginning in the Apostolic Tradition and never changed her Apostolic nature, continuing as *"one"* *"first-born and truthful Church,"* *"the real ancient, in which are incorporated those who are by good intention just,"* and which *"the many heresies attempt to divide."*   Contrary to those who have turned to heresies, we (the Orthodox) who keep to the Apostolic Tradition, say that there is only one ancient and catholic Church, which unites in one faith, by the Will of God, those of different periods.[2526]

The Holy Apostles received the Teachings from the Lord, Who is the actual Truth and they, by God's Inspiration, preserved it and gave it to the Church, being *"the pillar and ground of the Truth."*[2527]   The Church developed this Truth and gave to it formalities, clarifying the Divine Revelation according to the needs of the faithful, never adding to or subtracting from it, but preserving it unchanged in its essence and remaining in the Teachings of the Holy Apostles. On these foundations the Orthodox Church is infallible as is evident in her protection and preservation of Apostolic Tradition, as a Covenant entrusted to her, *"not subtracting or decreasing,"* nor adding any human embellishments. She *"rightly divides the word of the Truth"*[2528] against any heretic who dares to doubt the pure Teachings according to the admonition: *"O Timothy!   Guard what was committed to your trust."*[2529]

The infallibility of the Orthodox Church does not rely on the revelation of new truths, that were not revealed by Christ or His Apostles, but on the infallible development, expression and transmission of the revealed Truths, which are the Treasures of the Covenant that were entrusted to the Church.   The Divine Enlightenment that preserves this infallibility, differentiates from the God-inspiration that motivated the Prophets and the Holy Apostles when they were writing their God-inspired books, and which compose the Canon of the Holy Scriptures.   This Covenant of the Divine Revelation was treasured within the Church and was

---

[2525] St Irenaeus, *Heresies,* book I, ch. 10, §§1, 2, in Migne, *P.G.,* 7, 549. Cf. Ibid, in Hadjephraimides, pp. 64-65.
[2526] Clement the Alexandrian, *Stromata*, VII, ch. XVII (298), in *B*, v. 8, p. 298.
[2527] Gal. 2:15. Cf. Frangopoulos, *Christian Faith*, pp. 186-187. Mitsopoulos, *Themata*, pp. 254-255.
[2528] 2 Tim. 2:15.
[2529] 1 Tim. 6:20.

preserved undefiled by her, being interpreted infallibly and remaining unchangeable.

This infallibility of the Church was assured by our Lord and Saviour Jesus Christ, the Son of God, when He promised His Holy Apostles that, through them and to the whole Church, He will be with them *"all the days till the end of this age."*[2530] He also promised to send the Holy Spirit to them, *"the Spirit of Truth, Who will teach and remind them of all things"*[2531] that the Lord said to them, and to guide them *"to all Truth."*[2532] These promises of the Lord are not irrelevant and the indestructibility and the immortality of the Church is based upon His assurance that *"the gates of Hades shall not prevail against"*[2533] her. How can it be possible for lies and errors to enter into a Divine and Eternal institution? How can the gates of Hades not prevail against the Church, if lies were to prevail within her? For this reason St Paul calls the Church *"the pillar and ground of the Truth.*[2534]

CHAPTER THREE
THE ORGANISATION OF THE CHURCH

Question 307: What is the special Order and Ministry of the Church?

Answer: According to the Holy Evangelists our Lord *"appointed twelve, that they might be with Him and that He might send them out to preach and to have power to heal sicknesses and to cast out demons."*[2535] Besides the twelve Apostles who composed the close circle, Christ *"appointed seventy others also, and sent them two by two before His face into every city and place where He Himself was about to go."*[2536]

To the Twelve and to all those who were in the upper room the Lord, for the first time after His Resurrection from the dead, said: *"Peace to you! As the Father has sent Me, I also send you."*[2537] *"Receive the Holy Spirit. If you forgive the sins of any, they are forgiven them; if you retain the sins of any, they are retained."*[2538] Before His Ascension into Heaven He gave the Command: *"Go therefore and make disciples of all the nations, Baptizing them in the Name of the Father and of the Son and of the Holy Spirit,*

[2530] Matth. 28:20.
[2531] John 14:26.
[2532] John 16:13.
[2533] Matth. 16:18.
[2534] Gal. 2:15.
[2535] Mark 3:14-15. Cf. Matth. 10:1-4 and Luke 6:12-16.
[2536] Luke 10:1.
[2537] John 20:21.
[2538] John 20:22-23.

teaching them to observe all things that I have Commanded you; and lo I Am with you always, even to the end of the age,"[2539] signifying that the Commandment and the Authority given to the Holy Apostles will remain within the Church forever. Because the Holy Apostles would also pass away from this life, St Paul assured that the Lord gave to the Church *"some Apostles, some Prophets, some Evangelists, and some Pastors and Teachers, for equipping of the Saints for the work of ministry, for edifying of the Body of Christ."*[2540]

The Holy Apostles who received the Command and the Authority of the Ministry within the Church that was established by Divine Right directly from Christ and afterwards was passed down to the hierarchy, believed that *"through Him we have received Grace and Apostleship for obedience to the Faith among all nations for His Name,"*[2541] as being *"servants of Christ and stewards of the Mysteries of God"*[2542] and as receiving from Him *"the ministry of reconciliation."*[2543] Practising according to the Lord's Command the Authority that was given to them, they *"went out and preached everywhere,"*[2544] fixing by the Inspiration of the Holy Spirit, laws and orders for the faithful, which referred to the keeping of Mosaic Law,[2545] ecclesiastic worship[2546] and the living together of married couples,[2547] etc. They imposed disciplinary authority,[2548] performed the Divine Mysteries[2549] and, through the laying on of the hands, bestowed the *charismata* of the Holy Spirit and the authority of ecclesiastic *diakonia*.[2550] Thus, it is witnessed by the ancient practice of the Church that *"God has appointed these in the church: first Apostles, second Prophets, third Teachers, after that Miracles, then Gifts of healing, helps, administrations, varieties of tongues"*[2551] and gave diverse other Gifts, Ministries and activities.[2552] Right from the beginning a special order was established to practice throughout all future generations the threefold Office of Christ, Who, being the Head of the Church, gives her this Authority.

[2539] Matth. 28:19-20.
[2540] Ephes. 4:11-12.
[2541] Rom. 1:5.
[2542] 1 Corinth. 4:1.
[2543] 2 Corinth. 5:18.
[2544] Mark 16:20.
[2545] Acts 15:28.
[2546] 1 Corinth. 14:26-34.
[2547] 1 Corinth. 7:2-16.
[2548] 1 Corinth. 5:3-5. 2 Corinth. 13:10.
[2549] Acts 2:41, 42, 46; 20:7. 1 Corinth. 1:14, 17. Acts 8:15.
[2550] Acts 6:6; 14:23. 1 Tim. 1:14. 2 Tim. 1:6.
[2551] 1 Corinth. 13:28.
[2552] 1 Corinth. 12:4, 5, 6.

Question 308: Is there equality in the special Order and Ministry?

Answer: In the Orthodox Church the Order of Priesthood is not a special separate body from that of laymen. This differentiation is by *"the law of equality"* and for the purpose that both the ruler and the subject *"be placed and mixed together, and that which is inferior and that which is superior, to be as one member"* of the same Body *"and by the harmony of the Spirit to be reconciled and joined in one perfect Body, worthy of Christ Who is our Head."*[2553] This union, in one inseparable and unified Body of rulers and subjects, is the main goal of the establishment of this special Order in the Church. It also gives a special nature to the ecclesiastic authority, creating equality among all the members of the Church, because all are members of the mystical Body of Christ[2554]

According to St John Chrysostom, in the Church *"there is neither typhus of the rulers nor servility of the subjects, but a spiritual principal, which overrules this, to seek the most hardworking"* *"and not to seek more honours."* Under no circumstances must the subjects, and even more importantly, the rulers, forget that *"as one house must the Church live, as one Body to dispose all; as the Baptism is one."* The rulers and for the subjects there is *"one table,"* at which, with equal rights, both sit, *"and one Source"* which waters both, *"and one Creation and one Father."*[2555] Determining elsewhere the boundaries of the authority of the Elders upon the faithful, he proclaimed what St Paul said: *"Not that we have dominion over your faith, but are fellow workers for your joy; for by faith you stand."*[2556] He who gives advice speaks from his own experience without enforcing his opinion upon the one who listens but leaves him to be the ruler of his choice of what he has heard. He then urges the rulers to avoid disregarding *"those who advise, whether they are from the subjects, or from the poor,"* nor to demand those things which they, as rulers, introduce, *"those completely to hold,"* nor to say: *"Why are you calling me for advice, since you do not listen to what I say? For these words are not of an advisor but of a tyrant."*[2557]

All despotic and tyrannical inclinations must be completely avoided as alien to the pure ecclesiastical Authority that the Lord established. It is not only manifested by His words that strongly distinguished between the rulers

---

[2553] St Gregory of Nyssa, *Homily* 32, § 11, in Migne, *P.G.,* 36, 185. Ibid, *2 Apologetic,* § 3, in Migne, *P.G.,* 35, 409.

[2554] Cf. Mitsopoulos, *Themata,* pp. 263-264.

[2555] St John Chrysostom, *Homily* 18, § 3, in Migne, *P.G.,* 61, 527-528.

[2556] 2 Corinth. 1:24.

[2557] St John Chrysostom, *To Ephesians,* Homily 11, § 5, in Migne, *P.G.,* 62, 87.

of the world and the Apostles as rulers in the Church, proclaiming that *"whoever desires to become great among you, let him be your servant. And whoever desires to be first among you, let him be your slave."*[2558] It was also dignified by the example which the Lord Himself made by washing the feet of His Apostles [2559] and thereby teaching them that in exercising their authority, they should be as servants to those whom they would serve.[2560] St Paul characterising the nature of Apostleship proclaims: *"Let a man so consider us as servants of Christ and stewards of the Mysteries of God"*[2561] and *"ourselves as your bondservants for Jesus' sake."*[2562] He also urges all saying: *"Therefore let no one boast in men. For all things are yours: whether Paul or Apollos or Cephas, or the world or life or death, or things present or things to come – all are yours."*[2563] By the use of the expression *"all are yours,"* he abolishes the typhus (pride) of the teachers. The Apostles were obliged to the faithful, for they became Teachers and Apostles because of them, having received the Grace of Apostleship. By using the phrase *"stewards of the Mysteries of God,"* he draws the attention of each one who is in the ecclesiastic *d i a k o n i a*, *"not to demand as a despot, but to administrate as a good steward. Because the steward is to administrate well the things; and not to act as a despot, but on the contrary to be a despot of his own."* The assurance that the Apostles were *"servants of Christ"* is proclaimed by the Apostle Paul as he is *"a minister"*[2564] and *"a bondservant"*[2565] to those who accept the Gospel.[2566]

Question 309: Where does the equality of all originates?

Answer: The union of all in one Body, rulers and subjects, and the dependence of all upon the one Divine Head as the Source of Life, creates, as we have mentioned, equality among the members. The differentiation and inequality in the distribution of the *c h a r i s m a t a* is a necessary condition to create the one Body of Christ St Paul, by numbering these *charismata*, placing first the Apostles, second the Prophets, third the

---

[2558] Matth. 20:26-27.
[2559] John 13:3-12.
[2560] John 13:13-17.
[2561] 1 Corinth. 4:1.
[2562] 2 Corinth. 4:5.
[2563] 1 Corinth. 3:21-22.
[2564] Col. 1:23.
[2565] Rom. 1:1.
[2566] St John Chrysostom, *To 1 Corinthians, Homily 10, § 2,* in Migne, *P.G.,* 61, 83. Ibid, *To 2 Corinthians, Homily 8, § 3,* in Migne, *P.G.,* 61, 456. Ibid, *To Acts, Homily 37, § 3,* in Migne, *P.G.,* 60, 266. Ibid, *To the Ascension, Homily 2, § 12,* in Migne, *P.G.,* 52, 784.

Teachers,[2567] with whom he joins the shepherds,[2568] declared openly that whatever he said about the *charismata* in his Epistles, have the same effectiveness on the administrating order and ecclesiastic instruments within the Church that have been entrusted with its administration. St Paul stresses the unequal distribution of the *charismata*.[2569] The Source from Whom these *charismata* are poured forth is always one and the same: the Holy Spirit Who distributes *"to each one individually as He Wills."*[2570]

Besides, without this differentiation in the distribution of the *charismata,* it would not have been possible to form the one Body because, if all had the same *charisma* and all were Apostles or Prophets or Shepherds, they would all be *"one part and not a body."* Now, *"because everyone does not have the same charisma, for this reason they are one Body. Being a Body, all are one and do not differ from one another as being one Body."* *"This difference"* in the *charismata* is what *"makes the equality"* because, if it did not exist, they would not be all one Body. *"Not being a Body, they would not be equal. For the equality is achieved because of the one Body. And as in the human body the eye cannot say to the rest of members 'I have no need of you,' for the hands need one another, and the feet support one another, and the eyes in agreement have the conception of light,"* in a similar manner and in the Mystical Body of Christ there can be no excuse for those *"who have received higher charismata to boast against those have received lesser, as though they have no need of them."* For *"the lesser charisma is necessary, and without it the fullness of the Church is hobbled."* As in the human body it cannot be said that *"one of the members makes the body by itself"* without being united to the rest of the members, likewise in the Church he who has the *charisma* of being a Bishop cannot alone compose the Body of the Church.[2571]

All together each individual's *charisma* must be united to one another in order that in the communion of life, each individual's *charisma* becomes common to the others, and the differences of the *charismata* through the unity of all Gifts, compose the one perfect Body, and all together fulfill the Body of Christ

---

[2567] 1 Corinth. 12:28.

[2568] Ephes. 4:11.

[2569] 1 Corinth. 12:4-6.

[2570] 1 Corinth. 12:11.

[2571] Zigabinos, *To 1 Corinthians 12:29-30.* Kalogeras, *Maria,* I, p. 320. St John Chrysostom, *1 Corinthians,* Homily 30, § 3, in Montfaucon, v. 10, p. 319. St John of Damascus, *To 1 Corinthians,* in Migne, *P.G.,* 95, 672. St Ecumenius, *To 1 Corinthians,* in Migne, *P.G.,* 118, 821-824. St Basil, the Great, *Epist.* 203, § 3, in Migne, *P.G.,* 32, 741. St John Chrysostom, *1 Corinthians,* Homily 31, § 1, in Migne, *P.G.,* 61, 257. 1 Corinth. 12:14-26.

It is clear that the Clergy do not compose a separate Church, apart and above the rest of the Body of Church. The Church is one and undivided, the one Mystical Body of Christ Our Lord, the God-Man and Saviour, did not call Himself "*Church,*" but in the New Testament He is her "*cornerstone,*" her "*Head,*" whereas the Church is called His "*Body*" and His "*fullness.*" Neither is the company of the Twelve Apostles is ever called "*Church.*" They are called: "*foundations,*" "*pillars*" and "*Elders*" of the Church and even the foundations and pillars are parts of the same Divine Building.

Question 310: What is the spiritual and mystical Priesthood?

Answer: Besides all the above, under no circumstances should anyone deny that the clergymen in the Church consist of a special body, having special duties and rights, being vested with Divine Justice and having special Authority, as well as being incorporated within the Body of the Church. And as members of the Church they have a special place within the Body of the Church, united inseparably to all the members, under the same Life-giving Head and the same Holy Spirit as the rest of all the members. They have an honourable role in the Church, just as the eye has in the body.[2572] And even the supreme Elders of the Orthodox Church, who are the Bishops with the honourable title of '*Patriarch*,' without ceasing to be rulers, have the same spiritual needs as the least of the faithful and must also be cleansed and nourished by the Life-giving Mysteries. They do not perform the Divine Mysteries in order that only the faithful receive Life and have Communion with the Divine Grace through them, but that they themselves may receive the saving Grace as equal among all members.

With this meaning in mind, we can speak of the general and Spiritual Priesthood that each and every faithful possesses, without disregarding the special and Mystical Priesthood that God has given to the Church, which is necessary for the perfection of the Divine Mysteries and the administration of the Divine Ministry in the Body of Christ

The Priesthood, according to Orthodox Tradition, consists of a Mystery that transmits a special *charisma* to those who are Ordained. It can never be said that the Hierarchy are practicing the threefold Office of the Lord as simple agents or representatives of the faithful in the Church and not as a special body established in the Church by Divine Authority. Now this does not prevent us from referring to all the faithful as consisting of a

---

[2572] St John Chrysostom, *To Ephesians 1:23*, in Migne, *P.G.,* 62, 20. St Ecumenius, in Migne, *P.G.,* 118, 821.

379

'Holy Priesthood,'[2573] because they have been Regenerated in Christ and due to their incorporation and union with Him, they participate in His threefold Office. They are being Called to be crucified together with Him and to be raised together with Him in the new Life as Priests, each one offering everyday of his own body the logic and *"spiritual sacrifice acceptable to God."*[2574] Since we have been Regenerated through Christ and have become by Grace brothers of Christ.[2575] We are the generation of Christ; we have been sowed by Christ.[2576]

Hence immediately after Baptism, through which we are Regenerated and have become the family of Christ, we receive the Mystery of Holy Chrismation. *"We are called Christians because we have received Holy Chrismation,"* which in the Old Testament was given to the Priests and to the Kings as a *"symbol."* The Kings and Prophets of the Old Testament *"it was typical; but for us is not typical, but truthful, because we have been Chrismated by the Holy Spirit,"* and thus *"we are called Christians confirming through the Regeneration the name."*[2577]

St John Chrysostom gives a more complete report of the results which we receive from the Mystery of Holy Chrismation.[2578] He observed also that: *"In this way you become King and Priest and Prophet through Baptism; King by throwing down all the evil deeds and slaughtering the sins; Priest by presenting yourself to God and offering as a sacrifice the body and being slaughtered; Prophet by learning about the future things to come and becoming a nation and being sealed."*[2579]

Another opinion, according to which we become partakers of the threefold Office of Christ, is our incorporation into Christ and the reception and vestment of Christ through Baptism. Thus St Augustine proclaims that *"we all are Priests, because we are members of the one Priest."*[2580]

Our incorporation into the Body of the High and Eternal High Priest makes each faithful a Priest of his own body, becoming simultaneously for himself a sacrificer and the sacrificial victim, being crucified together with

---

[2573] 2 Peter 2:5.

[2574] 2 Peter 2:5.

[2575] Aristides, *Apology,* ch. XV, § 1. St Justin, the philosopher and martyr, *Dialogue,* 116, 117, 1, **B,** v. 3, p. 316.

[2576] Theophylactus of Bulgaria, *To 1 Peter 2:9,* in Trempelas, *Dogmatique,* v. II, p. 378. Kalogeras, *Maria,* II, p. 533. Didymus the Blind, *To 1 Peter,* in Migne, *P.G.,* 39, 1763.

[2577] St Cyril of Jerusalem, *Catechesis Mystagia,* 3, § 6, in Migne, *P.G.,* 33, 1093.

[2578] 1 Corinth. 2:9.

[2579] St John Chrysostom, *To 2 Corinthians,* Homily 3, § 7, in Montfaucon, v. 10, p. 529.

[2580] St Augustine, *De civitate Dei,* I, XX, c. X, in migne, *P.L.,* 41, 676. Cf. Ibid, *Quaestionum evangeliorum,* 2, 40, in migne 35, 1355. Ibid, *Sermo* IV, in migne, *P.L.,* 54, 148.

Christ Living in the Newness of Life in Christ, he offers to God a sacrifice of a humble spirit, a living sacrifice, logical and Holy.[2581]

It is true that only those who have the special Priesthood (Bishops, Presbyters and Deacons) have the Authority to celebrate and to offer the Holy Mysteries. None of the laymen may give Holy Communion or consecrate the Holy Chrismation, nor pass down Priesthood through Ordination, nor forgive sins, nor perform any other Holy Mysteries. But this does not prove that the faithful are deprived of the general Priesthood.

The Holy Mystery of Priesthood is one, but has three degrees. Having in the one and undivided Priesthood three levels, the ground upon which is based and grows the Mystical Priesthood, is the spiritual or general Priesthood of the faithful, who together with the Clergy compose the royal Priesthood. And the Mystical Priesthood presupposes and has as its basis, the Spiritual Priesthood. This is the reason why anyone who is not Baptised cannot be Ordained because he has to first enter into the general or Spiritual Priesthood. Consequently, not only do the faithful not compete against those in the special Priesthood, but it is necessary for them to cooperate with them in order to achieve the Work of Salvation.

CHAPTER FOUR
THE ORTHODOX CHURCH AS THE COMMUNION OF SAINTS

Question 311: What do we mean by the term *"Communion of Saints"*?

Answer: The term *"Communion of Saints"* was first used to signify the common participation and Communion of the Faithful in the Holy things.[2582] It was used in one fragment of interpretation of the Apostolic Creed, which was commonly accepted in the West. It was believed that Nicetas, Bishop of Remeziana (about 375), introduced this term. After the forth century the term was used in the French churches, either because of the influence of the Catechesis of St Cyril of Jerusalem or because of Nicetas' writings that were influenced by St Cyril's Catechesis.[2583] In the Eastern Orthodox Church the Apostolic Creed remained unknown while the Nicene Creed (Nicene-Constantinople) prevailed. *"The 'Communion of Saints' of the Church is the Alpha and Omega of all the creative Economia of God."* [2584]

[2581] Cf. St John Chrysostom, *To Romans,* Homily 20, §§ 1 and 2, in Montfaucon, v. 9, pp. 727 and 728. St Gregory of Nazianzus, *Homily 2 Apology,* § 45, in Migne, *P.G.,* 35, 497.

[2582] *Explanatio symboli,* n. 10, in migne, *P.L.,* 52, 871. Mitsopoulos, *Themata,* pp. 235-237.

[2583] Cf. Bernad, "de Theologie", v. III, p. 450. Briggs, *Symbolics,* p. 78.

[2584] Evdokimov, *Orthodoxia,* p. 166.

The union of each member with Christ within this Communion that perfects their unity and solidarity, is achieved through faith in Christ and the renunciation of one's old self, thoughts, intentions, desires and, generally speaking, through the new Supernatural Life, which leads to Theosis (Deification) in Christ The more we separate ourselves from our egoistical demands and desires, the more we form Christ within us. We become more harmonious and equal to one another. According to the Lord's Prayer the Faithful must consist of a unity undivided, internal and solid, consistent with the Prototype of the unity between Christ and His Father. Through the unity between them and the Holy Trinity, as our Lord said, *"that they may be one in Us"*[2585] and thus become *"partakers of the Divine Nature."*[2586] Christ, by referring to Himself as *"the True Vine,"*[2587] regards those who believe in Him as being like branches that are inseparably dependant and united to one and same Root, which nourishes them with Divine Grace, thereby strengthening them and making them spiritually fruitful. Thus, all the Faithful, being united with Christ and through Christ to one another.[2588]

The uprooting of the egoism by each individual and his Regeneration in Christ consists of a Work that requires continuous struggle and effort. Without these endeavours the Faith that leads us to Christ could be corrupted or fade away. Then we find ourselves in a state of complete alienation or separation from the Unity and Love of the Church.

According to the aforementioned, the main characteristic and manifestation of the Communion of Saints is the strengthening of True Faith and the Unity of Oneness of Mind and Love. This is what St Paul meant when writing to the Ephesians, exhorting them to strive *"to keep the Unity of the Spirit in the bond of Peace"*[2589] proclaiming that the Unity *"which the Spirit unitesthose who are different in kind and manner"* is also preserved through Peace that consists of the bond *"by which we are united to one another and to God."* The strengthening of True Faith in the living Members of the Communion of Saints is due to the fact that they pray together, one for the other *"through mutual Faith"*[2590] and each one, seeing the Faith of the other, is *"comforted and rejoices and supported."*[2591] Furthermore, they share the Knowledge of the Saving Truth

---

[2585] John 17:21.

[2586] 2 Peter 1:4.

[2587] John 15:1-8.

[2588] St Basil the Great, *About the judgment of God,* ch. 4, in Migne, *P.G.,* 31, 660.

[2589] Ephes. 4:3.

[2590] Rom. 1:12.

[2591] Kalogeras, *Maria,* II, p. 36. Ibid, *Maria,* I, p. 12. St John Chrysostom, *To Ephesians,* in Migne, *P.G.,* 63, 73. Theophylactus of Bulgaria, *Epist. to Romans 1:12,* in Migne, *P.G.,* 124, 348. St Basil the Great, *Epist.* 90, in Migne, *P.G.,* 32, 473.

admonishing,[2592] teaching, preaching and warning one another so *"that they may present every man perfect in Christ Jesus."*[2593]

This solidarity of the Members, which is shown at first as compassion towards the suffering and ill whereby the strong uphold those *"weak in faith"*[2594] with humility, mourns the fall of others.[2595] Therefore they teach those in error with *"a spirit of gentleness"*[2596] working together with love. They become servants *"to all"*[2597] in order to *"heal the souls of those who are ill."*[2598] Secondly, this solidarity is shown in the use of the Charismata (Gifts) in the service to others and the common structure of the Church *"for the equipping of the Saints for the Work of Ministry"* and *" for the edifying of the Body of Christ."*[2599] Having an excess of Charisma is difficult and demands more effort for the sake of others.[2600] Thirdly, this solidarity is shown by our Prayers for one another.

Question 312: Are the prayers for one another an expression of solidarity?

Answer: The fact that prayers for one another are seriously expressed, the solidarity and help for each another is understood when one takes into consideration, on the one hand, that through these prayers those who are in charge can *"through extensive prayer to the Lord assist"* those Brethren who are in danger,[2601] whereas, on the other hand, that even from the Old Testament prayers for one another were introduced as in the case of Abraham who *"standing before the Lord"* asked Him about the salvation of any righteous in the cities of Sodom and Gomorrha should any be found.[2602] Furthermore, Moses prayed to calm the Anger of God against the Israelites[2603] and likewise Samuel prayed *"to the Lord."*[2604] In the New Testament our Lord Jesus Christ Commands us to address our prayers to the Heavenly God, addressing Him as *"our Father"*[2605] because we are

---

[2592] Rom. 15:14. 2 Thess. 3:15.
[2593] Col. 1:28. 1 Thess. 5:14.
[2594] Rom 14:1.
[2595] 1 Corinth. 5:2. 2 Corinth. 12:21.
[2596] Gal. 6:1. Kalogeras, *Maria,* I, p. 278.
[2597] 1 Corinth. 9:19.
[2598] Kalogeras, *Maria,* I, p. 278.
[2599] Ephes. 4:12.
[2600] St John Chrysostom, *To Ephesians,* Homily 11, §§ 1-2, in Migne, *P.G.,* 62, 81-82.
[2601] Ibid.
[2602] Gen. 18:23-33.
[2603] Ex. 32:11-14.
[2604] 1 Samuel (1 Kings) 7:5 and 12:19.
[2605] Matth. 6:9.

members of one and same Family. St Paul not only addressed prayers for all those to whom he wrote[2606] but he also sought their prayers[2607] and advised them to always pray *"with all prayer and supplication in the Spirit, being watchful to this end with all perseverance and supplication for all the Saints."*[2608] And St James, the Brother of our Lord Jesus, urged the Faithful to Confess their trespasses *"to one another and pray for one another"* so that they *"may be healed"* for *"the effective, fervent Prayer of a Righteous man avails much."*[2609]

Question 313: What is the solidarity between the Militant and the Triumphant Church?

Answer: As we have mentioned before, the Triumphant Church in Heaven is part of the Militant Church on earth. Death is unable to disrupt the relationship of the Militant Church or to dull the feelings of love and compassion of the living towards their brethren.[2610] Origen correctly observed that *"the chief of all Virtues"* according to the words of Christ is *"the love towards our neighbour."* It is necessary to remember that those Saints who have fallen asleep have more love *"towards those who still struggle in life"* than for those who *"are still in the human weakness and co-struggling with the lowest."*[2611] It is natural then, that we have a relationship with them since the bonds of Love between them and us are not abolished but rather strengthened and exalted because of the separation. Consequently, between the Triumphant and Militant Church a mutual relationship exists, which is manifested mainly in the Prayers of one another.

In many Eastern Orthodox Prayers, it is evident that the Divine Eucharist is offered, not merely in general for all who have fallen asleep, such as the *".Patriarchs, Prophets, Martyrs, Confessors"* and *"especially for our Most Blessed and Ever Virgin Mary, the Glorious Prophet and Forerunner John the Baptist, the Holy and glorious Apostles"* but also for all others who have departed this life.

No one can deny that the Commemoration of those who have become perfect and Sanctified is done triumphantly, with gratitude for the Grace and Glory offered by God to His Saints. The Orthodox Church highlights Saints

---

[2606] Rom. 1:9.
[2607] Rom. 15:30. 2 Corinth. 1:11. Phil. 1:19. Philem. 22. Col. 4:2-4. 2 Thess. 3:1-2.
[2608] Ephes. 6:18.
[2609] James 5:16.
[2610] Mitsopoulos, *Themata,* pp. 244-245.
[2611] Origen, *About prayer,* 11, 2, in Migne, *P.G.,* 11, 449.

as being the Victorious and Glorious Army of the Lord for whom His Sacrifice on the Cross was not offered in vain.

As the Militant Church expresses Her Love and Her unbreakable bonds with the Triumphant Church, likewise, hoping upon that bond of Love, She relies on the prayers of the Saints in Heaven, which are nothing else than the Prayers of the Triumphant Church. Our Lord Jesus Christ assured us that *"there is Joy in the Presence of the Angels of God over one sinner who repents."*[2612] This clearly demonstrates the interest of those who are in Heaven in those who are still struggling on earth under the Flag (the Cross) of Christ Holy Scripture repeatedly refers to Angels who present *"the remembrance of prayer"* of those on earth *"before the Holy One"*[2613] as well as *" golden bowls full of incense, which are the prayers of the Saints."*[2614] The saints who have reposed pray to God for Israel.[2615] Henceforth Origen, based upon these verses, concluded that *"not only the High Priest.."* and Lord Jesus Christ *"prays with those who purely pray"* but furthermore *"in Heaven, the Angels rejoice for the Repentance of one sinnerand also the souls of the Saints who had fallen asleep."*[2616]

This is something natural for those who have reposed because, when they were alive on this earth, they besought the prayers of their companions within the Militant Church, praying for them as well. It is then natural too that when they departed this life, they did not forget nor cease to ask for whatever they prayed for and thus they fulfilled this Act as their brotherly duty.[2617]

Question 314: How it is possible for the Saints in Heaven to be informed of our needs or to have knowledge of our prayers and petitions?

Answer: It is commonly accepted that *"although* (the Saints) *by their own do not know, nor hear our Prayers, but nevertheless through Revelation and Divine Grace which God richly granted them, they know and hear"*[2618] which is similar to the Prophets who, while *"being in the body knew the things in Heaven through which they foretold the things to come."*[2619]. For the Holy Saints of the Orthodox Church this manner of communication is

---

[2612] Luke 15:10.

[2613] Tobit 12:12.

[2614] Rev. 5:8. Rev. 8:3-4.

[2615] II Macc. 15:12-16.

[2616] Origen, *About prayer,* 11, § 1, in Migne, *P.G.,* 11, 448.

[2617] Kritopoulos, in Karmires, *The dogmatics,* v. II, p. 548.

[2618] Mogilas, III, 52, in Karmires, *Τα The dogmatics,* v. II, p. 679.

[2619] Dositheus of Jerusalem, *Confession,* Term VIII, in Karmires, *The dogmatics,* v. II, p. 751.

the Revelation of the All-present and All-knowing Holy Spirit Who reveals to His servants whatever He wishes[2620] them to know.

Christ is the only *"Mediator between God and man."*[2621] He is the only One Who can mediate directly for us with God the Father. However, we do not call upon the Saints as Mediators, but rather as Ambassadors and Supplicants to God. We do not call upon them as gods, but as our Brethren and friends of God who request Divine Assistance for us. That does not imply that they help us by means of their own power, nor that God owes them something as He certainly does not owe anyone anything at all. Instead they are able to assist us only according to the honesty with which God has granted them according to His Great Mercy and Love.[2622] Therefore, this Invocation is based upon the obligation that the Faithful have to pray for one another and upon the God-inspired assurance that the *"fervent Prayer of a Righteous man avails much."*[2623]

Hence the beneficial influence of the Triumphant Church supports the Militant Church on earth. However, it cannot overcome the limits of the influence and help of one another that is manifested by the members of Christ from their Communion. Consequently, those in Heaven recognise those who are worthy of God's favour while they cannot assist anyone who is alienated from God. Only those who are worthy and who faithfully serve God may receive their intercessory Prayers and assistance. Therefore myriads of Holy Powers pray together with those who, with good will, pray to God for Higher Things.[2624] In the public Prayers of the Faithful, not only Christ our Lord and Saviour is present but also the Angelic Powers as well as the souls of the Saints and those who have fallen asleep. The Presence of the Angelic World can be understood when one remembers that there is a Guardian Angel for each Faithful who has been entrusted to guard and to protect them.[2625] Thus, together with the Faithful who gather together in Prayer, their Guardian Angels also gather so that in the gathering of the Saints there is a double gathering of the Church, which consists of both mankind and Angels.[2626]

According to the Teachings of the Orthodox Church concerning Guardian Angels we conclude that the Saints in Heaven and generally the members of the Church Triumphant pray for their Brethren on earth,

---

[2620] Kritopoulos, *Confession,* ch. 17, in Karmires, *The dogmatics,* v. II, p. 549.

[2621] 1 Tim. 2:5.

[2622] Cf. Dositheus of Jerusalem, *Confession,* Term VIII; Kritopoulos, *Confession,* ch. 17; Mogilas, III, 52, in Karmires, *The dogmatics,* v. II, pp. 751, 549 and 679.

[2623] James 5:16.

[2624] Origen, *Against Celsus,* XIII, 64, in **B,** v. 10, p. 222.

[2625] Psalm 33(34):7. Gen. 48:16.

[2626] Origen, *About prayer,* 31, 5, in Migne, *P.G.,* 11, 553.

invisibly and silently encouraging, strengthening and urging them in their struggle against sin. Although they manifest their favour and care for them under no circumstances can they transmit Grace to them from their own Grace. Saints do not possesses Divine Grace due to their own nature. It is bestowed upon the Faithful only by Christ Who grants the Treasures of Grace unrestricted and sufficiently by means of which not only we on earth but even the Perfected Just in Heaven are Saved.

PART SIX

THE HOLY MYSTERIES
AS WAYS OF DIVINE GRACE, WHICH INCORPORATE US IN GOD'S KINGDOM

CHAPTER ONE
THE HOLY MYSTERIES AS THE MEANS OF DIVINE GRACE

Question 315: Are the ways of Divine Grace are God-instituted rites?

Answer: The term *"ways of Grace"* is not found in Holy Scripture but generally prevails in Christian Theological literature signifying the God-instituted Rites, which as Divine Gifts lead towards piety and the Newness of Life in Christ Through these Rites Divine Grace is transmitted to the faithful, which regenerates them and makes them grow *"to the measure of the stature of the fullness of Christ."*[2627] These Mysteries are characterized as being God-instituted because they were instituted by our Lord and Saviour Jesus Christ, the Son of God, Who is the Leader of the Orthodox Church. From Him and His Sacrifice on the Holy Cross, they received Supernatural and Sanctifying Attributes.

And it is true that only two of the Holy Mysteries, that of Holy Baptism and Holy Eucharist, were instituted directly by our Lord and Master. However, taking into consideration that the rest of the Holy Mysteries were passed down to the Church by the Holy Apostles, once again their institution is Attributed indirectly to the same Lord, since His Disciples, in organizing the Church, always had as their guideline the inseparable Teachings of Christ, to Whom they always wanted to prove themselves as faithful co-workers, stewards and guardians.

Besides, in the words and actions of our Lord, we find the central core around which all Holy Mysteries were formed through the Enlightenment of

---

[2627] Ephes. 4:13.

the Holy Spirit Who guided the Holy Apostles to complete understanding of the Teachings of the departed Master. Thus, in the words of Christ concerning the insoluble marriage,[2628] the Authority of the keys of Heaven[2629] with which He vested His Apostles and the practice of the *"anointing with oil* (of the sick) *in the Name of the Lord,"*[2630] we find the Divine foothold and the Holy Mysteries of Marriage, Confession and Repentance, Priesthood, Chrismation and Unction.

When we assign the Institution of the Holy Mysteries to the Lord, we must keep in mind that this Institution comes down to the determination of the details of the order of the Mystical Rites. Nonetheless, if we then accept that the Lord promised the Apostles the Grace of the Holy Spirit through a certain relationship, leaving the Guidance of the Helper Who alone would remind and teach them *'all'* the saving Truth in order to organize the visible part of certain Mysteries, once again the Divine Institution of the Holy Mysteries remains unassailable.[2631]

According to the above, since the Holy Mysteries were instituted by our Lord and Saviour Jesus Christ, the Son of God, and were determined by Him as ways of granting and transmitting Divine Grace, it is obvious that the use of these Mysteries is necessary and absolutely essential.

Assuredly, we cannot say that the Holy Spirit is limited by these Mysteries to the extent that in extraordinary situations He cannot grant His Gifts and Graces without them. On the contrary, it is accepted that the Holy Spirit is the Ruler of all and even without these Mysteries He can act. This is manifested when the Holy Apostles were Regenerated and finally Ordained by the descent of the Holy Spirit upon them on the Day of Pentecost, thus proving that *"the Saviour baptized the Apostles in the Holy Spirit and fire,*[2632] *when 'suddenly there came a sound from Heaven, as of a rushing mighty wind.*[2633]*"*[2634] This is also manifested in the case of Cornelius the centurion[2635] and all those in his house: *"while Peter was still speaking these words, the Holy Spirit fell upon all those who heard the Word."*[2636] Even in the Tradition of the Orthodox Church, at the time of Martyrdom when a Catechumen was not yet received in the Church through the Holy Mystery of Baptism, by the calling upon the Name of the Holy

---

[2628] Matth. 19:6.
[2629] Matth. 16:19; 18:18. John 20:22-23.
[2630] James 5:14.
[2631] Androutsos, *Dogmatique,* p. 296.
[2632] Matth. 3:11.
[2633] Acts 2:2.
[2634] St Cyril of Jerusalem, *Catechesis,* III, § 9, in Migne, *P.G.,* 33, 440.
[2635] Acts 10:1-48.
[2636] Acts 10:44.

Trinity as their blood was flowing, they were Baptized with their own blood. This type of Baptism is called the *'Baptism of Martyrdom'* and is considered as the most perfect and honorable way of Baptism, as imitating the Baptism of Christ on the Cross.[2637] There is also a *"Baptism in the air"* which is still in use within the Orthodox Church, according to which new born babes who are in danger of dying are Baptised if no Priest is available. The Orthodox parents or doctor or nurse or any layman regardless of age or sex, may Baptise the new born by raising it up and down three times in the air, calling upon the Name of the Father and of the Son and of the Holy Spirit. These extraordinary ways of Baptism reveal that the Holy Spirit is not restricted by any typical orders.

Nevertheless, the Holy Spirit uses these Mysteries according to the Divine definition and institution, as ways to transmit Divine Grace, which regenerates and creates the new Creation. Thus they are essential and necessary for the incorporation of all men into the spiritual Body of Christ, in order to progress and grow in the Newness of the Life in Christ and to be Sanctified within the Church. Thus, the Holy Mysteries are the main channels and means of Divine Grace.

Question 316: What other secondary ways do we have?

Answer: Concerning prayer, we shall note that no one is allowed to ignore its importance and power since our Lord and Saviour Jesus Christ, the Son of God, urges us to: *"Ask, and it will be given to you; seek, and you will find; knock, and it will be opened to you. For everyone who asks receives, and he who seeks finds, and to him who knocks it will be opened"*[2638] and *"how much more will your Father Who is in Heaven give good things to those who ask Him?"*[2639] Even the major part of the Holy Mysteries consists of prayer but it is obvious, as in the case of the centurion Cornelius, that prayer prepares the soul at first to receive the work of Divine Grace, guiding it to the Faith, the Saviour and the Baptism. When the faithful through Baptism and the Mysteries of Holy Chrismation and Eucharist are incorporated into the spiritual Body of Christ, they receive through it the special Power, of which our Lord assured us, that *"in that day"*[2640] when the Holy Spirit, through His descent will inaugurate the New Age of Grace by which we will participate through the Holy Mysteries, *"you will ask in My*

[2637] Matth. 20:22-23.
[2638] Matth. 7:7-8.
[2639] Matth. 7:11.
[2640] John 16:23.

Name"[2641] and "*the Father Himself Who loves you*"[2642] "*.will give you in My Name, because you have loved Me, and have believed*"[2643] in Me. As the prayers and alms of Cornelius could not assure him Salvation in Christ without receiving Baptism, likewise for every man prayer prepares him to receive Divine Grace, which transmits Adoption and Regeneration to him by receiving the Holy Mysteries.

The same can be applied to the preaching of the Divine Word. No one can deny that the Grace of the Holy Spirit influences the hearing of Divine preaching, stimulating their interest and enlightening them with the understanding of the Teachings, as in the case of St Lydia, the "*seller of purple from the city of Thyatira*" when "*the Lord opened her heart to heed the things spoken by Paul.*"[2644] St Paul declared that "*faith comes by hearing, and hearing by the Word of God.*"[2645] St Peter also assured us that the Orthodox Christians "*having been born again, not of corruptible seed but incorruptible, through the Word of God which lives and abides forever.*[2646] St James, the Brother of God, urged us: "*Therefore lay aside all filthiness and overflow of wickedness, and receive with meekness the implanted Word, which is able to save your souls.*"[2647] The Epistle to the Hebrews presents "*the Word of God*" to be "*living and powerful, and sharper than any two-edged sword, piercing even to the division of soul and spirit, and of joints and marrow, and is a discerner of the thoughts and intents of the heart.*"[2648]

The Word of God spread through preaching into the hearts of those who listen, remains fruitless if the action of Divine Grace of the Holy Mysteries is not added to the advice given by the preaching. For without participation in them, no matter how much man is moved by the hearing of the Divine Word, he will remain alien to Christ and the Salvation through His Blood.[2649] The preaching of St Peter on the Day of Pentecost clearly informs us of this. Those who "*were cut to the heart*" were urged by St Peter and the rest of the Holy Apostles, to "*repent, and let every one of you be Baptized in the Name of Jesus Christ for the remission of sins; and you shall receive the Gift of the Holy Spirit.*"[2650] After Baptism they received

---

[2641] John 16:26.
[2642] John 16:27.
[2643] John 16:23.
[2644] Acts 16:14.
[2645] Rom. 10:17.
[2646] 1 Peter 1:23.
[2647] James 1:21.
[2648] Heb. 4:12.
[2649] Androutsos, *Symbolique*, p. 282. Leeming, *Principles*, p. 5.
[2650] Acts 2:37, 38.

forgiveness of their sins and the Gift of the Holy Spirit. It is obvious then, that, if they had not been Baptised, the hearing of the Divine Word of God would not have had any effect upon them.

On the one hand the hearing or reading of the Divine Word of God influences mankind according to the skills of those who preach or the writers who interpret the Word; whereas, on the other hand, it influences them according to their capability of receiving, hearing or reading the Word of God and their willingness to accept and practice it. The preachers are not always the leaders of the Apostles, nor is it the work of all to become preachers. Nevertheless, Divine Grace, which is granted through the Holy Mysteries, is not influenced by moral status or worthiness of the officiator because at that moment God Himself is the One Who is celebrating the "*Mystagogia.*" In addition, the effectiveness of the Mysteries is manifested not only to those intellectuals who participate in them, but to infants as well, and generally speaking, to all those who do not oppose the Grace of God. This, however, does not apply to the hearing of the Word because only those who are in a position to follow it, can benefit from it.

Question 317: Are the Holy Mysteries Gifts?

Answer: According to the above, the Word of God can be considered only as secondary and to be numbered generally among the ways of Divine Grace. The Divine Mysteries instituted by Christ Himself and His Holy Apostles, are the only methods of Sanctification within the Church.

Truly, prayer and preaching of the Word of God are found in the Old Economia. Prayer was exercised not only in the public worship of the Synagogue, but also in private and was addressed by all the God-lovers and all levels of the faithful. The Book of Psalms is a book of prayers. The Word of God appears to be preached by God-called and God-inspired men, Patriarchs and Prophets - all those who appeared from the time of Noah and Moses until Malachi - and was read in the Temple of the Lord and in the Synagogues.

The Divine Mysteries are the exclusive inheritance of the New Economia of the Divine Grace, according to which, after the Death, Resurrection and Ascension into Heaven of our Lord and Saviour Jesus Christ, the Son of God, the Holy Spirit was sent into the world.

The Mysteries in the Old Testament are mentioned as such: the Circumcision, the Paschal Lamb, the Bread of Prothesis, the Rites of Cleanliness and Purification and the Sacrifices of Atonement. All these can be characterized only as types and shadowy prefigurations of the Holy

Mysteries of the New Testament, which have real and Divine effectiveness and which are more elevated than the prototypes.[2651]

Thus, the Jewish Rites of Purification through the washing with water could not free any one from sin, but only from the stains of the body and for the cleanliness of the flesh,[2652] not Sanctifying spiritually. On the contrary, our Baptism is much greater, filled with Divine Grace, for it frees one from sin and cleanses the soul through the Gift of the Holy Spirit. Circumcision prefigures the *"circumcision made without hands, by putting off the body of the sins of the flesh, by the circumcision of Christ, buried with Him in Baptism."*[2653] The circumcision of the Old Testament worked towards the putting aside of the flesh, whereas Baptism is the putting aside of sins, while the anointing through Holy Chrismation that Orthodox Christians receive, is the symbol according to which, in the Holy Scriptures, kings and Prophets were anointed. Although for them it worked typically, for Orthodox Christians it works truly because we are actually anointed by the Holy Spirit. In the Old Testament there was also the Bread of Preparation or Prothesis, but it came to an end, whereas according to the New Testament the Heavenly Bread and the Saving Cup Sanctify the soul and body. The basin that was in the Temple also symbolised Baptism. So how can they be compared to our Divine Mysteries? Consider the differences that separate the Passover of the Old Testament to that of the Lamb of God, Who takes up the sins of the world, and Whose Sacrifice on the Cross was offered once and for all as an Everlasting Sacrifice. Our Passover[2654] consists of ". *Christ, our Passover* (Who) *was Sacrificed for us."*[2655]

Question 318: Do the Holy Mysteries receive their power from Christ's Sacrifice?

Answer: It was necessary to present the Sacrifice offered for us by the Lamb of God and then to receive the Gift of the Holy Spirit. Before Christ was Crucified and Ascended into Heaven *"the Holy Spirit was not yet given,*

[2651] St Augustine, *In Psalm LXXIII*, 2, in migne, *P.L.*, 36, 931. Bartmann, *Theologue Dogmatique*, v. II, p. 267.

[2652] St John Chrysostom, *To the holy and saving Baptism of our Saviour Jesus Christ*, in Migne, *P.G.*, 49, 366.

[2653] Col. 2:11-12. Cf. Rom. 2:25-29; 3:1, 30; 4:9-12; 15:8. 1 Corinth. 7:19. Gal. 2:7-9, 12; 5:6, 11; 6:15. Ephes. 2:11. Phil. 3:3-5. Col. 3:11.

[2654] St Ecumenius, *To Hebrews* 9, 13, in Migne, *P.G.*, 119, 337. Kalogeras, *Maria*, 2, 406. St John Chrysostom, *To the holy and saving Baptism of our Saviour Jesus Christ*, in Migne, *P.G.*, 49, 366. Ibid, *To Genesis*, Homily 39, § 5, in Migne, *P.G.*, 53, 368. St Cyril of Jerusalem, *Catechesis*, XXI, § 6, in Migne, *P.G.*, 33, 1193 and 1100. Ibid, *Catechesis*, III, § 5, in Migne, *P.G.*, 33, 433.

[2655] 1 Corinth. 5:7.

because Jesus was not yet glorified."[2656]   It was to be poured forth from on High after the Cross because before then, we were enemies,[2657] having sinned and consequently, were deprived of the Gift of God.   When the Sacrifice was offered for us, not only did we receive the Enlightenment of the Holy Spirit as did the Prophets of the Old Testament, but He now dwells and abides within us causing us to become temples of God contrary to the Prophets, of whom none ever became a temple of God.[2658] Consequently, the Source from which the Divine Mysteries of the New Testament receive their supernatural Power, which is distributed to those who partake of them, is the Sacrifice on the Cross of our Lord and Saviour Jesus Christ, Who reconciled us to God the Father[2659] and Who became the reason for sending the Holy Spirit into the world, by Whom we were "*Anointed*" and "*Sealed*" giving "*us the Spirit in our hearts as a guarantee.*"[2660]

St Cyril of Jerusalem accepts that the outpouring of the Blood and Water from the Side of Christ are symbols of the Saving Baptism and from which the Church was born, "*as Eve was made from the side of Adam, likewise are we from the Side of Christ.*"[2661]

CHAPTER TWO
THE MEANING AND NATURE OF THE MYSTERIES
(SACRAMENTS)

Question 319: What is the Meaning of the term "*Mystery*"?

Answer: The first meaning of the term "*Mystery*" is derived from the Greek verb "*μύειν*" (meaning "*to close the eyes or the mouth as instruments of transmitting or seeing the hidden things*") according to which it is "*a hidden and Mystic Thing.*" During the Roman period the term signified the Militant Oath that soldiers vowed at their Enlistment in the Roman Army and which was generally referred to as the "*Sacramentum.*" In Roman Law the term "*Sacramentum*" means the Covenant that was placed in the temples by those who disputed it.

In Holy Scripture, in both Old and New Testaments, the term is used 45 times. It means the secret Will of God that is related to the Salvation of

---

[2656] John 7:39.
[2657] Rom. 5:10.
[2658] St John Chrysostom, in Migne, *P.G.,* 59, 284.   St Cyril of Alexandria, in Migne, *P.G.,* 73, 757.
[2659] Rom. 5:10. 2 Corinth. 5:18-20.
[2660] 2 Corinth. 1:21, 22.
[2661] St Cyril of Jerusalem, *Catechesis*, XII, § 11, in Migne, *P.G.,* 33, 788.

mankind *"according to the Revelation of the Mystery kept secret since the world began but now made manifest by the Prophetic Scriptures made known to all nations, according to the Commandment of the Everlasting God."*[2662] In other cases it refers to a hidden and symbolic institution, such as that of Marriage symbolising the Union of Christ with the Church[2663] or some kind of narration, such as in the case of King Nabuchodonosor[2664] or a certain symbolic name, such as the Mystery of the Seven Stars mentioned in the Book of Revelation,[2665] or even the Mystery of the name of the great city of Babylon.[2666] In any case, nowhere in Holy Scripture is the term *"Mystery"* used, meaning a Sacred Rite by means of which Supernatural Divine Grace of the Holy Spirit is transmitted through material symbols.

St Ignatius of Antioch proclaimed that the Death of our Lord Jesus Christ is *"the Mystery"* of our Salvation because *"through Him and His Death (which some deny), the Mystery through which we came to believe, and because of which we patiently endure, we might be found to be Disciples of Jesus Christ, our only Teacher."*[2667]

Tertullian also used the term generally, referring to Christian Teaching as a *"Mystery,"* especially the Teaching concerning the Holy Trinity as well as the whole Christian Faith and and the entire Work of Salvation. Furthermore he spoke of Holy Baptism and Eucharist as Mysteries.[2668]

Question 320: What are the external & internal aspects of the Holy Mysteries?

Answer: Although the Mystery has an external and perceptible aspect, simultaneously it includes an internal and Supernatural Reality, which is not conceivable or understandable to our physical senses as only through Faith is it accepted. The Mystery is the visible Sign of the invisible Grace of God, which is outpoured upon the Faithful having been instituted by our Lord Jesus Christ whereby each Faithful receives Divine Grace.[2669] It consists of the natural and the Supernatural.[2670] It is the material symbol that upholds

---

[2662] Rom. 16:25-26.

[2663] Ephes. 5:32.

[2664] Daniel 2:18, 27 and 30.

[2665] Rev. 1:20.

[2666] Rev. 17:5.

[2667] St Ignatius, *To Magnesians,* 9, 1, in Lightfoot, *Apostolic Fathers,* p. 95.

[2668] Tertullian, *Praescriptione haereticorum,* XX, in migne, *P.L.,* 2, 20. Ibid, *Adversus Praxeam,* II and XXX, in migne, *P.L.,* 2, 180 and 220. Ibid, *De Baptismo,* 13, in migne, *P.L.,* 1, 323. Ibid, *Adversus Marcianem,* IV and XXXIV, in migne, *P.L.,* 2, 442. Ibid, *De resurrectuion carne,* C, IX, in migne, *P.L.,* 1, 806. Ibid, *De coron. militiae,* III, in migne, *P.L.,* 2, 79.

[2669] Mogilas, A, 99, in Karmeris, *The dogmatics,* p. 635.

[2670] Dositheus of Jerusalem, *Confession,* ch 15, p. 39.

the immaterial Grace of God, which works towards the Salvation of man.[2671] Holy Mystery is not restricted to special Ceremonies alone but extends to all Divine Truths of Christian Faith.

St John Chrysostom explained that Divine Mystery is those things that are normally unseen but which, through Faith *"we see differently and we believe differently."*[2672]

This combination of sensual and material with invisible and spiritual aspects within the Mysteries corrrespond completely to the fact that man consists of both matter and spirit. As he consists of two elements, body and soul, he receives double Purification: the spiritual through the invisible aspects and the physical through the body.[2673] God wanted to grant His Grace not only invisibly - although this was not impossible for Him to do because for anything He Wills He does – but through some visible Signs as well, thereby assuring His Promises to His Elect. Because mankind consists of two elements, God granted two methods of transmitting His Divine Grace - through matter and through the Holy Spirit.[2674]

Question 321: Are the Holy Mysteries symbols & bestowers of Divine Grace?

Answer: Thus the Mysteries are Signs and Ways, Symbols and Bestowers of Divine Grace. In these spiritual and Supernatural nature rule over the perceptible and material. The Mysteries are perceptible Signs that symbolise the invisible Divine Grace, which is transmitted to the Faithful and which stimulate their Faith assuring the Truthfulness of Divine Promises. Hence the *"Bath through Water"* can be characterised as being symbolic *" of the Washing of the soul, which cleans every stain of evil."* Furthermore, in Baptism we symbolically *" insinuate the three day Burial of Christ.."* and being Baptised *"we do not die in reality, nor we are buried, nor we are really raised having been crucified, but the imitation is in image."* It can be said of the transmission of the Body and Blood of our Lord in the Divine Eucharist that *"in the type of the bread the Body is offered to you and in the type of the wine is the Blood of Christ is given to you."*[2675]

[2671] St Athanasius of Paros, *Epitome*, p. 344, in Jugie, *Theologia*, v. II, p. 14.

[2672] St John Chrysostom, *To 1 Corinthians*, Homily 7, § 1, in Migne, *P.G.*, 61, 55-56.

[2673] St Cyril of Jerusalem, *Catechesis*, III, § 4, in Migne, *P.G.*, 33, 429.

[2674] Kritopoulos, in Karmeris, *The dogmatics*, v. II, p. 524.

[2675] Origen, *To John* VI, § 17, in Migne, *P.G.*, 14, 257. St Cyril of Jerusalem, *Catechesis Mystagogia*, II, §§ 4 and 5, in Migne, *P.G.*, 33, 1081. Ibid, *Catechesis Mystagogia*, IV, § 3, in Migne, *P.G.*, 33, 1100.

Considering that the elements that are used in the Holy Mysteries remain unchanged in their nature, even after the Blessing and Perfection of Divine Mystery, we must not be surprised when the bread used in the Divine Eucharist is referred to, especially before its Consecration, as the *"Image of the Body of the Only Begotten"* and be assured that indeed *"this Bread is the Image of the Holy Body"*[2676] or that the elements used for the Consecration are called *"antitypes of the Body and Blood of Christ"*[2677] However, even after the Consecration we hear some Holy Fathers stating that *"we are Commanded to eat not bread and wine but the antitype of the Body and Blood of Christ.."*[2678] and they generally speak of *"antitypes of the precious Body and Blood."*[2679]

The Mysteries are real ways, active bestowers and channels of Divine Grace, through which and by which it is transmitted to those who partake of it. They are the Mysterious Energies[2680] and Actions of God within the Church for the Salvation of the world.

Question 322: What is the internal aspect of the Holy Mysteries?

Answer: The Mysteries include spiritual acts and conditions, as well as essential words of consecration that instituted the Mysteries[2681].

Concerning the internal and invisible side of the Mystery it must be noted, that all the Holy Mysteries offer to those who partake of them the sanctifying Grace of the Holy Spirit, which either regenerates them and strengthens them in the new life in Christ (Baptism, Chrismation), either nourishes and gives life to them through their union with Christ (Divine Eucharist), either offers to them the healing of the wounds of their souls and bodies (Repentance, Unction), either making them capable and strengthening them to serve in the various diakonia of the Church (Priesthood), or exalting and sanctifying their union in life (Marriage).[2682]

The Holy Mysteries have their Supernatural Attributes not because of the worthiness of those who officiate them or of those who partake of them. Their holiness and truth derives from Christ Who instituted them.[2683]

[2676] Report of Serapion, in Rauschen, *Fiorilegium,* p. 29.

[2677] In the Divine Liturgy of St Basil, the Great, before the consecration.

[2678] St Cyril of Jerusalem, *Catechesis Mystagogia,* V, § 20, in Migne, *P.G.,* 33, 1124.

[2679] St Gregory of Nazianzus, *Homily 8, To his sister Gorgonia,* § 18, in Migne, *P.G.,* 35, 809. *Apostolic Diatagae,* V, 14, 7, in *B,* v. 2, p. 85; VI, 30, 2, *B,* v. 2, p. 116; VII, 25, 4, *B,* v. 2, p. 125.

[2680] St Irenaeus, *Heresies,* book II, ch. 30, § 7, in Migne, *P.G.,* 7, 820. Cf. Ibid, in Hadjephraimides, pp. 177-178.

[2681] Androutsos, *Dogmatique,* p. 297. Ibid, *Symbolique,* p. 289.

[2682] Cf. Scheeben, *Les Mystères,* p. 576.

[2683] St Augustine, in migne, *P.L.,* 43, 559.

Receiving their Supernatural Attribute from our Lord and Saviour Jesus Christ, the Son of God, they have the Divine Grace that characterises or symbolises each one separately and transmits Divine Grace to those who do not resist or oppose to them.

When we say, that the Holy Mysteries contain Divine Grace, we do not mean that this Divine Grace is contained within them as the water in a container but rather that they are contained within them in power as the result of their cause. Except the Holy Mystery of the Divine Eucharist, in which the change of the used elements – bread and wine- takes place in reality. The Mysteries are instruments which transmit the Divine Grace of God to those who partake of them, as this is manifested by Holy Scriptures by the use of the terms *"of"* and *"through"*. Our Lord and Saviour Jesus Christ, the Son of God, taught us saying: *"Most assuredly, I say to you, unless one is born of water and the Spirit, he cannot enter the kingdom of God."*[2684] St Paul emphasied *"not by works of righteousness which we have done, but according to His mercy He saved us, through the washing of regeneration and renewing of the Holy Spirit,"*[2685] and he added *"that He might sanctify and cleanse her with the washing of water by the word."*[2686] Elsewhere it is assured *"that through the laying on of the apostles' hands the Holy Spirit was given"*[2687] to those who were Baptised and transmit *"the gift of God"* – the charisma of the *Diakonia* - to St Timothy *"through the laying on of, the hands"*[2688] of St Paul. The Mysteries are the instruments and channels through which the Divine Grace of God is granted and transmitted to the faithful.

In relation to the way of the dwelling and transmission of the Divine Grace in the Divine Mysteries one must never forget the image, which our Lord and Saviour Jesus Christ used concerning the action of the Holy Spirit saying: *"The wind blows where it wishes, and you hear the sound of it, but cannot tell where it comes from and where it goes. So is everyone who is born of the Spirit."*[2689] In other words *"as the wind cannot be seen, although it gives a sound"* likewise and *"even more the action of the Spirit cannot fall under the laws of nature, nor to the rules of bodily birth, nor to any of such things."*[2690] Consequently, the ways by which the Divine Grace

---

[2684] John 3:5.
[2685] Tit. 3:5.
[2686] Ephes. 5:26.
[2687] Acts 8:18.
[2688] 2 Tim. 1:6.
[2689] John 3:8.
[2690] St John Chrysostom, *To John,* Homily 26, in Migne, *P.G.,* 59, 155.

is transmitted within the Divine Mysteries remains inconceivable, unspoken and always a mysterious Mystery to all intellectual.

God Himself Acts in the Holy Mysteries transmitting His Divine Grace bringing an essential change to the receiving soul. The power and result of the Mystery derives not from any human factor but from its Divine Institution and Power. The Holy Mysteries have their perfection not in their use but even before their use. Neither are they perfected because of the faith of the faithful.[2691] To receive the Gifts of the Holy Mysteries it is required to have faith as an indispensable pre-requirement but neither the faith, the good will nor the devotion of the partaker is the cause of the Gift and Grace of God within the Mystery. The Mystery has within it and from it the Supernatural Power and Grace to Act either way for the Salvation of those who with faith and piety receive it or for the condemnation of those who with ungodliness approach it.

The Grace of God is offered not because of the work of the Celebrant or of the one who partakes of it ('*ex opera operantis*'), but from its own Energy, from the Power within it ('*ex opera operato*'), through the exact work of the Mystery itself as the instrument of Divine Grace.[2692] It is true that these terms used by the Scholastics remained unknown to the Orthodox Theology of the Eastern Orthodox Church to such extent that some Orthodox Theologians rejected this teaching.[2693]

Question 323: What is the indelible Seal of Divine Grace?

Answer: The Greek Fathers speak of Baptism as the "*Holy Seal indelible*" and "*Mystical Seal*" through which the one who is Baptised becomes known to the Master and is numbered amongst "*the Holy and logic flock of Christ..*" and "*is sealed with the Seal made without hands*" and "*Seal unbreakable.*"[2694]

The terms "*to seal*" and "*seal*" are used. Even in the Service the celebrant invokes the words: "*Seal of the Gift of the Holy Spirit. Amen.*" The use of this invocation is believed to be from the "*Catecheses*" of St Cyril of Jerusalem who taught that after Baptism "*the Seal was given for the communion of the Holy Spirit*" when "*the Holy Myrrh is anointed upon the forehead and the other parts of the body*" of the newly Illuminated who

---

[2691] Dositheus of Jerusalem, *Confession,* Term XV, in Karmeris, *The dogmatics*, v. II, p. 758.

[2692] Trempelas, *Dogmatique,* v. III, p. 23.

[2693] Androutsos, *Dogmatique,* p. 312.

[2694] St Cyril of Jerusalem, *Pre-catechesis,* §§ 16 and 17; Ibid, *Catechesis,* I, § 2, in Migne, 33, 360, 365 and 372. St Basil, *To Baptism*, § 5, in Migne, *P.G.,* 31, 433. *Apostolic Orders*, III, § 6, in Migne, 1, 797. Leeming, *Principles,* p. 155.

"become the anointed ones receiving the antitype of the Holy Spirit, because they are images of Christ"[2695]

The Holy Fathers of the Orthodox Church used of the term *"Seal"* in relation to the Mysteries of Holy Chrismation and Baptism based upon the following New Testament teachings, according to which: *"In Him you also trusted, after you heard the word of truth, the gospel of your salvation; in Whom also, having believed, you were sealed with the Holy Spirit."*[2696] *"Now He Who establishes us with you in Christ and has anointed us is God, Who also has sealed us and given us the Spirit in our hearts as a guarantee."*[2697] St Paul urged the Christians *"not to grieve the Holy Spirit of God, by Whom you were sealed for the Day of Redemption."*[2698]

Generally, it can be said for all the Holy Mysteries that within them the Action of the Divine Grace is purely creative and that the Holy Spirit is He Who acts and recreates through the Holy Mysteries perfecting all those who partake of them without any need of repeatition. This refers to all Holy Mysteries in which the Holy Spirit acts with the same Divine Power.

The form of the Seal which is imprinted through the Holy Mysteries, as well as how their prints cannot be removed, especially in the Holy Mystery of Baptism, remain unintelligible.[2699] Who can understand the Actions of God? Who can understand with his limited mind the movements of the Holy Spirit? Who can comprehend the unutterable ways of Regeneration and Recreation of the Newness of Life in Christ?

Question 324: Are the Holy Mysteries necessary?

Answer: From all the above is obvious the necessity of the Holy Mysteries. Since they were instituted by our Lord and Saviour Jesus Christ, the Son of God, and were assigned as the ways through which the Divine Grace, which regenerates and sanctifies the faithful. It is also obvious that the abstention from Holy Communion and Repentance results to the privation of Salvation. The Lord clearly proclaimed that Baptism is the only way for one to become member of God's Kingdom. He taught that *"unless one is born of water and the Spirit, he cannot enter the kingdom of God"*[2700] and concerning

---

[2695] Ibid, *Catechesis*, XVIII and XXI, § 1, in Migne, *P.G.*, 33, 1056, 1088.

[2696] Ephes. 1:13.

[2697] 2 Corinth. 1:21-22.

[2698] Ephes. 4:30.

[2699] Dyobouniotes, *The Mysteries,* p. 26. Androutsos, *Dogmatique,* p. 314. Trempelas, *Dogmatique,* v. III, p. 29.

[2700] John 3:5.

Holy Communion He stated that *"unless you eat the flesh of the Son of Man and drink His blood, you have no life in you."*[2701]

The case of the thief on the cross[2702] who entered Paradise without partaking of the Holy Mysteries, the Holy Apostles receiving of the Holy Spirit through the breathing of Christ[2703] and the descent of the Paracletus upon the Disciples on the Day of Pentecost[2704] by which they received the Authority of forgiving or not the sins, were exceptional and unique necessary for their regeneration and their fulfillment of their mission. These cases are extraordinary events, which were performed by our Lord and Saviour Jesus Christ, the Son of God. The only thing which is manifested through these examples is that God can save man in different ways or to strengthen him for a mission to which He calls him. Under no circumstances it is permissible to predetermine where and when and how God should Act.

The differentiation of the Holy Mysteries in '*compulsory*' and '*at will*' (marriage and Priesthood) is inaccurate because all the Holy Mysteries are necessary. It remains on the good will of the faithful to choose between marriage and celibacy. In the case where we chooses Marriage then it is necessary to sanctify our union through the Holy Mystery of Marriage. The same applies if one wishes to enter the Mystery of Priesthood.[2705]

CHAPTER THREE
THE PERFECTION OF THE HOLY MYSTERIES

Question 325: What is the perfection of the Holy Mysteries?

Answer: In order that a Holy Mystery is perfected and bears the saving fruits of its energy the following are prerequisites: The Mystery, besides the extraordinary cases of Baptism, is not permitted to be celebrated by lay faithful but only by a canonical ordained bishop or Priest The validity and authority of the Holy Mystery does not depend on the moral status, way of life, worthiness or unworthiness of the celebrant, because according to the common teachings of the Holy Fathers of the Orthodox Church, Christ is the One Who celebrates all the Holy Mysteries through the celebrant who becomes His instrument. It is required for the celebrant to act willingly in order to perfect the Mystery according to the Rites of the Orthodox Church.

[2701] John 6:53.
[2702] Luke 23:43.
[2703] John 20:22-23.
[2704] Acts 2:2-4.
[2705] Trempelas, *Dogmatique,* v. III, p. 31.

The bishop or Priest must be canonical and not in heresy or in schism. Mysteries performed outside the Orthodox Church, in communities of heretics or schismatics, are invalid. Such events must be performed canonically.

Question 326: Who have the authority to perfect the Holy Mysteries?

Answer: It has been mentioned in previous chapters that all faithful who are canonically baptised are members of the One Body of our Lord and Saviour Jesus Christ, the Son of God, and comprise the Royal Kingdom but not all have the authority to perform the Holy Mysteries. Only those who have the special gift of Priesthood with unbroken Apostolic Succession, bishops and Priests,[2706] are capable of officiating the Holy Mysteries. Just as deacons, although having received the first level of Priesthood, cannot celebrate any of the Holy Mysteries, likewise the laity, who, although they comprise the Royal Kingdom,[2707] have neither the authority nor the capability of performing the Holy Mysteries except in extreme necessity. As for example, when death is impending upon an infant they may perform the Holy Mystery of Baptism as long as they are not in heresy or schism. Bishops and Priests, when celebrating the Holy Mysteries are not the main celebrants but only instruments of God through whom the invisible great High Priest, Jesus Christ, Who is inseparable from His Mystical Body, His Church, Sanctifies and Perfects the Holy Mysteries.

Christ Himself is He Who offers the Sacrifice without the shedding of blood, and Who is being offered. The bishop or Priest calls upon the Holy Spirit to sanctify the offerings on the Altar and change them into Christ's precious Body and Blood. In addition during the Consecration and the Transmission of the Mystery, the celebrant gives his place to Christ Who Sanctifies the Mysteries, making the bread and the cup the Body and Blood of Christ The celebrant avoids referring to himself by saying *"I baptise"* or *"I anoint"* or *"I ordain"* but rather uses the terms *"the servant of God"* is baptised, sealed, crowned, ordained, etc and gives his place to the invisible Lord.

[2706] Jeremias, in Karmeris, *The dogmatics,* p. 406. Mogilas, (A 109, A 107), in Karmeris, *The dogmatics,* pp. 640 and 638.
[2707] Rev. 1:6.

Question 327: Can the unworthiness of the officiator affect the validity of the Holy Mysteries?

Answer: The Orthodox Church supports the opinion that neither the private life nor the unworthiness of the clergymen could affect the Holiness and Power of the Holy Mystery in any way.

St John Chrysostom stressed that, if the Divine Grace *"seeks everywhere the worthy ones"* there will be neither *"Baptism, nor Body of Christ."* But now *"through the unworthy God acts"* and under no circumstances is the Grace of Baptism damaged because of the unworthy life of the Priest. *"God acts through all, even if they are unworthy"* and this is because He seeks the salvation of the people. For, when He sent out the disciples to preach, and *"through Judas* (although unworthy) *He acted."* Also, concerning the false prophets who were prophesying in God's name, *"He says: 'I never knew you; depart from Me, you who practice lawlessness'*[2708], *and others had cast out demons."*[2709] If God acted through such unworthy persons in order to benefit His people how *"much more will He act through the Priests?"* He urged strongly *"that no one should be scandalized by examining the life of the Priest"* and reminds the faithful that the Grace *"that God grants"* *"should not be dependent on the virtue of the Priest"* for *"no man introduces it, but Grace is the work of God and God is He Who leads us to mystagogy."* He concludes that *"if we were to examine the life of the rulers, we should then ordain the teachers and the up will be down, and the feet will be up and the head down."*[2710]

St Isidorus of Pelusium stated that *"no one is harmed by receiving"* the Mysteries through the *"unworthy"* and under no circumstances *"are the precious Mysteries spoiled"* even if the officiator *"Priest is the worst of all sinners"*. He reminds us about the raven by which the Prophet Elijah was fed.[2711] As in the case of that great Prophet, God was feeding him through an unclean instrument, likewise within the Church the unclean Priests do not prevent, because of their sins, the Grace of God to regenerate us and to lead us to mystagogy[2712].

[2708] Matth. 7:23
[2709] Matth. 7:22.
[2710] St John Chrysostom, *To 1 Corinthians*, Homily 8, § 1, in Migne, *P.G.*, 61, 69. Ibid, *To 2 Timothy*, Homily 2, §§ 3 and 4, in Migne, *P.G.*, 62, 610 and 612.
[2711] 1 Samuel (I Kings) 17:6.
[2712] St Isidorus of Pelusion, *Epist.s*, book III, Epist. 340, in Migne, *P.G.*, 78, 1000.

Question 328: Is the Holy Mysteries officiated by the Church perfect?

Answer: If the private life of the Priest and his unworthiness under no circumstances prevents the action of the Holy Spirit to perfect the Holy Mysteries, it is necessary and an important term, that the officiator has to have the good will, to perform whatever the Orthodox Church performs in the Holy Mysteries and to invocate and repeat the same words and movements as well as the prayers which the Orthodox Church uses. For the Priest sanctifies the Mysteries by the power of the Holy Spirit.[2713] To this aim, right from the beginning, it was the practice that the officiator Priest after preparation vested himself with special vestments in order to perform any of the Mysteries and in order that through these he will separate himself from the daily and common life and be prepared for the sacred diakonia. It is also worthy to note, that in all the Holy Mysteries there is a preparatory part, prayers and invocations during the service. In order that the Holy Mystery be considered valuable, it must keep the form and the words of invocation and prayers which the Orthodox Church has established, not because they act as some kind of magic instruments, but because they express the faith and the opinion of the Orthodox Church and describe the full character of that which the Church performs and aims to transmit through the performed Mystery the Divine Grace of God.

Hence, the validity of the Mystery is not affected if the officiator prays carelessly or indifferently and even celebrates the Holy Mysteries without faith. It is enough that he celebrates the Divine Mysteries exactly as the Holy Orthodox Church received them from her Founder. For his impiety and indifference, the Priest is responsible and accountable before God, Who invisibly performs the Holy Mysteries. The unfaithfulness of the Priest cannot eliminate the effectiveness and power of the Holy Mysteries. Since he still remains within the Church and is not separated from her Head by renouncing the Orthodox faith, he can perform the Mysteries, although within his soul he remains alien to the Divine Grace.

The keeping of the order within the Holy Mysteries is necessary and indispensable in expressing the Church's opinion and faith. Again, if someone performs exactly the liturgical type of the one Holy Orthodox Church, but expresses a different faith, then the Mysteries are invalid, although the external form is correct.

[2713] Mogilas, A' 100, in Karmeris, *The dogmatics,* v. II, p. 635.

Question 329: Are the mysteries of the heretics valid?

Answer: The Orthodox Church takes into consideration the fact that the mysteries of the heretics were performed outside the One, Holy, Catholic and Apostolic Church and are considered invalid. St Cyprian, expressed in his writings that *"outside the Church there is no salvation."* This opinion was the general belief and principal of the first Church. What was accepted for the validity of the Holy Mystery of Baptism was also accepted for all the Holy Mysteries, and especially for that of Ordination. The heretics by breaking away from the true Faith they alienated themselves from the perfection of the Holy Spirit and consequently could not transmit the fullness of the Holy Spirit.[2714]

Question 330: Are the mysteries of the schismatics valid?

Answer: It was not only the heretics who departed and separated themselves from the original Body of Christ, but also the schismatics. Consequently, it was natural that the mysteries which were officiated by them, although they were performed exactly as in the Orthodox Church, and officiated by bishops or Priests who were previously ordained canonically but afterwards had split, these mysteries were considered invalid by the Orthodox Church.

In order for a Mystery to be valid, it is not enough that it is officiated canonically according to the Rites of the ancient Church or by a clergyman who was canonically ordained, but it is essential that the clergyman has to be in communion of Faith with the Orthodox Church. A bishop or Priest who is separated through heresy or schism from the true Church, breaks the line of Apostolic Succession, falls from the Grace of the Priesthood, alienates himself from the perfection of the Holy Spirit and becomes once again a layman who has no authority to baptize. In other words any mystery which is officiated outside the Orthodox Church can be under no circumstances recognized as valid.

The fact that the canonically ordained bishop or Priest remains an instrument of Divine Grace, of which the only source and treasury is the Church. We must never forget that the canonically ordained through Divine Grace which was transmitted to him, makes him for life an instrument for diakonia of the Divine Word and steward of the Divine Mysteries. The

---

[2714] Ibid, *Epist.* 24, in migne, *P.L.,* 20, 549. Gelasianus, *Sacramentarium,* in migne, *P.L.,* 74, 1145 and 1147. Johannis Papae, *Epist.* 267, in migne, *P.L.,* 136, 887. Paschalis Papae, *Epist. to the archbishop of Magentia,* in migne, *P.L.,* 163, 175.

mysteries which are officiated by heretics or schismatics or by defrocked Orthodox clergymen are not only illegal, but invalid and powerless and consequently must be repeated canonically.

Question 331: What does the term *"Economia"* mean?

Answer: *"Economia"* (dispensation) is the temporary deviation from the accurate practice of the Church in order to achieve a greater benefit.[2715] St Cyril of Alexandria uses the example of sailors who, when they are out at sea and face the winter storms, they empty the ship of its cargo, in order to save the whole ship and the crew; likewise the Church, when required, uses *"Economia"*, in order not to suffer damage but to accomplish greater benefit.[2716] *"Economia"* is used not to deviate from the essential correctness of the Church, but in order to achieve greater benefits or to avoid greater damage.

If *'Economia'* is used for extraordinary reasons and deviates from the Church's correctness, it is obvious that this does not create a permanent condition but is an exception to the rule and for a specific case only (*"jus singulare"*). It lasts briefly, in order that those who are outside of the Orthodox Church enter her bosom, as when a door is opened and immediately closed, in order that the Church's accuracy is not disturbed.[2717] *'Economia'* cannot at first and in advance be offered to all the members of the Orthodox Church; neither can it be said that the Orthodox Church is obliged to recognize as valid the mysteries of those outside the Orthodox Body.

Through *"Economia"* the Orthodox Church completes, gives life and grants the Gift and the Charismata of the Holy Spirit to those who were not previously canonically included within the body of the Church because when "a *heretic returns to Orthodoxy he corrects the previous error and heresy is removed; the Baptism by the anointing with Holy Myrrh, the ordination by the laying on of the hands*"[2718]. *"Economia"* can also be exercised even to members of the Church who require special dispensation for some reason or another. In this case the Canons (Laws) of the Church are set aside but only for that moment. *"Economia"* can only be applied to the Canons of the Orthodox Church which have been established by the Fathers under the inspiration of the Holy Spirit and can be regarded as

---

[2715] St Cyril of Alexandria, *Epist. 46 to Gennadius,* in Migne, *P.G.,* 77, 319.
[2716] Ibid, *Epist. 46 to Gennadius*, in Migne, *P.G.,* 77, 320. Ibid, *Epist.* 87, in Migne, *P.G.,* 77, 376.
[2717] Trempelas, *Dogmatique,* v. III, p. 49.
[2718] St Justin, the philosopher and martyr, *Answer 14 to the Orthodox,* in Migne, *P.G.,* 6, 1282.

flexible. But under no circumstances can *"Economia"* be applied to the Dogma of the Church which is the Revelation of God to His Church.

CHAPTER FOUR
THE NUMBER OF THE HOLY MYSTERIES

Question 332: What are the number of the Holy Mysteries?

Answer: Each Holy Mystery is witnessed in the New Testament as having its institution either directly from our Lord and Saviour Jesus Christ, the Son of God, the Founder and Head of His Church, or indirectly through His Holy Apostles and Disciples. Each Holy Mystery is a special way and main pipeline by means of which Divine Grace is transmitted to the faithful within the Church. In the New Testament we do not find any specific number[2719] concerning the Holy Mysteries.

The Apostolic Fathers and the Apologists mention two main Holy Mysteries, which introduce the faithful to the Church and incorporate him within Christ - those of Holy Baptism and Holy Eucharist. The Apostolic Fathers also mentioned ordinations of bishops and deacons,[2720] confession of the sins[2721] and the Holy Mystery of Marriage, which was conducted *"with the consent of the bishop"* so *"that the marriage may be in accordance with the Lord and not due to lustful passions."* [2722]

Origen spoke of the confession of sin committed against Priests, in order to expose the sin and to request the proper medicine to cure it[2723]. He also combined repentance as well as the laying on of hands with the use of oil and prayer, according to the teaching of St James.[2724] Furthermore in the *"Euchologion"* (Prayer Book) of St Serapion three prayers for Ordination are found, two prayers *"concerning the offered oil"* of which the one concerns *" the offered oils"* and the second *" the oil of the ill."*[2725] Thus all those Sacred Ceremonies which were used within the entire Orthodox Church were numbered as Holy Mysteries. St Augustine assured that

---

[2719] See: Meyendorff, *Theology,* pp. 191-192.
[2720] *Didache,* 15, 1, in Lightfoot, *Apostolic Fathers,* p. 157. St Clement of Rome, *1st Corinthians,* 7, 4-8, 1-5; 42, 4-5; 44, 2, in Lightfoot, *Apostolic Fathers,* p. 32-33, 51, 52.
[2721] *Didache,* 4, 14 and 14, 1-3, in Lightfoot, *Apostolic Fathers,* pp. 152 and 157. *Barnabas,* 19, 12, in Lightfoot, *Apostolic Fathers,* p. 186. St Clement of Rome, *1st Corinthians,* 51, 3 and 52, 1, in Lightfoot, *Apostolic Fathers,* p. 57.
[2722] St Ignatius, *To Polycarp,* 5, 2, in Lightfoot, *Apostolic Fathers,* p. 117.
[2723] Origen, *In Leviticus,* II, 4, in Migne, *P.G.,* 12, 418. Cf. Ibid, *To Psalm* 37(38), homily II, § 6, in Migne, *P.G.,* 12, 1386.
[2724] James 5, 14-15.
[2725] Serapion, in Trempelas, *Dogmatique,* v. III, p. 60.

"whatever the universal Church upholds were not laid down by Holy Synod, but were always practised and correctly believed as having been passed down by Apostolic authority."[2726]

Question 333: What other attempts for numbering the Holy Mysteries?

Answer: In the East some attempts were made to number the Holy Mysteries. At first in the writings that were believed to be by St Dionysius the Aeropagite, the Holy Mysteries of *"Illumination"* or Baptism, *"the Gathering or Communion,"* *"the Rite of Myrrh"* (Chrismation or Confirmation) and *"the Hierarchal Orders"* (Priesthood) are explained. Also amongst the Holy Mysteries the *"Mystery for those who have sacredly fallen asleep"* (Funeral Rite) and the tonsuring of Monks are numbered. In this catalogue according to St Dionysius, of the six Mysteries only four are characterised as *"Hierarchal Mysteries:"* *"Divine and Sacred Symbols,"* *"perceptible images of the Heavenly,"* *"Divine and Holy Symbols,"* *"the perceptibly sacred intellectual images"* and especially the Holy Eucharist which is called *"Divine and perfect Mystery"* and *"Ceremony of Ceremonies."*[2727]

St Theodore the Studite numbered the Mysteries up to six although from his biography we learn that at his death he participated in the Mystery of Holy Unction. In another letter he himself bore witness to the custom of the Christians of confessing.[2728] Thus during the 9th century neither the term *"Mystery"* ceased to be used in its general meaning nor was the final list of Holy Mysteries completed.

Peter Abelardus (+1142) numbers the Mysteries up to six including Marriage. After him, Peter Lombardus (+1160) presented the final list of seven Mysteries in his work *"Sententiae"* and referred to them as the Mysteries of the New Law listing them as follows: Baptism, Chrismation, Eucharist, Repentance, Unction, Ordination and Marriage. Later different Provincial Synods[2729] in agreement proclaimed that the number of Holy Mysteries is seven.

Afterwards in the Synod of Lyon in the year 1274, those who participated from the East, the leader of whom was the Orthodox Emperor

---

[2726] St Augustine, *De Baptismo contra Donatus,* IV, 24, § 31, in migne, *P.L.,* 43, 174.

[2727] St Dionysius, *Ecclesiastic hierarchy,* I, §§ 1 and 5; II, §§ 1 and 2, in Migne, *P.G.,* 3, 372, 376, 392, 397, 424 and 425.

[2728] St Theodore the Studite, *Epist.,* book II, 165, in Migne, *P.G.,* 99, 1524. Ibid, *The life of Theodore of Studites*, II, 67, in Migne, *P.G.,* 99, 325. Ibid, *Epist.,* book II, 162, in Migne, *P.G.,* 99, 1845, 1504-1516.

[2729] The Provincial Synods of Durham in 1217, of Oxford in 1222, of Ratisbonne in 1235, of Valentia 1255 and of Cemon in 1247.

Michael Palaiologos, accepted the Confession of Faith of Pope Clement IV without any hesitation, in which the Holy Mysteries are seven. Three years later, in April 1277, the Patriarch of Constantinople, John Bekkos, repeated the list of Holy Mysteries in the same order as that of Lyon. In the second half of the 13th century, a Monk by the name of Job, in his work concerning the Holy Mysteries, added to the list the Tonsuring of Monks and Repentance combined with Holy Unction, although he distinguishes the two Holy Mysteries from one another.[2730] In this manner, in his list, the Mysteries remained seven. In the Orthodox Church, in contemporary times, the Theologians express the abovementioned opinion in their writings.[2731]

Question 334: What are the mysterious Ceremonies?

Answer: The term *"Mystery"* has also a wider meaning and includes some other ceremonies in the Mysteries as well. These ceremonies are similar to the Holy Mysteries and transmit Divine Grace invisibly through words and the use of matter as the Holy Mysteries but have not been Divinely instituted by Christ or by His Apostles. They are not essential for man's Salvation such as the Holy Mysteries. They were introduced by the Holy Fathers of the Orthodox Church according to the authority of our Lord and Saviour Jesus Christ, the Son of God, Who assured and promised that *"if two of you agree on earth concerning anything that they ask, it will be done for them by My Father in Heaven. For where two or three are gathered together in My Name, I Am there in the midst of them."*[2732] Furthermore, these Ceremonies are similar to the Holy Mysteries and for this reason they are called Mysterious (*"sacramentaux," "sacramentalis," "sacramentalien"*). They were distinguished into *"consecrations"* and *"benedictions,"* both referring to persons or lifeless things and places.

1. THE HOLY MYSTERY OF BAPTISM

Question 335: What is the Mystery of Holy Baptism?

Answer: Baptism is the Holy Mystery in which man through three immersions and elevations within and out of water and the invocation of the name of the three Persons of the Holy Trinity is regenerated by the Holy

---

[2730] Codex 61, Supplem. Graeci Paris, fol. 239, in Trempelas, *Dogmatique*, v. III, p. 62.
[2731] Cf. Mogilas (A' 98); Kritopoulos (ch. 5); Dositheus of Jerusalem, *Confession*, (Term 15), in Karmeris, *The dogmatics*, pp. 635, 388, 526, 757, 690 and 580.
[2732] Matth. 18:19-20.

Spirit and becomes the New Creation in Christ.[2733] St Paul refers to it as *"the washing of regeneration and renewing of the Holy Spirit."*[2734] Divine Grace descents upon the water giving to Baptism the cleanliness from sins and the power of regeneration. Baptism offers the Newness of Life in Christ, implants them in the Orthodox Church, which is the only Canonical Body of Christ, and offers to them the right to participate in all the Holy Mysteries. This Holy Mystery has been described by many names and each one clarifies it. Thus Baptism was called *"Illumination," "Bath," "Charisma," "Gift," "Vestment of Immortality," "Seal," "Phylacterion," "Vehicle to Heaven,"* etc.

The importance of this Holy Mystery is manifested by Holy Scripture through the prototypes and prefigures of the Old Testament. The baptism of St John the Forerunner and Baptist prepared the God-given Baptism of the Messiah through repentance. The importance of this Mystery is evident from the fact that it was instituted shortly before His glorious Ascension by the Son of God Who is our Lord, Master and Saviour. He commanded His Holy Apostles and Disciples to evangelise the entire world *"baptising"* those who believe in the Name of the Father and of the Son and of the Holy Spirit.[2735] Simultaneously He threatened all those who disbelieve and would not be baptised with condemnation.[2736]

2. THE MYSTERY OF HOLY CHRISMATION

Question 336: What is the Mystery of Holy Chrismation?

Answer: The Holy Mystery of Chrismation is given immediately after the Holy Mystery of Baptism by the Anointing and Signing of the Cross on the different parts of the one who has been baptised to transmit the Strength and various Gifts or Charismata of the Holy Spirit.[2737] These Gifts are necessary for the strengthening and arming of those who have been baptised in order to grow and perfect them in the Newness of Life in Christ It is an individual and separate Holy Mystery the nature and meaning of which is clarified by the different names applied to it. The Divine institution is evident from the

---

[2733] Cf. Damalas, *Catechesis,* pp. 82-83. Frangopoulos, *Christian Faith,* pp. 193-196. For the biblical interpretation of the Holy Mystery see: Labadarios, *Explanation,* Johannesburg, 1990. Ibid, *Sermons,* v.1 , pp.99-110. Meyendorff, *Theology,* pp. 192-195. Georgopoulos, *Anthology,* pp. 9-17.

[2734] Tit. 3:5. Cf. Evdokimov, *Orthodoxia,* pp. 368-370. Kefalas, *Catechesis,* pp. 180-181.

[2735] Matth. 28:19.

[2736] Mark 16:16.

[2737] Cf. Plato of Moscow, *Orthodox Teaching,* p. 148. Evdokimov, *Orthodoxia,* pp. 374-388. Kefalas, *Catechesis,* pp. 182-183. Frangopoulos, *Christian Faith,* pp. 197-199. Mitsopoulos, *Themata,* p. 312. Labadarios, *Sermons,* v. 1, pp. 111-114. Georgopoulos, *Anthology,* pp. 17-20.

promises of our Lord and Saviour Jesus Christ, the Son of God, concerning the richness of the Gifts or Charismata of the Holy Spirit bestowed upon the faithful. It is clearly witnessed by the laying on of hands of the Holy Apostles that followed Baptism for the purpose of transmitting the Holy Spirit to the faithful as well as by the Apostolic Proclamations of assurance, anointing and engagement of the Holy Spirit.. The Apostolic Proclamations refer to the inner Visitation and Action of the Holy Spirit but they do not exclude the external use according to ancient Ecclesiastic Tradition of oil.

3. THE MYSTERY OF HOLY EUCHARIST

Question 337: What is the Mystery of Holy Eucharist?

Answer: The Holy Eucharist is the Mystery of the Orthodox Church in which the presence of our Lord and Saviour Jesus Christ is real and essential. The bread and wine are offered as a Sacrifice without the shedding of blood and in remembrance of that unique Sacrifice that was offered on the Cross once and for all. The Holy Eucharist is offered as the Life-giving food and communion to all the faithful. Thus, the Holy Eucharist has two aspects, according to which it is a Mystery as well as a Sacrifice. These two aspects are manifested through the many and various names ascribed to Eucharist by Holy Scripture and Sacred Tradition of the Orthodox Church. Through these names the Mystery is exalted. It nourishes the souls of the faithful and unites them through the one Bread and the one Body to Christ and to one another. As a Sacrifice it is a re-enactment, without the shedding of blood, mysteriously and realistically of that Blood offered on the Cross by the High Priest Since in this Holy Mystery the exact Body and Blood of our Lord and Saviour Jesus Christ, the Son of God, is offered for eating and drinking, its supreme and special importance is obvious. It becomes the centre of all other Holy Mysteries and Christian Life. Therefore, as the greatest of all New Testament Holy Mysteries, it is prefigured in the Old Testament and undoubtedly was directly instituted by our Lord and Saviour Jesus Christ, the Son of God.[2738]

[2738] Cf. Kefalas, *Catechesis,* pp. 183-186. Frangopoulos, *Christian Faith,* pp. 199-201. Dositheus of Jerusalem, *Confession,* ch, 17, part 4, pp. 51-58. Mitsopoulos, *Themata,* pp. 315-320. Labadarios, *Sermons,* pp. 17-18, 69-81. Sophrony, *His Life,* pp. 87-90. Meyendorff, *Theology,* pp. 201-210. Georgopoulos, *Anthology,* pp. 20-42. Schmemann, *EchariSt The Mystery of the Kingdom,* translated by Joseph Roelides, Athens, 2000.

4. THE HOLY MYSTERY OF REPENTANCE

Question 338: What is the Mystery of Holy Repentance?

Answer: Repentance is the God-instituted Mystery, in which the officiator (Bishop or Priest), in the Name of the Lord, forgives the sins of the faithful that were committed after Holy Baptism and who, with sincere intention, decide to change their sinful ways and follow a virtuous life.[2739] The importance and necessity of this Holy Mystery are obvious when one recalls the weakness of human nature and that man easily tends towards evil from his youth. After his Regeneration, man is not immediately raised to the Perfection of Christ but gradually and through constant struggle, abolishes the remaining sinful tendencies and desires. Repentance cleanses the faithful from all stain of sin committed after Baptism. It is the Holy Mystery that was instituted by God's Kindness and *Philanthropia* as He does not want the death of a sinner but rather that he repents and lives.

5. THE HOLY MYSTERY OF PRIESTHOOD

Question 339: What is the Mystery of Holy Priesthood?

Answer: Priesthood is the Holy Mystery that was instituted by our Lord and Saviour Jesus Christ, the Son of God, by which, through the prayers with the laying on of the hands of a Bishop upon the head of an Ordained person, Divine Grace enabling him to practice the services of each level of Priesthood with authority is transmitted to him. [2740] The Priesthood comprises a special order within the Church distinguished by three different ranks or levels: Deacon, Presbyter and Bishop. The Divine institution of the Holy Mystery of Priesthood is witnessed by Holy Scripture, not only by the practice and Teachings of the Holy Apostles, but also by the election of the Holy Apostles by Christ.

[2739] Cf. Plato of Moscow, *Orthodox Teaching,* pp. 155-157. Evdokimov, *Orthodoxia,* pp. 388-394. Kefalas, *Catechesis,* pp. 186-187. Frangopoulos, *Christian Faith,* pp. 208-210. Mitsopoulos, *Themata,* p. 320. Labadarios, *Sermons,* v. 1, pp. 115-123. Sophrony, *His Life,* pp. 71-76. Meyendorff, *Theology,* pp. 195-196. Georgopoulos, *Anthology,* pp. 69-76. For more detail on this Holy Mystery see: Galanopoulos, *System,* Athens, 1960.
[2740] Cf. Plato of Moscow, *Orthodox Teaching,* pp. 157-158. Kefalas, *Catechesis,* p. 187. Frangopoulos, *Christian Faith,* pp. 212-213. Mitsopoulos, *Themata,* p. 322.

6. THE HOLY MYSTERY OF MARRIAGE

Question 340: What is the Mystery of Holy Marriage?

Answer: Marriage is the Holy Mystery in which, through the Blessing of the Church, the physical bond between man and woman is Sanctified.[2741] Husband and wife are joined for their lifetime in a Holy Communion of Life. Divine Grace restores the Blessing given to the first-formed and aims at the fulfilment of the Divine Plan as described in the Book of Genesis. Thus marriage is firstly the Divine Institution commanded by the Creator for the assistance of the one to the other of the first couple and the granting of the Divine Blessing for the multiplication of the human race for the filling of the earth. Marriage was instituted as a Mystery by our Lord and Saviour Jesus Christ, the Son of God, in the New Testament. The physical union of husband and wife was raised to the Image of the Mysterious Union of Christ with His Church in an insoluble and Holy Union, which secures Divine Grace given to those who enter into the Community of Marriage in order to achieve its high and sacred goals.

7. THE HOLY MYSTERY OF HOLY UNCTION

Question 341: What is the Mystery of Holy Unction?

Answer: The Holy Mystery of Unction is the Mystery in which, through the prayers with anointing with oil by the Presbyters of the Orthodox Church, the anointed one receives the Healing Grace of the Holy Spirit.[2742] This Divine Mystery received various names either because of the use of the oil and prayers or from the way it is celebrated. Finally, the Divine institution of this Holy Mystery is found in Holy Scripture, especially in the Epistle of St James the Adelphotheos (*"Brother of Christ"*) who urged the sick to call upon the Elders of the Church to anoint them with oil, accompanied by prayer.

[2741] Cf. Plato of Moscow, *Orthodox Teaching,* pp. 158-159. Evdokimov, *Orthodoxia,* pp. 394-401. Kefalas, *Catechesis,* pp. 187-188. Frangopoulos, *Christian Faith,* pp. 215-216. Mitsopoulos, *Themata,* pp. 324-326. Labadarios, *Sermons,* v. 1, pp. 89-92. Meyendorff, *Theology,* pp. 196-199.
[2742] Cf. Plato of Moscow, *Orthodox Teaching,* pp. 159-160. Kefalas, *Catechesis,* p. 188. Frangopoulos, *Christian Faith,* pp. 218-219. Mitsopoulos, *Themata,* p. 326. Meyendorff, *Theology,* p. 199. Georgopoulos, *Anthology,* pp. 77-81.

PART SEVEN

ESCHATOLOGY
OR
THE PERFECTION OF THE KINGDOM OF GOD
THE MIDDLE CONDITION

CHAPTER ONE
PARTIAL JUDGMENT

Question 342: What is the Middle Condition or Partial Judgment?

Answer: Physical death followed as the natural result of sin that first brought spiritual death. Death became a universal phenomenon and a common cup offered to all mankind, even to those who were justified through Christ, although they became free of spiritual death. Although the soul is separated from the body, as Holy Scripture teaches, it remains alive and in complete self-consciousness of its existence. According to the life one lived on earth, either in Virtue or in sinful passions, one's soul, after physical death, is placed in a condition according to its spiritual nature. In this middle condition each soul remains from the moment of its separation from this life until the Second Coming of Christ and the final Judgement of all. This period is known as the Partial Judgement, according to which the soul has a foretaste either of the good things of Paradise or it suffers torment in the darkness of Hades.[2743] As we can conclude, the Partial Judgement of each soul that takes place immediately after its departure from its body, as well as the foretaste of joy or pain, is distinguished from the Final and Universal Judgement, which will take place at the Second Coming of our Lord and Saviour Jesus Christ, the Son of God, after which the perfection of the Blessedness and Glory of the Just and the condemnation of the sinners into the Eternal Fire will follow.[2744]

Question 343: What is Death according to Holy Scripture?

Answer: Death according to Holy Scripture has three meanings:[2745]
1.   Physical or natural death is the end of this present life, which occurs through the separation of the soul from the body.

[2743] Dositheus of Jerusalem, *Confession,* ch. 18, pp. 95-96.
[2744] Cf. Kefalas, *Catechesis,* pp. 64-66. Frangopoulos, *Christian Faith*, pp. 223-224. Mitsopoulos, *Themata,* p. 92.
[2745] Mitsopoulos, *Themata,* pp. 92, 336.

2.   Spiritual or moral death, which occurs through the separation from God, caused by mortal sins, and finally

3.   Eternal death, which is the eternal separation of man from God and his condemnation into the endless punishment.

The last form of death is referred to by Holy Scripture as *"the second death, the lake of fire."*[2746]

The physical or natural death came into existence after the Offence of Adam - a natural, necessary and universal phenomenon. All men became mortal. No one can escape death, besides the two Prophets Enoch[2747] and Elijah[2748] who ascended alive into Heaven and who will taste death only when they will face the Anti-Christ before the glorious Second Coming of the Lord. In addition, St Paul assures us that *"we who are alive and remain shall be caught up together with them in the clouds to meet the Lord in the air. And thus we shall always be with Lord."*[2749]   *"Behold, I tell you a Mystery: We shall not all sleep, but we shall all be changed – in a moment, in the twinkling of an eye, at the last trumpet. For the trumpet will sound, and the dead will be raised incorruptible, and we shall be changed. For this corruptible must put on incorruption, and for this mortal must put on immortality."*[2750]

Question 344: Does the Soul exists after Death?

Answer: The body is dissolved as a material synthesis when separated from the soul that continues to exist, having an eternal nature.[2751] This Truth is based not only upon Theological arguments but also on philosophical proof that does not have absolute authority. This proof is as follows:

1.   The faith and hope of all nations that man continues to live after death (*"historical proof"*).

2.   The tendency of man for the absolute and infinite joy of the human soul that struggles in vain to achieve in this life that which can be realised in some other life (*"eschatological proof"*).

3.   From the nature of the soul as being simple and not subject to dissolution after physical death (*"ontological proof"*).

[2746] Rev. 20:14.
[2747] Gen. 5:24.
[2748] 2 Kings (4 Kings):2:11.
[2749] 1 Thess. 4:17.
[2750] 1 Corinth. 15:51-53.
[2751] Mitsopoulos, *Themata,* pp. 347-348.

4.　　　From the idea of justice that appears to be violated in this world as well as not being rewarded due to virtue being persecuted and injustice prevailing. Since we accept that God is Good and Just providing all things for the world, it is necessary to accept that He has just rewards in store for each man in another world *("moral proof")*.

The fact that the soul exists after death, preserving its full conscience and having an interest in those who continue to live in this life, as well as in the things that occur in this life, is witnessed not only in the Parable of the Rich Man and Poor Lazarus[2752] but also in other parts of Holy Scripture.[2753] In the Book of Revelation, the souls of those who were slaughtered unjustly appear under the Holy Altar of Heaven, crying out to the Lord and saying: *"How long, O Lord, Holy and True, until Thou judge and avenge our blood on those who dwell on the earth?"*[2754] Also the twenty-four Presbyters who represent the members of the Triumphant Church, being fully conscious, offer worship to the Living God and place their crowns before His Throne.[2755] Finally, the two Prophets, Moses and Elijah, representing the dead and the living respectively, appeared at the Transfiguration of our Lord. [2756] Furthermore, Christ assured us that: *"Abraham rejoiced to see His Day, and he saw it and was glad."*[2757]

Hence those who support the opinion that the soul falls into the sleep of death until the General Resurrection and Day of Judgement, and when the *Psychopannychia* have been condemned, are mistaken,[2758] although it is true that in many verses of Holy Scripture the terms *"sleep"* and *"fallen asleep"* are used to signify death.[2759] However these terms are used in relation to the body only, signifying the temporary rest in the tomb until, at the sound of the Trumpet of the Angel, all shall be Resurrected.

Question 345: Can we repent and struggle for virtue after this life?

Answer: Death is not the end of the life of the soul, nor does it weaken its self-conscience or the other Attributes and spiritual functions. Instead it marks the end of all efforts of repentance and correction of errors committed

---

[2752] Luke 16:19-31.
[2753] 1 Peter 3:19. John
[2754] Rev. 6:9-11.
[2755] Rev. 4:10; 5:8, 14.
[2756] Matth. 17:1-13. Mark 9:2-13. Luke 9:28-36.
[2757] John 8:56.
[2758] Origen, *To John,* v. XX, in *B*, v. 13, p. 254.
[2759] John 11:11. Acts 7:60; 13:36. 1 Corinth. 11:30; 15:6, 51. 2 Peter 3:4. Matth. 27:52. 1 Corinth. 15:18, 20. 1 Thess. 4:13-15.

in this life. The time of struggle for changing our ways of life and the achievement of virtues and deeds of Holiness is only during this lifetime and when it ends through death, the reward of the soul in its current moral condition in which death has found her, begins permanently and Eternally. Proof of this is obtained from the Parable of the Rich Man and Poor Lazarus[2760] as well as from many other words of our Lord, in addition to those recorded in the Epistles of the New Testament. Accordingly, the Rich Man and poor Lazarus were found by death to be in different spiritual conditions that separated them from each other by a great Chasm and although the Rich Man showed signs of repentance, his condition remained fruitless and no change or the smallest comfort could be offered to him.

According to the Parable of the Ten Virgins[2761] in which the five foolish Virgins showed awareness at the last moment, they remained excluded from the Wedding Festival. In conjunction with the instruction of the Lord to *"be ready, for the Son of Man is coming at an hour you do not expect,"*[2762] the same Truth is implied. Besides this, the Lord instructs us to *"strive to enter through the narrow gate, for many, I say to you, will seek to enter and will not be able. When once the Master of the House has risen up and shuts the door, you will begin to stand outside and knock at the door, saying, Lord, Lord, open for us, and He will answer and say to you, 'I do not know you, where you are from."*[2763] The combination of these two Teachings makes it clear that only in this life is the struggle for achieving virtue possible because if one has not prepared during this period, then one is excluded after death from the Kingdom of Heaven. St Paul also urged us: *"Behold, now is the acceptable time, now is the day of Salvation."*[2764] *"Therefore, as we have opportunity, let us do well to all, especially to those who are of the Household of Faith."*[2765]

St John Chrysostom observed that *"the period of life is the time to live accordingly, after the End Judgement and torment"*[2766] and consequently, while *"we are still in this life, it is possible to avoid the punishment by changing"* because once *" we depart there we will cry."*[2767] Elsewhere, interpreting the Parable of the Rich Man and Poor Lazarus, he noted that *"as long as we are here, we have good hope because if we depart to there, we*

[2760] Luke 16:19-31.
[2761] Matth. 25:1-13.
[2762] Matth. 24:44.
[2763] Luke 13:24-25.
[2764] 2 Corinth. 6:2.
[2765] Gal. 6:10.
[2766] St John Chrysostom, *To Matthew,* Homily 36, § 3, in Migne, *P.G.,* 57, 416.
[2767] Ibid, *To Psalm 9,* § 4, in Migne, *P.G.,* 55, 127.

are not rulers of repentance neither can we wash away the sins."[2768] In addition he raised the question: *"What hope, tell me, can you have after you depart with sins to there* (Hades) *where sins cannot be removed? For as long as they (the sinners) are here, there might be much hope of changing and becoming better; if they depart to Hades where there is nothing to gain from repentance, how can they not be worthy of lamentations?"*[2769]

Question 346: Is the character of the soul imprinted during this life time?

Answer: It is obvious that in this life man's behaviour imprints his permanent character on his soul according to his deeds, decisions and directions, so that in the after death Life he has been finally stabilized and cannot be changed due to the condition of his soul at the time of death that will also be his Eternal condition.

The Truth of the words of our Lord and Saviour and those of St Paul such as *"he who does not believe is condemned already"*[2770] and *"knowing that such a person is warped and sinning, being self-condemned"*[2771] is self-evident and as St Hippolytus observed: *"each one in which day he departs from this life has already been judged."*[2772]

Question 347: Who carry the souls in the afterlife?

Answer: Our Lord and Saviour Jesus Christ assured us that when Poor Lazarus died, his soul was *"carried by the Angels to Abraham's bosom"*[2773] while St John Chrysostom believed that *"not only the souls of the Just, but even the souls of those who are living in evil are carried there"* by the evil angels. Accordingly note what God said to the Foolish Rich Man: *"Fool! This night your soul will be required of you."*[2774] So, although *"Angels carried"* the soul of Poor Lazarus to Paradise, the soul of the foolish rich man *"was demanded by some frightful powers, sent for that purpose. And the one they carried out as a prisoner,"* while Poor Lazarus they *"surrounded as crowned with Victory."*[2775] In other words, according to the common Teachings of the Holy Fathers and ecclesiastic writers, when the

---

[2768] Ibid, *To Lazarus,* Homily 2, § 3, in Migne, *P.G.,* 48, 985.

[2769] Ibid, *To Philippians,* Homily 3, § 4, in Migne, *P.G.,* 62, 293.

[2770] John 3:18.

[2771] Titus 3:11.

[2772] St Hippolytus, *To Daniel 4:18,* in **B**, v. 6, p. 85.

[2773] Luke 16:22.

[2774] Luke 12:20.

[2775] St John Chrysostom, *To Lazarus,* Homily 2, § 2, in Migne, *P.G.,* 48, 984.

soul departs from this world it is surrounded by familiar spirits: the evil souls by evil spirits and the virtuous souls by good Angels.

The annoyance of the collection of taxes by tax-collectors, caused Origen to remark: "*I know other tax-collectors who, after our freedom from here, sit at the ends of the world and demand taxes and hold us if we have anything of theirs.*" He bases his opinion mainly on the last words of Christ: "*For the ruler of this world is coming, and he has nothing in Me*"[2776] and he wondered: "*What things we will have of those tax-collectors who will search everything, when someone they take instead of tax?*" Elsewhere he referred to the verse in the Gospel of St Luke that states: "*when you go with your adversary to the Magistrate, make every effort along the way to settle with him, lest he drags you to the Judge, the Judge delivers you to the Officer, and the Officer throws you into prison,*"[2777] which he interprets as:

1)   "*the Ruler*" being the leading Angel of each nation,
2)   "*the Adversary*" being one of the Angels,
3)   "*the Magistrate and Judge*" being our Lord Jesus Christ,
4)   "*the Officer*" being the one appointed to each man, whether Angel or demon, whom he refers to as "*the Adversary,*"[2778] because "*there are two Angels with man, one of Righteousness and one of wickedness.*"[2779]

It is obvious that this is a reference to the Judgement through which each soul will pass as she departs from this world.

St Athanasius the Great of Alexandria, narrating the life of St Anthony recalled one night when the hermit Father was called by Someone from Above to come out to witness something. As he came out he "*saw a huge, ugly and frightful giant reaching to the clouds and some, as with wings, trying to pass him by, but, stretching out his arms, he prevented them from passing him.*" Some passed by and ascended calmly although he snapped his teeth at them. "*As his mind was opened, he understood that that was the passing of the souls and the giant was the enemy who envies them and puts obstacles before those who are guilty, but those who did not submit to him, he could not hold back.*"[2780]

St Makarius the Egyptian, in his 22nd Homily, wrote that "*when the soul departs from the body, if she is responsible for sins, a group of demons*

[2776] John 14:30.
[2777] Luke 12:58.
[2778] Origen, *To Luke*, Homilies 23 and 35, in Migne, *P.G.*, 13, 1862 and 1892-1893.
[2779] *Shepherd of Hermas*, Mandate 6, 2, 1, in Lightfoot, *Apostolic Fathers*, p. 222.
[2780] St Athanasius, the Great, *Life and behaviour of holy father Anthony*, § 66, in Migne, *P.G.*, 26, 936-937.

and powers of darkness take her and hold her in their own place." On the contrary, *"with the holy servants of God, from now the Angels are awaiting and Holy spirits are surrounding and protecting them. And when they come out of their body, the Choir of Angels receives their souls in their own place."*[2781]

St Cyril of Alexandria, noted in his 14th Homily on the departure of the soul and the Second Coming, that when the soul of the Just departs *"she is held by the Holy Angels and passing through the air, she ascends Above."* On the way she meets the tax-collectors who guard the ascension of the souls by delaying them and putting obstacles in their paths as each tax-collector demon presents their own sins before them. There are five tax-collectors demons corresponding to the five senses of the body. In other words, there is the tax-collector of gossip, of the sins of the eyes, of the sins of evil hearing, of the sins of smelling and of the sins of feeling, each one presenting all sins that were committed while *"the Holy Angels who guide the soul, present whatever good they had done."*[2782]

Finally, St John of Damascus, taking into consideration the above Teachings of the Holy Fathers, draws our attention to the fear and terror that each and every one of us will experience *"when the soul will be separated from the body."* This fear is caused by *"an army and power of the enemy's forces [that] comes to us"* They are *"the rulers of the world of evil"* who *"in some way have the soul, presenting her all the sins, which were committed knowingly and in ignorance, from the time of our youth till that age, and they stand accusing her."*[2783]

According to St John there are four Divine Judgements: 1. The Just Judgement. 2. The Philanthropic Judgement. 3. The Beyond Love Judgement, and 4. The Condemnation Judgement, although frightful, whereby God in His Divine Justice distributes *"all Justice, in a just way decreeing those who have been judged."*

Question 348: Does the Partial Judgement differentiate from the General Judgement?

Answer: In Holy Scripture and in the Teachings of the Holy Fathers, we find some verses that confuse the Partial Judgement with that of the General Judgement,[2784] while the Just appear to be in the Hands of God immediately

---

[2781] St Makarius, *About two ways of departing from this life*, in Migne, *P.G.*, 34, 660.
[2782] St Cyril of Alexandria, *Homily XIV*, in Migne, *P.G.*, 77, 1073.
[2783] St John of Damascus, *About those who do not repent*, in Migne, *P.G.*, 96, 156. Ibid, *About those who have fallen asleep in the faith*, § 25, in Migne, *P.G.*, 95, 272.
[2784] Mitsopoulos, *Themata*, pp. 341-344.

after their departure from this life, enjoying the fullness of their rewards. Parallel to these, however, are other verses of Holy Scripture as well as the opinions of the Holy Fathers, according to which the Partial Judgement differentiates from the General Judgement that will occur before the entire Universe following the second Coming of Christ and the general Resurrection of all.

Thus in Hebrews it is written *"and as it is appointed for men to die once, but after this the Judgement."*[2785] According to this verse it is generally assured that death comes before Judgment, without revealing whether Judgement will follow immediately after death or after a long period.[2786] Nevertheless this verse does not eliminate the Middle Condition of the souls. Instead it refers to the General Judgment that will take place *"when the Son of Man comes in His Glory, and all the Holy Angels with Him, then He will sit on the Throne of His Glory. All the nations will be gathered before Him."*[2787] Obviously this General Judgement, according to which *"we must all appear before the Judgement Seat of Christ, that each one may receive the things done in the body, according to what he has done, whether good or bad"*[2788] and afterwards *"those who are on the left Hand of the Judge to go to Everlasting Punishment, but the Righteous into Eternal Life*[2789]*"* is indisputably distinguished in Holy Scripture from the Partial Judgement that occurs immediately after the departure from this life.

The Holy Fathers do not confuse the Partial Judgment with that of the General Judgement when they refer to the rewards that follow after death. They speak of the permanent and unchangeable condition of each soul when departing this life. They also refer to the foretaste of those things that await the souls of the Righteous and the sinners that will be awarded to each one, making the waiting period of the Just joyous but that of the sinners most wretched and full of torment. Finally, they contemplate the period between the departure of the soul from its body and the General Judgement.

Question 349: What atkes place at the separation of the Souls?

Answer: Although the difference between Partial and General Judgement is very clear, we must not forget that during the Partial Judgement the separation between righteous and sinners occurs immediately after the

---

[2785] Heb. 9:27.
[2786] Androutsos, *Dogmatique,* p. 412.
[2787] Matth. 25:31-32.
[2788] 2 Corinth. 5:10.
[2789] Matth. 25:46.

separation of the soul from its body and then remains in a special Condition (Middle Condition) until the Second Coming of Christ

Origen observed that when the soul departs from this world it is placed according to its spiritual value and deeds, either winning Eternal Life and Blessedness, or being delivered into Eternal Fire and perpetual punishments while awaiting the Resurrection in Immortality and glory of its body that "*is sown in corruption*" but "*raised in Incorruption.*"[2790,2791]

St Hippolytus, however, supported the opinion that all souls, the "*righteous and unjust*" following the separation from the body, descend to a common place referred to as "*Hades.*" Furthermore, he confesses that although all souls descend into "*that place*" they "*do not follow one way*" only because the Righteous "*are led to an illustrious Place*" referred to as "*the bosom of Abraham*" while "*the unrighteous are dragged to the left by angels who punish, until near Hell.*"[2792]

St John of Damascus, referring to the place that "*is thought to be* (of an) *intellectual and incorporeal nature,*" characterised it as "*an intellectual place*" because the incorporeal nature "*does not have shape*" with which " *to surround itself bodily and does not move in body, but intellectually.*" Thus "*the Angel does not move bodily in space, to be imprinted and shaped.*" Yet it is referred to as being "*in a place*" because they are intellectually present and not elsewhere. For this reason, incorporeal souls and Angels are described as intellectual beings wherever they are. "*For the soul cannot act in various places simultaneously, because this is only* (an Attribute) *of God Who is Ever-present and acts at the same time*" whereas the Angel, because of his nature, although able to act in and move quickly to various places " *is described in time and space, although intellectually.*"[2793]

The just and the sinners are in different situations in the Middle Condition because "*all good and God-loving souls, released from the body, remain conscious and in the sight of the Good, enjoying some kind of pleasure and moving towards their Master, avoiding the present life as being a prison.*"[2794] In contrast, the souls of the sinners "*think of the frightful Vision of the Fire with the waiting of the future Judgement*" and they are "*already suffering.*" Although "*they are separated from their bodies, yet they are not separated from their passions,*" carrying with them a fleshly stench. By not having the means with which to fulfil their sinful

---

[2790] 1 Corinth. 15:42.

[2791] Origen, *About principals,* I, 5, in Migne, *P.G.,* 11, 118.

[2792] St Hippolytus, *To Greeks,* homily I, in *B*, v. 6, p. 227.

[2793] St John of Damascus, *Exposition. About the place of God and that only the divine is indescribeable,,* I, 13, in Migne, *P.G.,* 94, 853.

[2794] St Gregory of Nazianzus, *To Caesarius,* homily 7, § 2, in Migne, *P.G.,* 35, 781.

desires that they indulged in with their bodies, they suffer even more. These wretched souls are far away from the King while the souls of the Righteous, *"either here or there, are with the King"* being *"even closer"* to Him after death.[2795]

The souls who have already departed this present life have not received their full reward or punishment, which will take place after the Universal Resurrection. After the Last Judgement sinners will suffer Eternal Fire and Punishments, whereas the Righteous will enjoy Eternal and Blessed Joy and will see God *"for now we see in a mirror, dimly, but then face to face. Now I know in part, but then I shall know just as I also am known."*[2796]

CHAPTER TWO
THE FORETASTE OF THE GLORY OF THE SAINTS
IN THE MILITANT CHURCH

Question 350: What do we mean by the teachings that the Sainst foretaste their glory in the Militant Church?

Answer: From the moment of their departure from this present life, the righteous foretaste the glory and honour of Perfection (Theosis) in Heaven, which they shall receive as their eternal and inalienable reward following the Universal Resurrection and Judgement. This fact is witnessed to by Holy Scripture and the Teaching of Holy Tradition. The Militant Church honours the Martyrs and Saints by either building temples upon their tombs celebrating their *"birthday"* (i.e. *"the day of their Martyrdom"*) or by naming churches in honour of them. The faithful address petitions to the Saints as being the true friends of God Who, through them and their Holy Relics, performs wonders and miracles in order to glorify them within His Church as they glorified Him within their lives. This honourable veneration is expressed through the honour shown to the Holy Icons and relics of Holy men and women of all ages, who proved and manifested in their lives the Life of Christ This veneration is not a worship offered to gods because we Orthodox Christians worship only One God, Father, Son and Holy Spirit, but is a veneration of honour to the direct friends of God.[2797]

[2795] St John Chrysostom, *To Philippians*, Homily 3, § 3, in Migne, *P.G.*, 62, 203. Athenagoras, *Deputation*, 31, in **B**, v. 4, p. 307. Androutsos, *Symbolique*, pp. 398-399.

[2796] 1 Corinth. 13:12. St Cyril of Alexandria, *To John 19:30*, in Migne, *P.G.*, 74, 669. St Irenaeus, *Heresies*, book V, ch. 31, § 2, in Migne, *P.G.*, 7, 1209. Cf. Hadjephraimides, p. 414.

[2797] Cf. Plato of Moscow, *Orthodox Teaching*, pp. 182-183. Dositheus of Jerusalem, *Decree VIII*, in Link, *Apostolic Faith Today*, pp. 56-57.

Question 351: Why do we honour of the Saints?

Answer: Because the Saints are God's friends they have been honoured much by us.[2798]   For, he who does not honour the King's friends does not honour the King.   For, he who does not love the King's friends does not love the King.   *"Now to the King eternal, immortal, invisible, to God who alone is wise, be honour and glory forever and ever"*[2799].   The Saints not only loved God but gave their entire life and existence to Him and became His eyes, ears, mouth, hands and feet presenting all their bodily members and soul to Him as Holy vessels and home in which the Holy Trinity dwells. Our Lord and Saviour Jesus Christ, the Son of God, assured us, saying: *"If anyone loves Me, he will keep My word; and My Father will love him, and We will come to him and make Our home with him."*[2800]   The Saints became imitators of God as St Paul teaches us saying *"therefore, be imitators of God as dear children."*[2801]   Also our Lord assured us once again that *"he who receives you receives Me, and he who receives Me receives Him who sent Me."*[2802]   St Paul teaches us that *"glory, honour, and peace to everyone who works what is good."*[2803]

This teaching of the Holy Scriptures was clarified by the practice of the Orthodox Church from ancient times through the teachings and proclamations of the Holy Fathers and Scholars of our Church.   Thus the *Martyrdom of St Polycarp,* one of the most ancient testimony saved to our times, assures us that the Christians of Smyrna gathered together *"with joy and gladness to celebrate the birthday of his* (St Ignatius) *Martyrdom in commemoration of those who have already fought in the contest, and for the training and preparation of those who will do so in the future."*[2804]

St Basil the Great observed that *"it is honourable and by us"* in this life and before the Universal Judgement and Resurrection that the Martyrs and the rest of the Saints *"enjoy the engagement"* of the glory due to them.[2805]   This honour offered by the Church to the Saints is distinguished from the worship offered only to God.[2806]

[2798] Dositheus of Jerusalem, *Confession,* queSt 4, 104.

[2799] 1 Tim. 1:17.

[2800] John 14:23.

[2801] Ephes. 5:1.

[2802] Matth. 10:40.

[2803] Rom. 2:10.

[2804] *The Martydom of Polycarp,* 18, 3, in Lightfoot, *Apostolic Fathers,* p. 142.

[2805] St Basil the Great, *To Barlaam martyr,* Homily 17, § 1, in Migne, *P.G.,* 31, 484. Cf. Fragkopoulos, *Christian Faith,* pp.227-230.

[2806] Cf. Dositheus of Jerusalem, *Confession,* queSt 4, p. 105. Mitsopoulos, *Themata,* pp.358-362.

It is obvious that this honour towards the Martyrs and Saints was expressed on the one hand with the building of temples in their names and usually upon their tombs; whereas, on the other hand through the festive gathering during the anniversary of their *"birthday"* (day of departure from this life). During this day they were reading Holy Scripture and narrating the lives and achievements of the Martyr or Saint who pleased God and with festive psalms the ceremony ended with the Divine Eucharist.[2807]

Question 352: What is the true meaning of the honour to the Saints?

Answer: The Saints are honoured and this honour offered to them was clarified within written sources which expressed the belief of the entire Orthodox Church, in the homilies and writings of the Holy Fathers and Scholars and in the Decrees of Canons of the Holy Councils.

St Basil the Great characterised *"the honour towards the Martyrs and their fellow servants"* as *"the proof of the favour towards the Master."* Through the narration of the lives *"of those who are distinguished in piety"* he supported the opinion that *"we glorify first the Master through the servants."*[2808]

St John of Damascus expressing the opinion of all the Holy Fathers and Scholars concluded that we must honour *"the Saints as friends of Christ, as children and heirs of God."* According to the proclamation of the fourth Evangelist that whoever received Christ *"to them He gave the right to become children of God"*[2809] and the assurance of the Saviour Who said *"you are My friends."*[2810] In addition, he proclaimed that *"the Saints are gods and rulers and kings not by nature, but as they overruled the passions and kept unchanged the Divine image and as having been united to God according to their choice and having received as inhabitants within them the Grace, which He is by Nature. Should we then not honour the servants and friends and sons of God?"* Determining furthermore the ways according to which it is proper to honour the Saints, he said: *"Yes, we must honour, by building temples to God in their names, presenting offerings, glorifying their memories and enjoying spiritually, in psalms and hymns and spiritual odes. They are the living pillars and images becoming the imitators of the virtues".* Naming and counting those who must be honoured

---

[2807] St Gregory of Nyssa, *To the martyr Theodorus,* Homily I, in Migne, *P.G.,* 46, 785. *Apostolic Orders,* VI, 30, § 2, in *B*, v. 2, pp. 165 and 116. St Cyprian, *Epist.* 34, in migne, *P.L.,* 4, 331-337.
[2808] St Basil the Great, *To the forty Martyrs,* Homily 19, § 1, in Migne, *P.G.,* 31, 508. Ibid, *To the martyr Gordius,* Homily 18, § 1, in Migne, *P.G.,* 31, 492.
[2809] John 1:12.
[2810] John 15:14.

"the Theotokos as mainly and truly the Mother of God, the prophet John as the Forerunner and Baptist, the Apostle and Martyr" then the *"Apostles, prophets, shepherds and teachers, the Martyrs of the Lord and our Holy fathers, the god-bearing ascetics the prophets, patriarchs, just who were before and had foretold about the appearance of the Lord."*[2811]

As the climax of the testimonies from Holy Tradition we present the 4th Act of the 7th Ecumenical Council according to which *"we were taught to honour and glorify first and above the Theotokos, who is higher than all the heavenly powers, the Holy and angelical powers, the blessed and all-complimentary Apostles, the glorious prophets, and the victorious Martyrs who suffered for Christ and the Holy and god-bearing teachers and all the Holy men, and to ask for their interventions, as being able to familiarise us to God the King of all."*[2812]

Question 353: Why do we ask for the mediation of the Saints?

Answer: In the Old Testament concerning the invocation of the mediation of the Saints, God appeared urging Abimelech, king of Gerara, who was struck by illness because he took Sarah, forcing him to return her to Abraham *"for he is a prophet, and shall pray for you, and you shall live; but if you restore her not, know that you shall die and all yours."*[2813] Elsewhere God instructed Eliphaz the Thaemanite and his two friends who sinned by having *"not said anything true before"* the Lord, to go to Job *"and he shall offer a burnt-offering for"* them.[2814] In other cases we see Samuel being asked by the people of Israel not to cease *"crying to the Lord"* for them to *"save"* them.[2815]

In the New Testament St Paul beseeched the prayers and petitions of the Christians. Writing to the Thessalonians he noted *"brethren, pray for us."*[2816] In another case writing from Rome to the Ephesians he beseeched the *"supplication of all the Saints"* to pray for him *"that utterance may be given to"* him.[2817] The same request is repeated to the Colossians[2818] *"helping together in prayer for"* him.[2819]

[2811] St John of Damascus, *Exposition. About the honour to the saints and their relics,* IV, 88, 15, in Migne, *P.G.,* 94, 1164-1168.

[2812] 4th Act of the 7th Ecumenical Council, in Harduin, *Acta counciliorum,* IV, p. 265. Mogilas, A, 40 and C, 52, in Karmeris, *The dogmatics,* v. II, pp. 613, 679, 770. Fytrakis, *Relics,* pp. 28-31, 35, 64-68, 78-81, 104-108.

[2813] Gen. 20:7.

[2814] Job 42:7, 8 and 9.

[2815] I Samuel (I Kings):7:8, 9.

[2816] 1 Thess. 5:25.

[2817] Ephes. 6:18, 19.

Question 354: How are the Saints informed of our prayers and requests?

Answer: Holy Scriptures speak repeatedly of the servants of God who are alive and through supernatural visions and revelations are informed about the hidden things in the depths of the heart of others, or about events which took place in distant lands. St Peter was informed about the secret agreement between Ananias and Sapphira who *"lied to the Holy Spirit and kept back part of the price of the land for"* themselves.[2820] Elisaie received full knowledge of what happened to Giezi when he ran to Naiman and received in the ignorance of the prophet *"a talent of silver, and two changes of raiment"*[2821] as well as about the secret plans of the king of Syria, which he *"announced to the king of Israel."*[2822]

In addition Holy Scripture assures us that the Charisma of foreseeing was given to the servants of God. Jacob *"having looked up, he saw the host of God encamped; and the angels of God met him."*[2823] Many Holy men were caught up in an inconceivable, spiritual way out of their bodies or were found within their bodies in direct communication with the heavenly places.[2824] Thus the Prophet Isaiah saw *"the Lord sitting on a high and exalted throne"* surrounded by Seraphim crying out and saying *"Holy, Holy, Holy, is the Lord of hosts: the whole earth is full of His glory."*[2825] Ezekiel stood before *"the glory of the Lord"* and fell on his knees before the *"throne"* and the Cherubs stood on the right side.[2826] In the New Testament St Paul was caught up to the third Heaven where he heard *"inexpressible words, which it is not lawful for a man to utter."*[2827] Also St John the Apostle and Evangelist became *"in the Spirit"*[2828] and saw *"the four living creatures"*[2829] and *"the twenty-four elders"*[2830] *"each having a harp, and golden bowls full of incense, which are the prayers of the Saints."* When the Lamb *"had taken the scroll"*[2831] which was *"written inside and on the back,*

[2818] Col. 4:3.
[2819] 2 Corinth. 1:11.
[2820] Act 5:3.
[2821] 2 Kings (4 Kings) 5:20-27.
[2822] 2 Kings (4 Kings) 6:11-13.
[2823] Gen. 32:1.
[2824] 2 Corinth. 12:1-5.
[2825] Is. 6:1-3.
[2826] Ez. 2:2:1-8; 10:1.
[2827] 2 Corinth. 12:4.
[2828] Rev. 1:10; 4:2.
[2829] Rev. 4:6, 8, 9; 5:6, 8, 11, 14; 6:1, 3, 5, 7; 7:11; 15:7; 19:4.
[2830] Rev. 4:4, 10; 5:8, 11, 14; 6:1; 7:11; 11:16; 19:4.
[2831] Rev. 5:8.

sealed with seven seals"[2832] and had received revelations about "*the things which you have seen, and the things which are, and the things which will take place after this.*"[2833]

From the above the faithful Orthodox Christian is informed by the All-wise and Almighty God Who is All-present and knows all. God is rich in His Ways through which He reveals to His servants those things which are far from them and the things which are or will take place in this world.[2834]

Question 355: What does Holy Tradition teach on the mediation of the Saints?

Answer: Regarding the teachings on the intervention of the Saints in the Tradition of the Orthodox Church,[2835] it is worthy to recall the advice of Origen to his friend Ambrosius. He urges Ambrosius, who was facing Martyrdom, to overcome his hesitation concerning his children and advises that he will be more beneficial to them "*after his departure*" rather than "*if he remained with them*" because "*then and more officially he will love them and will be closer praying for them.*"[2836]

St Ambrosius proclaimed that the Martyrs can pray for our sins, whose own sins have been washed with blood. They are our protectors, the overseers of our lives and deeds, whom we are not ashamed to acknowledge as our intercessors.[2837]

St John Chrysostom supports the opinion that the Saints have favour before God. "*For the Martyrs were not slaughtered for us. Yet, we run for their honour. If we run together with those who were slaughtered for Christ's sake , what will He do in return?*"[2838] Explaining the reason why we receive blessings from the relics of Saints he observed "*as the soldiers show their wounds, which they received in battle, to the king and they speak to him, likewise these who were beheaded whatever they ask from the heavenly King they will receive.*"[2839]

St Hieronymus concerning the honour and intervention of the Saints and Martyrs, supported the argument that, if when they were alive they had the need to pray for themselves and they could also pray for others, how

---

[2832] Rev. 5:1.

[2833] Rev. 1:19.

[2834] Kritopoulos, in Karmeris, *The dogmatics*, v. II, p. 548.

[2835] Dositheus of Jerusalem, *Confession*, ch. 8, p. 32. Mitsopoulos, *Themata*, pp. 362-365.

[2836] Origen, *To Martyrdom*, 38, in **B**, v. 9, p. 59.

[2837] St Ambrosius, *De viduis*, c. 9, § 55, in migne, *P.L.*, 16, 264.

[2838] St John Chrysostom, *To Genesis*, Homily 44, § 2, in Migne, *P.G.*, 54, 408.

[2839] Ibid, *To the martyr Julianus*, § 3, in Migne, *P.G.*, 50, 576.

much more could they do this after they have received the crowns, the victories and the triumphs?[2840]

Question 356: Why do we Orthodox honour the holy relics of the Saints?

Answer: The honour towards the Martyrs and Saints was expressed especially in the honour towards their relics[2841] and in whatever items or clothes they had used. Thus it is mentioned in the *Martyrdom of Polycarp* that this Holy man removed his clothes the last moment, when he was ready to be received by the fire, so *"when the pyre was prepared, he took off all his clothes and removed his belt; he also tried to take off his shoes, though not previously in the habit of doing this, because all the faithful were always eager to be the first to touch his flesh. For he had been treated with all honour on account of his Holy life even before his grey hair appeared."*[2842]

The fact that the Church offered liturgical honour to the relics of the Saints was not a discrimination of the faithful between Saints and non-Saints, but the belief of the ancient Orthodox Church was that Christ manifested Himself in the Martyr in a special way and through him He was revealing His power and victory over death.[2843] The relics of the Martyr are a testimony for the Church, a proof of Christ's final Victory.[2844]

St Cyril of Jerusalem explained that the above example occurred *"not only to honour the souls of the just"* but also their bodies. *"In the bodies of the just there is power"* since *"the dead body of the prophet became a work of life and gave life to that which had died, that itself remained among the dead."*[2845]

St John Chrysostom, reminding us about the narration of the Prophet Elisha, observed that not only the bodies *"but the relics of the Saints are full of Grace."* Because if, before the Holy Spirit dwelt within the Church of Christ, during the period of the Old Testament at the time of the prophet Elisaie, *"this happened and his case was touched by the dead and the bonds of death were loosened and he returned back from the dead, how much more now, when we have greater Grace, when the action of the Spirit is much more"* will the faithful stretch his hand to touch the case which

---

[2840] St Hieronymus, *Contra Vigilant,* § 6, in migne, *P.L.,* 23, 359.

[2841] Bryennios, *Paralipomena,* ch. XI, p. 80.

[2842] *The Martyrdom of Polycarp,* 13, 2, in Lightfoot, *Apostolic Fathers,* p. 140.

[2843] Schmemann, *The Church Praying,* p. 234. Cf. Grabar, *Martyrium,* I, p. 29.

[2844] Schmemann, *The Church Praying,* p. 234.

[2845] St Cyril of Jerusalem, *Catechesis,* 18, § 16, in Migne, *P.G.,* 33, 1036-1037.

contains the Holy relics and *"will receive from it much power."*[2846] St John Chrysostom stressed that these Holy relics were received by the Antiochians *"with crowns"* not only by them alone *"but by all the cities from Rome"* to Antioch they were *"accompanied praising the victor, glorifying the athlete, mocking the devil."*[2847]

These testimonies should be considered natural expressions of the members of the Orthodox Church since they are based upon Holy Scriptures and Holy Tradition. The power of Grace, which emanates from the tombs of the Holy Martyrs and Saints, is confirmed by the multitude of miracles, which take place when one approaches with faith and piety.

Question 357: Why do we honour the Holy Icons?

Answer: Concerning the honouring veneration of the Holy Icons,[2848] St Basil the Great in his confession to Julian observed that *"the characters of the Saints' Icons I honour, which is not forbidden by the Holy Apostles, but in all our churches they are painted"* and the prohibitions in the Old Testament are not absolute. In the second commandment of the Ten Commandments we are instructed: *"You shall not make to yourself an idol, nor likeness of anything, whatever things are in the heaven above, and whatever are in the earth beneath, and whatever are in the waters under the earth."*[2849] But, the same Lord and God instructed Moses to make images of Cherubs.[2850] Elsewhere God instructed Moses to *"make a serpent and it came to pass that whenever a serpent bit a man, and he looked on the brazen serpent, he lived."*[2851] The king and prophet Solomon, when he made the *"Sea"* or the *"basin,"* he made *"twelve oxen under the sea"*[2852] and *"between the projections were lions, and oxen, and cherubs."*[2853] But, these images of the Cherubs were not to be worshipped, but mainly to remind the Israelites, that this place is Holy and that you who enter in should be Holy.

This prohibition was not renewed in the New Testament by the Law-giver, our Lord and Saviour Jesus Christ, the Son of God, for as He renewed and fulfilled[2854] the Law of the Old, He Himself gave the new Law of the

---

[2846] St John Chrysostom, *Praise to Ignatius the Theophorus,* § 5, in Migne, *P.G., 50,* 595.

[2847] St John Chrysostom, *To the Theophorus Ignatius,* § 5, in Migne, *P.G., 50,* 594.

[2848] Dositheus of Jerusalem, *Confession,* quest. 4, pp. 104-105, 106.

[2849] Ex. 20:4.

[2850] Ex. 25:18-22.

[2851] Num. 21:8-9.

[2852] 2 Kings (3 Kings) 7:25.

[2853] 2 Kings (3 Kings) 7:29.

[2854] Matth. 5:17.

New Covenant speaking with authority and saying: *"You have heard that it was said to those of old But I say to you."*[2855]

From the first centuries of Christianity in the Catacombs, the Christians used to draw designs either of events or persons with symbolic meaning such as the anchor, lamb, pigeon, fish, etc., with allegoric meaning relating to the parables of Christ (the Vine, the Good Shepherd, the Harp Player, etc.), from Scriptures (Noah in the Ark, the resurrection of Lazarus, Daniel, Jonah, the Three Children in the fire, Moses striking the rock, etc.) or of the Lord, the Theotokos and the Saints which are from the 3rd and 4th century and the oldest from the end of the 1st century.

St Gregory of Nyssa informs us of how rapidly the use of Holy Icons was spread during the 4th century. He stressed the benefits which one receives by seeing the Holy Icons because they teach the Christian.[2856]

St John Chrysostom spoke of the sign of the Holy Cross and informed us that *"everyone continuously signs themselves with the sign of the Cross on their members,"* that is on the forehead and *"everywhere one can see (the sign of the Cross), in the homes, in the market, in the deserts, in the roads, in the mountains, in the sea and ships and islands, in the beds, in the clothes, in the arms, in silver vessels, in the walls, everywhere being shined and spread."*[2857]

St Basil the Great in his speech to the Martyr Barlaam, called upon the *"luminous painters"* to *"magnify the achievements of the Holy Martyrs,"* with their skills and colours makings the Icon of the commander general and Martyr. Elsewhere, he spoke of the sameness of the Essence of the Holy Trinity and the equality of the Son to the Father and described prophetically the reason upon which the veneration of the Icons is based observing that *"the honour of the Icon goes to the prototype."*[2858]

In the Church History intense struggles were known in the Orthodox Church against the blasphemous Iconoclasts (the breakers of Icons) concerning the correct veneration of the Holy Icons. The end to this period was given by the 7th Ecumenical Synod which took place in Nicene of Bithynia (787), which proclaimed, that with the sign of the precious and life-giving Cross to have the precious and Holy Icons, which with colours and mosaic and other matter are made with skill in the Churches of God, on the Holy items and vestments, walls and boards, houses and roads. The Holy Synod declared that *"the Icon of our Lord and God and Saviour Jesus*

[2855] Matth. 5:21-22; 27-28; 31-32; 33-34; 38-39; 43-44.
[2856] St Gregory of Nyssa, *To the martyr Theodorus,* in Migne, *P.G.,* 46, 737.
[2857] St John Chrysostom, *Proof to Jews and Greeks, that Christ is God,* § 9, in Migne, *P.G.,* 48, 826.
[2858] St Basil the Great, *To the martyr Barlaam,* Homily 17, § 3, in Migne, *P.G.,* 31, 484. Ibid, *About the Holy Spirit,* ch. XVIII, § 45, in Migne, *P.G.,* 32, 149.

Christ and of the blessed Theotokos, noble angels, and all the Saints and Holy men." Explaining the benefit which one receives from the vision and honour of the Holy Icons the Holy Synod added that *"as much as one looks at the painted representations, even more those who watch recall and desire the memory of the prototypes."* Determining the boundaries in which one should move concerning the honour to the Holy Icons, it concludes that we must *"kiss and venerate,"* not offering true worship, which is only given to the Divine Nature, but in the same manner to the sign of the precious and Life-giving Cross and the Holy Gospels and the rest of the Holy items. *"For, the honour of the Icon passes to the prototype and he who venerates the Icon venerates the hypostasy of him who is described."*[2859]

The defender of the Holy Icons is considered to be St John of Damascus[2860] who expressed his opinions in the following arguments:

1. Without ignoring the Invisibility and absolute Immatteriality of God, he emphasised that *"if to depict the soul is helpless how much more God Who gave to the soul the immatterial?"* He proclaimed that *"I depict God Who is invisible not as invisible, but as having become visible for us, partaking of flesh and blood; I do not depict the invisible Deity, but I depict the flesh of God which was seen."*[2861]

2. But the question: *"Is it allowed to make and use these Icons?"* Many opposed the making and the use according to the prohibitions of the Old Testament. But these prohibitions were not absolute because in the Old Testament, according to the instruction of God, images were made by the *"work of man's hands and in the likeness of Cherubim. How then can you forbid by law, those which the law commands to make? If for the law you forbid the Icons, forbid also the Sabbath and circumcision, but know, if you keep the Law, Christ has benefitted us nothing."* Strengthening his argument with another argument, this Holy Father added: *"The ancient Israel did see God, we see the glory of the Lord with an uncovered face."* For the Jews *"because of the danger of falling into idolatry, the Law was given"* forbidding the making of images. *"We (the Orthodox), to whom was given to flee the error of superstition, were made clear with God, knowing the truth and worshipping only God and being enriched in the true knowledge of God and becoming perfect and passing by the infancy, we are no longer under a supervisor, having received the distinctive habit from*

[2859] Mansi, XIII, p. 380. Karmeris, *Τα Δογματικά,* v. I, pp. 203-204.

[2860] Trempelas, *Encyclopaedia,* pp. 41-42.

[2861] St John of Damascus, *1st Apologeticus to those who slander the holy icons*, Homily I, §§ 14, 16, in Migne, *P.G.,* 94, 1236. Ibid, *3rd Apologeticus to those who slander the holy icons Homily,* Homily III, § 25, in Migne, *P.G.,* 94, 1345.

God and knowing what is that which is depicted and what is indescribable in an Icon."[2862]

3. The veneration of Holy Icons is taught by the Tradition of the Orthodox Church. *"Do not make new laws"* neither *"move the eternal boundaries, which your fathers have placed. For they did not deliver the ecclesiastic law only in writings, but in some unwritten tradition."*[2863]

4. The Icons of God are everywhere. First in the Holy Trinity, the Son is *"the natural and unchangeable living image of the invisible God." "They are images and examples in God of what He is, that is His eternal Will. These images and examples were called by Dionysius predestinations. For in His Will, all were characterised by Him predestined and which will take place before their birth, as if someone wanted to build a house but first he designs the plan in his mind."* In the visible creation *"the visible things are the images of the invisible and shapeless"* and *"since the creation of the world, His invisible Attributes are clearly seen.*[2864] *For we see images in Creation that dimly declare to us the Divine manifestations."* All the Old Testament is a type and image of the New Testament.[2865]

St John of Damascus proved that the use of Holy Icons is permissable. He then proceded to clarify the problem between the use of the terms *"worship"* (of God) and *"veneration"* (of Holy Icons.) He confronted the argument that the veneration of Holy Icons is an act of respect towards the prototype depicted on matter. Whereas worship belongs to God alone. He stressed that: *" I do not worship the matter, I worship the Creator of matter Who became for me matter and in matter dwelt and through matter worked my Salvation."*[2866]

St John determining the nature of the veneration of Holy Icons distinguished the different types of worship and veneration. First, he determined and numbered the ways of worship and veneration, which are *"the only proper ways for us to worship the nature of God."* Then he clarified the veneration (respect) which is showed to the *"creatures, through*

[2862] St John of Damascus, *1st Apologeticus to those who slander the holy icons*, Homily I, § 16, in Migne, *P.G.*, 94, 1248. Ibid, *3rd Apologeticus to those who slander the holy icons Homily* III, § 8, in Migne, *P.G.*, 94, 1328. Ibid, *1st Apologeticus to those who slander the holy icons*, Homily I, §§ 6-8, .in Migne, *P.G.*, 94, 1248. Ibid, *2nd Apologeticus to those who slander the holy icons*, Homily II, §§ 7, 8, in Migne, *P.G.*, 94, 1284.

[2863] Ibid, *1st Apologeticus to those who slander the holy icons*, Homily I, § 23. Ibid, *2nd Apologeticus to those who slander the holy icons*, Homily II, § 16, in Migne, *P.G.*, 94, 1257.

[2864] Rom. 1:20.

[2865] St John of Damascus, *1st Apologeticus to those who slander the holy icons*, Homily I, §§ 9-13 and Homily III, § 18-23, in Migne, *P.G.*, 94, 1240.

[2866] St John of Damascus, *1st Apologeticus to those who slander the holy icons*, Homily I, § 16 and Homily II, §§ 13 and 14,.in Migne, *P.G.*, 94, 1245.

and in which God worked our Salvation" such as *"the mountain of Sinai, the manger, the cave, Golgotha, the wood of the Cross, etc."* Furthermore he continued to emphasise that *"all the Holy temples of God and everything which God is called upon are venerated, not because of their nature, but because they are vessels of the Divine Actions."* However, *"I respect and venerate Angels, men and all matter which are partakers of Divine Action."* Nevertheless *"we must worship nothing as God, but rather only Him Who is by Nature God and we are obliged to offer Him all worship and honour."* Consequently, we offer honouring veneration to Holy Icons and generally to all Sanctified persons or things as *"the veneration and worship"* is strictly reserved for God. *"The veneration of worship"* belongs only to God and is *"that which is presented out of respect and honour."* *"We venerate the Icons, not offering veneration to the matter, but through them to those who are depicted on them. For the honour of Icon goes to the prototype, as St Basil said."*[2867]

The Holy Father proceeded further to explain the benefits that we receive from Holy Icons. At first, he emphasised that *"the Icon is a reminder and what the letters of the books are for those who are initiated, the Icon is for the illiterate; what the word is to hearing, the Icon is for the sight."* *"For this reason God commanded the making of the Ark out of wood that does not decay and the placing therein of the tablets and the rod and the golden pot which contained manna as a reminder of the events and the prototypes of the future."* *"For the Icons were placed as reminders, not as gods, but as reminders of Divine Actions."* *"How then should we not depict the saving sufferings of Christ our God, so that when my son asks me to explain, I shall say, that God the Word became Man and through Him all nature was restored to its first blessedness."* In addition, we depict the achievements of *"those who followed in the footsteps of the Lord"* so as *"to be anointed with zeal by imitating them."* Their examples are represented with skill and colours and being seen with our eyes, they stimulate the desire in us to imitate them. Holy Icons are vessels and channels of Divine Grace for the faithful.[2868]

[2867] St John of Damascus, *Homily* III, §§ 33-36, 40. Ibid, *Homily* I, §§ 8, 14, 16 and 21; *Homily* II, § 11; in Migne, *P.G.,* 94, 1352 and 1356.
[2868] St John of Damascus, *Homily* I, §§ 17, 18 and 21, in Migne, *P.G.,* 94, 1248, 1249, 1252, 1264. Ibid, *Exposition of the Orthodox Faith,* IV, § 16, in Migne, *P.G.,* 94, 1172.

Question 358: What was the decision of the 7th Ecumenical Council concerning the veneration of the holy Icons?

Answer: In 786, a Church Council was convened by Empress Irene in Constantinople in order to restore the veneration of Holy Icons that had been destroyed by soldiers of the Imperial Guard. When these rebellious regiments were replaced by loyal Orthodox troops who were transferred to the capital from Thrace, Empress Irene was able to secure the triumph of Orthodoxy. In 787, a Council consisting of 350 Orthodox Bishops, presided over by the Orthodox Patriarch Tarasius of Constantinople, assembled in Nicene. It annuled the decisions of the Council of 754, which were declared as heresy, and solemnly restored the veneration of Holy Icons. The Doctrine of the Seventh Ecumenical Council on the veneration of Icons, reads as follows:

"We define with all accuracy and care that the venerable and Holy Icons be set up like the form of the venerable and Life-giving Cross, inasmuch as matter consisting of colours and of small stones and of other material is appropriate in the Holy Church of God, on sacred vessels and on vestments, on walls, on panels, in houses and on roads, as well as the Image of our Lord and God and Saviour Jesus Christ, that of our undefiled Lady, the Holy Mother of God, those of the Angels worthy of honour, and those of all Holy and pious men. For the more frequently they are seen by means of painted representation, the more those who behold them are aroused to remember and to desire the prototypes and to give them salutation, honour and veneration (ασπασμόν καί τιμητικήν προσκύνησιν), but not the true worship (τήν αληθινήν λατρείαν) of our faith which benefits only the Divine Nature; and to offer them both incense and candles in the same way as to the form of the venerable and Life-giving Cross and to the Holy Books and to other sacred objects, as was the custom even of the ancients."

CHAPTER THREE
THE PERFECTION OF ALL
THE END OF THE AGE AND THE SECOND COMING OF THE LORD

Question 359: What is the Doctrine of the End of the Age?

Answer: The assurance of the End of the Age is derived from the mortality of Creation, which falls under the law of unpreventable mortality. Holy

Scripture stresses the fact that *"the form of this world is passing away."*[2869] The term *"form"* implies that all *"the things of this present world have appearance and have nothing permanent or secure."*[2870] At other times it proclaims that *"the End of all things is at hand"*[2871] and that *"the Day of the Lord will come as a thief in the night."*[2872]

The End of this present Age was foretold by Holy Scripture. It will take place suddenly and unexpectedly with the Second Coming and appearance of our Lord and Saviour Jesus Christ, the Son of God, Who will come to *"judge the living and the dead"*[2873] on the Day that is referred to by Holy Scripture as the *"last Day,"*[2874] *"the Day of our Lord Jesus Christ,"*[2875] *"the Day,"*[2876] *"the Day of the Lord Jesus,"*[2877] *"the Day of Christ,"*[2878] *"the Day of Judgement"*[2879] and *"the Day of the Son of Man."*[2880] Because this Coming of the Lord will be glorious and visible to everyone throughout the world, it is called His *"Coming,"*[2881] *"Appearing,"*[2882] *"when His glory is revealed,"*[2883] etc.

The Coming of the Lord is frequently mentioned in the Old Testament. The Prophets foretold that *"the Lord will come as fire and His chariots as a storm to render His vengeance with wrath, and His rebuke with a flame of fire. For with the fire of the Lord all the earth shall be judged, and all flesh with His sword: many shall be slain by the Lord."*[2884] They spoke of the *"great and glorious Day of the Lord"*[2885] *"for the great Day of the Lord is near, it is near, and greatly hastens; the sound of the Day of the Lord is made bitter and harsh. A mighty Day of wrath is that Day, a Day of affliction and distress, a Day of desolation and destruction, a Day of gloominess and darkness, a Day of cloud and vapour, a Day of the trumpet and cry against the strong cities, and against the high towers."*[2886] *"For,*

[2869] 1 Corinth. 7:31.
[2870] St Ecumenius, *To 1 Corinthians*, in Migne, *P.G.*, 118, 740.
[2871] 1 Peter 4:7.
[2872] 2 Peter 3:10.
[2873] 2 Tim. 4:1.
[2874] John 6:39; 11:24; 12:48.
[2875] 1 Corinth. 1:8; 5:5.
[2876] 1 Corinth. 3:13.
[2877] 1 Corinth. 5:5.
[2878] Phil. 1:10.
[2879] 1 John 4:17.
[2880] Luke 17:24. Cf. St Symeon, *Euriskomena,* Homily LVII, pp. 287-301.
[2881] Matth. 24:3. 2 Thess. 2:8.
[2882] 1 Tim. 6:14. 2 Tim. 4:1. Tit. 2:13.
[2883] 1 Peter 4:13.
[2884] Is. 66:15-16
[2885] Joel 2:31.
[2886] Zeph. 1:14-18.

behold, a Day comes burning as an oven, and it shall consume them; and all the aliens, and all that do wickedly, shall be stubble: and the Day that is coming shall set them on fire, said the Lord Almighty."[2887] "*I beheld until the thrones were set, and the Ancient of Days sat; and His raiment was white as snow, and the hair of His head as pure wool: His throne was a flame of fire, and His wheels burning fire. A stream of fire rushed forth before Him: thousand thousands ministered to Him, and ten thousands of myriads attended upon Him: the Judgement sat, and the books were opened.*"[2888]

The prophecies of the Old Testament concerning Christ's Coming was initially fulfilled with His first Coming, the Incarnation of the Word of God and His appearance in the form of a servant and habitation amongst men. During this period the Lord did not come "*to condemn the world, but that the world through Him might be Saved.*"[2889] The Judgement and Condemnation of men is due to their the Salvation that our Lord and Saviour offers to the entire world. Therefore, "*he who believes in Him is not condemned, but he who does not believe is condemned already, because he has not believed in the Name of the Only Begotten Son of God.*"[2890]

Our Lord and Saviour Jesus Christ, the Son of God, condemned Satan, the ruler of this world, who tempted the Lord in the desert but who was defeated.[2891] Thus Christ entered into the "*strong man's house*" having "*first* (bound) *the strong man*" before plundering "*his house.*"[2892] Furthermore, before His sufferings, our Lord warned us that "*the ruler of this world is coming, and he has nothing in Me.*"[2893] Christ explained that Satan was already "*judged*"[2894] and "*cast out*"[2895] from Heaven, although his authority had received a deadly blow due to the Sacrifice of the crucified Lord, it was not yet completely destroyed. The fulfillment of the first Appearance of Christ and the Judgement of the works of men as well as the complete abolishment of the devil's works will take place at the Second Coming of the Lord, when He will come "*in His glory, and all the Holy Angels with Him.*"[2896] With the "*flame of fire*" He will punish take revenge

---

[2887] Mal. 4:1.
[2888] Daniel 7:9-14.
[2889] John 3:17.
[2890] John 3:18.
[2891] Matth. 4:1-11. Mark 1:12-13. Luke 4:1-13.
[2892] Matth. 12:29.
[2893] John 14:30.
[2894] John 16:11.
[2895] John 12:31.
[2896] Matth. 25:31.

those who did not know God and who did not obey His Gospel[2897] *"because they did not receive the love of the truth, that they might be Saved."*[2898]

Since the time of His Sermon on the Mount our Lord and Saviour Jesus Christ, the Son of God, referred to His Second Coming[2899] by very clearly stating that " *in that Day many will say to* (Him) *'Lord, Lord, have we not prophesied in Thy Name, cast out demons in Thy Name, and done many wonders in Thy Name?"* He warned us that He *"will declare to them, 'I never knew you; depart from Me, you who practice lawlessness!"*[2900] Then in the Lord's Prayer, He advised every disciple to address all petitions to our Heavenly Father, in the expectation that *"Thy Kingdom come."* Therefore the prayers of the first Christian Community were based on the sayings: *"Even so, come, Lord Jesus"*[2901] and *"may Grace come, and may this world pass away. Hosanna to the God of David. If anyone is Holy, let him come; if anyone is not, let him repent. Maranatha! Amen."*[2902]

The Lord referred to the prophesy of Daniel,[2903] which refers to His glorious Second Coming. He assured that after the tribulations of the world, all nations *"will see the Son of Man sitting at the Right Hand of the Power, and coming with the clouds of Heaven"*[2904] and *"all the Angels"*[2905] will accompany Him as witnesses of the Universal Judgement.[2906] Thus the Lord repeatedly assured us that He will appear again in all His Glory and Power, visible to the sight of all, even to sinners, manifesting the Majesty of His Kingship.[2907] To manifest this Royal Majesty our Lord compared Himself to *"a certain nobleman who went into a far country to receive for himself a Kingdom and to return."*[2908] Referring to the Judgement that will follow His Second Coming, He revealed that He will separate the just from the sinners, just *"as a shepherd divides his sheep from the goats."*[2909] He also assured us that He *"will send out His Angels, and they will gather out of His Kingdom all things that offend, and those who practise lawlessness and will cast them into the furnace of fire."*[2910] When teaching His Disciples and

---

[2897] Daniel 7:9, 10.
[2898] 2 Thess. 2:8.
[2899] Matth. 5:1-7:29.
[2900] Matth. 7:22-23.
[2901] Rev. 22:20.
[2902] *Didache,* 10, 6, in Lightfoot, *Apostolic Fathers,* p. 155.
[2903] Daniel 7:9-14.
[2904] Mark 14:62.
[2905] Matth. 25:31.
[2906] Matth. 24:29-31.
[2907] Rev. 1:7.
[2908] Luke 19:12.
[2909] Matth. 25:32.
[2910] Matth. 13:41-42.

the Jews concerning His Second Coming, He used the analogy of the dragnet, which *"was cast into the sea"* and gathered *"some of every kind, which when it was full, they drew to shore; and they sat down and gathered the good into vessels. But threw the bad away."*[2911] In the fourth Holy Gospel Christ referring to the faithfulness of St John the Evangelist, assured St Peter that: *"If I Will that he remains until I come, what is that to you? You follow Me."*[2912] Elsewhere, Christ proclaimed that the Father *"has given Him Authority to execute Judgement because He is the Son of Man"*[2913] whereas, on the contrary, He assured that *" the hour is coming in which all who are in the graves will hear His Voice and come forth – those who have done good, to the resurrection of life, and those who have done evil, to the resurrection of condemnation."*[2914] Furthermore, he taught that the Will of God the Father is *"that of all He has given"* to the Son *"should lose nothing, but should raise it up at the last Day"*[2915] and *"everyone who sees the Son and believes in Him may have everlasting life."*[2916]

In addition the two chapters in the Holy Gospel of St Matthew[2917] refer to the events of the future during the last Days to come and which will take place before the Second Coming. They also refer to the preparation and watchfulness that one should have in order to receive the Lord as the Heavenly Bridegroom Who will suddenly arrive *"at an hour you do not expect,"*[2918] so as to be able to enter the Wedding Festival with Him in His Kingdom. Nevertheless, in all the promises and prophecies concerning the Second Coming of the Lord, we have one unchangeable Truth:

That Christ will come as King of the Heavenly Kingdom vested with all His Glory.

The Lord made this declaration when He was in the form of a Servant dwelling among us and even after His glorious Ascension into Heaven, the fulfillment of His Prophecies concerning the catastrophe of Jerusalem and the falling of the world of idolatry. Each one of these manifestations of the Power and Glory of our Lord, consist of prophetic words and prefigurations of His Second Coming

---

[2911] Matth. 13:47-48.
[2912] John 21:22.
[2913] John 5:27
[2914] John 5:28-29.
[2915] John 6:39.
[2916] John 6:40.
[2917] Matth. 24 and 25.
[2918] Matth. 24:44.

In all the writings of the Holy Apostles, they urged the faithful to have their hope in and to await the Second Coming of the Lord. He who renounces this Truth uproots the whole structure of Apostolic Theology.

St Peter addressing the Jews *"in the porch which is called Solomon's"*[2919] proclaimed that, according to the Eternal Plan of God, *"Heaven must receive until the times of restoration of all things, that which God has spoken by the mouth of all His Holy Prophets since the world began"*[2920] and which will follow the Repentance of Israel.[2921] In this case the Second Coming of Christ is combined with the instruction of repentance of Israel, whereas elsewhere St Peter projected it as joy *"to the extent that you partake of Christ's sufferings, that when His glory is revealed, you may also be glad with exceeding joy."*[2922] St Peter in his 2nd Epistle spoke of the hope and promises urging the faithful: *"that scoffers will come in the last days But the heavens and the earth which are now preserved by the same word are reserved for fire until the Day of Judgement and perdition of ungodly men But the Day of the Lord will come as a thief in the night, in which the heavens will pass away with a great noise, and the elements will melt with fervent heat; both the earth and the works that are in it will be burnt up."*[2923]

St Paul repeatedly projected to the faithful that *"the Day of our Lord Jesus Christ"* is the Day *"waiting for the revelation"* of the Lord[2924] Who, when He comes, *"will both bring to light the hidden things of darkness and reveal the counsels of the hearts."*[2925] This Day of Christ's Coming is desirable for every Orthodox Christian because *"when Christ Who is our Life appears"* we *"also will appear with Him in glory"*[2926] enjoying *"the crown of righteousness, which the Lord, the Righteous Judge, will give to all who have loved His appearing.. on that Day."*[2927] Meeting the Lord Who will come from the Heavens we will be inseparable from Him, living with Him for all Eternity.

Regardless of how desirable the Day of the Lord is, it will be frightful and catastrophic for *"those who did not know God, and on those who do not obey the gospel of our Lord Jesus Christ"* because *"these shall*

[2919] Acts 3:11.
[2920] Acts 3:21.
[2921] Acts 3:11-26.
[2922] 1 Peter 4:13.
[2923] 2 Peter 3:2-14.
[2924] 1 Corinth. 1:7.
[2925] 1 Corinth. 4:5.
[2926] Col. 3:4.
[2927] 2 Tim. 4:8. 1 Thess. 4:15-17.

be punished with everlasting destruction from the Presence of the Lord and from the Glory of His Power."[2928] Hence St Paul stressed the obligation and the need of the faithful to "*establish their hearts blameless in holiness before our God and Father at the coming of our Lord Jesus Christ with all His Saints.*"[2929] St Peter speaking of "*times of refreshing*"[2930] did not expressed a different oppinion of that which St Paul assured saying that "*the Lord will appear a second time, apart from sin, for salvation.*"[2931]

St Jude wrote that the Lord is coming "*to execute Judgement on all, to convict all who are ungodly among them of all their ungodly deeds which they have committed in an ungodly way, and of all the harsh things which ungodly sinners have spoken against Him.*"[2932]

St James encouraging the faithful urged them to: "*Establish their hearts, for the coming of the Lord is at hand.*" "*Behold, the Judge is standing at the door!*"[2933] St John also urged to "*abide in Him, that when He appears, we may have confidence and not be ashamed before Him at His coming*"[2934] and in the book of Revelation he proclaimed that "*every eye will see Him, even they who pierced Him. And all the tribes of the earth.*"[2935]

The essential part of the prophetic promise and hope, which refers to the Second Coming of Christ, is the agreement of all the voices of Prophets and Apostles. Concluding the Apostolic testimonies we refer to the assurance given by the Holy Angels on the Day of Christ's Ascension into Heaven: "*Men of Galilee, why do you stand gazing up into heaven? This same Jesus, who was taken up from you into heaven, will so come in like manner as you saw Him go into heaven.*"[2936]

Question 360: What is the Doctrine of the End of the Age according to Holy Tradition?

Answer: In the *Didache* we read: "*Watch over your life: 'do not let your lamps go out, and do not be unprepared, but be ready, for you do not know the hour when our Lord is coming'*[2937] *For in the last Days the false prophets and corrupters will abound, and the sheep will be turned into*

[2928] 2 Thess. 1:8, 9.
[2929] 1 Thess. 3:13.
[2930] Acts 3:19.
[2931] Heb. 9:28.
[2932] Jude 15.
[2933] James 4:8, 9.
[2934] 1 John 2:28.
[2935] Rev. 1:7.
[2936] Acts 1:11.
[2937] Mark 13:35, 37. Matth. 24:42, 44. Luke 12:35, 40.

wolves, and love will be turned into hate. For as lawlessness increases, they will hate and persecute and betray one another.[2938] *And then the deceiver of the world will appear as a son of God and 'will perform signs and wonders,'*[2939] *and the earth will be delivered into his hands, and he will commit abominations the likes of which have never happened before. Then all humankind will come to the fiery test, and 'many will fall away' and perish; but 'those who endure' in their faith 'will be saved'*[2940] *And 'then there will appear the signs'*[2941] *of the truth: first the sign of an opening in heaven, then the sign of the sound of a trumpet,*[2942] *and third, the resurrection of the dead – but not of all; rather, as it has been said, 'The Lord will come, and all his saints with him.'*[2943] *Then the world 'will see the Lord coming upon the clouds of heaven.*[2944],[2945]

St Cyril of Jerusalem proclaimed that the Lord "*is coming at the End of this world with glory during the last Day.*" The "*second from the previous much beauty*" will not be "*humbled*" as the first but "*glorious.*" Because "*in the previous He suffered the humiliation of the Cross*" in "*the second He is coming accompanied and glorified by an army of Angels; He is coming not to be judged, but to judge those who judged Him.*" "*He is coming upon the clouds of heaven and angelic trumpets will then sound*" and not only glorious, but and "*..the descent of the Master will be frightful.*"[2946]

Finally, St John of Damascus emphisied that the Lord "*is coming from heaven, as the Holy Apostles saw Him ascending into Heaven, perfect God and perfect Man with glory and power.*"[2947]

Question 361: Is the time of the Second Coming known?

Answer: The Second Coming of our Lord and Saviour Jesus Christ, the Son of God, is the most certain event which will take place. But the time of His Coming remains unknown.[2948] Although our Lord repeatedly was asked about the time of His Coming by the Holy Apostles, He sated that "*It is not for you to know times or seasons which the Father has put in His own*

[2938] Matth. 24:10-12.
[2939] Mark 13:22.
[2940] Matth. 24:10, 13.
[2941] Matth. 24:30.
[2942] Matth. 24:31. 1 Corinth. 15:52. 1 Thess. 4:12.
[2943] Zech. 14:5. 1 Thess. 3:13.
[2944] Matth. 24:30.
[2945] *Didache,* 16, 1-8, in Lightfoot, *Apostolic Fathers,* p. 158.
[2946] St Cyril of Jerusalem, *Catechesis,* XV, §§ 1, 2, 9, in Migne, *P.G.,* 33, 869.
[2947] St John of Damascus, *Catechesis,* IV, 26, in Migne, *P.G.,* 94, 1217. Mogilas, in Karmeris, *The dogmatics,* v. II, p. 619.
[2948] Bryennios, *Paralipomena,* ch. XLI, v. III, p. 122.

authority."[2949]   Christ as a perfect Man ignores the time, as He proclaimed saying: *"But of that Day and hour no one knows, not even the Angels of Heaven, but My Father only."*[2950]

St Paul presented this truth of Christ's Coming saying: *"For you yourselves know perfectly that the Day of the Lord so comes as a thief in the night."*[2951]   St Peter also used this example saying: *"But the Day of the Lord will come as a thief in the night, in which the heavens will pass away with a great noise, and the elements will melt with fervent heat; both the earth and the works that are in it will be burned up."*[2952]   This example of the *"thief"* was used by the Lord, who instructed His Disciples to be watchful, because as the owner of the house does not know *"what hour the thief would come"*[2953] likewise and the disciples and all the faithful ignore *"what hour the Lord is coming."*[2954]   Both Holy Apostles draw the attention on the event, that, when men *"say, 'Peace and safety!' then sudden destruction comes upon them, as labor pains upon a pregnant woman. And they shall not escape."*[2955]   The Lord also compared the time of His Second Coming to the times of Noah saying: *"As the Days of Noah were so also will the coming of the Son of Man be. For as in the Days before the flood, they were eating and drinking, marrying and giving in marriage, until the Day that Noah entered the ark, and did not know until the flood came and took them all away, so also will the coming of the Son of Man be."*[2956]   According to our Lord and the Holy Apostles, it is not for us to ask about the time of the Second Coming, but rather to be watchful, alert and always ready to receive the Master.[2957]

Question 362: What are the Signs before the Second Coming?

Answer: Although the Second Coming of our Lord will take place in an unknown time, *"as a thief in the night,"* some events will prepare the ground for His Appearance.[2958] These events comprise *"the signs of His Coming, and the End of the Age,"*[2959] which foretold the Coming of the Lord. *"When*

[2949] Acts 1:7.
[2950] Matth. 24:36. Mark 13:32.
[2951] 1 Thess. 5:2.
[2952] 2 Peter 3:10.
[2953] Matth. 24:43.
[2954] Matth. 24:42.
[2955] 1 Thess. 5:3.
[2956] Matth. 24:36-39.
[2957] Cf. Plato of Moscow, *Orthodox Teaching,* p. 129. Mitsopoulos, *Themata*, p.374
[2958] Cf. Plato of Moscow, *Orthodox Teaching,* pp. 129-130. Evdokimov, *Orthodoxia*, pp. 401-404. Mitsopoulos, *Themata*, pp. 374-377.
[2959] Matth. 24:3.

you see all these things, know that it is near – at doors."[2960] The Lord spoke of these signs shortly before His sufferings and they are clearly prophetic.[2961]

According to the above these signs can be as follows:

a) The preaching of the Holy Gospel in the entire world.[2962]

b) St Paul revealed in his Epistle to the Romans that when *"the fullness of the Gentiles has come in,"* then also *"Israel will be saved,"*[2963] believing in the Gospel and acknowledging Jesus as the true Messiah, Christ and Saviour. Many times the return of Israel is linked with the return of the Prophet Elijah. The Prophet Malachi first spoke of the coming of Elijah. He spoke that the future Messiah will have a *"messenger who will survey the way before"* him[2964] and he names him as *"Elijah the Thesbite."* *"And behold, I will End to you Elijah the Thesbite, before the great and glorious Day of the Lord comes: who shall turn again the heart of the father to the son, and the heart of a man to his neighbour, lest I come and smite the earth grievously."*[2965] During the time of our Lord, the awaiting of the return of the Prophet Elijah was a general belief among the Jews. The Angel foretold to the Prophet Zachariah about his son, St John the Forerunner and Baptist, saying that *"he will also go before Him in the spirit and power of Elijah."*[2966] Christ assured saying that *"But I say to you that Elijah has come already, and they did not know him but did to him whatever they wished."*[2967]

c) The Lord instructed, that a great Apostasy will take place before His Second Coming.[2968] The false-prophets *"will deceive many."*[2969] Increasing indifference, enslavement to materialism and the pleasures of the present life will prevail as these conditions were *"in the Days of Noah, so it will be also in the Days of the Son of Man: They ate, they drank, they married wives, they were given in marriage, until the Day that Noah entered the ark, and the flood came and destroyed them all. Likewise as it was also in the Days of Lot: They ate, they drank, they bought, they sold, planted, they built; but on the Day that Lot went out of Sodom it rained fire and*

[2960] Matth. 24:33.
[2961] Matth. 24. Mark 13:1-37. Luke 21:5-36.
[2962] Matth. 24:14.
[2963] Rom. 11:25, 26.
[2964] Mal. 3:1
[2965] Mal. 4:5-6.
[2966] Luke 1:17.
[2967] Matth. 17:12.
[2968] Plato of Moscow, *Orthodox Teaching,* p. 129.
[2969] Matth. 24:5.

brimstone from heaven and destroyed them all. Even so will it be in the Day when the Son of Man is revealed."[2970] Regardless of the tribulations and temptations, by which the Divine providence searched to brings right and the return of the lawless generation, it remained hard and unbent and unrepentant. "*They blasphemed the God of heaven because of their pains and their sores, and did not repent of their deeds.*"[2971]

The increasing of sin create a greater misery, which is accompanied by an anxiety and hopelessness. This was described by the Lord saying: "*There will be signs in the sun, in the moon, and in the stars; and on the earth distress of nations, with perplexity, the sea and the waves roaring; men's hearts failing them from fear and the expectation of those things which are coming on the earth, for the powers of the heavens will be shaken. Then they will see the Son of Man, coming in a cloud with power and great glory. Now when these things begin to happen, look up and lift up your heads, because your redemption draws near.*"[2972] Thus the prophecy of St Paul will be fulfilled according to which the Lord's Day will not come "*unless the falling away comes first, and the man of sin is revealed, the son of perdition.*"[2973]

d) The peak of the Apostasy, misery and anxiety will be the coming of the Antichrist According to *Didache* "*in the last Days the false prophets and corrupters will abound, and the sheep will be turned into wolves, and love will be turned into hate. For as lawlessness increases, they will hate and persecute and betray one another.*[2974] *And then the deceiver of the world will appear as a son of God and 'will perform signs and wonders,'*[2975] *and the earth will be delivered into his hands, and he will commit abominations the likes of which have never happened before.*"[2976] The Divine Evangelist John characterized as "*Antichrist*" "*every spirit that does not confess that Jesus Christ has come in flesh*"[2977] and assured that "*many false prophets have gone out into the world.*"[2978]

St John of Damascus observed, "*in a special way the Antichrist is called, he will come at the End of the Age.*"[2979] "*Unless the falling away comes first, and the man of sin is revealed, the son of perdition, who*

[2970] Luke 17:26-30.
[2971] Rev. 16:11.
[2972] Luke 21:25-28. Cf. Matth 24:29-31. Mark 13:24-27.
[2973] 2 Thess. 2:3.
[2974] Matth. 24:10-12.
[2975] Mark 13:22.
[2976] *Didache,* 16, 3-4, in Lightfoot, *Apostolic Fathers,* p. 158.
[2977] 1 John 3:3.
[2978] 1 John 3:1.
[2979] St John of Damascus, *Exposition. About the Anti-Christ,* IV, 99, 26, in Migne, *P.G.,* 94, 1217.

opposes and exalts himself above all that is called God or that is worshiped, so that he sits as God in the temple of God, showing himself that he is God."[2980]

The Holy Fathers of the Orthodox Church accepted the Antichrist as "*some knowledgeable and wise person, who pretends to have wisdom and philanthropia*" not as the incarnation of the devil but "*a man by nature, who will receive all the power of the devil. And as God and Saviour took up our human nature and was able to work through it the salvation, likewise and Satan will chose a man to give him all his power to deceive men.*" "*The devil does not become man according to the Lord's incarnation*" but the devil dwells in a man "*the future free-will the lawless God foreseeing consents that the devil inhabits in him.*" He will work great things and wonders and will show admirable signs, but these will be "*false and deception of magic signs and wonders of lies and not real.*" "*Because the father of lies, Satan in person will act through him, to make the multitudes to believe the dead as risen, and the limp walking and the blind seeing, without the healing taking place.*" Through these he will attempt to prove that he is god and "*will oppose God and will destroy the gods and will command to worship him instead of God.*" He will appear to the Jews "*as the Christ which they await.*" "*He will deceive*" many "*and when prevailing he will persecute the Church of God and will manifest all his evilness*" and "*all the human lawlessness will surpass of those who in the pass were unjust and ungodly, murderers and unmerciful and especially will be against the Christians.*"[2981] Some of the Holy Fathers support the opinion that the Antichrist will come not from the Christians, but from the Jews. He will be worshipped by all those Jews who have not accepted Christ as the Son of God and Messiah as well as by all those who denied the True Christian Faith (heretics) and he will demand the rebuilding of the Temple of Solomon.[2982]

e) According to the teachings of our Lord and Saviour Jesus Christ, the Son of God " *you will hear of wars and rumors of wars. See that you are not troubled; for all these things must come to pass, but the End is not yet. For nation will rise against nation, and Kingdom against Kingdom. And there will be famines, pestilences, and earthquakes in various places. All these are the beginning of sorrows. Then they will deliver you up to*

[2980] 2 Thess. 2:3-4.

[2981] St Cyril of Jerusalem, *Catechesis,* XV, § 12, in Migne, *P.G.,* 33, 885. Theodoretus of Cyrus, *To 2 Thessalonians 2:4,* in Migne, *P.G.,* 82, 664. St John of Damascus, *Catechesis,* IV, 26, in Migne, *P.G.,* 94, 1217. St John Chrysostom, *To 2 Thessalonians 2:4,* in Migne, *P.G.,* 62, 482.

[2982] St John of Damascus, *Exposition. About the Anti-Christ,* IV, 99, 26, in Migne, *P.G.,* 94, 1217. St Cyril of Jerusalem, *Catechesis,* XV, § 12, in Migne, *P.G.,* 33, 889, 893.

tribulation and kill you, and you will be hated by all nations for My name's sake. And then many will be offended, will betray one another, and will hate one another. Then many false prophets will rise up and deceive many. And because lawlessness will abound, the love of many will grow cold. But he who endures to the End shall be saved. And this gospel of the Kingdom will be preached in the entire world as a witness to all the nations, and then the End will come."[2983] St Peter said as "*the world that existed perished, being flooded with water*" so "*the heavens and the earth which are now preserved by the same word, are reserved for fire until the Day of Judgement,*"[2984] because "*the Day of the Lord will come as a thief in the night, in which the heavens will pass away with a great noise, and the elements will melt with fervent heat; both the earth and the works that are in it will be burned up.*"[2985]

Question 363: What is the Millennium and its true meaning?

Answer: The Second Coming of our Lord and Saviour Jesus Christ, the Son of God, and the End of the world will happen simultaneously. The teaching concerning the reign of Christ is mentioned in the Book of Revelation,[2986] according to which the Lord our God will rule on earth for one thousand years. During this period the devil will be bound but before, a great battle will take place against the Church and he, his angels and all his evil followers will be defeated (Armagedon). Hence the teaching concerning the Millennium came forth, which was taught by Cerinthus,[2987] Papias,[2988] Irenaeus,[2989] Tertullian[2990] and some of the Apologists.[2991] However, this theory was opposed by Gaius in Rome, Origen,[2992] St Dionysius of Alexandria,[2993] Methodius of Olympus,[2994] St Gregory of Nazianzus,[2995] St

---

[2983] Matth. 24:6-14.
[2984] 2 Peter 3:6, 7.
[2985] 2 Peter 3:10.
[2986] Rev. 20:1-15. Cf. Mitsopoulos, *Themata*, pp. 378-383.
[2987] Eusebius, *Church History*, III, 28, 2, in Migne, *P.G.*, 20, 273.
[2988] Ibid, *Church History*, III, 39, 12, in Migne, *P.G.*, 20, 300.
[2989] St Irenaeus, *Heresies*, book V, chs. 32-35, in Hadjephraimides, pp. 414-423.
[2990] Tertullian, *Instit.*, VII, 17.
[2991] St Justin, the philosopher and martyr, *Dialogue*, 80, 81, in *B*, v. 3.
[2992] Origen, *About Principals*, II, 11, 2, in Migne, *P.G.*, 11, 241 and 242.
[2993] Eusebius, *Church History*, VII, 24, 4, in Migne, *P.G.*, 20, 693.
[2994] Methodius, *Symposium*, IX, 1, 5, in Migne, *P.G.*, 18, 176.
[2995] St Gregory of Nazianzus, *Epist. 102 to Cledonius*, in Migne, *P.G.*, 37, 197.

Basil the Great,[2996] St Epiphanius,[2997] St Hieronymus[2998] and St Augustine.[2999]

Today, the misinterpretation of the Millennium is supported by the heresies of the Rebaptists and Jehovah Witnesses who believe that Christ will rule materially for one thousand years, establishing an earthly government. Briefly, in their false teachings, they renounce the Holy Trinity, the Son, the Holy Spirit, the Church, the Holy Mysteries and the Saints and have adopted all the old and contemporary heresies which Satan has developed in order to mislead men into Eternal Condemnation.

We must never forget that the teachings of the Book of Revelation are under a veil of Divine Mystery. Consequently, we can accept:

1. The period of one thousand years is obviously symbolic and must be considered in the light of the Apostolic Teachings that *"with the Lord one day is as a thousand years, and a thousand years as one day."*[3000] The Holy Gospel will prevail on earth and for a long period the Will of God will rule among men. Thus the Church will be found triumphantly accomplishing all her goals on earth. The teachings concerning the Biblical Millennium is a prophecy of the final victory of Christianity within the boundaries of time. During that period Satan will be bound because, although evil will not have been completely abolished, it will have been restricted and weakened. The nations and governments will be Enlightened by the Will of God. Science and Art will serve Christian thought and find their ideal expression. The fullness of all the Gifts of the One, Holy, Catholic and Apostolic Eastern Orthodox Church will become universal and new, submitting the different religious confessions under one Holy Christian Faith which will uphold the True Teachings of our Lord Jesus Christ, the Son of God. All the followers of Christ will acknowledge one Leader of their Faith Who is the Head of the Church. They will have one and the same Faith and Love in order to grow together.

2. This Millennium will end because everything under the sun in this world will come to an end. After this period Satan, who will be bound but not destroyed, will once again become free and he will fight against all the Powers of Heaven. However, the Saving Power of Christ at His Second

---

[2996] St Basil, the Great, *Epist.* 263, 4, in Migne, *P.G.,* 32, 980. Ibid, *Epist.* 265, 2, in Migne, *P.G.,* 32, 988.
[2997] St Epiphanius, *Panarion, Heresy* 77, §§ 36-37, in Migne, *P.G.,* 42, 697.
[2998] St Hieronymus, *Comm. in Isaiah* XXX, 26; LIV, 11; LV, 3; LVIII, 14, in migne, *P.L.,* 24, 362, 561, 550, 597.
[2999] St Augustine, *De civitate Dei,* XX, 7, in migne, *P.L.,* 41, 667.
[3000] 2 Peter 3:8.

Coming will utterly destroy Satan's power and will condemn him and all his evil servants. Even nature itself will be regenerated and will glorify the Lord. After the Last Judgement the faithful will enjoy the extreme Blessedness of God's Kingdom, whereas the ungodly, unbelievers and unrepentant sinners will be cast out into Eternal Condemnation.

However, once again, we must keep in mind that the Book of Revelation is the only prophetic Book of the New Testament and many things are hidden under a veil of Divine Mystery, which can only be revealed by the same Holy Spirit Who inspired St John the Apostle and Evangelist. Any attempts to interpret this Holy Book without the Holy Spirit, the guidance of the Holy Fathers of the Orthodox Church accompanied by humility, prayer and acknowledgment of our weakness will consequently lead to dangerous misinterpretations.

The Holy Spirit warns us by saying: *"I testify to everyone who hears the words of the prophecy of this Book: if anyone adds to these things, God will add to him the pledges that are written in this Book; and if anyone takes away from the words of the Book of this prophecy, God shall take away his part from the Book of Life, from the Holy City, and from the things that are written in this Book. He who testifies to these things says: 'Surely, I Am coming quickly.'"*[3001]

CHAPTER FOUR
THE RESURRECTION OF THE DEAD

Question 364: What is the Doctrine of the Resurrection of the Dead?

Answer: The Doctrine of the Resurrection of the dead is completely Christian. According to the ancient world of idolatry, although we find some philosophic opinions expressing the belief in the immortality of the soul, the idea of giving life to bodies in graves was a completely alien concept. This is evident when St Paul addressed the Greeks on Areopagos (the Hill of Ares), preaching the unknown God to the Athenians.[3002] The belief is expressed from a Christian point of view in the Epistle to the Hebrews whereby *"the Doctrine of Baptism, of Laying on of Hands, of Resurrection of the dead, and of Eternal Judgement"*[3003] had to be taught in order to familiarise those who believed in Christ For St Paul it was

---

[3001] Rev 22: 18 – 20.
[3002] Acts 17:16-34.
[3003] Heb. 6:2.

unacceptable and completely irresponsible for any Christian who believes in Christ to renounce the Universal Resurrection of the dead.[3004]

In the Old Testament we find some belief in the Resurrection stressing specifically the descent of souls into Hades whereas only in Job[3005] do we find the belief of the Resurrection. The Prophets Isaiah,[3006] Ezekiel[3007] and Hosea[3008] use the imagery of the Resurrection of bodies to express the ethnic restoration from the death of slavery to the Resurrection of freedom of Israel. The use of this imagery proves that hope of the dead rising from death was not strange to them. Daniel spoke quite literally of *"many who sleep in the dust of the earth shall awake, some to Everlasting Life, and some to reproach and Everlasting Shame."*[3009] In the Book of Maccabees, the seven brothers who were martyred, believed in the Resurrection of only the Just.[3010]

During the time of our Lord, the belief in the Resurrection appears to have been generally widespread. Christ assured St Martha, the sister of St Lazarus: *" your brother will Rise again"* to which she replied: *"I know that he will Rise again in the Resurrection at the Last Day."*[3011] In the Book of Acts we realise that although the Pharisees believed in the Resurrection, the Sadducees did not.[3012] In addition, we can conclude that the Pharisees had very materialistic hopes of the Resurrection from the tricky question they put to Christ regarding seven brothers who took the same wife. Answering them our Lord declared: *"For in the Resurrection they neither marry nor are given in marriage, but are like Angels of God in Heaven."*[3013]

Our Lord guaranteeing the Immortality of the soul, implied the receiving of its body and urged His Disciples to be attentive and *"not to fear those who kill the body but cannot kill the soul. But rather fear him who is able to destroy both soul and body in Hell."*[3014] Christ also spoke of the Reward of those who show hospitality to *"the poor, the mained, the lame, the blind"* because they *"will be Blessed"* and *"shall be repaid at the Resurrection of the Just."*[3015] In the Gospel of St John, our Lord explicitly warned: *"the Hour is coming in which all who are in the graves will hear*

[3004] 1 Corinth. 15:12-20.
[3005] Job 19:25-26.
[3006] Is. 26:19. Cf. St Irenaeus, *Heresies,* book V, ch. 34, § 1-4, in Hadjephraimides, pp. 418-420.
[3007] Ez. 27:1-14.
[3008] Hos. 13:14.
[3009] Daniel 12:2.
[3010] II Maccabees 7:9, 14, 23; 12:43, 44.
[3011] John 11:23, 24.
[3012] Acts 23:8.
[3013] Matth. 22:30.
[3014] Matth. 10:28.
[3015] Luke 14:13, 14.

His Voice and come forth – those who have done good, to the Resurrection of Life, and those who have done evil, to the Resurrection of Condemnation."[3016] Furthermore He proclaimed *"that of all"* that the Father *"has given Me, I should lose nothing, but should Raise it up at the Last Day. And this is the Will of Him Who sent Me, that everyone who sees the Son and believes in Him may have Everlasting Life; and I will Raise him up at the Last Day."*[3017] Hence, *"whoever eats"* Christ's *"Flesh and drinks"* His *"Blood has Eternal Life"* and as Promised, He *"will raise him up at the Last Day."*[3018]

After Christ, the Holy Apostles taught the Resurrection of the dead in their Sermons and as a result, the Sadducees accused them of and condemned them for proclaiming the belief in *"the Resurrection of the dead"*[3019] through their Teachings of Christ.

St Paul in his Epistles exalted the inseparable Communion of Christ with the faithful who comprise His Mystical Body, by assuring that *"if the Spirit of Him Who Raised Jesus from the dead dwells in you, He Who Raised Christ from the dead will also give Life to your mortal bodies through His Spirit Who dwells in you,"*[3020] *"knowing that He Who Raised up the Lord Jesus will also Raise us up with Jesus."*[3021] Thus our Lord and Saviour Jesus Christ, the Son of God, *"will transform our lowly body that it may be conformed to His Glorious Body."*[3022] St Paul mocked the Corinthians who doubted the Resurrection of the dead.[3023] *"For the Lord Himself will descend from Heaven with a shout, with a voice of an Archangel, and with the Trumpet of God. And the dead in Christ will Rise first. Then we who are alive and remain shall be caught up together with them in the clouds to meet the Lord in the air. And thus we shall always be with the Lord."*[3024]

In the Book of Revelation it is written: *"Then I* (John) *saw a great white Throne and Him Who sat on it, from Whose Face the earth and the Heavens fled away. And there was found no place for them. And I saw the dead, small and great, standing before God, and Books were opened. And another Book was opened, which is the Book of Life. And the dead were Judged according to their works, by the things which were written in the*

[3016] John 5:28-29.
[3017] John 6:39-40.
[3018] John 6:54.
[3019] Acts 4:2; 17:32; 24:15, 21; 26:23.
[3020] Rom. 8:11.
[3021] 2 Corinth. 4:14.
[3022] Phil. 3:21.
[3023] 1 Corinth. 15:12-20.
[3024] 1 Thess. 4:16-17.

Books. The sea gave up the dead who were in it, and Death and Hades delivered up the dead who were in them. And they were Judged, each one according to his works. Then Death and Hades were cast into the Lake of Fire. This is the Second Death. And anyone not found written in the Book of Life was cast into the Lake of Fire."[3025]

Question 365: What is the Doctrine of the Resurrection of the Dead according to Holy Tradition?

Answer: St Clement used examples from nature to illustrate the Resurrection of the dead: "*Let us consider, dear friends, how the Master continually points out to us the coming Resurrection of which He made the Lord Jesus Christ the Firstfruit when He Raised Him from the dead.*"[3026] He also urged: "*Let none of you say that this flesh is not Judged and does not Rise again,*" for "*we will receive our reward in this flesh.*"[3027]

In the *Epistle of Barnabas* it is stressed that "*the one who does*" "*the Lord's Commandments*" "*will be glorified in the Kingdom of God; the one who chooses their opposites will perish together with his works. This is why there is a Resurrection; this is why there is recompense.*"[3028]

St Polycarp of Smyrna typified as "*the first-born of Satan*" all those "*who do not confess that Jesus Christ has come in the Flesh*" characterising them as " '*Antichrist*'[3029] and whoever does not acknowledge the Testimony of the Cross 'is of the devil;'[3030] and whoever twists the saying of the Lord to suit his own sinful desires and claims that there is neither Resurrection nor Judgement – well, that person is the first-born of Satan.*"[3031]. In the prayer that he offered to God, he stressed: "*I bless Thee because Thou hast considered me worthy of this day and hour, that I might receive a place among the number of the Martyrs in the Cup of Thy Christ, to the Resurrection to Eternal Life, both of soul and of body, in the Incorruptibility of the Holy Spirit.*"[3032]

St Justin the Philosopher and Martyr believed that we as Christians "*hope that those who are dead and placed in the ground will receive their own bodies again.*" "*In death and in the burial*" "*the human bodies, as*

[3025] Rev. 20:11-15.

[3026] St Clement of Rome, *1ˢᵗ Corinthians,* 24, 1, in Lightfoot, *Apostolic Fathers,* p. 42.

[3027] Ibid, *2ⁿᵈ Corinthians,* 9, 1 and 5, in Lightfoot, *Apostolic Fathers,* p. 72.

[3028] *Barnabas,* 21, 1, in Lightfoot, *Apostolic Fathers,* p. 187.

[3029] Cf. 1 John 4:2-3.

[3030] Cf. 1 John 3:8.

[3031] St Polycarp of Smyrna, *To Philippians,* 7, 1, in Lightfoot, *Apostolic Fathers,* p. 126-127.

[3032] *Martyrdom of Polycarp,* 14, 2, in Lightfoot, *Apostolic Fathers,* p. 141.

seeds, are spread in the earth, and unless God commands it, are impossible to Rise and Vest with Immortality."[3033]

The belief in the Resurrection of the dead was included in the Nicene Creed: "*I look for the Resurrection of the dead and the Life of the world to come.*"

Question 366: What is the consequence of our union with Christ?

Answer: The Resurrection of the dead is an inseparable part of the summing up of everything in Christ.[3034] St Paul stressed that in Baptism *"we were buried with Him through Baptism into death, that just as Christ was Raised from the dead by the Glory of the Father, even so we also should walk in Newness of Life. For if we have been united together in the likeness of His death, certainly we also shall be in the likeness of His Resurrection, knowing this, that our old man was crucified with Him, that the body of sin might be done away with, that we should no longer be slaves of sin. For he who has died has been freed from sin. Now if we died with Christ, we believe that we shall also live with Him, knowing that Christ, having been Raised from the dead, dies no more. Death no longer has dominion over Him. For the death that He died, He died to sin once for all; but the Life that He lives, He lives to God. Likewise you also reckon yourselves to be dead indeed to sin, but alive to God in Christ Jesus our Lord.*"[3035] Since we become one Body with Christ, it is natural that His Resurrection is the beginning of the Resurrection of all those who believe in Him and are united with Him. There cannot be a Resurrection of the Head without the Resurrection of the whole Body. The bodies of all Orthodox Christians are the members of Christ's "*Body, of His Flesh and His Bones*"[3036] as well as being temples of the Holy Spirit.[3037] The Resurrection of our bodies from the dead is a consequence of this exaltation[3038] because "*if the Spirit of Him Who raised Jesus from the dead dwells in you, He Who raised Christ from the dead will also give life to your mortal bodies through His Spirit Who dwells in you.*"[3039]

According to the above, the Resurrection of the dead is a natural result of our union with Christ and the indwelling of the Holy Spirit within us.

[3033] St Justin, the philosopher and martyr, *1 Apology,* 18, 6 and 19, 4, in **B**, v. 3, p. 171.
[3034] Cf. Frangopoulos, *Christian Faith,* p. 235. Mitsopoulos, *Themata,* pp. 386-388.
[3035] Rom. 6:4-11.
[3036] Ephes. 5:30. 1 Corinth. 6:15.
[3037] 1 Corinth. 6:19.
[3038] 1 Corinth. 6:14.
[3039] Rom. 8:11.

The renouncement of this belief contradicts faith in the Truth of being united with Christ as one Holy Body.

Question 367: What will be the nature of the human body after the Resurrection?

Answer: According to the belief of the Orthodox Church the nature of the body after the general Resurrection of the dead will be *"the same and not the same"*[3040] as when it was placed in the tomb.[3041] Theodorus of Mopsuestias added that *"as glass is* (made) *from sand"* but is no longer like sand *" but something else; and the wheat likewise is"* no longer *"seed, but wheat; likewise in the Resurrection"* the body becomes *"a better body."*[3042]

The new body resulting from the Resurrection of the dead is not a new creation nor is it organically related to the previous one although between the two there a commonality as well as a difference like that between the seed and the wheat or between the sperm and the infant.[3043]

The different elements of which the body is composed and which decomposed in the tomb, will be gathered together once again and a new body will be reconstructed. Even though man may ignore or forget where these elements have been buried, God does not ignore or forget because He knows everything. God has the Knowledge and the Power to Raise the bodies *"with equal opulence"* uniting the different elements *"again to their own parts and particles"* even if they have been scattered everywhere.[3044]

Although the Risen body will be *"the same"* as that which the soul had when it departed from this life, because of the new Attributes which it will receive, it will *"not be the same"* in the opinion of the Divine Chrysostom.[3045] This is neither impossible nor contradictory according to God's Divine Almightiness. The human body is raised by God in a Mysterious way: *"the body is sown in corruption, and it is raised in Incorruption. It is sown in dishonour, it is raised in Glory. It is sown in*

[3040] St John Chrysostom, *To 1 Corinthians,* Homily 41, § 2, in Migne, *P.G.,* 61, 356, 357. Cf. St Basil the Great, *To Psalm 41(42),* § 1, in Migne, *P.G.,* 29, 388. Ibid, *To Psalm 114(115),* § 5, in Migne, *P.G.,* 29, 492. Origen, *To Psalm* I, § 5, in Migne, *P.G.,* 12, 1093-1096. Ibid, *Against Celsus,* V, 23, in *B,* v. 10, p. 27. Ibid, *About Principals,* II, 10, 3, in Migne, *P.G.,* 11, 236. St Gregory of Nyssa, *About the creation of man,* ch. XXVII, in Migne, *P.G.,* 44, 225-228. Bryennios, *Paralipomena,* ch. VII, v. III, p. 77.
[3041] St John Chrysostom, *To 1 Corinthians,* Homily 41, § 2, in Migne, *P.G.,* 61, 356, 357. Plato of Moscow, *Orthodox Teaching,* pp. 162-163.
[3042] Theodorus of Mopsuestias, in Trempelas, *Dogmatique,* v. III, p. 468.
[3043] Mitsopoulos, *Themata,* pp. 388-389.
[3044] Cf. Athenagoras, *About resurrection,* ch. 2, 3, in *B,* v. 1, pp. 312-313. Tertullian, *Apologeticus,* in migne, *P.L.,* 1, 525. St Cyril of Jerusalem, *Catechesis,* 18, §§ 1-2, in Migne, *P.G.,* 33, 1020-1021.
[3045] St John Chrysostom, *To 1 Corinthians,* Homily 41, § 2, in Migne, *P.G.,* 61, 356, 357.

weakness, it is raised in Power. It is sown a natural body, it is raised a spiritual body."[3046]   Since the new environment and the condition into which men shall enter after the Resurrection will be alien to the mortality and the density of this present world, it is thus necessary for the risen bodies to be adapted so that they may exist in this new environment and condition. It is impossible for human nature to participate in the Heavenly things unless it is transformed so that the natural body is vested with Immortality. How this will take place remains a Mystery known only to God.

Our Lord and Saviour Jesus Christ first informed us of this transformation by assuring us that " *in the Resurrection they neither marry nor are given in marriage, but are like Angels of God in Heaven*"[3047] "*nor can they die anymore, for they are equal to the Angels.*"[3048]   In addition, St Paul declared that *"God will destroy both" "foods for the stomach and the stomach for foods."*[3049]

Nonetheless, the Resurrected body will be spiritual although "*it is sown a natural body, it is Raised a spiritual body.*"[3050] According to St John Chrysostom it will be spiritual either because the Holy Spirit will remain for ever in the bodies of the Just or it will be the power of the soul governed continuously by the Holy Spirit. It may even be spiritual because it shall become lighter or rather because of all these facts combined.[3051]

Origen thought that the body will be "*airy*" and without the weaknesses of the flesh.   He supported the opinion that at the time of the change, it will become like the bodies of Angels: airy and light.[3052]

Finally, the Resurrected body is characterised as "*glorious.*"[3053]   Our Lord said that "*the Righteous will shine forth as the sun in the Kingdom of their Father.*"[3054] The Lord's Transfiguration on Mount Tabor, as well as the Heavenly Light that surrounded St Paul when the Lord appeared to him after His Resurrection, gives us some idea of this "*glorious*" change, which awaits the Righteous according to St Paul.[3055] Although the nature of those who will be glorified is one aspect of the Resurrection, there will be many levels and differences of Offices as well for those who will be condemned.

[3046] 1 Corinth. 15:42-44.
[3047] Matth. 22:30.
[3048] Luke 20:36.
[3049] 1 Corinth. 6:13.
[3050] 1 Corinth. 15:42-44.
[3051] St John Chrysostom, *To 1 Corinthians*, Homily 41, § 3, in Montfaucon, v. 10, p. 454.
[3052] Origen, *To Matthew*, v. 17, §§ 29 and 30, in *B*, v. 14, pp. 193 and 197. Ibid, *Against Celsus*, III, 41, 42, in *B*, v. 9, pp. 206 and 207.
[3053] Scheeben, *Les Mystères*, p. 657.
[3054] Matth. 13 :43.
[3055] 1 Corinth. 15:38-53.

While the bodies of the Righteous will shine as stars brighter than the sun, the sinners will be in Darkness[3056] and despite everyone rising from the dead for Eternity, having their own bodies, they will not have the same conditions because all unrepentant sinners " *will receive an Eternal body, which will suffer the punishments of sins, not being consumed by the Eternal Fire.*"[3057]

CHAPTER FIVE
THE UNIVERSAL JUDGEMENT

Question 368: What does the Church teach concerning the Universal Judgement according to Holy Scripture and Holy Tradition?

Answer: In the Old Testament the idea of Judgement is one that causes catastrophe and destruction such as the Great Flood, the annihilation of Sodom and Gomorrah, the ten plagues of Egypt and the various punishments suffered by the Israelites in Egypt and Canaan. This idea developed gradually and thereby Divine Revelation gained the acceptance of those to whom God reveals Himself. If, since the Judgement in the Old Testament appears at first as a direct Punishment of certain acts or circumstances, during the period of the Prophets the Divine Revenge against human error appears to be reserved for a certain Day of Judgement, when all nations will be Judged and as a consequence it will develop into a Day of Catastrophe. On that Day "*man and cattle* [will] *be cut off; let the birds of the air and the fishes of the sea be cut off; and the ungodly shall fail, and I will take away the transgressors from the face of the land, said the Lord.*"[3058] "*It shall come to pass in that Day, said the Lord of Hosts, that I will utterly destroy the names of the idols from off the land, and there shall be no longer any remembrance of them: and I will cut off the false prophets and the evil spirit from the land.*"[3059] "*For behold, in those days and in that time, when I shall have turned the captivity of Judah and Jerusalem, I will also gather all the Gentiles, and bring them down to the Valley of Josaphat, and will plead with them there for My people and My heritage Israel, who have been dispersed among Gentiles; and these Gentiles have divided My land, and cast lots over My people, and have given their boys to harlots, and sold their girls for wine, and have drunk.*"[3060] This Judgement shall include

---

[3056] Zigabinos, *To Matthew*, in Migne, *P.G.*, 129, 416. St Gregory of Nyssa, *To Hexaemeros*, § 24, in Migne, *P.G.*, 44, 116. Theodoretus of Cyrus, *To 1 Corinthians 15:41*, in Migne, *P.G.*, 81, 365.
[3057] St Cyril of Jerusalem, *Catechesis*, 18, § 19, in Migne, *P.G.*, 33, 1040.
[3058] Zeph. 1:2-3.
[3059] Zach. 13:2.
[3060] Joel 3:1-3.

Israel who will be Judged according to his works that " *the righteousness of the Righteous shall not deliver him, in the day wherein he errs: and the iniquity of the ungodly shall not harm him, in the day wherein he turns from his iniquity, but the righteous erring shall not be able to deliver himself.*"[3061] "*For, behold, the Lord will come as Fire, and His chariots as a storm to render His Vengeance with Wrath, and His Rebuke with a Flame of Fire. For with the Fire of the Lord all the earth shall be Judged, and all flesh with His Sword: many shall be slain by the Lord.*"[3062]

The Prophet Daniel presents the "*Ancient of days*" as sitting on a Throne, which "*was a Flame of Fire, and His wheels burning Fire*" being ministered to by "*thousand thousands*" and "*ten thousands of myriads attended upon Him*" in order to Judge the works of each man according to the "*Books*" which "*were opened*" transmitting to Him " *the Dominion, and the Honour, and the Kingdom*" to Judge "*all nations, tribes, and languages.*"[3063]

The Prophet Isaiah simultaneously foresaw the first Coming and the Second Coming of the Lord: "*the Day of Lord is near, and destruction from God shall arrive.*"[3064] "*For behold! The Day of the Lord is coming which cannot be escaped, a Day of Wrath and Anger, to make the world desolate and to destroy sinners out of it.*"[3065] "*For the Heavens shall be enraged, and the earth shall be shaken from her foundatio, because of the fierce Anger of the Lord of Hosts, in the day in which His Wrath shall come.*"[3066]

The Lord had no need to essentially change or to perfect the Teachings of the Prophets concerning the Day of Judgement. He joined the Teachings of the Prophets concerning the Final Judgement of each man with the Final Judgement of all the nations. Thus in His speech on the Mount He stated: "*Many will say to Me in that Day, 'Lord, Lord, have we not prophesied in Thy Name, cast out demons in Thy Name, and done many wonders in Thy Name? And then I will declare to them, 'I never knew you; depart from Me, you who practice lawlessness.*"[3067] He specifically mentioned the "*Day of Judgement*" in which "*it will be more tolerable for Tyre and Sidon*"[3068] and on which Day men shall "*give account*" "*for every idle word*"[3069] "*for the Son of Man will come in the Glory of His Father with His Angels, and then

---

[3061] Ez. 33:12.
[3062] Is. 66:15-16.
[3063] Daniel 7:9-12.
[3064] Is. 13:6.
[3065] Is. 13:9-11.
[3066] Is. 13:13.
[3067] Matth. 7:22-23.
[3068] Matth. 11:22.
[3069] Matth. 12:36.

He will reward each according to his works."[3070] Christ will Judge all nations, since *"all nations will be gathered before Him."*[3071]

Our Lord refers to this Day of Judgement in His Parables of the Wheat and Tares,[3072] the Dragnet,[3073] the Ten Virgins,[3074] the Ten Talents,[3075] the King *"who wanted to settle accounts with his servants,"*[3076] the Labourers[3077] as well as the Royal Wedding.[3078] Furthermore, our Lord systematically referred to this Day in His eschatological speeches addressed to His Apostles and Disciples shortly before His Sufferings.[3079] As in the Book of Daniel whereby the *"Ancient of old"* appears at first as the Judge but then transmits the *"dominion"* to the *"Son of Man,"* likewise in the Teachings of Christ. In some cases, the Heavenly Father *"Who sees in secret, will Himself reward"* those who do *"charitable deeds"*[3080] or pray,[3081] or confess Him before men,[3082] while in others, the Lord appears as the Lord of the Entrance of the Kingdom of Heaven. He excludes all those who have worked evil and lawlessness,[3083] with Authority as the Son of Man Who sends before Him His Angels *"to gather out of His Kingdom all things that offend, and those who practice lawlessness, and will cast them into the Furnace of Fire. There will be wailing and gnashing of teeth. Then the Righteous will shine forth as the sun in the Kingdom of their Father"*[3084] The Son of Man *"will come in the Glory of His Father with His Angels"* to *"reward each according to his works."*[3085] He *"will appear in Heavencoming on the clouds of Heaven with Power and great Glory"*[3086] and will Judge all nations. He will Condemn the sinners *"into the Everlasting Fire prepared for the devil and his angelsbut the Righteous into Eternal Life."*[3087] Thus, *"the Father Judges no one, but has committed all*

[3071] Matth. 25:32.
[3072] Matth. 13:24-30; 36-43.
[3073] Matth. 13:47-50.
[3074] Matth. 25:1-13.
[3075] Matth. 25:14-30.
[3076] Matth. 18:23-35.
[3077] Matth. 20:1-16.
[3078] Matth. 22:2-14.
[3079] Matth. 24:1-25:1-46. Mark 13:1-37. Luke 21:5-36.
[3080] Matth. 6:4.
[3081] Matth. 6:6.
[3082] Matth. 10:32-33.
[3083] Matth. 18:34-35.
[3084] Matth. 13:41-43.
[3085] Matth. 16:27.
[3086] Matth. 24:30.
[3087] Matth. 25:31-46.

Judgement to the Son"[3088] *"and has given Him Authority to execute Judgement also because He is the Son of Man."*[3089] Truly the Lord Judging as Man, *"Judges as He hears"* from the Father and *"does nothing on His own."* Consequently He Judges *"as if the Father Himself was the Judge."*[3090] However, Christ Judges us because He is closer to our humanity and because He gave us the Laws and Suffered for our Salvation, thereby being the only proper Judge of all mankind.

Furthermore, the Holy Apostles repeated the Teachings of our Lord. St Peter testified that Jesus Christ is *"ordained by God to be Judge of the living and the dead."*[3091]

St Paul assured us that God has appointed a Day on which *"the Lord Jesus Christ, will Judge the living and the dead at His Appearing and His Kingdom."*[3092] He presented that Day as a *"Day of Wrath and Revelation of the Righteous Judgement of God, Who will render to each one according to his deeds; Eternal Life to those who by patient continuance in doing good, seek for glory, honour and immortality; but to those who are self-seeking and do not obey the Truth, but obey unrighteousness – indignation and wrath, tribulation and anguish, on every soul of man who does evil."*[3093] Parallel to this, he characterises this Appearance as a Revelation of *"the Lord Jesus"* will be *"revealed from Heaven with His mighty Angels in flaming Fire These shall be punished with Everlasting Destruction from the Presence of the Lord and from the Glory of His Power when He comes in that Day to be Glorified in His Saints and to be admired among all those who believe."*[3094]

The *Epistle of Barnabas* literally assures us that *"the Son of God, Who is Lord and is destined to Judge the living and the dead, suffered in order that His Wounds might give us Life."*[3095]

St Cyril of Jerusalem declared on the one hand that Christ *"is coming not to be judged again, but to Judge those who judged Him"* whereas on the other hand he stressed that the Father Himself does not Judge anyone as He *"gave all to the Son, not alienating Himself from the Authority, but Judging through the Son. Through the nod of the Father, the Son Judges. For there*

[3088] John 5:22.
[3089] John 5:27.
[3090] St John Chrysostom, *To John 5:30,* in Migne, *P.G.,* 59, 225.
[3091] Acts 10:42.
[3092] 2 Tim. 4:1.
[3093] Rom. 2:5-9.
[3094] 2 Thess. 1:7-10.
[3095] *Barnabas,* 7, 2, in Lightfoot, *Apostolic Fathers,* p. 170.

are no other nods of the Father or of the Son" as it is *"one and the same."*[3096]

There is no doubt that the Judgement will be in all Justice, for God will Judge the entire world with Justice[3097] and without partiality. He *"will render to each one according to his deeds."*[3098] Subsequently, all the secret works of men will be revealed because He Who sits on the Throne of Judgement is He Who always knows and seeks the hearts of men.[3099] The Lord *"will both bring to light the hidden things of darkness and reveal the counsels of the hearts"*[3100] *"in the Day when God will Judge the secrets of men"*[3101] demanding an account not only for the offences of the Law, but for every word and every deed they neglected to do, for *"to him who knows to do good and does not do it, to him it is sin."*[3102] *"And the dead were Judged according to their works, by the things which were written in the Books."*[3103]

Question 369: What are the Punishments?

Answer: The Punishments that will be bestowed by the Judge on the condemned,[3104] can be categorized as either negative and positive, or internal and external. The Eternal Punishment are:

1. First, being deprived of all God's Grace.
2. Secondly, the positive and internal Punishment, whereby the guilt of the conscience and awareness of guilt will be like an *"unsleeping worm"* that will eat at hearts, distressing them forever.
3. Thirdly, the external Punishment, according to which the soul will suffer Eternal pain of the Fire, sadness, external Darkness and communion with the evil spirits.[3105]

If one just considers the Divine Wrath resulting in the alienation of those who will be condemned by God Who is the only True Source of all Peace and Blessedness, and who will be deprived of the Vision of the

---

[3096] St Cyril of Jerusalem, *Catechesis,* XV, §§ 1 and 25, in Migne, *P.G.,* 33, 869.
[3097] Plato of Moscow, *Orthodox Teaching,* p. 126.
[3098] Rom. 2:6.
[3099] Heb. 4:12-13.
[3100] 1 Corinth. 4:5.
[3101] Rom. 2:16.
[3102] James 4:17.
[3103] Rev. 20:12.
[3104] Cf. Plato of Moscow, *Orthodox Teaching,* pp. 165-166. Evdokimov, *Orthodoxia,* pp. 443-447. Frangopoulos, *Christian Faith,* pp. 235-236. Mitsopoulos, *Themata,* pp. 397-403.
[3105] Mesoloras, *Symbolique,* v. II, p. 129.

Divine Glory of the Holy Trinity, this alone should be considered as an unbearable Punishment!

The negative aspect of the future Condemnation is inseparably united to the positive aspect. Primarily, there will be the disgrace that will overcome sinners due to having *"before their eyes their sins for all Eternity.."* for which they will be condemned to *"hard punishment"* *"the pain and the disgrace of which are really Eternal."*[3106]

Undoubtedly, the descriptions of the Punishments by the Holy Fathers as mentioned above, do not differ from those revealed by our Lord and Saviour Jesus Christ, the Son of God, when He spoke of the Punishments that await the ungodly after the Final Judgement. Expressions such as *"outer darkness,"* the *"weeping and gnashing of teeth,"* the *"Everlasting Punishment,"* *"Hell,"* *"the Fire that shall never be quenched,"* the *"Worm which does not die"* and *"torment of Flame,"*[3107] are a few of those that our Lord Himself used to describe the Eternal Punishments.

The exact nature of these Punishments is unknown since they occur in the After Life, which is beyond human senses and invisible.[3108] It may vaguely be perceived by means of the Parable of the Rich Man and Poor Lazarus,[3109] according to which the Rich Man found himself in Hell, *"being in torments"*[3110] and completely deprived from all the good things that he had enjoyed in this present life. His heart was enslaved by earthly things and the vanity of the pleasures of the flesh, which he could no longer satisfy. He was in the midst of a fiery Furnace that caused him terrible thirst and great anxiety. Also in this Parable, our Lord referred to a *"place of torment"*[3111] that is separated by *"a great gulf"* from the place of the Righteous.[3112] In addition to all this, our Lord spoke of *"the Everlasting Fire prepared for the devil and his angels."*[3113]

"Hell," *"Everlasting Fire"* or *"the Outer Darkness"*[3114] is a spiritual condition that God created not for man, but because of Satan and his angels being stubbornly unrepentant. This condition is real, unchangeable and eternal, since the Will of God is Eternal and Unchangeable. No one can adequately describe this condition that is beyond any human understanding, not even St Paul who was *"caught up in Paradise and heard inexpressible*

[3106] St Basil the Great, *To Psalm 33(34)*, §§ 4 and 8, in Migne, *P.G.*, 29, 364 and 372.
[3107] Matth. 8:12; 25:46. Mark 9:45-48. Luke 16:24.
[3108] 1 Corinth. 13:12.
[3109] Luke 16:19-31.
[3110] Luke 16:23.
[3111] Luke 16:28.
[3112] Luke 16:26.
[3113] Matth. 25:41.
[3114] Kefalas, *Catechesis,* pp. 242-243.

words, which it is not lawful for a man to utter."[3115] Similarly, should anyone enter into Hell, he would be completely unable to express the terrifying things he might see, hear or feel.

Question 370: What is the condition of the Righteous?

Answer: The Blessedness that awaits the Righteous, filling hearts with an inexpressible Joy and Happiness, will be due to the assurance that they have been Saved forever.[3116] The positive aspect of the future inheritance of the Righteous is expressed as *"Paradise of God,"* where *"the Tree of Life is in the midSt.."*[3117] and in which *"inexpressible words"* are heard, *"which it is not lawful for a man to utter."*[3118] This Eternal Life is also described as the *"City of God,"* *"the Holy City, New Jerusalem, coming down out of Heaven from God, prepared as a bride adorned for her husband,"*[3119] or as *"the Tabernacle of God"* that is with men and where He *"will dwell with them"*[3120] Furthermore it is described as the *"Father's house"* which has *"many mansions"*[3121] as well as being proclaimed as *"the Bride, the Lamb's wife"*[3122] that has *"the Glory of God."*[3123] Other descriptions of Eternal Life are: as the future City that has *"no temple in it, for the Lord God Almighty and the Lamb are its Temple;"*[3124] *"Assembly and Church of the Firstborn who are Regenerated in Heaven;"*[3125] *"an Inheritance incorruptible and undefiled;"* that *"does not fade away, reserved in Heaven;"*[3126] *"Kingdom of Heaven;"*[3127] *"Kingdom of God;"*[3128] *"Kingdom of the Father of the Lord"*[3129] or *"Kingdom prepared for the Blessed"*[3130] wherein the Lord will not only drink from the new Cup with His Disciples,[3131] but they *"shall also*

[3115] 2 Corinth. 12:4.
[3116] Cf. Plato of Moscow, *Orthodox Teaching,* pp. 164-165. Evdokimov, *Orthodoxia,* pp. 441-443. Mitsopoulos, *Themata,* pp. 393-397.
[3117] Rev. 2:7.
[3118] 2 Corinth. 12:4.
[3119] Rev. 20:2.
[3120] Rev. 20:3.
[3121] John 14:2.
[3122] Rev. 21:9.
[3123] Rev. 21:11.
[3124] Rev. 21:22.
[3125] Heb. 12:23.
[3126] 1 Peter 1:4.
[3127] Matth. 4:17; 5:3, 10, 20; 13:24, 31, 44, 47; 16:19; 18:23; 19:12; 20:1; 22:2; 23:13; 25:1, 14
[3128] Luke 14:15. Matth. 19:24; 21:31
[3129] Matth. 26:29
[3130] Matth. 25:34.
[3131] Matth. 26:29.

reign with Him."[3132]   No words can describe the perfect beauty of the Heavenly Things that await the Righteous who will partake in the Divine Nature of our Lord, watching and enjoying the Glory of the Holy Trinity, our True and Only God.

In God's Kingdom there is no fear, hunger or illness. No one is in pain, angry or flamed by desire because all these passions have been wiped away. No one will age because all will be vested with Immortality and Everlasting Joy, living together with the Angels, Archangels and all the higher Heavenly Powers. There will be no war or rebellion. There will only be the agreement of and harmony with the Saints and the oneness of mind.[3133]

The factor and cause of this Blessedness that the Saints experience, is referred to as "*Deification*" or "*Theosis*" that begins in this world. The final Purpose of the Lord's Incarnation is to lead fallen mankind towards the inheritance of the Kingdom of Heaven so that we may enjoy Divine Blessedness and be Deified. The term "*Deification*" or "*Theosis*" of our human nature and Deification of the Just, is understood as men becoming through this Deification "*partakers of the Divine Nature.*"[3134] While human nature is not abolished, being absorbed by the infinite Divine Nature, it partakes according to its limitations in the Life and Glory of God. Each of the Righteous, preserving his own personality and being, is raised up to approach the Divine but remaining always limited.

In the Divine Incarnation of the Word and Son of God, the second Person of the Holy Trinity took up the whole human nature, without sin, and was united with her in one Person and in one Hypostasy, His two Natures remaining "*unmixed and their Attributes unchangeable; and the Flesh was Deified, but it did not change its own Nature.*"[3135] Incomparably and to a greater degree the Deification of the Righteous, in which each one preserves his own personality, is clearly distinguished from the three Persons of the Holy Trinity because human nature is not in essence united to the Divine Nature. Human nature continues to remain human and within its own limits. However, by Grace and not by nature, it unites with the Divine Nature, participating in the Divine Life and Glory. The Word as the Infinite God "*alone has Immortality, dwelling in Unapproachable Light, Whom no man has seen or can see*"[3136] but the Deified nature of man is united with

---

[3132] 2 Tim. 2:12.
[3133] St John Chrysostom, *To the fallen Theodorus*, I, § 11, in Migne, *P.G.*, 47, 291.
[3134] 1 Peter 1:4.
[3135] St John of Damascus, *Catechesis*, III, 17, in Migne, *P.G.*, 94, 1069.
[3136] 1 Tim. 6:16.

Him, thereby comprising His Divine and Mystic *"Body"* which is *" the fullness of Him Who fills all in all."*[3137]

This union, in which the Divine and Infinite Nature of God the Word, although Hypostatically united with the human nature of the God-Man to which we are also united, remains unapproachable to us. We cannot be united in essence to it. This remains a *"Great Mystery."*[3138] Nevertheless, our Union as members of the Church with Christ begins in this life, from the moment of our Baptism into Christ Consequently, it is perfected in that Blessed condition, becoming the Source of the new Holy and Divine Life that gives Life to the whole Body. The reason for the exaltation of the body into the *"Glory and Majesty"*[3139] of God is its Union and Communion with Christ, Who is *"the Peace of God, which surpasses all understanding"* and which *" will guard"* *"hearts and minds through Christ Jesus."*[3140]

According to St John the Apostle, Evangelist and Theologian, *"it has not yet been revealed what we shall be, but we know that when He is revealed, we shall be like Him, for we shall see Him as He is."*[3141] Furthermore, only by seeing Him as He is will create a great Joy, just as at the time of the Lord's Transfiguration when the two Prophets Moses and Elijah appeared before the Lord on Mount Tabor and St Peter said to our Lord Jesus: *"Lord, it is good for us to be here."*[3142] The Vision of the Divine Glory makes all those who see participators, as St Paul taught us by saying that *"we all, with unveiled face, beholding as in a mirror the Glory of the Lord, are being transformed into the same image from glory to Glory, just as by the Spirit of the Lord,"*[3143] and the Lord said: *" the Righteous will shine forth as the sun in the Kingdom of their Father."*[3144]

Our Lord and Saviour Jesus Christ, in His prayer addressed to His Father shortly before His Sufferings, asked Him *"that they all may be one, as Thou, Father, are in Me, and I in Thee; that they also may be one in Us."*[3145] He asked the Father to grant that all who belong to Him become *"one to another in the sameness of soul and the unity of the spirit, not disagreeing, but all having the same mind."* As the Son *"is by nature and truly one with His Father"* likewise also we *"become the same generation to another through the intension having the unity of the Son to the Father."* In

---

[3137] Ephes. 1:23.
[3138] Ephes. 5:32.
[3139] Psalm 44(45):3.
[3140] Phil. 4:7.
[3141] 1 John 3:2.
[3142] Matth. 17:4.
[3143] 2 Corinth. 3:18.
[3144] Matth. 13:43. Zigabinos, *To Matthew,* in Migne, *P.G.,* 129, 416.
[3145] John 17:21.

the blessed condition all the righteous will be united in one and will copy the unity of the Holy Trinity, as far as possible to their human capability, *"for it is impossible to become equal to it"* and they shall live according to the blessed life of the Holy Trinity.

CHAPTER SIX
THE END AND THE RENEWAL OF THE WORLD

Question 371: What are the teachings of the End and the Renewal of the World?

Answer: According to Holy Scripture and the Tradition of the Orthodox Church, this present world will come to an end. This end, which takes place at the same time as the Universal Resurrection of the dead and Universal Judgement, must not be considered as being the abolishment and destruction of the world but its renewal and recreation.[3146] This recreation of the world remains a mystery that falls under the Plan of Creation, which is hidden in the Omnipotent Will of the Creator. The only certainty is that this New Creation is the *"new heavens and new earth in which righteousness dwells"*[3147] as well as the Kingdom of God which is the Church of the firstborn. The power and authority of death and mortality will be abolished and sin will no longer enter. After *"the end, when Christ delivers the Kingdom to God the Father, when He puts an end to all rule and all authority and power."*[3148] He remains the centre of the union of His people.[3149] *"Now when all things are made subject to Him, the Son Himself will also be subject to Him Who put all things under Him, that God may be all in all."*[3150]

Question 372: What do the Holy Scripture teach on the End and the Renewal of the World?

Answer: In the Old Testament we find prophecies referring to the catastrophe of the world, its recreation and its change.[3151] The Prophet Isaiah proclaimed: *" all the powers of the heavens shall melt, and the sky shall be rolled up like a scroll: and all the stars shall fall like leaves from a*

[3146] Mitsopoulos, *Themata*, pp. 403-405.
[3147] 2 Peter 3:13.
[3148] 1 Corinth. 15:24.
[3149] 1 Corinth. 15:25.
[3150] 1 Corinth. 15:28.
[3151] Psalm 101(102):26-27.

vine and as leaves fall from a fig-tree."[3152] "*For there shall be a new heaven and a new earth: and they shall not at all remember the former, neither shall they at all come into their mind.*"[3153]

Initially in the New Testament, our Lord repeatedly assured us that "*heaven and earth shall pass away, but one jot or one tittle will by no means pass from the law until all is fulfilled.*"[3154] He foretold great tribulations, according to which "*the sun will be darkened, and the moon will not give its light; the stars will fall from heaven, and the powers of the heavens will be shaken*"[3155] "*and on earth distress of nations, with perplexity, the sea and the waves roaring; men's hearts failing them from fear and the expectation of those things which are coming on the earth, for the powers of the heavens will be shaken.*"[3156] However, Christ did not fail to reassure His Apostles, and through them His Orthodox Church, that He would be with them "*even to the end of the age.*"[3157]

St Paul, on the other hand, taught that all Creation "*was subjected to futility, not willingly, but because of Him Who subjected it in hope; because the Creation itself also will be delivered from the bondage of corruption into the glorious liberty of the children of God. For we know that the whole Creation groans and labours with birth pangs together until now. Not only that, but we also who have the firstfruits of the Spirit, even we ourselves groan within ourselves, eagerly waiting for the adoption, the redemption of our body.*"[3158] Furthermore, "*the Lord Jesus is revealed from Heaven with His mighty Angels, in flaming fire taking vengeance on those who do not know God, and on those who do not obey the Gospel of our Lord Jesus Christ.*"[3159]

St Peter spoke in more detail of this fire verifying that "*the heavens and the earth which are now preserved by the same word, are reserved for fire until the Day of Judgement and perdition of the ungodly men.*"[3160] "*But the Day of the Lord will come as a thief in the night, in which the heavens will pass away with a great noise, and the elements will melt with fervent heat; both the earth and the works that are in it will be burnt up.*"[3161]

[3152] Is. 34:4. Is. 51:6.
[3153] Is. 65:17.
[3154] Matth. 5:18; 24:35. Mark 13:31. Luke 16:17; 21:33.
[3155] Matth. 24:29.
[3156] Luke 21:25-26.
[3157] Matth. 28:20.
[3158] Rom. 8:20-23.
[3159] 2 Thess. 1:7-8.
[3160] 2 Peter 3:7.
[3161] 2 Peter 3:10.

"Nevertheless we, according to His Promise, look for a new heaven and a new earth in which righteousness dwells."[3162]

Parallel to this, St John the Apostle, Evangelist and Theologian, in the Book of Revelation, saw that with the Resurrection of the dead and the following Judgement *"the earth and the heaven fled away"* from the Face of Him Who sat on the Throne. *"And there was found no place for them."*[3163] *"Now I saw a new heaven and a new earth, for the first heaven and the first earth had passed away."*[3164] *"Then He Who sat on the Throne said, 'Behold, I make all things new."*[3165]

Question 373: What does the Tradition of the Church teach concerning the Renewal of the World?

Answer: The *Epistle of Barnabas* emphasises that *"when His Son comes, He will destroy the time of the lawless one and will judge the ungodly and will change the sun and the moon and the stars, and then He will truly rest on the seventh day."*[3166]

St Clement of Rome stressed that *" you know that 'the Day' of Judgement is already 'coming as a blazing furnace,'*[3167] *and 'some of the heavens will dissolve'*[3168] *and the whole earth will be like lead melting in a fire, and then the works of men, the secret and the public, will appear."*[3169]

The *Shepherd of Hermas* emphasises *" they will fit into another much inferior place, but not until they have been torment and fulfilled the days of their sins. And they will be transferred for this reason only, that they received the righteous word. And then it will happen that they will be transferred out of their torments they will not be save, because of their hard-heartedness."*[3170]

St Justin the Philosopher and Martyr distinguished the prophesy of Moses whereby the *"fire"* *"has been kindled out of My wrath; it shall burn to hell below; it shall devour the land; it shall set on fire the foundations of the mountains."*[3171]

[3162] 2 Peter 3:13.
[3163] Rev. 20:11.
[3164] Rev. 21:1.
[3165] Rev. 21:5.
[3166] *Barnabas,* 15, 5, in Lightfoot, *Apostolic Fathers,* p. 182.
[3167] Cf. Mal. 4:1.
[3168] Cf. Is. 34:4.
[3169] St Clement of Rome, *2nd Corinthians,* 16, 3, in Lightfoot, *Apostolic Fathers,* p. 76.
[3170] *Shepherd of Hermas,* Vision III, 15, 6, in Lightfoot, *Apostolic Fathers,* p. 206.
[3171] Deut. 32:22.

St Cyril of Jerusalem taught that *"the end of the world takes place and this world which is born will be regenerated."* This is necessary due to the numerous sins, which polluted the Creation.[3172]

St John Chrysostom with reference to Psalm 101(102) and Isaiah, observed that as those who inhabit the earth will not perish but *"will change to immortality."* likewise the Creation.[3173]

Question 374: Why do we proclaim our Lord as the Eternal King?

Answer: In this new condition, our Lord and Saviour Jesus Christ, the Son of God, will be the Eternal King Whose Kingdom will have no end. St Paul informed us that at the end, *"when He delivers the Kingdom to God the Father, when He puts an end to all rule and all authority and power"*[3174] and *"when all things are made subject to Him, then the Son Himself will also be subject to Him Who put all things under Him, that God may be all in all."*[3175] The Archangel Gabriel assured the Ever Virgin Mary and Theotokos that her Son and Lord *"will reign over the house of Jacob forever, and of His Kingdom there will be no end."*[3176] Daniel spoke of His Kingdom.[3177] *"Your throne, O God, is forever and ever."*[3178]

The above verses agree by proclaiming the same Truth, which was incorporated in the Nicene Creed: *"and His Kingdom shall have no end."* Thus, the Son will reign over all and it is said that He is the *Pantocrator* (Almighty) King and His Kingdom shall have no end. Furthermore, our Lord reigns over the hearts of all the Orthodox Christians who willingly submit themselves to His Divine Will. This Kingdom has as its principal the words of the Lord Who said: *"Ask of Me, and I will give You the nations for Your inheritance, and the ends of the earth for Your possession."*[3179] Until the moment He submits the Kingdom to His Father, *"He must do the duties of a king; in other words to fight the enemies, enter into alliance with His own; the ones to conquer and the others to free thus He makes the work of submitting us under His Kingdom."* When this submission has been completed, *"His work of ruling over us ends."* *"Then, after these nothing is needed; for the Kingdom is without rebellion."*

[3172] St Cyril of Jerusalem, *Catechesis,* XV, § 3, in Migne, *P.G.,* 33, 873 and 876.
[3173] St John Chrysostom, *To Romans,* Homily 14, § 5, in Migne, *P.G.,* 60, 530.
[3174] 1 Corinth. 15:24.
[3175] 1 Corinth. 15:28.
[3176] Luke 1:33.
[3177] Daniel 7:14.
[3178] Heb. 1:8.
[3179] Psalm 2:8.

When the Salvation of the Church and the people of the Lord Jesus are completed, it will no longer be necessary for the God-Man to act as our High Priest and Mediator, neither to struggle as King and Head of His Church, which no longer be Militant but the one Triumphant and glorious. Having thus submitted Himself to the Will of God the Father Who sent Him to the human race, He will present His Church to Him, submitting her and Himself according to His humanity and as the Head of His Church.[3180]

Our Lord and Saviour Jesus Christ, the Son of God, fulfilling the work which the Father gave Him, remains forever the God-Man and the *"firstborn among many brethren."*[3181] He is the first among those who are in His image and is *"the Lamb"* Who *"leads them to the living fountain of waters."*[3182] He is the *"Light"* which *"illuminates"* the City of God,[3183] the Mediator between God and man, Who with the Father is One and through His humanity is united with the human race as the Head of His Church. He is the Eternal Light and Life for the glorious Church, granting Life to all those who believe in Him. *"They shall see His Face, and His Name shall be on their foreheads."*[3184]

Thus, our Lord and Saviour Jesus Christ, the Son of God, in the Kingdom to come, will be exalted above all and will be glorified with the Father and the Holy Spirit for all Eternity. *"And the Spirit and the bride say, 'Come!' And let him who hears say, 'Come!' And let him who thirsts come. Whoever desires, let him take the water of Life freely."*[3185]

"The Grace of our Lord Jesus Christ be with all the Saints. Amen."[3186]

[3180] St John Chrysostom, *To 1 Corinthians,* Homily 39, § 6, in Migne, *P.G.,* 61, 341.
[3181] Rom. 8:29.
[3182] Rev. 7:17.
[3183] Rev. 21:23.
[3184] Rev. 22:4,
[3185] Rev. 22:17.
[3186] Rev. 22:21.

BIBLIOGRAPHY.

Acta = Acta Sanctorum, April III, Junii V, September VII, October XII, Apend. XVI - XVII.

Achelis, *Die ältesten Quellen* = H. Achelis, *Die ältesten Quellen des oriental Kirchen rechts,* v. I, *Die Canones Hippoliti,* Λειψία, 1891.

Androutsos, *Dogmatique* = Chrestos Androutsos, *Dogmatique of the Orthodox Eastren Church,* Athens, 1907.

Androutsos, *Symbolique* = Chrestos Androutsos, *Symbolique from an Orthodox view,* 3rd Ed., Thessalonica, 1963.

George, Abbot, *The Deification as the purpose of man's life",* Holy Monastery of St Gregorios, Mt. Athos, Greece, 2001.

Arseniev, *Mysticism* = Nicholas Arseniev, *Mysticism & the Eastern Church,* New York, 1979.

B = Liberary of the Greek Fathers, ed. Apostoliki Diakonia.

Balanos, *Orthodox Cat.* = D. Balanos, *Orthodox Catechesis,* Athens, 1920.

Balanos, *Is Theology Science* = D. Balanos, *Is Theology Science?* Athens, 1906.

Balanos, *Crisis* = D. Balanos, *Crisis of the Dogmatique of Chrestos Androutsos,* Anatypon, In Jerusalem, 1907.

Bartmann, *Theologie Dogmatique* = Bartmann Bernard, *Precis de Theologie Dogmatique traduit par M. Gautier,* v. I and II, Mulhouse, 1951.

Bernard, «de Theologie » = P. Bernard, «de Theologie », in *Vacant et Mangenot Dictionary,* v. III.

Bolotow, «Day» = B. Bolotow, "Day and year of the martyrdom of the Evangelist Mark", (in Russian), journal of the Academy Petersburg, v. LXXIII, 1893).

Bonnet, *Acta* = M. Bonnet, *Acta apostolorum apocrypha,* v. III, Leipzig, 1903.

Boulgareos, *Theologicon* = Eugenios Bolgareos, *Theologicon,* Venice, 1872.

Bratsiotes, «The meaning» = P. Bratsiotes, "The meaning of the doctrine in the Orthodox Theology", journal *Theology,* v. 28, t. 4.

Briggs, *Symbolics* = Ch. Briggs, *Theological Symbolics*, Edinburg, 1914.

Bryennios, *Paralipomena* = Bryennios, *Paralipomena* = Joseph Bryennios, *Paralipomena,* v. III, 2nd Ed., Thessalonica, 1991.

Cicero, *Quaestiones academicae.*

Cleopa, *The Truth* = Elder Cleopa of Romania, *The Truth of our Faith,* Thessalonica, 2nd Ed., 2002.

Connoly, "On the text" = D. H. Connoly, "On the text of the baptismal Creed of Hippolytus", in Journal of theological Studies, v. XXV, 1924.

Damalas, *About Principals* = N. M. Damalas, *About Principals.*

Damalas, *Catechesis* = N. M. Damalas, *Orthodox Catechesis*, Athens, 1877.

Daniélou, *The first,* – Jean Danielou & Henri Marrou, *THE CHRISTIAN CENTURIES. The first Six Hundred Years,* v. 2, 5th edition, Essex, 1983.

Demistas, *Alexandria* = Margarites Demitsas, *History of Alexandria. Description geographical, historical, literature, political, ecclesiastical and archaeological, from the foundation of the city till its conquer by the Arabs,* Athens, 1885.

Dictionary = *A Dictionary of Christian Biography, Literature, Sects and Doctrines; being a continuation of the Dictionary of the Bible,* volume I. A-D, edited by Smith William and Wace Henry, London, 1877.

Dositheus, *Confession* = Dositheus, Patriarch of Jerusalem, *Confession of the Orthodox Fath,* ed. Regopoulos, Thessalonica, 1983.

Duchesne, *Histoire* = L. Duchesne, *Histoire anciencede l' Eglise,* Paris, 1908.

Durand, *Inspiration* = A. Durand, *Inspiration de la Bible*, in A. d' Ales, Dict. Apolog., v. 2, col. 900.

Dyobouniotes, *The mysteries* = K. Dyobouniotes, *The mysteries of the Eastern Orthodox Church from dogmatic view.*

Dyobouniotes, *Dogmatique of Chr. Androutsos* = K. Dyobouniotes, *Criticism of the Dogmatique of Chr. Androutsos.*

Evdokimov, *Orthodoxia* = Παύλου Ευδοκίμοοφ, *Η Ορθοδοξία,* Θεσσαλονίκη, 1972. (in Greek).
(Paul Endokimov, *Orthodoxia,* Thessalonica, 1972).

Evdokimov, *Icon* = Paul Endokimov, *The technic of the Icon. Theology of the Beauty,* Thessalonica, 1972.

Feidas, *The 1ˢᵗ Ecumenical Council* =Feidas Blasios, *The 1ˢᵗ Ecumenical Council.* Athens, 1974.

Felten, *Marcus* = J. Felten, *Marcus*, in the dictionary of Wetzer – Welte's *Kirchenlexikon,* τ. VIII.

Frangopoulos, *Christian Faith* = Athanasius Frangopoulos, Our *Christian Faith. (What we believe) – Public Dogmatique,* 12ᵗʰ ed., Athens, 1999.

Fuller, *The anointing* = F. W. Fuller, *The anointing of the Sick in Scripture and Tradition,* London, 1904.

Fytrakis, *Relics* = Andreas I. Fytrakis, *Relics and tombs of the martyrs during the first three centuries.*

Galanopoulos, *System* = Meletius Galanopoulos, Metropolitan of Kythera, *System of Holy Confession,* Athens, 1960.

Galites, *Interpretations* = George Ant. Galites, *Interpretations of the New Testament. Universety studies,* 5ᵗʰ Ed., Thessalonica, 1982.

Gavin, *Orthodox Thought* = Frank Gavin, Rev., *Some Aspects of Contemporary Greek Orthodox Thought,* London, 1923.

Georgopoulos, *Anthology* = Georgopoulos, *Anthology of the Seven Mysteries,* Thessalonica, 1996.

Gialourakis, *Egypt* =Manolis Gialourakis, *The Egypt of the Greeks. Brief History of the Greeks of Egypte,* Athens, 1967.

Grabar, *Martyrium* = A. Grabar, *Martyrium· recherches sur le culte des reliques et l' art chrétien antique,* v. I-II, Paris, College de France, 1946.

Harduin, *Acta counciliorum* = J. Harduin, *Acta Counciliorum,* Paris, 1715.

Harnack, *Dogmengeschichte* 5 = A. Harnak, *Lehrbuch der Dogmengeschichte* 5, v. I.

Harnack, *Mission* = A. Harnack, *Die Mission und Ausbreitung des Christentums in den ersten drei Jahrhunderten,* Leipzig, 1902.

Hastoupis, *Introduction* =Athanasius P. Hastoupis, *Introduction to the Old Testament,* Athens, 1981.

Hagenbach, *History* = R. K.A. Hagenbach, *A History of Christian Doctrines,* translated by E. H. Plumptre, v. I-III, Edinburgh, 1883.

Hauler, *Didascaliae Apostolorum* = Ed Hauler, *Didascaliae Apostolorum fragmenta veronensia latina.*

Jugie, *Theologia*= M. Jugie, *Theologia Dogmatica Christianorum Orientalium*, v. I-V, Parisiis, 1926-1935.

Kalogeras, *Maria* = I. Kalogeras, *Mary the Ever-Virgin Theotokos according to the orthodox faith,* Thessalonica, 1958.

Karabidopoulos, *Apocrypha* = Ioannis Karabidopoulos, *Apocrypha Christian Texts B. Apocrypha Acts-Epistoles-Revelations,* Thessalonica, 2004.

Karmeris, *Synopsis* = I. Karmeris, *Synopsis of the Dogmatique teaching of the Orthodox Catholic Church.*

Karmeris, *The dogmatics* = I. Karmeris, *The Dogmatic and Symbolic books of the Orthodox Catholic Church,* volumes I & II, Athens, 1952, 1953.

Karmeris, *The descent of Christ into Hades from an Orthodox view,* Athens, 1939.

Katsonis, *The canonical* = Hieronymus Kotsonis, *The canonical view about the communication with the heterodox.*

Kefalas, *Immortality* = St Nektarios Kefalas, Metropolitan of Pentapolis, *The Immortality of the soul and Holy Commemorations,* Athens.

Kefalas, *Catechesis* = St Nektarios Kefalas, Metropolitan of Pentapolis, *Orthodox Holy Catechesis,* 4th Ed., Thessalonica, 2001.

Kefalas, *Christology* = St Nektarios Kefalas, Metropolitan of Pentapolis, *Christology,* Athens, 1992.

Kefalas, *Ecumenical Synods* = Kefalas, Metropolitan of Pentapolis, *The Ecumenical Synods. About the Holy Icons,* Thessalonica, 1972).

Knowles, *The Middle Ages* = David Knowles & Dimitri Obolensky, *THE CHRISTIAN CENTURIES. The Middle Ages,* v. 2, 5th edition, Essex, 1983.

Kyrillos II, «Le voyage». = Kyrillos II, Patriarche Copte-Catholique d' Alexandrie, «Le voyage de St Marc en Egypte», *Bulletin de la Societe Khediviale de Geographie, Ve Series, No 7,* Le Caire, 1900, σελ. 381-406.

Labadarios, *Explanation* = Panteleimon Labadarios, Archimandrite (today Archbishop of Pelusium), *The Explanation of the Holy Sacraments of Holy Baptism and Holy Chrismation according to the Eastern Orthodox Church,* Johannesburg, 1989.

Labadarios, *Marriage* = Panteleimon Labadarios, Archimandrite (today Archbishop of Pelusium), *The Explanation of the Holy Sacrament of Marriage,* Johannesburg, 1990.

Labadarios, *Sermons* = Panteleimon Labadarios, Archimandrite (today Archbishop of Pelusium), *Hellenic South African Orthodox Sunday Sermons,* v. 1, Johannesburg, 1989.

Labadarios, *Sermons* = Panteleimon Labadarios, Archimandrite (today Archbishop of Pelusium), *Hellenic South African Orthodox Sunday Sermons,* vs. 2-3, Johannesburg, 1992.

Lagrange, "L' ange" = M. S. Lagrange, "L' agne de Jahve" in Revue biblique, 1903.

Leeming, *Principals* = Bernard Leeming, *Principals of Sacramental Theology,* London, 1955.

Lightfoot, *Apostolic Fathers* = J. B. Lightfoot and J. R. Harmer, *The Apostolic Fathers,* edited and revised by M. W. Holmes, 2nd Edition, U.S.A., 2000.

Lightfoot, *AF* = J. B. Lightfoot, *The Apostolic Fathers, Part I: S. Clemetn of Rome.* 2d. ed., 2 vols.; *Part II: S. Ignatius. S. Polycarp.* 2d ed., 3 vols., London: Macmillan, 1890, 1889; reprinted Grand Rapids: Baker, 1981.

Link, *Apostolic Faith Today* = Edited by Hans-Greorg Link, *Apostolic Faith Today. A Handbook for Study,* Faith and Order Paper No. 124, World Council of Churches, Geneva.

Lipsius, *Die apokryphen, v. III* = R. A. Lipsius, *Die apokryphen Apostelgeschichten und Apostellegenden,* Braunschweig, τόμ. III, 1890.

Loofs, *Nestoriana* = F. Loofs, *Nestoriana fragmenta vatia,* Halle, 1905.

Lossky, *Theology* = Vladimir Lossky, *Orthodox Theology. An Introduction.* New York, 1989.

Mai, *Spicilegium romanum* = Severi Antiocheni, *Liber adversus Julianum Halicarnassensem*, Mai, *Spicilegium romanum,* Rome, 1844.

Macaire, *Histoire* = Georges Macaire, *Histoire de l' Eglise d' Alexandrie depuis St Marc jusqu'a nos jours,* Le Caire, 1894.

Mazarakis, *Contribution* = Gerasimos Mazarakis, *Contributuion to the History of the Orthodox Church in Egypt,* Alexandria, 1932.

Makarios, *Enchiridion* = Makarios, Metropolitan of Moscow, *Enchiridion of the Dogmatic Theology according to the Orthodox Faith in Christ,* translated in Greek by Neophytos Pagida, Archimandrite, Athens, 1882.

Martensen, *Dogmatique* = Martensen, *Dogmatique,* traduite par G. Ducros, Paris, 1879.

Mansi = Mansi, Sacrorum Conciliorum nova et ampilissima Collection, vs. 1-53, Paris, 1901-1927.

Mesoloras, *Practical Theology* = I. E. Mesoloras, *Practical Theology,* Athens, 1911.

Mesoloras, *Symbolique* = I. E. Mesoloras, *Symbolique of the Orthodox Catholic Church,* Athens, 1911.

Meyendorff, *Theology* = John Meyendorff, *Byzantine Theology. Historical trends and doctrinal themes,* New York, 1987.

Meyendorff, *Legacy* = John Meyendorff, *The Byzantine Legacy in the Orthodox Church,* New York, 1982.

Miclosich, *Acta* = F. Miclosich and I. Müller, *Acta et diplomata Graeca Medii Aevi,* v. I.

Migne, *P.G.* = Accurante J.- P. Migne, *Patrologie Cursus Completus seu bibliotheca universalis, integra, uniformis, commoda, oeconomica, omnium SS. Patrum, Doctorum Scriptorumque Ecclesiasticorum, sive Latinorum, sive Graecorum, Patrologiae Graece,* Parisiis, 1857-1894.

Mitsopoulos, *Themata* = Nicholaos Mitsopoulos, *Themata of Orthodox Dogmatique Theology*, Athens, 1983.

Moehler, « Symbolique » = Moehler, «La Symbolique », traduit de l' Allemand par F. Lachat, vs. I-III, Bruxelles, 1853-1859.

Mouratides, *The essence* = K. Mouratides, *The essence and the regime of the Church according to the teaching of John Chrysostom,* Athens, 1958.

Ott, «Precis» = L. Ott, «Precis de Theologie Dogmatique», traduit par M. Grandclaudon, Paris, 1955.

Oosterzee, *Dogmatics* = Van Oosterzee, *Christian Dogmatics,* translated by I. Waston & M.Evansa,London, 1891.

Owen, *Theology* = Robert Owen, *Atreatise of Dogmatic Theology,* London, 2nd edition, 1887.

Papadopoulos, *History* = Chrysostom Papadopoulos, Archbishop of Athens, *History of the Church of Alexandria (60-1934),* Alexandria, 1935.

Papadopoulos, «Mark» = Chrysostom Papadopoulos, Archimandrite, "The First Days of the Church of Alexandria. The Evangelist Mark. John Mark as companion of the Apostles", *Ecclesiasticos Pharos,* vol. 4, 2nd Year, Alexandria, 1909.

Pedalion = The Rudder (Pedalion) of the Metaphorical ship of the one Holy Catholic and Apostolic Church of the Orthodox Christians or all the Sacred and Divine Canons of the Holy Councils, Ecumenical as well as Regional, and of individual Divine Fathers, as Embodied in the original Greek text, for the sake of authenticity, and explained in the vernacular by way of rendering them more intelligible to the less educated, By Agapius, a Hieromonach and Nicodemus, a Monk, Published by the Orthodox Christian Educational Society, Illinois, USA, 1957

Plato, *Orthodox Teaching* = Plato, Metropolitan of Moscow, *Orthodox Teaching,* translated by Adamantios Koraes according to the 4th edition of the year 1851. Published by Bas. Regopoulos, Thessalonica, 1995.

Polybius, III.

Popovic, *Ecumenism* = Archim. Justinus Popovic, Professor of the University of Belgrad, *Orthodox Church and Ecumenism,* 1974.

Romanides, *Dogmatique* = John S. Romanides, Protopresbyter, Prof., *Dogmatique and Symbolique Theology of the Orthodox Catholic Church,* vs. I and II, 4th ed., Thessalonica, 1999.

Pomazansky, *Theology* = Michael Pomazansky, Father, *Orthodox Dogmatic Theology,* United States, 1994.

Rauschen, *Fiorilegium* = G. Rauschen, *Fiorilegium Patristicum Fasc.*, VII editio altera Bonnae, 1914.

Rhosse, *System* = Rosse Zekos, *System of the Dogmatique of the Orthodox Catholic Church,* Athens, 1903.

Richardson, *Fathers* = C. C. Richardson, ed. *Early Christian Fathers,* Philadelphia: Westminster, 1953; reprinted New York: Macmillan, 1970.

Scheeben, *Les Mystères* = Scheeben I. M., *Les Mystères du Christianisme,* translated by A Kerkvorde. J. Tixeront, *Histoire des Dogmes,* vol. I-III, Paris, 1924, 1928.

Schmaus, "Mariology" = Michael Schaus, "Mariology", in *Encyclopedia of Theology. The Concise Sacramentum Mundi,* pp. 893-905, edited by Karl Rahner, New York, 1975..

Schmemann, *Eucharist* = Fr. A. Schmemann, *EuchariSt The Mystery of the Kingdom,* translated by Joseph Roelides, Athens, 2000.

Schmemann, *The Church Praying* = Fr. A. Schmemann, *The Church Praying,* Translated by Protopresbyter Demetrios Tzermpos, 2nd Ed., Athens, 2003.

Sidarous, *Patriarcats* = Sesostris Sidarous, *Les Patriarcats dans l' Empire Ottoman et specialement en Egypte,* Paris, 1907.

Siskos, *Organosis* = Anthimos Siskos, Archimandrite, Theologian – Lawyer, *The Organosis of the Church of Alexandria,* Alexandria, 1937.

Sollerii, "De sancti" = Johannis Baptistae Sollerii S.J. "De sancti Marci apostolatu et obitu Disseretatio", *Acta Sanctorum,* vol. Junii V.

Sophrony, *His Life* = Archimandrite Sophrony, *His Life is Mine,* St Vladamir's Seminary Press, New York, 1977.

St Irenaeus, *Heresies* = St Irenaeus Bishop of Lyon, *Heresies,* Translated by Irenaeus Hadjephraimides, Archimandrite, Introduction – Translation-Notes, Thessalonica, 1991.

St John Chrysostom, *Priesthood* = St John Chrysostom, *Homilies about Priesthood. Introduction-Text-Translation-Comments,* by Panagiotes Chrestou, Thessalonica, 1960.

St Symeon, *Euriskomena* = St Symeon the New Theologian, *Euriskomena,* Thessalonica, 1977.

Stefanides, *Eccl. History* = B. Stefanides, *Church History.From the beginning till today.* Athens, 4th ed., 1978.

Theodorou, *Christological*= A. Theodorou, *The Christological term and teaching of Cyril of Alexandria and Theodorus of Cyrus.*

The Orthodox Study Bible = *The Orthodox Study Bible. New Testament and Psalms.* King James Version. Published by St Athanasius Orthodox Academy, U.S.A., 1993.

Tillemont, *Memoires* = Tillemont, *Memoires pour servir a l' histoire ecclesiastique des six premiers siecles,* τόμ. II, Paris, 1701.

Tischendorf, *Apocrypha* = Tischendorf, *Acta apostolorum apocrypha,* Lipsiae, 1851.

Tixeront, *Histoire* = J. Tixeront, *Histoire des Dogmas,* vs. I-III, Paris, 1924, 1928.

Trempelas, *Dogmatique* = Panagiotes N. Trempelas, *Dogmatique of the Orthodox Catholic Church*, volumes I-III, Athens, 1978.

Trempelas, *Encyclopaedia* = Panagiotes N. Trempelas, *Encyclopaedia of Theology,* Athens, 1980.

Trempelas, *The laymen in the Church* = Trempelas, *The laymen in the Church, "The royal Priesthood",* Athens, 1976.

Trempelas, *Small Euchologion* = Trempelas, *Small Euchologion,* vs. I and II, Athens, 1998.

Tsakonas, *Paracletus* = Basilios G. Tsakonas, *The Teaching of the Evangelist John about the Paracletus. (Under the view of the general Biblical Pneumatology)*, Athens, 1978.

Ware, *Way* = Bishop Kallistos Ware, *The Orthodox Way,* London, Oxford, 1987.

Xenophon, *Anabasis* = Ξενοφῶντος, *Κύρου Ανάβασις.*

Zogheb, *Etudes* = Alexander Max De Zogheb, *Etudes sur l' ancienne Alexandrie. L' Eglise d' Alexandrie,* Paris, 1909.

INDEX

PART ONE

GOD

CHAPTER ONE

CHAPTER TWO

CHAPTER THREE

CHAPTER FOUR

THE DIVINE ATTRIBUTES IN RELATION TO THE WAY OF THE DIVINE EXISTENCE

CHAPTER FIVE

THE DIVINE ATTRIBUTES IN RELATION TO THE WAY OF GOD's ENERGY

CHAPTER SIX

THE DOCTRINE OF THE TRIUNE GOD

CHAPTER SEVEN

THE TRINITARIAN DOCTRINE

CHAPTER EIGHT

THE CHARACTERISTICS OF THE DIVINE HYPOSTASES'S ATTRIBUTES

CHAPTER NINE

THE HYPOSTATIC ATTRIBUTES IN RELATION TO THE IDENTITY OF THE DIVINE ESSENCE

PART TWO

THE CREATION

PART ONE

CHAPTER ONE

THE CREATION OF THE WORLD

I. GOD THE CREATOR OF ALL

II. THE CREATION FROM NOTHINGNESS

III. THE CREATION IN RELATION TO TIME

IV. THE CHARACTERISTICS OF GOD'S CREATIVE ACTION

II. THE GOVERNMENT OF GOD IN RELATION TO MAN'S FREEDOM AND SYNERGY

PART TWO

THE SPIRITUAL WORLD

CHAPTER FIVE

THE WORLD OF THE ANGELS

CHAPTER SIX

THE FALLEN ANGELS

CHAPTER SEVEN

THE ORIGINE OF MAN AND HIS PRIMITIVE CONDITION

I. THE CREATION OF MAN

II. THE ELEMENTS OF MAN

CHAPTER EIGHT

THE FALL AND ITS RESULTS

I. THE TEMPTER, THE FIRST DISOBEDIENCE & DIRECT CONSEQUENCES

CHAPTER TWO

PREPARATION OF SALVATION BY DIVINE PROVIDENCE

CHAPTER THREE

THE INCARNATION OF THE WORD

CHAPTER FOUR

THE SAVIOUR

THE DIVINITY OF JESUS CHRIST

CHAPTER FIVE

THE HUMAN NATURE OF CHRIST

CHAPTER SIX

THE HYPOSTATIC UNION OF THE TWO NATURES IN THE ONE PERSON JESUS CHRIST

CHAPTER SEVEN

THE RESULTS OF THE HYPOSTATIC UNION

CHAPTER ELEVEN

THE OFFICE OF CHRIST AS KING

CHAPTER TWELVE

THE MOTHER OF GOD

PART FOUR

MAN IN GOD'S KINGDOM

CHAPTER ONE

DEFINITION AND NECESSITY OF THE DIVINE GRACE

CHAPTER TWO

THE UNIVERSALITY OF GOD'S GRACE AND IT'S RELATIONSHIP TO MAN'S FREEDOM

CHAPTER THREE

THE UNITED WORK OF GRACE

CHAPTER FOUR

THE PREPARATION OF JUSTIFICATION

CHAPTER FIVE

THE ESSENCE OF THE JUSTIFICATION

CHAPTER SIX

THE CONDITION OF JUSTIFICATION

PART FIVE

THE ORTHODOX CHURCH AS THE KINGDOM OF GOD ON EARTH

CHAPTER ONE

MEANING, DIVINE INSTITUTION AND THE NECESSITY OF THE CHURCH

CHAPTER TWO

THE ATTRIBUTES OF THE CHURCH

CHAPTER THREE

THE ORGANISATION OF THE CHURCH

CHAPTER FOUR

THE ORTHODOX CHURCH AS THE COMMUNION OF SAINTS

PART SIX

THE HOLY SACRAMENTS AS WAYS OF DIVINE GRACE, WHICH INCORPORATES US IN GOD'S KINGDOM

CHAPTER ONE

THE HOLY SACRAMENTS AS THE MEANS OF DIVINE GRACE

CHAPTER TWO

THE MEANING AND NATURE OF THE MYSTERIES (SACRAMENTS)

CHAPTER THREE

THE PERFECTION OF THE HOLY MYSTERIES

CHAPTER FOUR

THE NUMBER OF THE HOLY MYSTERIES

1. THE HOLY MYSTERY OF BAPTISM

2. THE HOLY MYSTERY OF HOLY CHRISMATION

3. THE HOLY MYSTERY OF EUCHARIST

4. THE HOLY MYSTERY OF REPENTANCE

5. THE HOLY MYSTERY OF PRIESTHOOD

6. THE HOLY MYSTERY OF MARRIAGE

7. THE HOLY MYSTERY OF UNCTION

PART SEVEN

ESCHATOLOGY OR THE PERFECTION OF THE KINGDOM OF GOD

THE MIDDLE CONDITION

CHAPTER ONE

PARTIAL JUDGMENT

CHAPTER TWO

THE FORETASTE OF THE GLORY OF THE SAINTS IN THE MILITANT CHURCH

CHAPTER THREE

THE PERFECTION OF ALL THE END OF THE AGE AND THE SECOND COMING OF THE LORD

CHAPTER FOUR

THE RESURRECTION OF THE DEAD

CHAPTER FIVE

THE UNIVERSAL JUDGEMENT

CHAPTER SIX

THE END AND THE RENEWAL OF THE WORLD